DISABILITY DISCRIMINATION
LAW AND PRACTICE

Third Edition

DISABILITY DISCRIMINATION
LAW AND PRACTICE

Third Edition

Brian J Doyle LLB, LLM, PhD, *Barrister*
Chairman of Employment Tribunals
Sometime Professor of Law,
The University of Liverpool

JORDANS
2000

Published by
Jordan Publishing Limited
21 St Thomas Street
Bristol BS1 6JS

British Library Cataloguing-in-Publication Data
A catalogue record for this book is available from the British Library.

ISBN 0 85308 568 4

Typeset by Mendip Communications Limited, Frome, Somerset
Printed by MPG Books, Bodmin, Cornwall

DEDICATION

In memory of my mother, Mary Doyle

PREFACE

It is four years since the last edition of *Disability Discrimination: Law and Practice*. As I noted in the preface at that time, that edition was effectively the second edition of *Disability Discrimination: The New Law* which had been published in early 1996 (shortly after the Disability Discrimination Act 1995 had received Royal Assent). This is thus the third edition of that book.

Looking back at the first edition, I am struck by how little material – other than the Disability Discrimination Act 1995 itself – any author had to play with in attempting to make judgements about how the Act would be interpreted and what it would mean in practice. Writing that edition was akin to tight-rope walking without a safety net. However, by the time of the second edition, the substantive provisions of the Act were beginning to be brought into force and the statutory guidance, regulations and codes of practice were appearing. That at least allowed the second edition (published in late 1996) to interpret the law with the aid of a safety harness. Yet lawyers bred in the British common law tradition are never truly at ease with the interpretation of statutes until there is some case-law with which to negotiate the high wire of legislative intention. Now, within a relatively short space of time, a substantial body of first instance and appellate decisions has emerged. Indeed, the Court of Appeal has already directly considered the meaning of the Act's provisions on four occasions (in *Clark v TDG Ltd t/a Novacold*, in *MHC Consulting Services Ltd v Tansell*, in *Kapadia v London Borough of Lambeth* and in *R v Powys County Council, ex parte Hambidge*). Further parts of the Act have also been brought into force in tandem with associated guidance or codes of practice. A new Disability Rights Commission is also open for business.

I hope that, as a result, the interpretation and observations offered in this new edition are more confident, less tentative and more strongly rooted in the legal pragmatism which is the product of hard cases being subjected to litigation. However, it is also clear (as is explained in Chapter 1) that the law is not standing still. Future reform of the 1995 Act is probable; further testing case-law is in the pipeline; developments in the European Union are likely to add new ingredients to the domestic recipe; and the Human Rights Act 1998 will give the mixture an extra stir. This might be the last edition of a book on *Disability Discrimination* which can afford to focus so centrally upon a single Act (the Disability Discrimination Act 1995). I suspect that by the time of the next edition it may be necessary to retitle this work *Disability Rights: Law and Practice*.

As with previous editions, I have incurred a number of debts in writing this book. At various times in the last four years I have acted as an adviser or contributor to the work of the National Disability Council (NDC), the Disability Access Rights Advisory Service (DARAS), the Disability Rights Task Force (DRTF) and the Disability Discrimination Act Representation and Advice Project (DDARAP). Together with Nigel Meager and his colleagues at the

Institute of Employment Studies, I was also part of the research team which monitored the working of the 1995 Act for the NDC and the Department for Education and Employment. It was a privilege to be involved with the implementation of the Act in so many ways and I am very grateful to my colleagues in these ventures for the insights which I have gleaned therefrom. My thanks are also due to Michael Rubenstein, Elaine Aarons, Owen Warnock, Jenny White, Caroline Gooding and others with whom I have shared conference platforms in recent years and who have enhanced my understanding of this difficult area of law. As always, thanks are due to Stephen Honey and his colleagues at Jordans who have been encouraging and forbearing during the long gestation period of this new edition.

I have attempted to state the law as I understand it to be on 1 August 2000.

BRIAN DOYLE
August 2000

CONTENTS

Dedication   v
Preface   vii
Table of Cases   xv
Table of Statutes   xxi
Table of Statutory Instruments   xxxiii
Table of European and UN Legislation   xxxvii
Table of Codes of Practice and Guidance   xxxix
Table of Abbreviations   xliii

Chapter 1   INTRODUCTION   1
             1.1   Background   1
             1.2   Disability Discrimination Act 1995   5

Chapter 2   DISABILITY AND DISABLED PERSON   7
             2.1   Introduction   7
             2.2   Meaning of 'disability' and 'disabled person'   8
             2.3   Impairment   9
                   Physical impairment   10
                   Mental impairment   11
                   Sensory and other impairments   12
             2.4   Ability to carry out normal day-to-day activities 13
             2.5   Substantial adverse effect   15
                   Meaning of 'substantial'   15
                   Recurring conditions   17
                   Progressive conditions   18
                   Severe disfigurement   19
                   Effect of medical treatment   20
             2.6   Long-term adverse effect   22
                   Past disability and long-term adverse effect   23
             2.7   Persons deemed to be disabled   23
             2.8   Past disabilities   24
             2.8   Future reform   25

Chapter 3   EMPLOYMENT AND CONTRACT WORK   27
             3.1   Introduction   27
             3.2   General prohibition on discrimination in
                   employment   28
                   Employment   29
                   Employment at an establishment in Great
                   Britain   29
                   Exclusion of small businesses   30
                   Other exemptions   32

3.3   Discrimination in employment   34
        Exceptions   36
        Pre-employment health screening   37
3.4   Meaning of discrimination   39
        Less favourable treatment   40
        Reason related to disability   43
        Employment advertisements   45
        Discrimination by association   47
3.5   Defence of justification   47
        Performance-related pay   51
        Agricultural wages   51
3.6   Duty to make reasonable adjustments   52
        Discrimination and the duty to make
        reasonable adjustments   52
        When does the duty to make reasonable
        adjustments arise?   53
        Arrangements   54
        Physical features of premises   55
        Substantial disadvantage   55
        The duty illustrated   56
        What are reasonable steps to take?   59
        To whom is the duty owed?   61
        Discrimination, justification and reasonable
        adjustments   63
3.7   Occupational pension schemes   64
        Employers' obligations   64
        Trustees of occupational pension schemes   65
3.8   Insurance benefits provided to employees   67
3.9   Discrimination against contract workers   69
        Introduction   69
        Unlawful discrimination   71
        Contract work and reasonable adjustments   72
3.10   Enforcement, remedies and procedures   73
3.11   Disabled Persons (Employment) Acts   74
3.12   Other employment legislation   75
        Employment in local government   75
3.13   Future reform   76

Chapter 4   TRADE ORGANISATIONS   77
4.1   Introduction   77
4.2   Meaning of 'trade organisation'   78
        Organisation of workers   78
        Organisation of employers   79
        Other organisations   80
4.3   Discrimination by trade organisations   80
        Discrimination against applicants for
        membership of trade organisations   81

		Discrimination by trade organisations against existing members	81
	4.4	The meaning of discrimination by trade organisations	82
		Discrimination and less favourable treatment	82
		Discrimination and the duty to make adjustments	83
		Discrimination and victimisation	83
	4.5	Duty to make adjustments	84
		When does the duty arise?	84
		To whom is the duty owed?	85
		What are reasonable steps?	86
		The duty illustrated	87
	4.6	Defence of justification	88
		Less favourable treatment	88
		Failure to make adjustments	89
		Justification illustrated	89
	4.7	Enforcement and remedies	90
Chapter 5		GOODS, FACILITIES AND SERVICES	91
	5.1	Introduction	91
		Timetable	91
		Code and regulations	92
		Part III of the DDA 1995 outlined	92
	5.2	Provision of services	93
		Services	93
		Goods and facilities	94
		Service providers	95
		Manufacturers and designers	95
		Private members' clubs	96
		To whom the service is provided	96
		Excluded services	96
	5.3	Unlawful discrimination	97
		Refusal to provide goods, facilities or services	97
		Standard or manner of service	97
		Terms on which service is provided	98
		Failure to make reasonable adjustment	98
	5.4	Meaning of discrimination	98
		Less favourable treatment	99
		Indirect discrimination	102
	5.5	Duty to make reasonable adjustments	103
		Introduction	103
		Practices, policies or procedures	105
		Physical features	106
		Auxiliary aids and services	109
	5.6	Justification	110
		Subjective opinion and objective reasonableness	111
		Conditions for justification defence	112
		Insurance services	116

		Guarantees	117
		Deposits	117
	5.7	Enforcement, remedies and procedures	118
Chapter 6		PROPERTY, PREMISES AND LEASES	119
	6.1	Introduction	119
	6.2	Discrimination in relation to premises	120
		Unlawful acts of discrimination	120
		Person with power to dispose of any premises	122
		Premises and tenancy	123
		Exemption for small dwellings	123
		Meaning of discrimination	125
		Victimisation	127
		Enforcement and remedies	128
	6.3	Alterations to premises occupied under leases	128
		The duty to make reasonable adjustments to premises	128
		The problem of leases	129
		The effect of the DDA 1995 premises occupied under leases	130
		Employment and trade organisation cases	132
		Procedure and remedies	134
		Goods and services cases	136
		Management and disposal of premises	137
Chapter 7		EDUCATION	139
	7.1	Introduction	139
	7.2	Education and anti-discrimination law	139
		Disability Rights Task Force	143
	7.3	Education and policy-making	143
		Schools	144
		Teacher Training Agency	145
		Further education colleges and institutions	145
		Further education funding councils	147
		Local education authorities	147
		Universities and higher education institutions	148
Chapter 8		PUBLIC TRANSPORT	151
	8.1	Introduction	151
		Transport services and Part III of DDA 1995	151
		Transport employers and Part II of DDA 1995	152
		Public transport and Part V of DDA 1995	152
	8.2	Taxis	152
		Taxi accessibility regulations	153
		Taxis to be covered by the regulations	154
		Exemption regulations	155
		Swivel-seat regulations	156

		Duties of taxi drivers towards disabled passengers	156
		Taxi accessibility at designated transport facilities	159
		Application to Scotland and Northern Ireland	160
		Implementation	160
	8.3	Public service vehicles	160
		PSV accessibility regulations	161
		Accessibility certificates	163
		Type approval certificates	164
		Offences and exemptions	165
		Implementation	166
	8.4	Rail vehicles	167
		Rail vehicle accessibility regulations	167
		Offences	170
		Regulated rail vehicles	170
		Exemptions	171
	8.5	Aviation and shipping	172
Chapter 9		INSTITUTIONAL FRAMEWORK	175
	9.1	Introduction	175
	9.2	Disability Rights Commission	176
		Status	177
		Staffing of the Commission	177
		Commissioners	177
		Functions and powers	178
		Assistance in relation to proceedings	180
		Formal investigations	181
		Non-discrimination notices	185
		Action plans	188
		Agreements in lieu of enforcement action	191
		Persistent discrimination	192
		Disclosure of information	193
		Enforcement of court orders	193
		Offences	194
		Service of notices	194
	9.3	Codes of practice	195
	9.4	Guidance on meaning of disability	197
	9.5	Application to the Crown	199
	9.6	Application to Parliament	200
	9.7	Regulations and orders	201
Chapter 10		LIABILITY AND REMEDIES	203
	10.1	Causes of action	203
		Discrimination	203
		Victimisation	204
	10.2	Legal liability	206
		Aiding unlawful acts	206
		Liability of employers	207
		Liability of principals	208

		Statutory authority	209
		National security	210
	10.3	Employment cases	211
		Statutory questionnaire	211
		Employment tribunal proceedings	213
		Time-limits	214
		Conciliation	215
		Compromises or settlements	217
		Restriction on publicity	219
		The hearing and decision	220
		Remedies	221
		Declaration of rights	221
		Compensation and interest	221
		Unfair dismissal compensation and disability discrimination	223
		Recommendations	225
		Future reform	226
	10.4	Services and premises cases	227
		Proceedings in the county court or sheriff's court	227
		Time-limits	227
		Conciliation	228
		Settlements	229
		Remedies	230
Appendix I		DISABILITY DISCRIMINATION ACT 1995	231
Appendix II		DISABILITY RIGHTS COMMISSION ACT 1999	309
Index			333

TABLE OF CASES

References are to paragraph numbers.

AB v South Western Water Services Ltd, *sub nom* Gibbons v South Western
Water Services Ltd [1993] QB 507, [1993] 2 WLR 507, [1993] 1 All ER
609, CA   10.3.31

AM v WC and SPV [1999] ICR 1218, [1999] IRLR 410, (1999) IDS Brief
B641/3, EAT   10.2.2, 10.2.4

Abbey Life Assurance Co Ltd v Tansell [2000] IRLR 387, (2000) IDS Brief
661/5, CA; *sub nom* MHC Consulting Services Ltd v Tansell [1999] IRLR
677, (1999) IDS Brief B649/8, EAT   3.9.2

Aldred v Nacanco [1987] IRLR 292, CA   10.2.5

Alexander v Home Office [1988] 1 WLR 968, [1988] 2 All ER 118, [1988]
IRLR 190, CA   10.3.31

Amies v Inner London Education Authority [1977] 2 All ER 100, [1977] ICR
308, [1977] 1 CMLR 336, EAT   10.3.10

Anyanwu v South Bank Students' Union [2000] ICR 221, [2000] IRLR 36,
(1999) IDS Brief B650/3, CA   10.2.2

Applin v Race Relations Board [1975] AC 259, [1974] 2 WLR 541, [1974] 2 All
ER 73, HL   5.2.7

Arboshe v East London Bus & Coach Co Ltd (1999) EAT/877/98   3.6.11

Aziz v Trinity Street Taxis Ltd [1988] 3 WLR 79, [1988] ICR 534, [1988] IRLR
204, CA   10.1.8

BP Chemicals Ltd v Gillick [1995] IRLR 128, EAT   3.9.3

Balgobin and Francis v Tower Hamlets London Borough [1987] ICR 829,
[1987] IRLR 401, (1987) 84 LS Gaz 2530, EAT   10.2.6

Barclays Bank plc v Kapur [1991] 2 AC 355, [1991] 2 WLR 401, [1991] 1 All
ER 646, [1991] ICR 208, HL   10.3.10

Barker v Westbridge International Ltd (2000) EAT/1180/98   2.1.4

Baynton v Saurus General Engineers Ltd [2000] ICR 375, [1999] IRLR 604,
(1999) IDS Brief B646/5, EAT   3.5.1, 3.5.6, 3.5.7, 3.6.23

Bilka-Kaufhaus GmbH v Karin Weber von Hartz (C-170/84) [1987] ICR 110,
[1986] IRLR 317, [1986] 2 CMLR 701, ECJ   3.5.5

Boddington v Lawton [1994] ICR 478, (1994) *The Times*, February 19   4.2.3

Bradford City Metropolitan Borough Council v Arora [1991] 2 QB 507, [1991]
2 WLR 1377, [1991] 3 All ER 545, [1991] IRLR 165, CA   10.3.31

British Airways Engine Overhaul Ltd v Francis [1981] ICR 278, [1981] IRLR 9,
EAT   10.1.8

British Gas plc v Sharma [1991] ICR 19, [1991] IRLR 101, (1990) *The Times*,
October 11, EAT   10.3.39

British Sugar plc v Kirker [1998] IRLR 624, EAT   3.3.8, 3.4.4, 3.4.5, 3.4.8, 3.6.13

Broadbent v Crisp [1974] 1 All ER 1052, [1974] ICR 248, [1974] ITR 147   4.2.3

Butterfield v Rapidmark Ltd t/a 3 MV (1998) EAT 131/98   3.6.3

Buxton v Equinox Designs Ltd [1999] ICR 269, [1999] IRLR 158, (1998) *The
Times*, December 3, EAT   10.3.28

Calder v James Finlay Corporation Ltd [1989] ICR 157n, [1989] IRLR 55,
    EAT   10.3.10
Carrington v Helix Lighting [1990] ICR 25, [1990] IRLR 6, (1990) 87(1) LSG
    30, EAT   10.3.5
Charter v Race Relations Board [1973] AC 868, [1973] 2 WLR 299, [1973] 1
    All ER 512, HL   5.2.7
Chief Constable of Lincolnshire Police v Stubbs [1999] ICR 547, [1999] IRLR
    81, (1999) IDS Brief B630/3, EAT   10.2.5
Chief Constable of West Yorkshire Police v Khan [2000] IRLR 324, [2000] TLR
    185, (2000) IDS Brief 660/12, CA   10.1.8, 10.3.31
Clark v Novacold Ltd [1999] 2 All ER 977, [1999] ICR 951; *sub nom* Clark v
    TGD Ltd t/a Novacold [1999] IRLR 318, CA; [1998] IRLR 420,
    EAT   3.1.1, 3.1.2, 3.3.8, 3.4.1, 3.4.8, 3.4.13, 3.6.3, 3.6.7, 4.4.2, 5.1.2, 5.4.5, 5.4.7
Clymo v Wandsworth London Borough Council [1989] ICR 250, [1989] IRLR
    241, [1989] 2 CMLR 577, EAT   3.3.7
Colt Group Ltd v Couchman [2000] ICR 327, EAT   3.2.8
Conservative and Unionist Central Office v Burrell [1982] 1 WLR 522, [1982]
    2 All ER 1, [1982] STC 317, CA   4.2.4
Construction Industry Training Board v Labour Force Ltd [1970] 3 All ER 220,
    [1970] ITR 290, (1970) 9 KIR 269, DC   3.9.1
Coote v Granada Hospitality Ltd (No 2) [1999] ICR 942, [1999] IRLR 452,
    EAT   3.3.8
Cornelius v University College of Swansea [1987] IRLR 141, (1987) 131 SJ 359,
    (1987) 84 LS Gaz 1141, CA   10.1.8

Daley v Allied Suppliers Ltd [1983] ICR 90, [1983] IRLR 14, (1983) 80 LS Gaz
    213, EAT   3.9.1
Deane v London Borough of Ealing [1993] ICR 329, [1993] IRLR 209, EAT   10.4.6,
                                                                                          10.3.31
Del Monte Foods Ltd v Mundon [1980] ICR 694, [1980] IRLR 224, EAT   3.4.12
DPP v Marshall [1998] ICR 518, [1999] IRLR 494, EAT   10.3.11
Dockers' Labour Club and Institute Ltd v Race Relations Board [1976] AC 285,
    [1974] 3 WLR 533, [1974] 3 All ER 529, HL   5.2.7

Enterprise Glass Co Ltd v Miles [1990] ICR 787, EAT   10.2.4

Foster v Hampshire Fire and Rescue Service (1998) 43 BMLR 186, EAT   2.1.4
Foster v South Glamorgan Health Authority [1988] ICR 526, [1988] IRLR 277,
    EAT   10.3.11
Furniture, Timber and Allied Trades Union v Modgill; PEL v Modgill [1980]
    IRLR 142, EAT   4.4.3

Gilbert v Kembridge Fibres Ltd [1984] ICR 188, [1984] IRLR 52, (1984) 134
    NLJ 256, EAT   10.3.14
Gittins v Oxford Radcliffe NHS Trust (2000) EAT/193/99   2.3.8
Glasgow City Council v Zafar. *See* Zafar v Glasgow City Council
Goodwin v The Patent Office [1999] ICR 302, [1999] IRLR 4, EAT   2.1.2, 2.2.2, 2.3.5,
                                                                       2.4.2, 2.5.3, 2.5.14, 3.1.2
Greenwood v British Airways plc [1999] ICR 969, [1999] IRLR 600, (1999) IDS
    Brief B647/5, EAT   2.1.1, 2.6.3

Hampson v Department of Education and Science [1991] AC 171, [1990] 3
    WLR 42, [1990] 2 All ER 513, [1990] IRLR 302, HL, [1989] IRLR 69, CA   3.5.5,
    10.2.9

Hanlon v University of Huddersfield (1998) EAT 166/98   3.6.19

Hardie v CD Northern Ltd [2000] ICR 207, [2000] IRLR 87, (2000) IDS Brief
    655/3, EAT   3.2.8

Harris (Representative of Andrews) v Lewisham and Guy's Mental Health NHS
    Trust [2000] IRLR 320, (2000) IDS Brief 660/7, CA   10.3.7

Harrods Ltd v Remick [1997] IRLR 583, (1997) *The Times,* July 22, CA   3.9.1

Hawkins v Ball and Barclays Bank plc [1996] IRLR 258, EAT   10.3.11

Heasmans (a firm) v Clarity Cleaning Co Ltd [1987] ICR 949, [1987] IRLR
    286, (1987) 137 NLJ 101, CA   10.2.5

Heggison v A & W Bernard (2000) EAT/1276/99   3.4.13

Heil v Rankin [2000] IRLR 334, [2000] TLR 224, CA   10.3.31

Heinz (HJ) & Co Ltd v Kenrick [2000] ICR 491, [2000] IRLR 144, (2000) IDS
    Brief 657/3, EAT   3.1.2, 3.4.13, 3.5.7, 3.6.13, 3.6.23, 5.4.7, 5.4.8

Hillingdon London Borough Council v Commission for Racial Equality. *See* R v
    Commission for Racial Equality ex parte Hillingdon London Borough
    Council

Home Office v Evans 18 November 1993, unreported, DC   4.2.3

Humphries v Environment Agency (1999) EAT/24/95   3.6.11

Hutchinson v Westward Television Ltd [1977] ICR 279, [1977] IRLR 69,
    (1976) 12 ITR 125, EAT   10.3.11

Irving and Irving v Post Office [1987] IRLR 289, CA   10.2.5

Jones v Tower Boot Co Ltd [1997] 2 All ER 406, [1997] ICR 254, [1997] IRLR
    168, CA   10.2.5

Kapadia v London Borough of Lambeth [2000] IRLR 14, (1999) IDS Brief
    B645/11, EAT, 9 June 2000, unreported, CA   2.1.4, 2.5.13, 2.5.14

Kelly v Northern Ireland Housing Executive; Loughran v Northern Ireland
    Housing Executive [1998] 3 WLR 735, [1998] ICR 828, [1998] IRLR 593,
    HL   3.2.4

Kenny v Hampshire Constabulary [1999] ICR 27, [1999] IRLR 76, EAT   3.6.7

Kent County Council v Mingo [2000] IRLR 90, (2000) IDS Brief 657/5, EAT   3.6.13

King v The Great Britain-China Centre [1992] ICR 516, [1991] IRLR 513,
    (1991) *The Times*, October 30, CA   3.4.5, 10.3.5

Kirby v Manpower Services Commission [1980] 1 WLR 725, [1980] 3 All ER
    334, [1980] IRLR 229, EAT   10.1.8

Lancashire County Council v Mason [1998] ICR 907, EAT   3.2.1, 10.2.7

Law Hospital NHS Trust v Rush (2000) EAT/842/99   2.4.2

Littlewoods Organisation plc v Traynor [1993] IRLR 154, EAT   10.3.10

London Borough of Hammersmith and Fulham v Farnsworth (2000)
    EAT/461/99   3.4.13

London Borough of Hillingdon v Morgan (1999) IDS Brief B649/10, EAT   3.1.2,
    3.6.11, 3.6.13, 3.12.2

London Underground Ltd v Bragg (1999) EAT/847/98   2.1.4, 2.4.2, 2.5.2, 2.5.7

Loughran v Northern Ireland Housing Executive. *See* Kelly v Northern Ireland
    Housing Executive; Loughran v Northern Ireland Housing Executive

MHC Consulting Services Ltd v Tansell. *See* Abbey Life Assurance Co Ltd v
  Tansell
Midland Cold Storage Ltd v Turner [1972] 3 All ER 773, [1972] ICR 230, 116
  SJ 783, NIRC   4.2.4
Mirror Group Newspapers v Gunning [1986] 1 WLR 546, [1986] 1 All ER 385,
  [1986] ICR 145, CA   3.2.3, 3.9.1
Morganite Electrical Carbon Ltd v Donne [1988] ICR 8, EAT   10.3.34
Morse v Wiltshire County Council [1998] ICR 1023, [1998] IRLR 352, (1998)
  44 BMLR 58, EAT   3.6.5, 3.6.14
Motherwell Railway Club v McQueen [1989] ICR 418, EAT   10.3.34
Mulligan v Commissioner for Inland Revenue (1999) EAT/691/99   3.6.11
Murphy v Sheffield Hallam University (2000) EAT/6/99   3.4.9
Murray v Powertech (Scotland) Ltd [1992] IRLR 257, EAT   10.3.31

Nagarajan v London Regional Transport [1999] 3 WLR 425, [1999] 4 All ER
  65, [1999] ICR 877, [1999] IRLR 572, HL   3.4.9, 10.1.8
Nelson v Tyne and Wear Passenger Transport Executive [1978] ICR 1183,
  (1978) 122 SJ 642, EAT   10.3.40
Noone v North West Thames Regional Health Authority (No 2) [1988] ICR
  813, [1988] IRLR 530, CA   10.3.39

O'Neill v Symm & Co Ltd [1998] ICR 481, [1998] IRLR 233, EAT 2.3.8, 3.4.13, 5.4.7,
                                                                                                  5.4.8
O'Shea (CJ) Construction Ltd v Bassi [1998] ICR 1130, EAT   3.9.1
Oxford v Department of Health and Social Security [1977] ICR 884, [1977]
  IRLR 225, (1977) 12 ITR 436, EAT   10.3.6

Post Office v Adekeye [1997] ICR 110, [1997] IRLR 105, (1996) 93(46) LSG
  29, CA   3.3.8
Post Office v Jones [2000] ICR 388, EAT   3.5.7, 3.6.5, 3.6.22, 3.6.23, 10.2.9, 10.3.38
Prestige Group plc, Re; Commission for Racial Equality v Prestige Group plc
  [1984] ICR 473, HL   9.2.15

Quinlan v B & Q plc (1998) IDS Brief 614, EAT 1386/97   2.1.4

R v Commission for Racial Equality ex parte Hillingdon London Borough
  Council [1982] AC 779, [1982] 3 WLR 159, [1982] IRLR 424, HL   9.2.15
R v Entry Clearance Officer Bombay ex parte Amin [1983] 2 AC 818, [1983] 3
  WLR 258, [1983] 2 All ER 864, HL   5.2.2
R v Powys County Council ex parte Hambidge (No 2) [2000] TLR 196, (2000)
  The Times, March 16, CA   5.4.5
R v Secretary of State for Employment ex parte Equal Opportunities
  Commission [1995] 1 AC 1, [1994] 2 WLR 409, [1994] 1 All ER 910,
  [1994] ICR 317, [1994] IRLR 176, HL   3.5.5, 9.2.6
Rainey v Greater Glasgow Health Board [1987] AC 224, [1986] 3 WLR 1017,
  [1987] 1 All ER 65, [1987] ICR 129, [1987] IRLR 26, HL   3.5.5
Read v Tiverton District Council and Bull [1977] IRLR 202, IT   10.2.4
Rice v Fon-A-Car [1980] ICR 133, EAT   3.9.1
Ridout v TC Group [1998] IRLR 628, EAT   3.1.2, 3.6.21
Rose v Bouchet [1999] IRLR 463   5.6.4, 5.6.5, 6.2.14

Sheehan v Post Office Counters Ltd [1999] ICR 734, EAT   3.2.3
Sheriff v Klyne Tugs (Lowestoft) Ltd [1999] ICR 1170, [1999] IRLR 481,
    (1999) IDS Brief B645/3, CA   10.3.31
Simon v Brimham Associates [1987] ICR 596, [1987] IRLR 307, CA   3.4.12
Sougrin v Haringey Health Authority [1991] ICR 791, [1991] IRLR 447, EAT 10.3.10
Swithland Motors plc v Clarke [1994] ICR 231, [1994] IRLR 275, EAT   10.3.10

Tanna v Post Office [1981] ICR 374, EAT   3.9.1
Taylor v Lifesign Ltd (2000) EAT/147/98   3.2.6
Thornhill v London Central Bus Co Ltd (2000) EAT/463/99   2.4.1

Vicary v British Telecommunications plc [1999] IRLR 680, (1999) IDS Brief
    B650/7, EAT   2.1.2, 2.2.1, 2.4.2, 2.5.2, 2.5.4, 2.5.13
Virdee v ECC Quarries Ltd [1978] IRLR 295, IT   10.3.5

Waters v Metropolitan Police Commissioner [1997] ICR 1073, [1997] IRLR
    589, (1997) *The Times*, July 21, CA   10.1.8
Wiltshire Police Authority v Wynn [1981] QB 95, [1980] 3 WLR 445, [1980]
    ICR 649, CA   4.2.3
Writers' Guild of Great Britain v British Broadcasting Corporation [1974] 1 All
    ER 574, [1974] ICR 234, NIRC   4.2.3

Zafar v Glasgow City Council; *sub nom* Glasgow City Council v Zafar [1997] 1
    WLR 1659, [1998] ICR 125, [1998] IRLR 36, HL   3.4.5

TABLE OF STATUTES

References are to paragraph numbers.

Access to Medical Reports Act
1988 — 3.3.12
Agricultural Wages Act 1948
s 5 — 3.5.9
Agricultural Wages (Scotland)
Act 1949
s 5 — 3.5.9
Americans with Disabilities Act
1990 (USA) — 1.1.2, 1.1.5

British Transport Commission
Act 1949
s 53 — 9.5.4
Broadcasting Act 1990 — 5.2.2
Broadcasting Act 1996 — 5.2.2
Building Act 1984
s 122 — 3.6.15

Charities Act (Northern Ireland)
1964 — 3.2.13
Chronically Sick and Disabled
Persons Act 1970
s 2(1) — 5.4.5
Civic Government (Scotland) Act
1982
s 20(2A) — 8.2.14
Contempt of Court Act 1981
s 15 — 9.2.36
County Courts Act 1984
s 55 — 9.2.36
(1)–(4) — 9.2.36
Courts and Legal Services Act
1990 — 10.3.17
Criminal Justice and Public
Order Act 1994
s 126 — 4.2.3
s 127 — 9.5.4
Crown Proceedings Act 1947
Pts II–V — 9.5.1
s 20 — 9.5.1
s 23 — 9.5.1
s 44 — 9.5.1

Disability Discrimination Act
1992 (Australia) — 1.1.2
Disability Discrimination Act
1995
Pt I — 1.2.2, 2.1.2, 10.1.7
Pt II — 1.2.2, 2.1.1, 2.5.7, 2.6.3, 2.8.1,
3.1.2, 3.2.3, 3.2.4, 3.2.6,
3.2.13, 3.2.14, 3.3.1, 3.3.11,
3.4.1, 3.6.1, 3.7.1, 3.7.5,
3.7.8, 3.8.3, 3.9.6, 3.10.1,
3.10.2, 3.10.3, 4.1.1, 4.2.3,
4.2.6, 4.4.1, 4.7.1, 5.2.2,
5.4.1, 5.4.5, 5.4.7, 5.5.3,
5.5.10, 5.6.3, 5.6.4, 6.1.2,
6.2.5, 7.1.1, 7.2.3, 8.1.4,
9.2.6, 9.2.9, 9.2.15, 9.2.19,
9.2.31, 9.2.34, 9.3.4, 9.3.6,
9.5.2, 9.5.3, 9.5.4, 9.6.2,
10.1.2, 10.1.4, 10.1.5,
10.2.12, 10.3.1, 10.3.4,
10.3.5, 10.3.7, 10.3.15,
10.3.26, 10.3.29, 10.4.4
Pt III — 1.2.2, 2.8.1, 3.3.11, 3.7.5, 3.8.3,
3.8.4, 3.9.4, 4.1.2, 4.2.6,
4.2.7, 4.4.1, 4.6.4, 5.1.2,
5.1.3, 5.1.4, 5.2.2, 5.2.4,
5.2.6, 5.2.7, 5.2.8, 5.2.9,
5.3.1, 5.4.1, 5.4.2, 5.4.5,
5.4.6, 5.4.8, 5.5.2, 5.5.3,
5.6.2, 5.6.3, 5.6.4, 5.6.6,
5.7.1, 6.1.1, 6.1.2, 6.2.13,
6.2.17, 6.3.2, 6.3.5, 6.3.15,
7.1.1, 7.2.2, 7.2.3, 7.2.4,
7.2.5, 7.2.6, 7.2.7, 7.2.8,
7.3.5, 8.1.2, 8.1.3, 8.1.4,
8.5.1, 9.2.6, 9.2.9, 9.2.15,
9.2.19, 9.2.31, 9.2.34, 9.3.4,
9.3.6, 9.6.2, 10.1.3, 10.1.4,
10.1.5, 10.2.11, 10.2.12,
10.3.8, 10.4.1, 10.4.2, 10.4.4,
10.4.5, 10.4.6, 10.4.7, 10.4.9,
10.4.10, 10.4.11
Pt IV — 7.1.1, 7.3.1, 7.3.6, 8.5.1, 10.4.4
Pt V — 8.1.1, 8.1.5, 8.2.6, 8.2.15, 10.4.4
Pt VI — 1.2.2, 9.1.1
Pt VII — 1.2.2

Disability Discrimination Act
  1995 – *cont*

ss 1–3	1.2.2
s 1	2.1.2, 2.2.1., 2.8.3, 7.3.7
(1)	2.1.2, 2.4.1, 2.5.1, 3.5.5
(2)	2.1.2
s 2	2.1.2, 2.7.2, 7.3.7
(1)	2.8.1, 3.2.1
(2)	2.6.4, 2.8.1, 3.6.9
(4), (5)	2.8.2
s 3	2.1.2, 9.4.1, 9.7.1, 10.2.4
(1)	9.4.1
(2)	9.4.2
(3)	2.1.2, 9.4.1
(4), (5)	9.4.3
(6)	9.4.4
(7), (8)	9.4.4
(9)	9.4.4, 9.7.1
(10)	9.4.4
(11)(a), (b)	9.4.1
(12)	9.4.1, 9.4.4
ss 4–6	3.7.7, 3.9.3
ss 4–7	10.1.2, 10.3.7
ss 4–11	3.9.5
ss 4–18	1.2.2
s 4	3.2.1, 3.3.1, 3.5.6, 3.6.3, 3.6.22, 3.8.1, 3.8.6, 3.9.3, 10.1.2, 10.1.4, 10.2.7
(1)	3.4.2, 3.9.5, 10.1.2
(a)	3.3.2, 3.3.13, 3.4.2
(b)	3.3.3
(c)	3.3.4, 3.4.16
(2)	3.4.2, 3.7.1, 3.9.4, 3.9.5, 10.1.2
(a)	3.3.5, 3.8.1
(b), (c)	3.3.6, 3.8.1
(d)	3.3.8
(3)	3.3.9, 3.3.10, 3.8.1, 3.9.4, 3.9.5
(a)–(c)	3.3.10
(4)	3.3.6, 3.3.9, 3.5.8, 3.9.4, 4.3.4, 6.2.5
(5)	3.3.1, 10.1.4, 10.1.7
(6)	3.2.1
s 5	2.5.2, 3.4.1, 3.4.6, 3.7.8, 3.8.6, 3.9.5, 4.4.1, 5.4.1, 6.3.1
(1)	3.4.1, 3.4.2, 3.4.11, 3.4.13, 3.6.3, 3.6.23, 5.4.7
(a)	3.4.3, 3.4.4, 3.4.8, 3.4.9, 3.4.11, 3.4.13, 3.5.1, 3.5.2, 3.5.6
(b)	3.4.8, 3.4.11, 3.5.1, 3.5.6, 3.5.7
(2)	3.4.1, 3.5.1, 3.5.6, 3.6.5, 3.6.22
(a), (b)	3.6.3

s 5(3)	3.5.1, 3.5.3, 3.5.4, 3.5.6, 3.5.7, 3.6.23
(4)	3.5.1, 3.5.6, 3.5.7, 3.6.3, 3.6.5, 3.6.22, 3.6.23
(5)	3.5.6, 3.5.7, 3.6.23, 5.6.3
(6)	3.1.2, 3.5.8, 3.5.9, 3.8.6
(7)	3.1.2
(a)	3.8.6
s 6	2.5.2, 3.3.7, 3.3.14, 3.4.1, 3.4.2, 3.4.8, 3.4.15, 3.5.3, 3.5.6, 3.5.9, 3.6.1, 3.6.3, 3.6.5, 3.6.8, 3.6.17, 3.6.22, 3.6.23, 3.9.5, 3.9.8, 4.5.1, 6.1.2, 6.3.6, 6.3.9, 8.1.4, 10.3.26, 10.3.38
(1)	3.5.5, 3.6.4, 3.6.5, 3.6.8, 3.6.9, 3.6.11, 3.6.14
(a)	3.4.2, 3.6.6
(b)	6.3.1
(2)	3.6.5, 3.6.11
(a)	3.6.6
(b)	3.6.6, 3.6.7
(3)	3.6.5, 3.6.7, 3.6.11, 4.5.6
(a)	6.3.1
(4)	3.6.5, 3.6.12, 3.6.16, 5.5.3, 6.3.1
(5)(a), (b)	3.6.19
(6)	3.4.11
(a), (b)	3.6.19
(7)	3.6.1
(8)	3.1.2, 3.6.12, 3.6.16, 4.5.5
(g), (h)	3.6.8
(9)	3.6.12, 3.6.16
(10)	3.1.2, 3.6.11
(11)	3.7.4, 3.8.7
(12)	3.6.22
s 7	3.4.17, 3.9.5
(1)	3.2.6, 3.2.7
(2)	3.2.9
(3)	3.2.9, 3.2.10
(4)	3.2.9
(5), (6)	3.2.10
(7)	3.2.10
(9), (10)	3.2.10
s 8	3.10.1, 3.10.3, 4.7.1, 6.3.13, 9.2.9, 9.2.34, 10.2.11
(1)	10.3.7
(2)	6.3.14, 10.3.26
(a)	10.3.27
(b)	10.3.29
(c)	10.3.37
(4)	10.3.31
(5)	10.3.40
(8)	10.3.8
s 9	3.10.2, 3.10.3, 4.7.1, 6.3.4, 6.3.8

Disability Discrimination Act
1995 – *cont*

s 9(1)	10.3.14
(c)	10.3.15
(2)(a)	10.3.14, 10.3.15
(b)	10.3.15
(3)(a)	10.3.16
(b)	10.3.19
(c)	10.3.20
(4)	10.3.17
(b), (c)	10.3.17
(4A)(a)–(d)	10.3.18
(4B)	10.3.17
(5)	10.3.18
s 10(1)	3.2.13
(a), (b)	3.2.13
(2)(a), (b)	3.2.14
(3)	3.2.13, 3.2.14
(4)	3.2.13
(5)	3.2.13
s 11	3.3.2, 3.4.14, 3.4.17, 10.3.7
(1)(a)–(d)	3.4.15
(e)(i), (ii)	3.4.15
(2)	3.4.16
(3)	3.4.15, 3.4.17
s 12	3.9.1, 3.9.2, 3.9.3, 3.9.5, 3.9.6, 3.9.7, 10.1.2, 10.1.4, 10.3.7
(1)	3.9.3, 3.9.4, 3.9.5, 10.1.2
(2)	3.9.4
(3)	3.1.2, 3.9.5, 3.9.8
(4)	3.9.5, 10.1.4, 10.1.7
(5)	3.9.3
(6)	3.9.1, 3.9.2
ss 13–15	10.3.7
s 13	4.1.1, 4.1.3, 4.2.1, 4.2.3, 4.3.1, 4.4.1, 4.4.5, 4.5.1, 4.7.1, 5.2.2, 5.2.7, 10.1.4
(1)	10.1.2
(a)	4.3.2
(b)	4.3.3
(2)	4.3.4, 10.1.2
(3)	4.4.5, 10.1.4, 10.1.7
(4)	4.2.1, 4.2.5, 4.2.6
ss 14–16	10.1.2
s 14	4.1.1, 4.1.3, 4.2.1, 4.4.1, 4.4.5, 4.7.1, 5.2.2, 5.2.7, 5.4.1
(1)	4.4.1, 4.4.2, 4.6.1
(a)	4.4.3
(b)	4.6.2
(2)	4.1.1, 4.4.1, 4.4.4, 4.5.1, 4.6.1
(b)	4.6.3
(3)	4.6.2
(4)	4.1.1, 4.6.3
(5)	4.1.1, 4.6.2
s 14(6)	4.6.2, 4.6.3
s 15	4.1.1, 4.1.3, 4.2.1, 4.4.1, 4.4.4, 4.4.5, 4.5.1, 4.5.6, 4.6.2, 4.6.3, 4.7.1, 5.2.2, 5.2.7, 6.1.2, 6.3.1, 6.3.6, 10.3.26
(1)	4.5.4
(a)	4.5.2
(b)	4.1.1, 4.5.3
(2)	4.5.2
(3)(a), (b)	4.5.5
(c)	4.5.5
(d), (e)	4.5.5
(4)(a), (b)	4.5.4
(5)	4.5.4
(6)	4.5.1
(7)	4.5.2, 4.5.3, 4.5.5
(8)	4.5.5
(10)	4.5.1
s 16	3.6.8, 3.6.22, 4.5.6, 6.1.2, 6.3.5, 6.3.10, 6.3.13, 10.1.2, 10.3.26
(1)	6.3.6
(a)	6.3.5
(b), (c)	6.3.6
(2)	6.3.8
(a), (b)	6.3.6
(c), (d)	6.3.6, 6.3.10
(2A)(i)–(iii)	6.3.7
(3)	6.3.5
(4)(a), (b)	6.3.6
s 17	3.3.11, 10.1.2
(1)	3.7.5
(a)	3.7.5
(b)	3.7.5
(3)	3.7.8
(4)	3.7.5
s 18	3.3.11, 3.8.1, 3.8.2, 3.8.4, 3.8.5, 10.1.2
(1)(a), (b)	3.8.2
(2)	3.8.3
(3)	3.8.3, 3.8.5
(4)	3.8.3
ss 19–21	1.2.2, 5.1.2, 5.4.1, 6.2.8, 6.2.13, 7.1.1, 7.2.2, 8.1.2, 8.1.3
s 19	3.8.3, 10.1.3, 10.1.4, 10.2.4
(1)	5.1.2, 5.3.5, 5.4.1, 5.5.2, 10.1.3
(a)	5.1.4, 5.3.2, 5.6.10
(b)	5.1.2, 5.1.4, 5.3.5, 5.5.2, 5.5.4, 5.5.12
(c)	5.1.4, 5.3.3, 5.6.11
(d)	5.1.4, 5.3.4, 5.4.5, 5.6.11, 5.6.12
(2)(a)	5.1.4, 5.2.1
(b)	5.2.4, 5.2.7

Disability Discrimination Act

1995 – *cont*

s 19(2)(c)   5.2.1, 5.4.5
   (3)   5.2.1, 5.2.3
      (h)   5.4.5, 7.2.4
   (4)   5.4.1, 10.1.5, 10.1.7
   (5)   4.2.7, 7.1.1
      (a)   5.2.9, 7.2.1, 7.2.2, 7.2.5
         (i)   7.2.2
         (ii)   7.2.2, 7.2.7
      (b)   5.2.9, 8.1.2, 8.5.1
      (c)   5.1.3, 5.2.9, 7.1.1, 7.2.5
   (6)   4.2.7, 7.2.2, 7.2.7
s 20   3.8.3, 4.4.1, 5.4.1, 5.6.14, 6.2.15,
                          6.3.2, 10.1.3
   (1)   5.1.2, 5.4.2, 5.4.7, 5.4.8, 5.5.1,
                                  5.5.2
      (a)   5.4.2, 5.4.5, 5.6.2
      (b)   5.4.8, 5.6.1
   (2)   5.1.2, 5.5.2, 5.5.4
      (b)   5.6.1
   (3)   5.4.8, 5.6.1
      (a)   5.6.1, 5.6.5
      (b)   5.6.1, 5.6.5
   (4)   5.4.8, 5.6.1, 5.6.6, 6.2.15
      (a)   5.4.8, 5.6.7
      (b)   5.6.8
      (c)   5.4.8, 5.6.10
      (d)   5.4.8, 5.6.11
      (e)   5.6.12
   (5)   5.6.13
   (7)   5.1.3, 5.6.9
   (8)   5.1.3, 5.6.1, 5.6.14
   (9)   5.5.2, 5.6.1
s 21   5.1.2, 5.1.4, 5.3.5, 5.5.2, 5.5.4,
       5.5.7, 5.5.10, 5.6.1, 5.6.5,
       6.1.2, 6.3.2, 6.3.6, 10.1.3,
                               10.4.11
   (1)   5.5.5, 5.5.6, 5.5.12
   (2)   5.5.7, 5.5.8, 5.5.9, 5.5.10,
                         5.5.12, 6.3.2
      (a)   5.1.2, 5.5.7, 5.5.14, 6.3.2,
                                   8.1.3
      (b)   5.1.2, 5.5.7, 5.5.14, 6.3.2,
                                   8.1.3
      (c)   5.1.2, 5.5.7, 5.5.14, 8.1.3
      (d)   5.5.7, 6.3.2
   (3)(a)   5.5.7
      (b)   5.5.10
   (4)   5.5.6, 5.5.13
      (a), (b)   5.5.12
   (5)(a)–(d)   5.5.5
      (e)   5.1.3, 5.5.8
      (f)   5.5.8

s 21(5)(g)   5.5.13
      (h)   5.1.3, 5.5.13
   (6)   5.5.3
   (7)–(9)   5.5.3, 5.5.12
   (10)   5.5.2
ss 22–24   6.1.1, 6.1.2, 6.2.8, 6.2.10,
             6.2.13, 6.2.14, 6.2.17, 6.3.2,
                          6.3.19, 10.1.3
ss 22–28   1.2.2
s 22   6.2.10, 6.2.13, 6.2.14, 6.2.17,
                         10.1.4, 10.2.4
   (1)   6.2.1, 6.2.8, 6.2.9, 6.2.11,
                        6.2.12, 10.1.3
      (a)   6.2.2
      (b)   6.2.3
      (c)   6.2.4
   (2)   6.2.9
   (3)   6.2.1, 6.2.11, 10.1.3
      (a), (b)   6.2.5
      (c)   6.2.6
   (4)   6.2.1, 6.2.7, 6.2.11, 6.2.12,
                               10.1.3
   (5)   6.2.7, 10.1.4
   (6)   6.2.8, 6.2.9, 6.2.10
   (7)   6.2.17, 10.1.7
   (8)   6.2.10
s 23(1)   6.2.11
   (2)(a)–(c)   6.2.12
      (d)   6.2.11
   (3)–(5)   6.2.11
   (6), (7)   6.2.12
s 24   4.4.1, 5.6.4, 6.2.1, 6.2.13, 6.2.14,
                        6.2.15, 6.2.16
   (1)   6.2.13
      (a), (b)   6.2.14
   (2)   6.2.14
      (a), (b)   6.2.14
   (3)   6.2.15
   (4)   6.2.14
   (5)   5.1.3, 6.2.15, 6.2.16
ss 25–28   5.1.2, 6.2.18
s 25   5.7.1, 6.3.16, 9.2.9, 9.2.34, 10.2.11
   (1)   5.8.1, 10.4.1
   (2)   5.8.1, 10.4.10
   (3), (4)   5.8.1, 10.4.1
   (5)   5.8.1, 10.4.11
s 26   6.3.4, 6.3.8, 6.3.19
   (1)   10.4.7
   (2)   10.4.9
   (3)–(6)   10.4.8
s 27   5.5.7, 6.1.2, 6.3.5, 6.3.19, 10.1.3,
                               10.4.11
   (1)   6.3.6
      (a)   6.3.5

Disability Discrimination Act		s 39	8.2.16
1995 – *cont*		ss 40–45	8.3.2
s 27(1)(b), (c)	6.3.6	ss 40–48	8.3.1
(2)	6.3.8	s 40	8.3.8, 8.3.9, 8.3.16, 8.3.17, 9.7.1
(a)–(d)	6.3.6	(1)	8.3.3
(3)	6.3.5	(a), (b)	8.3.3
(4)(a), (b)	6.3.6	(2)	8.3.5
s 28	10.4.4, 10.4.5	(3)(a)–(c)	8.3.7
(1)	10.4.4, 10.4.5	(4)	8.3.7
(2)–(8)	10.4.5	(5)	8.3.2, 8.3.4
ss 29–31	1.2.2, 7.3.1	(6)	8.3.4, 9.7.1
s 29(1)	7.3.2	(7)	8.3.3, 8.3.10, 8.3.13
(2)	7.3.3	s 41	8.3.10, 8.3.14, 8.3.15, 8.3.16,
(3)	7.3.4		8.3.17, 9.7.1
s 30	7.3.8	(1)	8.3.15
(1)	7.3.6	(a), (b)	8.3.9
(2), (3)	7.3.7	(2)	8.3.10
(4)	7.3.10	(3)	8.3.9, 8.3.15
(5)	7.3.12	(4)	8.3.9
(6)	7.3.12, 7.3.13	s 42	8.3.9, 8.3.11, 8.3.15, 8.3.16,
(7), (8)	7.3.11		8.3.17, 9.7.1
s 31(1), (2)	7.3.12	(1)	8.3.11, 8.3.12
(3)	7.3.12, 7.3.13	(2)	8.3.11
ss 32–39	8.2.15	(3), (4)	8.3.13
ss 32–49	1.2.2	(5)	8.3.13
s 32	8.2.10, 8.2.13	(a)	8.3.11
(1)	8.2.2	(6)	8.3.11, 8.3.14
(2)(a)–(c)	8.2.3	(7)(a), (b)	8.3.14
(3), (4)	8.2.3	(8)	8.3.13
(5)	8.2.3, 8.2.4	s 43	8.3.16, 8.3.17, 9.7.1
s 33(1)–(4)	8.2.14	(1)–(3)	8.3.16
s 34	8.2.5, 8.2.8	s 44	8.3.12
(1)	8.2.5, 8.2.8	(1), (2)	8.3.12
(2), (3)	8.2.5	(3)–(6)	8.3.9, 8.3.13
(4)	8.2.5, 9.7.1	s 45	8.3.9, 8.3.12, 8.3.13
s 35	8.2.7, 8.2.8	(1)(a)	8.3.11
(1)–(4)	8.2.7	(b)	8.3.9
(5), (6)	8.2.8	s 46	8.4.1, 8.4.2, 8.4.6, 8.4.9
(7)	8.2.7, 8.2.8	(1)	8.4.2, 8.4.7
s 36	8.2.11, 8.2.13	(a), (b)	8.4.2
(1), (2)	8.2.9	(2)	8.4.2, 8.4.3
(3)	8.2.11	(a)–(g)	8.4.3
(a)–(e)	8.2.9	(3), (4)	8.4.6
(4)(a), (b)	8.2.10	(5)	8.4.2, 9.7.1
(5)	8.2.9	(a)–(c)	8.4.5
(6)	8.2.10	(6)	8.4.3, 8.4.5, 8.4.6, 8.4.7, 8.4.8,
(7)(a), (b)	8.2.11		8.4.9
(8), (9)	8.2.11	(7)	8.4.8
s 37	8.2.12, 8.2.13	(8), (9)	8.4.9
(1)(a), (b)	8.2.12	(10)	8.4.6
(2)–(4)	8.2.12	(11)	8.4.2
(5)–(8)	8.2.13	s 47	8.4.1, 8.4.10, 8.4.11
(9)–(11)	8.2.12	(1)–(5)	8.4.10
s 38(1)–(3)	8.2.11, 8.2.13	s 48	8.3.8, 8.4.6

Disability Discrimination Act
  1995 – *cont*
  s 48(1)–(3)   8.3.8, 8.4.6
  s 49   8.2.11, 8.2.13, 8.3.9, 8.3.13
  ss 50–70   1.2.2
  s 50(2), (3)   9.1.1
    (9)   9.1.2
    (10)   9.1.2
  ss 51–54   9.3.4
  s 51(1)   9.3.1
    (2)   5.1.3, 9.3.1
  s 52   9.3.1
    (2)   9.3.5
      (a), (b)   9.3.1
  s 53   4.1.1, 9.3.3
    (1)(a)   3.1.2
    (4)–(6)   3.1.2
  s 53A(1)   9.3.4
    (2)   9.3.4
    (3)–(5)   9.3.5
    (6)(a)   9.3.4
      (b), (c)   9.3.5
    (7)   9.3.5
    (8)   9.3.6
  s 55   3.3.1, 3.4.1, 3.9.5, 4.4.1, 5.4.1,
                  9.2.9, 10.1.4
    (1), (2)   4.4.5, 6.2.17, 10.1.5
    (3), (4)   10.1.6
  s 56   10.3.1, 10.3.2
    (1)   10.3.1
    (2)   10.3.2
    (3)(a)   10.3.4
      (b)(i), (ii)   10.3.5
    (4)   10.3.2
    (5)   10.3.4, 10.3.6
  s 57   3.2.2, 10.2.2, 10.2.4, 10.3.7
    (1)   10.2.2
    (2)   10.2.4, 10.2.7
    (3)   10.2.3
    (4)   10.2.3, 10.2.4
    (5)   10.2.3
  s 58   3.2.2, 10.2.2, 10.2.4, 10.3.7
    (1)   10.2.4
    (2), (3)   10.2.7
    (4)   10.2.3, 10.2.4
    (5)   10.2.6, 10.2.7
  s 59   4.5.7, 5.2.2, 5.5.10, 5.6.7, 10.2.8
    (1), (2)   10.2.8
    (3)   10.2.12
  s 60(1)   9.1.2
    (6)(b)   9.1.2
  s 61   3.1.3, 3.11.1
    (1)   3.11.1
    (7)   3.11.1

s 62(1)   10.3.21
s 63   10.3.24
s 64   9.5.1, 9.5.4
  (1)   3.2.12
    (a), (b)   9.5.1
  (2)   9.5.2
    (a)   9.5.3
  (3), (4)   9.5.1
  (5)   3.2.12, 4.2.3, 9.5.4
  (6)   3.2.12, 9.5.4
  (7)   3.2.12, 4.2.3, 9.5.4
  (8)   3.2.12, 9.5.2, 9.5.4
s 65(1)   9.6.1
  (2)–(4)   9.6.2
s 66(1)–(3)   9.5.3
s 67   3.7.8
  (1)   5.1.3, 8.3.17, 9.7.1
  (2)   5.1.3, 8.2.5, 8.3.4, 8.4.5, 9.7.1
  (3)   5.1.3, 8.2.5, 8.3.4, 8.4.5, 9.7.1
    (a), (b)   9.7.1
  (5)   9.7.1
  (6)   8.3.17, 9.7.1
  (7)   8.2.5, 8.3.4, 8.4.5
s 68   3.9.3
  (1)   2.3.6, 3.2.3, 3.2.5, 3.2.6, 3.4.1,
        3.9.1, 4.2.1, 4.2.3, 4.2.6,
       5.1.3, 6.2.5, 6.2.10, 8.2.5,
     9.7.1, 10.2.8, 10.3.9, 10.4.2
  (2)–(5)   3.2.5
s 70   3.1.3
  (3)   9.7.1
  (4)   3.12.1
  (6)   1.2.1, 3.2.1, 3.2.3
s 72   3.2.6
Schs 1–8   1.2.2
Sch 1   2.1.2, 2.2.1, 2.8.3, 7.3.7, 9.4.2
  para 1(1)   2.3.4, 2.3.5
    (2)   2.1.2, 2.3.4
      (a)   2.3.3
    (3)   2.3.3, 2.3.4
  para 2(1)   2.6.1, 2.6.4
    (2)   2.5.5, 2.6.3, 2.6.4
    (3)   2.5.5, 2.6.4
    (4)   2.1.2, 2.6.1
  para 3   2.3.3
    (1)   2.5.10
    (2)   2.1.2
    (3)   2.1.2, 2.5.11
  para 4   2.5.8
    (1)   2.4.1
    (2)   2.4.1
      (a)   2.1.2
  para 5   2.5.2
    (a)   2.1.2

Disability Discrimination Act
   1995 – *cont*
   Sch 1, para 6   2.3.2
                  (1), (2)   2.5.13
                  (3)(a), (b)   2.5.15
          para 7   2.1.3, 2.7.1, 3.11.1
                  (2)(a)   2.7.1, 2.7.2
                    (b)   2.7.2
                  (3)–(6)   2.7.1
                  (7)   2.7.1, 2.7.2
          para 8(1)   2.5.7
                  (a)   2.5.7
                  (2)   2.5.7
          para 49   2.7.1
   Sch 2   2.1.2, 2.7.2, 2.8.1, 7.3.7
          para 2   2.6.4, 2.8.1
          para 3   3.6.9
          para 4   3.6.19
          para 5   2.6.4
   Sch 3
          Pt I   3.10.3, 10.3.8
          Pt II   6.2.18
          para 1   3.10.1, 10.3.12
          para 2   3.10.1
                  (1), (2)   10.3.7
          para 3   3.10.1
                  (1)   10.3.9
                  (2)   10.3.11
                  (3)(a)–(c)   10.3.10
                  (4)   10.3.10
          para 4(1)(a)   10.2.11
                  (b)   10.1.28, 10.2.12
                  (2)   10.2.11, 10.2.12
          para 5(1), (2)   10.4.1
          para 6(1)   10.4.2, 10.4.6
                  (2)   10.4.6
                  (3)   10.4.2
                  (a)   10.4.3
                  (4)(b), (c)   10.4.3
                  (5)   10.4.3
          para 7   5.7.1, 10.4.10
          para 8(1)(a)   10.2.11
                  (b)   10.2.12
                  (2)   10.2.11, 10.2.12
   Sch 4   6.1.2, 6.3.5, 10.1.2, 10.1.3,
                        10.3.26, 10.4.11
          Pt I   3.6.8, 3.6.22, 4.5.6, 6.3.10,
                          6.3.13
          Pt II   5.5.7, 6.3.15, 6.3.19
          para 1   6.3.5, 6.3.13
          para 2(1)–(4)   6.3.14
                  (5)(a), (b)   6.3.14
                  (6)   6.3.14
                    (a)–(c)   6.3.14

Sch 4, para 2(7)   6.3.14
             (9)   6.3.14
          para 3   3.1.2, 6.3.10
          para 4   6.3.5
          para 5   6.3.15
          para 6(1)–(5)   6.3.16
          para 7(1)–(4)   6.3.17
               (5)(a), (b)   6.3.18
               (6)(a)–(c)   6.3.18
               (7), (8)   6.3.18
          para 8   6.3.16, 6.3.18
          para 9   6.3.5
   Sch 6   3.1.3
          para 5   3.12.1
                  (c)   3.12.2
   Sch 7   3.1.3, 3.12.1
          para 7(4)   3.2.13
   Sch 8   1.2.1
          para 2   9.4.1
                  (1)   2.1.2
          para 3   3.2.1
          para 4(3)   3.2.10
          para 7   3.2.14
                  (2)   3.2.14
                  (3)   3.2.13
          para 8   3.9.3
          para 9(1)   5.2.1
               (2), (3)   7.2.2
          para 12   5.7.1, 10.4.1
          para 14   10.4.4
          paras 16–23   8.2.16
          para 16(2)   8.2.4
          para 18   8.2.5
          para 19   8.2.7
          para 20   8.2.11
          para 21   8.2.13
               (3)   8.2.12
          para 24(1)   8.3.3
               (2)   8.3.2
               (3)   8.3.3
          para 25(1)   8.3.10
               (2)   8.3.9
          para 26   8.3.11
          para 27   8.3.16
          paras 28, 29   8.3.12
          para 30(1)   8.4.2
             (2), (3)   8.4.8
               (4)   8.4.2
          para 33   9.1.1
          paras 34, 35   9.1.1
          para 38   10.3.2
          para 39   10.2.8
          para 41   3.11.1
          para 44   9.5.1, 9.5.2

Disability Discrimination Act		s 9	9.3.4
1995 – *cont*		(1)	9.3.4, 9.3.5, 9.3.6
Sch 8, para 44(1)	9.5.1	(2)	9.3.5
(3), (4)	9.5.4	(3)	9.3.4
(4)(b)	9.5.1	s 10	10.4.5
para 47	3.2.3, 3.2.5	s 11	3.2.9
(1)	10.2.8	s 13(2)	9.2.6
para 50(1)	10.3.12	s 14(2)	9.3.4
(2)	10.2.11, 10.2.12	s 15	9.2.2
(4)	10.2.11	s 16(1)–(5)	9.2.1
Disability Rights Commission Act		s 17(1)–(4)	9.3.5
1999 1.2.1, 1.2.2, 3.2.11, 9.1.3, 9.2.1,		Sch 1	9.2.1
10.4.5		para 1	9.2.2
s 1(1)	9.2.1	para 2(1)–(3)	9.2.4
(2)	9.2.3	para 3(1), (2)	9.2.4
(3), (4)	9.2.1	para 4	9.2.4
s 2(1)	9.2.6, 9.2.12	para 5(a)–(c)	9.2.4
(a)–(c)	9.2.8	para 6(1), (2)	9.2.5
(2)–(5)	9.2.6	para 7	9.2.5
s 3(1), (2)	9.2.12	paras 8, 9	9.2.4
(3)	9.2.12, 9.2.31	para 10	9.2.3
(4)(a), (b)	9.2.13	(2)	9.2.3
(5)	9.2.12, 9.2.13	para 11	9.2.3
s 4	9.2.12, 9.2.15	para 12(1), (2)	9.2.7
(1)	9.2.19	para 13	9.2.7
(a)	9.2.20, 9.2.22	para 14(1), (2)	9.2.7
(b) 9.2.20, 9.2.21, 9.2.22, 9.2.23,		para 15	9.2.3, 9.2.8
9.2.24		para 16	9.2.8
(2)	9.2.20, 9.2.22	Sch 2	9.2.13
(3)	9.2.21	para 1(1), (2)	9.2.13
(a)	9.2.24	para 2(1), (2)	9.2.13
(b)	9.2.24, 9.2.29	para 3	9.2.13
(4)(a), (b)	9.2.24	para 4(1)	9.2.13
(5), (6)	9.2.19, 9.2.24	(2)(a)–(c)	9.2.13
s 5	9.2.12, 9.2.31	(3)	9.2.13
(1)	9.2.31	para 5	9.2.13
(2)(a)	9.2.32	Sch 3	9.2.31, 9.2.36, 9.2.37
(b)	9.2.33	Pt I	9.2.12
(i), (ii)	9.2.32	Pt II	9.2.15, 9.2.19
(3)	9.2.33	Pt III	9.2.15, 9.2.24
(4)(a)–(c)	9.2.32	para 1(1)	9.2.12
(5)(a), (b)	9.2.32	para 2	9.2.14
(6), (7)	9.2.33	(1)(a), (b)	9.2.14
(8)	9.2.33, 9.2.36, 9.2.37	(2)	9.2.14
(9)	9.2.33	(3)	9.2.14, 9.2.16
(10)	9.2.32	(4), (5)	9.2.14
(11), (12)	9.2.31	para 3	9.2.12
s 6(1)(a)–(c)	9.2.34	(1)	9.2.16
(2)–(5)	9.2.34	(a)	9.2.15
s 7	9.2.9	(b), (c) 9.2.15, 9.2.16
(1)(a), (b)	9.2.9	(2)	9.2.15
(2)–(5)	9.2.10	(3)(a), (b)	9.2.15
s 8	9.2.11	(4)–(9)	9.2.16
(1)–(5)	9.2.11	(10)	9.2.15

Disability Rights Commission Act
1999 – *cont*
Sch 3, para 4 — 9.2.37
    (1), (2) — 9.2.17
    (3)(a), (b) — 9.2.17
  para 5 — 9.2.37
    (1), (2) — 9.2.17
  para 6(1) — 9.2.18
    (2)(a), (b) — 9.2.18
    (3) — 9.2.18
  para 7(1)–(5) — 9.2.18
  para 8 — 9.2.19
    (1)–(5) — 9.2.19
  para 9 — 9.2.20
  para 10(1), (2) — 9.2.21
    (3)(a), (b) — 9.2.21
    (4) — 9.2.22
    (5)(a), (b) — 9.2.22
    (6), (7) — 9.2.22
  para 11(a), (b) — 9.2.23
  para 12(1)–(3) — 9.2.23
  para 13 — 9.2.23
  para 14(1) — 9.2.25
    (2) — 9.2.24
  para 15(1) — 9.2.25
    (2) — 9.2.25, 9.2.27
    (3) — 9.2.25
  para 16 — 9.2.25, 9.2.27
    (1) — 9.2.26
    (b) — 9.2.26
    (2)–(4) — 9.2.26
  para 17 — 9.2.26
    (1)–(4) — 9.2.27
  para 18(1)–(3) — 9.2.28
  para 19 — 9.2.25
  para 20 — 9.2.29
  para 21 — 9.2.37
    (1), (2) — 9.2.30
    (3) — 9.2.30, 9.2.37
    (4) — 9.2.30
  para 22(1)–(3) — 9.2.35
  para 23(1) — 9.2.36
    (2)(a)–(c) — 9.2.36
    (3), (4) — 9.2.36
  para 24(1), (2) — 9.2.37
  para 25(1)–(3) — 9.2.38
  para 26 — 9.2.12, 9.2.19, 9.2.24
Sch 5 — 9.3.4
Disabled Persons (Employment)
  Act 1944 — 2.1.3, 2.7.1, 2.7.2, 3.1.3, 3.2.6, 3.2.14, 3.2.15, 3.11.1, 3.12.1
  s 1 — 3.11.1

ss 6–14 — 3.11.1
s 15 — 3.2.14, 3.11.2
s 16 — 3.11.2
s 19 — 3.11.1
s 21 — 3.11.1
Disabled Persons (Employment)
  Act 1958 — 3.1.3
Disabled Persons (Employment)
  Act (Northern Ireland)
    1945 — 3.2.14, 3.2.15, 3.11.1
  s 15 — 3.2.14

Education Act 1944
  s 41 — 7.3.11
    (2A), (2B) — 7.3.11
Education Act 1993 — 7.3.2
  s 161(5) — 7.3.2
    (6), (7) — 7.3.3
  Sch 6, para 8 — 7.3.3
Education Act 1994
  s 1(4) — 7.3.8
Education Act 1996 — 7.2.1
  s 2 — 7.2.6, 7.3.11
  s 4(1), (2) — 7.2.2
  s 15 — 7.3.11
  s 133 — 3.2.1
  s 136 — 3.2.1
  s 317(5) — 7.3.2
    (6), (7) — 7.3.3
  s 508 — 7.2.6
  s 582(2) — 7.3.2, 7.3.3, 7.3.11
  Sch 13 — 3.2.1
  Sch 14 — 3.2.1
  Sch 38, Pt I — 7.3.2, 7.3.3, 7.3.11
Education (No 2) Act 1986
  s 30 — 7.3.3
Education (Scotland) Act 1980 — 7.2.1
  s 1(3) — 7.2.6
  s 135(1) — 7.2.2
Employment and Training Act
  1973
  s 2 — 5.2.1
Employment and Training Act
  (Northern Ireland) 1950
  ss 1, 2 — 5.2.1
Employment Equality Act 1998
  (Ireland) — 1.1.2
Employment Rights Act 1996 — 3.6.13, 10.3.36
  s 98 — 3.6.13
  s 99 — 3.4.1, 3.4.12
  s 104 — 10.1.4
  s 111 — 10.3.11
  s 113 — 10.3.34

Employment Rights Act 1996 –
  cont
  s 117(3)   10.3.34
    (4)(a)   10.3.34
    (5)(a), (b)   10.3.34
    (6)(a)–(c)   10.3.34
    (7), (8)   10.3.34
  ss 118–127   10.3.34
  s 126   10.3.35
  s 195   9.6.2
  s 203   10.3.15
Employment Rights (Dispute
  Resolution) Act 1998   10.3.33,
                            10.3.34, 10.3.35
  ss 9–10   10.3.15
Employment Tribunals Act 1996
  s 12(1)   10.3.21
    (2)   10.3.21
      (a)   10.3.22, 10.3.23
    (3)(a)–(c)   10.3.23
    (4)–(6)   10.3.23
    (7)   10.3.21, 10.3.22
  s 18   10.3.12
    (1)(c)   10.3.12
    (2), (3)   10.3.12
    (6), (7)   10.3.13
  s 32   10.3.24
  s 42(1)   10.3.12
Equal Pay Act 1970
  s 1(3)   3.5.5
Equal Status Act 1999 (Ireland) 1.1.2

Fire Services Act 1947   9.5.4
Further and Higher Education
  Act 1992   7.3.6
  s 5   7.3.7
    (6)(b)   7.3.7
    (7A)   7.3.7, 7.3.8
    (7B)   7.3.7, 7.3.8
  s 8(6), (7)   7.3.10
  s 62(7A), (7B)   7.3.12
  s 65(4A)   7.3.12
    (4B)   7.3.12, 7.3.13
  s 89(4)   7.3.8
Further and Higher Education
  (Scotland) Act 1992
  s 22   7.3.6
  s 37(4A), (4B)   7.3.12
  s 40(5)   7.3.12
    (6)   7.3.12, 7.3.13

Health and Safety at Work etc
  Act 1974
  s 12   10.2.10
Health and Social Services and
  Social Security Adjudications
  Act 1983
  s 17(2)   5.4.5
House of Commons
  Disqualification Act 1975
  Sch 2   9.5.2
Human Rights Act 1993 (NZ)   1.1.2
Human Rights Act 1998   1.1.3, 9.2.6
  s 6   9.2.15, 9.2.19, 9.2.31

Insurance Companies Act 1982   5.6.14
Interpretation Act 1978
  s 21   10.2.8
  Sch 1   10.3.7
Interpretation Act (Northern
  Ireland) 1954
  s 1(f)   10.2.8

Law Reform (Miscellaneous
  Provisions) Act 1934
  s 1(1)   10.3.7
Law Reform (Miscellaneous
  Provisions) (Scotland) Act
  1990
  Pt I   3.2.13
Legal Aid Act 1988   9.2.11
Legal Aid (Scotland) Act 1986   9.2.11
Local Government and Housing
  Act 1989   3.12.2
  s 7   3.12.1
    (2)(f)   3.12.2

Mental Health Act 1983
  Pt VII   5.6.9
  s 1(2)   2.3.6
Metropolitan Public Carriage Act
  1869   8.2.7
  s 6   8.2.4
Ministry of Defence Police Act
  1987
  s 1   9.5.4

National Health Service
  Community Care Act 1990
  s 47   5.4.5
Northern Ireland Act 1998
  Sch 13, para 16   1.2.1

Parks Regulation Act 1872	9.5.4
Pension Schemes Act 1993	3.7.6
Pension Schemes (Northern Ireland) Act 1993	3.7.6
Prison Act (Northern Ireland) 1953	
s 2(2)	9.5.4
Public Passenger Vehicles Act 1981	8.3.2, 8.3.9
Race Relations Act 1968	5.2.7
Race Relations Act 1976	3.1.1, 3.3.8, 3.4.9, 3.4.12, 3.5.5, 4.3.4, 5.2.2, 5.4.9, 9.2.15, 10.1.8, 10.3.29, 10.3.34, 10.3.39
Pt III	7.1.1
s 2	10.1.4
s 3(4)	3.4.8
s 4	3.2.1
s 7	3.9.1
s 10	3.2.4
s 11	4.1.3, 4.3.1
s 12	4.2.7
ss 20–27	5.1.2
ss 21–24	6.1.1
s 25	5.2.7
s 32	10.2.4
s 33	10.2.2
s 41	10.2.9
s 47	9.3.1
s 54(1)	10.3.7
s 56	10.3.26
(1)(c)	10.3.37
s 65	10.3.1
s 68(1)	10.3.9
(6)	10.3.11
(7)	10.3.10
s 72	10.3.15
s 75	9.5.1
s 75A	9.6.2
s 75B	9.6.2
Race Relations (Remedies) Act 1994	10.3.29
Rehabilitation Act 1973 (USA)	1.1.2
Representation of the People Act 1983	
s 18	7.2.4
Road Traffic Act 1988	
s 66A	8.3.9
Sale of Goods Act 1979	
s 61	5.2.3

School Standards and Framework Act 1998	
s 140(3)	7.2.2
Sch 31	7.2.2
Scotland Act 1998	8.2.14
Sex Discrimination Act 1975	3.1.1, 3.3.7, 3.3.8, 3.5.5, 4.3.4, 5.4.9, 10.1.8, 10.3.29, 10.3.34, 10.3.39
Pt III	7.1.1
s 4	10.1.4
s 5(3)	3.4.8
s 6	3.2.1
(7)	3.3.11
s 9	3.9.1
s 11	3.2.4
s 12	4.1.3, 4.3.1
s 13	4.2.7
ss 29–36	5.1.2
ss 30–32	6.1.1
s 41	10.2.4
s 42	10.2.2
s 56A	9.3.1
s 63(1)	10.3.7
s 65	10.3.26
(1)(c)	10.3.37
s 74	10.3.1
s 76(1)	10.3.9
(5)	10.3.11
(6)	10.3.10
s 77	10.3.15
s 85	9.5.1
s 85A	9.6.2
s 85B	9.6.2
Special Constables Act 1923	
s 3	9.5.4
Teaching and Higher Education Act 1998	
s 38	7.2.2
Town Police Clauses Act 1847	
s 37	8.2.4
Trade Union and Labour Relations (Consolidation) Act 1992	4.5.7
Pt I, ch IV	4.5.8
s 1	4.2.2
s 47	4.5.8
s 48	4.5.8
s 51	4.5.8
s 122	4.2.5
s 288	10.3.15
s 296	4.2.3, 4.2.5

Trade Union Reform and   Transport and Works Act 1992   8.4.7,
    Employment Rights Act   8.4.8
    1993
  s 39   10.3.15

TABLE OF STATUTORY INSTRUMENTS

References are to paragraph numbers.

Building Regulations 1991, SI 1991/2768
  Sch 1, Part M   3.6.15
Building Standards (Scotland) Regulations 1990, SI 1990/2179   3.6.15
Building Standards (Scotland) Amendment Regulations 1993, SI 1993/1457   3.6.15
Building Standards (Scotland) Amendment Regulations 1994, SI 1994/1266   3.6.15

Civil Procedure Rules 1998, SI 1998/3132   2.2.2
  Pt 35 Experts and Assessors   2.2.2
  Pt 35 Practice Direction – Experts and Assessors   2.2.2

Departments (Northern Ireland) Order 1999, SI 1999/283 (NI 1)   1.2.1
Disability Discrimination (Abolition of District Advisory Committees) Order
  1997, SI 1997/536   9.1.2
Disability Discrimination (Description of Insurance Services) Regulations
  1999, SI 1999/2114   3.8.5
Disability Discrimination (Employment) Regulations 1996, SI 1996/1456   3.1.2
  reg 2   3.5.8, 3.6.8, 3.6.15, 6.3.9
  reg 3   3.5.8, 3.6.17
    (1)(a), (b)   3.5.8
    (2), (3)   3.6.10
  reg 4   3.7.7, 3.7.8
    (1)–(3)   3.7.2
  reg 5   3.7.3, 3.7.7, 3.7.8
  reg 6(a), (b)   3.5.9
  reg 7(1)–(3)   3.9.8
  reg 8   5.5.10
    (1)(a)   3.6.15
    (2)   3.6.15
  reg 9   3.6.8
  regs 10–15   6.3.14
  reg 10   6.3.9
  reg 11   6.3.11
    (1)–(4)   6.3.10
  reg 12(a)–(c)   6.3.11
  reg 13(1), (2)   6.3.11
  reg 14(1)(a)–(d)   6.3.12
    (2)   6.3.11
  reg 15   6.3.9
Disability Discrimination (Employment) Regulations (Northern Ireland)
  1996, SR 1996/419   3.1.2
Disability Discrimination (Exemption for Small Employers) Order 1998, SI
  1998/2618   3.2.8
  art 2   3.2.6

Disability Discrimination (Guidance and Code of Practice) (Appointed Day)
     Order 1996, SI 1996/1996
   para 2   9.4.2
   para 3   3.1.2
Disability Discrimination (Meaning of Disability) Regulations 1996, SI 1996/
     1455   2.1.2, 2.2.1
   reg 2   2.3.3
   reg 3(1), (2)   2.3.3
   reg 4(1)   2.3.4
      (2), (3)   2.3.3
   reg 5   2.5.2, 2.5.11
   reg 6   2.4.4, 2.5.2
Disability Discrimination (Meaning of Disability) Regulations (Northern
     Ireland) 1996, SR 1996/421   2.1.2
Disability Discrimination (Questions and Replies) Order 1996, SI 1996/2793   10.3.3
   reg 2   10.3.3
   reg 3   10.3.4
   reg 4(a)–(d)   10.3.3
   reg 5   10.3.3
   Schs 1, 2   10.3.3
Disability Discrimination (Repeal of s 17 of, and Sch 2 to, the Disabled
     Persons (Employment) Act 1944) Order 1998, SI 1998/565   9.1.2
Disability Discrimination (Services and Premises) Regulations 1996, SI 1996/
     1836   3.8.3, 5.1.3
   reg 1(2)   5.6.14
   reg 2   5.6.14
      (1)   5.6.14
      (2)(a)–(c)   5.6.14
   reg 3(2)–(4)   5.6.14
   reg 4   5.6.14
   reg 5(1)   5.6.15
      (2)(a)–(c)   5.6.15
      (3)   5.6.15
   reg 6   5.6.16
      (1)   5.6.16
      (2)(a)–(c)   5.6.16
   reg 7(1)   6.2.16
      (2)(a)–(d)   6.2.16
   reg 8   5.6.9, 6.2.15
   reg 9   5.2.9, 7.2.5
      (1)(a)   7.2.6
         (b)   7.2.7, 7.2.8
         (c)   7.2.7
         (d)(i), (ii)   7.2.7
      (2)   7.2.7
         (a), (b)   7.2.7
Disability Discrimination (Services and Premises) Regulations 1999, SI 1999/
     1191   5.1.3
   reg 3   5.5.8
   reg 4   5.5.14
Disability Discrimination (Sub-leases and Sub-tenancies) Regulations 1996, SI
     1996/1333   6.2.10
   reg 4   6.3.5
      (a)   6.3.5

Disability Discrimination (Sub-leases and Sub-tenancies) Regulations 1996 –
  cont
  reg 4(b)   6.3.7
Disability Discrimination Act 1995 (Commencement No 3 and Saving and
  Transitional Provisions) Order 1996, SI 1996/1474
  art 2(3)   3.1.2
  art 3   3.1.2, 3.11.1
  Sch, Pt III   3.1.2
Disability Discrimination Act 1995 (Commencement No 6) Order 1999, SI
  1999/1190   4.5.1
Disability Rights Commission Act 1999 (Commencement No 1 and
  Transitional Provisions) Order 1999, SI 1999/2210   9.2.1
Disability Rights Commission Act 1999 (Commencement No 2 and
  Transitional Provisions) Order 2000, SI 2000/880   9.2.1
Disability Rights Commission (Time Limits) Regulations 2000, SI 2000/879   9.2.12,
      9.2.24

Education (Disability Statements for Further Education Institutions)
  Regulations 1996, SI 1996/1664   7.3.8
  reg 2   7.3.8
Education (Modification of Enactments Relating to Employment) Order
  1998, SI 1998/218   3.2.1, 10.2.7
Education (Northern Ireland) Order 1996, SI 1996/274
  Pt II   7.2.1
Education and Libraries (Northern Ireland) Order 1986, SI 1986/594   7.2.2
Equal Opportunities (Employment Legislation) (Territorial Limits)
  Regulations 1999, SI 1999/3163   3.2.5
Employment Appeal Tribunal Rules 1993, SI 1993/2854   10.3.24
  r 23A   10.3.24
Employment Appeal Tribunal (Amendment) Rules 1996, SI 1996/3216   10.3.24
Employment Tribunals (Constitution and Rules of Procedure) Regulations
  1993, SI 1993/2687   10.3.8
  Sch 1   10.3.21
  r 2(3)   10.3.12
  r 10   10.3.25
  r 14   10.3.21
    (1A)   10.3.21
    (1B)   10.3.21
  r 20(7)   10.3.12
Employment Tribunals (Constitution and Rules of Procedure) (Amendment)
  Regulations 1994, SI 1994/536   10.3.8
Employment Tribunals (Constitution and Rules of Procedure) (Amendment)
  Regulations 1996, SI 1996/1757   10.3.8, 10.3.21
Employment Tribunals (Constitution and Rules of Procedure) (Scotland)
  Regulations 1993, SI 1993/2688   10.3.8
  Sch 1
  r 14   10.3.21
    (1A)   10.3.21
    (1B)   10.3.21
Employment Tribunals (Constitution and Rules of Procedure) (Amendment)
  (Scotland) Regulations 1994, SI 1994/538   10.3.8
Employment Tribunals (Constitution and Rules of Procedure) (Amendment)
  (Scotland) Regulations 1996, SI 1996/1757   10.3.8
Employment Tribunals (Interest on Awards in Discrimination Cases)
  Regulations 1996, SI 1996/2803   10.3.32

Fire Services (Northern Ireland) Order 1984   9.5.4

Industrial Tribunals (Northern Ireland) Order 1996, SI 1996/1921   10.3.12

Occupational Pension Schemes (Internal Dispute Resolution Procedures)
    Regulations 1996, SI 1996/1270   3.7.7

Public Service Vehicles (Conduct of Drivers, Inspectors, Conductors and
    Passengers) Regulations 1990, SI 1990/1020   8.3.6

Race Relations (Questions and Replies) Order 1977, SI 1977/842   10.3.1
Rail Vehicle Accessibility Regulations 1998, SI 1998/2456   8.4.2, 8.4.4, 8.4.11
    reg 2(1)   8.4.7
    reg 3(1)   8.4.7
    regs 4–8   8.4.4
    reg 9   8.4.4, 8.4.5
    reg 10   8.4.4
    reg 11   8.4.4, 8.4.5
    regs 12–14   8.4.4
    reg 15   8.4.4, 8.4.5
    regs 16–24   8.4.4
Rail Vehicle (Exemption Application) Regulations 1998, SI 1998/2457   8.4.11
    regs 3, 4   8.4.11
    Sch   8.4.11
        para 11   8.4.11
Road Traffic (Northern Ireland) Order 1981   8.3.2
    art 61   8.2.4

Sex Discrimination and Equal Pay (Remedies) Regulations 1993, SI 1993/
    2798   10.3.29
Sex Discrimination (Questions and Replies) Order 1975, SI 1975/2048
    (amended by SI 1977/844)   10.3.1

Transfer of Functions to the Scottish Ministers etc Order 1999, SI 1999/1750
    art 2, Sch 1   8.2.14
Transport and Works (Guided Transport Modes) Order 1992, SI 1992/3231   8.4.7

TABLE OF EUROPEAN AND UN LEGISLATION

References are to paragraph numbers.

EC Charter of Fundamental Social Rights of Workers, adopted on 9.12.1989
  art 26   1.1.4
EC Council Recommendation on the Employment of Disabled People 86/
  376/EEC, of 24 July 1986, OJ L225/43 of 12.8.1986   1.1.4
EC Protocol on Social Policy (February 1992)
  Social Chapter Agreement
  art 2   1.1.4
EC Council Resolution on Equality of Opportunity for People with
  Disabilities of 20 December 1996, OJ 97/C12/01   1.1.4
EC Treaty (Treaty of Rome)
  Art 13   1.1.4
  Art 141   3.5.5
EC Council Resolution on the 1999 Employment Guidelines   1.1.4
European Convention for the Protection of Human Rights and Fundamental
  Freedoms   1.1.3
  Draft Protocol No 12   1.1.3
UN Declaration on the Rights of Disabled Persons, General Assembly
  Resolution 3447 (XXX), 9 December 1975   1.1.3
UN Standard Rules on the Equalization of Opportunities for Persons with
  Disabilities, General Assembly Resolution 48/96, 20 December 1993   1.1.3

TABLE OF CODES OF PRACTICE AND GUIDANCE

References are to paragraph numbers.

Code of Practice: Duties of trade organisations to their disabled members and applicants (1999)	4.1.1
para 1.4	4.1.1
para 2.1	4.2.7
para 2.2	4.2.4
para 2.3	4.2.6
paras 3.1–3.8	4.5.1
para 3.2	4.1.2
para 4.2	4.3.4
para 4.5	4.4.5
paras 5.1–5.5	4.4.2
paras 6.1–6.19	4.5.1
paras 6.3, 6.4	4.5.2
paras 6.5–6.7	4.5.4
paras 6.8–6.19	4.5.5
paras 7.1–7.9	4.6.1
para 7.2	4.6.2
paras 7.5–7.7	4.6.3
paras 7.8, 7.9	4.5.7
paras 8.1–8.3	4.7.1
Annex 3	4.7.1
Code of Practice for the elimination of discrimination in the field of employment against disabled persons or persons who have had a disability (1996)	2.2.2, 3.1.2
Chs 5, 6	3.6.6, 3.6.11
para 1.3	3.1.2
para 2.2	3.4.9, 3.6.1
para 2.6	3.2.8
para 3.3	3.6.14
para 4.2	3.4.3
para 4.3	3.4.4, 3.4.6
para 4.6	3.5.4, 3.5.5
para 4.7	3.6.23
para 4.9	3.6.23
para 4.11	10.2.4
paras 4.12–4.14	3.6.4
para 4.15	3.6.8
para 4.16	3.6.6, 3.6.8
para 4.17	3.6.9
para 4.18	3.6.17
para 4.20	3.4.18, 3.6.11
paras 4.21–4.32	5.5.3
paras 4.22–4.27	3.6.16, 3.6.17
paras 4.23, 4.24	3.6.18

Code of Practice for the elimination of discrimination in the field of
    employment against disabled persons or persons who have had a
    disability (1996) – *cont*

paras 4.28–4.33	3.6.16
para 4.28	3.6.18
para 4.31	3.6.18
para 4.34	3.6.23
paras 4.35–4.39	3.6.15, 5.5.10
para 4.41	6.3.9, 6.3.13
paras 4.42–4.46	6.3.10
para 4.47	6.3.7
para 4.48	6.3.9, 6.3.10, 6.3.11
para 4.52	3.5.9
paras 4.53–4.54	10.1.8
paras 4.55–4.59	10.2.4
para 4.57	3.6.20
para 4.57 *et seq*	3.4.13, 5.4.8
paras 4.58–4.64	3.6.20
paras 4.62–4.63	10.2.4
para 4.65	3.6.18, 10.2.8
para 4.66	3.12.2
para 5.2	3.3.2
para 5.3	3.3.2
para 5.4	3.3.2
paras 5.5, 5.6	3.3.14
paras 5.7–5.9	3.4.15
para 5.10	3.3.14, 3.6.20
para 5.11	3.3.14, 3.6.20
paras 5.12–5.26	3.3.2
para 5.20	3.3.14, 3.6.20
para 5.21	3.3.2
para 5.22	3.3.2
paras 5.23, 5.24	3.3.15
para 5.26	3.4.9, 3.6.1
para 5.27	3.3.3, 3.3.5
para 5.28	3.3.5, 3.5.8, 3.6.17
para 5.29	3.5.8, 3.6.17
para 6.2	3.3.5
para 6.3	3.3.5
paras 6.4–6.7	3.3.6
para 6.7	3.6.12
para 6.8	3.3.10
para 6.9	3.7.7
paras 6.10–6.12	3.7.2
paras 6.10–6.16	3.7.7
para 6.14	3.7.2
para 6.15	3.7.3
para 6.16	3.7.4
para 6.17	3.8.4, 3.8.5
para 6.18	3.8.1
paras 6.19–6.21	3.6.7, 3.6.13
paras 6.19–6.23	3.3.8
paras 7.1–7.8	3.9.1

Code of Practice for the elimination of discrimination in the field of
  employment against disabled persons or persons who have had a
  disability (1996) – *cont*

para 7.5	3.9.7
para 7.6	3.9.7, 3.9.9
paras 7.7, 7.8	3.9.6
paras 7.9–7.13	4.1.1

Code of Practice on the Identification and Assessment of Special Educational
  Needs   7.2.1
Code of Practice on Schools Admissions   7.2.1
Code of Practice: Rights of Access: Goods, Facilities, Services and Premises 5.1.3,
                                                                            5.2.1

Ch 1	5.1.3
Chs 2–4	5.3.1
Ch 4	5.5.3
Ch 8	6.1.1
paras 2.4–2.5	5.4.2
para 2.13	5.2.1, 5.2.2
para 2.16	5.2.4
paras 2.18–2.20	7.2.5
para 2.19	7.2.8
paras 2.21–2.22	8.1.3
paras 2.23–2.24	5.2.7
paras 2.25–2.26	5.2.6
paras 3.3–3.11	5.4.2
paras 3.4–3.7	5.4.3
paras 3.8–3.10	5.4.4
para 3.9	5.4.5
paras 3.11–3.14	5.3.2
paras 3.15–3.16	5.3.3
para 3.17	5.3.4
para 3.18	5.4.2
paras 4.7–4.9	5.5.4
paras 4.10–4.12	5.5.3
paras 4.16–4.17	5.5.3
paras 5.2–5.8	5.5.6
para 5.3	5.5.5
paras 5.5–5.8	5.5.5
paras 5.9–5.11	5.5.7
paras 5.13–5.14	5.5.7
paras 5.15–5.35	5.5.13
paras 5.19–5.20	5.5.14
para 6.7	5.6.4, 5.6.5, 6.2.14
para 6.8	5.6.5
paras 6.10–6.12	5.6.7
para 6.12	5.6.3
paras 6.13–6.14	5.6.8
para 6.15	5.6.9
para 6.16	5.6.3
paras 6.17–6.19	5.6.10
para 6.19	5.6.3
paras 6.20–6.22	5.6.11
para 6.22	5.6.3
para 6.23	5.6.12

Code of Practice: Rights of Access: Goods, Facilities, Services and Premises –
   cont
   para 6.24   5.6.13
   paras 6.25–6.26   5.5.3
   para 6.26   5.6.3
   paras 7.2–7.8   5.6.14
   paras 7.9–7.13   5.6.15
   paras 7.14–7.19   5.6.16
   para 8.5   6.2.14
   para 8.6   6.2.13
   para 8.7   6.2.8
   paras 8.8–8.9   6.2.10
   paras 8.10–8.11   6.2.9
   para 8.13   6.2.2
   para 8.14   6.2.3
   para 8.15   6.2.4
   paras 8.16–8.22   6.2.11
   paras 8.24–8.25   6.2.5
   paras 8.26–8.27   6.2.6
   para 8.28   6.2.11
   para 8.29   6.2.7
   para 8.30   6.2.11
   paras 8.31–8.34   6.2.14
   paras 8.35–8.37   6.2.15
   paras 8.38–8.43   6.2.16
   paras 9.2–9.5   6.2.17, 10.1.8
   paras 9.8–9.10   10.2.4
   para 9.12   10.2.8
Guidance on matters to be taken into account in determining questions
   relating to the definition of disability (1996) 2.1.2, 2.1.3, 2.1.4, 2.2.1, 2.2.2, 2.4.2,
                                                                                  9.4.2
   Pt I, para 10 *et seq*   2.3.2
      para 11   2.3.3
      para 12   2.3.7
      para 13   2.3.4
      para 14   2.3.5
   Pt II
      para A1   2.5.2
      paras A2–A6   2.5.3
      paras A7–A9   2.5.4, 2.5.6, 2.5.13
      para A10   2.5.3
      paras A12, A13   2.5.14
      para A14   2.5.15
      para A17   2.5.10
      para B1   2.6.3
      para B2   2.6.3
      para B3   2.5.6
      para B4   2.5.6
      para B5   2.5.6, 2.6.3
      para B7   2.5.6, 2.6.3
      para B8   2.6.3
      para B9   2.6.4
      para C2   2.4.3
      para C3   2.4.3, 2.4.5
      paras C5–C21   2.5.1
      paras C14–C21   2.4.1
Tribunal Procedure Rules
   rule 6   2.1.1

TABLE OF ABBREVIATIONS

1994 Green Paper	*A consultation on government measures to tackle discrimination against disabled people* (July 1994)
1995 White Paper	*Ending discrimination against disabled people* (Cm 2729: January 1995)
ACAS	Advisory, Conciliation and Arbitration Service
CANDO	Careers Advisory Network on Disability Opportunities
CRE	Commission for Racial Equality
DARAS	Disability Access Rights Advisory Service
DDA 1995	Disability Discrimination Act 1995
DDARAP	Disability Discrimination Act Representation and Advice Project
DPTAC	Disabled Persons Transport Advisory Committee
DRC	Disability Rights Commission
DRCA 1999	Disability Rights Commission Act 1999
DRTF	Disability Rights Task Force
DRTF Report	*From Exclusion to Inclusion: A Report of the Disability Rights Task Force for Disabled People*
EAT	Employment Appeal Tribunal
ECHR	European Convention on Human Rights
Employment Code of Practice	*Code of practice for the elimination of discrimination in the field of employment against disabled persons or persons who have a disability* (1996, London: HMSO)
EOC	Equal Opportunities Commission
ERA 1996	Employment Rights Act 1996
ETA 1996	Employment Tribunals Act 1996
FEFC	Further Education Funding Council for England
Guidance	*Guidance on matters to be taken into account in determining questions relating to the definition of disability* (1996, London: HMSO)
HEFCE	Higher Education Funding Council for England
HEFCW	Higher Education Funding Council for Wales
ILO	International Labour Organisation
IMO	International Maritime Organisation
LEA	local education authority
NACEDP	National Advisory Council on the Employment of Disabled People
NDC	National Disability Council
NIDC	Northern Ireland Disability Council
PSV	public service vehicle
Rights of Access Code of Practice	*Code of Practice: Rights of access: goods, facilities, services and premises* (1999, London: HMSO)

RRA 1976	Race Relations Act 1976
SDA 1975	Sex Discrimination Act 1975
SEN	special educational needs
SHEFC	Scottish Higher Education Funding Council
Trade Organisations Code of Practice	*Code of Practice: Duties of trade organisations to their disabled members and applicants* (1999, London: HMSO)
TULR(C)A 1992	Trade Union and Labour Relations (Consolidation) Act 1992
UN	United Nations
WHO	World Health Organization

Chapter 1

INTRODUCTION

1.1 BACKGROUND

1.1.1 Volumes of research provide long-established evidence that disabled people in the UK face discrimination and barriers to equal participation and opportunity in education, employment, health and social services, housing, transport, the built environment, leisure and social activities, and civic rights.[1] Yet successive governments have been reluctant or unwilling to recognise that the disadvantage and experience of many disabled people could be explained by discrimination and negative attitudes.[2] If disability discrimination was recognised as a phenomenon, then inevitably the argument would be raised that anti-discrimination legislation would be too complex to draft and uncertain in its application.[3] Two years before his government introduced a disability discrimination Bill, a former premier felt it necessary to state that his government had 'no plans to introduce generalized anti-discrimination legislation because we foresee problems in both approach and implementation'.[4] The preferred approach was to eliminate unjustified discrimination by education and persuasion, supported by specific legislation to target particular problems.

---

1 The most cogent and comprehensive account of this research is to be found in Barnes, *Disabled People in Britain and Discrimination: A Case for Anti-Discrimination Legislation* (Hurst & Company/British Council of Organizations of Disabled People, London, 1991).
2 Although see the limited concessions in Department of Employment, *Employment and Training for People with Disabilities: Consultative Document* (Department of Employment, London, 1990) at p 16.
3 Department of Employment, *Employment and Training for People with Disabilities: Consultative Document* (Department of Employment, London, 1990) at paras 5.14–5.15.
4 HC Deb, vol 217, col 485 (Mr J Major) 22 January 1993.

1.1.2 Beyond Parliament, however, disabled people themselves were arguing for anti-discrimination legislation. The disability rights movement was especially inspired by the comprehensive and universal civil rights agenda set for disabled people in the United States enshrined in the Americans with Disabilities Act 1990. That statute built upon the earlier limited provisions of the Rehabilitation Act 1973.[1] In 1992, the Australian federal government passed its Disability Discrimination Act 1992 (adding to comparable laws at state level) and, the following year, New Zealand's Human Rights Act 1993 explicitly addressed the civil rights of disabled citizens. Canada had also long experimented in its human rights codes in attempting to legislate for the mischief of disability discrimination. More recently still, Ireland has introduced its Employment Equality Act 1998 and Equal Status Act 1999, both statutes directly addressing the rights of disabled persons.[2] These comparative examples (and others besides) demonstrated that anti-discrimination legislation could be framed and might be made to work with the necessary political will.[3]

---

1 See Gooding, *Disabling Laws, Enabling Acts: Disability Rights in Britain and America* (Pluto Press, London, 1994).

2 These Acts followed upon an influential report of Ireland's Commission on the Status of People with Disabilities (*A Strategy for Equality*) and an earlier unsuccessful attempt at introducing disability rights legislation which had been declared unconstitutional by the Irish Supreme Court.

3 See Quinn et al, *Disability Discrimination Law in the United States, Australia and Canada* (Oak Tree Press/National Rehabilitation Board, Dublin, 1993); Doyle, *Disability, Discrimination and Equal Opportunities: A Comparative Study of the Employment Rights of Disabled Persons* (Mansell Publishing, London, 1995). See also Doyle, 'Defining disability rights: comparative perspectives' in Disability Rights Task Force, *From Exclusion to Inclusion: A Report of the Disability Rights Task Force on Civil Rights for Disabled People* (DfEE, London, 1999) Annex C.

1.1.3 International legal standards had also provided some comfort for advocates of disability rights. The International Labour Organisation (ILO) had established minimum labour standards for persons with physical and mental disabilities.[1] The United Nations (UN) Declaration on the Rights of Disabled Persons also provided a touchstone for equal rights and anti-discrimination principles.[2] It pre-dated the UN's Decade of Disabled Persons which ended in 1992 and which witnessed many of the legislative developments in other industrial democracies already alluded to. The Council of Europe is also considering amendments to the European Convention on Human Rights which would establish a general prohibition on discrimination in the enjoyment of any right set forth by law and which might encompass disability.[3] However, perhaps the most tangible evidence of the fruits of the UN Decade are the UN Standard Rules on the Equalization of Opportunities for Persons with Disabilities.[4] The Standard Rules set the framework and establish the principles for nation States to adopt domestic anti-discrimination and equal opportunities legislation.

---

1 See ILO Convention No 159 and Recommendation No 168 (1983). Note also ILO Convention No 99 (1955).

2 General Assembly Resolution 3447 (XXX) 9 December 1975.

3 Council of Europe, Draft Protocol No 12 to the European Convention on Human Rights (ECHR) and Draft Explanatory Report (June 1999). Neither the Draft Protocol nor the Convention specifically mentions 'disability', but there is a general prohibition against discrimination based on 'other status' in the enjoyment of ECHR rights. The staged implementation of the Human Rights Act 1998 throughout the UK during 1999 and 2000 is likely to result in greater use being made of the ECHR and its jurisprudence in domestic tribunals and courts. It remains to be seen what impact, if any, this will have on disability rights. See further: Daw, *Human Rights and Disability: The Impact of the Human Rights Act on Disabled People* (NDC/RNID, London, 2000).

4 General Assembly Resolution 48/96, 20 December 1993. See Degener and Koster-Dreese (eds), *Human Rights and Disabled Persons: Essays and Human Rights Instruments* (Martinus Nijhoff Publishers, Dordrecht, 1995). See also Doyle, 'Disabled workers' rights, the Disability Discrimination Act and the UN Standard Rules' (1996) 25 *Industrial Law Journal* 1–14.

1.1.4 The law of the European Union (EU) and European Communities (EC) also provides some assistance to the disability rights movement. The EC adopted a soft law measure in the form of the 1986 Recommendation on the Employment of Disabled People,[1] while Article 26 of the EC Charter of Fundamental Social Rights of Workers expressed the right of disabled people to expect Member States to take steps to improve their social and professional integration.[2] However, there has always been doubt about the legal competence of the EU/EC to legislate for the social rights of disabled Europeans, although a legal basis for such legislation can be found in the Treaty provisions.[3] Nevertheless, the European Commission's 1994 White Paper on Social Policy heralded a clear intention to introduce anti-discrimination legislation (perhaps in the form of a directive) addressing the question of disability.[4] The 1996 Inter-Governmental Conference provided the opportunity to revise the EU/EC treaties to achieve that end.[5]

1　Council Recommendation 86/376/EEC (24 July 1986), OJ L225/43 (12 August 1986).
2　Adopted by 11 of the then 12 Member States (excluding the UK) at Strasbourg on 9 December 1989. See also Article 2 of the Social Chapter Agreement annexed to the EC Protocol on Social Policy (February 1992).
3　See Waddington, *Disability, Employment and the European Community* (MAKLU, Ontwerp, 1995). See also *Invisible Citizens: Disabled Persons' Status* in the European Treaties (Secretariat of European Day of Disabled Persons 1995, Brussels, 1995).
4　EC Commission, *European Social Policy: A Way Forward for the Union* (COM (94) 333 final) (EC Commission, Luxembourg, 1994).
5　Now EC Treaty, Article 13 and Proposed Council Directive Establishing a General Framework for Equal Treatment in Employment and Occupation (1999). See further, for example, European Commission, *Equality of Opportunity for People with Disabilities: A New European Community Disability Strategy* (COM 406 final, 1996); Council Resolution of 20 December 1996 on Equality of Opportunity for People with Disabilities (OJ 97/C12/01); *Mainstreaming Disability within EU Employment and Social Policy* (DG V Services Working Paper); *Employment and People with Disabilities* (Report of the Special Meeting of the High Level Group on Disability, Brussels, October 1997); European Commission, *Raising Employment Levels of People with Disabilities: The Common Challenge* (European Commission Working Paper, 1998); Council Resolution on the 1999 Employment Guidelines.

1.1.5　None the less, it has not been European, international or comparative pressure which has brought about a sea-change in government attitude towards disability discrimination legislation in the UK. Rather, it has been domestic political forces that have been at work. Backbench parliamentarians first introduced a private members' Bill modelled after the Americans with Disabilities Act in the 1991–92 parliamentary session. This was the Civil Rights (Disabled Persons) Bill. Similar Bills were introduced in subsequent sessions but, without frontbench support, failed to make progress, despite cross-party approval. When, in 1993–94, another Civil Rights (Disabled Persons) Bill completed the Committee stage in the House of Commons for the first time, disability rights activists were optimistic that the Bill would reach the statute book. However, the Bill was defeated at Report stage by procedural means in May 1994.[1]

1　HC Deb, vol 242, cols 960–1017 and vol 243, cols 1077–1102.

1.1.6　Then, in July 1994, a Green Paper was published setting out proposals for limited law reform to prevent discrimination against disabled people in the labour market and in access to goods and services.[1] This was followed in January 1995 by a White Paper committing the then Conservative Government to legislate to end discrimination against disabled people in employment, access to goods and services, transport and education.[2] Simultaneously, a Disability Discrimination Bill was published as the vehicle for implementing many (but not all) of the proposals contained in the White Paper. It is perhaps noteworthy that neither the Bill nor the Government statements of policy which prefaced it make any mention of an intention to legislate in conformity with European or international developments. This was purely a domestic initiative.

---

1   *A Consultation on Government Measures to Tackle Discrimination Against Disabled People* (Department of Social Security, 1994).
2   *Ending Discrimination Against Disabled People* Cm 2729 (HMSO, London, 1995).

1.1.7   Moving the Third Reading of the Disability Discrimination Bill in the House of Commons on 28 March 1995,[1] the then Minister for Social Security and Disabled People, Mr William Hague, claimed:

> 'It is a landmark Bill. It is the only comprehensive Bill for disabled people ever introduced by a British Government. It will mark the United Kingdom out as one of the world leaders and the leader in Europe in the move towards comprehensive anti-discrimination legislation for disabled people. It is a profound measure with significant implications for every part of the economy . . . It sets this country on a clear, workable and unambiguous course to ending discrimination against disabled people. It will make a genuine difference to the opportunities and lives of millions of our fellow citizens . . .'[2]

Five years and a change of government later, the Disability Discrimination Act 1995 (DDA 1995) remains as the foundation stone of disability discrimination law. The new Labour Government (elected in May 1997) promised comprehensive civil rights legislation for disabled people. It established a task force to examine the question. The Disability Rights Task Force reported in December 1999, but it is not expected that its recommendations will result in any major reforms of the 1995 Act or the introduction of civil rights legislation before the next election.[3] The Act has also been the subject of much research and analysis which will undoubtedly inform future reform.[4]

---

1   The complete legislative history of the Bill is as follows:
    House of Commons: 1st Reading (12 January 1995); 2nd Reading (24 January 1995: HC Deb, vol 253, cols 147–239); Committee (31 January 1995 to 28 February 1995: HC Deb, Standing Committee E); Report (27 and 28 March 1995: HC Deb, vol 257, cols 697–799 and cols 840–904); 3rd Reading (28 March 1995: HC Deb, vol 257, cols 904–928).
    House of Lords: 1st Reading (29 March 1995); 2nd Reading (22 May 1995: HL Deb, vol 564, cols 800–815 and 830–892); Committee (13, 15 and 27 June 1995: HL Deb, vol 564, cols 1640–1718, 1723–1784, 1895–1954 and 1975–2054; HL Deb, vol 565, cols 608–680 and 686–744); Report (18 and 20 July 1995: HL Deb, vol 566, cols 114–141, 168–186, 205–280 and 386–476); 3rd Reading (24 October 1995: HL Deb, vol 566, cols 969–1080).
    The Bill as amended was further considered by the House of Commons (31 October 1995: HC Deb, vol 265, cols 109–179) and the House of Lords (6 November 1995: HL Deb, vol 566, cols 1581–1602). The Bill received Royal Assent on 8 November 1995.
2   HC Deb, vol 257, cols 904 and 928. See the similar comments made by the lead Minister in the House of Lords (HL Deb, vol 566, col 1070).
3   Disability Rights Task Force, *From Exclusion to Inclusion: A Report of the Disability Rights Task Force on Civil Rights for Disabled People* (DfEE, London, 1999). See also: Better Regulation Task Force, *Anti-Discrimination Legislation* (May 1999).
4   See, for example, Whitfield, *The Disability Discrimination Act: Analysis Data From an Omnibus Survey* (Department of Social Security, In House Report, 30 July 1997); CCH Editions Ltd,

The New Law on Disability Discrimination: Survey of Employers' Responses (CCH, 1997); Incomes
Data Services Ltd, *Disability and Employment: Law and Company Practice* (IDS, London, 1998);
CCH Editions Ltd, *More Honoured in the Breach? A Survey of the Impact of the Disability
Discrimination Act* (CCH, 1998); Meager, Doyle et al, *Monitoring the Disability Discrimination Act
1995* (DfEE Research Report RR119, 1999); Meager and Hibbert, 'Disabled people in the
labour market: findings from the DfEE baseline survey', *Labour Market Trends* (September
1999); Bruyère, *A Comparison of the Implementation of the Employment Provisions of the Americans
with Disabilities Act in the United States and the Disability Discrimination Act in Great Britain*
(Cornell University, 1999).

1.2 DISABILITY DISCRIMINATION ACT 1995

1.2.1 The long title of the Act seeks:

'to make it unlawful to discriminate against disabled persons in connection with
employment, the provision of goods, facilities and services or the disposal or
management of premises; to make provision about the employment of disabled
persons; and to establish a National Disability Council.'

In fact, the Act also makes provision in respect of education and public
transport. Subsequently, the Disability Rights Commission Act 1999 has
disestablished the National Disability Council.[1] With the exception of some of
the provisions on public transport, the 1995 Act is largely in force. The Act is
expressed in language which appears to suggest that its substantive provisions
apply only to England and Wales and to Scotland. However, the provisions of
the 1995 Act are also extended to Northern Ireland.[2]

---

1 See Chapter 9.
2 DDA 1995, s 70(6). The application of the Act in Northern Ireland has effect to the extent
   of (and subject to the textual modifications set out in) DDA 1995, Sch 8 as amended by the
   Northern Ireland Act 1998, Sch 13, para 16. Where appropriate, these are indicated in the
   text below. See also Departments (Northern Ireland) Order 1999, SI 1999/283 (NI 1) which
   renames some of the Northern Ireland government departments. This is reflected in the
   text.

1.2.2 Part I of the Act addresses the problem of defining the meaning of
'disability' and 'disabled person'.[1] Part II deals with the issue of discrimination
in the employment field, including contract work and trade organisations.[2]
Discrimination in non-employment areas is approached in Part III of the Act.
This embraces the measures outlawing discrimination in relation to goods,
facilities and services,[3] as well as discrimination in relation to the disposal and
management of premises.[4] Education and transport have been expressly
excluded from the anti-discrimination formula contained in Part III of the
Act. Instead, the statute's preferred approach in respect of education is to
place educational institutions and funding bodies under specific duties to
provide information about educational opportunities available to disabled
pupils and students.[5] So far as concerns public transport, the Act resembles
enabling legislation, empowering the relevant Minister to lay regulations
to define standards of accessibility for disabled people to taxis,

public service vehicles and trains.[6] The Act (as amended) contains its own institutional framework.[7]

---

1   DDA 1995, ss 1–3 and Schs 1–2. These are key provisions of the legislation and are considered in detail in Chapter 2.
2   Ibid, ss 4–18 and Schs 3–4. See Chapters 3–4 and 10.
3   Ibid, ss 19–21, 25–28 and Schs 3–4. See Chapters 5 and 10.
4   Ibid, ss 22–28 and Schs 3–4. See Chapters 6 and 10.
5   Ibid, ss 29–31. See Chapter 7.
6   Ibid, ss 32–49. See Chapter 8.
7   Ibid, Parts VI–VII (ss 50–70 and Schs 5–8) and Disability Rights Commission Act 1999. See Chapter 9.

Chapter 2

DISABILITY AND DISABLED PERSON

2.1 INTRODUCTION

2.1.1 The twin concepts of 'disability' and 'disabled person' are central to the operation of disability discrimination law. These are the terms that determine who has rights and expectations under the DDA 1995. Only someone who can satisfy the definition of disabled person within the meaning of the legislation can enjoy the protection of its framework.[1]

---

1 In a Part II case, for example, it will be open to an employment tribunal to treat the question of disability as being an issue suitable for a preliminary hearing under rule 6 of the tribunal procedure rules: *Greenwood v British Airways plc* [1999] IRLR 600.

2.1.2 Part I of the Act (ss 1–3) and Schs 1 and 2 to the Act furnish definitions of 'disability' and 'disabled person'. A 'disabled person' is defined as 'a person who has a disability'.[1] A person has a disability if he or she has a physical or mental impairment which has a substantial and long-term adverse effect on his or her ability to carry out normal day-to-day activities.[2] These provisions are supplemented by regulations[3] and by the statutory guidance issued by the Secretary of State under s 3 (referred to hereafter as the 'Guidance').[4] The Guidance does not impose any legal obligations in itself and is not designed to be an authoritative statement of law. Nevertheless, an employment tribunal or court is required to take account of the Guidance, where relevant, when determining certain questions arising from the statutory definition of disability.[5]

---

1 DDA 1995, s 1(2).
2 Ibid, s 1(1). Note that the definition is also extended to include persons who had such a disability in the past (s 2 and Sch 2). See **2.8**.
3 Disability Discrimination (Meaning of Disability) Regulations 1996, SI 1996/1455 which came into force on 30 July 1996 and made under the authority of Sch 1, paras 1(2), 2(4), 3(2)–(3), 4(2)(a) and 5(a). See also Disability Discrimination (Meaning of Disability) Regulations (Northern Ireland) 1996, SR 1996/421.
4 *Guidance on matters to be taken into account in determining questions relating to the definition of disability* (1996, London: HMSO). In Northern Ireland, the power to issue s 3 guidance is vested in the Department of Enterprise, Trade and Investment (Sch 8, para 2(1)) and a separate edition of the Guidance has been issued there.
5 See s 3(3) and *Goodwin v The Patent Office* [1999] IRLR 4 EAT. As to the legal status of the Guidance, see **9.4**. The Guidance is likely to be of assistance in marginal cases. It is not to be used in a literal fashion to reach conclusions that overturn the obvious impression of someone as being disabled within the meaning of the Act: *Vicary v British Telecommunications plc* [1999] IRLR 680.

2.1.3 Considerable care must be exercised in any attempt to use existing definitions of disability employed in other legal contexts (such as social welfare or social security law) as a means of identifying disabled persons protected under the DDA 1995. In order to enjoy protection from disability discrimi-nation, applicants or claimants must bring themselves fairly and squarely within the definitional provisions of 1995 legislation and the statutory Guidance. However, with that necessary caveat, it is likely that many (but not all) individuals who satisfy the definition of disability or disabled person in other statutory contexts will be able to do so under disability discrimination law. Indeed, in one particular case – that of a person registered as disabled under the Disabled Persons (Employment) Act 1944 at specified times – there is a deeming provision by which the existing status of an individual as a legally recognised disabled person is preserved for that purpose.[1]

---

1   DDA 1995, Sch 1, para 7. See **2.7**.

2.1.4   The burden of proof that a complainant was a disabled person at the time of the alleged act of discrimination lies with the complainant. An applicant or claimant in tribunal or court proceedings under the Act will be expected to lead evidence which relates to his or her status at the time of the events which have given rise to the complaint. This is a question of fact and provided the tribunal or court directs itself carefully as to the statutory definition, considers the Guidance, and weighs the evidence appropriately, it is unlikely that its decision on this question will be interfered with on appeal, unless on grounds of perversity.[1]

---

1   See *Quinlan v B & Q plc* (1998) IDS Brief 614, EAT and *Foster v Hampshire Fire and Rescue Service* (1998) 43 BMLR 186, EAT. A tribunal cannot simply ignore uncontested medical evidence: *Kapadia v London Borough of Lambeth* [2000] IRLR 14 (confirmed by the Court of Appeal, 9 June 2000, unreported). Equally, it is inadvisable for a tribunal to conduct its own tests of the status or extent of an applicant's disability: *London Underground Ltd v Bragg* (1999) EAT/847/98. Knowledge of the disability by the defendant is not an ingredient of the test of whether there is a disability or not: *Barker v Westbridge International Ltd* (2000) EAT/1180/98.

2.2   MEANING OF 'DISABILITY' AND 'DISABLED PERSON'

2.2.1   As already noted, a 'disabled person' is a person who has a 'disability' and a person has a 'disability' if he or she has a physical or mental impairment which has a substantial and long-term adverse effect on his or her ability to carry out normal day-to-day activities.[1] It might be useful to take account of what the legislature hoped to achieve in defining the protected class in this way. The apparent intention was to create a common sense definition which fitted the generally accepted perception of what is a disability and who is a disabled person, and which provided certainty and avoided vagueness.[2] It was thought that the definition, and the legislation which it underpins, would not be credible if it embraced individuals who were not fairly or generally recognised as disabled. The government of the day believed that the definition would cover the vast majority of the 6.5 million disabled persons in Britain identified by the 1988 Office of Population Census and Surveys report.[3]

---

1   DDA 1995, s 1 (subject to the provisions of Sch 1, the statutory Guidance and the Disability Discrimination (Meaning of Disability) Regulations 1996, SI 1996/1455).
2   HC Deb Standing Committee E, col 73. However, tribunals and courts must be aware that a relatively small proportion of disabled people are visibly disabled and should avoid

approaching this issue with a stereotypical image of a disabled person as someone who uses a wheelchair or has severely impaired mobility: *Vicary v British Telecommunications* [1999] IRLR 680.
3 Martin, Meltzer and Elliott, *The Prevalence of Disability Among Adults: OPCS Surveys of Disability in Great Britain Report 1* (1988, London: HMSO). More recently, it has been estimated that approximately 11.7 million adults (20 per cent of the population) are covered by the Act: Whitfield, *The Disability Discrimination Act: Analysis of Data from an Omnibus Survey* (1997, London: Department of Social Security).

2.2.2 The Employment Appeal Tribunal in *Goodwin v The Patent Office*,[1] a decision equally relevant in non-employment cases, has set out the correct approach to the question of whether an applicant is a disabled person within the meaning of the Act. The tribunal (or court) should look carefully at what the parties say in the documents setting out the claim and the defence.[2] Whether the issue of disability is in contention should be identified before the hearing and standard directions or a directions hearing will often be appropriate. Where expert evidence is to be called, advance notice should be given to the other party and a copy of any expert report provided.[3] Above all, the tribunal (or court) should adopt an inquisitorial or interventionist approach to the question of disability, while a purposive approach to the construction of the statute should be taken so as to construe the language of the Act in a way which gives effect to Parliament's intention. Explicit reference should always be made to any relevant provision of the Guidance or Code of Practice, but without creating an extra hurdle over which the applicant (or claimant) must jump. The tribunal (or court) should look at the evidence by reference to four different conditions:

(1) Does the applicant have an impairment?
(2) Does it have an adverse effect on the ability to carry out normal day-to-day activities?
(3) Is the adverse effect substantial?
(4) Is the adverse effect long term?

Each of these elements of the definition of disability is considered in turn below.

1 [1999] IRLR 4, EAT.
2 In the context of employment tribunal proceedings, these will be the originating application and notice of appearance.
3 In non-employment proceedings, account will have to be taken of Civil Procedure Rules 1998, Part 35 and the associated Practice Direction on expert evidence.

2.3 IMPAIRMENT

2.3.1 The term 'impairment' is vital to an understanding of the concept of disability. Yet it is not defined in the legislation. A literal interpretation of the word would suggest a condition of weakness, injury or damage, but the term has a more precise meaning in medical circles. The World Health Organization (WHO) 1980 classification of impairment, disability and handicap defines impairment as 'any loss or abnormality of psychological, physiological, or anatomical structure or function'.[1] The tenor of the parliamentary debates on the DDA 1995 suggests that the intention was to base the framework of disability discrimination law upon a medical model of disability. In that regard, the WHO definition may be a helpful one (although not necessarily one that would be embraced by disabled people themselves).

---

1   World Health Organization, *International Classification of Impairments, Disabilities and Handicaps: A Manual of Classification Relating to the Consequences of Disease* (1980, Geneva: WHO).

2.3.2   The Guidance anticipates that in many cases there will be no dispute over whether or not a person has an impairment. It makes clear that the question of how an impairment was caused is not a relevant consideration. However, the Guidance does not go any further in explaining the term 'impairment'.[1]

---

1   Guidance, Part I, para 10 et seq. Note that an impairment includes one which is controlled or corrected by medical treatment, medication, prosthesis, auxiliary devices or other aids: DDA 1995, Sch 1, para 6. See **2.5.12** et seq.

Physical impairment

2.3.3   The term 'physical impairment' is also not defined or further explained in the DDA 1995.[1] However, an addiction to (including dependency upon) alcohol, nicotine or any other substance does not amount to an impairment for the purposes of the Act.[2] That does not prevent, for example, liver disease resulting from alcohol dependency or abuse from counting as an impairment, even though alcoholism itself would not be so treated.[3] This exclusion also does not prevent an addiction which was originally the result of administration of medically prescribed drugs or other medical treatment from amounting to an impairment, all other things being equal.[4] So, for example, an addiction to pain-killers, to sedatives or to a mood-altering drug may amount to an impairment provided that the drug in question was *medically prescribed* and not simply bought over-the-counter without prescription or otherwise acquired. Seasonal allergic rhinitis (a form of severe hay fever) is also treated as not amounting to an impairment.[5] In this case, however, account might be taken of the condition so far as it aggravates the effect of another condition which does amount to an impairment (for example, a breathing impairment, such as asthma).[6]

---

1   Although note that the Act treats a severe disfigurement as a relevant impairment in defined circumstances (see Sch 1, para 3 and the more detailed discussion of this provision at **2.5.10**). Many commonly accepted conditions (such as orthopaedic impairments, cerebral palsy, epilepsy, muscular dystrophy, multiple sclerosis, cancer, heart disease, diabetes and tuberculosis) will almost invariably qualify as impairments.
2   Disability Discrimination (Meaning of Disability) Regulations 1996, SI 1996/1455, regs 2 and 3(1) made under DDA 1995, Sch 1, para 1(2)(a) and (3). This regulation-making power provides flexibility to deal with future medical developments and to resolve problems of interpretation that arise through case-law or medically disputed or controversial conditions: HC Deb Standing Committee E, cols 105 and 109.
3   Guidance, Part I, para 11.
4   Disability Discrimination (Meaning of Disability) Regulations 1996, SI 1996/1455, reg 3(2).
5   Ibid, reg 4(2).

6   Disability Discrimination (Meaning of Disability) Regulations 1996, SI 1996/1455, reg 4(3).

Mental impairment

2.3.4   The term 'mental impairment' is only partly defined in the Act and then not in a particularly helpful way.[1] The Guidance is of little further assistance, indicating that the term refers to 'a wide range of impairments relating to mental functioning, including what are often known as learning disabilities (formerly known as "mental handicap")'.[2] Clearly, it is intended that learning, psychiatric and psychological impairments are to be included,[3] but regulation-making powers have been used to exclude certain anti-social disorders and addictions.[4] To that end, the conditions of a tendency to set fires, to steal or to physical or sexual abuse of other persons, together with the conditions of exhibitionism and voyeurism, are treated as not amounting to impairments.[5]

1   See DDA 1995, Sch 1, para 1(1) discussed below.
2   Guidance, Part I, para 13.
3   Although, as already noted, addiction to alcohol, nicotine or any other substance has been excluded (whether this amounts to a mental or a physical impairment). See **2.3.3**.
4   HC Deb Standing Committee E, cols 72 and 105.
5   Disability Discrimination (Meaning of Disability) Regulations 1996, SI 1996/1455, reg 4(1) made under DDA 1995, Sch 1, para 1(2)–(3). See HC Deb Standing Committee E, col 109.

2.3.5   A mental impairment *includes* 'an impairment resulting from or consisting of a mental illness' – but only if 'the illness is a *clinically well-recognised* illness'.[1] What amounts to a clinically well-recognised illness will be a question of fact for the decision of a tribunal or court. This will clearly call for expert medical evidence in tribunal or court proceedings where there is any doubt about whether or not an apparent mental illness is well-recognised by medical opinion. In difficult cases, tribunals may be called upon to choose between opposing medical expert evidence. Clearly, merely *some* degree of recognition in *some* quarters of medical opinion will not be sufficient. General medical recognition of the condition as a mental illness will be called for and there is room for lengthy medical and legal dispute about whether a claimant is clinically mentally impaired. The EAT in *Goodwin v The Patent Office* recommends that, where there is doubt as to whether a mental illness counts as a disability or not, reference should be made to the WHO *International Classification of Diseases*.[2]

1   DDA 1995, Sch 1, para 1(1) (emphasis added).
2   [1999] IRLR 4, EAT. See also Guidance, Part I, para 14 to the same effect.

2.3.6   The definition of 'mental impairment' used in the 1995 Act is not the same as that used in other mental health legislation.[1] The fact that an impairment would be a mental impairment for other purposes does not prevent it from being a mental impairment under the 1995 Act, but it is not to be treated as automatically so. Nevertheless, mental impairments (including learning disabilities) that are not mental illnesses are covered by the disability discrimination legislation. Similarly, persons with recognised mental illnesses are treated as disabled persons under the DDA 1995. This will include individuals experiencing schizophrenia, manic depression, severe and extended depressive psychoses and a range of other conditions recognised by clinical psychiatrists and psychologists. However, the Act is not intended to cover 'moods or mild eccentricities', 'obscure conditions unrecognised by reputable clinicians' and 'mild or tendentious' conditions. At the same time, 'arrested or incomplete development of the mind, psychopathic disorder and any other disorder or disability of mind' do fall within the 1995 definition of mental impairment, provided they are conditions which have attracted clinical recognition,[2] and unless otherwise excluded by regulation.[3]

1   DDA 1995, s 68(1). See, for example, Mental Health Act 1983, s 1(2).
2   HC Deb Standing Committee E, cols 103–105.
3   See **2.3.4**.

Sensory and other impairments

2.3.7   Are individuals with sensory impairments embraced by the definition of physical or mental impairment used in the DDA 1995? Sensory impairments include deafness, other hearing impairments or loss, blindness, partial sightedness and dual sensory impairments (such as combined loss of speech and hearing). It is clear that the legislature intended that persons with sensory impairments should be covered by the legislation:

> 'The terms physical and mental are intended to be seen in their widest sense and should comprehensively cover all forms of impairment ... [A] third category, in addition to physical and mental impairment, might imply that those categories are not all-embracing ... Sensory conditions would generally be covered as physical conditions or, exceptionally, in cases such as hysterical deafness, as mental conditions.'[1]

That is as clear an expression of legislative intention as one could hope to receive and, should there be any doubt whether or not an individual who has a sensory impairment is entitled to bring proceedings under the Act, reference should be made to the legislative history of the measure. In any event, the Guidance makes it plain that the concept of a physical or mental impairment includes sensory impairments, such as those affecting sight or hearing.[2]

1   HC Deb Standing Committee E, col 71.
2   Guidance, Part I, para 12.

2.3.8   Nevertheless, there remains some ground for doubt and argument about what impairments are of a physical or mental nature, and undoubtedly there will be difficult cases where the point will be taken in litigation. For example, the condition of chronic fatigue syndrome (so-called 'ME') is one which is not universally recognised in medicine but, where it is, there is doubt about whether its origins are physical, viral or psychological.[1] Similarly, there is disagreement about whether epilepsy is a physical disability (because of its physical manifestations) or a mental disability (because of its origins as a disturbance in the brain). It cannot be imagined that the legislation will not afford protection against discrimination to persons with epilepsy, despite this dichotomy, whereas doubt will almost certainly be cast upon whether individuals with other conditions (such as 'stress', pre-menstrual tension, obesity and so-called 'repetitive strain injury') are within the protected class. It is important to note that the DDA 1995 does not recognise the concept of a generic disability. In each case, the individual will have to show how his or her condition and its effects fit into the definitional framework erected by the statute.[2]

---

1 The condition was recognised as amounting to a disability for the individual applicant in *O'Neill v Symm & Co Ltd* [1998] IRLR 233, EAT, where the tribunal at first instance placed reliance upon expert evidence and the WHO *International Classification of Diseases.*

2 See for example: *Gittins v Oxford Radcliffe NHS Trust* (2000) EAT/193/99 (bulimia is not a generic disability; it is the effects of bulimia on the individual applicant which are in issue.

2.4 ABILITY TO CARRY OUT NORMAL DAY-TO-DAY ACTIVITIES

2.4.1 A person is a disabled person only if possessing an impairment that has an adverse effect, of the degree required, upon that person's 'ability to carry out normal day-to-day activities'.[1] An impairment is treated as affecting the ability of the person concerned to carry out normal day-to-day activities *only* if it affects one of the following:[2]

– mobility;
– manual dexterity;
– physical co-ordination;
– continence;[3]
– ability to lift, carry or otherwise move everyday objects;
– speech, hearing or eyesight;
– memory or ability to concentrate, learn or understand;
– perception of the risk of physical danger.

The Guidance explains what is meant by the scope of the eight listed activities,[4] and this is not reproduced here.

---

1 DDA 1995, s 1(1).

2 Ibid, Sch 1, para 4(1). Note the power to make regulations under Sch 1, para 4(2). No regulations have been made at the time of writing.

3 A rare example is *Thornhill v London Central Bus Co Ltd* (2000) EAT/463/99 (an unduly frequent desire to urinate, which did not lead to incontinence, was not a disability).

4 Guidance, Part II, paras C14–C21.

2.4.2 It is clear that it is the effect upon the complainant (and not persons generally) that matters. The EAT in *Goodwin v The Patent Office* has given important guidance on this question:

> 'What the Act is concerned with is an impairment on the person's *ability* to carry out activities. The fact that a person can carry out such activities does not mean that his abilities to carry them out has not been impaired ... In order to constitute an adverse effect, it is not the doing of the acts which is the focus of attention but rather the ability to do (or not do) the acts ... The focus of attention required by the Act is on the things that the applicant either cannot do or can only do with difficulty, rather than on the things the person can do.'[1]

This should mean that, contrary to trends in some of the early first instance decisions, a claimant should find it relatively easy to establish his or her status as a disabled person, despite having adopted means of neutralising the effects of a disabling condition or environment.[2]

---

1   [1999] IRLR 4, EAT. Expert evidence of what the applicant or claimant can and cannot do (and the circumstances of that capability) will be important. Often this will be in the form of a report or evidence from a medical specialist (such as a consultant or occupational health professional). However, the tribunal (or a court) must not delegate the decision as to what are normal day-to-day activities to the expert witness. That is a judicial decision, to be arrived at using basic common sense, and in the light of the evidence, the statute and the Guidance: *Vicary v British Telecommunications plc* [1999] IRLR 680.

2   But there is a 'Catch-22' for many applicants in arguing that they are sufficiently disabled to be covered by the Act, but not so disabled as to be prevented from carrying out, for example, the duties of employment. See *London Underground Ltd v Bragg* EAT/847/98. The proper test of whether a person is able to carry out normal day-to-day activities is not to be judged by reference to whether or not the person is carrying out a prescribed job of work: *Law Hospital NHS Trust v Rush* (2000) EAT/842/99.

2.4.3   However, the reference to the effect which an impairment has upon the ability to carry out normal day-to-day activities is designed to exclude mild or trivial conditions from the scope of the DDA 1995. For example, individuals with temporary and non-chronic conditions, such as sprains or influenza, most obviously fall outside the boundaries of the statute.[1] Moreover, a person who, because of some physical or mental limitation, is effectively excluded from participating in a specialised activity or pursuit – which the majority of people would be incapable of enjoying in any event – enjoys no protection under the Act. Thus, a person with colour blindness, who is disqualified from being a commercial airline pilot, cannot usually be said to experience adverse effects on his or her ability to carry out normal day-to-day activities. A person who is left-handed will be disabled in using industrial machinery designed for right-handed use, but left-handedness is not usually recognised as a disability. An individual with a poor educational record because of comparatively low or average intelligence will be effectively disqualified from aspiring to the position of heart surgeon, but the majority of the population can be said to be 'disabled' to that extent also. It is not thought that colour blindness, left-handedness or indifferent educational attainment are within the scope of the Act.[2] It is also not intended that activities which are normal only for a particular person or group of people should be included. Account must be taken of how far the activity is normal for most people and carried out by most people on a daily or frequent and fairly regular basis.[3]

---

1   This is also underlined by the 'substantial and long-term adverse effect' formula discussed at **2.5**.

2   See further: Guidance, Part II, para C3.

3   See Guidance, Part II, para C2.

2.4.4   Where a child under six years of age has an impairment which does not have an effect on the child's ability to carry out one of the listed normal day-to-day activities, the impairment is nevertheless to be taken to have a substantial and long-term adverse effect on the child's ability to carry out normal day-to-day activities if it would normally have such an effect on the ability of a person aged six years or over.[1]

1 Disability Discrimination (Meaning of Disability) Regulations 1996, SI 1996/1455, reg 6.

2.4.5 Although the DDA 1995 covers clinically well-recognised mental illnesses, it might be difficult for persons with such illnesses to be able to show that they have an adverse effect on normal day-to-day activities, as those activities are defined in the Act. In the employment sphere, many mental illnesses might have an adverse effect upon a person's full working capacity, but work is not one of the listed normal day-to-day activities.[1]

1 See Guidance, Part II, para C3.

2.5 SUBSTANTIAL ADVERSE EFFECT

2.5.1 To satisfy the definition of a disability, the putative disabled person must demonstrate that he or she has a physical or mental impairment 'which has a substantial and long-term adverse effect' on the ability to carry out normal day-to-day activities.[1] The statutory Guidance specifically refers to the matters which a court or tribunal ought to take into account when determining whether an impairment has a substantial adverse effect on a person's ability to carry out normal day-to-day activities or whether such an impairment has a long-term adverse effect. Without intending to weaken the definition of disability or to exclude particular impairments,[2] it gives examples in four particular circumstances:[3]

(1) effects which it would be reasonable to regard as substantial adverse effects in relation to particular activities;
(2) effects which it would not be reasonable to regard as substantial adverse effects in relation to particular activities;
(3) substantial adverse effects which it would be reasonable to regard as long term;
(4) substantial adverse effects which it would not be reasonable to regard as long term.

By these means, the Guidance assists the present discussion by illustrating and exemplifying how the statutory definition works in practice.

1 DDA 1995, s 1(1).
2 See the assurance given at HC Deb Standing Committee E, col 124.
3 See Guidance, Part II, paras C5–C21. It is not proposed to replicate those examples here.

Meaning of 'substantial'

2.5.2 Whether an impairment has a substantial adverse effect upon a person is not explained in the DDA 1995.[1] It was intended that minor impairments should not provide a cause of action. The use of the word 'substantial' is designed to ensure that trivial conditions are beyond the scope of the legislation.[2] For example, persons with a minor vision impairment (such as 20/40 vision) might find it difficult to show that their impairment has a substantial adverse effect of the kind required by the statute.[3] The Guidance confirms that a substantial effect is one that is more than minor or trivial. It indicates that the requirement that an adverse effect be substantial is designed to reflect the general understanding of disability as being a limitation going beyond the normal differences in ability between people.[4] In the final analysis, however, what is and what is not a 'substantial' adverse effect will be a matter for judicial interpretation of the statutory language, albeit assisted by the provisions of the Guidance and any appropriate regulations.[5]

---

1   The word 'substantial' is also used, for example, in the employment provisions of ss 5 and 6 and there is no suggestion that this should be interpreted in different ways in different contexts. See the discussion of this question in Chapter 3 below.
2   HC Deb Standing Committee E, col 114; HC Deb, vol 566, col 174.
3   Someone whose hearing impairment merely requires them to view television with the volume up and results in occasional difficulty in hearing speech may have difficulty in showing substantial adverse effect. See the *obiter dicta* in *London Underground Ltd v Bragg* EAT/847/98.
4   Guidance, Part II, para A1. For an example of where an employment tribunal mistakenly gave the word 'substantial' its ordinary dictionary definition, rather than following the Guidance, see *Vicary v British Telecommunications plc* [1999] IRLR 680 (ability to prepare vegetables, cut up meat and carry a tray held on appeal to be all examples of normal day-to-day activities, as were various DIY and household tasks, so that an inability to carry out these functions was regarded as 'obviously' amounting to a substantial adverse effect on the ability to carry out normal day-to-day activities). It is for the tribunal (or the court) to assess what adverse effects are substantial or not.
5   DDA 1995, Sch 1, para 5 provides that regulations may be made to provide for an effect of a prescribed kind on the ability of a person to carry out normal day-to-day activities to be treated as being (or, alternatively, as not being) a substantial adverse effect. No general regulations have been made under this power; but see the Disability Discrimination (Meaning of Disability) Regulations 1996, SI 1996/1455, reg 5 (on tattoos and body piercing, discussed at **2.5.11**) and reg 6 (on babies and young children under six years of age, discussed at **2.4.4**).

2.5.3   The Guidance states that, in judging whether the adverse effects of an impairment upon a normal day-to-day activity are substantial, account should be taken of the time taken to carry out the activity and the way in which the activity is carried out.[1] If the impairment adversely affects the speed or manner in which that person can perform a particular activity in comparison with other persons, that is a relevant consideration. Environmental considerations will also be important (for example, the effect which temperature or stress has upon the impairment).[2] It will also be appropriate to take account of the cumulative effects of an impairment.[3] For example, someone with mild cerebral palsy may experience only minor effects upon any of a number of the listed normal day-to-day activities, but the aggregate effect may be quite disabling and should be treated as so under the Act.[4] The cumulative effect of two or more impairments might also produce the substantial adverse effect on normal day-to-day activities called for by the statute – even if, in isolation, each impairment could not be said to have such an effect.[5]

1 Guidance, Pt II, paras A2–A3.
2 Ibid, para A10. The EAT has said that, in judging whether an impairment has a *substantial* adverse effect, a tribunal may take into account how the applicant appears to the tribunal to manage, 'although tribunals will be slow to regard a person's capabilities in the relatively strange adversarial environment as an entirely reliable guide to the level of ability to perform normal day-to-day activities' (*Goodwin v The Patent Office* [1999] IRLR 4, EAT).
3 Ibid, para A4.
4 Ibid, para A5 and see the examples provided there.
5 Ibid, para A6.

2.5.4 Account should also be taken of how far a person might reasonably be expected to modify their behaviour so as to prevent or reduce the adverse effects of an impairment on normal day-to-day activities.[1] For example, a person with a condition which manifests itself as an allergic reaction to certain substances might reasonably be expected to take steps to avoid those substances. To that extent, that person could not be said to experience a substantial adverse effect upon his or her normal day-to-day activities and would no longer satisfy the definition of disability. However, such avoidance or coping strategies must be subject to a test of reasonableness and might produce second order disabling effects in themselves. In any event, it must be recognised that such strategies might break down at times of stress and that must be weighed in the balance.[2]

1 Guidance, Pt II, paras A7–A9.
2 Ibid, para A8. Note also para A9 discussed at **2.5.13**. It is also the case that the fact that a person is able to mitigate the effects of a disability does not mean that they are not disabled within the meaning of the legislation: *Vicary v British Telecommunications plc* [1999] IRLR 680.

Recurring conditions

2.5.5 The DDA 1995 provides that if an impairment is one which has had a substantial adverse effect on a person's ability to carry out normal day-to-day activities, but subsequently ceased to have that effect, it will be treated as continuing to have such a substantial adverse effect (that is, during any intervening period of remission or good health) 'if that effect is likely to recur'.[1] This is an essential provision which recognises that there are many impairments whose effects upon day-to-day activities fluctuate. In the case of epilepsy or multiple sclerosis, for example, the underlying condition is constant, but the adverse effects of the condition are variable, with periods of impairment or disability alternating with periods of good health and normal activity. Such conditions are within the Act.[2] Nevertheless, seasonal allergic rhinitis, a condition whose effects are recurring and can be substantial for a brief time, has been excluded by regulation.[3]

1 DDA 1995, Sch 1, para 2(2). The likelihood of an effect recurring shall be disregarded in circumstances which may be prescribed in regulations (Sch 1, para 2(3)). No such regulations have been made to date.
2 HC Deb Standing Committee E, col 113.
3 See **2.3.3**.

2.5.6 In respect of an impairment or condition with recurring effects, the Guidance states that an effect is likely to recur if 'it is more likely than not that the effect will recur'.[1] If the effects are likely to recur beyond 12 months after the first occurrence, then they are to be treated as long term.[2] However, in judging the likelihood of recurrence, account should be taken of all the circumstances, including any reasonable expectation that the person concerned should take steps to prevent the recurrence.[3]

---

1 Guidance, Part II, para B3. It is likely an event will happen if it is more probable than not that it will happen: ibid, para B7.
2 Ibid, para B4.
3 Ibid, para B5 applying much the same behavioural expectations as were discussed at **2.5.4** (and see Guidance, Part II, paras A7–A9).

Progressive conditions

2.5.7 Special provision is made for persons with progressive conditions (such as 'cancer, multiple sclerosis, muscular dystrophy or infection by the human immunodeficiency virus').[1] Where a person has a 'progressive condition' and, as a result of that condition, he or she has an impairment which has (or had) an effect on his or her ability to carry out normal day-to-day activities, but that effect is not (or was not) a *substantial* adverse effect, such a person is treated as having an impairment which has such a substantial adverse effect if the condition is likely to result in that person having such an impairment in the future.[2]

---

1 DDA 1995, Sch 1, para 8(1)(a). This list is not intended to be exhaustive. Regulations may provide (for the purposes of this provision only) that conditions of a prescribed description are to be treated as being or not being progressive conditions (Sch 1, para 8(2)). No such regulations have been made to date.
2 Ibid, para 8(1). However, the double-edged nature of this sword is that a degenerative condition might be seen as undermining an applicant's claim in a Part II case to be employable (with or without adjustments) for the future. See *London Underground Ltd v Bragg* EAT/847/98. The answer must be that this is a question that goes to remedy rather than to establishing liability for discrimination.

2.5.8 It is apparent from the parliamentary debates that the legislature did not intend that this provision should protect individuals from discrimination where they possess asymptomatic conditions (for example, a person diagnosed as HIV positive but without manifest symptoms of the virus or a related illness):[1]

> 'We recognise that there is a need to protect people where the effect of the condition is not yet substantial but is expected to be so in the future. That is why the [Act] specifically includes people with progressive conditions as soon as there are any effects on their ability to carry out normal day-to-day activities. However, we do not believe that it would be right to include people with conditions which may remain latent, possibly for a considerable number of years ... The Disability Discrimination [Act] is designed to protect people who have, or ... have had, an actual disability. It is not a general anti-discrimination [Act] nor a general health discrimination [Act]. If we extend it to cover people who may develop a disability at some unspecified time in the future we will undermine the effectiveness of the [Act] by creating uncertainty about who is covered.'[2]

A symptomless illness or condition is not an impairment which has yet affected one of the designated normal day-to-day activities.[3]

---

1   HL Deb, vol 566, col 1061.
2   Ibid, vol 564, col 1682.
3   DDA 1995, Sch 1, para 4.

2.5.9   Despite the inclusive tone of the statute's treatment of progressive conditions, the wording of the Act makes it plain that it is to be the *future* effects of a *presently existing* progressive condition only which the law intends to embrace. A person whose medical status or condition merely indicates that it is likely that he or she might suffer from a progressive condition *in the future* is not treated as having an impairment with substantial adverse effects on ability to carry out normal day-to-day activities. Thus the 'progressive conditions' provision does not include within the protection of the Act individuals who merely have a genetic or other predisposition to (or risk of) a progressive condition in the future. Individuals who have undergone a medical test which indicated that they have a predictive propensity to develop an impairment at a later date (such as Usher syndrome, Huntingdon's chorea, Alzheimer's disease or multiple sclerosis) are not protected from disability discrimination at this point. The Act also does not protect individuals who have a mistaken or erroneous reputation as a person who has (or had) a disability or might do so in the future.

Severe disfigurement

2.5.10   An impairment which consists of a severe disfigurement is treated as having a substantial adverse effect on the ability of the person concerned to carry out normal day-to-day activities.[1] The assessment of the severity of a disfigurement is a matter of degree and account may be taken of where on the body the feature in question is to be found.[2] The inclusion of severe disfigurements within the definition of disability for the purposes of the Act is important. Persons with facial port wine stains, other birth marks, severe burns or scalds, and other disfiguring signs face discrimination based upon aesthetic appearance.[3] Such an impairment is rarely disabling in itself. Rather the disability experienced by disfigured individuals is as a result of society's reaction to perceived imperfection. This is a rare example of the legislation acknowledging a social model of disability rather than a purely medical one.

---

1   DDA 1995, Sch 1, para 3(1).
2   Guidance, Part II, para A17. The implication is that a facial disfigurement is more likely to pass the test of severity than one hidden by a person's clothing.
3   The Guidance also refers to scars, limb or postural deformation or diseases of the skin (Part II, para A17).

2.5.11   Whilst the Act does not automatically exclude deliberately acquired severe disfigurements, it does provide for their potential exclusion by regulations.[1] Regulations stipulate that a severe disfigurement is not to be treated as having a substantial adverse effect on the ability of the person concerned to carry out normal day-to-day activities if it consists of a tattoo (which has not been removed) or body-piercing for decorative or other *non-medical purposes* (including any object attached through the piercing for such purposes).[2] For the moment, the regulations do not make any further exclusions and it should be noted that there is no general exclusion of deliberately acquired disfigurements (such as facial or bodily scarring caused by self-mutilation or self-administered injury).[3]

---

1   DDA 1995, Sch 1, para 3(3).
2   Disability Discrimination (Meaning of Disability) Regulations 1996, SI 1996/1455, reg 5. *Quaere* whether a severe disfigurement resulting from an attempt to remove a tattoo would also be excluded? It is suggested that it would not be so excluded.
3   HC Deb Standing Committee E, cols 110–111.

Effect of medical treatment

2.5.12   Does a person whose disability is controlled, corrected or adjusted by medical treatment, or by the use of medication, auxiliary devices or other aids, remain a person with an impairment for the purpose of protection against disability-related discrimination? In a strict sense, such a person might no longer be said to have an impairment which has an adverse effect on normal day-to-day activities. Yet, at the same time, the underlying condition or impairment remains and the person is disabled to the extent that the method of control or correction will involve residual or second order effects and inconveniences. Equally, such a person might experience continuing adverse treatment at the hands of others who might continue to regard that person as disabled. That might be the case illustratively where an individual walks with the aid of a prosthesis or is mobile with the assistance of a motorised wheelchair.

2.5.13   The DDA 1995 provides that an impairment which would be likely to have a substantial adverse effect on the ability of the person concerned to carry out normal day-to-day activities, but for the fact that measures are being taken to treat or correct it, is nevertheless to be treated as continuing to be an impairment amounting to a disability.[1] The legislation gives examples of measures treating or correcting an impairment as including 'medical treatment and the use of a prosthesis or other aid'.[2] The Act does not define what is meant by 'medical treatment', but the EAT has held that counselling sessions with a consultant clinical psychologist constitute such treatment.[3] If a disabled person is advised by a medical practitioner to behave in a certain way in order to reduce the impact of a disability, that might count as treatment to be disregarded under this provision.[4] Provided that the impairment would have had a substantial adverse effect on a person's ability to carry out normal day-to-day activities *but for* the fact that it has been treated or controlled or corrected in the manner described, then it is also to be treated as continuing to have such a substantial adverse effect even though no such effect is actually experienced because of such treatment or control or correction. An example of such an impairment might include insulin-controlled diabetes or medication-regulated epilepsy. A further illustration would be hearing loss improved by a hearing aid.

1 DDA 1995, Sch 1, para 6(1).
2 Ibid, para 6(2).
3 *Kapadia v London Borough of Lambeth* [2000] IRLR 14 (confirmed by the Court of Appeal, 9 June 2000, unreported). Similarly, 'aid' is not defined, but the EAT has offered the *obiter* view that this refers 'to aids such as zimmer frames or sticks or wheelchairs and not to household objects' (such as automatic can openers): *Vicary v British Telecommunications* [1999] IRLR 680.
4 Guidance, Pt II, para A9, and thus that behaviour should not be taken into account at all under paras A7–A8 (see **2.5.4**).

2.5.14 The Guidance states that this provision applies even if the measures in question result in the effects being completely under control or not at all apparent.[1] The question of whether or not a person has an impairment which has a substantial adverse effect upon the ability to carry out normal day-to-day activities is to be answered by reference to what would be the effect of the impairment or condition but for the treatment, aid or medication.[2] The EAT has said that a tribunal (or court) should examine how an applicant's abilities have been affected whilst on medication (or, by analogy, any other medical treatment). It should then consider the 'deduced effects': that is, what effects would there have been *without* the medication (or other medical intervention) and whether those effects are clearly more than minor or trivial.[3]

1 Guidance, Part II, para A12.
2 Ibid, para A13.
3 See *Goodwin v The Patent Office* [1999] IRLR 4 and *Kapadia v London Borough of Lambeth* [2000] IRLR 14 (confirmed by the Court of Appeal, 9 June 2000, unreported).

2.5.15 However, this provision does not extend to the impairment of a person's sight, to the extent that the impairment is, in the particular person's case, 'correctable by spectacles or contact lenses'.[1] Individuals with spectacles or contact lenses which compensate for an impairment to their sight do not usually regard themselves as disabled and are not treated as such for the purposes of the Act. The use of the word 'correctable' seems to suggest also that an individual who has a sight impairment, but does not use spectacles or contact lenses that might otherwise correct the sight loss, would not qualify as a 'disabled person'. In other words, this provision of the Act only embraces involuntary disabilities. This might mean that a person who chooses not to take basic, non-surgical remedial action to correct a vision impairment cannot claim protection of the Act. The statute does not suggest that a sight impairment correctable by surgical techniques is presently excluded from the coverage of the legislation. However, the Guidance states that the only effects on ability to carry out normal day-to-day activities to be considered are *those which remain* when spectacles or contact lenses are used (or would remain if they were used).[2] There would seem to be some room for confusion here which will call for judicial resolution.

1 DDA 1995, Sch 1, para 6(3)(a). Regulations may also provide that this exception be extended to other impairments: Sch 1, para 6(3)(b). No such regulations have been made to date.

2.6   LONG-TERM ADVERSE EFFECT

2.6.1   The DDA 1995 is more expansive in its explication of what amounts to long-term effects of an impairment. It provides that the effect of an impairment is 'long term' if:

–   it has lasted for at least 12 months; or
–   the period for which it lasts is likely to be at least 12 months; or
–   it is likely to last for the rest of the life of the person affected.[1]

The intention is to exclude from the protection of the anti-discrimination principle those persons whose impairment or disability is merely short term or temporary.[2]

1   DDA 1995, Sch 1, para 2(1). Regulations may prescribe circumstances in which an effect
    which would not otherwise be long term is to be treated as a long-term effect or an effect
    which would otherwise be long term is not to be treated as a long-term effect (Sch 1,
    para 2(4)). No such regulations have been made to date.
2   HC Deb Standing Committee E, col 70.

2.6.2   Suppose that an employee suffered a sudden onset of deafness and was dismissed within six months of medical diagnosis. Would the employee have redress under the law, all other things being equal? Even though at the time of dismissal the impairment had not lasted at least 12 months, nevertheless the employee should be able to show that the period for which the hearing impairment is likely to last is at least 12 months, and so the employee would be enabled to seek a remedy. However, a person refused access to a restaurant because he has a broken leg in plaster, or because she exhibits obvious signs of German measles, would not have redress because the impairments or conditions in question do not have, or are not likely to have, long-term effects.[1] How does the Act treat a person diagnosed as having a terminal illness with a prognosis that he or she would not live for more than a few months and less than 12 months?[2] Could such a person be lawfully refused, for example, provision of goods or services in a shop or restaurant? Terminal illnesses are within the definition and, in this case, the impairment can reasonably be expected to last for the rest of the life of the person affected.

1   See further HC Deb Standing Committee E, cols 77–78.
2   HC Deb Standing Committee E, col 78.

2.6.3   The Guidance states that, in judging whether the adverse effects of an impairment are long term, it is not necessary for the effect to be the same throughout the period in question. The effect may be variable or progressive. Provided the impairment continues to have (or is likely to have) an adverse effect on ability to carry out normal day-to-day activities throughout the period, there is a long-term effect.[1] The Guidance also states:

> 'In assessing the likelihood of an effect lasting for any period, account should be
> taken of the total period for which the effect exists. This includes any time before

the point when the discriminatory behaviour occurred as well as time afterwards. Account should also be taken of both the typical length of such an effect on an individual, and any relevant factors specific to this individual (for example, general state of health, age).'[2]

Note, however, that provision is also made for recurring effects.[3] If the adverse effects are likely to recur beyond 12 months after the first occurrence, they are to be treated as long term.[4] It is likely that an event will happen if it is more probable than not that it will happen.[5]

---

1 Guidance, Part II, paras B1–B2.
2 Ibid, para B8. See *Greenwood v British Airways plc* [1999] IRLR 600 to the effect that an employment tribunal in a Part II case should consider the adverse effects of the applicant's condition up to and including the date of the hearing. *Quaere* whether that is what para B8 means? *Greenwood* is a curious case where it would seem that the act of disability discrimination complained of triggered a recurrence of the applicant's disability which had appeared to have been successfully treated or at least under control.
3 See Sch 1, para 2(2) and the discussion at **2.5.5–2.5.6**.
4 Guidance, Part II, para B5.
5 Ibid, para B7.

Past disability and long-term adverse effect

2.6.4   Some modification of the meaning of 'long-term effect' is necessary in order to accommodate the inclusion of past disabilities.[1] When dealing with the question of whether a person with a past disability has experienced a long-term adverse effect on ability to carry out normal day-to-day activities, the effect of an impairment is a long-term effect if it has lasted for at least 12 months.[2] Where an impairment ceases to have a substantial adverse effect on a person's ability to carry out normal day-to-day activities, it is to be treated as continuing to have that effect if that effect recurs.[3]

---

1 By virtue of DDA 1995, s 2(2) and Sch 2, para 2.
2 DDA 1995, Sch 2, para 5 modifying Sch 1, para 2(1)–(3).
3 See Guidance, Part II, para B9.

2.7   PERSONS DEEMED TO BE DISABLED

2.7.1   There is no implicit assumption that a court or tribunal would regard a certification of a person as disabled under other disability legislation as conclusive or persuasive of their status under the DDA 1995. However, the Act contains one exceptional case in respect of a person who was a 'registered disabled person' under the Disabled Persons (Employment) Act 1944 (or its Northern Ireland equivalent) – a so-called 'Green Card' (in Northern Ireland, a 'Blue card') holder.[1] A person who was on the register maintained under the 1944 Act on 12 January 1995, and who remained registered on 2 December 1996, is 'deemed to have a disability'. That person is treated as a disabled person for the purpose of the application of any provision of the 1995 Act for 'the initial period'.[2] The certificate of registration is treated as conclusive evidence, in relation to the person with respect to whom it was issued, in respect

of the matters certified and, unless the contrary is shown, its validity is entitled
to be taken at face value.[3]

---

1   DDA 1995, Sch 1, para 7. For the modification of these provisions in the Northern Ireland
    context see Sch 1, para 49. Prescribed descriptions of persons might also be deemed to have
    disabilities and to be disabled persons for the purposes: Sch 1, para 7(5), (6). No such
    prescription has been made to date.
2   Ibid, para 7(2)(a).
3   Ibid, paras 7(3)–(4) and 7(7).

2.7.2   However, this deemed status only lasted for the so-called 'initial
period'.[1] This was a period of three years beginning on 2 December 1996 and
which ended on 1 December 1999.[2] Such a person will now need to meet the
statutory definition of 'disabled person' contained in all its detail in the 1995
Act and any accompanying guidance and regulations. In practice, that might
not be an insurmountable task for a person who qualified under the 1944 Act
and whose conditions and circumstances remain unchanged or comparable. In
any event, such a person was regarded as being a person who had a disability,
and thus to have been a disabled person, during the initial period.[3] This means
that they should be able to rely upon the extension of the Act to include
persons who have had a disability in the past.[4]

---

1   DDA 1995, Sch 1, para 7(2)(a).
2   Ibid, para 7(7).
3   Ibid, para 7(2)(b).
4   Ibid, s 2 and Sch 2 as discussed at **2.8**.

2.8   PAST DISABILITIES

2.8.1   Parts II and III of the DDA 1995 (discrimination in relation to
employment, contract work, trade organisations, goods, facilities, services and
premises) apply pari passu in relation to a person 'who has had a disability' as if
that person was a person who has that disability at the present or relevant time.[1]
The thinking behind this provision is as follows:

> 'It has become clear that people who have had a disability, although they may be no
> longer disabled as such, share with people who are currently disabled, a need for
> protection against discrimination in relation to their disability ... It is clearly a very
> important part of the whole process of recovery that someone who has been
> disabled is able not only to participate fully in employment and social activities but
> to feel confident in doing so ... In addition, we have been persuaded that it is not
> always possible to tell when a person has fully recovered from a disability and when
> the condition is no longer likely to recur.'[2]

It ensures consistency of treatment between persons who are presently disabled
and those individuals who have recovered from the same condition.[3]

---

1   DDA 1995, s 2(1). The substantive provisions of the Act are appropriately modified (s 2(2)
    and Sch 2). In particular, references in Parts II and III of the Act to a disabled person are
    also to be read as references to a person who has had a disability (Sch 2, para 2).
2   HL Deb, vol 564, col 1655.

2.8.2   In a case of alleged discrimination against a person who complains of an act based upon past disability, it does not matter that the relevant provisions of the DDA 1995 were not in force when that person was actually experiencing the disability in question. The question of whether a person had a disability at a particular time is determined as if the relevant provisions of the DDA 1995 which were in force at the time of the discriminatory act had been in force at the relevant time (ie when the person had the disability in issue).[1] Furthermore, the past disability in question might have been experienced at a time before the passing of the new legislation.[2]

1   DDA 1995, s 2(4).
2   Ibid, s 2(5).

2.8.3   The inclusion of past disabilities within the protection of the DDA 1995 is an important concession and provides a potential remedy for those persons who are discriminated against because of their history or record of disability. For example, a person with a history of depression or mental or emotional illness might be unreasonably excluded from employment opportunity but would otherwise have no cause of action unless the individual was suffering from the depression or mental or emotional illness at the time when the employment opportunity was denied. However, it is important to note that, where a person seeks to rely upon the status of being 'a person who has had a disability', it will still be necessary for that person to show that, at the relevant time in the past, he or she had a physical or mental impairment which had a substantial and long-term adverse effect on his or her ability to carry out normal day-to-day activities.[1]

1   Within the meaning of DDA 1995, s 1 and Sch 1.

2.9   FUTURE REFORM

In its final report in December 1999, the Disability Rights Task Force made a number of recommendations for the future reform of the definition of disability in the DDA 1995.[1] In particular, it recommends the extension of the definition to cover both people with cancer (as soon as it has a significant consequence on a person's life) and those with asymptomatic HIV (from diagnosis). Furthermore, it proposes that the definition should be reviewed to ensure that there is an appropriate and comprehensive coverage of mental health conditions under the Act. The Task Force would also like to see persons with severe but short-term conditions included (such as those with heart attacks, strokes or depression). Whether government will react positively to these recommendations remains to be seen.

1   Disability Rights Task Force, *From Exclusion to Inclusion: A Report of the Disability Rights Task Force for Disabled People* (1999, London: DfEE) Chapter 3.

Chapter 3

EMPLOYMENT AND CONTRACT WORK

3.1 INTRODUCTION

3.1.1 Part II of the DDA 1995 addresses the problem of discrimination against persons with disabilities in the field of employment. To a limited extent, it is modelled on similar provisions in the Sex Discrimination Act 1975 (SDA 1975) and the Race Relations Act 1976 (RRA 1976). Where the statutory language is common or identical, case-law under that legislation will be instructive. However, there are important differences between the DDA 1995 and the earlier statutes. In particular, the 1995 Act does not distinguish explicitly between direct and indirect forms of discrimination; uses a different comparative basis for detecting discrimination; contains a more broadly applicable justification defence; imposes a positive duty upon employers to accommodate disabled persons; and does not apply to small businesses (as defined). The Court of Appeal has expressly warned against approaching the 1995 Act with assumptions and concepts familiar from experience of the earlier equal opportunities statutes.[1]

---

1 *Clark v TDG Ltd t/a Novacold* [1999] IRLR 318, CA.

3.1.2 Part II of the DDA 1995, so far as it affects employment and contract work, came into force on 2 December 1996.[1] It is subject to regulations amplifying (and sometimes narrowing) the provisions on employment discrimination.[2] A code of practice (referred to hereafter as 'Employment Code of Practice') has been issued by the Secretary of State under s 53(1)(a). It provides guidance and assistance to employers in respect of their obligations under Part II.[3] It does not impose legal obligations of itself and is not intended to be an authoritative statement of law. However, it is admissible in proceedings before an employment tribunal or court, and these bodies must take into account any provision of the Employment Code of Practice which appears to be relevant to the determination of a question in those proceedings.[4]

---

1 Disability Discrimination Act 1995 (Commencement No 3 and Saving and Transitional Provisions) Order 1996, SI 1996/1474, art 2(3) and Sch, Part III subject to the saving and transitional provisions set out in art 3.
2 Disability Discrimination (Employment) Regulations 1996, SI 1996/1456 which came into force on 2 December 1996 and which were made under powers conferred by DDA 1995, ss 5(6)–(7), 6(8) and (10), and 12(3), and Sch 4, para 3. See also Disability Discrimination (Employment) Regulations (Northern Ireland) 1996, SR 1996/419.
3 *Code of Practice for the elimination of discrimination in the field of employment against disabled persons or persons who have had a disability* (1996, London: HMSO). The Employment Code of Practice came into force on 2 December 1996 by virtue of the Disability Discrimination (Guidelines and Code of Practice) (Appointed Day) Order 1996, SI 1996/1996, para 3. A separate (but essentially identical) Employment Code of Practice covers Northern Ireland,

reflecting the different institutional context of the province, and also came into force on
2 December 1996.
4   Employment Code of Practice, para 1.3 and DDA 1995, s 53(4)–(6). See generally, **9.3**. See
also: *Ridout v TC Group* [1998] IRLR 628, EAT; *Goodwin v The Patent Office* [1999] IRLR 4,
EAT; *London Borough of Hillingdon v Morgan* (1999) EAT/1493/98 27 May (unreported);
Clark v TDG Ltd t/a Novacold [1999] IRLR 318, CA and *HJ Heinz Co Ltd v Kenrick* [2000] IRLR
144, EAT.

3.1.3   The DDA 1995 repealed the statutory disabled workers' quota scheme
and the reserved occupations under the Disabled Persons (Employment) Acts
1944 and 1958, and made consequential amendments to other statutory
provisions affecting disabled employment rights or opportunities.[1]

1   DDA 1995, ss 61 and 70, and Sch 6 and 7. See **3.11–3.12**.

3.2   GENERAL PROHIBITION ON DISCRIMINATION IN EMPLOYMENT

3.2.1   Section 4 of the DDA 1995 makes it unlawful, in relation to employment
at establishments in Great Britain and in Northern Ireland,[1] for an employer to
discriminate against disabled persons.[2] As the section explains, this covers both
discrimination against disabled applicants in the recruitment and selection
process, as well as discrimination against disabled employees while in an
employer's employment.[3] The ministerial view is that:

> 'The [Act] prohibits an employer from discrimination against a disabled person in
> recruitment of new employees or against disabled employees. It uses broad and
> comprehensive general wording – as in race discrimination legislation – to cover all
> aspects of the recruitment process and the employment relationship. There is no
> need to deal with specific circumstances and forms of discrimination.'[4]

1   See s 4(6) as modified by s 70(6) and Sch 8, para 3.
2   As defined and discussed in Chapter 2 above. Note that the employment provisions of the
Act apply in relation to a person who has had a disability in the same way as they apply in
relation to a person who has that disability (s 2(1)). The task of identifying the employer is
not usually problematic, but see *Lancashire County Council v Mason* [1998] ICR 907, EAT
(neither the school governors nor the local education authority held to be liable for an
alleged act of disability discrimination in employment selection arrangements in the context
of a state-maintained county school with a delegated budget subject to the Education Act
1996, s 136 and Sch 14, disapplying s 133 of and Sch 13 to that Act; but now see the
Education (Modification of Enactments Relating to Employment) Order 1998, SI 1998/
218).
3   This section is virtually identical to the similar provisions in SDA 1975, s 6 and RRA 1976, s 4.
4   HC Deb Standing Committee E, col 142.

3.2.2   The liability of an employer may be vicarious liability for the actions of
employees in the course of employment.[1] The employer's liability may be
shared with another person who knowingly aids in the commission of an
unlawful act of discrimination.[2] These concepts are discussed in more detail in
Chapter 10 below.

1   DDA 1995, s 58.

Employment

3.2.3   The term 'employment' has the same extended definition as used in other discrimination statutes. The DDA 1995 embraces discrimination in employment under a contract of service or a contract of apprenticeship, but it also includes employment under a contract personally to do any work.[1] This extended definition of employment is subject to any provision prescribed by regulations (no such prescription has been made to date).

1   DDA 1995, s 68(1). An almost identical definition of 'employment' (with the omission of the word 'any' before the word 'work') applies in Northern Ireland by virtue of s 70(6) and Sch 8, para 47 modifying s 68(1)). The dominant purpose of the contract must be the execution of personal work or labour: *Sheehan v Post Office Counters Ltd* [1999] ICR 734, EAT (sub-postmaster held not to be an employee within the protection of Part II of the DDA 1995). See generally: *Mirror Group Newspapers Ltd v Gunning* [1986] ICR 145, CA.

3.2.4   Whilst Part II of the DDA 1995 generally will cover employment by a partnership (all other things being equal), it does not extend to the business relationship of partners within a partnership.[1] Disabled persons have no right of action under the Act if they believe that they have been discriminated against by reason of their disability when seeking to enter a partnership as a would-be partner or while participating in a partnership in the capacity of partner. This may be simply a small anomaly, but it does seem rather strange that, for instance, a firm of solicitors may not generally discriminate against a disabled lawyer seeking articles or employment as an assistant solicitor, but can do so with impunity if that disabled lawyer, after some years of employment in the firm, were later to seek an equity partnership in the firm (*quaere* the position of a salaried partner?).

1   HC Deb Standing Committee E, cols 455–457. This is in contrast to SDA 1975, s 11 and RRA 1976, s 10. However, note the effect of a decision under the Northern Ireland fair employment legislation, to the effect that the extended definition of 'employment' is wide enough to cover the provision of services by a professional person and that a partner in a firm can bring a discrimination claim in respect of unlawful discrimination against the firm by a third party: *Loughran and Kelly v Northern Ireland Housing Executive* [1998] IRLR 593, HL.

Employment at an establishment in Great Britain

3.2.5   In relation to the phrase 'employment at an establishment in Great Britain' (and, by extension, Northern Ireland),[1] it is provided that, where an employee does his or her work *wholly* outside Great Britain (or Northern Ireland), that employment is not to be treated as being work at an establishment in Great Britain (or Northern Ireland).[2] Work is treated as done at the establishment *from* which it is done or *with* which it has the closest connection.[3] Employment on board a ship, aircraft or hovercraft is to be regarded as not being employment at an establishment in Great Britain, unless regulations prescribe otherwise in respect of particular cases.[4] Furthermore, regulations may provide that employment of a prescribed kind, or in prescribed circumstances, is to be regarded as not being employment at an establishment in Great Britain.[5]

---

1   See DDA 1995, ss 4(6) and 68(1)–(5) (as modified for Northern Ireland by Sch 8, para 47). References to Great Britain in this paragraph should be read as also including Northern Ireland.
2   DDA 1995, s 68(2) as substituted by Equal Opportunities (Employment Legislation) (Territorial Limits) Regulations 1999, SI 1999/3163 with effect from 16 December 1999.
3   Ibid, s 68(5).
4   Ibid, s 68(3). No regulations have been prescribed to date.
5   Ibid, s 68(4). No regulations have been prescribed to date.

Exclusion of small businesses

3.2.6   The employment provisions of the DDA 1995 do not apply in relation to certain small businesses. As originally enacted, this exclusion was set so as to benefit employers with fewer than 20 employees.[1] That threshold reflected the pre-existing requirement for the operation of the statutory quota scheme under the 1944 Act and the Government's concern to protect the small business sector from prescriptive regulation.[2] However, following a statutory review of the exclusion, from 1 December 1998 the limit was reduced so that the employment provisions of the DDA 1995 will apply to employers with 15 or more employees.[3] It is believed that the effect of the review was to bring an additional 45,000 employers (employing three-quarters of a million people) and 60,000 disabled employees within the scope of Part II of the Act.[4]

---

1   DDA 1995, s 7(1). Note the expanded definition of 'employment' (and by inference 'employee') in s 68(1). Part-time, temporary, seasonal or casual employees will count towards the measurement of the threshold, as will working directors. It will also be necessary to include any contract workers for whom the employer has potential liability under DDA 1995, s 12: *Taylor v Lifesign Ltd* (2000) EAT/1437/98.
2   See, for example, HC Deb, vol 257, cols 727–728. At the time, it was calculated that, despite the small employer exemption, the Act would cover 83 per cent of employees (HC Deb, vol 257, col 732).
3   Disability Discrimination (Exemption for Small Employers) Order 1998, SI 1998/2618, art 2 (amending DDA 1995, s 7(1) by substitution).
4   See DfEE Press Release 415/98 8 September 1998 and *The Disability Discrimination Act 1995: The Employment Provisions and Small Employers: A Review* (DfEE, 1998).

3.2.7   The question of whether an employer has fewer than 15 employees is to be answered by examining how many employees are employed by that employer on the day the alleged discrimination took place, rather than on the date of any litigation or judicial proceedings.[1] Problems of interpretation might arise, nevertheless, in cases where there is a series of discriminatory acts rather than one single incident of discrimination. In the Government's view, no liability can arise for any actions within a series of actions which occur while the employer has fewer than 15 employees, even if at other times the employer's workforce exceeds that threshold.[2] This scenario might be particularly relevant to small employers who rely upon a fluctuating workforce of seasonal, temporary or casual employees. Nevertheless, a discriminatory act committed while the employer employed fewer than 15 employees might have continuing effects and, if the employer subsequently began to employ 15 or more employees, liability might arise from a failure to correct the continuing effects of a previous discriminatory act for which no liability had otherwise arisen.[3]

1   HC Deb Standing Committee E, col 227.
2   Ibid, col 249.
3   Because of s 7(1).

3.2.8   The statute also does not define how the number of employees is to be determined in cases of associated employers or corporate groups. The implication appears to be that, unless a tribunal or court is prepared to lift the corporate veil, the separate legal entity within which the employee is employed is to be the unit of calculation. For the purpose of determining the small employer threshold, there seems to be no scope for adding together separate workforces employed by the same employer through parent, holding and subsidiary companies or via associated firms.[2] The Employment Code of Practice makes it clear that independent franchise holders are exempt if they employ fewer than 15 people even if the franchise network has 15 or more employees.[1]

1   Employment Code of Practice, para 2.6 (the code as published refers to the original
    threshold of 20 employees, but this has been clearly overtaken by the 1998 Order).
2   *Hardie v CD Northern Ltd* [2000] IRLR 87, EAT; *Colt Group Ltd v Couchman* [2000] ICR 327,
    EAT.

3.2.9   The present threshold figure of 15 employees may be further adjusted by ministerial order.[1] Before making such an order the Secretary of State shall consult the Disability Rights Commission and such organisations representing the interests of employers and of disabled persons in employment (or seeking employment) as he considers appropriate.[2] Before laying an order before Parliament, the Secretary of State must publish a summary of the views expressed to him in his consultations.[3] The power may not be used to substitute a different number *greater* than the original figure of 20.[4] It cannot be used to increase the exempted class.

1   Under DDA 1995, s 7(2) (as was the case in 1998).
2   Ibid, s 7(3) as substituted by Disability Rights Commission Act 1999 (DRCA 1999), s 11.
3   Ibid, s 7(4) as substituted by DRCA 1999, s 11.
4   Ibid, s 7(2).

3.2.10   As originally enacted, the Act committed the Secretary of State to review the small employer exemption threshold, at the latest, by 1 December

2000.[1] Any such review had to be completed within 9 months.[2] In conducting a review, the Secretary of State had to consult such organisations (as he or she considers appropriate) representing the interests of employers and of disabled persons in employment or seeking employment.[3] There was no obligation upon the Secretary of State to amend the small employer threshold following a review. Instead, the Act required the Secretary of State, should he or she decide not to make an amending order, to lay before Parliament a report summarising the results of the review and giving reasons for the decision not to make an order.[4] This had to be done not later than one year after the commencement of a review. The report had to include a summary of the views expressed to the Secretary of State in the statutory consultations.[5]

1   DDA 1995, s 7(5) as read with s 7(3). This requirement was fulfilled in the 1998 review.
2   Ibid, s 7(6).
3   Ibid, s 7(7).
4   Ibid, s 7(9). In Northern Ireland the Department of Enterprise, Trade and Investment must lay such a report before the Northern Ireland Assembly (Sch 8, para 4(3)).
5   Ibid, s 7(10).

3.2.11   Now, as a result of the reform of these provisions wrought by the Disability Rights Commission Act 1999, the procedure is considerably simpler.[1] The former requirement to hold a review of the threshold before amending it has been replaced by a requirement merely to consult the Disability Rights Commission and relevant representative organisations.

1   As described in **3.2.9**.

Other exemptions

3.2.12   Although the DDA 1995 applies to employment by the Crown, government departments, statutory bodies and statutory office-holders,[1] the employment provisions of the Act do not apply to employment as:[2]

–   a statutory office-holder (such as a police officer);
–   a member of the Ministry of Defence Police, British Transport Police, Royal Parks Constabulary or the United Kingdom Atomic Energy Authority Constabulary;
–   a prison officer (except custody officers);
–   a fire fighting member of a fire brigade;
–   a member of the naval, military or air forces of the Crown.

These exemptions and the wider question of the application of the Act to the Crown and to Parliament are considered in more detail in Chapter 9 below.

1   DDA 1995, s 64(1).
2   Ibid, s 64(5)–(8).

3.2.13   Exceptional treatment under Part II of the DDA 1995 is also given to charities.[1] The term 'charity' has the same meaning as in the Charities Act

1993.[2] Nothing in Part II of the DDA 1995 (the employment provisions) affects any charitable instrument which provides for conferring benefits on one or more categories of person determined by reference to any physical or mental capacity.[3] A charitable instrument is an enactment or other instrument (whenever taking effect) so far as it relates to charitable purposes.[4] Moreover, nothing in the employment provisions of the Act makes unlawful any act done by a registered or non-registered charity[5] in pursuance of any of its charitable purposes, so far as those purposes are connected with persons determined by reference to any physical or mental capacity.[6]

---

1   DDA 1995, s 10(1).
2   Ibid, s 10(3). In Northern Ireland, see the Charities Act (Northern Ireland) 1964 (by virtue of DDA 1995, Sch 8, para 7(3)).
3   Ibid, s 10(1)(a).
4   Ibid, s 10(3). In England and Wales (and Northern Ireland), charitable purposes are purposes which are exclusively charitable according to the law of England and Wales (and Northern Ireland) (s 10(4) and Sch 7, para 7(4)). In Scotland only (s 10(5)), charitable purposes are to be construed as if contained in the Income Tax Acts.
5   By virtue of s 10(3), in Scotland only, a recognised body for the purposes of Part I of the Law Reform (Miscellaneous Provisions) (Scotland) Act 1990.
6   DDA 1995, s 10(1)(b).

3.2.14   Special provision is also made for persons providing supported employment under the Disabled Persons (Employment) Act 1944 or the Disabled Persons (Employment) Act (Northern Ireland) 1945. Nothing in Part II of the DDA 1995 (the employment provisions) prevents a person who provides supported employment from treating members of a particular group of disabled persons (or persons who have had a disability in the past) more favourably than other persons in providing supported employment.[1] In this context, 'supported employment' means facilities provided or paid for under s 15 of the 1944 or 1945 Acts.[2] Furthermore, nothing in Part II of the DDA 1995 prevents the Secretary of State (or, in Northern Ireland, the Department of Enterprise, Trade and Investment) from agreeing to arrangements for the provision of supported employment which will (or may) have the effect of treating members of a particular group of disabled persons (or persons who have had a disability in the past) more favourably than other persons.[3]

---

1   DDA 1995, s 10(2)(a).
2   Ibid, s 10(3) and Sch 8, para 7.
3   Ibid, s 10(2)(b) and Sch 8, para 7(2).

3.2.15   The effect of these provisions is not to exclude persons employed under supported employment arrangements from the prohibition on disability-related discrimination per se. Rather, the intention is to allow employers providing supported employment to distinguish between different groups of disabled persons when extending supported employment opportunities. Providing supported employment opportunities for some disabled persons while excluding other persons with a disability would otherwise amount to less favourable treatment for a reason which related to those other persons' disability contrary to the Act. For example, an employer is allowed to create a supported employment environment for workers with sight impairments and to do so without needing to provide similar facilities for other disabled workers.

However, the supported employment in question must be within the frame-work provided by the 1944–45 legislation. Moreover, this does not excuse acts of disability-related discrimination elsewhere in the employer's workplace.

3.3   DISCRIMINATION IN EMPLOYMENT

3.3.1   Part II of the DDA 1995 is concerned with outlawing disability discrimination in employment. Disability discrimination does not take place in a vacuum. A complainant will need to show that the alleged act of disability discrimination falls within one of the prohibited acts of employment discrimi-nation set out in the Act. Section 4 makes it unlawful for an employer to discriminate against a disabled person (as defined in the Act) in specified circumstances.[1]

---

1   In the case of an act of victimisation which, by virtue of s 55, constitutes discrimination for the purposes of Part II, the categories of unlawful action or omission in s 4 also apply to discrimination against a person who is not disabled (s 4(5)).

3.3.2   First, it is unlawful for an employer to discriminate against a disabled person in the 'arrangements' which the employer makes for the purposes of determining to whom the employer should offer employment.[1] As intended, the concept of 'arrangements' has a wide meaning, and will cover job advertisements,[2] and the selection process (including job specifications, qualifications, the location and timing of interviews, the use of assessment techniques, the interview itself, and selection criteria).[3] For example, the inclusion of unnecessary or marginal requirements in a job specification, or blanket exclusions which do not take account of individual circumstances, can be discriminatory.[4] So too, if a disabled person is rejected for a job because he or she lacks a qualification specified by the employer, the rejection might be discriminatory if the lack of the particular qualification is related to that person's disability (for example, because of the effect of dyslexia). The employer would need to justify the stipulation of that qualification (for example, by reference to relevance and significance) or demonstrate that no reasonable adjustment in favour of the disabled applicant (for example, reallocating some duties to another employee or devising an alternative test of competence) could have been made.[5]

---

1   DDA 1995, s 4(1)(a).
2   Note also the particular provisions of s 11 discussed below at **3.4.14** et seq.
3   Employment Code of Practice, para 5.2. On the use of aptitude tests and other forms of assessment techniques in the recruitment process, see ibid, para 5.21. On the selection and interview process generally, see ibid, paras 5.12–5.26.
4   Ibid, paras 5.2–5.4 and note the examples provided there.
5   Ibid, para 5.22.

3.3.3   Secondly, it is unlawful for an employer to discriminate against a disabled person in the terms on which the employer offers that person employment.[1] The Employment Code of Practice reinforces this point.[2]

---

1   DDA 1995, s 4(1)(b).

2 Employment Code of Practice, para 5.27.

3.3.4 Thirdly, it is equally unlawful for an employer to discriminate against a disabled person by refusing to offer that person employment.[1] Discrimination by these means includes a deliberate failure or omission to offer employment to a disabled person, so that there does not have to be an express refusal to offer employment in order for potential discrimination to have occurred.

1 DDA 1995, s 4(1)(c).

3.3.5 Fourthly, in respect of a disabled person in an employer's employment, it is unlawful for an employer to discriminate against a disabled employee in the terms of employment which the employer affords to such an employee.[1] As the Employment Code of Practice notes, terms and conditions of service should not discriminate against disabled persons. That does not mean that an employer can never offer a disabled person a less favourable contract but, subject to any duty to make reasonable adjustments, the employer must be prepared to justify the differential.[2] The Employment Code of Practice also reminds employers that they must not discriminate in their induction procedures. If necessary, a newly recruited disabled employee may need an individually tailored induction programme.[3]

1 DDA 1995, s 4(2)(a).
2 Employment Code of Practice, paras 5.27–5.28 (and note the examples provided there).
3 Ibid, paras 6.2–6.3.

3.3.6 Fifthly, disability-based discrimination in employment opportunities is also caught.[1] It is unlawful for an employer to discriminate against a disabled employee in certain employment opportunities afforded to that person by the employer. The opportunities in question are exhaustively defined as promotion, transfer, training or the receipt of any other benefit.[2] Benefits include facilities and services[3] and, subject to what is said below, plainly includes entitlements to fringe benefits of employment (such as private health insurance provided to employees by the employer through an insurance company) and to occupational pensions.[4] In addition, it is unlawful for an employer to discriminate against a disabled person whom the employer employs where the employer refuses to afford the disabled employee any such opportunities as mentioned above.[5] A refusal in this context includes a deliberate omission to afford such opportunities to a disabled employee.

1 DDA 1995, s 4(2)(b).
2 The Employment Code of Practice states (para 6.7) that 'benefits' might include canteens, meal vouchers, social clubs and other recreational activities, dedicated car parking spaces, discounts on products, bonuses, share options, hairdressing, clothes allowances, financial services, healthcare, medical assistance/insurance, transport to work, company car, education assistance, workplace nurseries, and rights to special leave. Note the examples provided there. In respect of promotion, transfer and training, see paras 6.4–6.6.
3 DDA 1995, s 4(4).
4 HL Deb, vol 566, col 169. On occupational pensions and insurance benefits, see **3.7** and **3.8**.

5   DDA 1995, s 4(2)(c).

3.3.7   This ensures that discrimination in the form of a refusal to consider access to possible employment opportunities, facilities and benefits is prohibited as well as discrimination in access to existing employment opportunities, facilities and benefits. This circumvents the restrictive interpretation of the different, but parallel, provisions in the SDA 1975. In *Clymo v London Borough of Wandsworth*,[1] the EAT regarded an employer's refusal to consider a job share proposal as not amounting to indirect sex discrimination because that statute had to be construed as applying only to opportunities or facilities which were already in existence. Such a construction cannot be placed upon the DDA 1995 and would be simply inconsistent with an employer's quite separate duty to make reasonable adjustments to employment arrangements so as to accommodate disabled persons.[2]

1   [1989] IRLR 241.
2   DDA 1995, s 6.

3.3.8   Finally, it is unlawful for an employer to discriminate against a disabled employee by dismissing him or her,[1] or by subjecting that person to any other detriment.[2] The term 'any other detriment' is broadly based and will provide a catch-all for any other forms of employment discrimination against disabled persons if not already caught by the specific categories previously set out. In particular, it is likely that harassment of a disabled person because of his or her disability (or for a reason related to his or her disability) will fall within this provision.[3] However, these provisions are not apt to embrace post-employment discrimination on grounds of disability (such as a refusal to provide a reference or discrimination occurring during post-termination appeal proceedings).[4]

1   See Employment Code of Practice, paras 6.19–6.21. A potentially unlawful dismissal of a
    disabled employee might arise in the context of capability or absence (as in *Clark v TDG Ltd
    t/a Novacold* [1999] IRLR 318, CA), but might equally arise from an unfair redundancy
    selection exercise (as in *British Sugar plc v Kirker* [1998] IRLR 624, EAT).
2   DDA 1995, s 4(2)(d).
3   This is confirmed by the Employment Code of Practice, paras 6.22–6.23.
4   *Post Office v Adekeye* [1997] ICR 110, CA (a decision under the comparable wording of the
    RRA 1976). The decision in *Coote v Granada Hospitality Ltd (No 2)* [1999] IRLR 452, EAT
    construing the comparable provisions of the SDA 1975 in the light of EC law (and with the
    opposite result) does not assist here. Although the EAT in *Coote* cast doubt upon the
    reasoning in *Adekeye*, it is a decision of the Court of Appeal on identical provisions to those
    in the DDA 1995 and must be followed in DDA 1995 cases unless distinguishable or until
    overruled.

Exceptions

3.3.9   The prohibition on discrimination against disabled persons while in employment does not generally apply to discrimination in relation to benefits of any description if the employer is concerned with the provision of benefits of that description to the public.[1] For example, the employer might be a bank providing loans to the public and loans to its employees (perhaps at favourable rates of interest). Similarly, that prohibition does not apply if the employer is concerned with the provision of benefits of that description to a section of the public which includes the disabled employee in question (for example, a local authority providing welfare-related benefits to disabled persons in the community, including its own disabled employees). A benefit for this purpose includes facilities and services[2] and it is immaterial whether or not the benefit is provided for payment.

---

1   DDA 1995, s 4(3).
2   Ibid, s 4(4).

3.3.10   However, these exceptions do not apply in three cases.[1] First, discrimination is prohibited if the employer is concerned with the public provision of the relevant benefits, but that provision differs in a material respect from the provision of the benefits by the employer to the employer's employees.[2] Secondly, discrimination is prohibited if the employer is concerned with the public provision of the relevant benefits, but the provision of the benefits to the employee in question is regulated by the employee's contract of employment.[3] The application of these two cases might be seen at work in the illustrations given immediately above.[4] Thirdly, discrimination is prohibited if the employer is concerned with the public provision of the relevant benefits, but those benefits relate to training.[5]

---

1   DDA 1995, s 4(3). See Employment Code of Practice, para 6.8.
2   Ibid, s 4(3)(a).
3   Ibid, s 4(3)(b).
4   See **3.3.9**.
5   DDA 1995, s 4(3)(c).

3.3.11   These exceptions are designed to prevent unnecessary overlap with the provisions in Part III of the DDA 1995 outlawing discrimination in the provision of goods, facilities and services.[1] The intention is that if an employer offers goods, facilities or services to its employees in the same way as it offers them to members of the public, but disabled employees receive discriminatory treatment in that provision, then their right of action falls under Part III of the Act, if at all. Nevertheless, Part II of the Act will continue to apply to such discriminatory treatment if the provision of goods, facilities and services to the employer's employees is not identical to such provision to the public, or is an incident of the employment contract, or relates to training.[2]

---

1   There are similar exceptions in the SDA 1975, s 6(7).
2   See the special treatment of occupational pensions and other insurance-related benefits under ss 17–18 as discussed at **3.7** and **3.8**.

Pre-employment health screening

3.3.12   The DDA 1995 does not expressly address the question of pre-employment medical examinations and screening. Many employers utilise health-related questions in application forms or medical examinations as a pre-condition of employment. By screening employment applicants for disability or medical conditions, many employers effectively exclude a proportion of applicants from further competition in the selection process. An applicant with a disability might be prematurely excluded from further consideration and may lose the opportunity to demonstrate ability and merit. An attempt was made during the legislative process to prohibit pre-employment medical examinations or screening, but the amendments were rejected. The Government's view was that 'in general, employers should be free to use whatever recruitment procedures best meet their needs and to conduct medical examinations of employees where that seems appropriate'.[1] It was unwilling to forbid medical examinations or to limit inquiries about disability. Indeed, employers might find it necessary to question disabled applicants about a disability where such questions are designed to assist the disabled person in competing for employment opportunities.[2]

---

1   HC Deb Standing Committee E, col 151. Note also the protections provided in the Access to Medical Reports Act 1988.
2   See further: HL Deb, vol 564, cols 1935–1936.

3.3.13   Nevertheless, that does not mean that health screens and examinations might not fall foul of the Act. Medical examinations, inquiries, questions or screening would undoubtedly constitute 'arrangements' made for the purpose of determinng who should be offered employment.[1] If the effect of such arrangements was to amount to less favourable treatment of a disabled person for a reason related to disability, the employer would have to show that that treatment was justifiable. Even if all applicants and employees were medically examined, the effect might be to discriminate indirectly against disabled persons if the employer uses the evidence gleaned from the examination without further individualised inquiry as to the ability to do the job (including reasonable adjustments).

---

1   DDA 1995, s 4(1)(a).

3.3.14   The Employment Code of Practice provides some useful guidance in this area. It indicates that employers may stipulate essential health requirements for a job, provided that they are capable of justification and if it would not be reasonable to waive them in an individual case.[1] Equally, stating that certain personal, medical or health-related characteristics are desirable or preferred may be discriminatory, unless justifiable.[2] A related issue is whether an employer should ask about disability at all. While the Act does not prevent such a question, the Employment Code of Practice recommends that the question should only be asked if disability is, or may be, relevant to the ability to do the job.[3] It might be appropriate – in order to counteract the negative impression left by such a question – to include a positive statement welcoming applications from disabled persons.[4] In any event, asking about the effects of a disability might be necessary as part of the process of considering what reasonable adjustments might be made.[5]

---

1   Employment Code of Practice, para 5.5.
2   Ibid, para 5.6.
3   Ibid, para 5.20.

4 Employment Code of Practice, para 5.10.
5 Ibid, paras 5.11 and 5.20 (in order to comply with the employer's duty under DDA 1995, s 6).

3.3.15 While an employer can insist upon a disabled person having a pre-employment medical examination, the Employment Code of Practice warns employers that it may be discriminatory without justification to single out a disabled person (and not other applicants or employees) for a health check.[1] Employers are reminded that having a disability does not adversely affect a person's general health and, while medical evidence about a disability might justify an employment decision (for example, a dismissal or refusal of promotion), it cannot do so if the disability has little or no effect upon the person's ability to do the job.[2]

1 Employment Code of Practice, para 5.23 and see the examples given there.
2 Ibid, para 5.24.

3.4 MEANING OF DISCRIMINATION

3.4.1 For the purposes of Part II of the DDA 1995, an employer discriminates against a disabled person if:

– for a reason which relates to the disabled person's disability, the employer treats that person less favourably than the employer treats or would treat others to whom that reason does not or would not apply;
– the employer cannot show that the treatment in question is justified.[1]

This definition of discrimination is closely (but not exactly) related to the definition of *direct* discrimination in the sex and race discrimination statutes,[2] but with the addition of a justification defence which is normally an adjunct of *indirect* discrimination.[3] In addition, where an employer has failed to comply with a duty to make reasonable adjustments in relation to a disabled person,[4] the employer is deemed to have discriminated against the disabled person, unless the employer can show that the failure to comply with that duty is justified.[5] Where these conditions are satisfied, there is prima facie discrimination. This extended definition of discrimination is re-examined in greater depth below in the discussion of the duty to make reasonable adjustments.[6]

1 DDA 1995, s 5(1). By virtue of s 55, victimisation of a person in specified circumstances also amounts to discrimination.
2 However, the Court of Appeal's warning against the 1995 Act with assumptions and concepts familiar from experience of the earlier equal opportunities statutes should be heeded: *Clark v TDG Ltd t/a Novacold* [1999] IRLR 318, CA.
3 The formula of 'a reason which relates to the disabled person's disability' has much in common with the provisions in the Employment Rights Act 1996, s 99 dealing with dismissal on grounds of pregnancy or childbirth.
4 DDA 1995, s 6. The reference to a s 6 duty in s 5 rather obviously means any duty imposed by or under s 6 (s 68(1)).

3.4.2 The DDA 1995 does not set out a test or formula for indirect discrimination. However, in the Government's view, the statutory provisions:[1]

> '. . . already firmly cover – and are intended to cover – the use of standards, criteria, administrative methods, work practices or procedures that adversely affect a disabled person. That applies whether determining who should be employed or dismissed or establishing terms on the basis of which people are employed and their access to opportunities is structured.'[2]

Furthermore, the Minister has stated that:

> 'The broad term "arrangements" has been deliberately used[3] . . . to cover anything done by or for an employer as part of his recruitment process or in making available opportunities in employment.'[4]

This would in principle address work practices and procedures which have an indirectly adverse effect upon the employment opportunities of disabled persons. The Government clearly intended that indirect discrimination would be prohibited and that this should be underlined by the duty to make reasonable adjustments.[5]

1   DDA 1995, ss 4(1), 4(2) and 5(1).
2   HC Deb Standing Committee E, col 142.
3   DDA 1995, ss 4(1)(a) and 6(1)(a).
4   HC Deb Standing Committee E, col 142.
5   Under DDA 1995, s 6. HC Deb Standing Committee E, col 143.

Less favourable treatment

3.4.3 The key concept which underpins the meaning of unlawful discrimination is the idea of less favourable treatment. An employer discriminates against a disabled person only if the employer treats the disabled individual 'less favourably than' the employer 'treats or would treat others' to whom the reason which relates the disabled person's disability does not or would not apply.[1] This concept of less favourable treatment calls for a comparative approach. The question is how has the disabled person been treated in comparison with other persons to whom the reason relating to the disabled person's disability does not apply? If the treatment of the comparator is more favourable than the treatment of the complainant, one of the necessary (but not sufficient) criteria for establishing unlawful direct discrimination is in place. A number of points should be noted about this definition of discrimination.

1   DDA 1995, s 5(1)(a). See the example provided in the Employment Code of Practice at para 4.2.

3.4.4 First, it seems to admit the possibility that a disabled complainant could seek to show that he or she has been treated less favourably than a hypothetical (rather than an actual) comparator. The double use of the word 'would' supports that reasoning.[1] If this interpretation is correct, this is especially important where a disabled person has been refused or denied employment opportunities in a context which is not an immediately competitive one. For example, a disabled employee denied promotion would not need to show that a colleague was actually promoted instead. It might be sufficient to show that a similarly situated employee without disability would have been promoted in those circumstances.[2] Indeed, it was suggested by the EAT in *British Sugar plc v Kirker*[3] that, where an applicant can show that he or she was disadvantaged by reason of his or her disability, it may not be necessary at all to identify other employees (or applicants for employment) with whom to compare the treatment of the disabled person. The EAT in *Kirker* appeared to be applying a 'but for' test of discrimination: but for his or her disability would the disabled person have been treated in that way?[4]

---

1   DDA 1995, s 5(1)(a).
2   This reasoning appears to be supported by the Employment Code of Practice, para 4.3.
3   [1998] IRLR 624.
4   See further **3.4.8**.

3.4.5   Secondly, there will often be no 'smoking gun' or direct evidence of discrimination. As in sex and race discrimination,[1] it may be necessary to draw inferences of discrimination from the primary facts. Indeed, the EAT has held that an employment tribunal is entitled to consider how an employer treated the disabled person prior to the enactment of the DDA 1995 (that is, to draw inferences of discrimination from events occurring before 2 December 1996) in order to determine whether the treatment of the disabled person was influenced by the employer's perception of his or her value as an employee.[2]

---

1   See *King v Great Britain-China Centre* [1991] IRLR 513, CA and *Zafar v Glasgow City Council* [1998] ICR 125, HL.
2   *British Sugar plc v Kirker* [1998] IRLR 624, EAT.

3.4.6   Thirdly, the phrasing of the definition of discrimination will allow a disabled person to seek to show that he or she has been treated less favourably than another disabled person has been or would be. Section 5 does not necessarily call for an analysis of discriminatory behaviour which distinguished between disabled and non-disabled individuals. For example, two equally well-qualified applicants might be in competition for an employment vacancy. One has a physical disability and the other a mental disability. If, without interviewing both candidates and considering their respective merits, the employer automatically rejects the applicant with a mental disability, that action could form the basis of a complaint of disability-informed discrimination brought by the rejected applicant. Again, the employer might be able to justify the differential treatment, but the individual with a mental disability was entitled to be given due consideration.[1]

---

1   See Employment Code of Practice, para 4.3.

3.4.7   Fourthly, the actual or hypothetical comparison is between the disabled complainant and a comparator to whom the reason relating to the disabled complainant's disability does not or would not apply. It is important to note that the Act does not call for a simplistic comparison between a disabled person and a person who is not disabled or who does not have the disability in question (although that is how the Bill was originally drafted). The Government has considered that 'it is important to define the test correctly to avoid confusion and unnecessary litigation' and to ensure that the test 'correctly reflects the need to show that the treatment was for a reason relating to the disability and not necessarily the mere fact of disability'.[1] The Minister gave the example of two employees who cannot type: one because he or she is disabled with arthritis and the other, who is not disabled, because he or she has never been taught to type. If the disabled person with arthritis is refused employment as a typist, that is not discriminatory treatment, provided the non-disabled person (who has never been taught to type) is also refused employment in such a position. In a strict sense, the disabled person has been refused employment because of a reason related to disability (the inability to type being due to arthritis), but he or she has not been treated less favourably in comparison with the other person if the employer has rejected all candidates who cannot type. If the employer offers the position to someone who is able to type, on the face of it that may be less favourable treatment of the person with arthritis for a reason related to his or her disability, but, subject to the duty to make adjustments, the employer will probably be able to explain the treatment if typing skills are a requirement of the position applied for.

---

1   HL Deb, vol 566, col 1200.

3.4.8   Fifthly, and closely related to this last point, is the question of whether the basis of the comparison must be drawn widely or narrowly.[1] For example, if a disabled employee is dismissed for absenteeism including disability-related absences, with whom should the employee be compared for the purpose of establishing less favourable treatment? One possibility is to compare how the disabled employee has been treated relative to an employee also absent from work for the same length of time, but for a reason which is not related to disability. This would reflect the usual expectation in discrimination cases that like should be compared with like.[2] However, the DDA 1995 does not require the comparison to be based upon a consideration of the comparators in relevant circumstances which are the same or not materially different.[3] Thus a second possibility is to compare how the disabled employee (who is unable to perform the functions of his or her job) has been treated in comparison with other employees who were not absent from work at all (that is, who are performing the main function of their jobs). This focuses upon the reason for the treatment (that is, the reason for the dismissal) and not the reason for the absence which led to the dismissal. The disabled employee has been dismissed for absenteeism. Some of those absences are related to his disability, so the dismissal is for a reason (that is, absenteeism) which relates to the disabled person's disability. For the purposes of establishing less favourable treatment, the comparison must be with others to whom that reason (that is absenteeism) does not (or would not) apply. Attention would then switch to the employer's justification defence.[4] That is the approach favoured by the Court of Appeal in the *Novacold* case and is now the authoritative one.[5]

---

1   This in turn depends upon the interpretation to be placed upon the phrase 'that reason' where it appears in s 5(1)(a).

2   This was the approach taken by the EAT in *Clark v Novacold Ltd* [1998] IRLR 420.
3   Contrast SDA 1975, s 5(3) and RRA 1976, s 3(4).
4   Under DDA 1995, s 5(1)(b), subject to the duty to make adjustments under s 6.
5   *Clark v TDG Ltd t/a Novacold* [1999] IRLR 318, CA. The Court of Appeal did not comment upon the EAT's approach in *British Sugar plc v Kirker* [1998] IRLR 624 (see **3.4.4**). The 'but for' test in *Kirker* is not without the attraction of simplicity but *Novacold* navigates the statutory language more assuredly.

Reason related to disability

3.4.9   In order for unlawful discrimination to be established, any less favourable treatment of a disabled person by an employer must be 'for a reason which relates to the disabled person's disability'.[1] The employer's intention, purpose or motive for so acting is not relevant. However, there must be a nexus or causal connection between the discriminatory treatment and the complainant's disability.[2] For example, a disabled person who is refused or denied an employment opportunity because he or she does not have the necessary vocational qualifications, or is not the best person for the job on merit, has not been discriminated against contrary to the DDA 1995.[3] That person has been treated less favourably than the person who was awarded the employment opportunity, at least in the sense that his or her employment aspirations have been disappointed. Nevertheless, the reason for the apparently less favourable treatment is not that person's disability, but rather a reason which is unrelated to disability, namely merit or qualification.

1   DDA 1995, s 5(1)(a).
2   The test of causation under the DDA 1995 appears to be the same as that under the other discrimination statutes: *Murphy v Sheffield Hallam University* (2000) EAT/6/99. Was the person's disability the effective and predominant cause or the real and efficient cause of the less favourable treatment?: *Nagarajan v London Regional Transport* [1999] IRLR 572, HL (decided under the Race Relations Act 1976).
3   As the Employment Code of Practice puts it (para 2.2): 'The Act does not prohibit an employer from appointing the best person for the job. Nor does it prevent employers from treating disabled people more favourably than those without a disability'. See also ibid, para 5.26.

3.4.10   It is suggested that the concept of 'a reason which relates to the disabled person's disability' is a deliberately wide one and should be interpreted broadly. For example, a disabled employee whose disability worsens, creating difficulty in carrying out his work, might have been dismissed by an employer for incompetence or poor performance. However, although the reason for dismissal is a performance-related reason, it is also a reason related to the employee's disability – but for the employee's disability, his work performance would not have deteriorated and dismissal would not have resulted. The question will then arise as to whether the disabled employee has been treated less favourably than others to whom that reason does not apply and, if so, whether the employer can justify the treatment. Although the concept of 'a reason which relates to the disabled person's disability' may be at large, the question will arise as to whether it is essential to be able to show that the employer was aware of the disability. The issue of knowledge is a separate one from the issue of motive or intention (which is irrelevant). There are two possible views.

3.4.11   The first view is that the employer's knowledge of the disability is irrelevant. The test is whether, with the benefit of hindsight, it can be seen that the disabled person has been treated less favourably for a reason which is related to disability as a matter of fact. The argument is based upon the wording of the relevant statutory provision,[1] which is silent on the question of knowledge. In contrast, in the context of the duty to make reasonable adjustments,[2] there is an express requirement that the employer must know (or, at least, have reasonable means of knowing) that an applicant or an employee is a disabled person. If the statute, in one context, has made knowledge of disability relevant by express provision, then the statute must have intended by its silence, in another context, that knowledge of disability should be irrelevant. The question of the employer's knowledge or ignorance of the complainant's disability then goes to justification[3] rather than to the issue of prima facie discrimination.[4]

---

1   DDA 1995, s 5(1).
2   Ibid, s 6(6).
3   Ibid, s 5(1)(b).
4   Ibid, s 5(1)(a).

3.4.12   The second view is that the employer's knowledge (actual or constructive) is relevant. Can an employer be said to have treated a person less favourably 'for a reason which relates to' that person's disability if the employer did not know that the person was disabled? How can someone be said to have acted for a particular reason unless they are aware of the ingredients which inform that reason? This is not to say that an employer can deliberately ignore the available evidence or facts and thereby argue that it did not know that the person was disabled. Equally, the fact that the employer did not believe the person to be disabled, or did not understand the significance of the statutory definition, may not be an excuse. However, this second view does require the employer to have some knowledge that the person is disabled before it can be said that there has been discrimination for a reason related to disability. Support for this reasoning might be found in the judicial approach to pregnancy-related unfair dismissal.[1] In a case where the reason for the dismissal was that the employee was pregnant or for a reason connected with her pregnancy, it is necessary that an employer should have known that the employee was pregnant before it can be held that there was an automatically unfair dismissal.[2]

---

1   Employment Rights Act 1996, s 99.
2   *Del Monte Foods Ltd v Mundon* [1980] ICR 694, EAT. See also *Simon v Brimham Associates* [1987] IRLR 307, CA in the context of the RRA 1976.

3.4.13   How are these conflicting views to be reconciled? One division of the EAT has ruled that the employer's knowledge (actual or constructive) of the disability is relevant.[1] It reasoned that an employer cannot be said to have treated a person less favourably *for a reason which relates to* that person's disability if the employer did not know that the person was disabled. Knowledge of the material features of the disability will be enough, but not simply knowledge of one or other equivocal symptom. One possible ill-effect of that decision was that it might discourage employers from seeking information from applicants and employees which might lead to a disclosure of disability, despite the exhortations of the Employment Code of Practice to the contrary.[2] It is doubtful whether this view – that the word 'reason',[3] as a matter of causation, involves knowledge of the matter which is material – was compatible with the Court of Appeal's construction of DDA 1995, s 5(1) in *Clark v TDG Ltd t/a Novacold.*[4]

Subsequently, however, another division of the EAT has reconsidered the position in *H J Heinz & Co Ltd v Kenrick.*[5] Here the EAT rejected the view that DDA 1995, s 5(1) requires the employer to have knowledge of the disability or its material features and casts doubt upon whether *O'Neill* is correct. In *Kenrick*, the EAT rules that the test of the relationship between the alleged discriminatory treatment and a disability is objective (does the relationship exist?) rather than subjective (did the employer know that the relationship existed?). Furthermore, a reason related to disability is a broad concept which can include a reason which derives from how the disability manifests itself. The effect of *Kenrick* is that employers should pause to consider whether a proposed dismissal might be connected with a reason related to a disability (of which the employer might otherwise be unaware).[6] Nevertheless, the question of what the employer knew of the disability will still be relevant to the issue of justification and the duty to make reasonable adjustments. In the view of the present author, the reasoning in *Kenrick* is preferable to that in *O'Neill.*

---

1   *O'Neill v Symm & Co Ltd* [1998] IRLR 233, EAT. The employer might be treated as being seised with the knowledge by virtue of what was known to an employee or agent of the employer (such as a personnel officer or occupational health practitioner) at the relevant time.
2   See Employment Code of Practice, paras 4.57 et seq. See also **3.6.21**.
3   In DDA 1995, s 5(1)(a).
4   [1999] IRLR 318.
5   [2000] IRLR 144. See also *London Borough of Hammersmith and Fulham v Farnsworth* (2000) EAT/461/99.
6   As soon as factors exist which put the employer on guard (such as the employer's awareness that the employee had been receiving medical treatment), the employer must pause to determine whether a disability exists which requires to be addressed by the duty to make reasonable adjustments (for example, by not dismissing or taking other steps). The employer cannot rely upon its ignorance of the circumstances unless that is rationally based and if at the relevant time it would have been reasonable to have undertaken further investigation to discover the actual situation and to assess it in the light of the relevant law: *Heggison v A & W Bernard* (2000) EAT/1276/99.

Employment advertisements

3.4.14   Unlike sex and race discrimination legislation, the DDA 1995 does not make separate provision for the outlawing or prohibition of discriminatory employment advertisements.[1] However, employment tribunals are enabled to make assumptions about an employer's reason for refusing employment to a disabled person where the employer has published an advertisement suggest-ing that it will discriminate against disabled persons.[2] There are a number of conditions which must be satisfied before the tribunal can make such assumptions.

---

1 For the Government's reasoning on this point see HL Deb, vol 565, col 676.
2 DDA 1995, s 11.

3.4.15 First, and most obviously, the disabled person must have presented a complaint of disability discrimination to an employment tribunal and that complaint must be against the employer in question.[1] Secondly, the disabled person must have applied for employment with the employer[2] and the employer has refused to offer, or has deliberately not offered, the disabled person that employment.[3] Thirdly, the employer must have advertised the employment for which the disabled person has applied (whether before or after the disabled person applied for it).[4] Fourthly, and most crucially, the advertisement must have indicated (or might reasonably be understood to have indicated) that any application for the advertised employment would, or might, be determined to any extent by reference to the successful applicant not having any disability or not having any category of disability which includes the disabled person's disability.[5] Alternatively, the advertisement must have indicated (or might reasonably be understood to have indicated) that any application for the advertised employment would, or might, be determined to any extent by reference to the employer's reluctance to take any action of a kind mentioned in the employer's duty to make reasonable adjustments.[6]

---

1 DDA 1995, s 11(1)(c).
2 Ibid, s 11(1)(a).
3 Ibid, s 11(1)(b).
4 Ibid, s 11(1)(d). An advertisement for this purpose includes every form of advertisement or notice, whether to the public or not: s 11(3). An advertisement would include the internal publication of a vacancy only within an office or company: Employment Code of Practice, para 5.8. See generally ibid, para 5.7 and the example provided there. Note also that advertising a job might call for a reasonable adjustment (for example, providing information about the post in alternative media or formats): ibid, para 5.9.
5 Ibid, s 11(1)(e)(i).
6 Under DDA 1995, s 6. See DDA 1995, s 11(1)(e)(ii).

3.4.16 If all these conditions are satisfied, then the employment tribunal hearing the disabled person's disability discrimination complaint will assume, unless the contrary is shown, that the employer's reason for refusing employment to the disabled person was related to the complainant's disability.[1] In other words, where the employer has published a discriminatory advertise-ment, there is a rebuttable presumption that any subsequent less favourable treatment of the disabled person was for a reason related to the complainant's disability. The requirement that the less favourable treatment of a disabled person must be for a reason 'which relates to the disabled person's disability' will be presumed to have been satisfied.[2]

1 DDA 1995, s 11 (2).
2 Note, however, that this presumption operates only where the complaint is brought under
   DDA 1995, s 4(1)(c) and is that the employer has refused to offer, or has deliberately not
   offered, the disabled person the employment so advertised.

3.4.17 This is a difficult and convoluted provision. The definition of
'advertisement'[1] is broad enough to embrace job particulars or details sent to
would-be applicants as well as job advertisements placed in newspapers or other
media. The Government's intention is to prevent employers using job
advertisements as a means of discouraging disabled employment applicants.[2]
At the same time, however, it is not intended that this provision should prevent
employers from specifying reasonable or justifiable health or other ability
requirements, even if these might cause difficulties of compliance for persons
with disabilities.[3]

1 DDA 1995, s 11 (3).
2 HL Deb, vol 565, col 678. However, s 11 does not apply to exempted small businesses under
   s 7.
3 HC Deb Standing Committee E, cols 282–284.

Discrimination by association

3.4.18 The DDA 1995 does not explicitly address the problem of discrimination against non-disabled persons because of their association with (or
relationship to) a disabled person. In debate, the relevant Minister stated that it
was the Government's intention 'that the concept of reasonable adjustment
could include the need to make arrangements to take into account the
particular difficulties that carers face because of their caring responsibilities'.[1]
However, he later recanted and explained that the 'needs of carers might be
taken into account as a reasonable adjustment for a disabled person. If the
needs were such that a disabled person had to fit in with the position of a carer,
the carer's needs could be taken in as part of the reasonable adjustment'.[2]

1 HC Deb Standing Committee E, col 168.
2 Ibid, col 172. To this effect, see Employment Code of Practice, para 4.20.

3.5 DEFENCE OF JUSTIFICATION

3.5.1 An employer discriminates against a disabled person if there is less
favourable treatment of a disabled person for a reason related to the disabled
person's disability[1] and the employer cannot show that the less favourable
treatment is justified.[2] The burden of proof will be upon the employer who
relies upon a justification defence. Less favourable treatment is justified 'if, but
only if, the reason for it is *both* material to the circumstances of the *particular* case
and substantial'.[3] What is novel about this justification defence is that, in

contrast to the existing discrimination jurisdictions, this justification defence is available in both cases of direct and indirect discrimination. However, it is clear that the concept of justification used in the 1995 Act is different from that used under the race and sex discrimination legislation.[4]

---

1   DDA 1995, s 5(1)(a).
2   Ibid, s 5(1)(b). There is also a justification defence in s 5(2) (introduced at **3.4.1**) and this defence is explained in s 5(4). See the further discussion at **3.6.22**.
3   Ibid, s 5(3) with emphasis added.
4   See *Baynton v Saurus General Engineers Ltd* [1999] IRLR 604. The EAT described the statutory test of justification in the 1995 Act as 'unique'.

3.5.2   The first thing to note about the justification defence is that it goes beyond merely showing that a disabled person was treated less favourably than others for a reason unconnected with or unrelated to his or her disability. An employer will always be able to defend a discrimination complaint by proving that the alleged discriminatory act was not for a reason which relates to the disabled complainant's disability.[1] The justification defence clearly applies only where an employer *has* treated a disabled person less favourably for a disability-related reason. In other words, the DDA 1995 envisages that there will be cases where, despite the merit principle, an employer could take lawful account of a person's disability. For example, the disabled person might be otherwise well qualified for the position, but the evidence might support a real fear that there is a clear and unacceptable health and safety risk to the disabled worker or others, or that the disability will prevent the employee from attending work regularly and predictably. However, such conclusions must be based upon hard evidence and not merely assumptions or stereotypes.

---

1   That is implicit in the wording of DDA 1995 s 5(1)(a).

3.5.3   The justification defence is a particular, rather than general, defence. The use of the phrase 'if, but only if'[1] clearly limits the scope for justifying less favourable treatment of a disabled person for a reason related to disability. An employer might have no difficulty in subjectively justifying to itself or to other employers the discriminatory treatment of disabled persons, but that is not enough to satisfy the legislative test of justification. The Act does not admit a general defence of justification. Furthermore, where the employer is under a statutory duty to make reasonable adjustments,[2] the justification defence must take account of that duty. This is considered further below.[3]

---

1   In DDA 1995, s 5(3).
2   Under s 6.
3   See **3.6.22–3.6.23**.

3.5.4   The statutory defence of justification in s 5(3) requires the employer to show that the reason for the less favourable treatment of a disabled person, for a reason related to that person's disability, is both 'material' to the circumstances of the particular case and 'substantial'. This final version of the defence reduces the complexity inherent in earlier drafts of the Bill that eventually became the DDA 1995. The Government believes that it has provided 'a simpler and clearer test for reasons which would justify less favourable treatment'.¹ The defence of justification must take account of the circumstances of the particular case, including 'the type of job, the type of disability and its effects, the nature of the position being taken and many other factors'.²

---

1 HL Deb, vol 566, col 118.
2 Ibid, vol 566, col 19. See also Employment Code of Practice, para 4.6.

3.5.5 The proper interpretation of the terms 'material' and 'substantial' is crucial to an understanding of the justification defence. The word 'material' has been used in other discrimination law contexts.¹ It conveys a sense that the reason for the discriminatory treatment must be important, essential or relevant in the circumstances of the case. The word 'substantial' is also used in the DDA 1995 to measure the adverse effect that a person's disability has upon normal day-to-day activities.² In this context, 'substantial' denotes something that is more than minor or trivial. In the context of the employer's justification defence, however, a claimant might understandably contend that the word carries a weightier implication. It is suggested that the combination of the words 'material' and 'substantial' might be interpreted as producing a relatively high threshold for the operation of the justification defence. However, the Employment Code of Practice states that the justification defence 'means that the reason has to relate to the individual circumstances in question and *not just be trivial or minor*'.³ That suggests, not without some logic, that the term 'substantial' should be interpreted consistently wherever it appears in the Act and simply denotes something that is more than minor or trivial.

---

1 Treaty of Rome, Art 141; Equal Pay Act 1970, s 1(3) as amended. See generally: *Bilka-Kaufhaus v Weber von Hartz* [1986] IRLR 317, ECJ; *Rainey v Greater Glasgow Health Board* [1987] IRLR 26, HL. See also, in the context of the SDA 1975 and RRA 1976: *R v Secretary of State for Employment, ex parte EOC* [1994] IRLR 176, HL; *Hampson v Department for Education and Science* [1989] IRLR 69, CA.
2 DDA 1995, s 1(1). See **2.5.2**. See also its use in s 6(1) of the 1995 Act where it qualifies the disadvantage that must be faced by a disabled person before the employer's duty to make reasonable adjustments is triggered (**3.6.9**).
3 Employment Code of Practice, para 4.6 (emphasis added). Note the many examples given there of treatment that would not be justifiable.

3.5.6 At the time of writing, the justification defence has been the direct subject of appellate scrutiny in two authorities. In *Baynton v Saurus General Engineers Ltd*,¹ the EAT noted the statutory sequence for establishing justification in a 'less favourable treatment' claim of disability discrimination. That sequence can be represented as follows:

– the disabled person shows less favourable treatment for a reason related to disability;²
– that less favourable treatment is shown to amount to a potentially unlawful act;³
– the employer shows that the treatment is justified⁴ if the reason for the treatment is both material to the circumstances of the particular case and substantial;⁵
– *unless* the employer is also under a statutory duty to make a reasonable adjustment in relation to the disabled person;⁶
– *and* the employer fails without justification to comply with that duty;⁷

– *subject to* the treatment being justified *even if* the employer had complied with that duty.[8]

The EAT also held that, in applying the test of justification,[9] the interests of the disabled person and the interests of the employer must be weighed in the balance. All the circumstances of the case must be considered (including both those of the disabled person and those of the employer) and not simply the justificatory reason offered by the employer. This appears to emphasise not merely the objective nature of the justification defence, but also its even-handedness.

---

1   [1999] IRLR 604.
2   DDA 1995, s 5(1)(a).
3   Ibid, s 4 (for example, dismissal).
4   Ibid, s 5(1)(b).
5   Ibid, s 5(3).
6   Ibid, s 6.
7   Ibid, s 5(2) and (4).
8   Ibid, s 5(5).
9   Under s 5(3) and, by extension, under s 5(4).

3.5.7 Subsequently, another division of the EAT has re-examined the justification defence in *H J Heinz & Co Ltd v Kenrick*.[1] Whilst not ruling out the balancing exercise between the interests of the employer and the employee suggested in *Baynton*,[2] the EAT in *Kenrick* pointed to the comparatively limited requirements of DDA 1995, s 5(3) which provides both a necessary and sufficient condition for the operation of the defence. The justification defence is not a general test of reasonableness. In fact, the threshold for justification of disability-related less favourable treatment is a very low one. The treatment *is* justified (not merely *can* or *may* be justified) if the reason for it is both material to the circumstances of the case and substantial (in the sense of being more than minor or trivial).[3] However, the EAT recognised that, where there was also a duty to make reasonable adjustments, s 5(3) merely provides a necessary but *not* sufficient condition for justification, because the requirements of s 5(5) (would a reasonable adjustment have made any difference?) also have to be satisfied. The EAT suggested that, whenever a tribunal is moving towards a view that less favourable treatment is justified under a s 5(1)(b) and (3), it should reflect upon whether the employer was also under a s 6 duty to make reasonable adjustments. If so, and if the employer has failed to comply with that duty, and if that failure is itself unjustified in accordance with s 5(4), then the tribunal should consider whether the less favourable treatment would still have been justified *even if* the employer had complied with the duty to make reasonable adjustments.[4]

---

1   [2000] IRLR 144. See also *Post Office v Jones* [2000] ICR 388, EAT (justification cannot arise until it is subjectively claimed, but then the test is an objective one as to materiality and weight).
2   The EAT in *Kenrick* agreed with *Baynton* that the relevant circumstances include the circumstances of both the employer and the employee.
3   On the facts, the employer's treatment of the disabled employee was held not to be justified because there had not been an adequate consideration of alternative employment or shorter hours before he was dismissed for a disability-related period of absence.

4   DDA 1995, s 5(5). See **3.6.22–3.6.23**.

Performance-related pay

3.5.8   Special provision is made by regulations for a justification defence in relation to pay.[1] In this context, 'pay' means remuneration of any kind, including any benefit.[2] Less favourable treatment of a disabled person for a reason related to disability is to be taken to be justified if it results from the application to the disabled person of a term or practice under which the amount of a person's pay is wholly or partly dependent on that person's performance.[3] Thus employers are permitted to pay disabled employees according to performance (for example, by piece rates), including perform-ance as assessed by reference to any measure (whether relative or absolute) of output, efficiency or effectiveness in an employment.[4] But the term or practice in question must be one which is applied: (1) to all the employer's employees; or (2) to all of a class of the employer's employees which includes the disabled person but which is not defined by reference to any disability.[5] The employer cannot choose to pay disabled employees by performance if fellow workers of the same class are being paid a fixed time rate.

1   DDA 1995, s 5(6) and Disability Discrimination (Employment) Regulations 1996, SI 1996/
    1456, reg 3. See Employment Code of Practice, paras 5.28–5.29.
2   Ibid, reg 2. It suggested that the term 'benefit' should be construed widely in accordance
    with s 4(4) of the DDA 1995.
3   Ibid, reg 3(1)(a).
4   Ibid, reg 2. For the interaction of this provision with the s 6 duty to make adjustments, see
    3.6.10.
5   Ibid, reg 3(1)(b).

Agricultural wages

3.5.9   The Agricultural Wages Board is allowed to issue a permit to a disabled individual incapable of earning the minimum wage set by the Board.[1] The permit may set a lower minimum wage for that person and/or may vary other minimum terms and conditions (other than holidays) applicable to that worker. Paying such a worker a lower rate of pay might not be capable of justification under the DDA 1995 simply by reason of the permit unless regulations so stipulated. Accordingly, special provision is made by regulations so that less favourable treatment of a disabled person is to be taken to be justified to the extent that it relates to (and accords with) a matter within the terms and conditions of a permit granted to incapacitated persons under the agricultural wages legislation.[2] This does not allow employers in the agricul-tural sector to discriminate against disabled persons in employment matters other than pay and terms and conditions covered by a permit.[3]

1   Agricultural Wages Act 1948, s 5 and Agricultural Wages (Scotland) Act 1949, s 5.
2   DDA 1995, s 5(6) and Disability Discrimination (Employment) Regulations 1996, SI 1996/
    1456, reg 6(a). Failure to take a step otherwise required to comply with a s 6 duty to make
    reasonable adjustments is also to be taken to be justified if that step would relate to a matter

within the terms and conditions of the permit but would exceed the requirements of those terms and conditions (reg 6(b)).
3   Employment Code of Practice, para 4.52.

3.6   DUTY TO MAKE REASONABLE ADJUSTMENTS

3.6.1   What distinguishes the disability discrimination legislation from existing discrimination law is the explicit duty which the DDA 1995 places upon employers to make reasonable adjustments to work arrangements and the working environment so as to accommodate disabled persons.[1] This duty is an example of legally mandated positive action. It is not a requirement of reverse discrimination or positive discrimination requiring an employer to treat disabled persons more favourably than others. Nevertheless, there is nothing in Part II of the Act to prevent employers voluntarily affording disabled persons preferential treatment.[2] However, the duty to make reasonable adjustments for disabled persons might be viewed erroneously as mandatory positive discrimination. To address this, the Act states that, subject to the statutory duty upon employers to make adjustments for disabled persons, nothing in Part II of the Act (the employment provisions) is to be taken to require an employer to treat a disabled person more favourably than the employer treats or would treat others.[3]

1   DDA 1995, s 6.
2   Subject to what is said about local government employers at **3.12.1**. See Employment Code of Practice, paras 2.2 and 5.26.
3   DDA 1995, s 6(7).

3.6.2   The duty to make reasonable adjustments is an essential part of the prohibition on disability-related discrimination. Without employers being required to adjust working practices or policies and to modify physical features of premises, disabled persons would face potentially indirect discrimination in the labour market. Employers' requirements and conditions will frequently represent barriers to equal opportunity and might have a disproportionate adverse impact upon disabled individuals. As in race and sex discrimination law, unless employers are required to re-examine norms and standards established by reference to the predominant society or culture (the so-called 'able-bodied world'), historic discrimination and inequality of opportunity is merely perpetuated.

Discrimination and the duty to make reasonable adjustments

3.6.3   For the purposes of the employment provisions of the Act, an employer also discriminates against a disabled person if the employer has failed to comply with any duty[1] to make reasonable adjustments in relation to that disabled person,[2] unless the employer can show that the failure to comply with that duty is justified.[3] The Court of Appeal in *Clark v TDG Ltd t/a Novacold*[4] has confirmed that an action for disability discrimination by way of a complaint that the employer has failed to discharge a duty to make reasonable adjustments does not depend upon the applicant also bringing or succeeding in a claim of less favourable treatment discrimination.[5] Nevertheless, they are separate claims and should be dealt with explicitly as such by an employment tribunal.[6] Of course, it will also be necessary to show that the unjustified failure to make a reasonable adjustment is unlawful in that it results in a denial of employment opportunities, dismissal or other detriment.[7]

---

1   Under DDA 1995, s 6.
2   Ibid, s 5(2)(a).
3   Ibid, s 5(2)(b) and (4).
4   [1999] IRLR 318, CA.
5   Under DDA 1995, s 5(1).
6   *Butterfield v Rapidmark Ltd t/a 3 MV* (1998) EAT 131/98.
7   DDA 1995, s 4.

When does the duty to make reasonable adjustments arise?

3.6.4   The duty upon an employer to make reasonable adjustments may be triggered in two circumstances. The duty occurs where:

–   any 'arrangements' made by or on behalf of an employer, or
–   any 'physical features of premises' occupied by the employer,

place the disabled person concerned at a substantial disadvantage in comparison with persons who are not disabled.[1] In either of these cases, it is the duty of the employer to take such steps as it is reasonable, in all the circumstances of the case, for *that* employer to have to take in order to prevent the arrangements or features having that effect.[2]

---

1   DDA 1995, s 6(1).
2   See generally, Employment Code of Practice, paras 4.12–4.14.

3.6.5   In *Morse v Wiltshire CC*,[1] the EAT has provided important guidance to employment tribunals on the practical approach to the issues raised by the duty to make reasonable adjustments. The first question is whether, in the particular circumstances of the case, there is a duty to make reasonable adjustments imposed upon the employer.[2] If so, the next step is to inquire whether the employer has taken reasonable steps to prevent the 'arrangements' or 'physical features of premises' having the effect of placing the disabled person at a comparative substantial disadvantage. That necessitates asking whether the employer reasonably could have taken any of the steps set out in the statutory provisions as illustrating the kinds of adjustments which might be made.[3] In judging the reasonableness criterion, consideration will need to be given to whether any of the factors set out in the Act apply.[4] If the tribunal then finds that the employer has failed to comply with its statutory duty to make reasonable adjustments, the final question is whether the employer has shown that this failure is justified.[5] The emphasis in *Morse* is upon an objective test of whether the employer has discharged its duty to make reasonable adjustments. The employment tribunal is not simply concerned with the reasonableness of the employer's explanation. The tribunal can substitute its own judgment for that of the employer. It may not be sufficient for an employer simply to assert that adjustments were considered and thought to be unreasonable if the tribunal finds that there were other reasonable adjustments which could have been made by the employer.

---

1   [1998] IRLR 352, EAT.
2   By DDA 1995, ss 6(1) and 6(2).
3   Under DDA 1995, s 6(3). See **3.6.11**.
4   Ibid, s 6(4). See **3.6.16**.
5   Ibid, ss 5(2) and 5(4). If not, the tribunal should recommend that the employer conduct a fresh section 6 exercise: *Post Office v Jones* [2000] ICR 388, EAT.

Arrangements

3.6.6   The first situation where the duty arises is where any 'arrangements' made by or on behalf of an employer place the disabled person concerned at a substantial disadvantage in comparison with persons who are not disabled.[1] In this context, the term 'arrangements' means only:

–   arrangements for determining to whom employment should be offered;[2] or
–   any term, condition or arrangements on which employment, promotion, transfer, training or any other benefit is offered or afforded.[3]

Examples of such arrangements would include procedures for recruitment and selection or promotion (such as application forms, interviews or employment tests), and terms upon which employment opportunities are granted (such as insistence upon mobility or flexibility clauses or satisfaction of unreasonably high medical standards).[4]

---

1   DDA 1995, s 6(1)(a).
2   Ibid, s 6(2)(a).
3   Ibid, s 6(2)(b).
4   See Employment Code of Practice, para 4.16 and see generally Chapters 5–6 therein.

3.6.7   Although the use of the phrase 'arrangements on which employment … is … afforded' is capable of a wide construction,[1] it is not without its limitations. First, the Court of Appeal in *Clark v TDG Ltd t/a Novacold*[2] has confirmed that, while the duty to make adjustments does not apply to a dismissal as such, it does apply to the process leading to dismissal. Clearly, a decision to dismiss is capable of amounting to an arrangement 'on which employment … is … afforded' (and the term 'afforded' is wider than the term 'offered'). Moreover, the list of examples of reasonable adjustments[3] contains many illustrations of adjustments which are clearly relevant to the retention of a dismissed employee in lieu of his dismissal. The Employment Code of Practice (paras 6.19–6.21) also contemplates that an employer is under a duty to adjust arrangements so as to retain disabled employees or avoid termination of employment.[4] Secondly, the EAT in *Kenny v Hampshire Constabulary*[5] has held that not all 'arrangements' that might be necessary to enable a disabled person to work fall within the duty to make adjustments. The duty is not intended to cover everything an employer *could* do (for example, arranging transport to and from work or providing a personal carer to assist with the disabled person's personal needs while at work). Only job-related arrangements (such as the way a job is structured or organised) are covered.

1   DDA 1995, s 6(2)(b).
2   [1999] IRLR 318, CA.
3   DDA 1995, s 6(3).
4   Employment Code of Practice, paras 6.19–6.21.
5   [1999] IRLR 76, EAT.

Physical features of premises

3.6.8   The term 'physical feature of premises' is not statutorily defined, but regulations assist in the identification of what is and what is not a relevant feature.[1] The following are treated as physical features (whether permanent or temporary) of premises:

–   any feature arising from the design or construction of a building on the premises;
–   any feature on the premises of any approach to, exist from or access to such a building;
–   any fixtures, fittings, furnishings, furniture, equipment or materials in or on the premises;
–   any other physical element or quality of any land comprised in the premises.

For these purposes, a building means an erection or structure of any kind.[2] Thus, the physical features of a building do not only include the physical fabric and structure of a building. Features such as lighting, air conditioning, building materials, fixtures and fittings, furniture and equipment are also included. It is clear, however, that it is only the physical features of 'premises occupied by the employer' which are in scope.[3] The duty to make reasonable adjustments in respect of the physical features of premises does not extend to a disabled person's private house (for example, in the case of a homeworker) or to the premises of another employer which a disabled employee might have to visit in the course of employment (for example, a travelling sales executive visiting a customer's premises).[4]

1   Disability Discrimination (Employment) Regulations 1996, SI 1996/1456, reg 9 (made under DDA 1995, s 6(8)(g)–(h) and for the purposes of s 6(1)). Note also the Employment Code of Practice, para 4.15 and the example given at para 4.16.
2   Ibid, reg 2.
3   Note the provisions of s 16 and Part I of Sch 4 to the Act which will apply where an employer occupies premises under a lease which prevents or hinders alterations being made in pursuit of a s 6 duty to make adjustments. These provisions are discussed in detail in Chapter 6 below.
4   HL Deb, vol 566, col 184.

Substantial disadvantage

3.6.9   The duty to make reasonable adjustments arises only if the employment arrangements or physical features in question place the disabled person concerned 'at a *substantial* disadvantage in comparison with persons who are not disabled'.[1] The duty to make reasonable adjustments is an individualised duty. It arises only where the disabled person in question suffers a comparative disadvantage. It does not necessarily arise generally or in respect of a class or group of disabled persons. The use of the word 'substantial' appears to create quite a high threshold for the operation of the duty to make reasonable adjustments. The problematic nature of this term has been discussed above.[2] However, the intention appears to be to ensure that minor and trivial disadvantages do not cause the duty to be imposed on employers and that only disadvantages of substance will call for accommodations.[3] Furthermore, the duty is imposed only following a comparative assessment of the adverse effect of the arrangement or physical feature upon the disabled person. The comparators are persons who are not disabled (and, in the case of a person with a past disability, who have not had a disability).[4]

1   DDA 1995, s 6(1) with emphasis added.
2   See **3.5.5**.
3   HC Deb Standing Committee E, col 196. This is confirmed by the Employment Code of Practice, para 4.17.
4   See s 2(2) and Sch 2, para 3. The troublesome question of how the pool of comparison is to be drawn for this purpose must await judicial interpretation.

3.6.10   A term or practice under which the amount of a person's pay is wholly or partly dependent on that person's performance is not to be taken to place disabled persons at a substantial disadvantage.[1] But this does not affect the operation of the duty to make reasonable adjustments where any arrangements or physical features of premises otherwise place the disabled person at a substantial disadvantage and thereby cause reduced performance by him or her.[2]

1   By virtue of the Disability Discrimination (Employment) Regulations 1996, SI 1996/1456, reg 3(2).
2   Ibid, reg 3(3).

The duty illustrated

3.6.11   Unusually, the statute (rather than, as might be expected, an extra-statutory source such as a code of practice) exemplifies the kinds of steps which an employer may have to take in relation to a disabled person in order to comply with the duty to make reasonable adjustments:[1]

–   making adjustments to premises;
–   allocating some of the disabled person's duties to another person;
–   transferring the disabled person to fill an existing vacancy;[2]
–   altering the disabled person's working hours;
–   assigning the disabled person to a different piece of work;[3]
–   allowing the disabled person to be absent during working hours for rehabilitation, assessment or treatment;

– giving the disabled person training, or arranging for such training to be given;
– acquiring or modifying equipment;
– modifying instructions or reference manuals;
– modifying procedures for testing or assessment;
– providing a reader or interpreter;
– providing supervision.

This list is illustrative only of the types of adjustments that might be made and is not intended to be exhaustive.[4] However, these examples do not exist in a vacuum. The duty to make such adjustments arises only where the statutory conditions are satisfied.[5]

---

1 DDA 1995, s 6(3). Useful illustrations of what each of these adjustments might involve in practice are provided in the Employment Code of Practice, para 4.20 and throughout Chapters 5–6 thereof. There is also a power to expand the duty in future, if necessary, by secondary legislation (s 6(10)).

2 It is not suggested that the employer must create a vacancy but, if there is an existing vacancy, it might be reasonable to make adjustments to that vacancy so as to allow the disabled person to fill it. The EAT has noted that it is not for the employment tribunal to identify a particular vacancy which the disabled person could have been offered, but it is for the employer to show that it addressed its mind to this question: *London Borough of Hillingdon v Morgan* (1999) IDS Brief B649/10, EAT (if the matter had been approached correctly by the employer, would adjustments have enabled the employee to return to work?). If suitable alternative work is offered, even at a reduced wage, the employer may have satisfied the duty to make reasonable adjustments: *Arboshe v East London Bus & Coach Co Ltd* (1999) EAT/877/98 (unless an employee's wages would be protected or maintained in analogous circumstances?).

3 For example, this might include allowing a disabled worker to work from home during a period of rehabilitation or as part of a phased return to work. See generally: *London Borough of Hillingdon v Morgan* (1999) EAT/1493/98, 27 May (unreported).

4 Nor is it a checklist: *Humphreys v Environment Agency* (1999) EAT/24/95. However, once the employer has made reasonable adjustments (for example, to the method or structure of the job), the duty to make reasonable adjustments does not require the employer to accept reduced performance from the disabled employee (for example, by lowering the quantity or volume of work being demanded): *Mulligan v Commissioner for Inland Revenue* (1999) EAT/691/99.

5 DDA 1995, s 6(1)–(2) and see **3.6.4–3.6.10**.

3.6.12 During debate, the Minister confirmed that the examples of reasonable adjustments that might be undertaken could include the provision of a sign language interpreter, minicom facilities or alterations to working hours. Furthermore, a reasonable adjustment 'could be a modification to a working environment, to a term or condition of employment or to any similar matters relating to the employment'.[1] Where an employer has existing car parking facilities for employees, it might be a reasonable adjustment to allocate a dedicated car parking space to an employee with a mobility disability.[2] Support for such initiatives might be sought by employers from funds available under the Government's Access to Work scheme. However, the Minister also indicated that the taxpayer could not be expected to meet all the costs of reasonable adjustments. Employers are expected to take some financial responsibility, especially in respect of adjustments and costs relating to working hours and retraining.[3] It does not appear likely that a financial ceiling will be put on the concept of reasonable adjustment,[4] although regulatory powers could be used in the future if there was evidence that the statute was not working appropriately.[5]

---

1   HC Deb Standing Committee E, col 208.
2   HL Deb, vol 566, col 209. See Employment Code of Practice, para 6.7.
3   HC Deb Standing Committee E, col 209.
4   Although note DDA 1995, s 6(4) discussed at **3.6.16**.
5   Note the power to make regulations under s 6(8). Such regulations may, in particular circumstances, make provision by reference to the cost of taking the steps concerned in the duty to make reasonable adjustments (s 6(9)).

3.6.13   Nothing in the DDA 1995 creates an obligation to provide disability leave[1] nor a requirement upon employers to retain newly-disabled employees. However, an employee absent from work on account of disability or long-term chronic ill-health will be entitled to the benefit of the duty upon employers to make reasonable adjustments, as well as the specific protection of unfair dismissal law. The combined effect of disability discrimination law and unfair dismissal standards produces an obligation upon employers to hesitate before dismissing an employee on the grounds of disability or incapacity. At the very least, such an employer will need to consider what reasonable adjustments might be made for the employee and this might have the effect of prolonging his or her employment tenure or of leading to redeployment.[2] To enjoy statutory protection from unfair dismissal under the Employment Rights Act 1996, an employee must have one year's continuous employment with the dismissing employer (from 1 June 1999). There is no minimum service qualification required to bring a complaint of a disability-related, discriminatory dismissal under the DDA 1995. Disabled employees dismissed with less than one year's service must rely upon the DDA 1995 alone, but, for a longer-serving employee with a disability, a dual claim under the disability discrimination and unfair dismissal legislation may prove attractive.[3] The rather subjective 'band of reasonable responses' test in unfair dismissal is not the same as the more objective questions that have to be asked in disability discrimination cases.

---

1   HC Deb Standing Committee E, col 220.
2   See Employment Code of Practice, paras 6.19–6.21 (which makes it clear that an employer must not discriminate by dismissing an employee who becomes disabled or whose disability worsens or where the nature of employment changes). Many employers' existing redeployment policies (which tend to give preference to redundant workers) will be unable to deal sufficiently with the specific duty to make reasonable adjustments that arise in the context of disability. See, for example: *London Borough of Hillingdon v Morgan* (1999) EAT/1493/98, 27 May (unreported) and *Kent County Council v Mingo* [2000] IRLR 90, EAT. Treating a disabled worker as just another candidate for redeployment is likely to be insufficient.
3   In *British Sugar plc v Kirker* [1998] IRLR 624, the EAT has stressed the importance of a tribunal approaching both claims separately and distinctly. It does not inevitably follow that a discriminatory dismissal is an unfair dismissal: *H J Heinz Co Ltd v Kenrick* [2000] IRLR 144,

EAT. An unfair dismissal is not necessarily a discriminatory dismissal. However, the tribunal should carefully address the statutory test of an unfair dismissal contained in s 98 of the 1996 Act: *Kent County Council v Mingo* [2000] IRLR 90, EAT.

What are reasonable steps to take?

3.6.14 The duty upon the employer is to take only such steps as it is reasonable, in all the circumstances of the case, to take in order to prevent the arrangements or features having an adverse effect on the disabled person.[1] The employer is entitled to take account of all the circumstances when deciding what steps it would be reasonable to take. For example, it might be reasonable to weigh 'whether the benefit to the disabled person would be proportionate to the cost and the difficulty of the measures in question'.[2] On the other hand, in deciding whether to make a reasonable adjustment, there is no compulsion upon an employer to take advice.[3] However, a failure to take advice or to seek assistance (for example, from an occupational medical adviser or disabled employment adviser) before determining whether or not to make a reasonable adjustment could be taken into account by an employment tribunal in considering whether the employer had acted reasonably in the circumstances.[4] Equally, the test of reasonableness might need to take account of the extent to which the disabled person has co-operated with the employer who attempts to make a reasonable adjustment.

1 As described in DDA 1995, s 6(1). Note the objective nature of the test here. See *Morse v Wiltshire CC* [1998] IRLR 352, EAT and **3.6.5**.
2 HC Deb Standing Committee E, col 196.
3 But see Employment Code of Practice, para 3.3.
4 HC Deb Standing Committee E, col 222.

3.6.15 For the purposes of the statutory duty to make adjustments to premises occupied by an employer, it is *never* reasonable for an employer to have to take steps in relation to a disabled person to the extent that this would involve altering any physical characteristic (included within building works) which was adopted with a view to meeting the requirements for the time being of Part M of the building regulations[1] with regard to access and facilities for disabled people.[2] However, the physical characteristic in question must have met those requirements at the time the building works were carried out and must have continued substantially to meet those requirements which applied at the time the building works were carried out.[3] It might also be necessary to obtain statutory consents to an alteration (planning permission, listed building consent, etc) and an adjustment would not be a reasonable one to make if the occupier has applied for such consent and it has been refused. In such a case, the duty to make adjustments should take account of alternative ways of achieving a viable adjustment.[4]

1 Within the meaning of the Building Act 1984, s 122: Disability Discrimination (Employment) Regulations 1996, SI 1996/1456, reg 2. The latest version of Part M of the building regulations is now found in Sch 1 to the Building Regulations 1991, SI 1991/2768. In Scotland, the appropriate reference is to Part T of the Technical Standards for compliance with the Building Standards (Scotland) Regulations 1990, SI 1990/2179 issued by the Scottish Office in 1990 and subsequently amended in July 1993 and July 1994 (see SI 1993/1457 and SI 1994/1266).

2   Disability Discrimination (Employment) Regulations 1996, SI 1996/1456, reg 8(1)(a) and
    (2). See further the Employment Code of Practice, paras 4.35–4.36.
3   Ibid, reg 8(1)(b).
4   Employment Code of Practice, paras 4.37–4.39.

3.6.16   In determining whether it is reasonable for an employer to take a particular step in order to comply with the duty to make adjustments, regard is to be had, in particular, to the following matters:[1]

–   the extent to which taking the step would prevent the effect in question;[2]
–   the extent to which it is practicable for the employer to take the step;[3]
–   the financial and other costs which would be incurred by the employer in taking the step and the extent to which taking it would disrupt any of the employer's activities;[4]
–   the extent of the employer's financial and other resources;[5]
–   the availability to the employer of financial or other assistance with respect to taking the step.[6]

The Employment Code of Practice anticipates that other factors might be relevant, depending upon the circumstances, including the effect which an adjustment has upon other employees, any adjustments already made for other disabled employees, and the extent to which the disabled person is willing to co-operate with the employer's attempts to make an adjustment.[7] It may also be reasonable for an employer to have to make more than one adjustment.[8]

1   DDA 1995, s 6(4). Although there is a power in s 6(8) to make regulations which will be
    relevant when judging the reasonableness of requiring an employer to take a particular step
    in particular circumstances, including by reference to costs (s 6(9)), no such regulations
    have been made to date.
2   That is, the effect of an arrangement or physical feature placing the disabled person at a
    substantial disadvantage in comparison with persons who are not disabled. See Employment
    Code of Practice, para 4.22.
3   See ibid, para 4.23.
4   See ibid, paras 4.24–4.27. The significance of the cost of a step may depend in part on the
    value of the employee's experience and expertise to the employer, including factors such as
    resources (such as training) already invested in the employee and the employee's length of
    service, level of skill and knowledge, quality of relationships with clients and level of pay:
    ibid, para 4.25.
5   See ibid, paras 4.28–4.30. It is more likely to be reasonable for an employer with substantial
    resources to have to make a significantly costly adjustment than it would be for an employer
    with fewer resources.
6   See ibid, para 4.31.
7   Ibid, para 4.32. See generally para 4.21.
8   Ibid, para 4.33.

3.6.17   The above listed matters are the 'key criteria . . . in no particular order of priority' by which the reasonableness of an adjustment will be judged.[1] For example, if the only possible adjustments that could be made to aid the output of a disabled worker could result in no more than a small improvement in productivity, but at a price of cost or disruption, the adjustments might not be reasonable.[2] Similarly, if after reasonable adjustments have been made a disabled worker's productivity is below normal, where the worker is paid according to performance an employer would not be expected to make further adjustments by compensating the worker for the loss of performance-related pay.[3]

---

1 HL Deb, vol 566, col 184.
2 Ibid, cols 184–185. See Employment Code of Practice, paras 4.22–4.27.
3 This is the effect of the interaction of s 6 of the Act with reg 3 of the Disability Discrimination (Employment) Regulations 1996, SI 1996/1456. See the discussion at **3.5.8** and **3.6.10**. Note the Employment Code of Practice, paras 4.18, 4.22 and 5.28–5.29.

3.6.18   The Minister gave further illustrations.[1] It might not be reasonable for an employer (especially a small employer) needing an employee urgently to have to wait for an adjustment to be made to allow a disabled person to be employed.[2] An adjustment that would involve a breach of safety laws or fire regulations could not be reasonable.[3] The cost of the adjustment might also render it an unreasonable one to make, and cost will include use of staff and other resources, as well as direct monetary costs.[4] The employer's resources must be taken into account and it might be more reasonable for an employer with considerable resources to make a significantly costly adjustment than for an employer with fewer resources.[5] Moreover, a step is not unreasonable if there is available compensatory help from an outside organisation or from the disabled person. For example, the employer might not be expected to purchase specialist computer equipment adapted for use by a person with a sight disability, but such equipment might be available free of charge under the Access to Work scheme or from a disability charity. It would also be a reasonable adjustment to allow a disabled worker to use his or her own auxiliary aids or equipment at work.[6]

---

1 HL Deb, vol 566, col 185.
2 See Employment Code of Practice, para 4.23.
3 See ibid, para 4.65.
4 See ibid, para 4.24.
5 See ibid, para 4.28.
6 See ibid, para 4.31.

To whom is the duty owed?

3.6.19   In respect of arrangements for determining to whom employment should be offered, the duty to make reasonable adjustments is owed only to a disabled person who is, or who has notified the employer that he or she may be, an applicant for that employment.[1] The length of notice given by the disabled applicant to the employer might play a part in determining whether the employer has satisfied the duty to make reasonable adjustments. In any other case, the duty is owed to a disabled person who is an applicant for the employment concerned or who is an employee of the employer concerned.[2] More significantly still, the duty to make reasonable adjustments is not imposed upon any employer in relation to a disabled person *unless* the employer knows (or could reasonably be expected to know) that the disabled person concerned is, or may be, an applicant for the employment in question.[3] In any case, the duty to make reasonable adjustments is not imposed in relation to a particular disabled person *unless* the employer knows (or could reasonably be expected to know) that the disabled person concerned has (or has had) a disability and is likely to be placed at a substantial disadvantage in comparison with non-disabled persons because of any arrangements made by the employer or any physical features of the premises occupied by the employer.[4] The question of what the employer knew or could reasonably be expected to know is a question of fact for the tribunal,[5] and will vary from case to case.

1   DDA 1995, s 6(5)(a).
2   Ibid, s 6(5)(b).
3   Ibid, s 6(6)(a).
4   Ibid, s 6(6)(b) and Sch 2, para 4.
5   See *Hanlon v University of Huddersfield* (1998) EAT 166/98.

3.6.20   The Employment Code of Practice goes a little further than the DDA 1995. It suggests that an employer must do all that it could reasonably be expected to do to find out whether a person has a disability which is likely to place him or her at a substantial disadvantage.[1] Thus employers need to be proactive and will not necessarily escape liability by simply not asking whether a person has a disability and whether the effects of any disability call for an adjustment to be made.[2] The Employment Code of Practice recommends that employers should only ask disability-related questions if disability is, or may be, relevant to the ability to do the job,[3] but equally employers should be positive in welcoming applications from disabled persons.[4] Asking about the effects of a disability is seen as a necessary part of the process of considering what reasonable adjustments might be made for a disabled person.[5] In any event, if a person asks for an adjustment to be made, the employer will be entitled to ask for evidence that the person has a disability such as to trigger the statutory duty.[6] Moreover, because a reasonable adjustment may not work in practice without the co-operation of other employees, it may be necessary to reveal the fact of a person's disability (where otherwise not obvious) to some of that person's work colleagues (particularly supervisors or managers) *in confidence* (for example, where special assistance may be needed).[7] This should be done on a selective and 'need to know' basis, but employers should be careful not to commit a separate act of discrimination by revealing such information without consulting the disabled person first or without a legitimate management purpose in doing so.[8]

1   Employment Code of Practice, para 4.57 and see the examples quoted there. Of course, if a disabled person chooses to conceal a disability, that will lessen the possibility that the employer should be expected to carry out a reasonable adjustment, unless the circumstances are such that it would be reasonable for the employer to be expected to know of the disability without the necessity for revelation: ibid, para 4.61.
2   The fact that the employer might not know of a person's disability will make no difference if, for example, a personnel officer, line manager, or occupational health officer employed by the employer has that information. The knowledge of an employee or agent of the employer is the vicarious knowledge of the employer itself: ibid, paras 4.62–4.63.
3   Ibid, para 5.20.
4   Ibid, para 5.10.

5 Employment Code of Practice, paras 5.11 and 5.20.
6 Ibid, para 4.64.
7 Ibid, paras 4.58–4.59.
8 Ibid, para 4.60.

3.6.21 There does appear to be some onus on the applicant or employee to make known to the employer their need for a reasonable adjustment. However, in *Ridout v TC Group*,[1] the EAT indicated that disabled people should not have a duty imposed upon them to give to an employer a detailed account of their disability and its effects upon them, especially where this would lead only to an employer making adjustments which it would have been reasonable to make in any event. It is equally undesirable to expect employers to ask intrusive questions of disabled people which would not have been asked of a non-disabled person. A tribunal has to measure the extent of the duty to make a reasonable adjustment, if any, against the actual or assumed knowledge of the employer both as to the disability and its likelihood of causing the individual a substantial disadvantage in comparison with persons who are not disabled.

1 [1998] IRLR 628.

Discrimination, justification and reasonable adjustments

3.6.22 A failure, without justification, to comply with the statutory duty imposed on an employer to make reasonable adjustments in relation to a disabled person will amount to an act of discrimination by the employer.[1] A failure to comply with that duty is justified if, but only if, the reason for the failure is both material to the circumstances of the particular case and substantial.[2] A breach of the statutory duty is not otherwise an actionable breach of duty in itself but is merely an ingredient of the meaning of discrimination.[3]

1 DDA 1995, ss 5(2) and 6. The discrimination will be unlawful if it falls within s 4. A period in
   which the employer is assessing whether to make an adjustment could be reasonable or
   justifiable: *Post Office v Jones* [2000] ICR 388, EAT (a period of 11 weeks said to be
   inexplicable and unjustifiable).
2 Ibid, s 5(4). See **3.5**. Note the provisions of s 16 and Part I of Sch 4 to the DDA 1995 which
   will apply where an employer occupies premises under a lease which prevents or hinders
   alterations being made in pursuit of a s 6 duty to make adjustments. These provisions are
   discussed in detail in Chapter 6 below.
3 Ibid, s 6(12).

3.6.23 Where an employer has treated a disabled person less favourably for a reason which relates to disability,[1] but has unjustifiably failed to comply with a statutory duty to make reasonable adjustments,[2] then the less favourable treatment cannot be justified[3] unless the employer can show that it would have been justified even if the employer had complied with the duty to make a reasonable adjustment.[4] So an employer cannot be liable for a justifiable non-performance of a duty to make reasonable adjustments, while a failure to make reasonable adjustments cannot be unlawful if the failure is justifiable.[5] In other words, before an employer can seek to justify the less favourable treatment of a disabled person for a reason related to disability, it must first address its duty to make reasonable adjustments. The employer cannot rely upon a material and substantial reason for less favourable treatment if that reason could have been rendered immaterial or insubstantial by carrying out a reasonable adjustment.

---

1   Under DDA 1995, s 5(1).
2   Ibid, s 6 and s 5(4).
3   That is, by reference to a material and substantial reason under DDA 1995, s 5(3).
4   DDA 1995, s 5(5). See *Baynton v Saurus General Engineers Ltd* [1999] IRLR 604 and *H J Heinz Co Ltd v Kenrick* [2000] IRLR 144 (discussed at **3.5.6–3.5.7**). The matter should not be tackled *de novo* by the tribunal and without reference to the steps actually taken by the employer: *Post Office v Jones* [2000] ICR 388, EAT (tribunal should not carry out a 'quasi-section 6 exercise' based solely on the evidence tendered at the hearing).
5   HL Deb, vol 566, col 992. See the examples given in the Employment Code of Practice, para 4.7. See also paras 4.9 and 4.34.

3.7   OCCUPATIONAL PENSION SCHEMES

Employers' obligations

3.7.1   Part II of the DDA 1995 is capable of covering the actions of an employer who provides opportunities to employees for occupational pensions. In particular, discrimination against disabled persons in 'the terms of employment' and in the opportunities afforded for 'receiving any other benefit' is unlawful.[1] So, if an employer treated a disabled person less favourably than other employees in respect of access to or benefits from an occupational pension scheme (including the terms of membership) that might amount to an unlawful act of discrimination, unless capable of justification.

---

1   DDA 1995, s 4(2).

3.7.2   Special provision is made for benefits provided under an occupational pension scheme in respect of termination of service, retirement, old age, death, accident, injury, sickness or invalidity.[1] Where, by reason of the disabled person's disability (including any clinical prognosis flowing from the disability), the cost of providing any of the above benefits is likely to be substantially greater than it would be for a comparable person without that disability,[2] less favourable treatment of a disabled person is to be taken to be justified if it results from applying the eligibility conditions set for receiving any such benefit or from determining the amount of any such benefit.[3] Employers should first satisfy themselves (at the time the disabled person is considered for admission to the scheme) of the likelihood of there being substantially greater costs and this will usually require a combination of actuarial advice and medical advice.[4] Only the likelihood of a *substantial* additional cost should be regarded as a justification.[5]

---

1   Disability Discrimination (Employment) Regulations 1996, SI 1996/1456, reg 4(3).
2   Ibid, reg 4(2).

3 Ibid, reg 4(1).
4 See Employment Code of Practice, paras 6.10–6.11. The justification defence cannot be
   applied to a disabled *member* of the scheme unless a term was imposed at the time of
   admission: ibid, para 6.12.
5 Ibid, para 6.14 which suggests that 'substantial' means more than minor or trivial.

3.7.3 Moreover, less favourable treatment is also *always* to be taken to be
justified if an employer requires from a disabled person the same rate of
contribution to an occupational pension scheme as the employer requires
from its other employees (or from any class of employees which includes the
disabled person but which is not defined by reference to any disability).[1] This is
notwithstanding that the disabled person is not eligible under that scheme (for
a reason related to his or her disability) to receive a benefit or to receive a
benefit at the same rate as a comparable person (to whom the reason related to
disability does not apply). This provision allows employers to maintain uniform
rates of contributions to occupational pension schemes by requiring disabled
employees to pay the same rate of contributions as other employees even if not
eligible for some of the benefits.[2]

1 Disability Discrimination (Employment) Regulations 1996, SI 1996/1456, reg 5.
2 Employment Code of Practice, para 6.15.

3.7.4 Does the duty to make reasonable adjustments apply to employers in
repect of ensuring disabled persons have equal access to (and opportunities
under) an occupational pension scheme? The statutory duty to make
reasonable adjustments is disapplied in respect of any benefit under an
occupational pension scheme (including benefits in respect of termination of
service, or retirement, old age or death, or accident, injury, sickness or
invalidity).[1] So, for example, where a disabled person lawfully has been refused
access to an occupational pension scheme (or denied the right to full benefits
of the scheme) on actuarial grounds, there will be no obligation on the
employer to adjust the terms of employment so as to compensate for the loss of
the pension benefit by increasing the disabled employee's salary.[2]

1 DDA 1995, s 6(11). Future regulations may add to this list after consultation.
2 Employment Code of Practice, para 6.16. Nor will an employer have to make an adjustment
   for a disabled employee receiving less benefit because that person justifiably receives a lower
   rate of pay (for example, because of a performance-related payment system).

Trustees of occupational pension schemes

3.7.5 Occupational pension schemes are run and managed by trustees, rather
than by the employer. There would be nothing to prevent such schemes
containing rules that discriminated against disabled persons or disabled
employees (unless they were also caught by Part III of the DDA 1995). The
Government was concerned that disabled persons might be unfairly denied
access to an employer's pension scheme arrangements by the decisions of the
scheme trustees (and not simply by the actions of employers). To avoid this

state of affairs or doubt, the Act states that every occupational pension scheme shall be taken to include a provision to be referred to as 'a non-discrimination rule'.[1] The effect of this implied non-discrimination rule relates to the terms on which persons become members of the scheme and the terms on which members of the scheme are treated.[2] The non-discrimination rule also requires the trustees or managers of the occupational pension scheme to refrain from any act or omission which, if done in relation to a person by an employer, would amount to unlawful discrimination under Part II of the Act.[3] Moreover, the 'other provisions of the scheme' are to have effect subject to the implied non-discrimination rule.

---

1   DDA 1995, s 17(1).
2   Ibid, s 17(1)(a).
3   Ibid, s 17(1)(b). Note s 17(3) discussed below at **3.7.8**.

3.7.6   The effect of this provision is to imply an 'overriding' rule of non-discrimination against disabled persons into the rules of occupational pension schemes.[1] 'This means that any discriminatory decision taken by trustees will be contrary to the rules of the scheme' and any disabled person affected by such a discriminatory decision 'will be able to seek redress through the dispute resolution mechanisms which already exist for pension schemes'.[2] Nevertheless, 'where a disabled applicant has a pre-existing medical condition which is likely to increase the risk of ill-health retirement or death in service', employers should be able to take that factor into account in the same way as they would do in respect of an applicant who was not disabled.[3] In the same breath, however, the Minister made it patent that such decisions must be based upon sound actuarial and medical evidence or advice. It must not be presumed that disability has a direct or inevitable effect upon life expectancy or risk of ill-health retirement. Disabled employees have a rebuttable right to access to employers' pension schemes.

---

1   The term occupational pension scheme has the same meaning as used under the Pension Schemes Act 1993 or the Pension Schemes (Northern Ireland) Act 1993.
2   HL Deb, vol 566, cols 994–995.
3   Ibid, col 995.

3.7.7   These provisions effectively 'ride piggy-back' upon the provisions of ss 4–6 of the DDA 1995 and regs 4–5 of the Disability Discrimination (Employment) Regulations 1996. The guidance contained in the Employment Code of Practice also applies to trustees and managers of occupational pension schemes (with appropriate modifications) as they do to employers.[1] Thus, trustees and managers might incur liability,[2] or employ a justification defence,[3] in exactly the same way as an employer might do so in respect of pensions. The exclusion of the duty to make reasonable adjustments in this context is equally applicable.[4] However, whereas the employer's liability might be tested in an employment tribunal, a complaint against the trustees or managers of an occupational pension scheme must be pursued through the appropriate dispute resolution machinery for pension schemes. This is beyond the scope of the present book.[5]

---

1   Employment Code of Practice, para 6.9 and see paras 6.10–6.16.
2   See **3.7.1**.

3 See **3.7.2–3.7.3**.
4 See **3.7.4**.
5 See the Occupational Pension Schemes (Internal Dispute Resolution Procedures) Regulations 1996, SI 1996/1270.

3.7.8 Regulations may be made under Part II of the DDA 1995 in respect of occupational pension schemes.[1] Such regulations may make different provisions affecting trustees or managers of occupational pension schemes to those provisions which affect employers in relation to pension arrangements. Alternatively, regulations may make provision modifying the application to pension scheme managers or trustees of any regulations made under Part II or of any provisions of Part II so far as they apply to employers. No regulations have been made under this power at the time of writing.[2]

1 DDA 1995, s 17(3) (without prejudice to the powers to make orders and regulations as set out in s 67).
2 The only regulations that are relevant are the Disability Discrimination (Employment) Regulations 1996, SI 1996/1456, regs 4–5 made under s 5 of the Act. These have been discussed at **3.7.7**.

3.8 INSURANCE BENEFITS PROVIDED TO EMPLOYEES

3.8.1 Insurance benefits (such as private health insurance) offered to employees by an employer as an incident of a contract of employment are clearly within the scope of the prohibition on employment discrimination.[1] Section 18 makes special provision for the situation where an employer makes arrangements with an insurer for insurance-related benefits to be received by the employer's employees. This is designed to address discrimination by the insurance company as opposed to by the employer itself, and to the situation where the insurer treats disabled persons differently from others for non-actuarial reasons.

1 DDA 1995, s 4, subject to s 4(3) discussed at **3.3.10–3.3.11**. Section 4(2)(a)–(c) would seem particularly apposite. As to how the employment of a disabled person might affect the provision of liability insurance cover to the employer, see the Employment Code of Practice, para 6.18.

3.8.2 Section 18 applies in either of two circumstances. First, the section applies where a provider of insurance services enters into arrangements with an employer under which the employer's employees receive 'insurance services' provided by the insurer in question.[1] Secondly, where the insurer enters into an arrangement with an employer under which the employer's employees are given an opportunity to receive insurance services provided by the insurer, the section is equally applicable.[2] In both cases, it does not matter whether the employee–insurer arrangements cover all the employer's employees or only a class thereof.

1 DDA 1995, s 18(1)(a).

3.8.3   Disability-related discrimination in respect of the provision of insurance benefits to employees under an employer–insurer arrangement is made unlawful by an awkward cross-reference to the provisions of Part III of the DDA 1995 concerning the provisions of goods, facilities or services.[1] Part III establishes that it is unlawful to discriminate against a disabled person for a reason related to disability in respect of the provision of goods, facilities or services to members of the public unless the discrimination is capable of justification: for example, by reference to actuarial evidence. For the purposes of Part II of the Act, in the context of employment benefits, an insurer is treated as having discriminated unlawfully against a disabled person who is a 'relevant employee' if the insurer acts in relation to the disabled employee in a way which would be unlawful discrimination under Part III.[2] In other words, would the insurer have committed an act of discrimination if it was providing the service in question *to members of the public* and as if the insurance services in issue were being provided to the disabled person as a member of the public?

1   See ss 19–20 and Chapter 5 below. Account will be taken there of the insurance aspects of the Disability Discrimination (Service and Premises) Regulations 1996, SI 1996/1836.
2   DDA 1995, s 18(2). A 'relevant employee' is determined by whether the employer–insurer arrangement is designed to benefit the employer's employees generally or only a class of employee (s 18(3)). It includes a person who has applied (or is contemplating applying) for employment by the employer (s 18(4)).

3.8.4   This is an unhappy piece of statutory drafting. The Minister attempted to explain its intended effect as follows:

'The insurance company will act unlawfully against a disabled person under [s 18] if it treats him in a way which would be an act of discrimination under Part III if done by the company with regard to a member of the public. That means that refusal to insure a disabled employee, or levying a higher premium, will be unlawful unless it is justified; for example, where there are reasonable grounds for supposing that the disabled person represents a higher risk than normal.'[1]

As will be seen in Chapter 5 below, the circumstances in which a service provider might justify less favourable treatment of a disabled person are more subjective and flexible than the test for justification in the employment context. In the final analysis, however, disabled persons who suspect that they have been discriminated against in the provision of occupational insurance benefits would be entitled to take both the employer and the insurer to an employment tribunal.

1   HL Deb, vol 566, col 995. See further, Employment Code of Practice, para 6.17.

3.8.5   What 'insurance services' are covered by DDA 1995, s 18?[1] The prohibition on discrimination in relation to occupational insurance benefits encompasses the provision of benefits in respect of termination of service, retirement, old age, death, accident, injury, sickness or invalidity. The Minister confirmed that s 18 will apply to insurance services provided under a group scheme (such as permanent health insurance benefits).[2]

---

1   Section 18(3) provides for regulations to prescribe the description of insurance services caught by the section. The Disability Discrimination (Description of Insurance Services) Regulations 1999, SI 1999/2114, provide that 'Group Insurance' (as defined) is an insurance service for this purpose.
2   HL Deb, vol 566, col 1020 and see the Employment Code of Practice, para 6.17.

3.8.6   Of course, it might not be the insurer that has discriminated against the disabled employee. The employer might have refused admission to the insurance scheme, anticipating possible higher costs to itself if the benefits are to be bought for a disabled person. This might amount to discrimination unless justifiable.[1] Regulations may make provision as to the circumstances in which treatment is to be taken to be justified or not to be justified.[2] Particular provision may be made in such regulations by reference to the cost of affording any benefit.[3] No such regulations have been made at the time of writing. The Government at the time gave an assurance that it had in mind only serious or non-trivial costs as a ground for justifying less favourable treatment.[4]

---

1   DDA 1995, ss 4–5.
2   Ibid, s 5(6).
3   Ibid, s 5(7)(a).
4   HL Deb, vol 566, col 1000.

3.8.7   Moreover, ordinarily the employer cannot justify discrimination without first addressing the duty to make reasonable adjustments, but an employer has no duty to make reasonable adjustments to accommodate disabled persons in respect of occupational insurance benefits.[1] The duty to make reasonable adjustments does not apply in relation to any of a number of benefits payable in money or money's worth under a scheme or arrangement for the benefit of employees. The benefits in question are those in respect of termination of service, or retirement, old age or death, or accident, injury, sickness or invalidity. Future regulations may add to this list after consultation.

---

1   DDA 1995, s 6(11).

3.9   DISCRIMINATION AGAINST CONTRACT WORKERS

Introduction

3.9.1   Section 12 deals with discrimination by principals against contract workers in respect of the provision of contract work.[1] A 'principal' is a person (X) who makes work available ('contract work') for doing by individuals (Y) who are employed by another person (Z) who supplies them under a contract made with X.[2] A 'contract worker' is any individual (Y) who is supplied to the principal (X) under a contract made between X and Z for contract work to be done.[3] Because of the expanded definition of 'employment' in the DDA 1995,[4] it would seem logical that the statute should apply to contract workers whether or not they are employees of Z or are self-employed but providing personal services under a contract with Z. However, that is not made explicit.[5]

1   Similar provisions are to be found in the SDA 1975, s 9 and the RRA 1976, s 7. See generally, Employment Code of Practice, paras 7.1–7.8.
2   DDA 1995, s 12(6). The existence of a contract between X (the principal) and Z (the contractor-employer) for the supply of Y's labour is crucial. In *Rice v Fon-A-Car* [1980] ICR 133, EAT a taxi driver was not a contract worker simply because his services were supplied to customers through a central agency because the agency had no contractual relationship with the customers. However, in *Harrods Ltd v Remick* [1997] IRLR 583, CA, employees of concessionaires in a department store were treated as contract workers as they worked for the concessionaires but for the benefit of the store. See also: *CJ O'Shea Construction Ltd v Bassi* [1998] ICR 1130, EAT.
3   DDA 1995, s 12(6).
4   Ibid, s 68(1).
5   Doubts about the contractual status of such workers have been explored in the other discrimination jurisdictions. See *Construction Industry Training Board v Labour Force Ltd* [1970] 3 All ER 220; *Tanna v Post Office* [1981] ICR 374; *Mirror Group Newspapers v Gunning* [1986] ICR 145. See further *Daley v Allied Suppliers Ltd* [1983] ICR 90 (trainees engaged under contracts for training were not contract workers).

3.9.2   The EAT has breathed considerable life into the provisions of s 12 (and its equivalents in the other discrimination statutes) by its imaginative decision in *MHC Consulting Services Ltd v Tansell*.[1] Mr Tansell (T), a disabled person within the meaning of the Act, had formed Intelligents Ltd (I) as a vehicle for offering his computer skills and services to third parties. T had placed his name with MHC Consulting Services Ltd (MHC), an employment agency specialising in placing computer personnel with third parties. Abbey Life Assurance Co Ltd (AL) entered into a contract with MHC whereby MHC contracted to provide computer personnel to AL. In pursuance of that relationship, MHC placed T's services with AL and did so by entering into a contract with I for the supply of T's services to AL. However, it was alleged by T in proceedings brought under s 12 that AL rejected his services because of his disability.

Both the employment tribunal and the EAT concluded that T was not an employee of either AL or MHC. If he was an employee at all, then he was employed by I. The employment tribunal found that T was not a s 12 contract worker in his relationship with AL, but was a contract worker in his relationship with MHC. Its reasoning was that there was no direct relationship between T's employer (I) and the alleged principal (AL), but that there was such a relationship between I and MHC. As it was, MHC which had made work available to T (via I) through its contract with AL, MHC was a principal within s 12 and T's DDA action lay against MHC rather than AL.

This result was clearly an unattractive one for the EAT, not least because T's action against MHC was likely to be met with the defence that it had not treated him less favourably by reason of his disability and that, in view of its client's alleged refusal to take T's services, MHC would be able to justify its position. It sought a construction of the statutory provision so as to give 'effect to the general principle which applies in social legislation of this kind, namely that the statute should be construed purposively, and with a bias towards conferring statutory protection rather than excluding it'. The EAT ruled that T could proceed with his action against AL under s 12. T was employed by I which supplied T's services through MHC to AL. This amounted to an unbroken chain of contracts between the individual (T) and the end-user (AL). In these circumstances, the end-user is a principal within the meaning of s 12(6).

---

1   [1999] IRLR 677, subsequently upheld by the Court of Appeal *sub nom Abbey Life Assurance Co Ltd v Tansell* [2000] IRLR 387. The EAT observed that s 12 is not drafted with clarity.

Unlawful discrimination

3.9.3   It is unlawful for a principal, in relation to contract work done at an establishment in Great Britain,[1] to discriminate against a disabled person:

–   in the terms on which the principal allows the disabled person to do that work;
–   by not allowing the disabled person to do or continue to do the contract work;[2]
–   in the way the principal affords the disabled person access to any benefits or by refusing or deliberately omitting to afford the disabled person access to any benefits;
–   by subjecting the disabled person to any other detriment.[3]

These categories of unlawful acts are very similar to some of the categories contained in the DDA 1995, s 4 (discrimination against employment applicants and employees). However, they do not include discrimination in recruitment, selection, engagement and dismissal. Any disability-related discrimination in those areas will have been perpetuated by the employer rather than the principal for whom the contract work is to be done. A complainant would have a potential cause of action against the employer under ss 4–6.

---

1   The provisions of DDA 1995, s 68 about the meaning of 'employment at an establishment in Great Britain' are modified accordingly (s 12(5)). Section 12 applies by extension to Northern Ireland by virtue of Sch 8, para 8.
2   The principal may have unlawfully discriminated by refusing to take on the contract worker: *BP Chemicals Ltd v Gillick* [1995] IRLR 128, EAT.
3   DDA 1995, s 12(1).

3.9.4   As is the case in the parallel employment provisions,[1] the contract worker provisions[2] do not apply to benefits of any description if the principal is concerned with the provision (whether for payment or not) or benefits of that description to the public (or a section of the public including the contract worker) unless that provision differs in a material respect from the provision of the benefits by the principal to contract workers.[3] However, in such a case, a contract worker might have a cause of action under Part III of the DDA 1995.

---

1   DDA 1995, s 4(2)–(3).
2   Ibid, s 12(1).
3   DDA 1995, s 12(2). Benefits include facilities or services: DDA 1995, s 4(4).

3.9.5   Section 12 outlaws disability discrimination against contract workers by applying the provisions on employment discrimination[1] to a principal in respect of contract work as if the principal were (or would be) the employer of the contract worker and as if any contract worker supplied to do work for the principal were an employee of the principal.[2] In particular, the effect is that a principal may not discriminate against a contract worker for a reason related to disability,[3] is subject to a duty to make adjustments,[4] may take advantage of the defence of justification where it would be available to an employer in parallel circumstances, and may be exempted by the small business exception.[5]

1   DDA 1995, ss 4–11 (except s 4(1)–(3)).
2   Ibid, s 12(3). This 'piggyback' provision does not use s 4(1)–(3) because the circumstances of unlawful discrimination against contract workers is exhaustively set out in s 12(1).
3   In the way defined in DDA 1995, s 5 (including victimisation within s 55). See s 12(4).
4   Under DDA 1995, s 6.
5   Ibid, s 7.

3.9.6   The intention behind s 12 is to protect disabled persons 'working under employment business arrangements if a hirer either refuses to hire the disabled person or discriminates against the disabled person once he has begun working for the hirer'.[1] Such persons will be generally protected by Part II of the Act in respect of their relationship with their employer (perhaps an employment agency or labour supplier), provided their employer employs 15 or more employees.[2] Section 12 extends that protection as against a third party during the period when their services have been hired or contracted to the third party, but again only if that third party (the so-called 'principal') employs 15 or more employees.[3]

1   HL Deb, vol 566, col 221.
2   See Employment Code of Practice, para 7.7.
3   These provisions also apply to severely disabled workers supplied by a local authority or voluntary organisation to a host employer under the Supported Placement Scheme: Employment Code of Practice, para 7.8.

Contract work and reasonable adjustments

3.9.7   If the principal is subject to s 12, then it will have a duty to make adjustments to accommodate disabled contract workers, including a duty to co-operate as far as is reasonable with adjustments already made for the worker by the employment business.[1] However, what will be a reasonable adjustment for a hirer to make will depend upon its individual circumstances and the rather limited, short-term nature of the labour hiring relationship. For example, it might be unreasonable for a principal to have to make adjustments if the disabled contract worker is to be seconded to the principal for only a short time.[2] Also, in practice, it might be reasonable for the principal to allow an adjustment to be made in respect of the disabled contract worker, but for the employer-supplier to provide or pay for the necessary adjustment.

1   HL Deb, vol 566, col 222; Employment Code of Practice, para 7.6.
2   Employment Code of Practice, para 7.5. No indication is given of what would amount to a
    short period of time, although the example accompanying para 7.5 suggests that two weeks
    would certainly be such a period.

3.9.8   In a complex provision, regulations provide for the situation where a
contract worker is likely to be placed at a similar substantial disadvantage (for
the purposes of ss 6 and 12(3)) by arrangements made by or on behalf of all or
most of the principals to whom he or she is or might be supplied.[1] This also
covers the situation where a contract worker is likely to be placed at a similar
substantial disadvantage by premises occupied by all or most of the principals to
whom he or she might be supplied. In these situations, it is deemed to be
reasonable for the contract worker's employer to have to take such steps as are
within its power and as it would be reasonable for it to have to take if the
arrangements were made by it (or on its behalf) or the premises were occupied
by it (as the case may be).[2] In such a case, it is not reasonable for the principal to
whom the contract worker is supplied in these situations to have to take any step
which it is reasonable for the employer to have to take by virtue of this
provision.[3]

1   Disability Discrimination (Employment) Regulations 1996, SI 1996/1456, reg 7(1).
2   Ibid, reg 7(2).
3   Ibid, reg 7(3).

3.9.9   This might be best explained by adopting and modifying an example
provided in the Employment Code of Practice.[1] A disabled word-processor
operator employed as a contract worker by a clerical agency requires a special
keyboard as an adjustment for his or her disability. It can be anticipated that the
contract worker will require such a keyboard wherever she or he is sent to work
by the agency. It would be a reasonable step for the agency to supply the
word-processor operator with the special keyboard and it would not be
reasonable to expect any firm to whom that contract worker's services are
supplied to acquire a special keyboard. However, those firms would be under a
separate duty to co-operate with the adjustment made by the agency – for
example, by allowing the worker to carry and use the special keyboard at their
premises. They might also have a residual duty to make a reasonable
adjustment (for example, by ensuring that the keyboard can be made
compatible with their computer system, for example by installing the appropriate printer driver software).

1   Employment Code of Practice, para 7.6.

3.10   ENFORCEMENT, REMEDIES AND PROCEDURES

3.10.1   Section 8 of the DDA 1995 sets out the enforcement procedures and
remedies available when a claim of unlawful discrimination is made in respect
of employment opportunities or contract work. A complaint of unlawful
discrimination under Part II of the Act may be presented to an employment

tribunal within 3 months of the act complained of.[1] No other civil or criminal proceedings (except judicial review) may be brought.[2] A conciliation process will normally follow.[3] The usual remedy in a successful complaint will be compensation, including damages for injury to feelings and interest, but plaintiffs might also be entitled to seek a declaration as to their rights or a recommendation that the respondent should take reasonable action to obviate or reduce the adverse effect complained of.[4] An appeal from a decision of an employment tribunal on a point of law will be to the Employment Appeal Tribunal.

1   DDA 1995, Sch 3, para 3.
2   Ibid, Sch 3, para 2.
3   Ibid, Sch 3, para 1.
4   Ibid, s 8 passim.

3.10.2   Section 9 makes void any contract term or agreement which would contravene any part of Part II, limit or exclude the operation of any provision of Part II, or prevent any person from presenting a complaint to an employment tribunal. An exception is made for settlements of claims by conciliation or through a compromise agreement following independent legal advice.

3.10.3   The question of enforcement remedies and procedures in employment and contract work cases is considered in more detail in Chapter 10 below.[1] The failure to provide an institutional framework for the strategic enforcement of Part II of the Act is considered in Chapter 9.

1   And see generally, DDA 1995, ss 8–9 and Sch 3, Part I.

3.11   DISABLED PERSONS (EMPLOYMENT) ACTS

3.11.1   The DDA 1995 radically amended the Disabled Persons (Employment) Act 1944.[1] The 1944 Act was the foundation stone of disabled employment rights for half a century.[2] However, the introduction of anti-discrimination legislation led to a logical pruning and paring of the earlier statute. The obligation upon employers of 20 or more employees to maintain a statutory 3 per cent quota of registered disabled persons, the designated employment scheme for persons registered as handicapped by disablement (the so-called 'reserved occupations') and the register of disabled persons have been repealed.[3] As noted in Chapter 2, persons registered as disabled under the 1944 Act may have been entitled, under certain conditions and for an interim period, to be deemed to satisfy the definition of disabled person for the purpose of the 1995 Act.[4]

1   DDA 1995, s 61(1). The comparable amendments to the Disabled Persons (Employment) Act (Northern Ireland) 1945 are set out in a modified s 61 substituted by Sch 8, para 41. These will not be repeated here.
2   On the background, operation and ultimate failings of the 1944 legislation, see House of Commons Employment Committee, *The Operation of the Disabled Persons (Employment) Act 1944*

(HC Paper 389: April 1995) and the Government's reply to this report (HC Paper 667: July 1995).

3   DDA 1995, s 61 (7) repealing ss 1, 6–14, 19 and 21 of the 1944 Act with effect from 2 December 1996. Certain saving and transitional provisions are contained in the Disability Discrimination Act 1995 (Commencement No 3 and Saving and Transitional Provisions) Order 1996, SI 1996/1474, art 3.

4   Ibid, Sch 1, para 7.

3.11.2   Section 15 of the 1944 Act gives the Secretary of State (in Northern Ireland, the Department of Enterprise, Trade and Investment) power to make arrangements for the provision of supported employment to provide job opportunities for severely disabled people unable or unlikely to obtain or retain work in open employment. This power is retained but with consequential revisions occasioned by the 1995 Act. Similar consequential amendments are made to s 16 of the 1944 Act which gives preference under s 15 to ex-service men and women. These amendments or revisions are largely terminological and cosmetic and are not fully rehearsed here.

3.12   OTHER EMPLOYMENT LEGISLATION

Employment in local government

3.12.1   The Local Government and Housing Act 1989, s 7 requires all staff engaged by a local authority (or parish or community council) to be appointed on merit. Prior to the DDA 1995 Act, this was subject to the disabled quota provisions of the 1944 Act which allowed local government employers to ignore merit as an employment criterion in respect of persons registered as disabled under the 1944 legislation if the local authority in question was failing to meet the 3 per cent quota. As the DDA 1995 abolished the quota scheme, consequential amendments to the 1989 statute were made.[1]

---

1   DDA 1995, s 70(4), Sch 6, para 5 and Sch 7.

3.12.2   The effect of these amendments was to reinstate merit as an unchallenged employment criterion in local government. This casts doubt upon the ability of local authorities to discriminate positively in favour of disabled persons in employment policies where private sector employers would not be so prevented. For example, a local authority is no longer enabled to give disabled persons priority interviews and make appointments before the remainder of the field. However, the amendments to the 1989 Act make it transparent that, while local authorities must appoint on merit, that is always subject to the duty to make reasonable adjustments under the 1995 Act.[1] It is equally clear that there remains a number of steps of positive action that local government employers might lawfully take in respect of disabled persons. These steps will include preferential training, special recruitment drives to encourage applications from disabled persons (either individually or in general) and guaranteed interviews for all suitable disabled applicants.[2]

---

1   Local Government and Housing Act 1989, s 7(2)(f) as inserted by para 5(c) of Sch 6 to the
    1995 Act. See HC Deb, vol 265, col 120. See also Employment Code of Practice, para 4.66
    and *London Borough of Hillingdon v Morgan* (1999) IDS Brief B649/10, EAT.
2   HC Deb, vol 265, cols 120–121. See also Employment Code of Practice, para 4.66.

3.13   FUTURE REFORM

The Disability Rights Task Force has made a number of recommendations for
the future reform of the definition of disability in the DDA 1995.[1] It
recommends the abolition of the small business exemption and, short of that,
the measurement of the small business threshold by reference to the total
number of employees employed within a group of companies or associated
employers. Under its recommendations, the exclusions of statutory office
holders, police officers, prison officers, fire fighters and members of the armed
forces would also be ended. The Task Force wishes to see volunteers,
partnerships, qualifying bodies, and barristers and advocates expressly
included within the Act (but not employment within a private household). It
proposes that the public sector should have a duty to promote the equalisation
of oppportunities for disabled people in employment. The final report also
recommends that pre-employment screening for disability should only be
permitted in limited circumstances (for example, for monitoring purposes or
to establish the need for a reasonable adjustment). If the Task Force
recommendations were accepted, it would no longer be possible to justify a
failure to make a reasonable adjustment (the concept of what was a
'reasonable' adjustment being seen as a sufficient safeguard of the employer's
interests). There is as yet no indication as to if and when the Government will
act on these recommendations.

---

1   Disability Rights Task Force, *From Exclusion to Inclusion: A Report of the Disability Rights Task
    Force for Disabled People* (1999, London: DfEE) Chapter 5.

Chapter 4

TRADE ORGANISATIONS

4.1 INTRODUCTION

4.1.1 Although Part II of the DDA 1995 deals generally with discrimination against disabled persons in the field of employment, it also ensures that discrimination against disabled persons by trade organisations is outlawed.[1] The effect of these additional provisions is that:

> '... trade unions, employers' associations and analogous bodies would be covered by this [Act] in their relationship with their members or prospective members who are disabled or who have had a disability. Such organisations are already covered in the [Act] to the extent that they are employers. However, they are not covered by the access to services right because they are not providing services to members of the general public – just to their members.'[2]

A trade union or employers' associations will be covered by the employment provisions in Part II of the Act insofar as they employ persons within the meaning of the statute, unless they are not caught by the small employer exemption (which some smaller bodies could be).[3] For example, a full-time officer of a trade union or a clerical worker employed by a trade association will be an employee (or would-be employee) of a trade organisation and will be protected from disability discrimination under Part II.

---

1   DDA 1995, ss 13–15. These provisions came into force on 2 December 1996, except ss 14(2), (4)–(5) and 15 (relating to a trade organisation's duty to make reasonable adjustments) which came into force on 1 October 1999. However, s 15(1)(b) (reasonable adjustments and physical features of premises) is not expected to be in force before 2004. The Secretary of State has issued a code of practice under s 53 to support ss 13–15. See *Code of Practice: Duties of trade organisations to their disabled members and applicants* (1999, London: HMSO) referred to hereafter as 'Trade Organisations Code of Practice' (a separate, but essentially identical, Code covers Northern Ireland). The Code revises what is said about trade organisations in the Employment Code of Practice, paras 7.9–7.13 (see Trade Organisations Code of Practice, para 1.4).
2   HL Deb, vol 566, cols 224–225.
3   There is no exemption from ss 13–15 based upon size or numbers of members.

4.1.2 However, there is nothing in principle to prevent trade organisations also being caught by Part III of the Act (the provisions on goods and services) where they also provide services to the public (as well as to their members).[1] For example, a trade union which allows its premises to be used as a meeting place by groups other than those within the union's organisational structure or membership will be subject to the duties and non-discrimination requirements contained in Part III. An illustration might include the use of a trade union's offices for a meeting of a local political party or community action group. Similarly, if a trade or professional organisation allows its facilities to be used for social purposes (such as wedding receptions), open to individuals unconnected with that organisation, it will need to consider its Part III obligations.[2]

1   See Chapter 5 below and see Trade Organisations Code of Practice, para 3.2 (and example).
2   This is discussed in more detail in Chapter 5.

4.1.3   The separate provisions of the Act in respect of discrimination by trade organisations against disabled members or disabled applicants for membership is important.[1] These are largely self-contained measures and so warrant separate treatment.

1   DDA 1995, ss 13–15. Similar provisions are to be found in SDA 1975, s 12 and RRA 1976, s 11.

4.2   MEANING OF 'TRADE ORGANISATION'

4.2.1   Sections 13–15 of the 1995 Act apply generally to discrimination by 'trade organisations' and to the associated duties of such bodies. The term 'trade organisation' is defined as:

'... an organisation of workers, an organisation of employers or any other organisation whose members carry on a particular profession or trade for the purposes of which the organisation exists.'[1]

It is clear from this definition that these sections apply to three types of organisation:

(1)   organisations of workers;
(2)   organisations of employers;
(3)   other organisations.

Each is considered in turn.

1   DDA 1995, s 13(4). This definition is applicable for all the purposes of ss 13–15 by virtue of s 68(1).

Organisation of workers

4.2.2   First, trade unions are subject to the DDA 1995 in respect of rights of and to membership.[1] The Act does not use the term 'trade union', but simply refers to 'an organisation of workers' without further definition. Some assistance might be gleaned from the definition of 'trade union' used in trade union law.[2] That definition refers to a temporary or permanent organisation of workers whose principal purposes include the regulation of relations between workers and employers or employers' associations.[3] The Act does not say what the purposes of an organisation of workers must be in order to qualify for coverage.

1   HL Deb, vol 566, cols 224–229 passim.
2   Trade Union and Labour Relations (Consolidation) Act 1992, s 1.
3   See generally, *Harvey on Industrial Relations and Employment Law* (Butterworths), vol 2, Division M on which the following account draws.

4.2.3 A 'worker' for this purpose is a person who works (or seeks to work) under a contract of employment or under any other contract for the personal performance of any work or services (other than a professional and client relationship)[1] or in Crown employment.[2] This denotes that the term 'worker' is usually understood in a wider sense than the term 'employee'.[3] However, police officers are not 'workers', but office-holders, so that the Police Federation would not be an organisation of workers,[4] while the position of the Prison Officer's Association is ambiguous.[5] Part II of the Act does not apply to certain employments, including the police service and service as a prison officer and service in the armed forces,[6] so that this effectively overrides s 13.[7]

---

1 See *Writers' Guild of Great Britain v BBC* [1974] ICR 234; *Broadbent v Crisp* [1974] ICR 248; *Wiltshire Police Authority v Wynn* [1980] ICR 649.
2 TULR(C)A 1992, s 296.
3 Although that term is already given a broad definition in DDA 1995, s 68(1).
4 *Home Office v Evans* (Divisional Court, 18 November 1993, unreported).
5 *Boddington v Lawton* [1994] ICR 478; but cf Criminal Justice and Public Order Act 1994, s 126.
6 DDA 1995, s 64(5) and (7).
7 See **9.5.4**.

4.2.4 Of more significance is the term 'organisation'. Borrowing again from trade union law, it would appear that the term 'organisation' imports some notion of form, structure and stability, so that a mere loose association of workers would be insufficient.[1] The DDA 1995 does not appear to make a distinction between permanent or temporary organisations of workers. As a result, any branch or other division of a trade union might constitute an organisation of workers, including unofficial workplace co-ordinating committees. It was feared that the DDA 1995:

'... might render unions liable for any failure to make adjustments by an informal group of union members of whose existence the union's officers are unaware ... [including] groups of union members not recognising union rule books and with whom the national union does not communicate and who are given no powers or resources.'[2]

It is suggested that this concern is a real one given the wording of the Act and the lack of a definition of 'organisation of workers' in the statute.[3]

---

1 *Conservative and Unionist Central Office v Burrell* [1982] 1 WLR 522; cf *Midland Cold Storage Ltd v Turner* [1972] ICR 230.
2 HL Deb, vol 566, cols 226–227.
3 Note Trade Organisations Code of Practice, para 2.2.

Organisation of employers

4.2.5 Secondly, the Act embraces discrimination by 'an organisation of employers'.[1] Again, the statute clearly intends that 'employers' associations' should be within its purview, but that term is not utilised. Some assistance might be sought from the definition of 'employers' association' elsewhere.[2] Many of the same arguments and potential problems that have been visited in respect of trade unions above will arise here and will not be rehearsed a second time.[3]

---

1   DDA 1995, s 13(4).
2   TULR(C)A 1992, s 122 (and see the definition of 'employer' in s 296).
3   See **4.2.2–4.2.4**.

Other organisations

4.2.6   Thirdly, this legal regime applies equally to 'any other organisation whose members carry on a particular profession or trade for the purposes of which the organisation exists'.[1] The term 'profession' includes any vocation or occupation, while the term 'trade' encompasses any business.[2] It is suggested that this will capture professional bodies and trade associations which would not otherwise be classifiable as trade unions or employers' associations. For instance, The Law Society or Bar Council might be said to be an 'organisation whose members carry on a particular profession ... for the purposes of which the organisation exists' and this could also be said of analogous organising bodies in other professions or professional spheres. Similarly, trade associations or organisations will be subject to the duties and restraints contained in this part of the legislation (even if they might be simultaneously subject to other provisions in Parts II or III of the DDA 1995).

---

1   DDA 1995, s 13(4).
2   Ibid, s 68(1). Corporate members of trade organisations are not protected, even if a disabled person is a representative of a corporate member: Trade Organisations Code of Practice, para 2.3.

4.2.7   One area of some doubt concerns the position of bodies which issue qualifications or authorisations required for (or facilitating engagement in) a trade or profession.[1] Examples might include The Law Society, the Council of Legal Education or the General Medical Council. Such bodies might be excluded from Part III of the DDA 1995 if they fall within the exclusions in respect of education.[2] However, if they are not so excluded, they might be caught by Part III insofar as they provide services to the public. Further or alternatively, they might be caught by the trade organisations provisions of the legislation insofar as they might be a professional or trade organisation.[3]

---

1   See HL Deb, vol 566, col 226 and cf SDA 1975, s 13 and RRA 1976, s 12.
2   DDA 1995, s 19(5)–(6). See Chapters 5 and 7 below.
3   The Trade Organisations Code of Practice, para 2.1 assumes that The Law Society and other 'chartered professional institutions' are trade organisations because they exist for the purposes of the profession or trade which their members carry on.

4.3   DISCRIMINATION BY TRADE ORGANISATIONS

4.3.1   Section 13 of the DDA 1995 prohibits discrimination by trade unions, employers' organisations and analogous bodies for a reason related to disability in a similar way to the coverage of such discrimination on gender or racial grounds.[1] The section deals with discrimination in three forms:

(1) discrimination against applicants for membership;
(2) discrimination against existing members; and
(3) discrimination by way of victimisation.[2]

Discrimination is defined in s 14 and this is considered in more detail below.[3] Sections 13 and 14 are interdependent and must be read together. Section 14 determines whether an act of discrimination has occurred, while s 13 delineates what acts of discrimination are made unlawful.

1   SDA 1975, s 12; RRA 1976, s 11.
2   See **4.4.5**.
3   See **4.4** generally.

Discrimination against applicants for membership of trade organisations

4.3.2 It is unlawful for a trade organisation to discriminate against a disabled person 'in the terms on which it is prepared to admit him [or her] to membership of the organisation'.[1] For example, a trade union which made it a condition of membership that a disabled person should pay a higher membership fee or joining fee than other applicants for membership would almost certainly transgress this provision. Similarly, a professional body that would admit disabled persons to membership only after a longer period of apprenticeship or practice in the profession than in the normal case might also be in breach.

1   DDA 1995, s 13(1)(a).

4.3.3 It is also unlawful for a trade organisation to discriminate against a disabled person 'by refusing to accept, or deliberately not accepting, his [or her] application for membership'.[1] A trade association which selectively or consistently refused membership of the association to disabled persons engaged in the relevant trade commits a prima facie unlawful act. Similarly, a trade union which has received an application for membership from a disabled person, and *deliberately* fails to process that application, has committed a potential act of unlawful discrimination, even though it has not positively taken a step to reject the application. Its deliberate default in respect of the application might be tantamount to a non-acceptance.

1   DDA 1995, s 13(1)(b).

Discrimination by trade organisations against existing members

4.3.4 The DDA 1995 provides that it is unlawful for a trade organisation to discriminate against a disabled person who is a member of the organisation:[1]

–   in the way it affords him or her access to any benefits;[2]

- by refusing him or her access to any benefits;
- by deliberately omitting to afford him or her access to any benefits;
- by depriving him or her of membership;
- by varying the terms on which he or she is a member;
- by subjecting him or her to any other detriment.

In general, a trade organisation may not treat its disabled members as second-class members in respect of the rights and benefits of membership. This would include expulsion from membership where a non-disabled member would not be deprived of membership.

---

1 DDA 1995, s 13(2). This provision is analogous to similar provisions in the SDA 1975 and the RRA 1976.
2 The term 'benefits' includes 'facilities and services' (s 4(4)) and will include training facilities, welfare or insurance services, information about the organisation's activities, and assistance to members in an employer's disciplinary or dismissal procedure: Trade Organisations Code of Practice, para 4.2. Whether something is a benefit will depend upon the circumstances, including an organisation's rules and practice.

4.4   THE MEANING OF DISCRIMINATION BY TRADE ORGANISATIONS

4.4.1   The meaning of discrimination for the purposes of ss 13–15 of the DDA 1995 is found in a self-contained definition in s 14.[1] A trade organisation discriminates against a disabled person in three circumstances:

(1) unjustified less favourable treatment for a reason relating to the person's disability;[2] or
(2) unjustified failure to comply with a statutory duty to make a reasonable adjustment in relation to the disabled person;[3] or
(3) victimisation.[4]

This is virtually identical to the definition of discrimination in the context of employment and many of the points made about that definition will apply here.[5]

---

1 Cases under DDA 1995, Part III (ss 20 and 24) and s 5 in Part II are likely to be instructive. See the relevant treatment of these sections in Chapters 3, 5 and 6.
2 Ibid, s 14(1).
3 Ibid, s 14(2).
4 Ibid, s 55.
5 Ibid, s 5. See Chapter 3.

Discrimination and less favourable treatment

4.4.2   First, a trade organisation discriminates against a disabled person if, for a reason which relates to the disabled person's disability, it treats him or her less favourably than it treats (or would treat) others to whom that reason does not (or would not) apply *and* it cannot show that the less favourable treatment is justified.[1] The test of discrimination is a comparative one. How has the disabled person been treated by the trade organisation in comparison with a person to whom the reason relating to the disabled person's disability does not apply? This has been explored in some detail in the previous chapter and the analysis there is equally applicable here.[2]

---

1 DDA 1995, s 14(1).
2 See, in particular, the judicial analysis in *Clark v TDG Ltd t/a Novacold* [1999] IRLR 318, CA. See also Trade Organisations Code of Practice, paras 5.1–5.5 and the examples therein.

4.4.3 The important point to note is that discrimination by a trade organisation arises only if the organisation has treated a disabled member or would-be member differently from others 'for a reason which relates to the disabled person's disability'.[1] In other words, the person's disability or a reason connected with that disability must have been a factor in the differential treatment. For example, the fact that a trade union has provided a disabled member with poor representation or inadequate services is not enough.[2] The Act is not concerned with indifferent treatment as such, but with less favourable treatment connected with the prohibited ground, namely a person's disability. Similarly, if a trade union's rule book limits eligibility for membership of the union (for example, to workers working in a particular trade or industry or employed at a certain grade or level), a refusal to admit a disabled person to the union because he or she does not meet those eligibility conditions is not an act of prohibited discrimination.[3] A disabled nurse cannot seek to become a member of the National Union of Mineworkers and complain of disability discrimination when refused membership on eligibility grounds. That is, of course, subject to the proviso that a non-disabled person, similarly ineligible, was not or would not be admitted to membership of the organisation.

---

1 DDA 1995, s 14(1)(a).
2 See, for example, the race discrimination case of *Furniture, Timber and Allied Trades Union v Modgill* [1980] IRLR 142.
3 HL Deb, vol 566, cols 226–227.

Discrimination and the duty to make adjustments

4.4.4 Secondly, a trade organisation also discriminates against a disabled person if it fails to comply with its statutory duty to make adjustments imposed on it in relation to the disabled person *and* it cannot show that its failure to comply with that duty is justified.[1] The statutory duty to make adjustments is considered further below.[2]

---

1 DDA 1995, ss 14(2) and 15.
2 See **4.5**.

Discrimination and victimisation

4.4.5 Thirdly, a person (X) discriminates against another person (Y) if X treats Y less favourably than X treats or would treat other persons whose circumstances are the same as Y's and X has done so for one of a number of statutory reasons.[1] In essence, those statutory reasons relate to the fact, belief or suspicion that Y has exercised rights under the Act or assisted others to do so.

This is victimisation and protects the rights of both disabled and non-disabled persons.[2] An act of victimisation is treated as a discriminatory act and would provide the victimised person with a cause of action.[3] For example, a trade union member (whether a disabled person or not) who was disciplined by the trade union because he or she gave evidence in legal proceedings against the union brought under the DDA 1995 (for example, proceedings brought by a disabled person denied membership of the union for a reason allegedly related to disability) would have a separate right of complaint under the Act.

---

1   DDA 1995, s 55(1)–(2). See also Trade Organisations Code of Practice, para 4.5.
2   The ingredients of victimisation are explored in more detail in Chapter 10 below.
3   Under DDA 1995, ss 13–15 by virtue of s 13(3).

4.5   DUTY TO MAKE ADJUSTMENTS

4.5.1   Section 15 of the DDA 1995 places trade organisations under a statutory duty to make adjustments so as to accommodate disabled persons who are members or who are seeking membership.[1] This is not a general duty or a duty at large, but rather one which is owed to the particular disabled person concerned. Nevertheless, trade organisations need to keep this duty in mind and ought to take steps to ensure and to anticipate that the rights of disabled persons in relation to the organisation are not compromised.[2] Except within its own terms, the duty to make adjustments does not require trade organisations to treat disabled persons more favourably than they treat or would treat others.[3] It only imposes duties for the purpose of determining whether a trade organisation has discriminated against a disabled person. As we have seen, an unjustified failure to comply with a duty to make adjustments amounts to discrimination for the purposes of establishing liability for an unlawful act.[4] A breach of the duty is not otherwise actionable as such.[5]

---

1   The section came into force on 1 October 1999: SI 1999/1190. See generally, Trade Organisations Code of Practice, paras 6.1–6.19. It is very similar to the parallel duty upon employers to make adjustments under s 6 (see Chapter 3).
2   The Trade Organisations Code of Practice (paras 3.1–3.8) provides general guidance to trade organisations to avoid discrimination.
3   DDA 1995, s 15(6).
4   Ibid, s 14(2) for the purposes of s 13. See **4.4.4**.
5   Ibid, s 15(10).

When does the duty arise?

4.5.2   First, where 'any arrangements' made by (or on behalf of) a trade organisation place the disabled person concerned 'at a substantial disadvantage in comparison with persons who are not disabled', the organisation is under a duty 'to take such steps as it is reasonable, in all the circumstances of the case, for it to have to take' in order to prevent the 'arrangements' having the effect of placing the disabled person at a comparative substantial disadvantage.[1] This aspect of the duty to make adjustments came into effect on 1 October 1999.[2] The term 'any arrangements' applies only in relation to 'arrangements for determining who should become or remain a member of the organisation' and to any 'term, condition or arrangements on which membership or any benefit is offered or afforded'.[3] Whether something is an 'arrangement' will depend on the circumstances of the case and on the rules, procedure and customs of the organisation. However, it is likely that arrangements in relation to advertisements, application forms, interviews, provision of information to members, training facilities, welfare or insurance schemes, invitations to attend events, grievance procedures, and assistance to members in employers' disciplinary or dismissal procedures will be covered.[4]

1   DDA 1995, s 15(1)(a). The term 'substantial disadvantage' is likely to mean disadvantages which are more than minor or trivial: Trade Organisations Code of Practice, para 6.4.
2   The power to make regulations under s 15(7) to provide for the circumstances in which arrangements are to be taken (or are not to be taken) to have the effect of a comparative substantial disadvantage upon a disabled person has not been used to date.
3   DDA 1995, s 15(2).
4   Trade Organisations Code of Practice, para 6.3.

4.5.3   Secondly, where 'any physical feature of premises occupied by the organisation' places the disabled person concerned 'at a substantial disadvantage in comparison with persons who are not disabled', the organisation is under a duty 'to take such steps as it is reasonable, in all the circumstances of the case, for it to have to take' in order to prevent the 'feature' having the effect of placing the disabled person at a comparative substantial disadvantage.[1] This aspect of the duty to make adjustments is not yet in force and is not expected to come into effect until 2004.[2]

1   DDA 1995, s 15(1)(b).
2   The term 'physical feature of premises' is not statutorily defined, but this is expected to be the subject of clarification in regulations to be made under s 15(7).

To whom is the duty owed?

4.5.4   The duty to make reasonable adjustments is owed only to 'the disabled person concerned'.[1] In the case of arrangements for determining to whom membership should be offered, this means any disabled person who is an applicant for membership or who has notified the organisation that he or she may be an applicant for membership.[2] In any other case, 'the disabled person concerned' is a disabled person who is an applicant for membership or who is already a member of the organisation.[3] Furthermore, an organisation cannot be placed under a statutory duty to make adjustments if the organisation does not know (and could not reasonably be expected to know) that the disabled person in question is (or may be) an applicant for membership, or has a disability and is likely to be placed at a comparative substantial disadvantage by arrangements (or, in due course, physical features of premises).[4] A trade organisation might be unable to simply shut its eyes and claim ignorance of an applicant's or member's disability if it has constructive or vicarious knowledge of the relevant facts.[5]

1   DDA 1995, s 15(1).
2   Ibid, s 15(4)(a).
3   Ibid, s 15(4)(b).
4   Ibid, s 15(5).
5   Trade Organisations Code of Practice, paras 6.5–6.7.

What are reasonable steps?

4.5.5   When a trade organisation is considering what steps it would be reasonable to take, in all the circumstances of the case, in order to prevent arrangements (or, from 2004, physical features of premises) placing a disabled person at a comparative substantial disadvantage, particular regard is to be had to a number of criteria. These criteria will also be used by a tribunal or court in judging whether a trade organisation has discharged its statutory duty.[1] First, regard should be had to the extent to which taking a particular step would prevent the effect of substantial disadvantage.[2] Trade organisations are not expected to make adjustments that would not have any real benefit for the disabled person. Adjustments do not have to be made if they would not ultimately accommodate the rights of the person affected. Secondly, the organisation might consider the extent to which it is practicable for it to take the step in question.[3] A step which is impracticable or impossible to take is not a reasonable adjustment. Thirdly, regard must be had to the financial and other costs that would be incurred by the organisation in taking the step and the extent to which taking that step would disrupt any of its activities.[4] Clearly, there might be a point where the costs of making an adjustment outweigh the benefits of doing so, and disruption to the activities of the organisation is part of that analysis. Fourthly, however, account must be taken of the extent of the organisation's financial and other resources.[5] The cost of making an adjustment might be more easily absorbed by a larger or wealthier organisation than it might be by a smaller or impecunious body and the resources of the organisation as a whole should be considered.[6] Account must also be taken of the availability to the organisation of financial or other assistance (for example, government funding) with respect to taking the step.[7] Other factors might also be relevant.[8]

1   See the guidance provided in the Trade Organisations Code of Practice, paras 6.8–6.18. The power to make regulations to provide as to the circumstances in which it is reasonable (or not reasonable) for a trade organisation to have to take steps of a prescribed description, and as to what steps it is always (or never) reasonable for a trade organisation to have to take, has not been used to date (see s 15(7) by cross-reference to s 6(8)).
2   DDA 1995, s 15(3)(a). It may be necessary to consider the effect of a number of possible adjustments in combination: Trade Organisations Code of Practice, paras 6.9 and 6.19.
3   Ibid, s 15(3)(b). See Trade Organisations Code of Practice, paras 6.10–6.12.
4   Ibid, s 15(3)(c). See Trade Organisations Code of Practice, para 6.13. No regulations have been made to date under s 15(7) making provision by reference to the cost of taking the steps concerned (s 15(8)).
5   Ibid, s 15(3)(d).
6   Trade Organisations Code of Practice, paras 6.14–6.16.

7   DDA 1995, s 15(3)(e). See Trade Organisations Code of Practice, para 6.17.
8   Trade Organisations Code of Practice, para 6.18.

The duty illustrated

4.5.6   In contrast with the duty upon employers to make adjustments, there is no list[1] of examples of steps that trade organisations might take when complying with their statutory duty to make adjustments. The duty might be illustrated by a requirement on a trade union to ensure that, where it was reasonable, members with visual impairments could obtain union literature in Braille form or members with hearing disabilities had access to signers at union meetings.[2] A further example, which will be relevant from 2004, would be the need for trade organisations to ensure that the buildings which they occupy are physically accessible to members with disabilities, perhaps by widening doors, installing wheelchair ramps and considering the layout of meeting rooms.[3] These are good examples of the duty and may already represent best practice in many trade unions and other trade organisations. These examples are subject, of course, to the various tests of when the duty is owed and to whom, as discussed immediately above.

1   Such as that contained in s 6(3) in relation to employment.
2   HL Deb, vol 566, col 225.
3   Note the provisions of s 16 and Part I of Sch 4 to the DDA 1995 which will apply where a trade organisation occupies premises under a lease which prevents or hinders alterations being made in pursuit of a s 15 duty to make adjustments. These provisions are discussed in detail in Chapter 6 below.

4.5.7   An interesting question concerns the overlap between the duty to make adjustments and the democratisation provisions in trade union law.[1] Although employers' associations and trade or professional organisations are not subject to the same regulatory framework as trade unions, they too will need to consider how the DDA 1995 impinges upon their democratic processes and their relations with disabled members. Nothing in the Act makes unlawful any act done in pursuance of any enactment,[2] but this does not prevent trade unions from being subject to the Act when discharging their general obligations under trade union legislation. In particular, trade unions need to consider how to meet the stringent requirements upon unions in respect of ballots and elections whilst also complying with the duty to make reasonable adjustments for their disabled members.[3]

1   Contained in TULR(C)A 1992.
2   DDA 1995, s 59. See Trade Organisations Code of Practice, para 7.8.
3   Trade Organisations Code of Practice, para 7.9.

4.5.8   For example, elections to certain positions in a union are required to be conducted by secret postal ballot.[1] Union members must not be unreasonably excluded from candidature[2] and union members with a disability may be able to use the DDA 1995 to reinforce that right. The union is obliged to circulate election addresses for every candidate[3] and the DDA 1995 might require a union to ensure that Braille or large print versions of such addresses are made available. This could also be said about the scrutineer's report and the publication of the results of the ballot at the conclusion of the election process. Voting in the election is to be by means of a fully postal secret ballot and no other form of voting is acceptable.[4] The system of fully postal voting actually works to the benefit of disabled members, some of whom might otherwise have been at a substantial disadvantage under a non-postal or partly postal voting system. However, a trade union might consider that the DDA 1995 requires it to redesign the ballot paper so as to accommodate the needs of disabled members (especially those with visual or learning disabilities) whilst remaining within the form and content required by trade union law. Similar considerations in respect of the rights of trade union members with disabilities might also arise in respect of other aspects of trade union law relating to administration, elections, ballots before industrial action, union discipline, political fund resolutions and ballots, and so on.

---

1   TULR(C)A 1992, Part I, Chapter IV.
2   Ibid, s 47.
3   Ibid, s 48.
4   Ibid, s 51.

4.6   DEFENCE OF JUSTIFICATION

4.6.1   Discrimination is defined as being either less favourable treatment of a disabled person for a reason which relates to that person's disability or a failure to comply with a statutory duty to make reasonable adjustments.[1] In both instances, a trade organisation has a possible 'defence' of justification (although, strictly, the absence of justification is part of the ingredients of 'discrimination').[2]

---

1   DDA 1995, s 14(1)–(2).
2   See generally, Trade Organisations Code of Practice, paras 7.1–7.9.

Less favourable treatment

4.6.2   First, less favourable treatment of a disabled person for a reason related to that person's disability is discriminatory if the trade organisation 'cannot show that the treatment in question is justified'.[1] For this purpose, 'treatment is justified if, but only if, the reason for it is both material to the circumstances of the particular case and substantial'.[2] In this context, 'substantial' is likely to mean that the reason is more than minor or trivial.[3] However, if the trade organisation is under a statutory duty to make adjustments in relation to the disabled person (who has been less favourably treated for a disability-related reason) and it has failed without justification to comply with that duty, it cannot justify its treatment of the disabled person 'unless the treatment would have been justified even if the organisation had complied with' that duty.[4] In other words, before a trade organisation can seek to justify the less favourable treatment of a disabled person for a reason related to disability, it must first address its duty to make reasonable adjustments. The trade organisation cannot rely upon a material and substantial reason for less favourable treatment if that reason could have been rendered immaterial or insubstantial by carrying out a reasonable adjustment.[5]

1   DDA 1995, s 14(1)(b).
2   Ibid, s 14(3). No regulations have been made to date providing for the circumstances in which treatment is to be taken to be (or not to be) justified (s 14(6)).
3   Trade Organisations Code of Practice, para 7.2.
4   DDA 1995, s 14(5).
5   No regulations have been made to date providing for the circumstances in which failure to comply with a s 15 duty is to be taken to be (or not to be) justified (s 14(6)).

Failure to make adjustments

4.6.3   Secondly, a failure to comply with a statutory duty to make adjustments is discriminatory if the trade organisation 'cannot show that its failure to comply with that duty is justified'.[1] For this purpse, failure to comply with that duty is justified 'if, but only if, the reason for the failure is both material to the circumstances of the particular case and substantial'.[2] In this context, 'substantial' is likely to mean that the reason is more than minor or trivial.[3] It follows logically that, if the adjustment was not a 'reasonable' one to make, then there is no failure of the statutory duty which has to be justified.[4] However, if there was a 'reasonable' adjustment that could have been made, a trade organisation is unlikely to be able to justify a failure to make it if it has not made appropriate efforts to obtain information or advice that would have assisted it in making the adjustment.[5]

1   DDA 1995, s 14(2)(b).
2   Ibid, s 14(4). No regulations have been made to date providing for the circumstances in which failure to comply with a s 15 duty is to be taken to be (or not to be) justified (s 14(6)).
3   Trade Organisations Code of Practice, para 7.5.
4   Ibid, para 7.6.
5   Ibid, para 7.7.

Justification illustrated

4.6.4   The defence of justification in respect of discrimination against disabled persons by trade organisations is closely related to the parallel defence available to employers in respect of discrimination against disabled employees and applicants for employment.[1] An example of circumstances in which less favourable treatment of a disabled person by a trade organisation could be justified might be considered.[2] A trade union delegation visiting inaccessible premises not controlled by the union might be able to justify the omission from the delegation of a member who is a wheelchair user because of the inaccessibility of the premises. It would also seem that the member would have no alternative cause of action under the DDA 1995 against the controller of the inaccessible premises, unless the visit is to premises controlled by a service provider and the visit was for the purpose of being provided with goods or services or facilities within the meaning of Part III of the DDA 1995.

1   The reader is referred to the fuller discussion of those provisions in Chapter 3 where the
    analysis is equally applicable to the present discussion.
2   HL Deb, vol 566, col 225.

4.7   ENFORCEMENT AND REMEDIES

4.7.1   Unlawful acts of disability discrimination by trade organisations contrary to ss 13–15 of the DDA 1995 are subject to the provisions on enforcement,
procedure and remedies in Part II of the Act.[1] There is a right of action in the
employment tribunal in like manner to actions alleging disability discrimination in connection with employment or contract work.[2] It might also be
appropriate to attempt to resolve the matter within the trade organisation or by
alternative dispute resolution methods.[3]

1   DDA 1995, ss 8–9.
2   The reader is referred to the summary of those provisions in Chapter 3 and to the more
    detailed discussion in Chapter 10.
3   See generally, Trade Organisations Code of Practice, paras 8.1–8.3 and Annex 3.

Chapter 5

GOODS, FACILITIES AND SERVICES

5.1 INTRODUCTION

5.1.1 The 1994 Green Paper promised that consultation would take place on extending building regulations to ensure that physical barriers to access by disabled persons to public and domestic buildings would be removed or reduced. However, as the 1994 Green Paper acknowledged:

> '... removing physical impediments does nothing to banish the mental barriers of ignorance and prejudice. Making buildings easier to get into is of no avail if disabled people are kept outside because their appearance or behaviour is deemed too upsetting for other patrons or through misguided concern for their safety.'[1]

Instead, the 1994 Green Paper mooted a new right of access that would make it unlawful for providers of goods or services to treat an individual unfavourably because of that person's disability, except where there were physical barriers or genuine safety issues. In turn, the 1995 White Paper proposed the introduction of a right of access to goods and services for disabled persons,[2] prohibiting discriminatory behaviour, while requiring reasonable and readily achievable positive action to overcome physical and communication barriers impeding access by disabled persons. Exceptionally, the new right would not apply to transport vehicles or to educational establishments. It would also not apply where the supply of the goods or services in question would pose a risk to the health and safety of the disabled person or others.[3]

---

1 *A Consultation on Government Measures to Tackle Discrimination Against Disabled People* (July 1994) para 4.2 (referred to hereafter as '1994 Green Paper').

2 *Ending Discrimination Against Disabled People* (Cm 2729: January 1995) para 4.4 (referred to hereafter as '1995 White Paper').

3 1995 White Paper, para 4.6.

Timetable

5.1.2 These novel rights of access are set out in Part III of the DDA 1995.[1] The Major administration intended that there would be a long lead-in time for businesses to adapt to these new provisions, with these measures being brought into force in stages over a period as long as 10 years.[2] Although the current Labour Government has accelerated the timetable for implementation, at the time of writing not all aspects of the new rights have been given effect. The simple duties on service providers not to refuse service to a disabled person, and not to discriminate in the manner, standard or terms of service, came into force on 2 December 1996.[3] The next rights of access – requiring service providers to make reasonable adjustments to service delivery, short of physical alterations to premises – came into force on 1 October 1999.[4] The remaining duties to remove physical barriers are likely to be made effective in 2004.[5]

1   DDA 1995, ss 19–21. Enforcement of the DDA rights and related questions are dealt with in
    ss 25–28. Part III of the Act is broadly modelled after comparable provisions in SDA 1975,
    ss 29–36 and RRA 1976, ss 20–27. However, there are important and subtle differences
    between Part III of the DDA 1995 and the provisions of the earlier Acts: *Clark v TDG Ltd t/a
    Novacold* [1999] IRLR 318, CA.
2   HL Deb, vol 566, col 1031.
3   DDA 1995, s 19(1) (except s 19(1)(b)) and 20(1)).
4   Ibid, ss 19(1)(b), 20(2) and 21 (except s 21(2)(a)–(c)).
5   Ibid, s 21(2)(a)–(c). See Disability Rights Commission, *The Disability Discrimination Act 1995:
    New Requirements to Make Goods, Facilities and Services More Accessible to Disabled People from 2004:
    Consultations on a New Code of Practice, Regulations and Practical Guidance* (April 2000).

Code and regulations

5.1.3   Those provisions of Part III of the DDA 1995 which are in force are supported by a statutory Code of Practice.[1] The Code gives practical advice on how to comply with the legal duties in Part III and is designed to help both disabled persons and service providers to understand the law. However, it does not impose legal obligations and is not an authoritative statement of the law. It may be used in evidence in legal proceedings and a court must take account of it where relevant.[2] Regulations under Part III have also been issued and will be considered at appropriate points in the text below.[3]

1   *Code of Practice: Rights of Access: Goods, Facilities, Services and Premises* (1999, London: HMSO)
    referred to hereafter as the 'Rights of Access Code of Practice'. The Code is issued by the
    Secretary of State under DDA 1995, s 51(2) and is based on proposals made by the National
    Disability Council (in respect of which the present author acted as consultant). It revises and
    replaces an earlier version of the Code of Practice published in 1996. A separate, but largely
    identical, Code of Practice has been issued in Northern Ireland.
2   See **9.3**. See generally, Rights of Access Code of Practice, Chapter 1.
3   Disability Discrimination (Services and Premises) Regulations 1996, SI 1996/1836 (in force
    on 2 December 1996) and Disability Discrimination (Services and Premises) Regulations
    1999, SI 1999/1191 (in force from 1 October 1999). These regulations derive their authority
    from DDA 1995, ss 19(5)(c), 20(7)–(8), 21(5)(e), 21(5)(h), 24(5), 67(1)–(3) and 68(1).

Part III of the DDA 1995 outlined

5.1.4   The DDA 1995 applies to providers of goods, facilities or services.[1] It is unlawful for a service provider to discriminate against a disabled person by refusing to provide (or deliberately not providing) any service which it provides (or is prepared to provide) to members of the public;[2] or in the standard of service which it provides to the disabled person or the manner in which it provides it;[3] or in the terms on which it provides a service to the disabled person.[4] It is also unlawful for a service provider to discriminate by failing to comply with any statutory duty imposed on it to make reasonable adjustments in circumstances in which the effect of that failure is to make it impossible or unreasonably difficult for the disabled person to make use of goods, facilities or services.[5]

1   Referred to throughout this chapter as 'service providers'. References to providing a service
    include providing goods or facilities (s 19(2)(a)).

2   DDA 1995, s 19(1)(a).
3   Ibid, s 19(1)(c).
4   Ibid, s 19(1)(d).
5   Ibid, ss 19(1)(b) and 21.

5.2   PROVISION OF SERVICES

Services

5.2.1   For the purposes of the present analysis, the provision of services includes the provision of any goods or facilities.[1] The terms are not defined in the statute or the extra-statutory sources, but the DDA 1995 provides a non-exhaustive list of examples of services to which the legislation applies:[2]

–   access to and use of any place which members of the public are permitted to enter;
–   access to and use of means of communication;
–   access to and use of information services;
–   accommodation in a hotel, boarding house or other similar establishment;
–   facilities by way of banking or insurance or for grants, loans, credit or finance;
–   facilities for entertainment, recreation or refreshment;
–   facilities provided by employment agencies;
–   certain training facilities;[3]
–   the services of any profession or trade, or any local or other public authority.

The Rights of Access Code of Practice adds considerably to this list by way of illustration.[4] A wide range of establishments and businesses are covered by the rights of access. What is also clear is that it is irrelevant whether the goods, facilities or services are provided on payment or without payment.[5]

1   DDA 1995, s 19(2)(a).
2   Ibid, s 19(3).
3   Provided under Employment and Training Act 1973, s 2 or Employment and Training Act (Northern Ireland) 1950, ss 1–2 (see DDA 1995, Sch 8, para 9(1)).
4   Rights of Access Code of Practice, para 2.13.
5   DDA 1995, s 19(2)(c).

5.2.2   The illustrative list of services does not explicitly include access to civic rights and duties, health services, broadcasting, the judicial system and legal proceedings, careers services, trade unions and employers' associations, trade and professional associations, or qualifying bodies,[1] but many of these examples are implicitly covered.[2] The apparent legislative intention was 'to provide a universal, all-embracing right of non-discrimination against disabled people that is applicable to all providers of goods, facilities and services to the general public'.[3] The list of services is thus not exhaustive.[4] It seems to have been intended that, for example, facilities for telecommunication, the judicial system and legal proceedings,[5] broadcasting services,[6] medical and health services, and the constituency services of parliamentarians are covered.[7] However, where central or local government is acting in discharge of a statutory power or duty, there is a very strong argument – supported by case-law under comparable provisions[8] – that this does not entail the provision of a service (unless otherwise closely analogous to the kinds of services provided by a private sector undertaking) and thus is not covered by Part III of the DDA 1995.[9]

---

1   Trade unions, employers' associations, trade associations and professional associations are the subject of ss 13–15 of Part II of the DDA 1995. See Chapter 4 above.

2   Rights of Access Code of Practice, para 2.13.

3   HC Deb Standing Committee E, cols 290–291.

4   There is doubt about whether services provided by a company to its shareholders (for example, information and meetings) are caught by Part III. The Disability Rights Task Force (DRTF) has recommended that the Department of Trade and Industry should examine this issue as part of its fundamental review of company law. See *From Exclusion to Inclusion: A Report of the Disability Rights Task Force for Disabled People* (1999, London: DfEE) (DRTF Report) recommendation 6.11.

5   Part III of the DDA 1995 probably does not apply to service as a juror or witness: HL Deb, vol 566, cols 259–262.

6   As to the requirements of television companies (other than the BBC) in respect of teletext and subtitling services, note the provisions of the Broadcasting Acts 1990 and 1996 (and the guidelines published by the Independent Television Commission). See also HL Deb, vol 566, cols 269–271.

7   HC Deb Standing Committee E, cols 292–293; HL Deb, vol 564, col 1952.

8   See *R v Entry Clearance Officer Bombay, ex parte Amin* [1983] 2 AC 818 where, under the similar provisions of the RRA 1976, the House of Lords held that an immigration officer exercising powers under immigration rules was not providing a service to the subject of an immigration decision. See also DDA 1995, s 59 (discussed in Chapter 10).

9   The DRTF recommends that all functions of public authorities should be covered, subject only to careful consideration of the practical effect on those functions of the duty to make reasonable adjustments. It also recommends that the public sector should be under a statutory duty to promote the equalisation of opportunities for disabled people in the provision of services: DRTF Report, recommendations 6.12–6.13.

Goods and facilities

5.2.3   An everyday meaning of 'goods' as chattels or moveable property is probably intended and there seems no reason to import a definition from other statutory sources.[1] A refusal to supply goods which are in the nature of personal or moveable property will be covered. The literal meaning of 'facilities' suggests that the law is concerned with the provision of equipment or the physical means for doing something. For example, the provision of a telephone involves the provision of 'goods'; the supply of a link to the telecommunications network is the provision of a 'service'; while the means by which the service provider then bills the customer for the provision of the goods and service (and the medium by which the customer may settle that bill) would amount to 'facilities'. It may be that the distinction is merely artificial. The term 'facilities' simply embraces any matter not obviously amounting to goods or services.[2]

---

1   Sale of Goods Act 1979, s 61 defines goods as including 'all personal chattels other than things in action and money' excluding non-physical property (such as shares or intellectual property).

2   The illustrations in the DDA 1995 (s 19(3)) of what amounts to 'services' appear to
    encompass 'facilities'.

Service providers

5.2.4   Part III of the DDA 1995 applies to 'a provider of services'. A person is a
provider of services only if that person is concerned with the provision of
services 'to the public or to a section of the public'.[1] The use of the word
'person' will include legal entities (such as companies or local authorities) as
well as individuals or associations of individuals (such as trade unions or
partnerships). It is clear, for example, that in many circumstances Part III
embraces the provision of services to the public or community by local and
other public authorities.[2] In some cases, there might be more than one service
provider – for example, where services are provided from multiple-occupancy
premises (such as a department store or shopping centre) or appear to be
provided by more than one service provider (as in the case of a conference held
in an hotel) – and it is important to determine which service provider has
liability or whether such liability is shared.[3]

1   DDA 1995, s 19(2)(b).
2   HL Deb, vol 565, col 672. This must be subject to what is said in **5.2.2**.
3   Rights of Access Code of Practice, para 2.16 (and examples).

5.2.5   The service provider must also be 'concerned with the provision, in the
United Kingdom, of services to the public'. The meaning of this phrase is
unclear and potentially ambiguous. It is capable of meaning that the services
themselves must be provided within the UK (and thus, for example, an overseas
holiday would not be covered). Equally, it might mean that it is sufficient that
the service provider is based in the UK (even if the services themselves will be
used outside the UK). Given the territorial nature of statutory jurisdiction, it
seems likely that a British court would interpret this clause narrowly and in
favour of the former interpretation rather than the latter. That does not mean
that, for example, a British tour operator offering holidays abroad is entirely
untouched by the DDA. The brochure and booking services which it offers to
the public in the UK are services within the Act, even if the actual holidays
themselves may not be. This is a matter which awaits testing in litigation.

Manufacturers and designers

5.2.6   Part III of the DDA 1995 does not apply to manufacturers and designers,
unless they supply goods or services directly to members of the public.[1] While
such persons might wish to consider how to comply with the spirit of the
legislation, they are not directly subject to its letter. There is no obligation upon
manufacturers or producers of goods or services (who are not also direct
suppliers to the public) to consider the accessibility of the design, labelling or
packaging of those goods or services to disabled consumers. For example, there
is no legal obligation upon manufacturers under the Act to include any user
instructions bundled with goods or products in accessible formats (such as

Braille, large print or audio-visual medium) and there would appear to be no such duty placed upon the retail supplier either.[2]

---

1   HL Deb, vol 566, cols 241–242. See Rights of Access Code of Practice, paras 2.25–2.26.
2   Ibid, col 251.

Private members' clubs

5.2.7   Private members' clubs (and organisations such as trade unions) are not covered by Part III of the DDA 1995 because they do not provide services *to the public* or a section of the public.[1] Such clubs (and organisations) are free to discriminate against disabled persons seeking membership or access.[2] The Code of Practice defines a private club as one where membership is a condition of participation and where there is a genuine selection process (usually under the club's rules).[3] Nevertheless, even a private membership club will be subject to Part III obligations if it uses its premises to provide some services of a public nature. For example, a private golf club which provides facilities to non-members for wedding receptions may not lawfully discriminate against a disabled wedding guest.

---

1   DDA 1995, s 19(2)(b). See Rights of Access Code of Practice, paras 2.23–2.24.
    Discrimination by trade organisations (and bodies such as trade unions) is subject to DDA 1995, ss 13–15. See Chapter 4 above.
2   See the case-law to like effect under the now repealed provisions of the Race Relations Act 1968: *Dockers Labour Club and Institute Ltd v Race Relations Board* [1976] AC 285; *Charter v Race Relations Board* [1973] AC 885. Cf RRA 1976, s 25 and *Applin v Race Relations Board* [1975] AC 259.
3   See Rights of Access Code of Practice, para 2.24. The DRTF recommends that private clubs should be covered, but without extending coverage to private social arrangements: DRTF Report, recommendation 6.10.

To whom the service is provided

5.2.8   It is clear that Part III of the DDA 1995 addresses discrimination only in the provision of services to disabled persons as consumers themselves. It does not cover the provision of services to a disabled person as a representative of another person (for example as parent, guardian or carer). Equally, it does not directly address discrimination against a person because of that individual's relationship to or association with a disabled person (perhaps as a spouse, parent or friend). Members of a family who are refused service in a restaurant because they are accompanied by a disabled child have no remedy under the Act (although the child will also have been discriminated against and will have a cause of action which could be pursued on the child's behalf).

Excluded services

5.2.9   Part III of the DDA 1995 does not apply to education and transport.[1] The scope of this exclusion is clearly important and merits separate consideration in Chapters 7 and 8 below. The Act also provides that Part III will not apply to 'such other services' as may be prescribed by regulations.[2] No such regulations have been made to date.[3] It would appear that this was a precautionary piece of drafting and there has been no indication that this power will be used at any particular time or for any particular purpose.

---

1 DDA 1995, s 19(5)(a)–(b).
2 Ibid, s 19(5)(c).
3 Although regulations clarifying the scope of the exclusion of education have been made and will be considered further below: Disability Discrimination (Services and Premises) Regulations 1996, SI 1996/1836, reg 9.

5.3 UNLAWFUL DISCRIMINATION

5.3.1 Part III of the DDA 1995 provides that it is unlawful for a service provider to discriminate in a number of specified ways.[1]

---

1 See generally, Rights of Access Code of Practice, Chapters 2–4.

Refusal to provide goods, facilities or services

5.3.2 First, it is an unlawful act for a service provider to discriminate against a disabled person in refusing to provide, or deliberately not providing, to a disabled person any service which the service provider provides, or is prepared to provide, to members of the public.[1] For example, a theatre which refuses to admit a person with cerebral palsy because of that individual's disability might be committing an unlawful act of discrimination.[2]

---

1 DDA 1995, s 19(1)(a).
2 See the further examples in the Rights of Access Code of Practice, paras 3.11–3.14.

Standard or manner of service

5.3.3 Secondly, it is an unlawful act for a service provider to discriminate against a disabled person in the 'standard of service' which the service provider provides to the disabled person or by virtue of the 'manner in which' the service provider provides that service to the disabled person.[1] A restaurant which forces disabled customers to dine in a separate room unseen by other patrons might breach this provision.[2] A theatre which limits disabled patrons to matinee performances only might also fall foul of the Act, although there would be nothing to prevent a theatre arranging special matinee performances for disabled persons, provided they are free to book seats for other times also.[3] Similarly, providing inferior goods or services to disabled persons would be unlawful, although what would amount to *inferior* goods or services might be difficult to measure. For example, requiring wheelchair users to sit in a particular part of a theatre or restaurant when other customers or patrons have a comparatively free choice as to where they sit could be regarded as the provision of an inferior service.[4] Much will hinge upon the application of the defence of justification for the differential treatment in such cases,[5] but a service provider who adopts a deliberate policy to discourage disabled customers (for example, by deliberately surly, dilatory or inferior service) would have difficulty in justifying such discrimination.[6]

---

1   DDA 1995, s 19(1)(c).
2   1994 Green Paper, para 4.3.
3   See the further examples in the Rights of Access Code of Practice, paras 3.15–3.16.
4   1994 Green Paper, para 4.4; Rights of Access Code of Practice, para 3.15.
5   See **5.6**.
6   HL Deb, vol 566, col 267.

Terms on which service is provided

5.3.4   Thirdly, it is an unlawful act for a service provider to discriminate against a disabled person in the terms on which the service provider provides a service (or goods or facilities) to the disabled person.[1] An example of an act made unlawful by this provision would be a shop or entertainment outlet which charged higher prices for purchases by or admission to disabled persons in comparison with other customers.[2]

---

1   DDA 1995, s 19(1)(d).
2   1994 Green Paper, para 4.3. See the further examples in the Rights of Access Code of Practice, para 3.17.

Failure to make reasonable adjustment

5.3.5   Finally, it is also an unlawful act for a service provider to discriminate against a disabled person by failing to comply with a duty imposed on it by the Act[1] to make reasonable adjustments in circumstances in which the effect of the failure is to make it impossible or unreasonably difficult for the disabled person to make use of any goods, facilities or services provided to other members of the public.[2] This is a pivotal duty under the Act and calls for separate and detailed explication below.[3]

---

1   DDA 1995, s 21.
2   Ibid, s 19(1)(b). This provision came into force on 1 October 1999 (the remaining provisions of s 19(1) having been in force since 2 December 1996).
3   See **5.5**.

5.4   MEANING OF DISCRIMINATION

5.4.1   As has just been described, it is unlawful for a provider of services to 'discriminate' against a disabled person in a number respects in relation to goods, facilities and services.[1] However, it is not sufficient to show that a disabled person has been badly or unreasonably treated in the outcomes set out above. It is also necessary to show that this is the result of discrimination by the service provider. What does 'discriminate' mean for this purpose and in this context? The definition of discrimination in the context of Part III of the DDA 1995 is broadly similar to that used in Part II (discrimination in employment and contract work and by trade organisations).[2] It contains two alternative bases for establishing discrimination: broadly, less favourable treatment and a failure to make a reasonable adjustment.[3] The Act also treats 'victimisation' as unlawful discrimination for present purposes (this is dealt with further in Chapter 10).[4]

---

1   DDA 1995, s 19(1) and see **5.3**.
2   Ibid, s 20. Cf ss 5 and 14 (see Chapters 3–4 above). Decisions and judicial interpretation under ss 5 and 14 will be of assistance in applying the parallel definition in s 20, but care must be taken to ensure that in Part III cases direct reference is made to the wording of s 20 itself.
3   The DRTF has recommended that the existing categories of discrimination should continue: DRTF Report, recommendation 6.1.
4   DDA 1995, s 55. An act of victimisation will constitute an act of discrimination for the purposes of discrimination in relation to goods, facilities and services and will provide a cause of action, whether or not the person victimised is a disabled person. This is achieved on the face of ss 19–21 by virtue of s 19(4).

Less favourable treatment

5.4.2   A provider of services discriminates against a disabled person if, for a reason which relates to the disabled person's disability, the service provider treats the disabled person less favourably than the service provider treats (or would treat) others to whom the reason which relates to the disabled person's disability does not or would not apply, and the service provider cannot show that the less favourable treatment in question is justified.[1] Although this definition allows less favourable treatment to be 'justified', it is closely related to the concept of 'direct discrimination' used in other discrimination legislation. However, the use of the phrase 'for a reason which relates to the disabled person's disability' suggests a more flexible test of discrimination.[2] This phraseology makes 'it clear that if a disabled person is refused service – for example, in a café – for a reason connected with his disability, where non-disabled people are happily served', that will be a prima facie case of discrimination, subject to any 'defence' of justification.[3]

---

1   DDA 1995, s 20(1). See the Rights of Access Code of Practice, paras 2.4–2.5 and 3.3–3.11 (and the examples provided there). Part III of the Act does not prohibit positive action in favour of disabled people. Service providers may provide services to disabled people on *more* favourable terms: Rights of Access Code of Practice, para 3.18.
2   Ibid, s 20(1)(a).
3   HL Deb, vol 566, col 120. Strictly, justification is not a defence, but rather is one of the component parts of the definition of discrimination.

5.4.3   This concept of discrimination requires proof that the disabled person has been treated less favourably than other persons to whom the reason related to disability does not apply. This calls for a comparison of how the disabled person was treated relative to such other persons.[1] The question is not merely whether the disabled person has experienced poor, inadequate or substandard provision in respect of goods, facilities or services.[2] Rather the issue is whether there has been differential and unfavourable treatment of the disabled person in circumstances where other persons (to whom the reason related to disability does not apply) have not been so treated. The comparator is another member of the public (or a hypothetical member of the public).[3] This might include a person with a disability of a different kind from the complainant because the wording of the Act does not rule out the unlawfulness of differential treatment by service providers among disabled persons themselves.[4]

---

1 Rights of Access Code of Practice, para 3.4.
2 Ibid, para 3.5.
3 Ibid, para 3.7.
4 Ibid, para 3.6.

5.4.4   The less favourable treatment must be related to the disabled person's disability. While the intention, purpose or motive with which the service provider acted is irrelevant, there must be a causal connection between the discriminatory action and the complainant's disability. A disabled person who is refused admission to a cinema because he or she does not have the means to pay for entry, or who is refused service in a public house because he or she is drunk and disorderly, has not been discriminated against contrary to the DDA 1995.[1] The reason for the apparently less favourable treatment is not that person's disability, but rather a reason which is unrelated to disability. Indeed, in any event, in these illustrations it might be claimed that there has been no less favourable treatment at all, because the service provider might be able to show that any member of the public in like circumstances would have been treated in the same way.

---

1 Rights of Access Code of Practice, paras 3.8–3.10.

5.4.5   However, following the logic of the Court of Appeal's decision in the Part II case of *Clark v TDG Ltd t/a Novacold,*[1] it is essential when approaching less favourable treatment discrimination under Part III to identify the reason why the disabled person is being treated less favourably than others. For example, suppose that a disabled person has cerebral palsy which causes her difficulty with physical co-ordination when eating. She is refused further service in a restaurant because the service provider objects to the messy way in which she eats. That is a refusal of service; the refusal is because of the way in which the customer eats; that is a reason which is related to the customer's disability (because her eating habits are affected by her disability); no other customers have been refused service in the restaurant; and so this amounts to less favourable treatment for a reason related to disability. It would not be sufficient for the restaurant to claim that it would have refused service to anyone who was a messy eater. The DDA 1995 does not require the comparison to be based upon a consideration of comparators in relevant circumstances which are the same or not materially different.[2] This would be unlawful discrimination unless the restaurant can justify the treatment of the disabled customer.[3]

Nevertheless, in *R v Powys County Council, ex parte Hambidge (No 2),*[4] the Court of Appeal has taken a narrower approach to the concept of less favourable treatment for a reason related to disability under Part III of the DDA 1995 than was taken in *Clark* under Part II. The applicant was in receipt of disability living allowance and received home care services from the local authority.[5] The local authority introduced charges for home care services.[6] It did so by reference to three categories of service user: (A) those in receipt of income support only; (B) those in receipt of income support and either attendance allowance or disability living allowance; and (C) those not in receipt of income support (regardless of whether they were receiving any other benefits). Those in category (A) were not charged for home care services at all, while those in categories (B) and (C) were charged at differential rates. The applicant fell into category (B). She challenged the home care services charge by arguing that it amounted to less favourable treatment for a reason related to her disability.[7] Her argument was that the charges levied on category (B) were because those in category (B) had more income than those in category (A) and that the only reason for this was that those in category (B) received disability benefits by virtue of having a disability. The High Court and the Court of Appeal rejected the applicant's contention that this amounted to disability discrimination unless justified. The appellate court thought that it could not have been intended that such a case should be covered by s 20(1)(a). The charges were based upon means or income rather than disability status or disability benefits as such. The case is probably best explained as being one based upon its particular facts.

1 [1999] IRLR 318, CA.
2 See the Rights of Access Code of Practice, para 3.9.
3 The question of justification is addressed at **5.6**.
4 [2000] TLR 196.
5 Under National Health Service Community Care Act 1990, s 47 and Chronically Sick and Disabled Persons Act 1970, s 2(1).
6 Under Health and Social Services and Social Security Adjudications Act 1983, s 17(2).
7 Relying upon DDA 1995, ss 19(1)(d), 19(2)(c), 19(3)(h) and 20(1)(a).

5.4.6 Is it an essential ingredient of this limb of discrimination to be able to show that the service provider knew that the service user is a disabled person or that it was aware of the disability to which the reason for the alleged unlawful treatment is related? The question of whether the service provider knew that the service user (being treated in a way which is allegedly unlawful) was disabled is likely to be an especially keen one under Part III of the DDA 1995. For example, a disability might affect the appearance or behaviour of the disabled person, leading the service provider to believe honestly, but wrongly, that the service user is drunk or is engaging in threatening or unacceptable behaviour. Can a service provider be said to have treated a person less favourably for a reason which relates to that person's disability if the service provider did not know that the person was disabled?

5.4.7 The issue of knowledge has been raised in the context of the employment provisions of Part II of the DDA 1995.[1] The wording of s 20(1) is for all intents and purposes virtually identical to that of the parallel provisions in s 5(1). Under the employment provisions, the correct approach to the question of the knowledge of disability has divided opinion in the EAT.

One division of the EAT (under the former President, Morison J) has taken the view that an employer's knowledge of the disability is relevant.[2] An employer cannot be said to have treated a person less favourably *for a reason which relates to* that person's disability if the employer did not know that the person was disabled. Knowledge of the material features of the disability will be enough, but not simply knowledge of one or other equivocal symptom.[3] However, subsequently and more recently, another division of the EAT (under Lindsay J, the new President) has doubted the correctness of the earlier view.[4] According to the later opinion, as the wording of the relevant statutory provision is silent on the question of knowledge, the test is an objective one of whether the disabled person has been treated less favourably for a reason which is related to disability *as a matter of fact.* The subjective question of the employer's knowledge or ignorance of the complainant's disability might then go to the issue of justification.

---

1 See above at **3.4.10** et seq.
2 *O'Neill v Symm & Co Ltd* [1998] IRLR 233, EAT.
3 Whether this view is compatible with the Court of Appeal's construction of DDA 1995, s 5(1) in *Clark v TDG Ltd t/a Novacold* [1999] IRLR 318, CA is arguably questionable.
4 *H J Heinz Co Ltd v Kenrick* [2000] IRLR 144.

5.4.8   In the employment context, the latter view that knowledge of disability is not a requirement of establishing less favourable treatment discrimination is defensible both on policy grounds[1] and in the framework of an employer's recourse to a broadly defined concept of justification. However, in relation to provision of goods and services, a service provider will not usually be possessed of the same degree of actual or potential knowledge of an individual's disability as an employer might be. Unless the service user immediately informs the service provider that he or she is disabled and explains the effects of the disability, a service provider might make a snap decision (for example to refuse service) for a reason (for example, the appearance of being drunk) which later turns out to be a disability-related reason. Unlike the potential knowledge-based justification open to an employer, the service provider's justification 'defence' is narrowly defined and limited to the circumstances set out in Part III.[2] A literal interpretation of s 20(1) would suggest that knowledge of the disability is not relevant, but whether a court in a Part III case will interpret this provision in a services environment in the same way as it might be construed in an employment setting remains to be seen.[3]

---

1 See **3.4.13** and the Employment Code of Practice, para 4.57 et seq.
2 DDA 1995, s 20(1)(b), (3) and (4). See **5.6**. It would then be for the service provider to argue that it is enough that it reasonably believed that, for example, the disabled person's appearance or behaviour created a danger to health or safety (s 20(4)(a)) or would prevent other service users from being served (s 20(4)(c) or (d)).
3 There is also the possibility that the Court of Appeal will be asked in due course to choose between *O'Neill* and *Heinz* (see **5.4.7**).

Indirect discrimination

5.4.9   A service provider providing services subject to a requirement or condition which a smaller proportion of disabled persons than non-disabled persons can meet could be said to have indirectly discriminated against disabled persons if they suffer a detriment as a result and if the service provider cannot justify the imposition of the requirement or condition. The DDA 1995 does not contain an explicit prohibition on indirect discrimination in relation to services, unlike the comparable provisions of the SDA 1975 and the RRA 1976. This is because the 1994 Green Paper took the view that indirect discrimination would be 'more difficult to tackle effectively where disabled people are involved because disability occurs in many forms' and should not be the subject of legislation.[1] That view was reiterated in the 1995 White Paper which stated that 'a general prohibition of indirect discrimination ... could have unforeseen consequences which were unfairly burdensome for businesses'.[2] However, it was accepted that certain practices – which had an indirect effect upon the right of disabled persons to access to services – should be prevented. The White Paper gave the specific example of a service provider banning animals from its premises and the disproportionate adverse effect this would have on persons with visual impairments who rely upon guide dogs. This would be a case that would clearly call for reasonable practical adjustments or modifications to be made by the service provider. That leads us to a consideration of the duty to make reasonable adjustments.

---

1 1994 Green Paper, para 4.11.
2 1995 White Paper, para 4.5.

5.5 DUTY TO MAKE REASONABLE ADJUSTMENTS

Introduction

5.5.1 While many incidents of indirect discrimination in relation to goods, facilities or services will be caught by the 'less favourable treatment' formula,[1] the duty to make reasonable adjustments assumes even greater importance as a means to prevent (or to require the adjustment of) unjustified practices, rules, policies, requirements or conditions which have a harsh or adverse impact upon access by disabled persons. The 1995 White Paper proposed that it would not be enough simply to prohibit discriminatory behaviour. Legislation would also require 'positive action which is reasonable and readily achievable to overcome the physical and communication barriers that impede disabled people's access'.[2] This would mean that policies, practices and procedures which discriminated against disabled persons would have to be prohibited, unless fundamental to the nature of the business. Auxiliary aids and services (such as information on tape for blind customers or induction loops in places of entertainment for individuals with hearing disabilities) would have to be provided, if this was reasonable and readily achievable. Physical barriers might also have to be removed or alternative means of access be provided.

---

1 DDA 1995, s 20(1). See **5.4.2**.
2 1995 White Paper, para 4.4.

5.5.2 Accordingly, the DDA 1995 places a duty on service providers to amend policies, procedures and practices which prevent disabled persons using a service; to remove or alter physical barriers; and to provide auxiliary aids or services.[1] The statutory duty placed upon service providers to make reasonable adjustments to allow disabled persons meaningful access to the provision of services provided to the public is the keystone to the rights of access contained in Part III of the DDA 1995. A breach of the duty to make reasonable adjustments is not actionable in itself and a failure to observe the duty on the part of a service provider does not give an aggrieved disabled person a common law right in tort to sue for breach of a statutory duty. Nevertheless, the duty to make reasonable adjustments is important for determining whether a service provider has discriminated against a disabled person.[2] An *unjustified* failure to comply with a s 21 duty imposed upon a service provider in relation to a disabled person is treated as amounting to discrimination against the disabled person.[3] Such a failure is potentially an *unlawful* act of discrimination if the failure has the effect of making it 'impossible or unreasonably difficult' for the disabled person to make use of a service which the service provider provides (or is prepared to provide) to the public.[4]

---

1 DDA 1995, s 21.
2 Ibid, s 21(10).
3 Ibid, s 20(2).
4 Ibid, s 19(1)(b). The Act assumes that an action for a breach of the duty to make reasonable adjustments will be brought under the bespoke provision in s 19(1)(b). However, there seems to be no reason of statutory construction (reading ss 19(1), 20(2), 20(9) and 21 together) why such an action could not be brought within the other causes of action set out in s 19(1) (and where the threshold for action may not be so high). Similarly, it might be possible to pursue the breach via ss 19(1)(b) and 20(1) ('less favourable treatment' discrimination).

5.5.3 The revised Part III Code of Practice attempts to cast light upon the meaning of this complex provision.[1] For example, the DDA 1995 does not define what is meant by 'impossible or unreasonably difficult' in the context of the effect upon the accessibility of a service to a disabled person as a result of a failure to make a reasonable adjustment. Instead, the Code offers some factors (such as time, inconvenience, effort or discomfort entailed in using a service) which go to the question of what would be unreasonably difficult for a disabled person to have to endure when attempting to use a service.[2] Again, the statute does not say what are 'reasonable steps' in relation to the duty of the service provider to make adjustments. Filling the gap, the Part III Code borrows from the Employment Code of Practice.[3] What is a reasonable step for a service provider to have to take will vary according to the type of services being provided; the nature of the service provider and its size and resources; and the effect of the disability on the individual disabled person.[4] Other factors which may be relevant include the effectiveness of the steps; their practicability; financial and other costs;[5] disruption to the service provider's business; the extent of the service provider's financial and other resources (including any resources already expended on adjustments); and the availability of financial or other assistance.[6] A service provider with substantial financial resources may be expected to take greater steps than a service provider with fewer resources. On the other hand, steps need not be taken if these adjustments would fundamentally alter the nature of the service in question or would alter the nature of the trade, profession or business which the service provider runs or owns.[7]

1 Rights of Access Code of Practice, Chapter 4.
2 Ibid, paras 4.16–4.17. The DRTF considers that the trigger point for making a reasonable adjustment should be monitored to see whether it has been set too high: DRTF Report, recommendation 6.5.
3 Employment Code of Practice, paras 4.21–4.32. There is a noticeable and important difference here, however, in that the Employment Code builds upon the factors identified in s 6(4) in Part II of the DDA 1995 as being within the scope of the reasonable steps inquiry for the purposes of the employment-related duty to make adjustments. Part III contains no such statutory factors and so the Rights of Access Code strictly speaking is filling a vacuum.
4 Rights of Access Code of Practice, para 4.10.
5 The DDA 1995 allows for a future possibility that a service provider would not be required to take any steps incurring expenditure exceeding a prescribed maximum sum: s 21(7). Any prescribed maximum might be calculated by reference to criteria set out in s 21(8) and the regulations may provide for expenditure incurred by one service provider to be treated as incurred by another: s 21(9). There is no present intention to use this power.
6 Rights of Access Code of Practice, para 4.11 (and example) and para 4.12. The DRTF approved of these factors but recommended that they should be set out in legislation: DRTF Report, recommendation 6.2.
7 DDA 1995, s 21(6); Rights of Access Code of Practice, paras 6.25–6.26.

5.5.4 Moreover, the Code describes the duty to make reasonable adjustments as one arising in relation to disabled people generally. It counsels service providers to anticipate the requirements of disabled users of its services for reasonable adjustments to be made to the way in which its services are provided. Section 21 of the DDA 1995 thus contains an anticipatory duty which is owed to disabled people at large, but the breach of which gives rise to a potential individual cause of action.[1] The duty is also a continuing and evolving one.[2] What may be a reasonable adjustment today may cease to be so in the future, especially as technological development gathers pace.[3]

1 The description of the duty in s 21 speaks of its effect upon 'disabled persons' (in the plural), whereas ss 19(1)(b) and 20(2) – in defining what is unlawful discrimination – addresses 'the disabled person' (in the singular).
2 Rights of Access Code of Practice, paras 4.7–4.8. The DRTF approved of these principles, but recommended that they should be expressed in legislation in clearer terms: DRTF Report, recommendation 6.4.
3 Ibid, para 4.9.

Practices, policies or procedures

5.5.5 The first aspect of the duty to make reasonable adjustments arises where a service provider has a 'practice, policy or procedure' which makes it 'impossible or unreasonably difficult' for disabled persons to make use of goods, facilities or services which the service provider provides or is prepared to provide to other members of the public.[1] In such a case, it is the duty of the service provider 'to take such steps as it is reasonable, in all the circumstances of the case',[2] for the service provider to have to take 'in order to change' the policy, practice or procedure in question so that 'it no longer has' the effect described (that is, making it impossible or unreasonably difficult for disabled persons to access the goods, facilities or services in point).[3] This may simply involve waiving a practice, or amending or abandoning a particular policy (such as a dress code in a restaurant or a requirement of a driving licence as proof of identification) which create difficulty for people with certain kinds of disabilities.[4]

1　DDA 1995, s 21(1).
2　See Rights of Access Code of Practice, paras 5.5–5.8.
3　Regulations may make provision as to the circumstances in which it is reasonable (or not reasonable) for a service provider to have to take steps of a prescribed description (s 21(5)(a)–(b)). Moreover, such regulations may prescribe what is to be included or not included within the meaning of a 'practice, policy or procedure' (s 21(5)(c)–(d)). No such regulations have been made at the time of writing.
4　Rights of Access Code of Practice, paras 5.3 (and examples).

5.5.6　The DDA 1995 provides no further guidance or interpretation as to the meaning of the s 21(1) duty or its component parts. Neither the 1994 Green Paper nor the 1995 White Paper cast further light on this duty. The parliamentary debates on the draft legislation are also unhelpful. The Code of Practice is a little bit more expansive.[1] However, the wording of the subsection is relatively unambiguous and the duty to make reasonable adjustments set out there is not likely to give rise to many disputes of legal interpretation. One obvious example that is caught by this duty is the policy or practice of shops or places of entertainment which exclude access to dogs accompanied by their owners. Such a policy or practice will need to be revisited and exception made (as was often the voluntary position previously) for service animals accompanied by a disabled person.[2] Similarly, cinemas or restaurants which refuse or limit access to wheelchair-users have to rethink this practice.[3]

1　Rights of Access Code of Practice, paras 5.2–5.8.
2　Ibid, para 5.4 (example).
3　Thus, there is an obvious overlap with the duty to provide auxiliary aids and services which arise under s 21(4).

Physical features

5.5.7　The 1994 Green Paper referred to the fact that disabled persons cannot take access to non-domestic buildings for granted and pointed out that high steps, narrow doorways, and absence of lift access and aids to communication constituted typical physical barriers.[1] Accordingly, the second aspect of the duty to make reasonable adjustments applies where a physical feature makes it impossible or unreasonably difficult for disabled persons to make use of goods, facilities or services which a service provider provides or is prepared to provide to other members of the public.[2] Where a physical feature of this kind has the effect described, then there is a duty upon the service provider 'to take such steps as it is reasonable, in all the circumstances of the case', for the service provider to have to take in order to:

– remove the feature;[3]
– alter it so that it no longer has that effect;[4]
– provide a reasonable means of avoiding the feature;[5]
– provide a reasonable alternative method of making the service in question available to disabled persons.[6]

While the last of these aspects of this particular duty was brought into force on 1 October 1999,[7] the remaining aspects of the duties in respect of physical features are expected to be given effect in 2004.[8]

---

1   1994 Green Paper, para 3.3.
2   DDA 1995, s 21(2).
3   Ibid, s 21(2)(a) (not yet in force at the time of writing).
4   Ibid, s 21(2)(b) (not yet in force at the time of writing).
5   Ibid, s 21(2)(c) (not yet in force at the time of writing). Regulations yet to be enacted may prescribe matters which are to be taken into account in determining whether the providing of means to avoid a physical feature is 'reasonable' (s 21(3)(a)).
6   Ibid, s 21(2)(d) and which was brought into force on 1 October 1999. Regulations may prescribe matters which are to be taken into account in determining whether the providing of an alternative method of making the service available to disabled persons is 'reasonable' (s 21(3)(a)). When this subsection was brought into force in 1999, no such prescriptive regulations were made in support.
7   See Rights of Access Code of Practice, paras 5.13–5.14.
8   Rights of Access Code of Practice, paras 5.9–5.11 and see **5.1.2** above. Note that DDA 1995, s 27 and Sch 4, Part II (when in force) will make special provision where a service provider occupies its premises under lease. Where the lease or the lessor prevents or hinders the occupier in making adjustments to the premises so as to comply with a s 21 duty, these provisions will modify the effect of the lease and place duties upon the lessor. See Chapter 6.

5.5.8   By way of example in the statute itself, a 'physical feature' refers to a feature 'arising from the design or construction of a building or the approach or access to premises'.[1] However, regulations go further and for this purpose physical features include:[2]

–   any feature arising from the design or construction of a building on the premises occupied by the service provider;
–   any feature on those premises or any approach to, exit from or access to such a building;
–   any fixtures, fittings, furnishings, furniture, equipment or materials in or on such premises;
–   any fixtures, fittings, furnishings, furniture, equipment or materials brought onto premises (other than those occupied by the service provider) by or on behalf of the service provider in the course of (and for the purpose of) providing services to the public;
–   any other physical element or quality of land comprised in the premises occupied by the service provider.

All these features are covered whether temporary or permanent. A building means an erection or structure of any kind.[3]

---

1   DDA 1995, s 21(2).
2   Disability Discrimination (Services and Premises) Regulations 1999, SI 1999/1191, reg 3 made under DDA 1995, s 21(5)(e)–(f).
3   Ibid, reg 3.

5.5.9   It is worth noting that s 21(2) of the DDA 1995 appears to leave to the service provider the choice of steps to be taken to overcome the adverse effects of a physical feature. The subsection does not require the service provider to remove or alter the physical feature as a priority and does not require a hierarchical approach to adjustments to physical features. Thus, somewhat controversially, the effect of this provision is not wholly integrationist or inclusive. It permits (but does not require) a 'separate but equal' or segregated approach to the provision of services to disabled persons. For example, when the subsection is fully in force in 2004, if access to a museum is by a front entrance which could not be made accessible to wheelchair-users without rebuilding or physical alteration, it might be reasonable for the museum trustees to provide a wheelchair-accessible entrance at the side or back of the building. However, such alternative means of access to the building might not be reasonable where the disabled visitor has to negotiate rubbish bins or other detritus in the process.[1] In such a case, physical alterations to the main entrance might be the only reasonable solution.

---

1   HL Deb, vol 564, cols 2022–2023. Note also that the s 21(2) duty might not be triggered at all if another reasonable adjustment has ensured that the physical feature does not make it impossible or unreasonably difficult for disabled persons to use the service.

5.5.10   Regulations may exempt categories of service providers from the duty to make reasonable adjustments in respect of physical features only.[1] This power of exemption has not been used to date. If it was to be used in the future, then it is likely that it would be used to safeguard limited groups of service providers – such as occupiers of listed buildings[2] – who might otherwise be faced with a disproportionately heavy burden under s 21(2) or for whom it would not be possible or sensible to make physical alterations.[3] When the balance of the s 21(2) duties comes into force (as expected) in 2004, regulations may also have to make provision for the interplay between the building regulations, disability access standards for buildings and any duty to make an adjustment to the physical features of premises occupied by a service provider.[4]

---

1   DDA 1995, s 21(3)(b).
2   Who might be generally protected, in any event, by s 59 of the DDA 1995 (acts done in compliance with existing enactments, such as listed buildings regulations). That said, there is no general exemption for listed buildings from the application of the s 21 duties: HL Deb, vol 564, cols 2021–2024.
3   HC Deb Standing Committee E, cols 358–359.
4   See White Paper, paras 4.2 and 8.1. Some insight into how this question will be addressed might be gleaned from the way in which it has been handled under Part II of the DDA 1995 (the employment provisions). See Disability Discrimination (Employment) Regulations 1996, SI 1996/1456, reg 8; Employment Code of Practice, paras 4.35–4.39.

5.5.11   This aspect of the duty to make reasonable adjustments calls for some imagination from service providers. For example, a supermarket might reasonably consider whether the aisles between shelves or between the check-out tills are sufficiently wide to accommodate wheelchair-users. A restaurant might consider how its seating arrangements are designed, while an art gallery might reconsider the height at which exhibits are hung, in both cases so as to accommodate diners or art lovers who are wheelchair-users. Signage in public buildings is also counted as a physical feature and is often poorly designed or sited, without the needs of disabled persons in mind. The height and design of points of sale or service in stores, banks or post offices also frequently cause physical barriers between disabled customers and sales assistants. Lighting and ventilation in buildings might also be regarded as a 'physical feature', so that the needs of persons with vision or respiratory impairments might call for reasonable adjustments to be made in these areas. Often very little effort or modification is required to remove or ameliorate the ill-effects of physical barriers. Installing simple ramps or repositioning fixtures and fittings can often make a lot of difference for little or no expense. Other alterations might involve some cost, but with attendant benefits for all, as well as increased custom for the service provider. These might include widening entrance doors or installing two-way door hinges to assist wheelchair-users, creating designated parking spaces for disabled customers or removing high pile, low density carpeting to aid the mobility of customers using a prosthesis or walking aid.

Auxiliary aids and services

5.5.12 Where an 'auxiliary aid or service' would enable disabled persons to make use of a service which a service provider provides (or is prepared to provide) to members of the public, it is the duty of the service provider to take such steps as it is reasonable, in all the circumstances of the case, for the service provider to have to take in order to provide the auxiliary aid or service in question.[1] Where an 'auxiliary aid or service' would facilitate the use by disabled persons of such a service, the duty also arises.[2] In either case, a failure to comply with the duty is an act of unlawful discrimination if its effect is to make it impossible or unreasonably difficult for the disabled person to make use of any goods, facilities or services.[3]

---

1   DDA 1995, s 21(4)(a). Note how the trigger for this duty differs from the duties in s 21(1) and (2).
2   Ibid, s 21(4)(b).
3   Ibid, s 19(1)(b). In principle, the duty to provide auxiliary aids or services could be the subject of an expenditure cap formulated by regulations: s 21(7)–(9). No such cap has been introduced.

5.5.13 The term 'auxiliary aid or service' is exemplified by reference to the provision of information on audio tape or the provision of a sign language interpreter.[1] Further illustrations would include the provision of induction loops in theatres or cinemas, large print point of sales literature in shops or audio-visual telephones in hotel rooms for individuals with sensory impairments. However, in many cases, an auxiliary aid or service might amount to no more than the allocating of a particular member of staff to provide requested assistance to a disabled customer. For example, a blind customer in a self-service store might reasonably request that a store assistant should locate a particular item for purchase or should read out loud the description of goods from any product packaging. A training company organising a seminar for the legal profession would have to take reasonable steps to accommodate the known needs of disabled delegates attending the seminar (such as by providing a sign interpreter or a temporary induction loop system). It would need to choose the seminar location in a hotel or conference centre that was reasonably physically accessible for delegates with mobility disabilities.[2]

---

1   DDA 1995, s 21(4). Future regulations may provide as to things which are to be treated, or which are not to be treated, as auxiliary aids or services: s 21(5)(g)–(h).
2   See the general advice and the further illustrations given in the Rights of Access Code of Practice, paras 5.15–5.35.

5.5.14   Until the balance of the duties in relation to reasonable adjustments and physical features comes into force (as expected) in 2004,[1] regulations provide that devices, structures or equipment – the installation, operation or maintenance of which would necessitate making a permanent alteration to (or which would have a permanent effect on) the physical fabric of premises, fixtures, fittings, furnishings, furniture, equipment or materials – are not to be treated as auxiliary aids or services.[2] The effect is that, until 2004, service providers are not required to do (but are not prevented from doing) anything that would involve a permanent alteration to the physical fabric of premises (as broadly defined in the regulations) when providing an auxiliary aid.[3]

---

1   DDA 1995, s 21(2)(a)–(c).
2   Disability Discrimination (Services and Premises) Regulations 1999, SI 1999/1191, reg 4.
3   But see the positive advice on good practice given by the Rights of Access Code of Practice, paras 5.19–5.20.

5.6   JUSTIFICATION

5.6.1   A provider of services discriminates against a disabled person in a case of disability-related less favourable treatment discrimination if it cannot show that the 'treatment in question is justified'.[1] Similarly, a service provider also discriminates against a disabled person in a case where it fails to comply with a duty to make reasonable adjustments in relation to the disabled person if it cannot show that the 'failure to comply with that duty is justified'.[2] The discriminatory treatment of a disabled person (or a failure to comply with a duty to make reasonable adjustments[3]) will be justified only if, in the service provider's opinion, one or more statutory conditions are satisfied[4] and it is reasonable in all the circumstances of the case for the service provider to hold that opinion.[5]

---

1   DDA 1995, s 20(1)(b).
2   Ibid, s 20(2)(b).
3   Ibid, s 20(9) states that in s 20 (3), (4) and (8) 'treatment' includes a failure to comply with a s 21 duty. The DRTF recommends that the justification defence should be removed in the case of discrimination based upon a failure to comply with a duty to make reasonable adjustments and that the service provider should be able to rely only upon a set of expanded factors in the assessment of what is a 'reasonable' adjustment: DRTF Report, recommendation 6.7.
4   Ibid, s 20(3)(a).

5   DDA 1995, s 20(3)(b).

5.6.2   This justification defence is a novel one. First, discrimination law in the fields of sex, race and equal pay (and fair employment in Northern Ireland) does not contain an explicit justification defence to direct discrimination (as opposed to indirect discrimination). Secondly, it might be argued that a justification defence is implicit in the principle of direct discrimination, in the sense that a defendant can always seek to show that the less favourable treatment complained of was not based upon the protected characteristic of the claimant. However, the justification defence is only truly relevant when the protected characteristic of the claimant has played a part in the resultant discrimination, but there are factors or criteria present which nevertheless excuse what would be otherwise discriminatory treatment, impacts or effects. Under the DDA 1995, justification is relevant where a disabled person has been treated less favourably 'for a reason which relates to the disabled person's disability'.[1] In other words, a service provider may be allowed to justify discrimination in circumstances where the less favourable treatment has been informed by the complainant's disability. Thirdly, in existing discrimination legislation the justification defence in indirect discrimination is the subject of an objective test (albeit one of variable quality in the decided cases). Part III of the DDA 1995 bucks that trend.

---

1   DDA 1995, s 20(1)(a).

5.6.3   The justification defence also differs significantly from the parallel defence in Part II of the statute (the employment provisions). The Government's view was that 'service providers often have to take very quick and perhaps less informed decisions when serving someone [so that] an opinion-based approach remains appropriate'.[1] Unlike the employment provisions in Part II of the Act,[2] there is no suggestion that in cases of less favourable treatment discrimination a service provider cannot justify the treatment if a reasonable adjustment would have made a difference.[3] The Part III defence also exhaustively identifies the key reasons that might justify less favourable treatment of a disabled person by a service provider, whereas the defence is at large under Part II.

---

1   HL Deb, vol 566, col 119.
2   DDA 1995, s 5(5).
3   In the previous edition of this book the author attempted to suggest otherwise and now recants. The Rights of Access Code of Practice is largely silent on this point (but see paras 6.12, 6.16, 6.19, 6.22 and 6.26 on good practice).

Subjective opinion and objective reasonableness

5.6.4   The justification defence in Part III of the DDA 1995 is based upon a mixture of a subjective test and an objective test. Whilst an opinion-based approach has been seen as appropriate, 'the proper degree of objectivity is imposed because the opinion must be shown to be reasonably held'.[1] The dual subjective–objective nature of the defence has also been recognised judicially.[2] The Rights of Access Code of Practice also emphasises this point, acknowledg-

ing that a service provider does not have to be an expert on disability, but is
expected to take account of all the circumstances.[3]

---

1   HL Deb, vol 566, col 119.
2   *Rose v Bouchet* [1999] IRLR 463 (Sheriff Principal Nicholson QC) a case under the similar
    provisions in DDA 1995, s 24 (the justification defence for discrimination in the disposal or
    management of premises). The court did not think that assistance could be summoned
    from cases under Part II (the employment provisions).
3   Rights of Access Code of Practice, para 6.7. The circumstances will include the available
    information, whether it was possible to seek advice, and whether the disabled person's input
    was sought and taken account of. However, the need to seek further information or make
    further inquiry will vary with the circumstances, and it might be reasonable to expect the
    disabled person to volunteer further information: *Rose v Bouchet* (above).

5.6.5   The burden of proof is on the service provider. The service provider
must be able to show that, *at the time of* the act of alleged discrimination, it
actually held the opinion that one of the statutory conditions for the operation
of the defence was satisfied (a subjective test). The language and tense used in
the statutory provision[1] make it clear that it is the service provider's opinion at
the time of the discriminatory treatment that matters. An ex post facto
rationalisation of events will not be sufficient or permissible.[2] In practice, the
subjective test of opinion will not be difficult to pass. However, it must also be
shown that it is reasonable, in all the circumstances of the case, for the service
provider to hold that opinion (an objective test). Again, the test of the
reasonableness of the service provider's subjectively held opinion should be
judged in the light of the circumstances known at the time of the discriminatory
act.[3] The concept of reasonableness is one that tribunals and courts are very
experienced in applying. However, it will not be the reasonableness of the
opinion itself that matters. Rather the question is whether it was reasonable of
the particular service provider to hold that opinion in the particular
circumstances of the case and in respect of the particular disabled person who
is the subject of the less favourable treatment (or failure to comply with a s 21
duty).[4]

---

1   DDA 1995, s 20(3)(a).
2   This is confirmed in *Rose v Bouchet* (above). See also Rights of Access Code of Practice, paras
    6.7–6.8.
3   DDA 1995, s 20(3)(b).
4   The wording of s 20(3)(b) does not appear to admit a test of reasonableness based upon
    what a reasonable service provider faced with similar circumstances might have opined,
    although undoubtedly that will be a useful starting point.

Conditions for justification defence

5.6.6   The conditions, one or more of which (in the service provider's
reasonably held opinion) must be satisfied for the operation of the statutory
defence of justification, are set out exhaustively in the statute.[1] Some of these
conditions apply generally, but some apply only in the context of particular
forms of discrimination in relation to goods, facilities or services. The DDA

1995 contemplates five conditions or circumstances in which the justification defence might be operable.[2]

---

1   DDA 1995, s 20(4).
2   The DRTF was generally content with the limited categories of justification available in Part III of the DDA 1995. It recommended that there should be better guidance to service providers on the appropriate use of the 'health and safety' and 'greater cost' justifications, and that the operation of the justification defence should be monitored: DRTF Report, recommendation 6.6.

Health and safety

5.6.7   First, in any case, disability discrimination might be justified where the less favourable treatment (or failure to comply with a duty to make reasonable adjustments) is 'necessary' (not merely reasonably necessary) in order not to endanger the health or safety of any person.[1] This may include endangerment to the health or safety of the disabled person who is alleging discriminatory treatment. For example, a local authority recreation centre could be justified in refusing the use of its indoor climbing wall to a person with orthopaedic impairment, or in excluding a wheelchair user from its basketball league, on the ground of a risk to the health and safety of the individual or other participants. A swimming instructor might be justified in excluding a disabled person from a beginners' swimming class if, by having to focus most attention on the disabled learner, the safety of other members of the class would be put at risk.[2] It remains to be seen how narrowly this defence of justification will be interpreted and applied in practice. Health or safety risk is often relied upon by service providers as a blanket reason for excluding disabled persons from places of refreshment or entertainment (such as cinemas, theatres and restaurants). Inappropriate or unsupported reference is also frequently made to the requirements of fire regulations.[3] The use of the word 'necessary' calls for individual justification on the facts where a service provider seeks to rely upon health and safety as the grounds for compromising the civil rights of disabled persons.

---

1   DDA 1995, s 20(4)(a).
2   HL Deb, vol 566, col 1025. See the further examples in Rights of Access Code of Practice, paras 6.10–6.12.
3   Rights of Access Code of Practice, para 6.11. Restrictions produced by genuine requirements of local fire regulations will excuse otherwise discriminatory treatment by virtue of s 59 (actions done in pursuance of a statutory authority).

Incapacity to contract

5.6.8   Secondly, in any case, the less favourable treatment of a disabled person (or failure to comply with a duty to make reasonable adjustments) can be justified if the disabled person is incapable of entering into an enforceable agreement, or of giving an informed consent, and for that reason the treatment (or failure) is reasonable in that case.[1] This provision generated some concern on behalf of persons with mental disabilities who, it was feared, might suffer discrimination in the provision of services on the basis of a service provider's perception that they lacked full legal capacity to make a contract. The Government's view was that:

> 'If a service provider has a reasonably held belief that a contract with a disabled customer might be invalid, he must be allowed, under this measure, to refuse to enter into an agreement until it is reasonably clear that it would be enforceable, without the fear of being accused of discrimination.'[2]

That would allow a service provider to refuse to sell goods to, or to enter into a consumer credit agreement with, a disabled person if it holds a reasonably held opinion that the customer lacks or might lack legal capacity (whether by virtue of age or mental incapacity). The test here is whether it is reasonable to discriminate within the particular circumstances of the case.[3] The Government believed that this justification will apply only when the purchase of a product or service would normally be the subject of a written agreement or contract formality. It would thus apply in only a few cases (such as motor car hire purchase or consumer credit agreements).[4]

---

1   DDA 1995, s 20(4)(b); Rights of Access Code of Practice, paras 6.13–6.14.
2   HC Deb Standing Committee E, col 349.
3   HC Deb, vol 257, col 893.
4   Ibid, vol 257, col 350. It remains to be seen whether such cases are few (but what of contracts for holidays, which are typically made on written standard form conditions, for example, or car rental agreements?). It was doubted whether it would be reasonable for a shopkeeper to rely upon this exception when someone is buying a newspaper or confectionery (as opposed to a luxury car).

5.6.9   Regulations have been made to disapply this provision where another person is acting for the disabled person under an enduring power of attorney[1] or where, in Scotland, a *curator bonis*, tutor or judicial factor has been appointed in relation to the disabled person's property or affairs.[2]

---

1   Or functions conferred by or under Mental Health Act 1983, Part VII.
2   DDA 1995, s 20(7); Disability Discrimination (Services and Premises) Regulations 1996, SI 1996/1836, reg 8; Rights of Access Code of Practice, para 6.15.

Providing the service

5.6.10   Thirdly, where disability discrimination takes the form of a refusal (or deliberate omission) to provide to a disabled person any goods, facilities or services provided to members of the public,[1] such less favourable treatment (or failure to comply with a duty to make reasonable adjustments) might be justified if it is 'necessary' (not merely reasonably necessary) because the service provider would otherwise be unable to provide the goods, facilities or services to members of the public.[2] The 1995 White Paper gave as an example that it would no longer be possible to bar disabled persons from places of entertainment, but a coach training champion athletes would still be able to exclude the majority of the population from coaching classes.[3] The Government believed that it had introduced a strict test for the application of this defence and that it would apply 'only in circumstances in which, if a service provider were to serve a particular disabled person, he would not be able to continue to provide his service at all'.[4] However, the preferences of other customers are not a justification for discrimination.[5]

---

1   Under DDA 1995, s 19(1)(a).
2   DDA 1995, s 20(4)(c); Rights of Access Code of Practice, paras 6.17–6.19.
3   1995 White Paper, para 4.4 and see the examples in the Rights of Access Code of Practice, paras 6.17–6.18.
4   HC Deb Standing Committee E, col 354. The Minister could not think of a meaningful example of when this provision would be applicable and his opinion was that it would only apply in extreme and rare circumstances.
5   Rights of Access Code of Practice, para 6.18.

Standard of service

5.6.11   Fourthly, in a case where the discriminatory treatment (or failure to comply with a duty to make reasonable adjustments) arises in the standard of service provided to disabled persons, or the manner in which or terms on which the service provider provides goods, facilities or services to disabled persons,[1] that treatment may be justified if it is 'necessary' (not merely reasonably necessary) in order for the service provider to be able to provide the service to the disabled person or to other members of the public.[2] This is clearly linked to the third condition above and is likely to apply in exactly the same way, if at all. By way of illustration, a cinema which reserves seats at the end of rows for persons with mobility disabilities might rely upon this provision to justify what might amount to a differential standard or manner or service. Without making such arrangements, the cinema might argue that it could not admit such a disabled person at all without infringing fire regulations or otherwise causing greater inconvenience to other customers. Similarly, a museum which provides a daily guided tour of its exhibits might be justified in rostering a guide with sign language skills to assist deaf visitors on specified days of the week only.[3]

---

1   Under DDA 1995, s 19(1)(c)–(d).
2   DDA 1995, s 20(4)(d); Rights of Access Code of Practice, paras 6.20–6.22.
3   See the further examples in Rights of Access Code of Practice, paras 6.20–6.21.

Greater cost

5.6.12   Fifthly, if the service provider has discriminated in the terms on which goods, facilities or services are provided to a disabled person,[1] that discrimination is capable of being justified where the difference in such terms as between that disabled person and other members of the public 'reflects the greater cost' to the service provider in providing the goods, facilities or services to the disabled person.[2] The Government indicated that this measure is aimed at small businesses, in particular, and gave as an example a shoe maker asked to make a shoe for a disabled person to an unusual design or in an unusual fabric.[3] If that task would involve greater labour or special equipment and materials, it might be reasonable for the shoe-maker to charge the disabled customer a premium to reflect that.

---

1   Under DDA 1995, s 19(1)(d).
2   DDA 1995, s 20(4)(e); Rights of Access Code of Practice, para 6.23.
3   HC Deb Standing Committee E, col 357; HL Deb, vol 564, col 2009.

5.6.13   Taken literally, however, this last condition might be thought to justify a hotelier charging a disabled person a room supplement for providing a room adapted to take a wheelchair or with an audio-visual fire alarm. It might also be taken to justify a service provider charging blind customers for the additional cost of providing Braille or tape formats of sales literature and so on. Nevertheless, a service provider who attempts to pass on the costs of compliance with the Act to disabled persons (as opposed to spreading those costs across all customers or clients) would not be facilitated in doing so by this provision.[1] The Act does not permit surcharges upon disabled persons for extra expenses or opportunity costs incurred by service providers in complying with the legislation. Moreover, the Act explicitly provides that any increase in the cost of providing services to a disabled person, resulting from the service provider's compliance with the statutory duty to make reasonable adjustments, is to be disregarded for the purposes of the 'greater cost' justification.[2] A service provider is not able to pass the costs of complying with its duties under the 1995 legislation directly to a disabled customer.[3]

---

1   HC Deb Standing Committee E, col 357.
2   DDA 1995, s 20(5); Rights of Access Code of Practice, para 6.24.
3   HL Deb, vol 564, cols 2009–2010; HL Deb, vol 566, col 119.

Insurance services

5.6.14   The DDA 1995 contemplates that regulations might be made so as to provide for other circumstances in which less favourable treatment of a disabled person for a reason relating to disability could be deemed to be justified.[1] Regulations address the circumstances where, for a reason which relates to a disabled person's disability, a provider of insurance services (in connection with an insurance business[2] carried on by it) has treated a disabled person less favourably than it treats or would treat others to whom that reason does not or would not apply.[3] That treatment is to be taken as justified if it is based upon information which is relevant to the assessment of the risk to be insured and if it is reasonable having regard to the information relied upon and any other relevant factors.[4] The information, which might include actuarial or statistical data or a medical report, must be from a source upon which it is reasonable to rely.[5] This recognises that insurers may need to distinguish between individuals on the basis of the risks against which they seek to insure. The burden of proof will be upon the insurer to show that there was an additional risk associated with the disabled person which arises from his or her disability.[6]

1   DDA 1995, s 20(8).
2   Within the meaning of the Insurance Companies Act 1982.
3   Disability Discrimination (Services and Premises) Regulations 1996, SI 1996/1836, regs 1(2), 2(1) and 2(2)(a). See generally, Rights of Access Code of Practice, paras 7.2–7.8. The DRTF recommends that the special treatment of insurance services should continue: DRTF Report, recommendation 6.19.
4   Ibid, regs 2(1) and 2(2)(b)–(c).
5   Ibid, reg 2(2)(b).
6   Transitional provision is made for insurance policies incepted before 2 December 1996: ibid, regs 1(2) and 3(4). Any treatment in relation to an insurance policy which existed before that date is taken to be justified until they fall for renewal or review (except as part of a general reassessment of the pricing structure for a group of policies) on or after that date: reg 3(2),(3). Then they fall to be treated under s 20 and reg 2. Transitional provisions are also made in respect of cover documents and master policies: reg 4.

Guarantees

5.6.15   Regulations also deal with guarantees where, for a reason which relates to a disabled person's disability, a service provider treats that person less favourably in respect of a guarantee than it treats or would treat others to whom that reason does not or would not apply.[1] The guarantee, whether legally enforceable or not, must have been provided by the service provider. It must guarantee that the purchase price of services provided will be refunded if not of satisfactory quality or that services in the form of goods provided will be replaced or repaired if not of satisfactory quality.[2] The service provider must have refused to provide a replacement, repair or refund under the guarantee because damage (above the level at which the guarantee would normally be honoured) has occurred for a reason which relates to the disabled person's disability.[3] It must be reasonable, in all the circumstances of the case, for the service provider to refuse to provide a replacement, repair or refund under the guarantee.[4] If all these conditions are satisfied, the less favourable treatment is deemed to be automatically justified.[5] Accordingly, this provision deals with situations where a disabled person's disability results in higher than average wear or tear to goods or services supplied and where it would not be reasonable to expect service providers to honour a guarantee.[6]

1   Disability Discrimination (Services and Premises) Regulations 1996, SI 1996/1836, reg 5(1).
2   Ibid, reg 5(2)(a). A guarantee includes any document which has the effect referred to in reg 5(2)(a), whether or not so described: reg 5(3).
3   Ibid, reg 5(2)(b).
4   Ibid, reg 5(2)(c).
5   Ibid, reg 5(1).
6   See generally, Rights of Access Code of Practice, paras 7.9–7.13.

Deposits

5.6.16   Regulations also deal with the question of deposits in respect of goods and facilities.[1] The circumstances in which this special provision operates are as follows. Goods or facilities have been provided to a disabled person for which that person is required to provide a deposit which is refundable if the goods or facilities are returned undamaged.[2] The service provider has refused to refund some or all of the deposit because damage has occurred to the goods or facilities for a reason which relates to the disabled person's disability.[3] That damage is above the level at which the provider would normally refund the deposit in full.[4] If it is reasonable in all the circumstances of the case for the service provider to refuse to repay the deposit in full,[5] then that less favourable treatment (for a reason related to disability) is deemed to be justified.[6]

1   Disability Discrimination (Services and Premises) Regulations 1996, SI 1996/1836, reg 6.
2   Ibid, reg 6(2)(a).
3   Ibid, reg 6(2)(b).
4   Ibid, reg 6(2)(b).
5   Ibid, reg 6(2)(c).
6   Ibid, reg 6(1). See generally, Rights of Access Code of Practice, paras 7.14–7.19.

5.7   ENFORCEMENT, REMEDIES AND PROCEDURES

5.7.1   A claim of unlawful discrimination in relation to the provision of goods, facilities or services under Part III of the DDA 1995 is the subject of civil proceedings for tort in the county court (in England and Wales or Northern Ireland) or in reparation for breach of a statutory duty in the sheriff court (in Scotland).[1] The usual remedy will be damages (including injury to feelings),[2] but a claimant (or pursuer) might also seek a declaration or an injunction.[3] The question of enforcement procedures and remedies is considered in more detail in Chapter 10.

1   DDA 1995, ss 25(1), 25(3) and 25(4). The modification of s 25 for Northern Ireland is achieved in Sch 8, para 12.
2   Ibid, s 25(2). An upper limit to compensation may be prescribed under Sch 3, para 7. No such cap on compensation has been set to date.
3   Ibid, s 25(5).

Chapter 6

PROPERTY, PREMISES AND LEASES

6.1 INTRODUCTION

6.1.1 Part III of the DDA 1995 also makes it unlawful for landlords and other persons who are disposing of or selling property to discriminate against a disabled person.[1] Whilst it is not thought that discrimination against disabled persons is as widespread as racial discrimination once was in the property market, the Government felt sufficiently moved by at least one case of landlord discrimination against a disabled person to introduce an amendment to the Act during its progress as a Bill.[2] As the provisions on discrimination in relation to premises are a free-standing part of Part III of the Act, they warrant separate treatment in this chapter. However, much of the terminology used in relation to property discrimination echoes many of the concepts used elsewhere in the Act. Accordingly, decisions reached and precedents made in respect of other sections will be influential and of assistance in the interpretation of the law on discrimination in respect of premises.

---

1   DDA 1995, ss 22–24 (in force since 2 December 1996). These provisions mirror similar measures in the sex and race discrimination statutes, although they are not in identical terms: SDA 1975, ss 30–32; RRA 1976, ss 21–24. See generally, Rights of Access Code of Practice, Chapter 8.
2   HC Deb Standing Committee E, col 453.

6.1.2 The DDA 1995 also makes provision for the position where employers, trade organisations and service providers occupy premises under the terms of a lease. It was recognised that such parties might find it difficult to discharge a duty to make reasonable adjustments for disabled persons,[1] especially in respect of the physical features of premises, where the lease or the landlord prevented or hindered such adjustments. Accordingly, both Part II and Part III adjust the respective rights of the landlord and tenant to a commercial lease so as to accommodate the duties to make adjustments to premises.[2] As these provisions affect property interests, they are logically dealt with in this chapter.

---

1   Under DDA 1995, ss 6, 15 and 21 respectively.
2   DDA 1995, s 16 (in respect of employers and trade organisations) and s 27 (in respect of service providers), in both cases supplemented by Sch 4. However, there is no duty to make reasonable adjustments under ss 22–24 and so ss 16 and 27 (and Sch 4) do not extend to discrimination in relation to property or premises falling within the former sections.

6.2   DISCRIMINATION IN RELATION TO PREMISES

6.2.1   The DDA 1995 makes it unlawful for 'a person with power to dispose of any premises' to discriminate against a disabled person in one of a number of ways.[1] It is also unlawful for 'a person managing any premises' to discriminate against a disabled person 'occupying those premises' in a similar fashion.[2] Furthermore, the legislation deals with discrimination which arises by the withholding of a licence or consent required for the disposal of premises to a disabled person.[3]

---

1   DDA 1995, s 22(1). The meaning of discrimination in this context is set out in s 24.
2   Ibid, s 22(3).
3   Ibid, s 22(4).

Unlawful acts of discrimination

6.2.2   First, it is unlawful to discriminate 'in the terms' on which a person with power to dispose of premises offers to dispose of those premises to a disabled person.[1] For example, a landlord cannot seek to charge a higher rent for premises to a disabled tenant than the landlord would otherwise charge to a non-disabled lessee.

---

1   DDA 1995, s 22(1)(a); Rights of Access Code of Practice, para 8.13.

6.2.3   Secondly, it is unlawful to discriminate where a person with power to dispose of premises refuses to dispose of those premises to a disabled person.[1] This is a self-evident measure designed to prevent a disabled person from being denied the right to own a legal interest in property solely because of a disability. It is analogous with the illegitimacy of a property owner's action in refusing to sell or lease property to a member of an ethnic minority. It does not prevent the property owner from refusing to dispose of the property to a disabled person for reasons unconnected with that person's disability (for example, their inability to meet the purchase price or evidence that as a tenant they would be a bad credit risk).

---

1   DDA 1995, s 22(1)(b); Rights of Access Code of Practice, para 8.14.

6.2.4   Thirdly, it is unlawful for a person with power to dispose of any premises to discriminate against a disabled person in his or her 'treatment' of that disabled person 'in relation to any list of persons in need of premises of that description'.[1] This prohibition most obviously addresses discrimination against disabled persons in relation to housing association or local authority housing lists or those of private letting agencies. For example, a refusal to include a disabled person on a housing list, or the removal of that person from such a list, or a failure to accord that person proper priority in accordance with their ranking on the list might all be acts of unlawful discrimination. Similarly, allocating less desirable property to a disabled person on a housing list where a non-disabled person is more favourably treated would constitute a likely act of discrimination.[2]

1   DDA 1995, s 22(1)(c); Rights of Access Code of Practice, para 8.15.
2   The Act does not prohibit more favourable treatment or positive action in respect of disabled persons and housing lists.

6.2.5 Fourthly, it is unlawful for a person managing any premises to discriminate against a disabled person occupying those premises 'in the way' the person managing the premises 'permits the disabled person to make use of any benefits or facilities' or by 'refusing or deliberately omitting' to permit the disabled person to make use of any benefits or facilities.[1] Inclusion of a person managing any premises clearly broadens the scope of this provision which is not solely concerned with discrimination by property owners. A property management agency, accommodation agency, housekeeper, estate agent or rent collection service could all constitute parties who might be liable under this provision (and those that follow below).[2] The terms 'benefits or facilities' are not defined and there is no express intention to include 'services' within these terms.[3] However, the Code of Practice indicates that benefits or facilities include, for example, laundry facilities, access to a garden and parking facilities.[4]

1   DDA 1995, s 22(3)(a) and (b); Rights of Access Code of Practice, para 8.25.
2   Rights of Access Code of Practice, para 8.24.
3   DDA 1995, s 68(1) does not require a cross-reference to the definition used in s 4(4) for the purposes of Part II of the Act.
4   Rights of Access Code of Practice, para 8.25. For example, a property management agency, managing a residential block of flats on behalf of a landlord, may not discriminate by refusing a disabled tenant access to benefits or facilities, such as common garden or recreational areas.

6.2.6 Fifthly, it is unlawful for a person managing any premises to discriminate against a disabled person occupying those premises by 'evicting' the disabled person or by 'subjecting him [or her] to any other detriment'.[1] This does not prohibit the eviction of a disabled tenant in accordance with a lawful process where, for example, the disabled person has failed to pay rent or has breached the terms of the tenancy. Instead, it provides a disabled tenant, who has been evicted by a manager of premises because of a reason related to disability, an additional cause of action apart from any available under the law of landlord and tenant. The provision also obviously addresses harassment of a disabled tenant by the person managing the premises.

1   DDA 1995, s 22(3)(c); Rights of Access Code of Practice, paras 8.26–8.27.

6.2.7 Finally, it is unlawful for any person 'whose licence or consent is required' for the disposal of any premises 'comprised in ... a tenancy' to discriminate against a disabled person by withholding that licence or consent for the disposal of the premises to the disabled person.[1] In Scotland, this prohibition applies in respect of the disposal of any premises 'the subject of' a tenancy. This subsection applies to tenancies created before or after the passing of the Act.[2]

1   DDA 1995, s 22(4); Rights of Access Code of Practice, para 8.29.
2   Ibid, s 22(5).

Person with power to dispose of any premises

6.2.8   The phrase 'a person with power to dispose of any premises'[1] is not
defined in the Act. However, the word 'dispose' is defined,[2] and by this
circuitous route some light can be cast upon the class of person whose
potentially unlawful actions constitute the mischief at which this part of the Act
is aimed. A person with the power to dispose of premises includes a person who
has the power to grant a right to occupy the premises.[3] Where the premises are
comprised in or the subject of a tenancy, the relevant party will be the person
with the power to assign the tenancy or to sub-let or part with possession of the
premises or any part of them. The Act thus covers both the sale and lease of
premises and, by implication, any other form of legal disposal (for example, by
licence).[4]

1   As used in DDA 1995, s 22(1).
2   In DDA 1995, s 22(6) and see Rights of Access Code of Practice, para 8.7.
3   This does not include the hire of premises or the booking of rooms in hotels or guest
    houses (which would be covered by the services provisions of DDA 1995, ss 19–21): Rights of
    Access Code of Practice, para 8.7. The boundary between ss 22–24 and ss 19–21 will not
    always be clear.
4   *Quaere* whether the statute is also concerned with the disposal of premises by the operation
    of the law of succession or insolvency law.

6.2.9   The DDA 1995 does not automatically apply to private occupiers
disposing of premises by private agreement or transaction.[1] This is because the
statutory provisions preventing discrimination against disabled persons by a
person with a power to dispose of premises do not apply to 'a person who owns
an estate or interest in premises *and wholly occupies them*', unless further
conditions are satisfied.[2] So the statute does not make any discrimination
against a disabled person unlawful where a person with the power to dispose of
premises is the owner (or owns a legal interest in the premises), wholly occupies
the premises, and disposes of the premises by private agreement. However, the
statutory prohibitions will still apply if such a person uses the services of an
estate agent[3] or publishes an advertisement (or causes an advertisement to be
published)[4] for the purpose of disposing of the premises.[5] That would cease to
be a disposal by a purely private agreement.

1   See generally, Rights of Access Code of Practice, paras 8.10–8.11. The Disability Rights Task
    Force ('DRTF') saw no reason to interfere with this exemption. See *From Exclusion to
    Inclusion: A Report of the Disability Rights Task Force for Disabled People* (1999, London: DfEE)
    ('DRTF Report') recommendation 6.23.
2   DDA 1995, s 22(2) (emphasis added) for the purposes of s 22(1).
3   An 'estate agent' for this purpose is a person carrying on the trade or profession of
    providing services 'for the purpose of finding premises for persons seeking to acquire them
    or assisting in the disposal of premises': DDA 1995, s 22(6). That definition would appear to
    be wide enough to include not only an estate agent per se, but also an accommodation
    bureau or agency.
4   An 'advertisement' includes every form of advertisement or notice, whether to the public or
    not: DDA 1995, s 22(6). So the circulation to a small or select number of persons of the

details of premises for disposal would constitute an advertisement of the premises and would trigger the provisions prohibiting discrimination against disabled persons in the subsequent disposal.

5   DDA 1995, s 22(2) (these are the further conditions referred to above).

Premises and tenancy

6.2.10   The term 'premises' is not statutorily defined.[1] Nevertheless, the ordinary or literal meaning of the word 'premises' suggests that the DDA 1995 is concerned with legal and equitable interests in houses, lands, tenements and buildings, while the Act makes no apparent distinction between commercial and non-commercial (or domestic) property. Thus the Act would appear to cover, for example, dwelling-houses, office blocks, flats, bed-sits, factory premises, industrial or commercial sites, agricultural land and so on – in other words, real property of any description.[2] The Act also clearly impinges upon the law of landlord and tenant.[3] A 'tenancy' means a tenancy created by a lease or sub-lease, by an agreement for a lease or sub-lease, by a tenancy agreement, or in pursuance of any 'enactment' (for example, a statutory tenancy).[4]

1   Except to the extent that s 68(1) of the DDA 1995 indicates that premises include land of any description and s 22(8) makes it clear that the Act is concerned only with premises in the UK.
2   Rights of Access Code of Practice, para 8.8.
3   DDA 1995, s 22 obviously and expressly applies to the granting of tenancies, their assignment and the right to sub-let.
4   Ibid, ss 22(6) and 68(1); Rights of Access Code of Practice, para 8.9. The Disability Discrimination (Sub-leases and Sub-tenancies) Regulations 1996, SI 1996/1333 do not apply to ss 22–24.

Exemption for small dwellings

6.2.11   Where certain cumulative conditions are satisfied, there is a statutory exemption[1] for small dwellings in respect of the provisions prohibiting discrimination against disabled persons in the disposal or management of premises[2] or by the withholding of a licence or consent for the disposal of premises.[3] The exemption is likely to apply to a multi-occupancy residential building with shared accommodation.[4] A necessary, but not sufficient condition for the operation of this exemption is that the premises must be 'small premises'.[5] Premises are 'small premises' if there is not normally residential accommodation on the premises for more than six persons in addition to the relevant occupier and any members of the relevant occupier's household.[6] Alternatively, premises are 'small premises' if the premises satisfy four conditions:[7]

(1)   only the relevant occupier and members of his or her household reside in the accommodation occupied by him or her;
(2)   in addition to the accommodation occupied by the relevant occupier, the premises must comprise residential accommodation for at least one other household;
(3)   the residential accommodation for each other household must be let (or available for letting) on a separate tenancy or similar agreement; and

(4) there must not normally be more than two such other households.

For example, a large house where the basement and an annex have been converted into self-contained residential dwellings or flats would satisfy these conditions if the owner also resides on the premises and there is an element of shared accommodation (other than for storage or access purposes).

---

1   DDA 1995, s 23(1). See generally, Rights of Access Code of Practice, paras 8.16–8.22, 8.28 and 8.30. The DRTF saw no reason to interfere with this exemption, except possibly to allow the threshold for its operation to be lowered: DRTF Report, recommendation 6.24.
2   Ibid, s 22(1) and (3).
3   Ibid, s 22(4).
4   Rights of Access Code of Practice, para 8.22.
5   DDA 1995, s 23(2)(d); Rights of Access Code of Practice, paras 8.20–8.21.
6   Ibid, s 23(3) and (5). A householder who has converted part of his or her dwelling-house into bed-sit accommodation would fall outside this exemption if such accommodation embraced more than six tenants.
7   Ibid, s 23(4).

6.2.12   The fact that the premises are a small dwelling is not enough. Three further conditions must also be satisfied. First, the relevant occupier must reside, and must intend to continue to reside, on the premises.[1] The use of the word 'reside' indicates that this exemption is only enjoyed in respect of dwelling-houses or other residential property and does not apply to commercial or industrial premises. A 'relevant occupier' means a person with the power to dispose of the premises[2] or the person whose licence or consent is required for the disposal of the premises.[3] In both cases, the relevant occupier will include 'a near relative'.[4] Secondly, the relevant occupier must be sharing accommodation on the premises with persons who reside on the premises and who are not members of the occupier's household.[5] This condition contemplates a multi-occupancy residential building with shared accommodation. This might include a large house, sub-divided into individually let bed-sits, with a resident landlord and shared accommodation, such as communal kitchens or bathrooms. Thirdly, the shared accommodation must not be storage accommodation or a means of access.[6] This underlines the last observation illustrating the notion of shared accommodation. It indicates that it is not enough that there is a common entrance door or passageway. Equally, the premises would not include shared accommodation only by virtue of there being a garage or cellar in which the tenants or occupiers may store their personal effects.

---

1   DDA 1995, s 23(2)(a) and (6).
2   In a case where s 22(1) would otherwise apply (discrimination in relation to the disposal of premises).
3   In any case where s 22(4) would otherwise apply (discrimination by withholding a licence or consent for the disposal of tenancy premises).
4   This term is exhaustively defined by s 23(7) to mean a person's spouse, partner, child, grandparent, grandchild, or brother or sister (whether of full or half blood or by affinity). The term 'partner' means the other member of a couple consisting of a man and a woman who are not married to each other but are living together as husband and wife. It only becomes necessary to identify whether someone is a partner if the relevant occupier is not

actually present on the premises when discrimination is alleged (for example, while
temporarily away on business): HL Deb, vol 564, col 2029.

5   DDA 1995, s 23(2)(b).

6   Ibid, s 23(2)(c).

Meaning of discrimination

6.2.13   The provisions of Part III of the DDA 1995 dealing with discrimination
in relation to premises include a self-contained definition of discrimination.[1]
This does not create a free-standing right to complain of discrimination and it
will be necessary to show that discrimination has occurred in a way which is
made unlawful.[2] While case-law on the meaning of discrimination as used
elsewhere in the statute will be instructive, care must be taken to ensure that an
action for alleged discrimination in the disposal or management of premises
satisfies the definition of discrimination for present purposes.[3] In particular,
there is no explicit duty to make reasonable adjustments for disabled persons in
the context of the disposal or management of premises. It remains to be seen
whether judicial interpretation of the meaning of discrimination will give rise
to an implicit duty of this nature.[4] The Code of Practice suggests not, although
it stresses that there is nothing in the Act to prevent positive action.[5] It also
notes that persons managing or disposing of premises (such as estate agents,
accommodation bureaux or management companies) may have parallel duties
as service providers and might be subject to a duty to make reasonable
adjustments to the way in which they provide their services in relation to
premises.[6]

1   DDA 1995, s 24.

2   That is, under DDA 1995, s 22. That is the effect of the opening words of s 24(1): 'For the
    purposes of section 22 ...'.

3   See the detailed discussion of the meaning of discrimination in Chapter 3 and Chapter 5.

4   The DRTF felt that the lack of a duty to make reasonable adjustments within ss 22–24 should
    be remedied. In particular, it recommended that there should be a duty on those covered
    by the disposal and management of premises provisions to make reasonable adjustments to
    policies, practices and procedures, and to provide auxiliary aids and services in the selling
    and letting process. It also recommended that covered persons should not be allowed to
    withhold consent unreasonably for a disabled person to make changes to the physical
    features of premises: DRTF Report, recommendations 6.25–6.27.

5   Rights of Access Code of Practice, para 8.6.

6   The boundary between ss 19–21 and ss 22–24 will not always be easily drawn, especially
    where the question of reasonable adjustments is being raised.

6.2.14   A person discriminates against a disabled person if, for a reason which
relates to the disabled person's disability, that person treats the disabled person
less favourably than that person treats (or would treat) others to whom that
reason does not or would not apply.[1] Such less favourable treatment for a
reason related to disability will amount to potentially *unlawful* discrimination[2] if
the alleged discriminator cannot show that the treatment in question is
justified.[3] The justification 'defence'[4] can only be made out if certain statutory
criteria are met.[5] First, the alleged discriminator must hold the opinion that

one or more statutory conditions are satisfied.[6] This is to be tested subjectively.[7] It must be shown that, at the time the treatment took place, *in the opinion* of the defendant (or defender) the treatment was necessary. It must be shown that this was an opinion held at that time and not an ex post facto rationalisation in the face of litigation. Secondly, it must be reasonable, in all the circumstances of the case, for that person to hold that opinion.[8] This calls for an objective assessment of all the relevant circumstances.[9] The objective reasonableness of the opinion may depend upon what information was available at the time, what further reasonable inquiries might have been made and what, if any, information has been proferred by the disabled person.[10]

1   DDA 1995, s 24(1)(a). See the discussion of the concept of disability-related less favourable treatment in Chapters 3 and 5 above. See also the examples given in Rights of Access Code of Practice, para 8.5.
2   For the purposes of DDA 1995, s 22.
3   DDA 1995, s 24(1)(b).
4   Strictly, the justification requirement is part of the definition of discrimination rather than an explicit defence.
5   DDA 1995, s 24(2). See generally Rights of Access Code of Practice, paras 8.31–8.34.
6   Ibid, s 24(2)(a).
7   *Rose v Bouchet* [1999] IRLR 463 (Sheriff Principal Nicholson QC). This decision is the only reported appellate decision under the provisions of ss 22–24 at the time of writing. It concerned the refusal to let a flat to a blind person accompanied by a guide dog. The refusal was said by the landlord to be motivated by a concern for the disabled person's safety because of a missing handrail on the steps leading to the flat's entrance. The Sheriff Principal did not think it helpful to engage the assistance of cases decided under the employment provisions of the Act when construing s 24.
8   DDA 1995, s 24(2)(b). Future regulations may amplify the circumstances in which it is reasonable (or not reasonable) for a person to hold the opinion that one or more of the statutory conditions are satisfied: s 24(4). No such regulations have been made at the time of writing.
9   *Rose v Bouchet* (above). On the facts, the landlord's opinion as to the safety issues arising from letting the flat to a blind person in the particular circumstances of the case was held to be objectively reasonable.
10 Ibid. See Rights of Access Code of Practice, para 6.7.

6.2.15 There are four possible statutory (and exhaustive) conditions about the satisfaction of which the alleged discriminator must hold a reasonably held opinion.[1] These conditions are very similar to the parallel conditions for the operation of the justification defence in respect of discrimination arising in the context of goods, facilities or services.[2] First, in any case, the person alleged to have discriminated may be able to justify less favourable treatment by showing that that person reasonably believed that the treatment was necessary in order not to endanger the health or safety of any person, including the disabled person.[3] Secondly, in any case, less favourable treatment might be justified by reference to a reasonably held opinion that the disabled person was incapable of entering into an enforceable agreement or of giving an informed consent and for that reason the treatment was reasonable in the particular case.[4] Thirdly, in a case where a person managing premises has treated a disabled occupier less favourably in the way in which that occupier is allowed to make use of any benefits or facilities,[5] the alleged discriminator might be able to show a reasonably held opinion that the discriminatory treatment was necessary in order for the disabled person (or occupiers of other premises forming part of the building) to make use of a benefit or facility.[6] Finally, in a case where a person managing premises has treated a disabled occupier less favourably by refusing (or deliberately omitting) to permit that occupier to make use of any benefits or facilities,[7] less favourable treatment might be justified by demonstrating a reasonably held opinion that the treatment was necessary in order for the occupiers of other premises forming part of the building to make use of the benefit or facility.[8]

---

1   DDA 1995, s 24(3). Future regulations may also provide for additional circumstances in which less favourable treatment of a disabled person is to be taken to be justified: s 24(5). No such regulations have been made at the time of writing.

2   Ibid, s 20(4). The justification defence in relation to the disposal or management of premises raises similar issues to those in respect of discrimination in the provision of goods, facilities or services. See Chapter 5 above for a more considered analysis of these issues.

3   Ibid, s 24(3)(a); Rights of Access Code of Practice, para 8.35.

4   Ibid, s 24(3)(b); Rights of Access Code of Practice, para 8.36. Note that the provisions on powers of attorney, etc contained in the Disability Discrimination (Services and Premises) Regulations 1996, SI 1996/1836, reg 8 do not apply to s 24 as they do to s 20 in the context of goods, facilities and services.

5   Ibid, s 22(3)(a).

6   Ibid, s 24(3)(c); Rights of Access Code of Practice, para 8.37.

7   Ibid, s 22(3)(b).

8   Ibid, s 24(3)(d); Rights of Access Code of Practice, para 8.37.

6.2.16   Regulations may provide for additional circumstances in which less favourable treatment of a disabled person is to be taken to be justified.[1] The only such provision to date affects deposits. It arises where a person with power to dispose of any premises ('the provider') grants a disabled person a right to occupy the premises, whether by a formal tenancy agreement or otherwise.[2] The provider may have required the disabled person to provide a deposit in respect of his or her occupation of the premises. The deposit is intended to be refundable at the end of the occupation provided that the premises and contents are not damaged.[3] Suppose that the provider refuses to refund some or all of the deposit because the premises or contents have been damaged for a reason which relates to the disabled person's disability.[4] If the damage is above the level at which the provider would normally refund the deposit in full,[5] and if it is reasonable in all the circumstances of the case for the provider to refuse to refund the deposit in full,[6] then that apparently less favourable treatment of the disabled person for a reason relating to his or her disability is deemed to be justified.[7]

---

1   DDA 1995, s 24(5).

2   Disability Discrimination (Services and Premises) Regulations 1996, SI 1999/1191, reg 7(2)(a). See generally Rights of Access Code of Practice, paras 8.38–8.43.

3   Ibid, reg 7(2)(b).

4   Ibid, reg 7(2)(c).

5   Ibid, reg 7(2)(c).

6   Ibid, reg 7(2)(d).

7   Ibid, reg 7(1) for the purposes of s 24.

Victimisation

6.2.17   For present purposes,[1] a person (X) also discriminates against another person (Y) if X treats Y less favourably than X treats (or would treat) other persons whose circumstances are the same as Y's, and X does so for one of a number of statutory reasons.[2] Those statutory reasons relate to the fact that Y has exercised (or is believed or suspected by X as having exercised or as intending to exercise) rights under the DDA 1995.[3] For example, Y may have brought proceedings against X or given evidence in respect of such proceedings. This is victimisation.[4] An act of victimisation amounts to discrimination.[5] A person (whether disabled or not) who is victimised in this way has a cause of action for an unlawful act in relation to the disposal or management of premises.[6] By way of illustration, if Y was employed by local authority X and brought a complaint of disability-related employment discrimination against X, it would be an act of discrimination if X then victimised Y by removing Y from the local authority's housing waiting list. In these particular circumstances, it is not strictly necessary that Y should be a disabled person. It is sufficient that he or she has been victimised for doing something in relation to the Act and has suffered a discriminatory act.

1   DDA 1995, ss 22–24 (as for Part III as a whole).
2   Ibid, s 55(1).
3   Ibid, s 55(2).
4   The concept of victimisation is explained in more detail in Chapter 10.
5   DDA 1995, s 22(7) for the purposes of ss 22–24.
6   As outlined in DDA 1995, s 22. See Rights of Access Code of Practice, paras 9.2–9.5.

Enforcement and remedies

6.2.18   The provisions in respect of disability-informed discrimination in the disposal or management of premises are enforced (and remedies are sought) in exactly the same way as complaints of discrimination in respect of the provision of goods, facilities and services.[1] Further discussion is pursued in Chapter 10.

1   The relevant provisions are contained in DDA 1995, ss 25–28 and Sch 3, Part II.

6.3   ALTERATIONS TO PREMISES OCCUPIED UNDER LEASES

The duty to make reasonable adjustments to premises

6.3.1   Where any physical features of premises occupied by an employer place a disabled person at a substantial disadvantage in comparison with non-disabled persons, it is the duty of the employer to take such steps as it is reasonable in all the circumstances of the case to take in order to prevent the physical feature in question having that effect.[1] That duty might require the employer to make adjustments to the premises, subject to considerations such as practicability, cost and resources.[2] An unjustifiable failure to consider or discharge that duty can amount to an act of unlawful discrimination.[3] A similar duty to make reasonable adjustments to any physical feature of premises occupied by a trade organisation is imposed upon such an organisation.[4]

1 DDA 1995, s 6(1)(b). The detail of this duty has been considered in Chapter 3.
2 Ibid, s 6(3)(a), (4).
3 Ibid, s 5.
4 Ibid, s 15. See Chapter 4.

6.3.2 In respect of Part III of the DDA 1995, a detailed duty to make reasonable adjustments is also placed upon service providers.[1] Where a physical feature of a building makes it impossible or unreasonably difficult for disabled persons to make use of a service provided to the public by a service provider, it is the duty of the service provider to make reasonable adjustments.[2] At the time of writing, that duty does not yet involve taking such steps as it is reasonable in all the circumstances of the case to take in order to remove the physical feature or to alter it or to provide a reasonable means of avoiding the feature, so that it no longer has the adverse effect referred to.[3] Those aspects of the duty are expected to come into force in 2004. At present, the service provider's duty in the above circumstances is to provide a reasonable alternative method of making the service available to disabled persons.[4] As with employers and trade organisations, a service provider's unjustified failure to discharge a duty to make reasonable adjustments to its premises in these ways is a potential act of discrimination.[5] There is no comparable duty to make reasonable adjustments to premises in respect of the disposal or management of premises.[6]

1 DDA 1995, s 21. See Chapter 5.
2 Ibid, s 21(2).
3 Ibid, s 21(2)(a)–(b).
4 Ibid, s 21(2)(d).
5 Ibid, s 20.
6 Ibid, ss 22–24 (discussed at **6.2**).

The problem of leases

6.3.3 The duty to make reasonable adjustments to premises is primarily imposed upon the employer, trade organisation or service provider that occupies those premises. Where that person owns the premises there can be no question that the person has a right to make alterations to the premises, subject only to planning, building and environmental regulation. In such a case, if there is a duty to make an adjustment, and if an alteration to the fabric or a physical feature of the premises would otherwise be a reasonable adjustment to make, then the occupier will be expected to take such steps, all other things being equal.

6.3.4 Nevertheless, many employers, trade organisations or service providers occupy premises as tenants under a commercial lease. A term or covenant in that lease might forbid or restrict alterations to the property or might permit such alterations only with the prior consent of the landlord. In that latter case, consent under the lease might not be forthcoming if the landlord reasonably or unreasonably withholds permission. In these circumstances, the employer, trade organisation or service provider might be unable to discharge its duty to a disabled person to make reasonable adjustments.[1] This could amount to an unlawful act of disability discrimination, although the restriction in the lease or the landlord's refusal to countenance an alteration to the occupied premises might bring a justification defence into play.

---

1   It is arguable (but uncertain) that a restrictive clause or covenant in a commercial lease, which prevents a tenant carrying out an alteration in pursuit of a duty to make a reasonable adjustment under the 1995 Act, is invalid as being a term of an agreement which limits the operation of the statute. See DDA 1995, ss 9 and 26. See also HL Deb, vol 566, col 1016.

The effect of the DDA 1995 upon premises occupied under leases

6.3.5   The DDA 1995 clarifies the relation between the potentially conflicting legal obligations of disability discrimination law and the law of landlord and tenant.[1] The effect may be to prevent landlords of commercial or industrial premises thwarting or undermining the objectives of the legislation. The relevant statutory provisions apply where an employer, trade organisation or provider of services ('the occupier') occupies premises under a 'lease'.[2] A 'lease' for this purpose includes a tenancy, sub-lease or sub-tenancy, and an agreement for a lease, tenancy, 'sub-lease' or 'sub-tenancy'.[3] The term 'sub-lease' means any sub-term created out of or deriving from a leasehold interest and 'sub-tenancy' means any tenancy created out of or deriving from a superior tenancy.[4] Where there are references in the statute[5] to a 'lessor', that reference is to be taken as referring to the lessor who is the occupier's immediate landlord in cases of an occupier occupying premises under a sub-lease or sub-tenancy.[6]

---

1   DDA 1995, ss 16 and 27 and Sch 4.
2   Ibid, ss 16(1)(a) and 27(1)(a).
3   Ibid, ss 16(3) and 27(3). The Act provides that regulations may further define the meaning of these terms.
4   Disability Discrimination (Sub-leases and Sub-tenancies) Regulations 1996, SI 1996/1333, reg 3. This applies for the purposes of s 16 only because s 27 (affecting Part III) is not yet in force. Regulations may also supplement or modify the provisions of ss 16 and 27 or Sch 4 in relation to cases where the occupier occupies premises under a sub-lease or sub-tenancy: Sch 4, paras 4 and 9.
5   DDA 1995, s 16 and Sch 4, para 1.
6   Disability Discrimination (Sub-leases and Sub-tenancies) Regulations 1996, SI 1996/1333, reg 4(a). Further modifications are made to s 16 and Sch 4 by reg 4, and these are referred to in the text below.

6.3.6   The statutory provisions apply if the effect of the lease would otherwise be that the occupier would not be entitled to make a particular alteration to the premises,[1] and if the alteration is one which the occupier proposes to make in order to comply with a statutory duty[2] to make reasonable adjustments.[3] If the terms and conditions of a lease impose conditions which are to apply if the occupier alters the premises, then the occupier is treated[4] as not being entitled to make the alteration.[5] Similarly, if the terms and conditions of the lease entitle the lessor to impose conditions when giving any consent to the occupier to alter the premises, the occupier is treated[6] as not being entitled to make the alteration.[7] If the above conditions are satisfied,[8] the Act provides that the lease shall have effect as if it provided for the occupier to be entitled to make the alteration with the written consent of the lessor.[9] In other words, a statutory term is implied into the lease or agreement at issue. The statutory term requires that, if the occupier wishes to make an alteration to the premises, the occupier must first make a written application to the lessor for consent.[10] Furthermore, the Act implies into the terms of the lease a requirement that, if a written application for consent is made by the occupier, the lessor will not withhold consent unreasonably.[11] In turn, the lessor is deemed to be entitled to make any consent the subject of reasonable conditions.[12]

---

1   DDA 1995, ss 16(1)(b) and 27(1)(b).
2   Under DDA 1995, ss 6 or 15 or 21.
3   DDA 1995, ss 16(1)(c) and 27(1)(c).
4   For the purposes of DDA 1995, ss 16(1)(b) and 27(1)(b).
5   DDA 1995, ss 16(4)(a) and 27(4)(a).
6   For the purposes of DDA 1995, ss 16(1)(b) and 27(1)(b).
7   DDA 1995, ss 16(4)(b) and 27(4)(b).
8   Ibid, ss 16(1) or 27(1).
9   Ibid, ss 16(2)(a) and 27(2)(a).
10   Ibid, ss 16(2)(b) and 27(2)(b).
11   Ibid, ss 16(2)(c) and 27(2)(c).
12   Ibid, ss 16(2)(d) and 27(2)(d).

6.3.7 Where the occupier occupies premises under a sub-lease or sub-tenancy, any superior lease under which the premises are held has effect (except to the extent to which it expressly so provides) in relation to the lessor and lessee who are parties to the superior lease as if it provided for the lessee to have to make a written application to the lessor for consent to the alteration.[1] If such an application is made, the superior lease has effect as if it provided for the lessor not to withhold its consent unreasonably and for the lessor to be entitled to make its consent subject to reasonable conditions.[2]

---

1   DDA 1995, s 16(2A)(i) inserted by the Disability Discrimination (Sub-leases and Sub-tenancies) Regulations 1996, SI 1996/1333, reg 4(b).
2   Ibid, s 16(2A)(ii)–(iii) inserted by the Disability Discrimination (Sub-leases and Sub-tenancies) Regulations 1996, SI 1996/1333, reg 4(b). In employment cases, see Employment Code of Practice, para 4.47.

6.3.8 Rather puzzlingly, the statutory wording appears to restrict the vigour of this otherwise quite far-reaching adjustment of the rights of commercial landlord and tenant. It is apparent that a lease is to have effect as modified by the statutory implied terms 'except to the extent to which it expressly so provides'.[1] The reference to 'it' must be taken to be a reference to the lease.[2] This suggests that the landlord might impose express terms in the lease that have the intent and effect of thwarting the statutory implications made in the lease. If that is right – and the author does not believe that this is what was intended – then it may be that such express terms would have to surmount the test of an invalid agreement.[3]

---

1   DDA 1995, ss 16(2) and 27(2).
2   It is possible that it is a drafting error and that the reference was intended to be to the sub-section rather than to the lease (the phrase 'except to the extent to which [the sub-section] expressly so provides' makes better sense).
3   DDA 1995, ss 9 or 26.

Employment and trade organisation cases

6.3.9   In employment cases, it is *not* reasonable for an employer to have to take a step in relation to premises occupied by it which would otherwise be required in order to comply with a statutory duty to make reasonable adjustments,[1] and which is contrary to the terms of any lease under which the employer occupies the premises, if:

–   the employer has applied to the lessor in writing to take the step;
–   the employer has indicated in writing that it proposes to take the step, subject to the lessor's consent, in order to comply with its statutory duty;
–   the lessor has withheld that consent; and
–   the occupier (employer) has informed the disabled person that it has applied for the consent of the lessor and that the lessor has withheld that consent.[2]

For the purposes of the employer's duty to make reasonable adjustments, where under any binding obligation an employer is required to obtain the consent of any person to any alteration of the premises occupied by the employer, it is *always* reasonable for the employer to have to take steps (*not* including an application to a court or tribunal) to obtain that consent and it is *never* reasonable for the employer to have to make that alteration before that consent is obtained.[3] In this context, a binding obligation means a legally binding obligation (not contained in a lease) in relation to the premises (whether arising from an agreement or otherwise).[4] An example of such an obligation would include a mortgage or a charge or, in Scotland, a feu disposition.[5]

---

1   Under DDA 1995, s 6.
2   Disability Discrimination (Employment) Regulations 1996, SI 1996/1456, reg 15. See further the Employment Code of Practice, para 4.41.
3   Ibid, reg 10. See further the Employment Code of Practice, para 4.48. Note also the possible effect of building regulations and statutory consents (see Chapter 3).
4   Ibid, reg 2.
5   Employment Code of Practice, para 4.48.

6.3.10   It is implied that the lessor will not withhold consent unreasonably,[1] although the landlord is entitled to make any consent the subject of reasonable conditions.[2] In employment cases, a lessor is to be taken to have withheld consent to an alteration where the lessor has received a written application by or on behalf of the occupier (employer) for consent to make the alteration and the lessor has failed within a period of 21 days (or such longer period as is reasonable) either:

– to reply consenting to or refusing the application; or
– to reply consenting to the application, subject to obtaining the consent of another person required under a superior lease or binding obligation (such as a mortgage or charge or, in Scotland, a feu disposition) *and* seeks that consent.[3]

If the lessor belatedly meets the above requirements, it shall be taken to have withheld its consent from the date of the failure to meet the requirements on time, but then shall be treated as having not withheld its consent from the time when it belatedly met the requirements.[4] A lessor is treated as not having sought the consent of another person (if so required) unless the lessor has applied in writing to that person indicating that the lessor's consent to the alteration has been applied for in order to comply with a statutory duty to make a reasonable adjustment and that the lessor has given its consent conditionally upon obtaining the other person's consent.[5]

---

1   DDA 1995, s 16(2)(c).
2   Ibid, s 16(2)(d). In which case, the occupier must carry out the alteration subject to that condition: Employment Code of Practice, para 4.42. As to when it would be reasonable or unreasonable to withhold consent, see ibid, paras 4.43–4.45. The question of what is a reasonable condition to consent is discussed below. See further the Employment Code of Practice, para 4.46.
3   Disability Discrimination (Employment) Regulations 1996, SI 1996/1456, reg 11(1)–(2) made under Sch 4, para 3 for the purposes of s 16 (and Sch 4, Part I). The period of 21 days begins with the day on which the application is received. See further the Employment Code of Practice, para 4.48.
4   Ibid, reg 11(3).
5   Ibid, reg 11(4).

6.3.11   In employment cases, a lessor withholds consent *unreasonably* where the lease provides that consent shall or will be given to an alteration of the kind in question.[1] Consent is also withheld *unreasonably* where the lease provides that consent shall or will be given to an alteration of the kind in question if the consent is sought in a particular way and that has been complied with.[2] Moreover, a lessor withholds consent *unreasonably* where the lessor is treated as withholding consent by virtue of reg 11 of the 1996 Regulations.[3] On the other hand, a lessor is regarded as acting *reasonably* in withholding consent where there is a binding obligation (for example, a mortgage or charge) requiring the consent of a third party to an alteration; the lessor has taken steps to seek that consent; and that consent has not been given or has been given subject to a condition making it reasonable for the lessor to withhold consent.[4] Alternatively, a lessor acts *reasonably* in withholding consent where the lessor is bound by an agreement allowing the lessor to consent to the alteration subject to a condition that the lessor makes a payment and that condition does not permit the lessor to make its consent subject to a condition that the occupier (employer) reimburse that payment.[5] If it would be *reasonable* for the lessor to withhold consent, but consent has nevertheless been given, it would be reasonable to impose a condition on that consent that upon expiry of the lease the employer (or any assignee or successor) must reinstate any relevant part of the premises to its prior state.[6]

---

1 Disability Discrimination (Employment) Regulations 1996, SI 1996/1456, reg 12(a).
2 Ibid, reg 12(b).
3 Ibid, reg 12(c). See **6.3.10**.
4 Ibid, reg 13(1). See further the Employment Code of Practice, para 4.48.
5 Ibid, reg 13(2).
6 Ibid, reg 14(2).

6.3.12 Where in employment cases the lessor gives consent to an alteration, but subject to a condition, such a condition is regarded as *reasonable* in all the circumstances if it is any of the following conditions (or a condition to a similar effect):

– the occupier must obtain any necessary planning permission (and any other consent or permission) required by or under any enactment;[1]
– the occupier must submit any plans or specifications for the alteration to the lessor for approval (provided the condition binds the lessor not to withhold approval unreasonably) and that the work is carried out in accordance with such plans or specifications;[2]
– the lessor must be permitted a reasonable opportunity to inspect the work when complete;[3] or
– the occupier must repay to the lessor the costs reasonably incurred in connection with the giving of the consent.[4]

---

1 Disability Discrimination (Employment) Regulations 1996, SI 1996/1456, reg 14(1)(a).
2 Ibid, reg 14(1)(b).
3 Ibid, reg 14(1)(c).
4 Ibid, reg 14(1)(d).

Procedure and remedies

6.3.13 In employment cases (and cases of discrimination by trade organisations), where an employment tribunal is considering a complaint of unlawful discrimination by an employer or trade organisation,[1] special provisions deal with a failure by an occupier to obtain consent to the alteration.[2] These apply where any question arises as to whether an employer or trade organisation occupying premises under a lease has failed to comply with its statutory duty to make a reasonable adjustment by failing to make a particular alteration to premises. In answering that question, the tribunal must ignore any constraint attributable to the fact that the employer or trade organisation occupies the premises under a lease, unless the occupier has applied to the lessor in writing for consent to make the alteration. The employer or trade organisation is denied recourse to a justification defence based upon the restrictive terms or covenants of a lease unless and until it has sought to obtain the landlord's consent to the making of the alteration despite that restriction.[3] In other words, the occupier of the premises cannot plead justification by pointing to the negative terms of a lease alone.[4] The occupier is expected to rely upon the statutory provisions[5] and to seek the landlord's consent to the alteration by means of written application.

---

1   DDA 1995, s 8.
2   See DDA 1995, Sch 4, Part I supplementing s 16.
3   DDA 1995, Sch 4, para 1.
4   Employment Code of Practice, para 4.41.
5   DDA 1995, s 16.

6.3.14   The sting in the tail of this provision is as follows. In employment tribunal proceedings, where a question arises about a duty to make a reasonable adjustment by an alteration to premises occupied under a lease, either the applicant or the occupier may request the tribunal to join (in Scotland, sist) the lessor as a party to the proceedings.[1] The tribunal must grant such a request if it is made before the hearing commences,[2] otherwise the granting of such a request is at the tribunal's discretion.[3] Such a request to join the lessor to proceedings cannot be made once the tribunal has determined the complaint.[4] If the lessor has been thus joined (or sisted) as a party to the tribunal proceedings, the tribunal has certain powers in relation to the lessor if certain conditions are satisfied. It may determine whether the lessor has refused consent to the alteration or consented subject to one or more conditions.[5] If so, the tribunal may then determine whether the refusal or any of the conditions was unreasonable.[6] Where the tribunal has so determined, it may take one or more steps.[7] The tribunal may make such a declaration as it considers appropriate or make an order authorising the occupier to make an alteration specified in the order.[8] This latter power is quite novel and is likely to prove important in practice. An order made under this power may require the occupier to comply with any conditions specified in the order.[9] Alternatively or additionally, the tribunal may order the lessor to pay compensation to the applicant.[10] Any step taken by the tribunal above may be in substitution for or in addition to the usual statutory remedies available against the respondent occupier employer or trade organisation.[11] However, if the tribunal decides to order the lessor to pay compensation to the applicant, it may not make a compensation order against the occupier (respondent).[12]

---

1   DDA 1995, Sch 4, para 2(1).
2   Ibid, Sch 4, para 2(2).
3   Ibid, Sch 4, para 2(3).
4   Ibid, Sch 4, para 2(4).
5   Ibid, Sch 4, para 2(5)(a).
6   Ibid, Sch 4, para 2(5)(b). The provisions of the Disability Discrimination (Employment) Regulations 1996, SI 1996/1456, regs 10–15 (discussed above) will be relevant to this exercise.
7   Ibid, Sch 4, para 2(6).
8   Ibid, Sch 4, para 2(6)(a) and (b).
9   Ibid, Sch 4, para 2(7).
10   Ibid, Sch 4, para 2(6)(c).

Goods and services cases

6.3.15   Similar, but slightly different, enforcement provisions are made in respect of a duty to make alterations to premises by providers of services.[1] These provisions are not yet in force (but will be brought into force when the duty to make reasonable adjustments to the physical fabric of premises in Part III cases is effective from 2004). Where any question arises as to whether a service provider occupying premises under a lease has failed to comply with a duty to make reasonable adjustments by failing to make a particular alteration to premises, any constraint attributable to the fact that the service provider occupies the premises under a lease must be ignored, unless the occupier has applied to the lessor in writing for consent to make the alteration.[2] This is a similar principle to that in employment cases.

1   DDA 1995, Sch 4, Part II.
2   Ibid, Sch 4, para 5.

6.3.16   A novelty is the provision for a reference to be made to the court where the lessor has refused consent for such an alteration to be made by the occupier.[1] A reference may also be made where the lessor has given consent to the alteration but has made the consent subject to one or more conditions. In both cases, the occupier must have applied in writing to the lessor for the necessary consent. In these circumstances, the occupier or a disabled person (who has an interest in the proposed alteration to the premises being made) may refer the matter to the county court.[2] It does not seem to be contemplated that such a reference can only be made where legal proceedings have been commenced.[3] These provisions would appear to provide for a preliminary clarification of the rights of the parties concerned by the court, even where litigation based upon a complaint of unlawful disability discrimination has not been initiated or contemplated. Where the matter has been referred to the court in this manner, the court shall determine whether the lessor's refusal was unreasonable or whether any conditions imposed upon consent are unreasonable.[4] If the court decides that the lessor's refusal of consent to the alteration (or any conditions imposed upon the consent) was unreasonable then the court may make an appropriate declaration at its discretion. It may also make an order authorising the occupier to make an alteration specified in the order.[5] Such an order may require the occupier to comply with specified conditions.[6]

1   DDA 1995, Sch 4, para 6(1). There is no equivalent in employment cases.
2   In Scotland, the sheriff court. See DDA 1995, Sch 4, para 6(2).
3   Under DDA 1995, s 25.
4   DDA 1995, Sch 4, para 6(3). Future regulations made under Sch 4, para 8 may assist here.
5   Ibid, Sch 4, para 6(4).
6   Ibid, Sch 4, para 6(5).

6.3.17   If litigation has been commenced, then in any court proceedings where a question arises about a duty to make a reasonable adjustment by an alteration to premises occupied under a lease, either the claimant (in Scotland, the pursuer) or the occupier may ask the court to join (in Scotland, sist) the lessor as a party to the proceedings.[1] The court must grant such a request if it is made before the hearing commences,[2] otherwise the granting of such a request is at the court's discretion.[3] Such a request to join the lessor to proceedings cannot be made once the court has determined the claim.[4] If the lessor has been joined (or sisted) as a party to the proceedings, then the court has certain powers in relation to the lessor if certain conditions are satisfied.

1   DDA 1995, Sch 4, para 7(1).
2   Ibid, Sch 4, para 7(2).
3   Ibid, Sch 4, para 7(3).
4   Ibid, Sch 4, para 7(4).

6.3.18   The court may determine whether the lessor has refused consent to the alteration at issue or whether the lessor has consented to the alteration but subject to one or more conditions.[1] If so, in either case, the tribunal may then determine whether the refusal (or any of the conditions) was unreasonable.[2] Where such a finding has been made, the court may make such a declaration as it considers appropriate or order the lessor to pay compensation to the claimant or pursuer.[3] Although this is not made explicit, it seems logical that any such remedy against the lessor may be made in addition to or instead of any remedy that the court would be able to make against the occupier who is the defendant (or defender) to the proceedings. However, if the court decides to order the lessor to pay compensation to the claimant or pursuer, it may not make a parallel compensation order against the occupier.[4] Moreover, the court is also given an additional or alternative power which might prove quite radical in practice. If the court has determined that the lessor's refusal of consent to (or conditions imposed upon) an alteration was unreasonable, it may make an order authorising the occupier to make an alteration specified in the order.[5] Such an order may require the occupier to comply with any conditions specified in the order.[6]

1   DDA 1995, Sch 4, para 7(5)(a).
2   Ibid, Sch 4, para 7(5)(b). Any future regulations made under Sch 4, para 8 will be relevant to
    this exercise.
3   Ibid, Sch 4, para 7(6)(a) or (c).
4   Ibid, Sch 4, para 7(8).
5   Ibid, Sch 4, para 7(6)(b).
6   Ibid, Sch 4, para 7(7).

Management and disposal of premises

6.3.19   The above provisions[1] do not apply to discrimination against disabled persons in relation to the disposal and management of premises.[2] This is because there is no parallel duty to make reasonable adjustments in that area as there is in respect of employment, trade organisations or services. There is no duty upon a private or domestic landlord to make or consent to changes or alterations to the property when a disabled person is seeking to become a tenant.[3] However, as previously noted, the provisions of s 26 may act to invalidate any prejudicial term within a main tenancy agreement, such as one seeking to prevent the tenant sub-letting the rented property to disabled persons.

1   DDA 1995, s 27 and Sch 4, Part II.
2   Under DDA 1995, ss 22–24.
3   HL Deb, vol 566, col 1016.

Chapter 7

EDUCATION

7.1 INTRODUCTION

7.1.1 Controversially, the DDA 1995 did not include access to education within the scope of its anti-discrimination provisions. Instead, in contrast to the position in discrimination law generally,[1] education was explicitly excluded from the scope of services for the purposes of Part III of the Act.[2] The controversial aspect of this exclusion is that education is recognised as being crucial to the aspirations of disabled persons to enjoy full and equal opportunities.[3] In many respects, the new right to freedom from discrimination in employment[4] will be undermined if educational opportunities are not equally available to disabled persons to enable them to compete with a well-qualified labour force as they seek to enter the competitive labour market. Nevertheless, the Act did address the question of access to education by means other than via the anti-discrimination framework contained in Part III of the Act. This was achieved in Part IV of the Act, provisions of which are now found elsewhere in the book (but discussed below).

---

1   See Part III of the SDA 1975 and RRA 1976.
2   DDA 1995, s 19(5). As to the provisions on services generally, see ss 19–21 and Chapter 5. This exclusion is subject to any provision to the contrary that may be made by regulations made by the Secretary of State (proviso to s 19(5)). At the time of writing, no such regulations have been made. The Secretary of State is empowered to exclude such other services as may be prescribed by regulations (s 19(5)(c)). It is not thought that this power will be used in the short term.
3   See generally, Disability Rights Task Force, *From Exclusion to Inclusion: A Report of the Disability Rights Task Force for Disabled People* (1999, London: DfEE) (DRTF Report) Chapter 4.
4   DDA 1995, Part II. See Chapter 3.

7.2 EDUCATION AND ANTI-DISCRIMINATION LAW

7.2.1 The 1994 Green Paper anticipated that the right of access to goods and services would not apply to educational facilities.[1] It was thought that provision for disabled pupils and students was already best served by being the subject of other legislation.[2] This disapplication of the new right of access was confirmed by the 1995 White Paper, which went on to promise fresh initiatives in respect of educational opportunities for disabled persons.[3] The exclusion of access to education from the right not to be discriminated against as a disabled person in relation to the provision of goods, facilities and services was enshrined in the DDA 1995.[4]

---

1   *A Consultation on Government Measures to Tackle Discrimination Against Disabled People* (July 1994) para 4.9.

2   As this book is a text on disability discrimination law, it is not proposed to explore the
    relevant law of education in any detail. See the Education Act 1996 (in England and Wales),
    the Education (Scotland) Act 1980 (together with Scottish Office Circular 4/96) and the
    Education (Northern Ireland) Order 1996, SI 1996/274 (Part II). See also the statutory *Code
    of Practice on the Identification and Assessment of Special Educational Needs* (Department for
    Education and Employment). See further, *Meeting Special Educational Needs: A Programme of
    Action* (Department for Education and Employment); *Shaping the Future of Special Education:
    An Action Programme for Wales* (Welsh Office); and *Code of Practice on Schools Admissions*
    (Department for Education and Employment).
3   *Ending Discrimination Against Disabled People* (Cm 2729: January 1995) para 4.6 and Chapter 6.
4   DDA 1995, s 19(5)(a).

7.2.2   First, the anti-discrimination provisions in Part III of the Act[1] do not apply to education which is funded or secured by a 'relevant body'.[2] A 'relevant body' is statutorily defined and means:[3]

–   a local education authority in England and Wales;
–   an education authority in Scotland;
–   the Funding Agency for Schools;
–   the Schools Funding Council for Wales;
–   the Further Education Funding Council for England;
–   the Further Education Funding Council for Wales;
–   the Scottish Further Education Funding Council;
–   the Higher Education Funding Council for England;
–   the Scottish Higher Education Funding Council;
–   the Higher Education Funding Council for Wales;
–   the Teacher Training Agency;
–   a voluntary organisation;
–   a body of a prescribed kind;[4]
–   an education and library board in Northern Ireland.[5]

Secondly, Part III of the Act does not apply to education 'provided at an establishment which is funded by' one of the relevant bodies listed above or which is funded by a Minister of the Crown (including the Treasury) or by the Department of Education for Northern Ireland.[6] Thirdly, those provisions of the Act do not apply to education provided at 'any other establishment which is a school' as defined.[7] This exclusion ensures that private educational establishments are treated on an equal footing with those in the public and maintained sectors.

1   DDA 1995, ss 19–21.
2   Ibid, s 19(5)(a)).
3   Ibid, s 19(6), as amended by the School Standards and Framework Act 1998, s 140(3) and
    Sch 31, and the Teaching and Higher Education Act 1998, s 38.
4   That is, one prescribed by regulations under the Act.
5   By virtue of DDA 1995, Sch 8, para 9(3).
6   DDA 1995, s 19(5)(a)(i) and Sch 8, para 9(2).
7   Ibid, s 19(5)(a)(ii) and Sch 8, para 9(2). A 'school' is one defined in the Education Act 1996,
    s 4(1)–(2); the Education (Scotland) Act 1980, s 135(1); or the Education and Libraries
    (Northern Ireland) Order 1986, SI 1986/594.

7.2.3   This is a comprehensive list of exclusions which will apply to schools, colleges and universities in the public sector or which are in receipt of public funds or which are wholly in the private sector. The effect of these provisions is to exclude education in pre-school institutions, primary schools, secondary schools, colleges and universities from the rights of access provided in the DDA 1995. Education does not count as the provision of goods, facilities or services for the purposes of the anti-discrimination measures in Part III of the Act. While employment in educational establishments will be within the prohibition on disability discrimination contained in Part II of the Act, the 1995 legislation does not touch upon educational opportunities or the rights of disabled pupils or students within such educational establishments. In particular, the aspirations of disabled children to mainstream education rather than segregated education are not addressed by the 1995 Act, nor is the right of disabled children or adults to physical access to and reasonable accommodation within educational institutions.

7.2.4   There is one lacuna (which may or may not have been intentional) in the exclusion of education from the anti-discrimination framework. The exclusion clearly applies only to 'education' per se. Although the term 'education' is not defined in the Act, it clearly does not extend to non-educational facilities or services which an educational establishment happens to provide alongside its curricular activities. For example, many schools and colleges allow the public to use their sporting facilities (such as swimming pools, playing fields and racquet sports arenas) with or without payment and outside the core scholastic timetable. Such arrangements necessarily involve the public provision of facilities or services which would be caught by Part III rather than by the exclusion of education. Schools are also often used as polling stations during local and central government elections, and it is possible that access to such buildings for this purpose would involve the provision of a facility to the public.[1] Of course, in both examples, it would be necessary to identify who the provider of the facilities or services was – but it would not matter whether it was the school authority itself or whether it was some other legal person merely using the educational premises under a licence or other legal relationship.[2]

---

1   Local authorities are, in any event, under a duty to review arrangements for polling stations, including disabled access, by virtue of the Representation of the People Act 1983, s 18. See also HL Deb, vol 564, cols 2005–2006.
2   Note DDA 1995, s 19(3)(h).

7.2.5   The Secretary of State has moved by regulation to exempt certain educational services from Part III.[1] In so doing, the regulations may have plugged some of the gaps in the attempted exclusion of education from the anti-discrimination framework of the Act. The regulations serve to exclude from Part III coverage of certain youth and community services provided by education authorities or voluntary organisations (such as the Scouts or Guides), the provision of facilities for research in certain circumstances, and some examination and assessment services.[2]

---

1   Insofar as they do not already fall within s 19(5)(a) of the DDA 1995, as explained at **7.2.1**. See the Disability Discrimination (Services and Premises) Regulations 1996, SI 1996/1836, reg 9 (in force 2 December 1996) made under s 19(5)(c).

2   Rights of Access Code of Practice, paras 2.18–2.20.

7.2.6   First,[1] Part III does not apply to services provided by a local educational authority (in Scotland, an education authority) in carrying out its functions under certain education legislation.[2] This relates to the statutory duty on an education authority to secure the provision for its area of adequate facilities for full-time or part-time further education suitable for the requirements of persons over compulsory school age. This includes vocational, social, physical and recreational training. It also includes organised leisure-time occupation – provided in connection with the provision of further education – in such organised cultural training and recreative activities as are suited to their requirements, for any persons over compulsory school age who are able and willing to profit by facilities provided for that purpose. Education authorities must give particular attention to persons with learning difficulties when exercising these functions. The regulations also cover the statutory duty placed on such authorities to secure that the facilities for further education include adequate facilities for recreation and social and physical training. An education authority may establish, maintain and manage camps, holiday classes, playing fields, play centres and other places (including playgrounds, gymnasiums and swimming baths) for this purpose, and may organise games, expeditions and other activities. The anti-discrimination provisions of Part III of the Act do not apply to these facilities or services.

1   Disability Discrimination (Services and Premises) Regulations 1996, SI 1996/1836, reg 9(1)(a).
2   Education Act 1996, ss 2 or 508; Education (Scotland) Act 1980, s 1(3).

7.2.7   Secondly,[1] Part III does not apply to the provision by a voluntary organisation of social, cultural and recreational activities and facilities for physical education and training where such activities are designed to promote the personal or educational development of persons taking part in them. Thirdly,[2] the provision of facilities for research (including the supervision of or guidance of research) at a relevant establishment is not covered by the provisions of Part III of the Act.[3] Fourthly,[4] those provisions do not embrace the assessment at a relevant establishment of pupils or students in connection with education provided to them by the establishment or by another relevant establishment. This also excludes the assessment at a relevant establishment of pupils or students to whom education has not been provided by the establishment where the assessment is undertaken.[5]

1   Disability Discrimination (Services and Premises) Regulations 1996, SI 1996/1836, reg 9(1)(b). The DRTF recommends the abolition of this exemption: DRTF Report, recommendation 4.18.
2   Ibid, reg 9(1)(c).
3   A 'relevant establishment' means an establishment funded by one of the bodies listed in **7.2.2** (except a body of a prescribed kind or, in Northern Ireland, an education and library board) or by a Minister of the Crown or any other establishment which is a school as defined: ibid, reg 9(2)(a) and (b) which cross-refer to DDA 1995, s 19(5)(a)(ii) and (6).
4   Disability Discrimination (Services and Premises) Regulations 1996, SI 1996/1836, reg 9(1)(d)(i) and see reg 9(2).

5   Disability Discrimination (Services and Premises) Regulations 1996, SI 1996/1836,
    reg 9(1)(d)(ii).

7.2.8   These are complex provisions and it remains to be seen how far the regulations operate wholly to exclude these services which are closely connected with the provision of education. However, it is suggested that these regulations are not wide enough to exclude from the scope of Part III a whole raft of services, facilities and activities which may be provided on school, college or university premises. In addition to the examples already given, student unions would not seem to be excluded,[1] while many colleges and universities allow their halls of residence to be used for conferences and self-catering holiday facilities open to the public during vacations and are thus subject to the Act.[2]

1   Unless they are caught by the Disability Discrimination (Services and Premises) Regulations
    1996, SI 1996/1836, reg 9(1)(b) (see **7.2.7**).
2   See the further examples given in Rights of Access Code of Practice, para 2.19.

Disability Rights Task Force

7.2.9   The Disability Rights Task Force regarded the lack of protection from unfair discrimination in education for disabled children as unacceptable, but rejected the simplistic solution of removing the education exclusion from the DDA 1995.[1] Instead, it recommends that providers of school education of all descriptions should be placed under a statutory duty not to discriminate unfairly against a disabled pupil, for a reason relating to his or her disability, in the provision of education. It also recommends that the pupil's parents should have a right of redress and that there should be a defence for *acceptable* less favourable treatment.[2] The Task Force goes further by advocating a statutory duty on school education providers to review policies, practices and procedures and to make reasonable adjustments to any that discriminate against or have an adverse impact upon disabled pupils.[3] Moreover, a duty to make reasonable adjustments – by taking reasonable steps to provide education by an alternative method – is suggested to overcome physical barriers which place disabled pupils at a substantial disadvantage in comparison with non-disabled pupils.[4] Furthermore, a right to adjustments to achieve physical access and access to the curriculum is urged.[5] Similar proposals affecting further, higher and adult education (and the Youth Service provision of local authorities) are also made.[6]

1   DRTF Report, p 48, para 14.
2   Ibid, recommendation 4.4.
3   Ibid, recommendations 4.5 and 4.6.
4   Ibid, recommendation 4.7.
5   Ibid, recommendation 4.10.
6   Ibid, recommendations 4.13 and 4.17.

7.3   EDUCATION AND POLICY-MAKING

7.3.1   Although the provision of education is not generally subject to the anti-discrimination principles in the DDA 1995, Part IV of the Act amended existing education legislation so as to encourage policy-making and action by educational institutions to promote the integration of disabled pupils and students.[1] These provisions apply to schools, colleges and universities.

---

1 See originally, DDA 1995, ss 29–31.

Schools

7.3.2 The DDA 1995 approached the task of improving educational opportunities and access for disabled pupils by amending the provisions of the Education Acts setting out the duties of governing bodies (in the case of county, voluntary or grant-maintained schools) and local education authorities (in the case of maintained nursery schools) in relation to pupils with special educational needs (SEN).[1] Information relating to pupils with SEN is required to be included in annual reporting mechanisms.[2] As the Government at that time explained:

> 'One of the major themes in the Education Act 1993 was that mainstream schools should play their full part in providing for pupils with special needs at every stage; and that a school's duties should be clarified through the code of practice for the identification and assessment of such children ... Local accountability is ensured through the requirement on schools to formulate and publish information about their policy for children with special needs, keeping parents and prospective parents informed. The publication of SEN policies will help to prevent the possibility that parents could feel inclined to send their child to a special school on the basis that they did not know enough about the SEN provision in local mainstream schools.'[3]

The 1995 reforms were intended to build upon that foundation.

---

1 See Education Act 1993, s 161(5); now Education Act 1996, s 317(5).
2 See originally, DDA 1995, s 29(1) now repealed by Education Act 1996, s 582(2) and Sch 38, Part I.
3 HL Deb, vol 564, cols 1993–1994.

7.3.3 Since 1 January 1997, the 'annual report' for each county, voluntary or grant-maintained school is required to include a report containing information as to the:

– arrangements for admission of disabled pupils;
– steps taken to prevent disabled pupils from being treated less favourably than other pupils;
– facilities provided to assist access to school by disabled pupils.[1]

The 'annual report' in question is a reference to the report to parents required to be prepared under the articles of government for the school.[2] This gloss upon the existing obligations of schools' governing bodies applies only in respect of pupils who are disabled persons within the meaning of the 1995 legislation,[3] whether or not they have a statutory SEN statement. It is intended that by these means schools which are inaccessible to disabled children will be required to admit it and to consider how they might be made accessible in a cost-effective way.[4] Parental rights might also be strengthened by giving dissatisfied parents a means to voice concerns about a school's non-compliance with its own stated policies through the existing local admissions appeals arrangements. The measures were hoped to encourage genuine and full integration of disabled pupils in mainstream education 'as far as possible'.[5]

1 Education Act 1993, s 161(6) as inserted by DDA 1995, s 29(2) (which was repealed by Education Act 1996, s 582(2) and Sch 38, Part I); see now Education Act 1996, s 317(6). See *School Prospectuses and Governors' Annual Reports* (DfEE Circulars 11/96 (primary schools) and 12/96 (secondary schools)).
2 In accordance with the Education (No 2) Act 1986, s 30 or the Education Act 1993, Sch 6, para 8. The cross-reference is made in the Education Act 1993, s 161(7) as inserted by DDA 1995, s 29(2) (which was repealed by Education Act 1996, s 582(2) and Sch 38, Part I). See now Education Act 1996, s 317(6), (7).
3 Education Act 1993, s 161(7) as inserted by DDA 1995, s 29(2) (which was repealed by Education Act 1996, s 582(2) and Sch 38, Part I). See now Education Act 1996, s 317(6), (7).
4 HL Deb, vol 564, col 1994.
5 Ibid, cols 1994–1995.

Teacher Training Agency

7.3.4 The Teacher Training Agency is the body which has responsibility for funding institutions providing teacher training. In exercising its functions, the Teacher Training Agency must have regard to the requirements of disabled persons.[1] Although this is not made clear, it is arguable that this will cover the needs of disabled persons entering the teaching profession as well as the training of teachers in respect of the needs of disabled pupils.

1 Education Act 1994, s 1(4) as inserted by DDA 1995, s 29(3).

Further education colleges and institutions

7.3.5 In justifying the exclusion of further and higher education from the services provisions of Part III of the DDA 1995, the Government at that time was said to be placing a high priority on widening access to colleges and universities,[1] but wished to consider the practical effects of inclusion and sought to avoid undermining the strategic role which the further and higher education funding councils play.[2] The Government elected for what it regarded as a coherent programme for encouraging access, enforceable through the existing complaints procedures rather than by litigation.[3] Nevertheless, it recognised that there was a genuine problem in guaranteeing access for disabled persons to educational opportunities in colleges and universities.

1 HL Deb, vol 564, col 1989.
2 Ibid, col 1989.
3 Ibid, col 1990.

7.3.6 The DDA 1995 amended the provisions of the Further and Higher Education Act 1992 which sets out the framework for further and higher education for disabled students (including those with learning disabilities) in

England and Wales. The amendments contained in the Act apply only to England and Wales and not to Scotland. Legislation already required Scottish colleges to submit development plans including information on provisions made for disabled students.[1] The 1992 statute 'requires the further education funding councils to act in a strategic manner to secure sufficient and adequate provision of further education'.[2] The councils must take particular account of the needs of the population in terms of location, equipment, aptitudes and abilities, and they have especial responsibilities in respect of disabled students. To those ends, the Further Education Funding Council for England (FEFCE) requires colleges to submit strategic plans, including analysis of local needs, and its funding methodology takes into account the needs of disabled students. Part IV of the DDA 1995 sought to build upon the existing strategy by amending the Further and Higher Education Act 1992.[3]

---

1   Further and Higher Education (Scotland) Act 1992, s 22.
2   HL Deb, vol 564, col 1990.
3   DDA 1995, s 30(1).

7.3.7   The funding councils for further education institutions and colleges are required to place conditions upon the financial support they give to such educational establishments.[1] In particular, the administration of funds by further education funding councils are subject to a new set of conditions for financial support given to further education colleges.[2] The new conditions are expressly without prejudice to the funding councils' existing powers to impose conditions on the granting of such financial support.[3] Those additional specific conditions require the governing body to publish annual 'disability statements' containing information about the provision of facilities for education made by the institution in respect of 'disabled persons' and may include conditions relating to the provision made (or to be made) by the institution with respect to disabled persons.[4]

---

1   Further and Higher Education Act 1992, s 5.
2   Ibid, s 5(6)(b) and (7A) as amended by DDA 1995, s 30(2).
3   Ibid, s 5(6)(b).
4   Ibid, s 5(7A) as inserted by DDA 1995, s 30(3). The phrase 'disabled persons' means only
    such persons as satisfy the definition of 'disabled person' in DDA 1995, ss 1–2 and Schs 1–2
    (see Chapter 2): Further and Higher Education Act 1992, s 5(7B) as inserted by DDA 1995,
    s 30(3).

7.3.8   The information to be contained in an annual disability statement about the provision of facilities made by further education institutions in England and Wales in respect of disabled persons is prescribed by regulations.[1] An annual disability statement must cover the following matters:[2]

–   policies of the institution relating to the provision of facilities for education;
–   names of a member or members of staff with special responsibility for disabled persons;
–   admission arrangements;

–   educational facilities and support, including academic and curriculum support, relevant staff expertise, and technology and equipment available;
–   additional support or special arrangements during examinations and assessments;
–   facilities and support associated with educational facilities and support, including counselling and welfare arrangements;
–   physical access to educational and other facilities.

The statement should also contain information about arrangements for handling complaints and (where applicable) appeals in respect of admission arrangements, educational facilities and support, additional support or special arrangements during examinations and assessments, facilities and support associated with educational facilities and support (including counselling and welfare arrangements), and physical access to educational and other facilities.

1   Education (Disability Statements for Further Education Institutions) Regulations 1996, SI 1996/1664 made under Further and Higher Education Act 1992, ss 5(7A)–(7B) and 89(4) as amended by DDA 1995, s 30. The Regulations came into force on 31 July 1996.
2   Ibid, reg 2.

7.3.9   These provisions do not give disabled students directly enforceable rights as such, but they will 'be able to seek redress from the councils on the rare occasions when provision fails to meet expectations raised by the information' contained in a statutory disability statement.[1] It would seem that ultimately a funding council could demand repayment of a grant paid to a college which fails to meet the new legislative requirements.

1   HL Deb, vol 564, col 1991.

Further education funding councils

7.3.10   Further amendments to the 1992 legislation build upon the strategic role of the further education funding councils. The funding councils are required to make an annual written report to the Secretary of State on the progress made during the previous year in the provision of further education for disabled students in their area and their plans for future provision of further education for disabled students.[1] It is envisaged that the funding councils will draw on existing review and planning mechanisms, as well as new information generated from the disability statements produced by colleges and the evidence being gathered by the FEFCE's committee on education and disability (the Tomlinson Committee).[2]

1   Further and Higher Education Act 1992, s 8(6) as inserted by DDA 1995, s 30(4). The term 'disabled students' refers only to students who are disabled persons under the DDA 1995: Further and Higher Education Act 1992, s 8(7) as inserted by DDA 1995, s 30(4).
2   HL Deb, vol 564, col 1991.

Local education authorities

7.3.11   The 1995 legislation also amended the functions of local education authorities (LEAs) in respect of further education in order to underpin the duties of colleges and funding councils.[1] Local education authorities are placed under a duty to publish disability statements at prescribed intervals.[2] Such statements must contain information (to be prescribed by regulations) about the provision of facilities for further education made by the LEA in respect of disabled persons within the meaning of the DDA 1995.[3] The intention is to ensure that courses provided by LEAs enjoyed 'parity of esteem' with FEFC-funded courses and that disabled students should be better informed about such locally provided courses.[4]

1 Education Act 1944, s 41 as amended by DDA 1995, s 30(7) (now repealed by Education Act 1996, s 582(2) and Sch 38, Part I). See now Education Act 1996, ss 2, 15 and 528.
2 Ibid, s 41(2A) as inserted by DDA 1995, s 30(8). The prescribed intervals will be dealt with in regulations (Education Act 1944, s 41(2B)). See now Education Act 1996, s 528.
3 Ibid, s 41(2B) as inserted by DDA 1995, s 30(8). See now Education Act 1996, s 528.
4 HL Deb, vol 566, cols 1032–1033.

Universities and higher education institutions

7.3.12 Prior to the DDA 1995, the Secretary of State provided mere guidance to the higher education funding councils that they should have regard to the needs of disabled students in universities and institutions of higher education. In a much debated change,[1] since 31 July 1996 the higher education funding councils for England, Wales and Scotland are now required to have regard to the requirements of disabled persons when exercising their statutory functions.[2] In both cases, the new statutory duty applies only in respect of disabled persons within the meaning of the DDA 1995.[3] The higher education funding councils are also empowered to make grants, loans or other payments to the governing body of a university or higher education institution conditional upon a requirement that the governing body should publish 'disability statements'.[4] This is without prejudice to the existing powers of the funding councils to impose conditions on governing bodies, except that the requirement to publish periodic disability statements is mandatory. Disability statements are to be published at intervals specified in the conditions subject to which grants, loans or other payments are made by a council.[5]

1 See, for example, HL Deb, vol 564, cols 874–876 and 1983–1986.
2 Further and Higher Education Act 1992, s 62(7A) as inserted by DDA 1995, s 30(5); Further and Higher Education (Scotland) Act 1992, s 37(4A) as inserted by DDA, s 31(1)–(2).
3 Ibid, s 62(7B) as inserted by DDA 1995, s 30(5); Ibid, s 37(4B) as inserted by DDA 1995, s 31(2).
4 Ibid, s 65(4A) as inserted by DDA 1995, s 30(6); Ibid, s 40(5) as inserted by DDA 1995, s 31(3).
5 Ibid, s 65(4B) as inserted by DDA 1995, s 30(6); Ibid, s 40(6) as inserted by DDA 1995, s 31(3).

7.3.13 A 'disability statement' is a statement containing information (specified in the conditions subject to which grants, loans or other payments are made by a council) about the provision of facilities for education and research made by the university or institution in respect of disabled persons (as defined in the DDA 1995).[1] The Higher Education Funding Council for England (HEFCE) and its Welsh and Scottish counterparts (HEFCW and SHEFC) have each issued a specification for disability statements required from institutions funded by each Council.[2] It is anticipated that a disability statement will be produced every three years, but should be updated and resubmitted where there have been significant changes.[3] Statements should be published and may be referred to in other publications (such as prospectuses).[4]

---

1   Further and Higher Education Act 1992, s 65(4B) as inserted by DDA 1995, s 30(6); Further and Higher Education (Scotland) Act 1992, s 40(6) as inserted by DDA 1995, s 31(3). It is clear that the 'facilities' referred to do not merely include *physical* facilities: HL Deb, vol 566, cols 278–279.
2   See HEFCE Circular 8/96 (May 1996); HEFCW Circular W96/43HE (June 1996); SHEFC Circular 47/96 (October 1996). See also: SHEFC, *Disability Discrimination and the Changing Legislative Context: Implications for the Scottish Higher Education Sector* (SHEFC Circular 9/99).
3   See, for example: HEFCE Circular 8/96, para 18.
4   Ibid, paras 20–21. The Internet is being used for dissemination purposes. The Careers Advisory Network on Disability Opportunities (CANDO) at Lancaster University is acting as a host for disability statements. See http://cando/lancs.ac.uk.

7.3.14   While a disability statement should describe facilities for education and research offered by a higher education institution to disabled persons, it is also designed to inform the funding council about such provision and to highlight good practice.[1] Although institutions are free to decide what facilities should be offered, they are encouraged to consider provision for disabled students and 'to plan strategically for future developments'.[2] Statements should be 'concise, informative and developmental'; may if necessary make reference to accessible secondary sources; and may need to be produced in alternative formats or media.[3] Statements should be structured so as to provide information under the headings of current policy, current provision, and future activity and policy development.

---

1   See, for example, HEFCE Circular 8/96, para 8.
2   Ibid, para 9.
3   Ibid, para 10.

7.3.15   As far as current policy is concerned, the statement should contain general information on policies and procedures relating to disabled students for:[1]

–   equal opportunities;
–   access and admissions;
–   examinations and assessments;
–   quality assessment, and monitoring and evaluation of support services;
–   staff development and training programmes;
–   provision of financial assistance to disabled students;
–   charging students for certain facilities.

If an institution does not have policies for the above areas, it should give an overview of its policies affecting disabled students.

---

1   See, for example, HEFCE Circular 8/96, paras 12–13. The date on which the policy or procedure became effective should also be stated. The HEFCW also includes complaints and appeals procedures in the list of existing policy: HEFCW Circular W96/43HE, para 8.

7.3.16 In connection with current provision, the statement should describe the nature and range of provision for disabled students, including:[1]

– names and titles (and contact details) of the co-ordinator and member of senior management responsible for disabled students;
– examples of the types of information, advice, services and materials available, and a broad picture of how the institution provides support;[2]
– academic services and support arrangements (for example, special provision for examinations and marking);
– information technology provision;
– a general description of the physical environment;
– specific information on medical facilities, transport, religious and spiritual worship, external services, and award ceremonies.

The statement should indicate any restrictions on services and facilities, and an indication of the number of disabled students at the institution.[3] Finally, the statement should outline plans for policy development and improvements to provision in the short to long term, covering at least the next 3 years.[4]

1   See, for example, HEFCE Circular 8/96, para 14.
2   The HEFCE circular poses some questions that might be addressed: ibid, para 14(b).
3   Ibid, paras 15–16.
4   Ibid, para 17.

7.3.17 The amendments to the powers of the higher education funding councils in respect of the administration of funds are designed to achieve the:

> '... intention that the [disability] statements would assist disabled students and funding councils generally in understanding the provision available for education and research in the particular institution ... The statements would thus go wider than simply including information about physical facilities. It will be a matter for the funding councils, in consultation, to determine how to specify the information needed in the statements to achieve that in a viable and cost-effective way ... [T]he provision of information will not *ipso facto* require any changes in the nature of the facilities offered by the institution.'[1]

This is apparently achieved without compromising the guarantees of academic freedom inherent in the 1992 legislation. There is nothing in the DDA 1995 which might require a university to change admissions arrangements, modify course structures or alter assessment programmes in order to meet the needs of disabled students. Moreover, nothing in a disability statement is intended to be used to pressurise universities or funding councils to change curriculum and admissions policies.[2] However, it is hoped that disability statements will concentrate the minds of universities and will encourage them to be receptive to the needs of disabled students.

1   HL Deb, vol 564, col 1993.
2   Ibid, vol 566, col 1036.

Chapter 8

PUBLIC TRANSPORT

8.1 INTRODUCTION

8.1.1 The 1994 Green Paper considered whether the proposed general right of access should be extended to facilities for transport or travel.[1] It anticipated that the new right would not require modifications to transport systems where existing physical barriers prevented access. The 1995 White Paper confirmed that the new right would not apply to transport vehicles but would apply to stations.[2] It suggested that further initiatives would take place outside the framework of the proposed disability discrimination legislation. In the event, the initiatives were taken in Part V of the DDA 1995. Part V is not fully in force at the time of writing.

---

1 *A Consultation on Government Measures to Tackle Discrimination Against Disabled People* (July 1994) para 4.5.
2 *Ending Discrimination Against Disabled People* (Cm 2729: January 1995) para 4.6.

Transport services and Part III of the DDA 1995

8.1.2 The goods, facilities and services provisions in Part III[1] do not apply to any service 'so far as it consists of the use of any means of transport'.[2] This means that the Part III rights of access to services may require transport providers to make some (but not all) of their facilities or services accessible without discrimination to disabled people. For example, facilities and services such as timetables, ticketing arrangements, booking facilities, waiting areas, toilet facilities, platforms and other public areas are subject to the anti-discrimination provisions of the DDA 1995. Transport providers must consider what reasonable adjustments might be made in order to ensure that disabled passengers enjoy effective access to such facilities or services.

---

1 DDA 1995, ss 19–21.
2 Ibid, s 19(5)(b) subject to any provision to the contrary in future regulations (no such regulations have been proposed to date).

8.1.3 However, Part III does not require buses, coaches, taxis, trains, aeroplanes, ferries, ships or other forms of public transport (including heritage vehicles) to be accessible without discrimination or to be accommodating of the needs of disabled passengers.[1] There may be other legal or extra-legal sources which assist disabled persons to achieve a right of access in respect of transport vehicles. For example, some local authorities already make the accessibility of taxis the subject of licensing conditions. Nevertheless, the DDA 1995 does not create a general right of transport accessibility. For example, hire car and breakdown recovery services are not fully subject to the Part III duty to make reasonable adjustments (so far as they consist of the use of a means of transport, such as the hire car itself or a breakdown relay vehicle). Furthermore, discriminatory behaviour on board a transport vehicle (such as refusal to serve a disabled person in a restaurant car of a train) is not unlawful. The Disability Rights Task Force has recommended that the exemption for transport operators from the pre-2004 rights of access[2] should be removed, and that car hire and breakdown recovery services should be brought within the fold.[3]

1   HL Deb, vol 566, col 463. See Rights of Access Code of Practice, paras 2.21–2.22.
2   That is, the provisions of ss 19–21 with the exception of s 21(2)(a)–(c). See Chapter 5.
3   Disability Rights Task Force, *From Exclusion to Inclusion: A Report of the Disability Rights Task Force for Disabled People* (1999, London: DfEE) (DRTF Report). See, ibid, recommendations 7.2 and 7.5.

Transport employers and Part II of the DDA 1995

8.1.4   The exclusion of transport services from Part III of the DDA 1995 does not prevent disabled persons from enjoying a right to equal employment opportunity under Part II of the Act in respect of transport employers. By way of illustration, a disabled bus driver would be entitled not to be discriminated against by the transport provider in its guise as employer. Ironically, that might call for modifications to be made to a vehicle if that would be a reasonable adjustment called for under the provisions of Part II.[1] For example, a driver with impaired hearing might be entitled to the installation of a simple audio-visual signalling system which indicated when a passenger wished to alight.

1   DDA 1995, s 6. See Chapter 3 above.

Public transport and Part V of the DDA 1995

8.1.5   Although transport systems are not fully covered by the anti-discrimination measures in the DDA 1995, the Act does empower the Government to enact new accessibility standards for public transport. These accessibility standards will apply to taxis, public service vehicles and rail vehicles. They apply only to land-based transport services and do not apply to aircraft or ferries. These are the measures set out in Part V of the Act which provides a statutory framework for accessibility regulations. Each of the methods of transport covered by Part V are now examined in turn.

8.2   TAXIS

8.2.1   While many local authorities have attempted to improve the accessibility of taxis to disabled passengers through licensing conditions, the Government took the view during the passage of the DDA 1995 that such a piecemeal approach had been tried and had failed. The sponsors of the DDA 1995 expressed their 'clear intention' to introduce 'provisions to require that, from days to be determined, taxis newly licensed must, as a condition of licence, be accessible to all disabled people, including those who use wheelchairs'.[1]

Whilst accepting that there had been criticism of the current models of wheelchair-accessible taxis, it was also made 'absolutely clear that we are not talking about a universal requirement for the current purpose-built taxi design'.[2]

---

1 HL Deb, vol 564, col 2034. A date for the implementation of the taxi accessibility standards was not indicated at the time: HL Deb, vol 566, cols 453–454.
2 Ibid, vol 564, cols 2034–2035.

Taxi accessibility regulations

8.2.2 The Secretary of State is given power by DDA 1995 to make 'taxi accessibility regulations'.[1] The purpose of the regulations is to secure that it is possible for disabled persons:

−   to get into and out of taxis in safety;
−   to be carried in taxis in safety and in reasonable comfort;
−   to be conveyed in safety into and out of taxis while remaining in their wheelchairs (where a wheelchair-user);
−   to be carried in taxis in safety and in reasonable comfort while remaining in their wheelchairs (where a wheelchair-user).

The regulations are intended to 'focus clearly on the needs of all disabled people and will be drawn up in close consultation with the Disabled Persons Transport Advisory Committee' (DPTAC). Design parameters will be defined based on research and experience to provide 'optimum levels of accessibility' and manufacturers will be expected to meet the new market demand so created.[2]

---

1 DDA 1995, s 32(1).
2 HL Deb, vol 564, col 2035.

8.2.3 Such taxi accessibility regulations may in particular require 'regulated taxis' to conform with regulations as to:

−   the size of door openings for passenger use;
−   the floor area of 'passenger compartments';[1]
−   the amount of headroom in passenger compartments; and
−   the fitting of restraining devices designed to ensure the stability of a wheelchair while the taxi is moving.[2]

Moreover, the regulations may require drivers of regulated taxis plying for hire (or under hire) to comply with regulations as to the carrying of ramps or other devices designed to facilitate the loading and unloading of wheelchairs.[3] The regulations might also require the driver of a regulated taxi, in which a disabled person in a wheelchair is being carried (while remaining in the wheelchair), to comply with regulations as to the position in which the wheelchair is to be secured.[4] The effect of these provisions is that taxi drivers must recognise their duty to carry disabled customers. It would not be lawful for drivers to refuse to pick up a disabled passenger in a wheelchair 'on the pretext . . . that they are not carrying the ramps'.[5] A failure to comply with such accessibility regulations by a driver plying for hire (or under hire) will be a criminal offence.[6]

---

1   The meaning of this term is to be prescribed in future regulations: DDA 1995, s 32(5).
2   Ibid, s 32(2)(a).
3   Ibid, s 32(2)(b).
4   Ibid, s 32(2)(c).
5   HL Deb, vol 564, col 2035.
6   DDA 1995, s 32(3). On summary conviction, a person guilty of such an offence will be liable to a fine not exceeding level 3 on the standard scale: s 32(4).

Taxis to be covered by the regulations

8.2.4   To what taxis will these new regulations and duties apply? The regulations will define which taxis are to be regulated for these purposes. However, the regulations can only apply to a 'taxi' as narrowly defined.[1] A 'taxi' for this purpose means only a licensed vehicle.[2] It does not include a taxi which is drawn by a horse or other animal. The effect is that any new accessibility standards for taxis will apply only to hackney cabs or so-called 'black cabs' and will not apply to private hire cars or 'minicabs'.[3] At the same time, it is not intended that the taxi trade will in future be expected to make universal use of the London-style black cab or that the legislation (when in force) will produce a universal purpose-built taxi design.[4]

---

1   DDA 1995, s 32(5).
2   That is, one licensed under the Town Police Clauses Act 1847, s 37 or the Metropolitan Public Carriage Act 1869, s 6. In Northern Ireland, a taxi is a vehicle licensed to stand or ply for hire under the Road Traffic (Northern Ireland) Order 1981, art 61 and which seats not more than eight passengers in addition to the driver: DDA 1995, Sch 8, para 16(2).
3   HL Deb, vol 566, col 451. The Disability Rights Task Force recommends that the Disability Rights Commission should consider mechanisms for increasing the availability of accessible private hire vehicles (including the carrying of registered assistance dogs): DRTF Report, recommendation 7.3.
4   Ibid, col 453.

8.2.5   In order 'to ensure an orderly transition to the new requirements without damaging the viability of the taxi trade',[1] taxi licensing authorities[2] shall not grant a taxi licence unless the taxi conforms with the relevant taxi accessibility regulations.[3] However, the licensing requirements by reference to any taxi accessibility regulations apply only to newly licensed taxis, as opposed to taxis with existing licences and seeking renewal.[4] The intention is to regulate only new entrants to the taxi trade (or newly acquired taxis). It does not prevent the re-licensing of non-accessible taxis provided that, subject to 28 days' grace, the new licence comes into force immediately on the expiry of the previous licence.[5] As the relevant Minister put it, this:

> 'provides that a licensing authority may, after a certain date, only license taxis which comply with the construction requirements that will be set out in the regulations ... We are also mindful of the need to protect the interests of the cab trade, much of which comprises small businesses. While it is reasonable to expect new taxis to be fully accessible, it would ... be unreasonable to require someone who had recently purchased and licensed a new non-accessible vehicle to dispose of it prematurely.'[6]

However, it is not intended that this exceptional treatment should continue indefinitely. The Secretary of State may provide by order that this exemption shall cease to have effect on a specified date.[7] The effect of such an order may be varied for different areas or localities.[8] Thus it is contemplated that there will be a future date beyond which no non-accessible vehicle can be re-licensed as a taxi. That date is to be the subject of consultation with the trade.

---

1   HL Deb, vol 564, col 2035.
2   See s 68(1) as to the meaning of this term.
3   DDA 1995, s 34(1).
4   Ibid, s 34(2). The provisions of s 34 are applied to Northern Ireland with appropriate substitutions: Sch 8, para 18.
5   HL Deb, vol 566, cols 440–441.
6   Ibid, vol 564, col 2035.
7   DDA 1995, s 34(3).
8   Ibid, s 34(4). By virtue of s 67(7), this is without prejudice to the generality of the powers to make regulations or orders by statutory instrument conferred by s 67(2)–(3).

Exemption regulations

8.2.6   It is hoped that these provisions will open up new markets for the taxi trade. However, it is acknowledged that compliance with the new standards could create difficulties. The Government recognised 'the enormously wide variations in types of area and of taxi use in this country'.[1] The 'strong presumption must be that, whatever the area, there will be now, or may be in the future, disabled people whose mobility would be enhanced by the availability of accessible vehicles'.[2] However, at the same time, the possibility that Part V of DDA 1995 'could jeopardise the viability of the trade in a particular area to the point at which there ceased to be taxi provision for anyone' was recognised.[3] The legislature wished to avoid that result.

---

1   HL Deb, vol 564, col 2036.
2   Ibid.
3   Ibid.

8.2.7   Accordingly, the Secretary of State may make 'exemption regulations' to enable taxi licensing authorities[1] to apply for an order to be exempt from the new licensing provisions.[2] This is so if the licensing authority believes that, having regard to 'circumstances prevailing in its area', the application of the licensing conditions would be 'inappropriate' and if their application would result in 'an unacceptable reduction in the number of taxis' in that area.[3] The exemption regulations may make particular provision and prescriptions requiring a licensing authority proposing to apply for an exemption order to carry out consultations,[4] to publish its proposal, to consider any representations made about the proposal (before it applies for an order), and to make its application in a prescribed form.[5] The Secretary of State must consider any application for an exemption order and consult the DPTAC (and any other persons the Secretary of State considers appropriate). Then the Secretary of State may make an exemption order (in the terms applied for or in such other terms as the Secretary of State considers appropriate) or refuse to make such an order.[6]

1   That is, a licensing authority responsible for licensing taxis in any area of England and Wales other than the area to which the Metropolitan Public Carriage Act 1869 applies: DDA 1995, s 35(7).
2   Ibid, s 35(1). Section 35 does not apply in Northern Ireland: ibid, Sch 8, para 19.
3   Ibid, s 35(3).
4   Including 'as a matter of course, disabled people and the taxi trade': HL Deb, vol 564, col 2036.
5   DDA 1995, s 35(2).
6   Ibid, s 35(4).

Swivel-seat regulations

8.2.8   Even if a taxi is exempted from the taxi accessibility regulations, there is still power to require an 'exempt taxi' to comply with 'swivel-seat regulations' as to the fitting and use of swivel seats in the taxi. The Secretary of State is given a power to make 'swivel-seat regulations' requiring any 'exempt taxi' plying for hire in an area in respect of which an exemption order[1] is in force to conform with provisions as to the fitting and use of swivel seats.[2] The term 'swivel seats' will be defined in regulations.[3] No further light on these proposed regulations is cast by the parliamentary debates on the legislation.[4]

1   That is, an order made under DDA 1995, s 35.
2   Ibid, s 35(5). An 'exempt taxi' is a taxi in relation to which s 34(1) would apply if there was not a s 35 exemption order in force: ibid, s 35(7). Note s 35(6) which cross-refers to s 34.
3   Ibid, s 35(7).
4   Although see HL Deb, vol 566, cols 1042–1043.

Duties of taxi drivers towards disabled passengers

8.2.9   Drivers of regulated taxis will be placed under new duties in respect of a taxi which has been hired by or for a disabled person in a wheelchair, or by a person who wishes to be accompanied by a disabled person in a wheelchair.[1] These duties (which are not yet in force) will be:

–   to carry in the taxi the passenger while he or she remains in the wheelchair;
–   not to make any additional charge for doing so;
–   to carry the wheelchair in the taxi if the passenger chooses to sit in a passenger seat; and
–   to take such steps as are necessary to ensure that the passenger is carried in the taxi in safety and in reasonable comfort.[2]

In addition, it will be the driver's statutory duty to give such assistance as may be reasonably required:

–   to enable the passenger to get into or out of the taxi;
–   to enable the passenger to be conveyed into and out of the taxi while in the wheelchair if the passenger wishes to remain in the wheelchair;
–   to load the passenger's luggage into or out of the taxi; and
–   to load the wheelchair into or out of the taxi if the passenger does not wish to remain in the wheelchair.[3]

A failure to comply with any of these duties without lawful excuse will be a criminal offence punishable upon summary conviction by a fine not exceeding level 3 on the standard scale.[4] However, there are certain defences and exemptions as follows.

---

1   DDA 1995, s 36(1).
2   Ibid, s 36(3)(a)–(d). The term 'the passenger' means the disabled person concerned and 'carry' means carry in the taxi concerned: s 36(2).
3   Ibid, s 36(3)(e).
4   Ibid, s 36(5).

8.2.10   The driver of a taxi is not required to carry more than one person in a wheelchair, or more than one wheelchair, on any one journey.[1] A taxi driver is not required to carry any person in circumstances in which it would otherwise be lawful for the driver to refuse to carry that person.[2] For example, a taxi driver could not be required to carry a disabled passenger where the taxi is already exceeding the number of passengers who may be carried in accordance with its licence. It will also be a defence to show that, even though the taxi conformed with any taxi accessibility regulations,[3] it would not have been possible for the wheelchair of the disabled passenger concerned to be carried in safety in the taxi.[4]

---

1   DDA 1995, s 36(4)(a) which also contemplates an exception in the case of a taxi of a prescribed description. No such prescription has been made at the time of writing.
2   Ibid, s 36(4)(b).
3   That is, under, ibid, s 32.
4   Ibid, s 36(6).

8.2.11   Provision is also made for the exemption of taxi drivers from these new statutory duties on medical grounds. A taxi licensing authority shall issue a driver with a certificate of exemption from the duties above if it is satisfied that it is appropriate to exempt the driver on medical grounds.[1] An exemption certificate may also be issued on the ground that the driver's physical condition makes it impossible or unreasonably difficult for him or her to comply with a taxi driver's duties imposed under DDA 1995.[2] The Government felt that this exception was important, especially for taxi drivers who themselves had a disability.[3] Provision is made for an appeal against a refusal to grant an exemption certificate.[4] The currency of the certificate of exemption shall be for such period as the licensing authority specifies on the certificate when issued.[5] Once an exemption certificate has been issued to a taxi driver, and so long as it remains in force, the driver is exempt from the statutory duties imposed,[6] provided an exemption notice (in a prescribed form and in a prescribed manner) is exhibited on the taxi.[7]

---

1   DDA 1995, s 36(7)(a). In Northern Ireland this power lies with the Department of the Environment: ibid, Sch 8, para 20. Provision is made in s 49 for criminal offences committed in connection with exemption certificates (for example, forgery or the making of false statements).

2   DDA 1995, s 36(7)(b).
3   HL Deb, vol 564, col 2036.
4   DDA 1995, s 38(1). Any person who is aggrieved by a refusal of a licensing authority to issue an exemption certificate under s 36 may appeal to the local magistrates court (or, in Northern Ireland, a court of summary jurisdiction) for the petty sessions area in which the licensing authority has its principal office: s 38(3). An appeal must be made within 28 days of the refusal: s 38(1). If the court allows such an appeal, it may direct the licensing authority to issue an exemption certificate and may specify the period of the currency of the exemption: s 38(2).
5   Ibid, s 36(8).
6   Under, ibid, s 36(3).
7   Ibid, s 36(9). The necessary prescriptions have yet to be made.

8.2.12   In order to address the problem of persons with sensory impairments (who use guide or hearing dogs) being refused access to taxis because they wish to be accompanied by their animal, DDA 1995 imposes additional duties on taxi drivers.[1] These duties arise where the taxi has been hired by or for a disabled person ('the passenger') accompanied by a guide dog or hearing dog.[2] The duties also apply where the taxi has been hired by a person who wishes to be accompanied in the taxi by a disabled person ('the passenger') accompanied by a guide or hearing dog.[3] The duties of a taxi driver in the above situations are to carry the disabled passenger's dog, allowing it to remain with the passenger in the taxi, and not to make any additional charge for so doing.[4] A breach of these duties is a criminal offence punishable on summary conviction by a fine not exceeding level 3 on the standard scale.[5] It is noteworthy that these duties apply to all taxis and not just to regulated taxis.

---

1   DDA 1995, s 37.
2   Ibid, s 37(1)(a) and (2). A guide dog is a dog trained to guide a blind person, while a hearing dog is a dog trained to assist a deaf person: ibid, s 37(11). Section 37 might also be applied by regulations in future to any other category of dog trained to assist a disabled person with a prescribed disability: ibid, s 37(9)–(10) and Sch 8, para 21(3). No such regulations or prescription have been made at the present.
3   Ibid, s 37(1)(b) and (2).
4   Ibid, s 37(3). The Disability Rights Task Force recommended that these provisions should be brought into force as soon as possible: DRTF Report, recommendation 7.4.
5   Ibid, s 37(4).

8.2.13   However, in the same way as an exemption may be made for the duties relating to the carrying of passengers in wheelchairs,[1] a licensing authority may exempt a driver from the duties in respect of a disabled passenger accompanied by a guide dog or hearing dog.[2] This is achieved by means of an exemption certificate if the licensing authority is satisfied that such exemption is appropriate on medical grounds.[3] In deciding that question, the authority must have particular regard to the physical characteristics of the taxi in question.[4] For example, this exemption might cover a driver who has a medical condition that is aggravated by dogs, such as an asthmatic condition or an allergy.[5] Provision is made for an appeal against a refusal to grant an exemption certificate.[6]

---

1   DDA 1995, s 36. Similar provisions are also made as to the issue and currency of a s 32 exemption certificate and the display of such certificate in the taxi: s 37(7)–(8).

2   DDA 1995, s 37.

3   Ibid, s 37(5). In Northern Ireland this power lies with the Department of the Environment: Sch 8, para 21. Provision is made in s 49 for criminal offences committed in connection with exemption certificates (for example, forgery or the making of false statements).

4   Ibid, s 37(6).

5   HL Deb, vol 564, col 2037.

6   DDA 1995, s 38(1). Any person who is aggrieved by a refusal of a licensing authority to issue an exemption certificate under s 37 may appeal to the local magistrates court (or, in Northern Ireland, a court of summary jurisdiction) for the petty sessions area in which the licensing authority has its principal office: s 38(3). An appeal must be made within 28 days of the refusal: s 38(1). If the court allows such an appeal, it may direct the licensing authority to issue an exemption certificate and may specify the period of the currency of the exemption: s 38(2).

Taxi accessibility at designated transport facilities

8.2.14   The Secretary of State may, by regulations, provide for the application of any provision of the DDA 1995 relating to taxis or taxi drivers (that is, those described above) to be extended to vehicles (or their drivers) used for the provision of services under 'a franchise agreement'.[1] These regulations may apply any such taxi provisions with such modifications as the Secretary of State considers appropriate.[2] A 'franchise agreement' is a contract entered into by the 'operator' of a 'designated transport facility' for the provision by the other party to the contract of 'hire car' services for members of the public using any part of the transport facility and which involves vehicles entering any part of that facility.[3] A 'designated transport facility' means any premises which form part of any port, airport, railway station or bus station which has been designated for the present purpose by an order made by the Secretary of State.[4] The 'operator' of such a facility means any person who is concerned with the management or operation of the facility.[5] The definition of 'hire car' will be prescribed by regulations.[6]

1   DDA 1995, s 33(2) as read with s 33(4). This power also applies to the potential extension of regulations made in pursuance of the Civic Government (Scotland) Act 1982, s 20(2A). Under the Scotland Act 1998, functions under this section are transferred to the Scottish Ministers (insofar as they are exercisable in or as regards Scotland) by the Transfer of Functions to the Scottish Ministers etc Order 1999, SI 1999/1750, art 2, Sch 1.

2   Ibid, s 33(3).

3   Ibid, s 33(1).

4   Ibid, s 33(4).

5   Ibid.

6   Ibid.

8.2.15   The intention behind this provision, when brought into force, is to ensure that 'taxis' (using that term here in the popular, loose sense) that ply for hire at airports, railway stations and other transport termini could be brought within the accessibility regime for taxis.[1] It is not designed to capture those taxis that already fall within the definition of a taxi regulated for any of the purposes of the taxi provisions of Part V of DDA 1995. They will already be subject to the new duties and standards. Instead, it is intended to embrace those taxis that are private hire cars or mini-cabs and which are entitled to provide car hire services to passengers under a monopoly contract or franchise with the operator of the transport terminus in question (such as, for example, the British Airports Authority at London Gatwick Airport).[2]

---

1   Created by DDA 1995, ss 32–39.
2   HC Deb, vol 265, cols 159–160.

Application to Scotland and Northern Ireland

8.2.16   On the face of DDA 1995, the new duties and statutory framework affecting taxis apply only in England and Wales. However, it is intended that the Civic Government (Scotland) Act 1982 will be amended so as to enable these provisions to be extended to Scotland by means of regulatory powers.[1] These new provisions also apply to Northern Ireland.[2]

---

1   DDA 1995, s 39.
2   With the appropriate modifications contained in DDA 1995, Sch 8, paras 16–23.

Implementation

8.2.17   In July 1997, various government departments jointly issued an informal consultation document covering the features which could be included in regulations and suggesting dates for implementation of the proposed regulations.[1] During the course of 2000, the Government is expected to commence formal consultation on the implementation of these proposals. The informal consultation document proposes that taxi accessibility regulations would come into force for newly licensed vehicles in January 2002. At the same time, interim regulations would come into force for previously licensed wheelchair-accessible taxis. By January 2012, all taxis would be required to comply with the main taxi accessibility regulations. It remains to be seen whether this timetable is to be adhered to in the light of the forthcoming formal consultation.

---

1   *The Government's Proposals for Taxis* (1997, London: DETR).

8.3   PUBLIC SERVICE VEHICLES

8.3.1   Introducing the provisions of DDA 1995 dealing with access to buses, coaches and rail services,[1] the relevant minister stated that they 'add up to a very significant change in the field of transport' and acknowledged that the transport industry had worked closely with the Department of Transport for many years 'to promote and encourage the introduction of better designs and operating practices to meet the needs of disabled people'.[2] Nevertheless, the Government at the time believed that legislation was necessary to continue progress towards an accessible transport system. At the same time, however, these new statutory measures are not retrospective and, when brought into force, will apply only to new vehicles.[3] It is intended to provide a legal framework compatible with existing transport requirements, but flexible enough to allow the introduction of new requirements that are workable and viable in a technical, operational and economic sense.

1   DDA 1995, ss 40–48.
2   HL Deb, vol 565, cols 714–715.
3   Ibid, vol 566, col 463. Heritage and replica vehicles are thus implicitly outside the new regime.

8.3.2   These provisions apply to 'public service vehicles' (PSVs).[1] A PSV is a vehicle adapted to carry more than eight passengers (in addition to the driver) and which is in public service.[2] These provisions will apply to buses and coaches of the required capacity offering a public transport service.

1   DDA 1995, ss 40–45.
2   Ibid, s 40(5) and Sch 8, para 24(2). See also the provisions of the Public Passenger Vehicles Act 1981 and the Road Traffic (Northern Ireland) Order 1981.

PSV accessibility regulations

8.3.3   After due consultation with the DPTAC and other representative organisations,[1] the Secretary of State is empowered to make 'PSV accessibility regulations'.[2] The purpose of such regulations is to secure that it is possible for disabled persons to get on to and off 'regulated public service vehicles' in safety and without unreasonable difficulty. In the case of disabled persons in wheelchairs, the regulations will seek to achieve this purpose while a disabled person remains in his or her wheelchair.[3] Furthermore, the regulations will attempt to secure that it is possible for disabled persons to be carried in 'regulated public service vehicles' in safety and reasonable comfort.[4]

1   DDA 1995, s 40(7) and Sch 8, para 24(3).
2   Ibid, s 40(1). The power to make such regulations in Northern Ireland is vested with the Department of the Environment: Sch 8, para 24(1).
3   Ibid, s 40(1)(a).
4   Ibid, s 40(1)(b).

8.3.4   As used in this context, a 'regulated public service vehicle' means a PSV to which the PSV accessibility regulations are expressed to apply.[1] This implies that the Secretary of State has discretion in defining which vehicles or kinds of public service are covered by the accessibility regulations. Moreover, the regulations may make different provisions with respect to different classes or descriptions of vehicle and with respect to the same class or description of vehicle in different circumstances.[2] For example, in the case of full-size single-deck buses, an access solution might be low floors, whereas, in the case of coaches, a lift might be appropriate.[3] It was anticipated that local and regional variations might also be necessary, as might flexibility of timescales for implementation.

1   DDA 1995, s 40(5).
2   Ibid, s 40(6). By virtue of s 67(7), this is without prejudice to the generality of the powers to make regulations or orders by statutory instrument conferred by s 67(2)–(3).

8.3.5   The PSV accessibility regulations may, in particular, make provision as to the construction, use and maintenance of regulated PSVs.[1] Such provision may include:

– provision as to the fitting of equipment to vehicles;
– equipment to be carried by vehicles;
– the design of such equipment;
– the fitting and use of restraining devices designed to ensure the stability of wheelchairs while vehicles are moving;
– the position in which wheelchairs are to be secured while vehicles are moving.

It is not intended that this list should be exhaustive.[2] The draft Public Service Vehicle Regulations published in 1999 address the following matters in relation to relevant PSVs and disabled passengers:

– boarding lifts and ramps;
– automatic kneeling systems;[3]
– steps;
– entrances and exits;
– handrails and handholds;
– floors and gangways;
– signs and markings;
– communication devices;
– lighting;
– wheelchair spaces and provisions;
– seats and priority seats;
– route and destination displays.

Draft regulations, when implemented, will also amend existing regulations on the conditions of fitness, equipment, use and certification of PSVs, and will place additional duties on PSV drivers and conductors with respect to wheelchair-users and disabled persons generally.

1   DDA 1995, s 40(2).
2   HL Deb, vol 565, col 716.
3   A system which enables a PSV to be raised and/or lowered relative to its normal height of travel.

8.3.6   Although frequent reference is made here to the needs of wheelchair-users, the accessibility regulations are intended to make provision for the needs of other disabled travellers, including those with sensory impairments (for example, by the use of colour contrast on handrails and seating, and improved lighting levels).[1] The general power to make codes of practice under the DDA 1995 might also be used to give guidance to transport staff on how to assist disabled persons (for example, in respect of audible announcements).[2]

1   HL Deb, vol 566, cols 459–460.
2   See the existing code of practice issued by the rail regulator (*Meeting the Needs of Disabled Passengers*). See also the Public Service Vehicles (Conduct of Drivers, Inspectors, Conductors and Passengers) Regulations 1990, SI 1990/1020, which make provision in respect of guide dogs on PSVs.

8.3.7 A regulated PSV shall not be used on the road unless it conforms with the provisions of any PSV accessibility regulations.[1] To do otherwise is a criminal offence punishable on summary conviction by a fine not exceeding level 4 on the standard scale.[2] It is also a criminal offence of like weight to contravene or fail to comply with any provision of the PSV accessibility regulations or to cause or permit a regulated PSV to be used on a road in non-conformity with such regulations.[3]

---

1   DDA 1995, s 40(3)(b).
2   Ibid, s 40(4).
3   Ibid, s 40(3)(a),(c).

8.3.8 Provision is made for offences committed by a corporate body.[1] If such an offence is committed with the consent or connivance of a director,[2] manager, secretary or other similar officer, then there is joint liability for the offence.[3] Joint liability may also arise where the offence is attributable to any neglect on the part of any such officers. The position is also the same where the offence is committed with the consent or connivance (or is attributable to any neglect on the part) of a person purporting to act in such a capacity. In addition, in Scotland only, an offence committed by a partnership or other unincorporated association in the above circumstances can lead to a partner or a person concerned in the management or control of the association incurring joint criminal liability.[4]

---

1   DDA 1995, ss 40 and 48.
2   Where the affairs of a corporate body are managed by its members, a director will include any such member: ibid, s 48(2).
3   Ibid, s 48(1).
4   Ibid, s 48(3).

Accessibility certificates

8.3.9 Without prejudice to the generality of the restraints and offences created above,[1] a regulated PSV shall not be used on a road unless a vehicle examiner[2] has issued an 'accessibility certificate'.[3] An 'accessibility certificate' is a certificate which certifies that the prescribed provisions of the PSV accessibility regulations have been satisfied in respect of the vehicle in question.[4] This will parallel the existing initial roadworthiness certification procedure for PSVs and it is envisaged that accessibility certificates will be issued at the same time as certificates of initial fitness.[5] A fee may be payable on application or issue.[6] If a regulated PSV is used on a road without an accessibility certificate, the operator of the vehicle is guilty of an offence and is liable on summary conviction to a fine not exceeding level 4 on the standard scale.[7]

---

1   By DDA 1995, s 40.
2   Appointed under the Road Traffic Act 1988, s 66A.
3   DDA 1995, s 41(1)(a). Provision is made for appeal to the Secretary of State against the refusal of a vehicle examiner to issue an accessibility certificate: s 44(3)–(6). A fee may be charged for such an appeal: s 45.

4   Provision is made in s 49 for criminal offences committed in connection with accessibility
    certificates (for example, forgery or the making of false statements).
5   HL Deb, vol 565, col 716 and vol 566, col 463.
6   DDA 1995, s 45(1)(b).
7   Ibid, s 41(3). This is subject to s 41(1)(b) and the provisions of s 42. See **8.3.13**. By virtue of
    s 41(4), the term 'operator' has the same meaning as in the Public Passenger Vehicles Act
    1981. The appropriate modification of s 41(3)–(4) for Northern Ireland is made by Sch 8,
    para 25(2).

8.3.10   After due consultation,[1] the Secretary of State may make further
regulations with respect to applications for accessibility certificates and their
issue.[2] Such regulations may also provide for the examination of vehicles in
respect of which applications have been made and in respect of copies of
certificates which have been lost or destroyed. At the time of writing, s 41 is not
in force and no accessibility certificate regulations have been made.

1   DDA 1995, s 40(7).
2   Ibid, s 41(2); in Northern Ireland, the Department of the Environment: Sch 8, para 25(1).

8.3.11   Where the Secretary of State[1] is satisfied that prescribed provisions of
the PSV accessibility regulations for the purposes of accessibility certificates
have been satisfied in respect of a particular vehicle, that vehicle may be given
approval on application and payment of a fee.[2] A vehicle approved in this
manner is referred to as a 'type vehicle'.[3] This provision will clearly apply to
vehicles produced in large numbers. The Secretary of State may at any time
withdraw approval of a type vehicle.[4]

1   In Northern Ireland, the Department of the Environment.
2   DDA 1995, ss 42(1) and 45(1)(a). In accordance with s 42(5)(a), the Secretary of State may
    make regulations with respect to applications for (and grants of) approval under s 42(1).
    Note the Northern Ireland modifications to s 42 contained in Sch 8, para 26.
3   Ibid, s 42(2).
4   Ibid, s 42(6).

8.3.12   If the Secretary of State refuses an application for the approval of a
vehicle,[1] provision is made for a review of that decision.[2] A request for review
must be made before the end of a period to be prescribed by regulations.[3] In
reviewing the original decision, the Secretary of State must consider any written
representations made by the applicant before the end of the prescribed
period.[4]

1   Under DDA 1995, s 42(1).
2   Ibid, s 44.
3   Ibid, s 44(1). The applicant for review must pay any fee fixed under s 45.
4   Ibid, s 44(2). The provisions appertaining to reviews, appeals and fees generally under
    ss 44–45 are modified for the purposes of Northern Ireland by Sch 8, paras 28–29.

Type approval certificates

8.3.13   If a person authorised by the Secretary of State has made a declaration
in the prescribed form that a particular vehicle conforms in design, construction and equipment with a type vehicle, then a vehicle examiner may issue 'an

approval certificate' to the effect that subsequent individual vehicles conform to the type vehicle.[1] The vehicle examiner may issue such an approval certificate after examining the vehicle to which the statutory declaration applies, if he or she thinks fit.[2] However, these provisions are clearly designed to avoid the need for each vehicle of the same type to be individually inspected.[3]

1 DDA 1995, s 42(3), (4) and (8). Regulations may make general provision in respect of approval certificates: s 42(5). Note the consultations requirements of s 40(7). Provision is made in s 49 for criminal offences committed in connection with approval certificates (for example, forgery or the making of false statements).
2 Ibid, s 42(4). Provision is made for appeal to the Secretary of State against the refusal of a vehicle examiner to issue an approval certificate: s 44(3)–(6). A fee may be charged for such an appeal: s 45.
3 HL Deb, vol 565, col 717.

8.3.14 If the Secretary of State withdraws approval of a type vehicle,[1] then a vehicle examiner may not issue any further approval certificates by reference to the type vehicle.[2] However, any approval certificate issued by reference to the type vehicle before such withdrawal of approval shall continue to have effect.[3]

1 Under DDA 1995, s 42(6).
2 Ibid, s 42(7)(a).
3 For s 41 purposes: ibid, s 42(7)(b).

Offences and exemptions

8.3.15 A regulated PSV vehicle shall not be used on a road unless it has an accessibility certificate[1] or unless, alternatively, an approval certificate[2] has been issued in respect of the vehicle.[3] Use of a regulated PSV in contravention of these alternative conditions is a criminal offence punishable on summary conviction by a fine not exceeding level 4 on the standard scale.[4]

1 Under DDA 1995, s 41.
2 Under, ibid, s 42.
3 Ibid, s 41(1).
4 Ibid, s 41(3).

8.3.16 These provisions[1] do not prevent the use of a regulated PSV on the road if the Secretary of State has by order authorised its use by reference to the class or description of the vehicle or by explicit specification.[2] This allows special operating authorisation for vehicles which do not comply with the PSV accessibility regulations and for which an accessibility or approval certificate is not in force. The Government recognised that there might be circumstances in which an individual vehicle or class of vehicles could not reasonably be expected to meet the full requirements of the new vehicle accessibility standards.[3] Such circumstances might be used to recognise the difficulty or undesirability of attempting to make vintage or heritage vehicles fully accessible.[4] Special authorisation may be given subject to specified restrictions or conditions[5] and even an order authorising the use of a vehicle in these circumstances may require it to conform with certain aspects of the PSV accessibility regulations, with specified modifications or exceptions.[6]

1   DDA 1995, ss 40–42.
2   Ibid, s 43(1). In Northern Ireland, the s 43 powers are vested in the Department of the Environment: Sch 8, para 27.
3   HL Deb, vol 565, col 717.
4   Ibid, vol 566, col 463.
5   DDA 1995, s 43(2).
6   Ibid, s 43(3).

8.3.17   Ordinarily, where the Secretary of State is given a power under the DDA 1995 to make an order, that power is exercisable by statutory instrument.[1] An exception is provided for[2] in respect of an order[3] by which the Secretary of State has authorised the use on roads of a regulated PSV which does not comply with the PSV accessibility regulations or which does not possess an accessibility or approval certificate.[4] Such an authorisation order need not be made by statutory instrument if it applies only to a specified vehicle or to vehicles of a specified person. Nevertheless, such an order is capable of being amended or revoked as if it was an order made by statutory instrument.[5]

1   DDA 1995, s 67(1).
2   Under, ibid, s 67(6).
3   Under, ibid, s 43.
4   Under, ibid, ss 40–42.
5   Ibid, s 67(6).

Implementation

8.3.18   In 1997, various departments issued an informal consultation document (including technical specifications) on the Government's proposals for buses and coaches under the DDA 1995.[1] This proposed various implementation dates for the application of the proposed PSV regulations. New large single-deck buses over 7.5 tonnes gross vehicle weight would be required to meet all accessibility requirements (including wheelchair access) by January 2000 and all other such vehicles by January 2015. New double-deck buses would be expected to meet accessibility requirements short of wheelchair access by January 2000 and full wheelchair access by January 2002, with all such vehicles meeting all access features by January 2017. New small buses and coaches carrying 22 or fewer passengers were to comply with accessibility standards short of wheelchair access by January 2000, with full wheelchair accessibility by January 2005. All such vehicles would be expected to be fully accessible by January 2015. New large coaches (carrying 23 or more seated passengers only) would be expected to meet the same implementation dates as small buses and coaches, with all large coaches fully accessible by January 2020.

1   *The Government's Proposals for Buses and Coaches* (1997, London: DETR).

8.3.19   However, in August 1999 a statutory consultation was embarked upon and draft regulations were published.[1] In the light of the informal consultation and the assessment of regulatory costs, the proposed implementation timetable is now slightly amended. Under the latest proposals, all new PSVs were to have met the accessibility requirements short of wheelchair access by January 2000, with the exception of new coaches (on local or scheduled timetabled services) with a seated capacity of 23 or more passengers, where the relevant date is January 2001. Full wheelchair accessibility is required of new PSVs from January 2000 for single-deck buses over 7.5 tonnes, from January 2001 for double-deck buses, and January 2005 for single-deck buses up to 7.5 tonnes and coaches with seating capacity of 23 or more passengers. Full accessibility is expected of all single-deck buses by January 2015, all double-deck buses by January 2017 and large coaches by January 2020. At the time of writing, the regulations remain in draft form and have not been laid before Parliament or brought into force. It is clear that the above timetable has already slipped.

---

1   See *Disability Discrimination Act 1995: The Public Service Vehicles Accessibility Regulations 1999; The Public Service Vehicles (Conditions of Fitness, Equipment, Use and Certification) (Amendment) Regulations 1999; The Public Service Vehicles (Conduct of Drivers, Conductors and Passengers) (Amendment) Regulations 1999: A Statutory Consultation* (1999, London: DETR).

8.4   RAIL VEHICLES

8.4.1   Although provision has already been made in railways legislation to ensure that rail transport operators have a duty to have regard to the needs of disabled passengers, the previous Conservative Government regarded the provision of accessible rail services as 'a key link in the transport chain'.[1] Relevant provisions of the DDA 1995 are intended to strengthen the existing legislative framework by addressing access to rail services, including light rapid transit and tram systems.[2]

---

1   HL Deb, vol 565, col 717.
2   DDA 1995, ss 46–47.

Rail vehicle accessibility regulations

8.4.2   The Secretary of State is empowered[1] to make 'rail vehicle accessibility regulations' after appropriate consultations.[2] The Rail Vehicle Accessibility Regulations 1998 came into force on 1 November 1998.[3] The purpose of the regulations is to secure that it is possible for disabled persons to get on to and off 'regulated rail vehicles' in safety and without unreasonable difficulty, and to be carried in such vehicles in safety and in reasonable comfort.[4] Moreover, the regulations may make provision for securing that it is possible for disabled persons in wheelchairs to get on to and off 'regulated rail vehicles' in safety and without unreasonable difficulty while remaining in their wheelchairs, as well as to be carried in such vehicles in safety and reasonable comfort while remaining in their wheelchairs.[5]

---

1   DDA 1995, s 46(1).
2   Ibid, s 46(11) and Sch 8, para 30(4). In Northern Ireland, the s 46 powers are vested in the Department of the Environment: Sch 8, para 30(1). Consultation upon the relevant regulations (discussed below) took place in May and June 1998. It took the form of the issue, by the Mobility Unit of the DETR, of draft regulations, together with a compliance cost assessment.

3   SI 1998/2456 made under DDA 1995, s 46(1),(2) and (5). The regulations will be supported
    in due course by non-statutory guidance for the railway industry indicating the scope of
    coverage of the regulations, detailed guidance on the regulatory requirements, best
    practice, how the exemption procedure works, and how the regulations will be enforced.
    Draft guidance was published for public consultation by the Mobility Unit of the DETR in
    March 2000.
4   DDA 1995, s 46(1)(a).
5   Ibid, s 46(1)(b).

8.4.3   The DDA 1995 anticipated that particular provision would be made in the rail vehicle accessibility regulations as to the construction, use and maintenance of 'regulated rail vehicles'.[1] Special provision might also be made in the regulations as to the fitting of equipment to rail vehicles; equipment to be carried by rail vehicles; the design of equipment to be fitted to or carried by rail vehicles; the use of equipment fitted to or carried by rail vehicles; the toilet facilities to be provided in rail vehicles; the location and floor area of the wheelchair accommodation to be provided in rail vehicles;[2] and assistance to be given to disabled persons.[3] While the statutory provisions make frequent reference to the needs of wheelchair-users, the accessibility regulations are intended to make provision for the needs of other disabled travellers, including those with sensory impairments (for example, by the use of colour contrast on handrails and seating, and improved lighting levels).[4]

1   DDA 1995, s 46(2).
2   The meaning of the term 'wheelchair accommodation' is defined by regulations: ibid,
    s 46(6).
3   Ibid, s 46(2)(a)–(g).
4   HL Deb, vol 566, cols 459–460.

8.4.4   It is not proposed to reproduce the content of the 1998 regulations here. Much of their provision is technical and detailed. However, in summary, the rail vehicle accessibility regulations cover requirements:

–   for the marking of doors, their warning devices and their controls;[1]
–   relating to steps on the exterior and in the interior of vehicles;[2]
–   relating to floors;[3]
–   for priority seating for the use of disabled persons;[4]
–   for request-stop controls in a tramcar, if the tramcar is fitted with such controls;[5]
–   relating to interior transparent surfaces;[6]
–   for handrails and for handholds fitted to the backs of seats;[7]
–   for the minimum force needed to operate a door handle;[8]
–   for audible and visual announcements inside and outside the vehicle including their use and contents;[9]
–   for any toilets which are fitted to a vehicle;[10]
–   the provision of wheelchair spaces, their dimensions and other requirements;[11]
–   the provision of wheelchair-compatible sleeping compartments;[12]
–   the provision of tables in wheelchair spaces, if other passengers have them;[13]

- the provision of wheelchair-compatible doorways and passageways to wheelchair spaces and wheelchair-compatible sleeping compartments;[14]
- relating to telephones for passengers' use;[15]
- for minimum internal door width;[16]
- for the provision of boarding devices, which may be lifts or ramps, and requirements relating to them;[17] and
- for catering services, if such services are available for other passengers,[18]

in each case, for the benefit of disabled persons.

---

1   Rail Vehicle Accessibility Regulations 1998, regs 4 and 5.
2   Ibid, reg 6.
3   Ibid, reg 7.
4   Ibid, reg 8.
5   Ibid, reg 9.
6   Ibid, reg 10.
7   Ibid, reg 11.
8   Ibid, reg 12.
9   Ibid, reg 13
10 Ibid, regs 14 and 20.
11 Ibid, regs 15–16.
12 Ibid, reg 17.
13 Ibid, reg 18.
14 Ibid, reg 19.
15 Ibid, reg 21.
16 Ibid, reg 22.
17 Ibid, reg 23.
18 Ibid, reg 24.

8.4.5   The statute anticipates that different provisions may be made in the regulations so as to differentiate between different classes or descriptions of rail vehicles and with respect to different 'networks'.[1] Similarly, different provision may be made in the rail vehicle accessibility regulations with respect to the same class or description of rail vehicle in different circumstances.[2] This apparently recognises that 'the design and use of rail vehicles will vary according to a range of factors' including locality, systems and uses. For example, the 1998 regulations do make differing provisions for tramcars as opposed to trains.[3] It seems also to be intended that there should be future flexibility so that the 'accessibility regulations do not undermine the historic character of heritage railways'.[4] In addition, different provision might be made to reflect the different operating conditions and vehicle design on different parts of the London Underground railway (for example, those lines which use tubes rather than orthodox tunnels to carry rail vehicles).

---

1   DDA s 46(5)(a),(c). The term 'network' means any permanent way or other means of guiding or supporting rail vehicles or any section of such a network: s 46(6).
2   Ibid, s 46(5)(b). By virtue of s 67(7), these powers are without prejudice to the generality of the powers to make regulations or orders by statutory instrument conferred by s 67(2)–(3).
3   See, for example, Rail Vehicles Accessibility Regulations 1998, regs 9, 11 and 15.
4   HL Deb, vol 565, col 718.

Offences

8.4.6 If a 'regulated rail vehicle' is used for carriage while not conforming with any appropriate provisions of the rail vehicle accessibility regulations, the 'operator'[1] commits a criminal offence punishable on summary conviction by a fine not exceeding level 4 on the standard scale.[2] A person uses a rail vehicle for carriage if that person uses it for the carriage of members of the public for hire or reward at separate fares.[3] Provision is made for offences committed by a body corporate.[4] If such an offence is committed with the consent or connivance of a director,[5] manager, secretary or other similar officer, then there is joint liability for the offence.[6] Joint liability may also arise where the offence is attributable to any neglect on the part of any such officers. The position is also the same where the offence is committed with the consent or connivance (or is attributable to any neglect on the part) of a person purporting to act in such a capacity. In addition, in Scotland only, an offence committed by a partnership or other unincorporated association in the above circumstances can lead to a partner or a person concerned in the management or control of the association incurring joint criminal liability.[7]

---

1   The person having the management of that vehicle: DDA 1995, s 46(6).
2   Ibid, s 46(3)–(4).
3   Ibid, s 46(10).
4   Ibid, ss 46 and 48.
5   Where the affairs of a body corporate are managed by its members, a director will include any such member: ibid, s 48(2).
6   Ibid, s 48(1).
7   Ibid, s 48(3).

Regulated rail vehicles

8.4.7 The key to an understanding of these access provisions is an appreciation of which rail vehicles are covered by the regulations. The rail vehicle accessibility regulations apply only to 'regulated rail vehicles'.[1] Thus the scope of the regulations is determined in the accessibility regulations themselves: the term 'regulated rail vehicle' is said to be 'any rail vehicle to which the rail vehicle accessibility regulations are expressed to apply'.[2] It is clear that the Secretary of State has maximum flexibility to determine which rail vehicles are to be included or excluded from the access requirements. The 1998 regulations apply to passenger-carrying vehicles used on railways, tramways, monorail systems or magnetic levitation systems ('regulated rail vehicles'),[3] which were first brought into use, or belong to a class of vehicle first brought into use, on or after 1 January 1999.[4]

---

1   DDA 1995, s 46(6).
2   Ibid, s 46(6).
3   Rail Vehicle Accessibility Regulations 1998, reg 3(1). In accordance with reg 2(1), 'railway' and 'tramway' have the same meaning as in the Transport and Works Act 1992; 'magnetic levitation' and 'monorail' have the meaning provided for in the Transport and Works (Guided Transport Modes) Order 1992, SI 1992/3231.

4   DDA 1995, s 46(1).

8.4.8   However, it is equally plain that the regulations can apply only to modes of passenger transport which satisfy the root definition of a 'rail vehicle': namely, a vehicle constructed or adapted to carry passengers on any railways, tramway or 'prescribed system'.[1] Except in Northern Ireland,[2] the terms 'railway' and 'tramway' have the same meaning as in the Transport and Works Act 1992. The use of the term 'prescribed system' means a transport system using a prescribed mode of guided transport within the meaning of the 1992 Act.[3]

---

1   DDA 1995, s 46(6). In Northern Ireland, the term 'rail vehicle' means a vehicle constructed or adapted to carry passengers by rail: Sch 8, para 30(2).
2   Ibid, Sch 8, para 30(3).
3   Ibid, s 46(7).

8.4.9   Yet, however the term 'rail vehicle' is defined, it is also clear that the accessibility standards do not apply to any rail vehicle (or class of rail vehicle) first brought into use on or before 31 December 1998.[1] At the time of the passage of these provisions, the Government at that time made it clear in debate that it intended to use the regulation-making powers only in respect of new railway rolling stock and that there was no intention to require modifications to any existing rolling stock.[2] However, the Disability Rights Task Force recommends that an end date by which all passenger rail vehicles should comply with the 1998 regulations should be introduced following consultation. It also recommends that the accessibility standards should be applied to the refurbishment of existing rolling stock.[3]

---

1   DDA 1995, s 46(6). The time at which a rail vehicle or class of rail vehicle is to be treated for s 46 purposes as first brought into use is determined by regulations made under s 46(8). Such regulations may provide for the disregarding of periods of testing or other prescribed periods of use: s 46(9).
2   HL Deb, vol 565, col 717.
3   DRTF Report, recommendation 7.1.

Exemptions

8.4.10   General provision is made for exemptions from the rail vehicle accessibility regulations.[1] After due consideration and consultation,[2] the Secretary of State (in Northern Ireland, the Department of the Environment) may make exemption orders[3] to authorise the use for carriage of any regulated rail vehicle of a specified description (or in specified circumstances) even though that vehicle does not conform with the appropriate provisions of the rail vehicle accessibility regulations. An exemption order may be made subject to specified restrictions or conditions.[4] The regulations may provide for procedural issues in respect of the application for, granting of, currency of or revocation of exemption orders.[5]

---

1   DDA 1995, s 47.
2   Ibid, s 47(3).
3   Ibid, s 47(1).

4   DDA 1995, s 47(4)–(5).
5   Ibid, s 47(2). It was not envisaged that the s 47 powers of exemption would be widely used: HL Deb, vol 565, col 718.

8.4.11   The Secretary of State has made the Rail Vehicle (Exemption Applications) Regulations 1998.[1] These regulations specify the manner in which applications for exemption from the Rail Vehicle Accessibility Regulations 1998 are to be made, including the information which is to be supplied with an application. An application must be in writing.[2] It must provide the following particulars with the application:[3]

–   name and address of applicant;
–   description of rail vehicle;
–   applicable circumstances of the exemption;
–   relevant requirements from which exemption is sought;
–   the technical, economic and operational reasons why exemption is sought;
–   the effect which the exemption would have on a disabled person's ability to use the rail vehicle so described;[4]
–   any measures which could be taken to enable disabled persons to use such rail vehicles if exemption is granted;[5]
–   any proposals for the later modification of such rail vehicles to secure compliance with the rail vehicle accessibility regulations within a stated period;
–   the period of exemption (unless permanent exemption is sought).

These regulations also make provision for the period and revocation of exemptions.[6] Numerous and various exemptions for particular descriptions of rail vehicles on particular rail systems have been sought and granted.[7]

1   SI 1998/2457 made under DDA 1995, s 47 and in force from 1 November 1998.
2   Ibid, reg 3.
3   Ibid, reg 3 and Schedule.
4   The meaning of 'use' is set out in the Schedule, para 11.
5   The meaning of 'use' is set out in the Schedule, para 11.
6   Ibid, reg 4.
7   The details of these exemption orders are not reproduced here.

8.5   AVIATION AND SHIPPING

8.5.1   The DDA 1995 does not directly address the rights of disabled people in respect of aviation or shipping services. Airports and passenger terminals are subject to Part III (on access to goods, facilities and services) insofar as they are providing facilities or services. However, aeroplanes, helicopters, airships, ferries, hovercraft, boats and ships are excluded from Part III, being 'the use of any means of transport'.[1] They are also not the subject of the framework for vehicle accessibility standards in Part V of the Act. The Disability Rights Task Force has welcomed steps being taken to develop a non-statutory code of practice on access for disabled people to air travel and suggests that the code (when developed) might be given statutory backing.[2] It also recommends a formal review, including the need for legislative provisions, for accelerating progress in compliance with the International Maritime Organisation (IMO) and DPTAC guidance on access for disabled people in the shipping industry.[3]

1   DDA 1995, s 19(5)(b).
2   DRTF Report, recommendation 7.8.
3   Ibid, recommendation 7.9.

Chapter 9

INSTITUTIONAL FRAMEWORK

9.1 INTRODUCTION

9.1.1   The DDA 1995 established the National Disability Council (NDC) and a separate Northern Ireland Disability Council (NIDC).[1] The primary duty of the NDC was to advise the Secretary of State on its own initiative or at the request of the Secretary of State on the following matters:[2]

–   matters relevant to the elimination of discrimination against disabled persons and persons who have had a disability;
–   measures which are likely to reduce or eliminate such discrimination;
–   matters related to the operation of the Act or of provisions made under the Act.

The Secretary of State was empowered to confer by order additional functions on the Council,[3] but this did not include any functions with respect to the investigation of complaints which might be the subject of proceedings under the Act.[4] This distinguished the NDC from the Equal Opportunities Commission (EOC) and the Commission for Racial Equality (CRE). It was clear that the Council was a purely advisory body, enabled to make recommendations only in respect of the matters or measures listed above.

---

1   DDA 1995, Part VI and Sch 8, paras 33–35.
2   Ibid, s 50(2).
3   Ibid, s 50(3).
4   Ibid, s 50(4).

9.1.2   As originally established, the NDC's power to give advice on its own initiative on matters relevant to the elimination of disability discrimination (or measures likely to reduce or eliminate such discrimination) did not include a power to give advice in respect of any matter relating to discrimination in the employment field.[1] However, these restrictions were to have effect only while there was in existence the National Advisory Council on the Employment of Disabled People (NACEDP) or any person appointed by the Secretary of State[2] to advise or assist him or her generally in connection with matters relating to the employment of disabled persons and persons who have had a disability.[3] These responsibilities would otherwise then pass automatically to the NDC. The NACEDP and district advisory committees were disestablished in April 1998 and the NDC then acquired an advisory role in respect of the employment of disabled people.[4]

---

1   DDA 1995, s 50(9).
2   Under ibid, s 60(1).
3   Ibid, s 50(10).

4   Disability Discrimination (repeal of s 17 of, and Sch 2 to, the Disabled Persons
    (Employment) Act 1944) Order 1998, SI 1998/565 made under DDA 1995, s 60(6)(b). See
    also: Disability Discrimination (Abolition of District Advisory Committees) Order 1997, SI
    1997/536.

9.1.3   Nevertheless, it was clear that the NDC was not a sibling of the EOC or
the CRE. It was not a rights agency to which individual complaints of
discrimination could be submitted. The NDC was a purely advisory body with a
limited remit and no powers of enforcement. In particular, unlike the
pre-existing commissions, the Council lacked the power to provide assistance
or advice to complainants, to conduct formal investigations into suspected acts
or patterns of discrimination, or to bring proceedings to enforce the Act on
behalf of complainants or in its own name. It also had no general power to
monitor and review the operation of the legislation. At the time of the passage
of the DDA 1995, the then Conservative Government rejected arguments for
the creation of a Disability Rights Commission, contending that such a
Commission would not work, might create a risk of a backlash against disability
rights and would not fit the social context of the late 1990s.[1] However, in 1997
the new Labour Government charged the newly established Disability Rights
Task Force with the job of developing proposals to create a Disability Rights
Commission. An interim report on the role and functions of a Commission was
presented in March 1998[2] and the Government responded with a White Paper.[3]
In turn, this led to the Disability Rights Commission Act 1999.

1   HL Deb, vol 565, cols 639–642 and vol 566, cols 408–410.
2   Disability Rights Task Force, *Recommendations to Government on the Proposed Role and Functions
    of a Disability Rights Commission* (March 1998). See also Disability Rights Task Force, *Moving
    Towards the Establishment of a Disability Rights Commission* (DRTF/1/98).
3   *Promoting Disabled People's Rights: Creating a Disability Rights Commission Fit for the 21st Century*
    (Cm 3977) (1998, London, HMSO).

9.2   DISABILITY RIGHTS COMMISSION

9.2.1   The Disability Rights Commission Act 1999 (DRCA 1999) establishes
the Disability Rights Commission (DRC).[1] The Act applies to England, Wales
and Scotland, but does not generally extend to Northern Ireland,[2] where
instead similar powers in respect of disability rights are exercised by the
Equality Commission for Northern Ireland. The DRC supersedes the NDC
which is now abolished.[3] It has functions similar to those of the EOC and CRE
(but with one important difference, as will be seen below at **9.2.31**). The DRC
opened for business on 25 April 2000.[4] While the Act leaves it free to set up
offices as appropriate (and it has established offices in London and in
Manchester, in the first instance), it is expected that it will ensure that it has at
least one office in each of England, Wales and Scotland.

1   DRCA 1999, ss 1(1) and 16(1). Schedule 1 to the Act makes provision for the Commission's
    constitution and related matters: s 1(3). The Act comes into force on such day as the
    Secretary of State may by order appoint (and different days may be appointed for different
    purposes): s 16(2),(3). See Disability Rights Commission Act 1999 (Commencement No 1
    and Transitional Provision) Order 1999, SI 1999/2210 and Disability Rights Commission Act
    1999 (Commencement No 2 and Transitional Provision) Order 2000, SI 2000/880.

2 DRCA 1999, s 16(4),(5).
3 Ibid, s 1(4).
4 From that date, the services previously provided by the Disability Access Rights Advisory Service (DARAS) were transferred to the DRC. The information and advice services which were provided by DARAS and the DDA Helpline have been merged to form the DRC Helpline. A conciliation service will continue to be run until the DRC outsources a replacement service.

Status

9.2.2 The DRC is a body corporate and is not the servant or agent of the Crown. It does not enjoy any status, immunity or privilege of the Crown. Its property is not to be regarded as property of or as held on behalf of the Crown.[1] The Act binds the Crown (but does not affect Her Majesty in her private capacity or in right of Her Duchy of Lancaster or the Duke of Cornwall).[2]

1 DRCA 1999, Sch 1, para 1.
2 Ibid, s 15.

Staffing of the Commission

9.2.3 The DRCA 1999 makes provision for the staffing of the DRC.[1] The DRC has a chief executive appointed by it, subject to the approval of the Secretary of State.[2] The DRC may also employ such other employees as it may appoint, subject to the approval of the Secretary of State as to numbers and terms and conditions of service.[3]

1 DRCA 1999, Sch 1, para 10. Financial provision for the expenses of the DRC is made in s 1(2) and there is a requirement on the DRC to keep proper accounts: Sch 1, para 15. The Government has provided the DRC with £25 million funding for its first two years (£3 million establishment costs, £11 million running costs for 2000/2001 and a similar sum for 2001/2002): DfEE Press Release 565/98 (4 December 1998).
2 In fact, the first appointment of a chief executive is made by the Secretary of State: DRCA 1999, Sch 1, para 10(2).
3 Employment with the DRC is subject to pension provision made under the Superannuation Act 1972, s 1 and Sch 1: DRCA 1999, Sch 1, para 11.

Commissioners

9.2.4 The DRC is to consist of not less than 10 and not more than 15 commissioners appointed by the Secretary of State.[1] In order to ensure the proper representation of disabled persons on the DRC, the Secretary of State may appoint as a commissioner a person who is not disabled (and has not had a disability) only if satisfied that after the appointment more than half of the commissioners will be disabled persons (or persons who have had a disability).[2] Thus it is intended that the majority of commissioners shall be disabled persons within the meaning of the DDA 1995. Commissioners hold and vacate office in accordance with the terms of their appointment.[3] A commissioner shall not be appointed for less than 2 or more than 5 years, although such a person may be reappointed.[4] A commissioner may resign by written notice to the Secretary of State.[5] The Secretary of State may also terminate the appointment of a commissioner if satisfied that, without the consent of the chairman of the DRC, the commissioner has failed to attend meetings of the DRC during a continuous period of 6 months beginning not earlier than 9 months before the termination.[6] The office of commissioner may also be ended if he or she has become bankrupt; has had his or her estate sequestrated; has made a composition or arrangement with (or granted a trust deed for) his or her creditors; or is otherwise unable or unfit to carry out the functions as a commissioner.[7] In special circumstances, a person who has ceased to be a commissioner might receive compensation on the direction of the Secretary of State.[8]

1   DRCA 1999, Sch 1, para 2(1). The DRC may pay to any commissioner such remuneration or expenses as the Secretary of State may determine: Sch 1, para 8. In like fashion, it may pay (or make provision for the payment of) pensions, allowances or gratuities to or in respect of any commissioner.
2   Ibid, Sch 1, para 2(2); but this provision does not apply in respect of the first three appointments to the office of commissioner: Sch 1, para 2(3).
3   Ibid, Sch 1, para 3(1).
4   Ibid, Sch 1, para 3(2).
5   Ibid, Sch 1, para 4.
6   Ibid, Sch 1, para 5(a).
7   Ibid, Sch 1, para 5(b)–(c).
8   Ibid, Sch 1, para 9.

9.2.5   One commissioner is to be appointed as chairman of the DRC by the Secretary of State.[1] Provision is also made for either one or two other commissioners as deputy chairmen. At least one of the persons holding office as chairman or deputy chairman should be a disabled person (or a person who has had a disability).[2] The chairman and deputy chairmen hold and vacate that office in accordance with the terms of their appointment; may resign by written notice to the Secretary of State; and shall cease to hold that office if they cease to be commissioners.[3]

1   DRCA 1999, Sch 1, para 6(1). The first chairman is Mr Bert Massie.
2   Ibid, Sch 1, para 6(2).
3   Ibid, Sch 1, para 7.

Functions and powers

9.2.6   The DRC has a number of general functions, including the following duties:[1]

–   to work towards the elimination of discrimination against disabled persons;[2]
–   to promote the equalisation of opportunities for disabled persons;
–   to take such steps as it considers appropriate with a view to encouraging good practice in the treatment of disabled persons; and
–   to keep under review the working of the Disability Discrimination Act 1995 and the Disability Rights Commission Act 1999.

Without limiting its powers, and for any purpose connected with the performance of its functions, the DRC may:[3]

- make proposals or give other advice[4] to any Minister of the Crown as to any aspect of the law or a proposed change to the law;[5]
- make proposals or give other advice to any government agency or other public authority as to the practical application of any law;
- undertake, or arrange for or support (whether financially or otherwise), the carrying out of research or the provision of advice or information.

It may also make charges for facilities or services made available by it for any purpose.[6]

1 DRCA 1999, s 2(1). The DRC will have *locus standi* to bring judicial review proceedings, *R v Secretary of State for Employment, ex parte Equal Opportunities Commission* [1994] ICR 317, HL.
2 The term 'disabled persons' includes persons who have had a disability; the term 'discrimination' means anything which is discrimination for the purposes of any provision of Part II or Part III of the DDA 1995 Act: DRCA 1999, s 2(5). In any event, expressions used in the 1999 Act have the same meaning as defined for the purposes of the 1995 Act: DRCA 1999, s 13(2).
3 DRCA 1999, s 2(2). The Explanatory Notes to the DRCA 1999 state that s 2(1)–(2) will enable the DRC to undertake a wide range of activities (including running conferences, seminars and workshops, providing advice and assistance on reasonable adjustments, and devising guidance for employers and service providers in particular sectors).
4 At the request of a relevant Minister, the DRC may be required to make proposals or give other advice on any specified matter. The Explanatory Notes to the DRCA 1999 state that s 2(2)–(3) will enable the DRC to give advice on amendments to the DDA 1995, the implementation of any relevant EU directive or the Human Rights Act 1998, or on other legislation where the needs of disabled persons are in issue (such as housing legislation).
5 DRCA 1999, s 2(3). The term 'the law' includes European Community law and the international obligations of the UK: DRCA 1999, s 2(5).
6 DRCA 1999, s 2(4).

9.2.7 The DRC may regulate its own procedure (including its quorum).[1] The validity of any proceedings of the DRC is not affected by a vacancy among the commissioners or by a defect in the appointment of a commissioner.[2] The DRC may delegate its powers. It may authorise any committee of the DRC or any commissioner to exercise such of its functions (other than functions relating to the conduct of a formal investigation) as it may determine.[3]

1 DRCA 1999, Sch 1, para 12(1). The quorum for meetings of the DRC shall in the first instance be determined by a meeting of the DRC attended by at least five commissioners: Sch 1, para 12(2).
2 DRCA 1999, Sch 1, para 13.
3 DRCA 1999, Sch 1, para 14(1). This does not affect any power of the DRC to authorise its employees to do anything on its behalf: Sch 1, para 14(2).

9.2.8 The DRC must submit to the Secretary of State an annual report on its activities during the previous accounting year.[1] The annual report must include (among other things):

- a report on anything done by the Commission, in the performance of its primary statutory functions,[2] jointly or otherwise in co-operation with any other organisation;

-   a general survey of developments in matters within the scope of the Commission's functions; and
-   proposals for the Commission's activities in the current year.

The Secretary of State shall lay a copy of the report before Parliament and arrange for such further publication as is considered appropriate.

---

1   DRCA 1999, Sch 1, para 16 (that is the year to 31 March: Sch 1, para 15).
2   That is, under DRCA 1999, s 2(1)(a)–(c).

Assistance in relation to proceedings

9.2.9   Provision is made in the DRCA 1999 for the DRC to provide assistance to individuals in relation to the bringing of actual or potential legal proceedings.[1] The power to provide such assistance applies to proceedings which an individual has brought (or proposes to bring) in an employment tribunal or county court (or, in Scotland, a sheriff's court)[2] in respect of a complaint or claim about unlawful discrimination under Parts II and III of the DDA 1995 (discrimination in the employment field and in respect of goods, facilities, services or premises).[3] Such assistance may also be provided in respect of proceedings of a prescribed description (being proceedings in which an individual who has or has had a disability relies or proposes to rely on a matter relating to that disability).[4]

---

1   DRCA 1999, s 7. This would include assistance to non-disabled persons using the victimisation provisions in DDA 1995, s 55.
2   That is, under DDA 1995, ss 8 or 25.
3   DRCA 1999, s 7(1)(a).
4   Ibid, s 7(1)(b). At the time of writing, no such prescription has been made.

9.2.10   Where the individual concerned applies to the DRC for assistance in relation to any relevant proceedings, the DRC may grant the application on any of the following grounds:[1]

-   that the case raises a question of principle;
-   that it is unreasonable to expect the applicant to deal with the case unaided (because of its complexity, because of the applicant's position in relation to another party or for some other reason);
-   that there is some other special consideration which makes it appropriate for the DRC to provide assistance.

If the DRC grants an application, it may:[2]

-   provide or arrange for the provision of legal advice;
-   arrange for legal or other representation (which may include any assistance usually given by a solicitor or counsel);[3]
-   seek to procure the settlement of any dispute;
-   provide or arrange for the provision of any other assistance which it thinks appropriate.

The DRC may authorise any employee of the DRC to exercise such of these functions as it may determine.[4]

---

1   DRCA 1999, s 7(2).
2   DRCA 1999, s 7(3).
3   This does not affect the law and practice as to who may represent a person in relation to any proceedings: DRCA 1999, s 7(4).
4   DRCA 1999, 7(5).

9.2.11   Provision is made for the recovery of expenses incurred by the DRC in providing assistance.[1] This may arise where the DRC has given an individual assistance under the provisions above in relation to any proceedings and any costs or expenses (however described) have become payable to that individual by another person in respect of the matter in connection with which the assistance is given.[2] A sum equal to any expenses incurred by the DRC in providing the assistance shall be a first charge for the benefit of the DRC on the costs or expenses concerned.[3] It does not matter whether the costs or expenses concerned are payable by virtue of a decision of a court or tribunal, an agreement arrived at to avoid proceedings or to bring them to an end, or otherwise.[4]

---

1   DRCA 1999, s 8. Provision may be made by regulations made by the Secretary of State for the determination of the expenses of the Commission in cases where this section applies: s 8(5). No such regulations have been made to date.
2   DRCA 1999, s 8(1).
3   DRCA 1999, s 8(2). By virtue of s 8(4), the charge thus created is subject to any charge under the Legal Aid Act 1988 and any provision in that Act for payment of any sum to the Legal Aid Board. It is also subject to any charge or obligation for payment in priority to other debts under the Legal Aid (Scotland) Act 1986 and any provision in that Act for payment of any sum into the Scottish Legal Aid Fund.
4   DRCA 1999, s 8(3).

Formal investigations

9.2.12   The DRC may conduct a formal investigation in two circumstances.[1] First, it may decide to conduct a formal investigation for any purpose connected with the performance of its statutory duties.[2] Secondly, it must conduct a formal investigation if directed to do so by the Secretary of State.[3] At any time, the DRC may decide to stop or to suspend the conduct of a formal investigation.[4] The Explanatory Notes to the DRCA 1999 suggest that the DRC's powers to conduct a formal investigation embrace three different kinds of investigation. A general investigation may be undertaken to find out what is happening in a particular sector of society or in relation to a particular kind of activity. In contrast, a named party investigation may confine the investigation to the activities of one or more named persons, who may be individuals or organisations.[5] In addition, a formal investigation might be used to monitor compliance with the requirements of a non-discrimination notice or a statutory agreement in lieu of enforcement proceedings.[6]

1   DRCA 1999, Sch 3, Part I has effect in respect of the conduct of formal investigations. See
    s 3(5) and Sch 3, para 1(1). The Secretary of State may make regulations making provision
    supplementing Part I in connection with any matter concerned with the conduct of formal
    investigations: DRCA 1995, Sch 3, para 26. See Disability Rights Commission (Time Limits)
    Regulations 2000, SI 2000/879.
2   Ibid, s 3(1) for the purposes of its duties under s 2(1).
3   Ibid, s 3(2) for the purposes of its duties under s 2(1).
4   Ibid, s 3(3). Such a decision requires the approval of the Secretary of State if the
    investigation is being conducted under a direction by the Secretary of State under s 3(2).
5   See ibid, Sch 3, para 3.
6   That is, under ibid, ss 4–5.

9.2.13   When conducting a formal investigation (of whatever kind), the DRC
may nominate one or more commissioners (with or without one or more
additional commissioners appointed for the purposes of the investigation) to
conduct the investigation on its behalf.[1] It may also authorise those persons to
exercise such of its functions in relation to the investigation (which may
include drawing up or revising terms of reference) as it may determine.[2] With
the approval of the Secretary of State, the DRC may appoint one or more
individuals as additional commissioners for the purposes of a formal investigation.[3] The DRCA 1999 makes provision for the appointment and tenure of
office of such additional commissioners.[4] An additional commissioner holds
office (and will vacate office or may be re-appointed) in accordance with the
terms of his or her appointment.[5] The DRC may not alter the terms of
appointment of an additional commissioner except with his or her consent and
with the approval of the Secretary of State.[6] It may pay such remuneration or
expenses to any additional commissioner – and pay (or make provision for the
payment of) pensions, allowances or gratuities in respect of any additional
commissioner – as the Secretary of State may determine.[7] Subject to the
approval of the Secretary of State, the DRC may terminate the appointment of
an additional commissioner if satisfied that, without reasonable excuse, the
commissioner has failed to carry out his or her duties during a continuous
period of three months beginning not earlier than six months before the
termination.[8] A commissioner's appointment may also be terminated if he or
she has become bankrupt, has had his or her estate sequestrated or has made a
composition or arrangement with (or granted a trust deed for) his or her
creditors.[9] Moreover, an appointment is terminable if an additional commissioner is otherwise unable or unfit to carry out his or her duties.[10] Otherwise,
the appointment will terminate at the conclusion of the relevant formal
investigation.[11] At the discretion of the Secretary of State, if there are special
circumstances which make it right that an additional commissioner should
receive compensation upon the termination or ending of the appointment, the
DRC may be directed to pay such compensation, as determined by the
Secretary of State.[12]

1   DRCA 1999, s 3(4)(a).
2   Ibid, s 3(4)(b).
3   Ibid, Sch 2, para 1(1).
4   Ibid, s 3(5) and Sch 2. An additional commissioner is not a servant or agent of the Crown:
    Sch 2, para 1(2).
5   Ibid, Sch 2, para 2(1). An additional commissioner may resign by notice in writing to the
    Commission: Sch 2, para 4(1).
6   Ibid, Sch 2, para 2(2).

7   Ibid, Sch 2, para 3.
8   Ibid, Sch 2, para 4(2)(a).
9   Ibid, Sch 2, para 4(2)(b).
10 Ibid, Sch 2, para 4(2)(c).
11 Ibid, Sch 2, para 4(3).
12 Ibid, Sch 2, para 5.

9.2.14 Before the DRC takes any steps in the conduct of a formal investigation, it must draw up terms of reference for the investigation.[1] Those terms of reference shall be drawn up (and may be revised[2]) either by the Secretary of State (after consulting the DRC) if the investigation is held at the direction of the Secretary of State or, in any other case, by the DRC.[3] The DRC must also serve or publish notice of the holding of the investigation and its terms of reference.[4] Where the terms of reference confine the investigation to activities of one or more named persons, that notice shall be served on each of those persons.[5] Where the terms of reference do not so confine the investigation, the notice shall be published in such manner as appears to the DRC appropriate to bring it to the attention of persons likely to be affected by it.[6]

1   DRCA 1999, Sch 3, para 2(1)(a).
2   If the terms of reference are revised, the provisions of DRCA 1999, Sch 3, para 2 apply again in relation to the revised investigation and its terms of reference: Sch 3, para 2(5).
3   Ibid, Sch 3, para 2(2).
4   Ibid, Sch 3, para 2(1)(b).
5   Ibid, Sch 3, para 2(3).
6   Ibid, Sch 3, para 2(4).

9.2.15 In the course of a formal investigation (whether or not the investigation has already begun), the DRC might propose to investigate whether:

–   a person has committed (or is committing) any unlawful act;[1]
–   any requirement imposed by a non-discrimination notice[2] served on a person (including a requirement to take action specified in an action plan[3]) has been or is being complied with;[4]
–   any undertaking given by a person in an agreement made with the DRC is being or has been complied with.[5]

In any of these instances, the DRC may not investigate any such matter unless the terms of reference of the investigation confine it to the activities of one or more named persons (and the person concerned is one of those persons).[6] In particular, the DRC may not investigate whether a person has committed (or is committing) any unlawful act unless it has reason to believe that the person concerned may have committed (or may be committing) the act in question,[7] or that matter is to be investigated in the course of a formal investigation into that person's compliance with any requirement or undertaking mentioned immediately above.[8]

1   DRCA 1999, Sch 3, para 3(1)(a). An 'unlawful act' is an act which is unlawful discrimination under the DDA 1995, Part II or III: DRCA 1999, Sch 3, para 3(10). It would also include any other unlawful act of a description prescribed in regulations for present purposes. No such prescriptive regulations have been made at the time of writing, but might include acts which breach the Human Rights Act 1998, s 6 as it affects disabled persons.
2   Ibid, s 4 and Sch 3, Part II.
3   Ibid, Sch 3, Part III.

4   Ibid, Sch 3, para 3(1)(b).
5   Ibid, Sch 3, para 3(1)(c).
6   Ibid, Sch 3, para 3(2).
7   Ibid, Sch 3, para 3(3)(a). See the case-law under comparable provisions in the RRA 1976:
    Hillingdon London Borough Council v Commission for Racial Equality [1982] AC 779, HL; *Re
    Prestige Group plc; Commission for Racial Equality v Prestige Group plc* [1984] ICR 473, HL.
8   Ibid, Sch 3, para 3(3)(b) (that is, in Sch 3, para 3(1)(b) or (c)).

9.2.16   The DRC shall serve a notice on the person concerned offering that person the opportunity to make written and oral representations about the matters being investigated.[1] If the DRC is investigating whether the person concerned has committed (or is committing) any unlawful act – otherwise than in the course of a formal investigation into that person's compliance with any requirement or undertaking[2] – the DRC shall include in this notice a statement informing that person that the DRC has reason to believe that that person may have committed (or may be committing) any unlawful act.[3] The DRC shall not make any findings in relation to any matter[4] without giving the person concerned (or a representative) a reasonable opportunity to make written and oral representations.[5] However, the DRC may refuse to receive oral representations made on behalf of the person concerned by a person (not being counsel or a solicitor) to whom the DRC reasonably objects as being unsuitable.[6] In such a case, it must give written reasons for its objection.[7]

1   DRCA 1999, Sch 3, para 3(4). Such a notice may be included in a notice of the holding of
    an investigation and the terms of reference required (by Sch 3, para 2(3)) to be served on
    named persons where the investigation is confined to the activities of such named persons:
    Sch 3, para 3(9).
2   That is, under ibid, Sch 3, para 3(1)(b) or (c).
3   Ibid, Sch 3, para 3(5).
4   That is, a matter mentioned in Sch 3, para 3(1).
5   Ibid, Sch 3, para 3(6).
6   Ibid, Sch 3, para 3(7). The Act does not define unsuitability.
7   Ibid, Sch 3, para 3(8).

9.2.17   As part of a formal investigation, the DRC may serve a notice on any person requiring that person to give such written information as may be described in the notice or to attend and give oral information about any matter specified in the notice, and to produce all documents in that person's possession or control relating to any such matter.[1] Such a notice may be served only on the written authority of the Secretary of State unless the terms of reference confine the investigation to the activities of one or more named persons and the person being served is one of those persons.[2] However, a person may not be required by such a notice to give information, or produce a document, which that person could not be compelled to give in evidence, or produce, in civil proceedings before the High Court (in England and Wales) or the Court of Session (in Scotland).[3] Furthermore, a person may not be required by such a notice to attend at any place unless the necessary expenses of a journey to and from that place are paid or tendered.[4] What if a person has been served with such a notice and that person fails to comply with it or the

DRC has reasonable cause to believe that that person intends not to comply with it?[5] In such circumstances, the DRC may apply to a county court (in England and Wales) or by summary application to the sheriff (in Scotland) for an order requiring the person concerned to comply with the notice or with such directions for the same purpose as may be contained in the order.[6]

---

1 DRCA 1999, Sch 3, para 4(1).
2 Ibid, Sch 3, para 4(2).
3 Ibid, Sch 3, para 4(3)(a).
4 Ibid, Sch 3, para 4(3)(b).
5 Ibid, Sch 3, para 5(1).
6 Ibid, Sch 3, para 5(2).

9.2.18 The DRCA 1999 entitles the DRC to make recommendations in the light of its findings in a formal investigation.[1] It may recommend that any person make changes in policies or procedures (or as to any other matter) with a view to promoting the equalisation of opportunities for disabled persons or persons who have had a disability.[2] It may also make recommendations to the Secretary of State for changes in the law or otherwise.[3] The DRC may make such recommendations before the conclusion of the formal investigation itself.[4] It must also prepare a report of its findings in any formal investigation.[5] That report must exclude any matter which relates to an individual's private affairs or any person's business interests if publication of that matter might, in the Commission's opinion, prejudicially affect that individual or person, and its exclusion is consistent with the Commission's duties and the object of the report.[6]

---

1 DRCA 1999, Sch 3, para 6(1).
2 Ibid, Sch 3, para 6(2)(a).
3 Ibid, Sch 3, para 6(2)(b).
4 Ibid, Sch 3, para 6(3).
5 Ibid, Sch 3, para 7(1). The report will be published: Sch 3, para 7(3),(4). The obligation to prepare and publish a report does not affect the Commission's power to issue a non-discrimination notice before a report is prepared or published: Sch 3, para 7(5).
6 Ibid, Sch 3, para 7(2).

Non-discrimination notices

9.2.19 In the course of a formal investigation, if the DRC is satisfied that a person has committed (or is committing) an unlawful act,[1] it may serve on that person a 'non-discrimination notice'.[2] Certain procedural requirements must be complied with.[3] The DRC must serve on the person concerned a notice informing that person that the DRC is considering issuing a non-discrimination notice (and of the grounds for doing so) and offering an opportunity to make written and oral representations.[4] It must also give the person concerned (or a representative) the opportunity to make oral and written representations within a period specified in the notice of not less than 28 days.[5] Moreover, the DRC may refuse to receive oral representations made on behalf of the person concerned by a person (not being counsel or a solicitor) to whom the DRC reasonably objects as being unsuitable.[6] In such a case, the DRC must give written reasons for its objection.[7]

---

1 An 'unlawful act' is an act which is unlawful discrimination under DDA 1995, Part II or III: s 4(5). It would also include any other unlawful act of a description prescribed in regulations for present purposes. No such prescriptive regulations have been made at the time of writing, but might include acts which breach the Human Rights Act 1998, s 6 as it affects disabled persons.
2 DRCA 1999, s 4(1). The provisions of Sch 3, Part II have effect in relation to non-discrimination notices: s 4(6). The Secretary of State may make regulations making provision supplementing Part II in connection with any matter concerned with the procedure for issuing non-discrimination notices: DRCA 1999, Sch 3, para 26.
3 By virtue of DRCA 1999, Sch 3, para 8(1), the DRC is prohibited from issuing a non-discrimination notice addressed to any person unless it has complied with the requirements of Sch 3, para 8.
4 Ibid, Sch 3, para 8(2).
5 Ibid, Sch 3, para 8(3).
6 Ibid, Sch 3, para 8(4). What amounts to unsuitability is not specified.
7 Ibid, Sch 3, para 8(5).

9.2.20 A non-discrimination notice must give details of the unlawful act which the DRC has found that the person has committed (or is committing).[1] It must also require that person not to commit any further unlawful acts of the same kind.[2] The notice may also include recommendations to the person concerned as to action which the DRC considers that person could reasonably be expected to take with a view to complying with that requirement.[3] On issuing a non-discrimination notice, the DRC must serve a copy on the person to whom it is addressed.[4]

---

1 DRCA 1999, s 4(1)(a).
2 Ibid, s 4(1)(b). If the finding is that the person is committing an unlawful act, the notice will require that person to cease doing so.
3 Ibid, s 4(2).
4 Ibid, Sch 3, para 9.

9.2.21 Provision is made for appealing against the issue of a non-discrimination notice. A person on whom a non-discrimination notice is served may appeal against any requirement imposed by the notice.[1] The appeal must be made within 6 weeks following the day on which the notice was served. In employment matters, the appeal lies to an employment tribunal; in non-employment matters, the appeal lies to a county court (in England and Wales) or a sheriff's court (in Scotland).[2] If the tribunal or court considers a requirement in a non-discrimination to be unreasonable, it may quash (in Scotland, recall) any requirement appealed against.[3] In the case of a requirement not to commit (or to cease committing) any further unlawful acts of the same kind as the DRC found to be committed (or is being committed),[4] the tribunal or court may quash (in Scotland, recall) the requirement if it considers that the Commission's finding was based on an incorrect finding of fact.[5]

---

1 DRCA 1999, Sch 3, para 10(1) (that is, a requirement under s 4(1)(b) or (3)).
2 Ibid, Sch 3, para 10(2).

3   Ibid, Sch 3, para 10(3)(a).
4   That is, a case falling under DRCA 1999, s 4(1)(b).
5   Ibid, Sch 3, para 10(3)(b).

9.2.22   Where a court or tribunal quashes (or recalls) a requirement, it may direct that the non-discrimination notice shall have effect with such modifications as it considers appropriate.[1] Such modifications may include the substitution of a requirement in different terms.[2] In the case of a requirement not to commit (or to cease committing) any further unlawful acts of the same kind as the DRC found to be committed (or is being committed),[3] the modifications may include modifications to the details of the unlawful act which the DRC has found has been committed or is being committed,[4] so far as necessary to describe any unlawful act on which the requirement could properly have been based.[5] If a tribunal or court allows an appeal against a non-discrimination notice without quashing (or recalling) the whole of the notice, the DRC may give notice to the person concerned and vary the non-discrimination notice. This can be done by revoking or altering any recommendation[6] or by making new recommendations.[7]

1   DRCA 1999, Sch 3, para 10(4). There is no right of appeal against a direction that a non-discrimination order shall have effect as modified by the tribunal or court: DRCA 1999, Sch 3, para 10(6).
2   Ibid, Sch 3, para 10(5)(a).
3   That is, a case falling under DRCA 1999, s 4(1)(b).
4   That is, under the terms of DRCA 1999, s 4(1)(a).
5   Ibid, Sch 3, para 10(5)(b).
6   Included in the notice in pursuance of the Commission's power under DRCA 1999, s 4(2).
7   Ibid, Sch 3, para 10(7).

9.2.23   A non-discrimination notice becomes final when any appeal against the notice is dismissed, withdrawn or abandoned or the time for appealing expires without an appeal having been brought.[1] It also becomes final when such an appeal is allowed without the whole notice being quashed (in Scotland, recalled).[2] The question of enforcement of a non-discrimination notice might then arise. A non-discrimination notice is enforceable during the period of 5 years beginning on the date on which the notice has become final.[3] During this period, the DRC may apply to a county court (in England and Wales) or by summary application to the sheriff (in Scotland) for an enforcement order. Such an application may be made if it appears to the DRC that the person concerned has failed to comply with any requirement imposed by the notice[4] or the DRC has reasonable cause to believe that the person concerned intends not to comply with any such requirement.[5] An enforcement order will require the person concerned to comply with the requirement or with such directions for the same purpose as are contained in the order.[6]

1   DRCA 1999, Sch 3, para 11(a). Provision is made in Sch 3, para 13 for the DRC to maintain a register of non-discrimination notices which have become final.
2   Ibid, Sch 3, para 11(b).
3   Ibid, Sch 3, para 12(1).

4   That is, under DRCA 1999, s 4(1)(b).
5   Ibid, Sch 3, para 12(2).
6   Ibid, Sch 3, para 12(3).

Action plans

9.2.24   A non-discrimination notice may require the person concerned to propose an 'adequate action plan',[1] with a view to securing compliance with a requirement in the notice not to commit further unlawful acts.[2] An 'action plan' is a document drawn up by the person concerned. It specifies action (including action the person has already taken) intended to change anything in that person's practices, policies, procedures or other arrangements which caused or contributed to the commission of the unlawful act concerned (or is liable to cause or contribute to a failure to comply with a requirement in the non-discrimination notice).[3] The action specified in an action plan may include ceasing an activity or taking continuing action over a period. An action plan is 'adequate' if the action specified in it would be sufficient to ensure, within a reasonable time, that the person is not prevented from complying with that requirement by anything in that person's practices, policies, procedures or other arrangements.[4] Once such an action plan has been proposed by that person and has become final, a non-discrimination notice may further require the person concerned to take any action which is specified in the plan (and which has not already been taken) at the time or times specified in the plan.[5]

1   An action plan is a plan subject to and in accordance with DRCA 1999, Sch 3, Part III. See s 4(3)(a),(6). The Secretary of State may make regulations making provision amending Part III in relation to the procedures for finalising action plans: DRCA 1999, Sch 3, para 26. See Disability Rights Commission (Time Limits) Regulations 2000, SI 2000/879.
2   DRCA 1999, s 4(1)(b). An 'unlawful act' is an act which is unlawful discrimination under DDA 1995, Part II or III: s 4(5). It would also include any other unlawful act of a description prescribed in regulations for present purposes. No such prescriptive regulations have been made at the time of writing.
3   DRCA 1999, s 4(4)(a).
4   Ibid, s 4(4)(b) and Sch 3, para 14(2).
5   Ibid, s 4(3)(b).

9.2.25   Where a person (referred to in the DRCA 1999 as 'P') has been served with a non-discrimination notice which has become final and includes a requirement for P to propose an action plan, further provision is made for a 'first action plan'.[1] P must serve the proposed action plan on the DRC within the period specified in the non-discrimination notice.[2] If P fails to do so, the DRC may apply to a county court (in England and Wales) or by way of summary application to the sheriff (in Scotland) for an order directing P to serve the proposed action plan within such period as the order may specify.[3] When P serves a proposed action plan on the DRC (either in response to the non-discrimination notice or to a court order), the action plan becomes final at the end of the prescribed period.[4] An action plan which has become final may be varied by written agreement between the DRC and P.[5]

1   DRCA 1999, Sch 3, para 14(1).
2   Ibid, Sch 3, para 15(1).

3 Ibid, Sch 3, para 15(2).
4 Ibid, Sch 3, para 15(3) unless the DRC has given notice to P under Sch 3, para 16 (dealt with in **9.2.26**).
5 Ibid, Sch 3, para 19.

9.2.26 The DRCA 1999 makes provision for the revision of a first proposed action plan at the invitation of the DRC where the DRC considers that a proposed action plan served on it is not an 'adequate' action plan. The DRC may give notice to P stating its view that the plan is not adequate. It may invite P to serve on the DRC a revised action plan which is adequate within a specified period.[1] In that notice, the DRC may include recommendations as to action which it considers might be included in an adequate action plan.[2] If P serves a revised proposed action plan on the DRC in response, the revised action plan supersedes the previous action plan and becomes final at the end of the prescribed period.[3] If P does not serve a revised action plan in response, the action plan previously served on the DRC becomes final at the end of the prescribed period.[4]

1 DRCA 1999, Sch 3, para 16(1).
2 Ibid, Sch 3, para 16(2).
3 Ibid, Sch 3, para 16(3) unless the DRC applies for an order under Sch 3, para 17 (dealt with in **9.2.27**).
4 Ibid, Sch 3, para 16(4) unless the DRC applies for an order under Sch 3, para 17 (dealt with in **9.2.27**).

9.2.27 The DRC might decide to take court action in relation to an inadequate action plan. If it considers that a proposed action plan served on it is not an adequate action plan, the DRC may apply to the county court (in England and Wales) or by way of summary application to the sheriff (in Scotland) for an order.[1] Such an application may not be made[2] unless a notice requiring the revision of the first proposed action plan[3] has been served on P by the DRC and P has not served a revised action plan in response within the specified period in the notice.[4] Where these requirements have been met, the court may make an order declaring that the proposed action plan in question is not an adequate action plan. The order may require P to revise the proposals and to serve on the DRC an adequate action plan within such a period specified in the order. The order may also contain such directions (if any) as the court considers appropriate as to the action which should be specified in the adequate action plan required by the order.[5] If the court does not make such an order, the proposed action plan otherwise becomes final at the end of the prescribed period.[6]

1 DRCA 1999, Sch 3, para 17(1).
2 Even where the action plan was served in compliance with a court order under DRCA 1999, Sch 3, para 15(2) (**9.2.25**).
3 That is, under DRCA 1999, Sch 3, para 16 (**9.2.26**).
4 DRCA 1999, Sch 3, para 17(2). The reference to the specified period in the notice is a reference to the provision in Sch 3, para 16(1)(b).
5 Ibid, Sch 3, para 17(3).

6   Ibid, Sch 3, para 17(4).

9.2.28   What is the position where a court order requires P to serve an adequate action plan on the Commission? In response to the order, P might then serve an action plan on the Commission.[1] That action plan becomes final at the end of the prescribed period, unless the DRC has applied to a county court (England and Wales) or to the sheriff (in Scotland) to enforce the order on the ground that the plan does not comply with the order and any directions of the court.[2] If the DRC makes such an application to the court, the action plan becomes final at the end of the prescribed period if the DRC withdraws its application or if the court considers that the action plan complies with the order.[3]

1   DRCA 1999, Sch 3, para 18(1).
2   Ibid, Sch 3, para 18(2).
3   Ibid, Sch 3, para 18(3).

9.2.29   If, during the period of five years (beginning on the date on which an action plan drawn up by P becomes final) the DRC considers that P has failed to comply with a requirement[1] to carry out any action specified in the action plan, it may apply to a county court (in England and Wales) or by summary application to the sheriff (in Scotland) for an order requiring P to comply with that requirement or with such directions for the same purpose as are contained in the order.[2]

1   Under DRCA 1999, s 4(3)(b).
2   Ibid, Sch 3, para 20.

9.2.30   The DRCA 1999 gives the DRC powers to obtain information in connection with the assessment or enforcement of action plans. This may be done for the purposes of determining whether an action plan proposed by P is an adequate action plan. It may also be done for the purposes of determining whether P has complied (or is complying) with the requirement to take the action specified in an action plan which has become final. The DRC may serve a notice on *any* person requiring that person to give information in writing, or copies of documents in that person's possession or control, which relates to any matters described in the notice.[1] However, a person may not be required to give information or produce a document which that person could not be compelled to give in evidence or produce in civil proceedings before the High Court (in England and Wales) or the Court of Session (in Scotland).[2] If the person in question fails to comply with the Commission's notice (requiring information), the DRC may apply to a county court (in England and Wales) or by summary application to the sheriff (in Scotland) for an order requiring the person concerned to comply with the notice or with such directions for the same purpose as may be contained in the order.[3]

1   DRCA 1999, Sch 3, para 21(1).
2   Ibid, Sch 3, para 21(2).

3   Ibid, Sch 3, para 21(3)–(4).

Agreements in lieu of enforcement action

9.2.31   The DRCA 1999 makes novel provision where the DRC has reason to believe that a person has committed (or is committing) an act made unlawful under the DDA 1995.[1] In such a case,[2] the DRC may enter into a written agreement with that person on the assumption that that belief is well founded. This may be done whether or not the person admits that the act in question was committed or is being committed.[3]

---

1   DRCA 1999, s 5(1),(12) and Sch 3. There is no comparable power enjoyed by the EOC or
    CRE. An 'unlawful act' is one which is unlawful discrimination under Part II or Part III of
    the DDA 1995 or any other unlawful act of a description prescribed by regulations for the
    purposes of the DRCA 1999, s 5(11). No such prescription has been made to date, but might
    in future include acts which breach the Human Rights Act 1998, s 6 as it affects disabled
    persons.
2   DRCA 1999, s 5 subject to s 3(3).
3   Ibid, s 5(1).

9.2.32   The agreement contemplated by this provision is an agreement in lieu of enforcement action.[1] The DRC must undertake not to take any 'relevant enforcement action' in relation to the unlawful act in question.[2] This means that the DRC must not begin a formal investigation into the commission by the person concerned of the unlawful act in question.[3] Alternatively, if such an investigation has begun,[4] the DRC must not take any further steps in the investigation of that matter.[5] Moreover, the DRC must not take any steps (or further steps) with a view to the issue of a non-discrimination notice based on the commission of the unlawful act in question.[6] In turn, the person concerned must undertake not to commit any further unlawful acts of the same kind (and, where appropriate, to cease committing the unlawful act in question).[7] In addition, that person must undertake to take such action[8] – that is, action intended to change anything in the practices, policies, procedures or other arrangements of the person concerned which caused or contributed to the commission of the unlawful act in question[9] or is liable to cause or contribute to a failure to comply with an undertaking not to commit any further unlawful acts of the same kind (and, where appropriate, to cease committing the unlawful act in question)[10] – as may be specified in the agreement.[11]

---

1   But this provision does not affect the Commission's powers to settle or compromise legal
    proceedings of any description: DRCA 1999, s 5(10).
2   DRCA 1999, s 5(2)(a).
3   Ibid, s 5(4)(a).
4   Whether or not the investigation is confined to that matter.
5   Ibid, s 5(4)(b).
6   Ibid, s 5(4)(c).
7   Ibid, 5(2)(b)(i).
8   Which may include ceasing an activity or taking continuing action over any period.
9   Ibid, s 5(5)(a).

10   Ibid, s 5(5)(b).
11   Ibid, s 5(2)(b)(ii).

9.2.33   The DRCA 1999 treats these undertakings as binding on the parties to the agreement.[1] Such an agreement may include terms providing for incidental or supplementary matters (including the termination of the agreement, or the right of either party to terminate it, in certain circumstances) and may be varied or revoked by agreement of the parties.[2] The agreement may not include any other terms or provisions, unless their inclusion is authorised by regulations made by the Secretary of State.[3] The agreement is designed to be enforceable at the initiative of the DRC. It may apply to a county court (in England and Wales) or by summary application to the sheriff (in Scotland) for an order if the other party to the agreement has failed to comply with any undertaking (mentioned above) or if the DRC has reasonable cause to believe that that party intends not to comply with any such undertaking.[4] The court's order may require the other party to comply with the undertaking or with such directions for the same purpose as are contained in the order.[5]

1   DRCA 1999, s 5(3). However, undertakings under s 5(2)(b) are only enforceable by the DRC as provided for in s 5(8).
2   Ibid, s 5(6).
3   Ibid, s 5(7). However, any provisions so authorised are not enforceable by the DRC in the manner contemplated by s 5(8) (**9.2.36**).
4   Ibid, s 5(8).
5   Ibid, s 5(9).

Persistent discrimination

9.2.34   The DRCA 1999 empowers the DRC to take court action if it believes that a person would commit further unlawful acts of disability discrimination. This power arises at any time within 5 years of a non-discrimination notice served upon the person becoming final.[1] The power also arises within 5 years of a final finding by a court or tribunal[2] that a person has committed an act which is unlawful discrimination for the purposes of any provision of Part II or Part III of the DDA 1995.[3] Moreover, the DRC is similarly empowered (and within the same time period) where there is a final finding by a court or tribunal in any other proceedings that a person has committed an act of a prescribed description.[4] In any of these cases, if it appears to the DRC that, unless restrained, the person concerned is likely to do one or more unlawful acts, the DRC may apply to a county court for an injunction (in England and Wales) or to the sheriff for an interdict (in Scotland) restraining the person from doing so.[5] If the court is satisfied that the application is well founded, it may grant the injunction or interdict in the terms applied for or in more limited terms.[6] The injunction or interdict is not confined to unlawful acts which have been the subject of the original non-discrimination notice or legal proceedings.

1   DRCA 1999, s 6(1)(a).
2   That is, in proceedings under DDA 1995, ss 8 or 25 (the provisions in respect of

discrimination in the employment field and those relating to goods, facilities, services and premises).
3 DRCA 1999, s 6(1)(b). A finding of a court or tribunal becomes final when an appeal against it is dismissed, withdrawn or abandoned or when the time for appealing expires without an appeal having been brought: s 6(5).
4 Ibid, s 6(1)(c),(4). No prescription has been made at the time of writing. There is an erroneous reference in s 6(1)(c) to s 6(4)(b). No such sub-section exists. It is assumed that this is a simple printing error and that the correct reference is to s 6(4).
5 Ibid, s 6(2).
6 Ibid, s 6(3).

Disclosure of information

9.2.35 No information given to the DRC by any person (referred to in the DRCA 1999 as 'the informant') in connection with formal investigations, non-discrimination notices, action plans and agreements in lieu of enforcement action shall be disclosed by the DRC or its past and present commissioners, additional commissioners or employees.[1] The restriction on disclosure does not apply to any disclosure made:[2]

– on the order of a court;
– with the informant's consent;
– in the form of a summary or other general statement published by the DRC which does not identify the informant or any other person to whom the information relates;
– in a report of the investigation published by the DRC;
– to a commissioner, an additional commissioner or an employee of the DRC, or, so far as is necessary for the proper performance of the DRC's functions, to other persons; or
– for the purpose of any civil proceedings to which the DRC is a party, or of any criminal proceedings.

A person who discloses information contrary to these provisions is guilty of an offence and liable on summary conviction to a fine not exceeding level 5 on the standard scale.[3]

1 DRCA 1999, Sch 3, para 22(1).
2 Ibid, Sch 3, para 22(2).
3 Ibid, Sch 3, para 22(3).

Enforcement of court orders

9.2.36 The DRCA 1999 makes provision for the enforcement of any court orders made as part of the Commission's functions or powers discussed above.[1] In England and Wales, in relation to a failure to comply with an order made by a county court, statutory provisions dealing with penalties for failure to give evidence will apply with modifications.[2] Any person who fails without reasonable excuse to comply with the order may be fined up to £1,000.[3] The county court, at its discretion, may direct that the whole or any part of that fine (after deducting costs) shall be applied to indemnify the DRC for expenses incurred or wasted in consequence of the failure to comply with the order.[4] In Scotland, where the sheriff finds a person to be in contempt of court in respect of a failure to comply with an order, the sheriff shall not commit the person to prison,[5] but may grant decree in favour of the DRC for such amount of any fine imposed for the contempt as appears to the sheriff to be appropriate in respect of the expense incurred or wasted by the DRC in consequence of the failure to comply with the order.[6] If the DRC applies to a county court (in England and Wales) or to the sheriff (in Scotland) to enforce a court order, the court may modify the order.[7]

---

1   That is (by virtue of DRCA 1999, Sch 3, para 23(1)), any order made by a county court or the sheriff under DRCA 1999, s 5(8) or Sch 3.
2   County Courts Act 1984, s 55.
3   Ibid, s 55(1) and (2) as substituted by DRCA 1999, Sch 3, para 23(2)(a). The provisions of s 55(3) of the 1984 Act are omitted for this purpose: DRCA 1999, Sch 3, para 23(2)(b).
4   County Courts Act 1984, s 55(4) (as substituted by DRCA 1999, Sch 3, para 23(2)(c)).
5   Notwithstanding the Contempt of Court Act 1981, s 15.
6   DRCA 1999, Sch 3, para 23(3).
7   Ibid, Sch 3, para 23(4).

Offences

9.2.37   The DRCA 1999 creates two offences in relation to the exercise by the DRC of its powers and functions.[1] First, a person who deliberately alters, suppresses, conceals or destroys a document required to be produced as part of a formal investigation,[2] or as part of the DRC's powers to seek information,[3] is guilty of an offence and liable on summary conviction to a fine not exceeding level 5 on the standard scale. Secondly, an identical offence is committed by a person who makes any statement which that persons knows to be false or misleading in a material particular (or recklessly makes a statement which is false or misleading in a material particular) when complying with a notice in relation to a formal investigation or the DRC's powers to seek information,[4] a non-discrimination notice, an agreement in lieu of enforcement or an order of a court.[5] Proceedings for these offences may be instituted against any person at any place at which the person has an office or other place of business, and against an individual at any place where he or she resides (or at which he or she is for the time being).[6]

---

1   DRCA 1999, Sch 3, para 24(1).
2   Under ibid, Sch 3, para 4 (or an order under para 5).
3   Under ibid, Sch 3, para 21 (or an order under para 21(3)).
4   Under ibid, Sch 3, paras 4 or 21.
5   Under ibid, s 5(8) or Sch 3.
6   Ibid, Sch 3, para 24(2).

Service of notices

9.2.38   Any notice required or authorised to be served on a person under the DRCA 1999 may be served by delivering it to that person, by leaving it at that person's proper address or by sending it by post to that address.[1] In the case of a corporation, the notice may be served on the secretary or clerk of that body. In the case of a partnership, the notice may be served on any partner or a person having control or management of the partnership business. In the case of an unincorporated association (other than a partnership), the notice may be served on any member of its governing body.[2] For present purposes, in the case of a corporation, its secretary or clerk, the proper address of any person is the address of its registered or principal office in the UK. In the case of an unincorporated association (other than a partnership) or a member of its governing body, the proper address is its principal office in the UK. In any other case, the proper address is the person's usual or last known address (whether of his or her residence or of a place where the person carries on business or is employed).[3]

---

1   DRCA 1999, Sch 3, para 25(1).
2   Ibid, Sch 3, para 25(2).
3   Ibid, Sch 3, para 25(3).

9.3   CODES OF PRACTICE

9.3.1   Under the DDA 1995, as originally enacted, there existed a rather labyrinthine process for producing codes of practice in support of the substantive legislation. When asked to do so by the Secretary of State, the NDC had a duty to prepare proposals for a code of practice dealing with matters referred to it by the Secretary of State.[1] In similar circumstances, the NDC could be asked to review an existing code of practice and, where appropriate, propose alterations to the code. In preparing a proposal for an original or amended code of practice, the NDC was required to consult any persons specified by the Secretary of State when requesting the Council to act.[2] The NDC was also required to consult such other persons (if any) as the Council considered appropriate.[3] However, the power to issue any codes of practice which had been prepared or reviewed by the NDC lay in the hands of the Secretary of State alone.[4]

---

1   DDA 1995, s 51(1). In Northern Ireland, the NIDC had a parallel duty at the behest of any department.
2   Ibid, s 52(2)(a).
3   Ibid, s 52(2)(b).
4   Ibid, ss 51(2) and 52.

9.3.2   The way in which the NDC could prepare or amend codes of practice to be issued by the Secretary of State was not so dissimilar from the power of the EOC or the CRE to issue codes of practice under the sex or race discrimination statutes.[1] All three bodies did not have the autonomous power to issue codes of practice and would first have to submit their proposals for the approval of the Secretary of State and Parliament. The noticeable difference, however, is that, unlike the EOC and the CRE, the NDC could not take the initiative to propose a draft code of practice and could act only at the request of the Secretary of State. Furthermore, under the DDA 1995, it was the Government which issued any codes of practice and not the NDC (cf the powers of the EOC and CRE).

---

1   See SDA 1975, s 56A and RRA 1976, s 47.

9.3.3   In the sex and race discrimination field, the statutory commissions alone have the power to prepare and issue codes of practice, albeit only with the necessary intervening ministerial and parliamentary approval. Under the original provisions of the DDA 1995, however, the Secretary of State could also issue codes of practice.[1] Such codes might contain such 'practical guidance' as he or she considers appropriate with a view to 'eliminating discrimination' against disabled persons (and persons who have had a disability) in the field of employment or 'encouraging good practice' in relation to the employment of disabled persons (and persons who have had a disability).

---

1   DDA 1995, s 53.

9.3.4   These provisions are now swept away by the DRCA 1999.[1] A considerably simpler and unified process for issuing codes of practice in the future is put in place.[2] The Secretary of State no longer has the power to issue or revise codes of practice under the DDA 1995. Instead, the DRC may prepare and issue codes of practice giving practical guidance to employers, service providers or other persons[3] on how to avoid discrimination or on any other matter relating to the operation of the provisions of the DDA 1995 on employment or goods, facilities, services and premises.[4] It may also issue such codes for the purpose of giving practical guidance to any persons on any other matter, with a view to promoting the equalisation of opportunities for disabled persons (and persons who have had a disability) or encouraging good practice regarding the treatment of such persons, in any field of activity regulated by the above provisions.[5] In addition, the DRC shall, when requested to do so by the Secretary of State, prepare a code of practice dealing with the matters specified in the request.[6]

---

1   The relevant provisions in DDA 1995, ss 51–54 are repealed by DRCA 1999, s 14(2) and Sch 5.
2   DRCA 1999, s 9. This does not affect the status of the three existing codes of practice: see Chapters 3–5. However, the revised code of practice issued in 1999 to support Part III of the DDA 1995 is likely to be replaced in due course in anticipation of the final rights of access coming into force in 2004.
3   To whom provisions of DDA 1995, Part II or Part III apply.
4   DDA 1995, s 53A(1) as inserted by DRCA 1999, s 9(1). A code of practice issued by the DRC comes into effect on such day as the Secretary of State may by order appoint: DDA 1995, s 53A(6)(a) as inserted by DRCA 1999, s 9(1).
5   The power to make codes of practice does not affect the Commission's general powers to give practical guidance on matters connected with its functions: DRCA 1999, s 9(3).
6   DDA 1995, s 53A(2) as inserted by DRCA 1999, s 9(1).

9.3.5   In preparing a code of practice, the DRC shall carry out such consultations[1] as it considers appropriate (which shall include the publication for public consultation of proposals relating to the code).[2] The DRC may not issue a code of practice unless a draft of it has been submitted to and approved by the Secretary of State and laid before both Houses of Parliament, and unless a 40-day period has elapsed without either House resolving not to approve the draft.[3] If the Secretary of State does not approve a draft code of practice, the DRC must be provided with a written statement of reasons.[4] A code of practice issued by the DRC may be revised in whole or part, and re-issued, by it.[5] A code may also be revoked by an order made by the Secretary of State at the request of the DRC.[6] Where the DRC proposes to revise a code of practice, it must follow the same procedures as for a new code.[7]

1 The DRC must maintain a list of the organisations it has consulted generally for the purposes of any of its functions: DRCA 1999, s 17(1),(3). The DRC shall make the list available to the public in whatever way it considers appropriate (subject to any charge it may impose): s 17(4). An organisation may be removed from the list if it has not been consulted generally in the 12 months preceding its removal: s 17(2).
2 DDA 1995, s 53A(3) as inserted by DRCA 1999, s 9(1). The DRC may treat any consultation undertaken by the NDC (under DDA 1995, s 52(2)) as being as effective for the purposes of s 53A(3) as if it had been undertaken by the DRC: DRCA 1999, s 9(2).
3 DDA 1995, s 53A(4) as inserted by DRCA 1999, s 9(1).
4 Ibid, s 53A(5) as inserted by DRCA 1999, s 9(1).
5 Ibid, s 53A(6)(b) as inserted by DRCA 1999, s 9(1).
6 Ibid, s 53A(6)(c) as inserted by DRCA 1999, s 9(1).
7 Ibid, s 53A(7) as inserted by DRCA 1999, s 9(1).

9.3.6 A failure to observe any provision of a code of practice does not of itself make a person liable to any proceedings. However, any provision of a code which appears to a court or tribunal to be relevant to any question arising in any proceedings[1] shall be taken into account in determining that question.[2]

1 Under DDA 1995, Part II or Part III.
2 Ibid, s 53A(8) as inserted by DRCA 1999, s 9(1).

9.4 GUIDANCE ON MEANING OF DISABILITY

9.4.1 The Secretary of State is empowered to issue statutory guidance about the matters which a court or tribunal ought to take into account when determining whether an impairment has a substantial adverse effect on a person's ability to carry out normal day-to-day activities or whether such an impairment has a long-term adverse effect.[1] A court or tribunal addressing these questions, for any purpose of the legislation, is obliged to take account of any statutory guidance issued by the Secretary of State which appears to it to be relevant.[2] If any such statutory guidance has been issued, the Secretary of State may from time to time revise the whole or any part of such guidance and reissue it.[3] The Secretary of State also has authority to revoke any guidance by order.[4]

1 DDA 1995, s 3(1). In Northern Ireland the power to issue s 3 guidance is vested in the Department of Economic Development (Sch 8, para 2).
2 Ibid, s 3(3) and (12).
3 Ibid, s 3(11)(a).
4 Ibid, s 3(11)(b).

9.4.2 The power to issue such statutory guidance is at large, but such guidance may give examples in four particular circumstances and in relation to particular activities:[1]

(1) effects which it would be reasonable to regard as substantial adverse effects;
(2) effects which it would not be reasonable to regard as substantial adverse;
(3) substantial adverse effects which it would be reasonable to regard as long-term;
(4) substantial adverse effects which it would not be reasonable to regard as long-term.

The then Minister for Disabled People gave an assurance in Committee that the guidance powers would not be used to weaken the definition of disability or to exclude particular impairments.[2] The guidance is intended to illustrate and exemplify rather than to exclude or limit the statutory definitions. The Secretary of State has issued statutory guidance on the meaning of disability which came into force on 31 July 1996.[3] The substance of this guidance has been considered in Chapter 2.[4]

---

1   DDA 1995, s 3(2). Further interpretative assistance is to be found in Sch 1 to the Act and in the discussion of the concept of 'disability' in Chapter 2.
2   HC Deb Standing Committee E, col 124.
3   *Guidance on matters to be taken into account in determining questions relating to the definition of disability* (1996, London: HMSO). The Guidance came into force on 31 July 1996 by virtue of the Disability Discrimination (Guidance and Code of Practice) (Appointed Day) Order 1996, SI 1996/1996, para 2. A separate edition of the Guidance has been issued in Northern Ireland.
4   See also: *Consultation on the Employment Code of Practice, Guidance on Definition of Disability and Related Regulations: An Analysis of the Responses* (1996, London: Department for Education and Employment).

9.4.3   In preparing a draft of any statutory guidance (or revised statutory guidance), the Secretary of State is required to consult such persons as he or she considers appropriate.[1] If the Secretary of State proposes to issue any statutory guidance (or to reissue any revised statutory guidance), he or she must first publish a draft of it, consider any representations which are made about the draft and, if the Secretary of State thinks it appropriate, may modify the proposals in the light of any of those representations.[2]

---

1   DDA 1995, s 3(4).
2   Ibid, s 3(5).

9.4.4   During the legislative process, concerns were expressed about parliamentary scrutiny of any statutory guidance to be issued or reissued by the Secretary of State. The then Government conceded that there was a strong case for making such guidance subject to the same parliamentary scrutiny as applied to codes of practice prepared under the DDA 1995, namely the negative resolution procedure.[1] Accordingly, if the Secretary of State decides to proceed with any proposed statutory guidance (or revised statutory guidance), he or she shall lay a draft of it before each House of Parliament.[2] If either House resolves not to approve the draft guidance within the next 40 days,[3] the Secretary of State shall take no further steps in relation to the proposed guidance,[4] although a new draft of the proposed guidance may be subsequently laid before Parliament.[5] If no such resolution is made within the 40-day period, the Secretary of State shall issue the guidance in the form of the draft proposal and the guidance shall come into force on a date to be appointed by order.[6]

1 HL Deb, vol 566, cols 122–123.
2 DDA 1995, s 3(6).
3 Calculated in accordance with DDA 1995, s 3(12).
4 Ibid, s 3(7).
5 Ibid, s 3(10).
6 Ibid, s 3(8)–(9).

9.5 APPLICATION TO THE CROWN

9.5.1 The DDA 1995 applies to any act or deliberate omission done by or for the purposes of a Minister of the Crown or government department in exactly the same way as it would apply to an act or omission done by a private person.[1] It also applies in like manner to an act or deliberate omission done on behalf of the Crown by a statutory body or a person holding a statutory office.[2] In short, the 1995 legislation applies to both the public and private sector.[3]

1 DDA 1995, s 64(1)(a). Parts II to V of the Crown Proceedings Act 1947 apply to proceedings against the Crown brought under the 1995 Act as they apply to Crown proceedings in England and Wales, in Northern Ireland and in Scotland under s 23 of the 1947 Act: DDA 1995, s 64(3)–(4) and Sch 8, para 44(1) and (4)(b). However, ss 20 and 44 of the 1947 Act (dealing with the removal of proceedings from the county court to the High Court or from the sheriff court to the Court of Session) are disapplied for this present purpose.
2 DDA 1995, s 64(1)(b).
3 Similar provisions are to be found in the SDA 1975, s 85 and RRA 1976, s 75. In Northern Ireland, s 64 is modified by the terms of Sch 8, para 44.

9.5.2 Part II of the DDA 1995 (outlawing discrimination against disabled persons in the employment field) applies to service for the purposes of a Minister of the Crown or government department (other than service of a person holding a statutory office) or on behalf of the Crown for the purposes of a person holding a statutory office or the purposes of a statutory body.[1] A 'statutory body' is one set up by or under an enactment and a 'statutory office' is construed accordingly.[2] The effect is to provide that civil servants are to be regarded as employees, but not a person holding a statutory office.[3] The kinds of office holders who might be thus excluded will include justices of the peace, by way of example, but a person employed by such an office holder is within the statute. The Disability Rights Task Force recommends that statutory office holders should be covered by civil rights legislation on employment.[4]

1 DDA 1995, s 64(2). Service for the purposes of a Minister of the Crown or government department does not include service in any office mentioned in the House of Commons Disqualification Act 1975, Sch 2 (that is, ministerial offices) or service as the head of a Northern Ireland department (s 64(8) and Sch 8, para 44).
2 DDA 1995, s 64(8).
3 HC Deb Standing Committee E, cols 441–442.
4 DRTF Report, recommendation 5.14.

9.5.3 However, a statutory office holder is not entirely excluded from the Act's protection. When making an appointment of a statutory office holder, the Minister or government department concerned must not act in a way which would contravene the employment provisions in Part II of the Act, as if the Minister or government department were acting as an employer.[1] So, in respect of an appointment of a person by a Minister or government department to an office or post, which would not otherwise be an employment within the meaning of Part II,[2] the anti-discriminatory principles of the Act will apply.[3]

---

1 DDA 1995, s 66(2).
2 Ibid, s 64(2)(a).
3 Ibid, s 66(1). However, regulations may prescribe that certain public appointments are to be outside this extended protection (s 66(3)). No such regulations have been made to date.

9.5.4 The DDA 1995 explicitly excludes service as a prison officer (with the exception of custody officers or prison custody officers),[1] a fire-fighting member of a fire brigade,[2] and service in the naval, military or air force from protection under Part II of the legislation (discrimination in employment).[3] The rationale for these exceptions is said to be that they involve positions calling for unusually demanding all-round requirements for fitness and stamina. The physical and mental capacity of recruits to these services is a matter of judgement for the recruiting authorities to make, without being hindered by the Act.[4] Police officers are implicitly outside the scope of the Act as they are neither employees under a contract of service nor are they Crown servants.[5] In any event,[6] Part II does not apply to service in the Ministry of Defence Police,[7] the British Transport Police,[8] the Royal Parks Constabulary,[9] or the United Kingdom Atomic Energy Authority Constabulary.[10] The Disability Rights Task Force recommends that all these occupations should be covered by civil rights legislation, although subject to safeguards.[11]

---

1   Within the meaning of the Criminal Justice and Public Order Act 1994, s 127 and the Prison Act (Northern Ireland) 1953, s 2(2).
2   Maintained in pursuance of the Fire Services Act 1947 or as defined in the Fire Services (Northern Ireland) Order 1984.
3   DDA 1995, s 64(5)–(8) and Sch 8, para 44(3)–(4).
4   HC Deb, vol 257, cols 894–895.
5   Within the meaning of DDA 1995, s 64.
6   Ibid, s 64(5).
7   Established under the Ministry of Defence Police Act 1987, s 1.
8   Established under the British Transport Commission Act 1949, s 53.
9   Established under the Parks Regulation Act 1872.
10 That is, the special constables nominated by the Authority under the Special Constables Act 1923, s 3.
11 DRTF Report, recommendations 5.15–5.16.

9.6 APPLICATION TO PARLIAMENT

9.6.1 The DDA 1995 applies to an act (or deliberate omission) done by (or for the purposes of) the House of Lords or the House of Commons.[1] In other words, the Act is equally applicable to Parliament as it would be to a private person. Nothing in any rule of law or the law or practice of Parliament prevents proceedings being instituted under the DDA 1995 against either of the Houses of Parliament in an employment tribunal or a court. Otherwise, parliamentary privilege would dictate that the Act would not apply to the legislature itself.

---

1   DDA 1995, s 65(1).

9.6.2   As far as the employment discrimination provisions of Part II of the DDA 1995 are concerned, the Corporate Officer of the House of Commons is to be treated as the employer of any person who is (or would be) a relevant member of the House of Commons staff.[1] In respect of discrimination in relation to the provision of goods, facilities or services to members of the public under Part III of the Act, the relevant provider of any services in question would be the Corporate Officer of the House of Commons and the Corporate Officer of the House of Lords respectively.[2] The two Houses provide a number of obvious services to visitors, such as refreshment facilities and information services. However, where the service at issue is the access to and use of any place in the Palace of Westminster which members of the public are permitted to enter (such as the public galleries in the debating chambers), the Corporate Officers of both Houses are treated as joint providers of such a service.[3] This makes it plain that physical access to the political process of the legislature itself is a matter that can be addressed and redressed under the relevant provisions of the DDA 1995.

---

1   DDA 1995, s 65(2) for the purposes of the Employment Rights Act 1996, s 195. There are similar concessions made under the sex and race discrimination legislation: SDA 1975, ss 85A–85B; RRA 1976, ss 75A–75B.
2   DDA 1995, s 65(3).
3   Ibid, s 65(4).

9.7   REGULATIONS AND ORDERS

9.7.1   The DDA 1995 makes provision in several places for the enactment of regulations and orders which amplify the substantive provisions of the new legislation. Any power under the Act to make regulations or orders is to be exercised by statutory instrument.[1] The term 'regulations' means regulations made by the Secretary of State.[2] Any such power may be exercised to make different provision for different cases, including different provision for different areas.[3] The power to make regulations and orders under the Act includes the power to make incidental, supplemental, consequential or transitional provisions.[4] That power is exercised by the Secretary of State as appears to him or her as expedient. The power to make regulations and orders may also provide for a person to exercise a discretion in dealing with any matter.[5] A statutory instrument made under the DDA 1995 is subject to annulment by a resolution of either House of Parliament.[6]

1   DDA 1995, s 67(1). An exception is provided for under s 67(6) in respect of an order under
    s 43 by which the Secretary of State may authorise the use on roads of a regulated public
    service vehicle (PSV) which does not comply with the PSV accessibility regulations or which
    does not possess an accessibility or approval certificate under ss 40–42 of the Act. See
    Chapter 8.
2   Ibid, s 68(1).
3   Ibid, s 67(2).
4   Ibid, s 67(3)(a).
5   Ibid, s 67(3)(b). Nothing in s 34(4) (licensing of taxis in compliance with taxi accessibility
    regulations) or s 40(6) (public service vehicle accessibility regulations) or s 46(5) (rail
    vehicle accessibility regulations) affects the powers conferred by s 67(2) or s 67(3) above.
6   Ibid, s 67(5). However, that annulment procedure does not apply to a statutory instrument
    made under s 3(9) (an order appointing the date on which any s 3 guidance as to the
    meaning of disability is to come into force) or under s 70(3) (an order appointing the date
    when the provisions of the Act come into force).

Chapter 10

LIABILITY AND REMEDIES

10.1 CAUSES OF ACTION

10.1.1 The DDA 1995 created a number of causes of actions. These have already been referred to in the discussion of the substantive law in earlier chapters of this book. However, it may be helpful to collect and revisit that information here. Broadly speaking, the DDA 1995 created seven potential causes of action based upon unlawful discrimination against disabled persons. The Act also provides that victimisation amounts to discrimination for its purposes.

Discrimination

10.1.2 First, it is unlawful for an employer to discriminate against a disabled person in the field of recruitment, selection and employment offers, and in relation to employment terms and opportunities, dismissal or the subjecting of a disabled person to any other detriment.[1] Secondly, it is unlawful for a principal to discriminate against a disabled person in relation to contract work.[2] Thirdly, it is unlawful for a trade organisation to discriminate against a disabled person in access to membership and in respect of the rights of membership.[3]

---

1 DDA 1995, s 4(1),(2). See generally ss 4–7 and Chapter 3. This liability is extended to trustees and managers of occupational pension schemes and providers of insurance services in the circumstances explained in ss 17–18. As has been explained in Chapter 6, liability might also arise in relation to the lessor of premises occupied under a lease (s 16 and Sch 4).
2 DDA 1995, s 12(1). This is in terms very similar to (but not identical with) those applicable to employers under s 4, while s 12 relies in general upon the provisions of Part II of the Act to amplify this liability. See Chapter 3.
3 DDA 1995, s 13(1),(2) as supplemented by ss 14–16 and Sch 4. See Chapter 4.

10.1.3 Fourthly, it is unlawful for a person to discriminate against a disabled person in relation to the provision of goods, facilities or services.[1] Fifthly, it is unlawful for a person with the power to dispose of any premises to discriminate against a disabled person in relation to the disposal or terms of disposal of premises or in the treatment of disabled persons in relation to waiting lists for premises.[2] Sixthly, it is unlawful for a person managing any premises to discriminate against a disabled person occupying those premises in relation to the way in which a disabled person is permitted (or not permitted) to use any benefits or facilities in relation to those premises, or by evicting the disabled person or subjecting him or her to any other detriment.[3] Seventhly, it is unlawful for any person whose licence or consent is required for the disposal of any premises comprised in or the subject of a tenancy to discriminate against a disabled person by withholding the licence or consent for the disposal of the premises to the disabled person.[4]

---

1   DDA 1995, s 19(1). This cause of action is amplified in the remaining sub-sections of s 19 and in the provisions of ss 20–21 and of Part III of the Act in general. See Chapter 5. The provisions of s 27 and Sch 4 will also be relevant where the service provider occupies premises under lease. See Chapter 6.
2   Ibid, s 22(1). See generally ss 22–24 and Part III. See Chapter 6.
3   Ibid, s 22(3). See generally ss 22–24 and Part III. See Chapter 6.
4   Ibid, s 22(4). See generally ss 22–24 and Part III. See Chapter 6.

Victimisation

10.1.4   For the purposes of Part II or Part III of the DDA 1995, a person also has a cause of action if he or she is victimised by another person in connection with the exercise of any rights contained within the Act.[1] The concept of liability arising from the victimisation of a person because he or she sought to exercise statutory rights is one which is established in discrimination law and in employment law generally.[2] The victimisation provisions in the DDA 1995 are drafted in a slightly different way from the other discrimination statutes, but the case-law under the comparable sections of the SDA 1975 and the RRA 1976 will be informative.[3]

---

1   DDA 1995, s 55. A cause of action is supplied here by cross-referencing s 55 with ss 4, 12, 13, 19 and 22. See ss 4(5), 12(4), 13(3), 19(4) and 22(5).
2   See, for example, SDA 1975, s 4; RRA 1976, s 2; ERA 1996, s 104.
3   HC Deb Standing Committee E, cols 425–426.

10.1.5   A person (A) discriminates against another person (B) if A treats B less favourably than A treats or would treat other persons whose circumstances are the same as B's and A does so for one of a number of reasons.[1] Those alternative reasons are:[2]

- B has brought proceedings against A or any other person (C) under the Act;
- B has given evidence or information in connection with proceedings brought by a person (D) against A or C under the Act;
- B has otherwise done anything under the Act in relation to A or any other person (C);
- B has alleged (expressly or impliedly) that A or C has contravened the Act;
- A believes or suspects that B has done or intends to do any of the above things.

The effect is to treat the listed forms of victimisation as amounting to acts of discrimination for the purposes of Part II or Part III of the DDA 1995.

---

1   DDA 1995, s 55(1).
2   Ibid, s 55(2).

10.1.6   However, victimisation of B by A in any of these circumstances is not made unlawful solely by virtue of the victimisation provisions if the less favourable treatment of B by A is because of an allegation made by B which was false and not made in good faith.[1] Furthermore, if the person being victimised (B) is a disabled person or a person who has had a disability, the disability in question is to be disregarded when comparing B's circumstances with that of any other person who is the comparator for judging A's less favourable treatment of B.[2] It is also clear that a tribunal or court could determine how B has been treated in comparison with a hypothetical comparator.[3]

---

1 DDA 1995, s 55(4).
2 Ibid, s 55(3).
3 HC Deb Standing Committee E, col 426.

10.1.7 Where B brings an action alleging unlawful discrimination by dint of victimisation in employment (or contract work) or by a trade organisation or in the provision of goods, facilities and services or in respect of the disposal (or management) of premises, it does not matter whether B is or is not a disabled person within the meaning of the Act.[1] Unlike the sex and race discrimination statutes, the DDA 1995 is asymmetrical. That is to say, it does not outlaw any act of reverse discrimination against non-disabled persons or more favourable treatment of disabled persons.[2] Similarly, it does not directly prohibit discriminatory treatment of a person because of his or her association or relationship with a disabled person. The victimisation provisions provide the only basis for a cause of action under the Act for a person who either does not satisfy the definition of a disabled person in Part I or who is not a disabled person at all.

---

1 DDA 1995, ss 4(5), 12(4), 13(3), 19(4) and s 22(7).
2 But note the position of local government employers discussed at **3.12**.

10.1.8 The victimisation provisions of the DDA 1995 will or should catch the following illustrations:[1]

– B, a disabled person, is dismissed by A (his or her employer) because B took A to an employment tribunal under the Act for refusing him or her access to a training opportunity or a promotion;
– B, a non-disabled person, is demoted and receives a cut in pay because he or she gave evidence in court proceedings brought under the Act against A (B's employer) by C (a disabled person) who had been refused service in A's restaurant because C was a wheelchair user;
– B, a disabled tenant of A (a local authority landlord), is evicted from his or her rented flat or removed from the housing list by A because B wrote to the local press complaining that A was failing to make provision under the Act to allow disabled persons physical access to the local community centre;
– B, a non-disabled activist on disability rights is refused entry to A's cinema because B had picketed the cinema alleging that it was physically inaccessible to disabled persons contrary to the Act.

However, judicial interpretation of the victimisation provisions of the SDA 1975 and RRA 1976 demonstrates that not all forms of apparent victimisation will be caught.[2]

1   See also Employment Code of Practice, paras 4.53–4.54 and Rights of Access Code of
    Practice, paras 9.2–9.5.
2   See, for example, *British Airways Engine Overhaul Ltd v Francis* [1981] IRLR 9, EAT (there
    must be a connection between B's actions, A's actions and the provisions of the Act); *Aziz v
    Trinity Street Taxis Ltd* [1988] ICR 534, CA (there must be a causal link between the
    victimisation and a protected act). However, it is not necessary to show conscious deliberate
    victimisation: *Nagarajan v London Regional Transport* [1999] ICR 877, HL (motive is irrelevant
    and victimisation might be inferred from subconscious acts). See also *Cornelius v University
    College of Swansea* [1987] IRLR 141, CA; *Kirby v Manpower Services Commission* [1980] ICR 420,
    EAT; *Waters v Metropolitan Police Commissioner* [1997] ICR 1073, CA; *Chief Constable of West
    Yorkshire Police v Khan* [2000] IRLR 324, CA.

10.2   LEGAL LIABILITY

10.2.1   The DDA 1995 established a number of ways upon which legal liability
for acts of unlawful discrimination can be based. In particular, provision is
made for the liability of employers and principals, and of those who aid
unlawful acts. There are also cases where there is an exemption from liability
which would otherwise arise (most notably in respect of the exceptions for
statutory authority and national security).

Aiding unlawful acts

10.2.2   A person who knowingly aids another person to do an act made
unlawful by the DDA 1995 is treated for the purposes of the legislation as having
done the same kind of unlawful act in his or her own right.[1] The effect is that a
person can become liable for a discriminatory act committed contrary to the
DDA 1995 merely by aiding and abetting the person who is primarily
responsible for the discriminatory conduct. For example, if a company's
personnel officer knowingly or deliberately discriminates against disabled
applicants for employment, the company will be primarily responsible under
the principle of statutory vicarious liability,[2] but the personnel officer may also
be liable,[3] having aided the company to commit the discrimination in question.
However, it is not commonplace for complainants to seek to make employees
or officers of a company (which has discriminated in the above circumstances)
jointly or individually liable in legal proceedings for their part in the act of
discrimination. Among other reasons, this is because of the difficulty of proving
that such a person 'knowingly' aided an unlawful act.[4] The mental element of
knowledge or intention is crucial. Furthermore, there may be little to be gained
in terms of remedies.

1   DDA 1995, s 57(1). This is modelled after like provisions in the other discrimination
    statutes: SDA 1975, s 42 and RRA 1976, s 33.
2   Under DDA 1995, s 58 (discussed below).
3   Under DDA 1995, s 57. See *AM v WC and SPV* [1999] IRLR 410, EAT.
4   *Anyanwu v South Bank Students' Union* [2000] IRLR 36, CA.

10.2.3   A person faced with an allegation of aiding another person to commit
a discriminatory act made unlawful by the legislation has an explicit defence.[1]
For present purposes, a person does not knowingly aid another to do an

unlawful act if he or she acts in reliance on a statement made to him or her by that other person. The statement must be to the effect that the discriminatory act would not be unlawful because of any provision of the Act and it must be reasonable to rely upon that statement. That other person is guilty of a criminal offence if he or she knowingly or recklessly makes such a statement which is false or misleading in a material respect.[2]

1 DDA 1995, s 57(3).
2 Ibid, s 57(4). A person guilty of that offence is liable upon summary conviction to a fine not exceeding level 5 on the standard scale (s 57(5)). An employer or principal cannot be made vicariously liable for such an offence committed by an employee or agent (s 58(4)).

Liability of employers

10.2.4 Anything done by a person in the course of his or her employment is treated for the purposes of DDA 1995 as also done by his or her employer, whether or not it was done with the employer's knowledge or approval.[1] This statutory principle of vicarious liability is an important inclusion because, for example, the Act speaks of unlawful acts committed by 'an employer',[2] 'a provider of services'[3] and 'a person with power to dispose' (of any premises).[4] It reflects similar provisions in other discrimination statutes.[5] The effect is to make the employer vicariously liable for the discriminatory actions of an employee during the course of employment. However, both the employer and the employee remain potentially liable, because the employee may have knowingly aided the employer in the commission of an unlawful act of discrimination.[6] The employee is not released from any individual liability that might arise. So, even though the employee might not be capable of committing an act of discrimination made unlawful by the Act, he or she may be deemed to have aided the employer's unlawful act.[7]

1 DDA 1995, s 58(1). See generally, Employment Code of Practice, paras 4.11, 4.55–4.59 and 4.62–4.63; Rights of Access Code of Practice, para. 9.8–9.10. By virtue of s 58(4), vicarious liability cannot extend to an offence committed under s 57(4).
2 Ibid, s 3.
3 Ibid, s 19.
4 Ibid, s 22.
5 SDA 1975, s 41; RRA 1976, s 32.
6 DDA 1995, s 57 (discussed at **10.2.2**). See under the SDA 1975: *Enterprise Glass Co Ltd v Miles* [1990] ICR 787, EAT; *AM v WC and SPV* [1999] IRLR 410, EAT.
7 This is because s 57(2) provides that an employee for whose act the employer is liable under s 58 shall be taken to have aided the employer to do the act. For an illustration of this under the SDA 1975, see *Read v Tiverton District Council* [1977] IRLR 202.

10.2.5 At common law, the meaning of 'in the course of employment' has been the subject of a long line of case-law[1] which establishes that it is insufficient that the act was done while on duty or that the occasion to commit the act was provided in the context of employment, but it is enough that the act that gave rise to the discriminatory conduct was authorised by the employer, although carried out in an unauthorised or prohibited fashion.[2] However, the common law principles on the meaning of 'in the course of employment' are not applicable to the statutory concept of vicarious liability.[3] The test of what will amount to 'in the course of employment' for the purposes of establishing vicarious liability for acts of disability discrimination is more flexible and is ultimately a question of fact for the tribunal.[4]

---

1   See, for example, *Irving and Irving v Post Office* [1987] IRLR 289, CA.
2   *Aldred v Nacanco* [1987] IRLR 292, CA; *Heasmans v Clarity Cleaning Co Ltd* [1987] IRLR 286, CA.
3   *Jones v Tower Boot Co Ltd* [1997] IRLR 168, CA.
4   See, for example, *Chief Constable of Lincolnshire Police v Stubbs* [1999] IRLR 81, EAT (vicarious liability for sexual harassment during work-connected social activities).

10.2.6   In a case founded upon the vicarious liability provision, an employer has a possible defence. The employer might escape vicarious liability (but not any liability faced in its own right) by proving that it took such steps as were reasonably practicable to prevent the employee from doing the act complained of or doing acts of the same description in the course of employment.[1] It may be sufficient to avoid vicarious liability by showing, for example, that the employer was unaware of the discriminatory acts being perpetrated by the employee and that there was proper and adequate staff supervision, including appropriate training and the dissemination of an anti-discrimination or equal opportunities policy.[2] The burden of proof will be upon the employer.

---

1   DDA 1995, s 58(5).
2   *Balgobin and Francis v London Borough of Tower Hamlets* [1987] IRLR 401, EAT (a sex discrimination case under comparable provisions).

Liability of principals

10.2.7   The statutory provision on vicarious liability also applies in part to the relationship of principal and agent. Anything done by a person as agent for a principal, and with the principal's express or implied authority, is treated for the purposes of the DDA 1995 as also done by the principal, whether the authority was given before or after the act in question.[1] Once again, this means that the principal is vicariously liable for the discriminatory actions of the agent and is jointly liable with the agent. The agent will be treated as having aided the principal to commit the unlawful act.[2] There is no defence available to the principal as there would be to an employer in a case of vicarious liability.[3]

---

1   DDA 1995, s 58(2)–(3). Whatever a person has power to do may be done by an agent. Without such a power vested in the principal, an agent has no power deriving from agency. See *Halsbury's Laws of England* Vol 1(2) 4th edn (1990) para 3. In a case brought under the DDA 1995, s 4 the governing body of a State-maintained school with a delegated budget was held not to be the agent of a LEA when committing an alleged act of disability discrimination in recruitment and selection arrangements because the LEA had no statutory power to carry out the governors' functions: *Lancashire County Council v Mason* [1998] ICR 907, EAT. But now see the Education (Modification of Enactments Relating to Employment) Order 1998, SI 1998/218.

2 By virtue of DDA 1995, s 57(2).
3 Under DDA 1995, s 58(5).

Statutory authority

10.2.8 The DDA 1995 contains an exception to liability in respect of statutory authority. Nothing in the 1995 legislation causes an act or deliberate omission to be made unlawful where that act or omission is done in any of the following circumstances:[1]

– in pursuance of any 'enactment';
– in pursuance of any 'instrument' made by a Minister of the Crown under any 'enactment';
– to comply with any condition or requirement imposed by a Minister of the Crown (whether before or after the passing of the Act) by virtue of any 'enactment'.[2]

An 'enactment' for this purpose will include an Act of Parliament, subordinate legislation (such as a statutory instrument) and any Order in Council,[3] whether passed or made before or after the date the DDA 1995 received Royal Assent.[4] An 'instrument' clearly refers to subordinate legislation made by a Minister under statutory delegated authority, whether made before or after the passing of the DDA 1995.

1 DDA 1995, s 59(1). See also Employment Code of Practice, para 4.65; Rights of Access Code of Practice, para 9.12.
2 In Northern Ireland, the relevant functions of a Minister of the Crown referred to in s 59 will be those of a Northern Ireland department (Sch 8, para 39).
3 DDA 1995, s 68(1) (and which cross-refers to the Interpretation Act 1978, s 21). Also included (by virtue of Sch 8, para 47(1)) is any statutory provision within the meaning of the Interpretation Act (Northern Ireland) 1954, s 1(f).
4 DDA 1995, s 59(2) (namely, 8 November 1995).

10.2.9 The use of the phrase 'in pursuance of' any enactment or instrument is deliberate. In the comparable provisions of race discrimination law,[1] the draftsman also used this term rather than the phrasing 'under' any enactment or instrument. This has led to a narrow interpretation of the exception by the courts. The exemption applies only to actions reasonably necessary to comply with a statutory obligation and not to acts done in exercise of a power of discretion conferred by the enactment or instrument.[2] The use of the word 'under' (contained originally in the 1995 Bill) may well have had the effect of inviting a wider interpretation of the statutory authority exemption. The result may have been that the exception would have applied to anything done under statutory authority, whether of a discretionary nature or not, and that would have gone some way towards undermining the objectives of the 1995 legislation. That possibility has apparently been excluded.

1 RRA 1976, s 41.
2 *Hampson v Department of Education and Science* [1990] IRLR 302 HL. See also, under the DDA 1995, *Post Office v Jones* [2000] ICR 388, EAT.

10.2.10   An example of how this exception might operate was given by a minister when the DDA 1995 Act was being enacted:

> 'Under s 12 of the Health and Safety at Work etc Act 1974, the Secretary of State is given the power to give the Health and Safety Commission directions about ways in which it carries out its functions. If one of those functions, in the Secretary of State's opinion, required the Commission to do something which adversely affected disabled people, it would not be unlawful and could not be challenged under the provisions of the [Act].'[1]

It was also made clear that it was important that the exception should apply to both existing and future enactments. This point was illustrated by reference to the hypothetical possibility that a future safety legislative provision might require employers to modify equipment for the protection of employee operators. As a result of that modification, a disabled person might find it no longer physically possible to operate the equipment. The exception ensures that, by refusing to remove or alter the modification, the employer would not be in breach of the duty to accommodate disabled persons under the DDA 1995. The new safety law would override the disability discrimination legislation to that extent alone, although other forms of reasonable adjustment might remain appropriate for the employee.[2]

---

1   HC Deb Standing Committee E, col 428. See also the examples in respect of alterations to the highway or to listed buildings given at HL Deb, vol 565, col 673.
2   There would be nothing to prevent a future enactment being made expressly subject to the DDA 1995.

10.2.11   In any proceedings in respect of discrimination in employment or contract work or by a trade organisation,[1] a certificate signed by or on behalf of a Minister of the Crown (or a Northern Ireland department) which certifies that any conditions or requirements specified in the certificate were imposed by a minister (or that department), and were in operation at or throughout a specified time, shall be conclusive evidence of the matters certified.[2] A document purporting to be such a certificate shall be received in evidence and, unless the contrary is proved, is deemed to be such a certificate.[3] Identical provision is made in respect of proceedings under Part III of the DDA 1995 in respect of goods, facilities, services and premises.[4]

---

1   Under DDA 1995, s 8.
2   Ibid, Sch 3, para 4(1)(a) and Sch 8, para 50(2).
3   Ibid, Sch 3, para 4(2).
4   Ibid, Sch 3, paras 8(1)(a) and 8(2) in respect of proceedings under s 25. The modification of this provision in the context of Northern Ireland is set out in Sch 8, para 50(4).

National security

10.2.12   Nothing in the DDA 1995 makes unlawful any act done for the purpose of safeguarding national security.[1] In proceedings under Part II before an employment tribunal or under Part III before a court, a certificate signed by or on behalf of a Minister of the Crown which certifies that an act specified in the certificate was done for the purpose of safeguarding national security is to be conclusive evidence of the matter certified.[2] A document purporting to be such a certificate shall be received in evidence and, unless the contrary is proved, is deemed to be such a certificate.[3]

---

1 DDA 1995, s 59(3).
2 Ibid, Sch 3, paras 4(1)(b) and 8(1)(b). In Northern Ireland, the relevant certificate must be signed by the Secretary of State (Sch 8, para 50(2)).
3 Ibid, Sch 3, paras 4(2) and 8(2).

10.3 EMPLOYMENT CASES

Statutory questionnaire

10.3.1 Provision is made for help for persons suffering disability discrimination in relation to employment.[1] This applies to a person ('the complainant') who considers that he or she may have been discriminated against by another person ('the respondent') in contravention of Part II of the DDA 1995 (discrimination in the employment field) and against whom the complainant may decide to make a complaint or has already done so.[2] This provision is modelled after similar provisions for assisting aggrieved persons to obtain information in cases of potential sex or race discrimination.[3] In such instances, a statutory questionnaire procedure has proved to be a useful device for assisting complainants in potential race or sex discrimination complaints in deciding whether to pursue proceedings and how best to frame the presentation of the complaint. It is likely to prove equally efficacious in disability discrimination cases.

---

1 DDA 1995, s 56.
2 Ibid, s 56(1).
3 SDA 1975, s 74; RRA 1976, s 65. The relevant provisions and forms in these jurisdictions are to be found in the Sex Discrimination (Questions and Replies) Order 1975, SI 1975/2048 (amended by SI 1977/844) and the Race Relations (Questions and Replies) Order 1977, SI 1977/842.

10.3.2 The Secretary of State is mandated to prescribe by order forms by which the complainant may question the respondent on the respondent's reasons for doing any relevant act or on any other matter which is or may be relevant.[1] These questionnaire forms may be used either before or after proceedings have been commenced. Forms may also be prescribed by which the respondent may (if the respondent so wishes) reply to any questions. The power to prescribe such forms is to be taken with a view to helping the complainant to decide whether, in the first place, to make a complaint against the respondent and, in the second place, to formulate and present the case in the most effective manner. The Secretary of State may also prescribe the period within which any questionnaire must be served on the respondent employer and the manner in which the questionnaire (and any reply) must be served.[2]

---

1   DDA 1995, s 56(2). In Northern Ireland, the Secretary of State's powers under s 56 are exercised by the Department of Economic Development (Sch 8, para 38).
2   DDA 1995, s 56(4).

10.3.3   The Secretary of State has complied with these requirements by issuing the Disability Discrimination (Questions and Replies) Order 1996.[1] The Order prescribes forms by which the complainant may question the respondent on its reasons for doing any relevant act (or on any other relevant matter) and by which the respondent may, if it wishes, reply to any questions.[2] A statutory questionnaire may be served upon the respondent by delivering it to the respondent; or by sending it by post to the respondent's usual or last known residence or place of business; or where the respondent to be served is acting by a solicitor, by delivering it at, or by sending it by post to, the solicitor's address for service.[3] Where the person to be served is a body corporate or is a trade union or employers' association, the questionnaire may be served by delivering it to the secretary or clerk of the body, union or association at its registered or principal office or by sending it by post to the secretary or clerk at that office.[4] The respondent may serve a reply on the complainant by delivering the reply, or sending it by post, to him or her at the address for reply as stated in the questionnaire.[5]

---

1   SI 1996/2793 which came into force on 2 December 1996.
2   Disability Discrimination (Questions and Replies) Order 1996, SI 1996/2793, reg 2 and Schs 1 and 2.
3   Ibid, reg 4(a)–(c).
4   Ibid, reg 4(d).
5   Ibid, reg 5.

10.3.4   A respondent employer faced with a statutory discrimination question-naire must consider very carefully how to reply to the questions, because the questions and any reply by the respondent are admissible in evidence in any subsequent tribunal proceedings under Part II of the DDA 1995.[1] However, this is subject to any enactment or rule of law regulating the admissibility of evidence in tribunal proceedings.[2] While the rules of evidence are not strictly applied in employment tribunals, the credibility of and compelling nature of evidence in such proceedings does depend upon the tribunal weighing and assessing such evidence in the light of those rules. Where a questionnaire was served before a complaint has been presented to a tribunal, a question is only admissible as evidence if it was served within 3 months of the alleged act of discrimination. Where it was served after a complaint has been presented to a tribunal, a question is admissible if it was served within 21 days of the presentation of the complaint (or, if it was served with the leave of a tribunal, within the period specified by that tribunal).[3]

---

1   DDA 1995, s 56(3)(a). It does not appear to matter whether the respondent's reply is in accordance with the prescribed forms or not.

2   Ibid, s 56(5).

3   Disability Discrimination (Questions and Replies) Order 1996, reg 3.

10.3.5   If, in the view of an employment tribunal in subsequent proceedings under Part II of the DDA 1995, the respondent deliberately omitted to reply to the questionnaire within a reasonable period without reasonable excuse, the tribunal may draw any inference which it considers it just and equitable to draw.[1] This might include an inference that an unlawful act of disability discrimination contrary to Part II of the Act has been committed by the respondent.[2] Similar adverse inferences may be drawn if the tribunal takes the view that the respondent's reply to a questionnaire is evasive or equivocal.[3]

1   DDA 1995, s 56(3)(b)(i). On the general power of tribunals to draw inferences of
    discrimination, see *King v The Great Britain-China Centre* [1991] IRLR 513, CA.

2   See, for example, the race discrimination case of *Virdee v ECC Quarries Ltd* [1978] IRLR 295.

3   DDA 1995, s 56(3)(b)(ii). See, for example, the sex discrimination case of *Carrington v Helix
    Lighting* [1990] IRLR 6, EAT.

10.3.6   The questionnaire procedure is without prejudice to any other enactment or rule of law regulating interlocutory and preliminary matters in proceedings before an employment tribunal.[1] This means that the ability to administer a statutory questionnaire to elicit replies to specific questions from a respondent is in addition to the tribunal's procedural powers in respect of further and better particulars, interrogatories and discovery.[2]

1   DDA 1995, s 56(5).

2   *Oxford v Department of Health and Social Security* [1977] ICR 884, EAT.

Employment tribunal proceedings

10.3.7   A complaint by any person that another person has unlawfully discriminated against him or her contrary to Part II of the DDA 1995[1] may be presented to an employment tribunal.[2] In fact, such a complaint of employment discrimination can be brought only via employment tribunal proceedings.[3] The employment tribunal will also have jurisdiction to hear complaints where the complainant alleges that another person is to be treated as having discriminated against him or her contrary to Part II of the Act. This expressly includes actions against a person who knowingly aids another to do an unlawful act contrary to Part II.[4] It also embraces actions based upon an act done by a person in the course of employment and which is to be treated as also done by that person's employer.[5] Furthermore, an act done by an agent with the authority of another person (the principal) is treated as being the act of the principal and will be equally actionable in the employment tribunal.[6]

1   The employment provisions contained in ss 4–7 and 11, the contract worker provisions in
    s 12 or the provisions touching trade organisations in ss 13–15.

2   DDA 1995, s 8(1) which is largely modelled after the similar provisions in SDA 1975, s 63(1)
    and RRA 1976, s 54(1). The term 'person' includes an individual, a body corporate and

unincorporated associations: Interpretation Act 1978, Sch 1. A complaint survives the death
of a complainant by virtue of Law Reform (Miscellaneous Provisions) Act 1934, s 1(1): *Harris
(Representative of Andrews v Lewisham and Guy's Mental Health NHS Trust)* [2000] IRLR 320,
CA.
3   The unlawfulness of any act by virtue of Part II of the statute does not give rise to any other
    civil or criminal proceedings (Sch 3, para 2(1)). However, this does not prevent the
    possibility of an application for judicial review being made in respect of an act made
    unlawful by the DDA 1995 (Sch 3, para 2(2)).
4   DDA 1995, s 57.
5   Ibid, s 58.
6   See generally **10.2**.

10.3.8   It is not intended to rehearse the constitution and procedures of the
employment tribunal here.[1] It is sufficient to note that proceedings are
commenced by presenting an originating application within the statutory
time-limits and that a respondent may then present a defence in the form of a
notice of appearance. Decisions of an employment tribunal are made
unanimously or by a majority. An appeal from a decision of an employment
tribunal may be made to the Employment Appeal Tribunal, on a point of law,
and from there to the Court of Appeal and the House of Lords. It might also be
noted that the employment tribunals are themselves subject to the Act and will
be covered by the rights of access to goods, facilities and services contained in
Part III of the Act.[2]

---

1   Their proceedings are governed by the Employment Tribunals (Constitution and Rules of
    Procedure) Regulations 1993, SI 1993/2687 as amended by SI 1994/536 and SI 1996/1757;
    in Scotland, see the Employment Tribunals (Constitution and Rules of Procedure)
    (Scotland) Regulations 1993, SI 1993/2688 as amended by SI 1994/538 and SI 1996/1758.
    See generally, Doyle *Employment Tribunals: The New Law* (1998, Bristol: Jordans). DDA 1995,
    Sch 3, Part I contains detailed further provisions concerning enforcement and procedures
    in respect of employment cases (s 8(8)). These provisions are considered below.
2   HC Deb Standing Committee E, col 279. See Chapter 5. Legal aid is not generally available
    in employment tribunal proceedings.

Time-limits

10.3.9   An employment tribunal shall not consider a complaint under the
DDA 1995 unless it is presented before the end of the period of 3 months
beginning when the act complained of was done.[1] The 3-month time-limit for
the presentation of a complaint is important as it goes to the question of the
jurisdiction of the employment tribunal to hear the complaint at all.

---

1   DDA 1995, Sch 3, para 3(1). An 'act' includes a deliberate omission (s 68(1)). This mirrors
    the identical provisions in SDA 1975, s 76(1) and RRA 1976, s 68(1). The case-law under
    those Acts will be instructive here and is referred to in the notes below.

10.3.10   Some confusion might arise as to when the 3-month time period
begins to run.[1] In the case of an isolated act of disability discrimination, the
presumption will be that time starts to run from the date of the act or the
omission itself. A deliberate omission is to be treated as done when the person
in question decided upon it.[2] Subject to rebutting evidence, a person is treated
as having decided upon an omission when he or she does an act inconsistent
with doing the omitted act or, in the absence of such inconsistent behaviour,
when the period expires within which he or she might reasonably have been

expected to do the omitted act if it was to be done.[3] However, in other cases, there is more flexibility in measuring the date upon which time starts to run. In the case of any act or omission which extends over a period of time, the 3-month limitation provision will not start to run until the end of the period in question.[4] Moreover, where the alleged unlawful act of discrimination is attributable to a term in a contract, time does not start to expire until the end of the contract. The unlawful act is said to extend throughout the duration of the contract.[5]

---

1 Compare the provisions of SDA 1975, s 76(6) and RRA 1976, s 68(7).
2 DDA 1995, Sch 3, para 3(3)(c).
3 Ibid, Sch 3, para 3(4). See, for example, *Swithland Motors plc v Clarke* [1994] ICR 231, EAT.
4 Ibid, Sch 3, para 3(3)(b). See *Amies v Inner London Education Authority* [1977] ICR 308, EAT and *Sougrin v Haringey Health Authority* [1991] ICR 791, EAT (distinguishes between continuing acts and continuing consequences); *Calder v James Finlay Corporation Ltd* [1989] IRLR 55, EAT (refusal of access to employment benefit throughout employment construed as continuing act of discrimination); *Littlewoods Organisation plc v Traynor* [1993] IRLR 154, EAT (a failure to remedy a discriminatory situation can be a continuing act of discrimination). On continuing acts of discrimination generally, see *Barclays Bank plc v Kapur* [1991] ICR 208, HL.
5 DDA 1995, Sch 3, para 3(3)(a).

10.3.11 Even where a complaint has been presented out of time, an employment tribunal may nevertheless entertain it if, in all the circumstances of the case, 'it considers that it is just and equitable to do so'.[1] This allows employment tribunals considerable discretion to admit late applications under the Act.[2] Tribunal decisions to extend the time-limit in such cases are rarely challengeable on appeal.[3] In the early years of the Act being in force, tribunals are likely to allow late complaints to proceed where the applicant was unaware of a cause of action or the time-limits governing it.[4]

---

1 DDA 1995, Sch 3, para 3(2).
2 *Hawkins v Ball* [1996] IRLR 258, EAT; *DPP v Marshall* [1998] ICR 518, EAT. Compare the similar provision in SDA 1975, s 76(5) and RRA 1976, s 68(6). Contrast the more restrictive provision in unfair dismissal cases under ERA 1996, s 111.
3 *Hutchinson v Westward Television Ltd* [1977] ICR 279, EAT.
4 See, for example, *Foster v South Glamorgan Health Authority* [1988] ICR 526, EAT.

Conciliation

10.3.12 The DDA 1995 anticipates that there will be an attempt to reach a conciliated settlement between the parties before a complaint proceeds to a hearing by an employment tribunal.[1] Provision is made for a copy of a complaint of disability discrimination to be sent to a conciliation officer of the Advisory, Conciliation and Arbitration Service (ACAS)[2] or, in Northern Ireland, the Labour Relations Agency.[3] In such a case, the conciliation officer must try to promote a settlement of the complaint, without a tribunal hearing, if requested to do so by both parties or if the conciliation officer considers that there is a reasonable prospect of a successful attempt to promote a settlement being made.[4] This latter provision allows the conciliation officer to be proactive, even if only one of the parties has requested a conciliatory intervention. Moreover, where a complaint has yet to be presented to an employment tribunal, but a person is contemplating presenting such a complaint, the conciliation officer shall try to promote a settlement if asked to do so by the potential complainant or potential respondent.[5]

---

1   See generally, Employment Tribunals Act 1996, s 18 replacing DDA 1995, Sch 3, para 1.
2   ETA 1996, ss 18(1)(c), (2) and 42(1). Note the provisions of rr 2(3) and 20(7) in Sch 1 to the Employment Tribunals (Constitution and Rules of Procedure) Regulations 1993, SI 1993/2687 relating to conciliation.
3   DDA 1995, Sch 8, para 50(1). See now the Industrial Tribunals (Northern Ireland) Order 1996, SI 1996/1921.
4   ETA 1996, s 18(2).
5   Ibid, s 18(3).

10.3.13   Two points about the conciliation stage are worth making here. First, the conciliation officer must consider the desirability of encouraging the parties to resolve the complaint by the use of appropriate available procedures for the settlement of grievances.[1] Especially in cases which have not yet resulted in an originating application, and where the complainant is in employment, a complaint might be more easily resolved by utilising the employer's internal grievance procedure, if any. Many employers have already adopted such procedures, either as an adjunct to disciplinary rules and practices, or as part of an equal opportunities policy or statement. Secondly, anything communicated to the conciliation officer during the course of the conciliation process is inadmissible in evidence in any subsequent proceedings before the employment tribunal, unless with the consent of the person who communicated that matter.[2]

---

1   ETA 1996, s 18(6).
2   Ibid, s 18(7).

10.3.14   If a conciliated settlement has been agreed with the assistance of an ACAS conciliation officer, the agreement will usually be recorded in writing using form COT3. An oral agreement would be equally valid, although obviously less certain.[1] A conciliated settlement will be a valid agreement and will not void[2] if it merely records an agreement not to institute proceedings or an agreement to discontinue proceedings before an employment tribunal.[3] Unless the conciliated settlement is otherwise challengeable or invalid, the employment tribunal will then have no jurisdiction to hear the complaint which is the subject of the conciliation. Even if a respondent reneges on an ACAS-brokered settlement, the complainant must sue on the agreement rather than seek to reopen the complaint.

---

1   *Gilbert v Kembridge Fibres Ltd* [1984] ICR 188, EAT.
2   By virtue of DDA 1995, s 9(1).

3   Ibid, s 9(2)(a).

Compromises or settlements

10.3.15   Apart from a settlement produced as a result of individual conciliation under the auspices of ACAS, what other possibilities arise to settle or to
compromise a complaint under the DDA 1995 without proceeding to an
employment tribunal hearing? Any term of an agreement which purports to
prevent any person from presenting a complaint to an employment tribunal
under Part II of the Act is prima facie void.[1] However, that does not apply
expressly to an agreement to discontinue or not to institute proceedings if that
agreement is the product of ACAS conciliation.[2] A settlement or compromise
agreement is also valid if three conditions are satisfied.[3]

1   DDA 1995, s 9(1)(c).
2   Ibid, s 9(2)(a).
3   Ibid, s 9(2)(b). Similar, but not identical, provisions are to be found in relation to
     compromise agreements introduced by the Trade Union Reform and Employment Rights
     Act 1993, s 39 in SDA 1975, s 77; RRA 1976, s 72; Trade Union and Labour Relations
     (Consolidation) Act 1992, s 288; and ERA 1996, s 203. All these measures have been
     amended by the Employment Rights (Dispute Resolution) Act 1998, ss 9–10. See Doyle
     Employment Tribunals: The New Law (1998, Bristol: Jordans), Chapter 4.

10.3.16   First, the complainant must have received 'advice from a relevant
independent adviser' as to the terms and effect of the proposed agreement not
to institute proceedings or to discontinue existing proceedings before the
employment tribunal.[1] The advice in question must highlight, in particular, the
effect of such agreement upon the complainant's ability to pursue the
complaint before an employment tribunal. In other words, the advice must
have made it clear that the settlement will generally prevent the complainant
resurrecting the complaint by seeking a hearing of the tribunal.

1   DDA 1995, s 9(3)(a) as amended. It is no longer necessary for there to have been
     independent legal advice from a qualified lawyer, thus allowing for compromise agreements
     to be settled by other categories of adviser (provided they are covered by indemnity
     insurance).

10.3.17   Advice is from 'a relevant independent adviser' if he or she is:[1]

–   a qualified lawyer;[2] or
–   an officer, official, employee or member of an independent trade union;
     or
–   working at an advice centre (whether as an employee or a volunteer); or
–   a person of a description specified in an order made by the Secretary of
     State.

In the case of an officer, official, employee or member of an independent trade
union (or an employee or volunteer at an advice centre), such a person is only a
relevant independent adviser if he or she has been certified in writing by the
trade union (or by the advice centre, as the case may be) as competent to give

advice and as authorised to do so on behalf of the trade union (or the advice centre).[3]

---

1   DDA 1995, s 9(4) as amended.
2   A 'qualified lawyer' is a barrister or advocate (whether in practice as such or employed to give legal advice), or a solicitor (holding a practising certificate): DDA 1995, s 9(4B) as amended. As a result of amendments introduced by the Employment Rights (Dispute Resolution) Act 1998, a person, other than a barrister or solicitor, who is an authorised advocate or authorised litigator (within the meaning of the Courts and Legal Services Act 1990) also counts as a 'qualified lawyer' for these purposes.
3   DDA 1995, s 9(4)(b),(c) as amended.

10.3.18   A person will not be a relevant independent adviser in relation to the complainant (or employee or worker) if he or she is employed by (or is acting in the matter for) the employer or an associated employer (or the other party or a person connected with the other party,[1] as the case may be).[2] In the case of advice being given by a trade union or advice centre, it is obviously the case that the advice would not be independent if the trade union or advice centre were a party to the complaint or proceedings.[3] Furthermore, in the case of advice given by an advice centre, the adviser will not be a relevant independent adviser if the complainant (or employee or worker) makes a payment for the advice received.[4] In addition, in the case of any other person who is of a description which has been designated as a relevant independent adviser by ministerial order, that adviser will also have to satisfy any conditions specified in the order in relation to the giving of advice.[5]

---

1   Any two persons are treated as connected or as associated employers if one is a company of which the other has control or if both are companies of which a third person has control. Control may be direct or indirect control. See DDA 1995, s 9(5) as amended.
2   DDA 1995, s 9(4A)(a) as amended.
3   Ibid, s 9(4A)(b) as amended.
4   Ibid, s 9(4A)(c) as amended.
5   Ibid, s 9(4A)(d) as amended.

10.3.19   Secondly, at the time when the advice was given to the complainant, there must have been in force a contract of insurance (or an indemnity provided for members of a profession or professional body) covering the risk of a claim by the complainant in respect of any loss that might arise as a consequence of the advice.[1] This is designed to protect the complainant from the consequences of negligent professional advice and provides the complainant with a secure alternative cause of action against the negligent adviser.

---

1   DDA 1995, s 9(3)(b) as amended.

10.3.20   Thirdly, the compromise or settlement agreement must be in writing, relate to the particular complaint, identify the legal adviser and state that the conditions above have been satisfied.[1]

---

1   DDA 1995, s 9(3)(c).

Restriction on publicity

10.3.21 Where evidence of a personal nature is likely to be heard by the employment tribunal hearing a complaint of disability discrimination, special provision is made for the restriction of publicity.[1] Evidence of a personal nature means any evidence of a medical or other intimate nature which might reasonably be assumed to be likely to cause significant embarrassment to the complainant if reported.[2] The Secretary of State is empowered to make regulations with respect to the procedure of employment tribunals so as to achieve this objective.[3] This is achieved by amending the employment tribunal procedural regulations.[4]

---

1 This provision was originally made in DDA 1995, s 62(1), but is now contained in ETA 1996, s 12(1).
2 ETA 1996, s 12(7).
3 Ibid, s 12(2). The tribunal procedure regulations already contained similar powers to make restricted reporting orders in respect of allegations of sexual misconduct: Employment Tribunals (Constitution and Rules of Procedure) Regulations 1993, SI 1993/2687 (Sch 1, r 14); Employment Tribunals (Constitution and Rules of Procedure) (Scotland) Regulations 1993, SI 1993/2688 (Sch 1, r 14).
4 Employment Tribunals (Constitution and Rules of Procedure) (Amendment) Regulations 1996, SI 1996/1757 which amend Employment Tribunals (Constitution and Rules of Procedure) Regulations 1993, SI 1993/2687, Sch 1, as previously amended, by introducing a new rule 14(1A) and 14(1B). A similar amendment is made in the Scottish Rules.

10.3.22 The new regulations empower the tribunal to make a 'restricted reporting order' on the application of the complainant or of its own motion.[1] A 'restricted reporting order' has the effect of prohibiting the publication in Great Britain (or Northern Ireland) of 'identifying matter' in a 'written publication' available to the public.[2] A written publication would obviously include a newspaper or magazine, but it also includes a film, a soundtrack and any other record in a permanent form.[3] A restricted reporting order will also have the effect of prohibiting the inclusion of any 'identifying matter' in a relevant radio or television programme for reception in Great Britain, or Northern Ireland, as the case may be.[4] This will effectively prevent the press and broadcast media from reporting any 'identifying matter' about the case. In this context, 'identifying matter' means any matter which is likely to lead members of the public to identify the complainant or any other persons named in the restricted reporting order.[5]

---

1 ETA 1996, s 12(2)(a).
2 Ibid, s 12(7).
3 Ibid, s 12(7).
4 Ibid, s 12(7).
5 Ibid, s 12(7).

10.3.23 A restricted reporting order has effect until the promulgation of the tribunal's decision in the case, unless the order is revoked earlier.[1] If the restricted reporting order is broken by a newspaper or periodical, the proprietor, editor or publisher of the newspaper or periodical is guilty of a summary offence punishable by a fine not exceeding level 5 on the standard scale.[2] Where the order is breached in a publication in any other form, the publisher of the matter shall be so liable.[3] Where the identifying matter is published in breach of a restricted reporting order by a radio or television broadcast, the broadcast company and the programme editor face criminal liability.[4] In any case, it is a defence to prove that, at the time of the alleged offence, the person charged was not aware (and neither suspected nor had reason to suspect) that the publication or programme in question was of (or included) the matter in question.[5]

---

1   ETA 1996, s 12(2)(a).
2   Ibid, s 12(3)(a).
3   Ibid, s 12(3)(b).
4   Ibid, s 12(3)(c).
5   Ibid, s 12(4). Note also s 12(5)–(6) which makes provision for offences of joint liability where the breach of a restricted reporting order is committed by a body corporate with the consent or connivance of (or attributable neglect of) a director, manager, secretary or other similar officer.

10.3.24   Provision is also made for the restriction of publicity on certain appeals from an employment tribunal to the EAT under the DDA 1995.[1] This applies to proceedings on an appeal against an employment tribunal's decision to make (or not make) a restricted reporting order in disability discrimination cases. It also applies in such cases on an appeal against any interlocutory decision of an employment tribunal in proceedings in which the employment tribunal has made a restricted reporting order which it has not revoked. It should be noted that the EAT does not otherwise have a general power to make a restricted reporting order in DDA proceedings. A new r 23A of the Employment Appeal Tribunal Rules 1993 provides that the EAT may, on the application of the complainant or of its own motion, make a restricted reporting order having effect, if not revoked earlier, until the promulgation of its decision. Before it makes a restricted reporting order, the EAT will give each party to the proceedings an opportunity to advance oral argument at a public hearing. Where the EAT makes a restricted reporting order, the EAT may direct that the order is to apply in relation to any other proceedings which are being dealt with by the EAT together with the appeal.

---

1   ETA 1996, s 32 (previously DDA 1995, s 63). The Employment Appeal Tribunal (Amendment) Rules 1996, SI 1996/3216 came into force on 10 January 1997 and give effect to s 32 by amending the Employment Appeal Tribunal Rules 1993, SI 1993/2854.

The hearing and decision

10.3.25   This is not the place to rehearse the practice and procedure of an employment tribunal hearing. The reader is referred to the usual sources. It is worth noting, however, that whereas a tribunal will usually give its written reasons for its decision in summary form (unless a party requests reasons in extended form), in a DDA case (as in race and sex discrimination cases) the tribunal must give extended reasons.[1]

1   Employment Tribunals (Constitution and Rules of Procedure) Regulations 1993, SI 1993/
    2687, Sch 1, r 10 (as amended).

Remedies

10.3.26   Where an employment tribunal finds that a complaint of unlawful disability discrimination in the employment field contrary to Part II of the DDA 1995 is well-founded, 'it shall take such of the following steps as it considers just and equitable':[1]

–   make a declaration as to the rights of the complainant and the respondent in relation to the matters to which the complaint relates;
–   order the respondent to pay compensation to the complainant;
–   recommend that the respondent take, within a specified period, action appearing to the tribunal to be reasonable, in all the circumstances of the case, for the purpose of obviating or reducing the adverse effect on the complainant of any matter to which the complaint relates.

This reflects the almost identical powers of employment tribunals in sex and race discrimination cases in relation to employment opportunities and rights.[2]

1   DDA 1995, s 8(2). Note also the possibility of a complainant having rights to compensation
    against a commercial landlord where an employer or trade organisation has been unable to
    comply with a s 6 or s 15 duty to make adjustments to premises (s 16 and Sch 4). See Chapter
    6.
2   SDA 1975, s 65; RRA 1976, s 56.

Declaration of rights

10.3.27   Where a complainant has successfully brought a disability discrimination application against a respondent employer, the very least that the disabled person will be entitled to is a declaration that he or she has suffered unlawful discrimination in certain particulars or that his or her rights have been unlawfully transgressed.[1] A declaration of the complainant's rights alone is likely to be appropriate in those cases where the complainant has suffered no measurable loss or where there is only a point of principle involved. A tribunal might occasionally use its declaratory powers to encourage the employer to take some positive step towards the successful complainant (such as offer employment to or reinstate him or her), although the legal effect of such a declaration is of doubtful value.

1   DDA 1995, s 8(2)(a).

Compensation and interest

10.3.28   In the other employment discrimination jurisdictions, compensation is frequently regarded as the primary remedy. Given the 1995 Act's emphasis upon employers' duties to make reasonable adjustments to accommodate disabled workers, it remains to be seen whether there will be a shift away (in DDA cases) from first reliance upon compensatory remedies and towards recommendations of positive action. The EAT has guided tribunals on the procedural approach to the assessment of compensation under the DDA 1995.[1] It is suggested that a separate remedies hearing will be appropriate. The parties' preparation for that hearing should be conducted under careful judicial management, often involving the giving of further directions and the exchange of statements of case and witness statements prior to the hearing. Where medical expert evidence is required (typically to assist the tribunal's findings as to the future employment prospects of the disabled applicant for the purpose of assessing future loss of earnings) the listing of the case may need to take account of the availability of the expert witness.

---

1   *Buxton v Equinox Design Ltd* [1999] IRLR 158, EAT.

10.3.29   Where a tribunal orders compensation to be paid in an employment discrimination case,[1] the amount of the compensation is calculated according to the principles applicable to the calculation of damages in claims in tort (or, in Scotland, in reparation for breach of a statutory duty).[2] In other words, disability discrimination compensation will be assessed like any claim for damages in tort and according to common law principles. Case-law under the parallel provisions of the SDA 1975 and the RRA 1976 will be instructive. Like those statutes as amended, there is no limit on the maximum amount of compensation that can be awarded for a breach of Part II of the DDA 1995.[3]

---

1   DDA 1995, s 8(2)(b).
2   Ibid, s 8(3).
3   For that reason, sex or race discrimination cases decided before the coming into effect of the Sex Discrimination and Equal Pay (Remedies) Regulations 1993, SI 1993/2798 (22 November 1993) and the Race Relations (Remedies) Act 1994 (3 July 1994) will not adequately reflect the true measure of damages to be awarded in such cases. Until those dates, tribunals could not award discrimination compensation exceeding £11,000.

10.3.30   A successful applicant will be entitled to be compensated for any actual financial or pecuniary loss up to the date of the tribunal decision, provided that it is caused by or attributable to the discriminatory act or omission. The tribunal may also be invited to calculate future or continuing losses within the award. The main head of damages is likely to be present or future loss of earnings which has resulted as a consequence of the act of discrimination. This will include loss of basic wages or salary, together with any fringe benefits (such as a bonus, commission, company car, private health insurance, pension entitlements, and so on) to which the individual would have been entitled but for the discriminatory action. The complainant will be subject to a duty to mitigate any loss.

10.3.31   The amount of compensation may also include compensation for injury to feelings, whether or not the award includes compensation under any other head.[1] It is suggested that such an element of damages will be appropriate (and easily implied without pleading) in most cases unless exceptional.[2] It will also include compensation for physical or psychiatric injury *caused by* an act of disability discrimination.[3] Aggravated damages may be awarded in exceptional cases where a respondent has acted in a high-handed, malicious, insulting or oppressive manner, but exemplary damages are now almost certainly not appropriate in disability discrimination claims because of recent developments in the common law.[4]

---

1   DDA 1995, s 8(4). Whether such awards are due for revaluation downwards following *Heil v Rankin* [2000] IRLR 334, CA and *Chief Constable of West Yorkshire Police v Kahn* [2000] IRLR 324, CA remains to be seen.
2   *Murray v Powertech (Scotland) Ltd* [1992] IRLR 257 EAT.
3   *Sheriff v Klyne Tugs (Lowestoft) Ltd* [1999] IRLR 481, CA. Such awards may be particularly relevant in DDA cases where the applicant's disability is a mental illness and which has been exacerbated by the act of discrimination.
4   See the thread of principle which has developed through the following cases: *Alexander v Home Office* [1988] IRLR 190, CA; *City of Bradford Metropolitan Borough Council v Arora* [1991] IRLR 165, CA; *AB v South Western Water Services Ltd* [1993] 1 All ER 609, CA; *Deane v Ealing London Borough Council* [1993] IRLR 209, EAT.

10.3.32   The DDA 1995 also provided for regulations to be made to give tribunals the power to award interest on an award of compensation and to specify how that interest is to be determined.[1] The Employment Tribunals (Interest on Awards in Discrimination Cases) Regulations 1996 provide for the award of interest in proceedings for payment of compensation under the DDA 1995.[2]

---

1   DDA 1995, s 8(6).
2   SI 1996/2803 (in force from 2 December 1996).

Unfair dismissal compensation and disability discrimination

10.3.33   The Employment Rights (Dispute Resolution) Act 1998 corrects two oversights resulting from the passage of the DDA 1995. These oversights concern cases which are found to give rise to liability for both unfair dismissal *and* disability discrimination. The 1998 Act makes provision to avoid the double recovery of compensation in such cases. It also provides for the availability of a higher additional award in disability discrimination cases where there has been a parallel finding of unfair dismissal followed by a re-employment order which has not been complied with.

10.3.34   Where an employment tribunal in unfair dismissal case makes a reinstatement or re-engagement order,[1] but the employer disobeys the order by refusing to re-employ the unfairly dismissed employee, the tribunal shall make an award of compensation for unfair dismissal,[2] plus an additional award of compensation to be paid by the employer to the employee.[3] An additional award will not be made if the employer satisfies the tribunal that it was not practicable to comply with the reinstatement or re-engagement order.[4] The appropriate amount of the additional award is usually between 13 and 26 weeks' pay.[5] However, the tribunal will award a higher additional award where the unfair dismissal was also found to be an act of unlawful discrimination within the meaning of the SDA 1975 and the RRA 1976.[6] The higher additional award in such cases is between 26 and 52 weeks' pay.[7] The 1998 Act amended the ERA 1996 so as to ensure that a higher additional award can also be made in cases where the unfair dismissal was found to be an act of unlawful discrimination under the DDA 1995.[8] This corrects an oversight in the 1995 Act and ensures that disability discrimination cases are treated on a par with race and sex discrimination cases.

---

1   Under ERA 1996, s 113.
2   Under ERA 1996, ss 118–127 and see s 117(8).
3   ERA 1996, s 117(3). As to how the tribunal should exercise its judicial discretion in fixing an additional award, see *Morganite Electrical Carbon Ltd v Donne* [1988] ICR 8, EAT; *Motherwell Railway Club v McQueen* [1989] ICR 418, EAT.
4   Ibid, s 117(4)(a) and see s 117(7).
5   Ibid, s 117(5)(b). A 'week's pay' is subject to the statutory maximum.
6   Ibid, s 117(6)(a)–(b).
7   Ibid, s 117(5)(a).
8   Ibid, s 117(6)(c) as amended.

10.3.35   In the case of an act which is *both* unfair dismissal *and* sex or race discrimination, recovery of the same loss under more than one provision is prohibited.[1] Where there is a successful complaint of unfair dismissal and also a finding of sex and/or race discrimination, the employment tribunal shall not award compensation, for example, under the heading of sex discrimination in respect of any loss or matter which has already been accounted for in the award of compensation for unfair dismissal. The effect is to prevent double, or even triple, recovery of a loss already compensated for in the tribunal's award. At the time of the passage of the DDA 1995, the need to take account of the risk of multiple recovery of loss in cases involving both unfair dismissal and disability discrimination was overlooked. The Employment Rights (Dispute Resolution) Act 1998 has remedied that oversight. Double recovery for the same loss is thus prevented, whether the question arises in the same proceedings before the tribunal in question or whether it arises in separate proceedings. For example, if the complainant has been dismissed and brought a successful unfair dismissal claim, it is likely that he or she will have been awarded compensation for loss of earnings to the date of the tribunal hearing and/or for future loss of earnings. A later tribunal considering a separate complaint of disability discrimination in respect of that dismissal must take account of the award for lost earnings when calculating any award under the DDA 1995.

---

1   ERA 1996, s 126.

10.3.36   However, problems are still likely to arise in respect of awards of loss of earnings. These will often be capped by the statutory maximum for an unfair dismissal compensatory award (currently £50,000). As there is no statutory limit to awards under the DDA 1995, it is in the complainant's interest to ensure that the award of lost earnings is dealt with explicitly under the DDA 1995 rather than the ERA 1996. What is not clear is what should happen where such an award has already been made under the unfair dismissal compensation provisions of the ERA 1996 and has then been capped by the statutory maximum? Is an employment tribunal considering making an award of loss of earnings under the DDA 1995 bound to decide that this is a loss which has already been taken into account in the earlier award (even though the amount of the loss has been artificially capped)? Alternatively, should the tribunal apportion the compensation awarded in the unfair dismissal claim and award the balance under the DDA 1995? The author is unaware of any judicial authority on this question, but expresses a preference for the latter approach, although it is not easily reconcilable with the statutory language.

Recommendations

10.3.37 Where the employment tribunal has upheld a complaint of disability discrimination in employment, it may recommend that the respondent take, within a specified period, action appearing to the tribunal to be 'reasonable', in all the circumstances of the case, for the purpose of obviating or reducing the adverse effect on the complainant of any 'matter' to which the complaint relates.[1] This mirrors the similar powers contained in sex and race discrimination statutes, except that here the action to be recommended must be 'reasonable' action, whereas in sex and race cases the action must be 'practicable'.[2] How the tribunals will interpret that difference of terminology, and what real effect it will have, still remains to be seen.

---

1   DDA 1995, s 8(2)(c).
2   SDA 1975, s 65(1)(c); RRA 1976, s 56(1)(c). Note also the use of the phrase 'act of discrimination' in these statutes where the simple word 'matter' appears in the 1995 Act. There does not appear to be any obvious consequence of this change in wording.

10.3.38 It is clear that the power to make recommendations may be used by the tribunal only to attempt to obviate or reduce the adverse effects of the discrimination on the complainant. This does not give the tribunal broader powers to effect changes for the benefit of a wider class of persons who are not party to the proceedings. The recommendation must be directed towards an individualised remedy rather than a class-based remedy. So the respondent employer cannot be ordered to review the wider effect of the discriminatory act nor to cease committing such an act in the future.[1] The tribunal's attention must be entirely focused upon making a recommendation which will counteract or reduce the discriminatory effect upon the complainant. This might include, for example, a recommendation that the employer should consider the complainant for the next available suitable vacancy or reconsider the training opportunities or career development of a disabled complainant already in the respondent's employment. It might also include a recommendation that the employer take steps that would amount to the making of reasonable adjustments to arrangements or the physical features of premises if this would be within that employer's statutory duty[2] and directed towards preventing a substantial disadvantage to the disabled complainant created by those unadjusted arrangements or physical features.[3]

---

1   But see the powers of the DRC discussed in Chapter 9.
2   Under DDA 1995, s 6.

3   But the EAT has suggested that the tribunal should simply recommend that the employer
    should take action to make reasonable adjustments within a specified time, rather than
    make a particular adjustment contended for: *Post Office v Jones* [2000] ICR 388, EAT.

10.3.39   It is a moot point whether the employment tribunal's statutory powers allow it to recommend that the disabled complainant should actually be engaged for or promoted to the next available suitable vacancy. Such a power was clearly not within the letter or spirit of the SDA 1975 or the RRA 1976 because the employer, in obeying such a recommendation, might then commit an act of unlawful positive or reverse discrimination.[1] That does not appear to be a problem under the DDA 1995 because the legislation is asymmetrical. The Act does not prohibit (but neither does it require) positive discrimination in favour of disabled persons, and a non-disabled person treated less favourably than a disabled person has no cause of action under the DDA 1995.

1   *Noon v North West Thames Regional Health Authority (No 2)* [1988] IRLR 530, CA; *British Gas plc
    v Sharma* [1991] IRLR 101, EAT.

10.3.40   If the respondent fails 'without reasonable justification' to comply with a recommendation made by an employment tribunal, the tribunal may, if it thinks it just and equitable, order the payment of compensation or increase the amount of a compensation order already made.[1] What will amount to 'reasonable justification' is clearly a question of fact and will vary from case to case.[2] For example, if a recommendation has been made to the effect that the complainant should be considered for promotion, but in the meanwhile he or she has lost their employment due to a genuine redundancy exercise, that would probably amount to a reasonable justification for the failure to comply with the recommendation. It is unlikely that justification could be advanced by reference to factors which are themselves made unlawful under the DDA 1995. So, for example, if the complainant was selected as a redundancy candidate only because he or she was a disabled person, that would not be a justifying reason.

1   DDA 1995, s 8(5).
2   *Nelson v Tyne and Wear Passenger Transport Executive* [1978] ICR 1183, EAT.

Future reform

10.3.41   In its final report, the Disability Rights Task Force made a number of recommendations for the future reform of employment tribunal powers and procedures in relation to the DDA 1995.[1] It suggested that employment tribunals should be able to order reinstatement or re-engagement in disability-related dismissal cases and be empowered to make enforceable recommendations regarding the future conduct of an employer found liable for discrimination. The Task Force recommended that the time-limits for completing the pre-proceedings statutory questionnaire should be fine-tuned and that, wherever possible, a tribunal hearing a DDA case should include at least one person with disability expertise. No action has been taken on these recommendations to date.

1   Disability Rights Task Force, *From Exclusion to Inclusion: A Report of the Disability Rights Task Force for Disabled People* (1999, London: DfEE) Chapter 3.

10.4   SERVICES AND PREMISES CASES

Proceedings in the county court or sheriff's court

10.4.1   Claims of disability discrimination arising under Part III of the DDA 1995 in respect of goods, facilities, services and premises are the subject of civil proceedings in the same way as any other claim in tort (or, in Scotland, in reparation for breach of a statutory duty).[1] Proceedings in England and Wales, and in Northern Ireland, may be brought only in the county court.[2] In Scotland, proceedings may be brought only in a sheriff's court.[3] No civil or criminal proceedings may be brought in respect of an act merely because the act is made unlawful under the provisions of Part III of the statute.[4] This does not prevent proceedings for judicial review arising in respect of any decision taken in relation to Part III.[5] It is likely that, in many instances, Part III cases will be brought under the small claims arbitration procedure.

1   DDA 1995, s 25(1).
2   Ibid, s 25(3) and Sch 8, para 12.
3   Ibid, s 25(4).
4   Ibid, Sch 3, para 5(1).
5   Ibid, Sch 3, para 5(2).

Time-limits

10.4.2   The limitation period for Part III claims is 6 months. A county court or sheriff's court shall not consider a Part III claim unless proceedings in respect of it have been instituted before the end of the period of 6 months beginning when the act complained of was done.[1] The court may consider a claim which is otherwise time-barred if, in all the circumstances of the case, the court considers that it is just and equitable to do so.[2]

1   DDA 1995, Sch 3, para 6(1) (but see **10.4.6**). An 'act' includes a deliberate omission (s 68(1)).
2   Ibid, Sch 3, para 6(3).

10.4.3   Similar questions about the operation of this limitation period are likely to arise as those in respect of the comparable provisions affecting employment cases. In particular, in the case of an isolated act of disability discrimination, the presumption will be that time starts to run from the the act or the omission itself. A deliberate omission is to be treated when the person in question decided upon it.[1] Subject to rebutting e\ person is treated as having decided upon an omission when he or s\ act inconsistent with doing the omitted act or, in the absen\

inconsistent behaviour, when the period expires within which he or she might reasonably have been expected to do the omitted act if it was to be done.[2] However, in other cases, there is more flexibility in measuring the date upon which time starts to run. In the case of any act or omission which extends over a period of time, the 6-month limitation provision will not start to run until the end of the period in question.[3] Moreover, where the alleged unlawful act of discrimination is attributable to a term in a contract, time does not start to expire until the end of the contract. The unlawful act is said to extend throughout the duration of the contract.[4]

---

1   DDA 1995, Sch 3, para 6(4)(c).
2   Ibid, Sch 3, para 6(5).
3   Ibid, Sch 3, para 6(4)(b).
4   Ibid, Sch 3, para 6(3)(a).

Conciliation

10.4.4   As originally enacted, the DDA 1995 empowered the Secretary of State to make arrangements for the provision of advice and assistance to persons 'with a view to promoting the settlement of disputes ... otherwise than by recourse to the courts'.[1] This advice and assistance service was available only in respect of disputes concerning the provision of goods, facilities or services, or in respect of the disposal or management of premises under Part III of the Act. It did not apply to cases of disability-related employment discrimination under Part II (including discrimination against contract workers or by trade organisations), nor to issues arising from the provisions in Parts IV and V concerning access to education and public transport.

---

1   DDA 1995, s 28(1) as orginally enacted. In Northern Ireland, the s 28 power was in the hands of the Department of Health and Social Services (Sch 8, para 14).

10.4.5   However, the DRCA 1999 amends the provisions of the 1995 legislation which made arrangements for the settlement of disputes under Part III.[1] Henceforth, the DRC may make arrangements with any other person for the provision of 'conciliation services' by (or by persons appointed by) that person in relation to disputes arising under Part III of the DDA 1995.[2] In deciding what arrangements (if any) to make, the DRC shall have regard to the desirability of securing, so far as reasonably practicable, that conciliation services are available for all disputes arising under Part III which the parties may wish to refer to conciliation.[3] No member or employee of the DRC may provide conciliation services in relation to such disputes.[4] The DRC must ensure that any such arrangements include appropriate safeguards to prevent the disclosure to members or employees of the DRC of information obtained by a person in connection with the provision of such conciliation services.[5] However, that does not apply to information relating to a dispute which is disclosed with the consent of the parties to that dispute.[6] Equally, it does not apply to information which is not identifiable with a particular dispute or a particular person, and is reasonably required by the DRC for the purpose of monitoring the operation of the arrangements concerned.[7] Anything communicated to a person while providing such conciliation services is not admissible in evidence in any proceedings (except with the consent of the person who communicated it to that person).[8]

---

1 DDA 1995, s 28 as substituted by DRCA 1999, s 10. The services previously provided by the Disability Access Rights Advisory Service (DARAS) were transferred to the DRC on 25 April 2000. The information and advice services which were provided by DARAS and the DDA Helpline have been merged to form the DRC Helpline. A conciliation service will continue to be run until the DRC outsources a replacement service.
2 DDA 1995, s 28(1) as substituted by DRCA 1999, s 10. The term 'conciliation services' means advice and assistance provided by a conciliator to the parties to a dispute with a view to promoting its settlement otherwise than through the courts: DDA 1995, s 28(8) as substituted by DRCA 1999, s 10.
3 DDA 1995, s 28(2) as substituted by DRCA 1999, s 10.
4 Ibid, s 28(3) as substituted by DRCA 1999, s 10.
5 Ibid, s 28(4) as substituted by DRCA 1999, s 10.
6 Ibid, s 28(5) as substituted by DRCA 1999, s 10.
7 Ibid, s 28(6) as substituted by DRCA 1999, s 10.
8 Ibid, s 28(7) as substituted by DRCA 1999, s 10.

10.4.6 Normally, civil proceedings for an alleged breach of the provisions of Part III of the DDA 1995 must be commenced within 6 months of the act of discrimination.[1] However, if the dispute concerned is referred for conciliation in pursuance of statutory arrangements made by the DRC before the end of the 6-month limitation period, then the limitation period within which civil proceedings must be commenced is extended by a further 2 months.[2]

---

1 DDA 1995, Sch 3, para 6(1).
2 Ibid, Sch 3, para 6(2) as amended.

Settlements

10.4.7 Any term in a contract for the provision of goods, facilities or services is void so far as it purports to require any person to do anything which would contravene any provision of (or made under) Part III of the Act.[1] This invalidating principle also applies to any term in any other agreement (which would presumably include a tenancy agreement or lease) that purports to have that effect. In like manner, a term in a contract or agreement which purports to exclude or limit the operation of any provision of Part III, or which seeks to prevent any person from making a claim under this part of the statute, is void.

---

1 DDA 1995, s 26(1).

10.4.8 The effect of such terms being voided is to make them unenforceable, but this does not apparently render the contract or agreement itself null and void. Instead, a person interested in an agreement containing such a void term may apply to a county court or a sheriff court for an order modifying the agreement to take account of the effect of the term being void.[1] The court may make such an order as it thinks just and this may include provision as respects any period before the order was made.[2] The court may not make any such order unless the affected parties have been given notice of the application (subject to any rules of court to the contrary) and have been afforded an opportunity to make representations to the court.[3]

---

1   DDA 1995, s 26(3).
2   Ibid, s 26(6).
3   Ibid, s 26(4)–(5).

10.4.9   This provision concerning the validity of contract terms does not prevent parties to a dispute under Part III of the DDA 1995 settling legal proceedings by an agreement on terms. A Part III claim by a person in civil proceedings may be settled by an agreement that has the effect of excluding or limiting the operation of any provision of Part III or prevents a person from pursuing or continuing a claim under the Act.[1] It cannot, of course, require any person to do anything that would contravene the statute.

---

1   DDA 1995, s 26(2).

Remedies

10.4.10   In any proceedings in respect of discrimination in non-employment cases under Part III of the DDA 1995, any damages awarded by the court in respect of discrimination found to be unlawful may include compensation for injury to feelings.[1] Such a head of damages may be awarded alone or in tandem with compensation for other heads of loss. However, the Act provides for the possibility that the amount of any damages awarded for injury to feelings shall not exceed a figure to be prescribed by regulations.[2] No such figure has been prescribed to date. If such a figure were to be prescribed in the future (which does not appear likely), it would not be a general ceiling on compensation that may be awarded in non-employment cases. It would be a limit only upon that element of any award that reflects injury to feelings.[3] The effect might be that any such limitation would ensure that the majority of litigation brought under Part III of the Act would be pursued through the county court small claims procedure for claims under £5,000 (as seems likely, in any event).[4]

---

1   DDA 1995, s 25(2).
2   Ibid, Sch 3, para 7.
3   HL Deb, vol 566, col 1065.
4   HL Deb, vol 565, cols 734–735.

10.4.11   Otherwise, the remedies available in civil proceedings under Part III are those which are available in the High Court or, in Scotland, the Court of Session.[1] In appropriate cases, therefore, a successful claimant (or pursuer) may be enabled to seek a declaration of his or her rights or an injunction to prevent further or continuing acts of discrimination.[2]

---

1   DDA 1995, s 25(5).
2   Note also the possibility of a claimant (or pursuer) having rights to compensation against a commercial landlord where a service provider has been unable to comply with a s 21 duty to make adjustments to premises (s 27 and Sch 4). This has been discussed in Chapter 6.

Appendix I

DISABILITY DISCRIMINATION ACT 1995
(1995 c. 50)

(AS AMENDED)

ARRANGEMENT OF SECTIONS

PART I

DISABILITY

Section		Page
1	Meaning of 'disability' and 'disabled person'	234
2	Past disabilities	234
3	Guidance	234

PART II

EMPLOYMENT

Discrimination by employers

4	Discrimination against applicants and employees	236
5	Meaning of 'discrimination'	236
6	Duty of employer to make adjustments	237
7	Exemption for small businesses	239

Enforcement etc.

8	Enforcement, remedies and procedure	239
9	Validity of certain agreements	240
10	Charities and support for particular groups of persons	242
11	Advertisements suggesting that employers will discriminate against disabled persons	242

Discrimination by other persons

12	Discrimination against contract workers	243
13	Discrimination by trade organisations	244
14	Meaning of 'discrimination' in relation to trade organisations	244
15	Duty of trade organisation to make adjustments	245

Premises occupied under leases

16	Alterations to premises occupied under leases	246

Occupational pension schemes and insurance services

17 Occupational pension schemes   247
18 Insurance services   247

PART III

DISCRIMINATION IN OTHER AREAS

Goods, facilities and services

19 Discrimination in relation to goods, facilities and services   248
20 Meaning of 'discrimination'   249
21 Duty of providers of services to make adjustments   250

Premises

22 Discrimination in relation to premises   252
23 Exemption for small dwellings   253
24 Meaning of 'discrimination'   253

Enforcement, etc.

25 Enforcement, remedies and procedure   254
26 Validity and revision of certain agreements   255
27 Alterations to premises occupied under leases   255
28 Conciliation of disputes   256

PART IV

EDUCATION

29 Education of disabled persons   256
30 Further and higher education of disabled persons   257
31 Further and higher education of disabled persons: Scotland   258

PART V

PUBLIC TRANSPORT

Taxis

32 Taxi accessibility regulations   258
33 Designated transport facilities   259
34 New licences conditional on compliance with taxi accessibility regulations   260
35 Exemption from taxi accessibility regulations   260
36 Carrying of passengers in wheelchairs   261
37 Carrying of guide dogs and hearing dogs   262
38 Appeal against refusal of exemption certificate   263
39 Requirements as to disabled passengers in Scotland   263

Public service vehicles

40 PSV accessibility regulations   264
41 Accessibility certificates   264
42 Approval certificates   265
43 Special authorisations   265
44 Reviews and appeals   266
45 Fees   266

Rail vehicles

46 Rail vehicle accessibility regulations   267
47 Exemption from rail vehicle accessibility regulations   268

Supplemental

48 Offences by bodies corporate etc.   269
49 Forgery and false statements   269

PART VI

THE NATIONAL DISABILITY COUNCIL

50 The National Disability Council   269
51 Codes of practice prepared by the Council   271
52 Further provision about codes issued under section 51   271

PART VII

SUPPLEMENTAL

53 Codes of practice prepared by the Secretary of State   272
53A Codes of practice   273
54 Further provision about codes issued under section 53   274
55 Victimisation   275
56 Help for persons suffering discrimination   275
57 Aiding unlawful acts   276
58 Liability of employers and principals   276
59 Statutory authority and national security etc.   277

PART VIII

MISCELLANEOUS

60 Appointment by Secretary of State of advisers   277
61 Amendment of Disabled Persons (Employment) Act 1944   278
****
64 Application to Crown etc.   279
65 Application to Parliament   280
66 Government appointments outside Part II   281
67 Regulations and orders   281

68 Interpretation   281
69 Financial provisions   283
70 Short title, commencement, extent etc.   283

SCHEDULES:
    Schedule 1—Provisions Supplementing Section 1   284
    Schedule 2—Past Disabilities   286
    Schedule 3—Enforcement and Procedure   287
        Part I—Employment   287
        Part II—Discrimination in Other Areas   288
    Schedule 4—Premises Occupied Under Leases   289
        Part I—Occupation by Employer or Trade Organisation 289
        Part II—Occupation by Provider of Services   290
    Schedule 5—The National Disability Council   292
    Schedule 6—Consequential Amendments   294
    Schedule 7—Repeals   295
    Schedule 8—Modifications of this Act in its Application to Northern
               Ireland   295

An Act to make it unlawful to discriminate against disabled persons in connection with employment, the provision of goods, facilities and services or the disposal or management of premises; to make provision about the employment of disabled persons; and to establish a National Disability Council.   [8 November 1995]

PART I

DISABILITY

1   Meaning of 'disability' and 'disabled person'

(1) Subject to the provisions of Schedule 1, a person has a disability for the purposes of this Act if he has a physical or mental impairment which has a substantial and long-term adverse effect on his ability to carry out normal day-to-day activities.

(2) In this Act 'disabled person' means a person who has a disability.

2   Past disabilities

(1) The provisions of this Part and Parts II and III apply in relation to a person who has had a disability as they apply in relation to a person who has that disability.

(2) Those provisions are subject to the modifications made by Schedule 2.

(3) Any regulations or order made under this Act may include provision with respect to persons who have had a disability.

(4) In any proceedings under Part II or Part III of this Act, the question whether a person had a disability at a particular time ('the relevant time') shall be determined, for the purposes of this section, as if the provisions of, or made under, this Act in force when the act complained of was done had been in force at the relevant time.

(5) The relevant time may be a time before the passing of this Act.

3   Guidance

(1) The Secretary of State may issue guidance about the matters to be taken into account in determining—

(a)   whether an impairment has a substantial adverse effect on a person's ability to carry out normal day-to-day activities; or

(b)   whether such an impairment has a long-term effect.

(2) The guidance may, among other things, give examples of—

(a)   effects which it would be reasonable, in relation to particular activities, to regard for purposes of this Act as substantial adverse effects;

(b)   effects which it would not be reasonable, in relation to particular activities, to regard for such purposes as substantial adverse effects;

(c)   substantial adverse effects which it would be reasonable to regard, for such purposes, as long-term;

(d)   substantial adverse effects which it would not be reasonable to regard, for such purposes, as long-term.

(3) A tribunal or court determining, for any purpose of this Act, whether an impairment has a substantial and long-term adverse effect on a person's ability to carry out normal day-to-day activities, shall take into account any guidance which appears to it to be relevant.

(4) In preparing a draft of any guidance, the Secretary of State shall consult such persons as he considers appropriate.

(5) Where the Secretary of State proposes to issue any guidance, he shall publish a draft of it, consider any representations that are made to him about the draft and, if he thinks it appropriate, modify his proposals in the light of any of those representations.

(6) If the Secretary of State decides to proceed with any proposed guidance, he shall lay a draft of it before each House of Parliament.

(7) If, within the 40-day period, either House resolves not to approve the draft, the Secretary of State shall take no further steps in relation to the proposed guidance.

(8) If no such resolution is made within the 40-day period, the Secretary of State shall issue the guidance in the form of his draft.

(9) The guidance shall come into force on such date as the Secretary of State may appoint by order.

(10) Subsection (7) does not prevent a new draft of the proposed guidance from being laid before Parliament.

(11) The Secretary of State may—

(a)   from time to time revise the whole or part of any guidance and re-issue it;

(b)   by order revoke any guidance.

(12) In this section—

   '40-day period', in relation to the draft of any proposed guidance, means—
      (a)   if the draft is laid before one House on a day later than the day on which it is laid before the other House, the period of 40 days beginning with the later of the two days, and
      (b)   in any other case, the period of 40 days beginning with the day on which the draft is laid before each House,
   no account being taken of any period during which Parliament is dissolved or prorogued or during which both Houses are adjourned for more than 4 days; and

'guidance' means guidance issued by the Secretary of State under this section and includes guidance which has been revised and re-issued.

PART II

EMPLOYMENT

Discrimination by employers

4 Discrimination against applicants and employees

(1) It is unlawful for an employer to discriminate against a disabled person—

    (a)   in the arrangements which he makes for the purpose of determining to whom he should offer employment;

    (b)   in the terms on which he offers that person employment; or

    (c)   by refusing to offer, or deliberately not offering, him employment.

(2) It is unlawful for an employer to discriminate against a disabled person whom he employs—

    (a)   in the terms of employment which he affords him;

    (b)   in the opportunities which he affords him for promotion, a transfer, training or receiving any other benefit;

    (c)   by refusing to afford him, or deliberately not affording him, any such opportunity; or

    (d)   by dismissing him, or subjecting him to any other detriment.

(3) Subsection (2) does not apply to benefits of any description if the employer is concerned with the provision (whether or not for payment) of benefits of that description to the public, or to a section of the public which includes the employee in question, unless—

    (a)   that provision differs in a material respect from the provision of the benefits by the employer to his employees; or

    (b)   the provision of the benefits to the employee in question is regulated by his contract of employment; or

    (c)   the benefits relate to training.

(4) In this Part 'benefits' includes facilities and services.

(5) In the case of an act which constitutes discrimination by virtue of section 55, this section also applies to discrimination against a person who is not disabled.

(6) This section applies only in relation to employment at an establishment in Great Britain.

5 Meaning of 'discrimination'

(1) For the purposes of this Part, an employer discriminates against a disabled person if—

    (a)   for a reason which relates to the disabled person's disability, he treats him less favourably than he treats or would treat others to whom that reason does not or would not apply; and

    (b)   he cannot show that the treatment in question is justified.

(2) For the purposes of this Part, an employer also discriminates against a disabled person if—

(a) he fails to comply with a section 6 duty imposed on him in relation to the disabled person; and

(b) he cannot show that his failure to comply with that duty is justified.

(3) Subject to subsection (5), for the purposes of subsection (1) treatment is justified if, but only if, the reason for it is both material to the circumstances of the particular case and substantial.

(4) For the purposes of subsection (2), failure to comply with a section 6 duty is justified if, but only if, the reason for the failure is both material to the circumstances of the particular case and substantial.

(5) If, in a case falling within subsection (1), the employer is under a section 6 duty in relation to the disabled person but fails without justification to comply with that duty, his treatment of that person cannot be justified under subsection (3) unless it would have been justified even if he had complied with the section 6 duty.

(6) Regulations may make provision, for purposes of this section, as to circumstances in which—

(a) treatment is to be taken to be justified;
(b) failure to comply with a section 6 duty is to be taken to be justified;
(c) treatment is to be taken not to be justified;
(d) failure to comply with a section 6 duty is to be taken not to be justified.

(7) Regulations under subsection (6) may, in particular—

(a) make provision by reference to the cost of affording any benefit; and
(b) in relation to benefits under occupational pension schemes, make provision with a view to enabling uniform rates of contributions to be maintained.

6 Duty of employer to make adjustments

(1) Where—

(a) any arrangements made by or on behalf of an employer, or
(b) any physical feature of premises occupied by the employer,

place the disabled person concerned at a substantial disadvantage in comparison with persons who are not disabled, it is the duty of the employer to take such steps as it is reasonable, in all the circumstances of the case, for him to have to take in order to prevent the arrangements or feature having that effect.

(2) Subsection (1)(a) applies only in relation to—

(a) arrangements for determining to whom employment should be offered;
(b) any term, condition or arrangements on which employment, promotion, a transfer, training or any other benefit is offered or afforded.

(3) The following are examples of steps which an employer may have to take in relation to a disabled person in order to comply with subsection (1)—

(a) making adjustments to premises;
(b) allocating some of the disabled person's duties to another person;
(c) transferring him to fill an existing vacancy;
(d) altering his working hours;
(e) assigning him to a different place of work;
(f) allowing him to be absent during working hours for rehabilitation, assessment or treatment;
(g) giving him, or arranging for him to be given, training;

(h)   acquiring or modifying equipment;
(i)   modifying instructions or reference manuals;
(j)   modifying procedures for testing or assessment;
(k)   providing a reader or interpreter;
(l)   providing supervision.

(4) In determining whether it is reasonable for an employer to have to take a particular step in order to comply with subsection (1), regard shall be had, in particular, to—

(a)   the extent to which taking the step would prevent the effect in question;
(b)   the extent to which it is practicable for the employer to take the step;
(c)   the financial and other costs which would be incurred by the employer in taking the step and the extent to which taking it would disrupt any of his activities;
(d)   the extent of the employer's financial and other resources;
(e)   the availability to the employer of financial or other assistance with respect to taking the step.

This subsection is subject to any provision of regulations made under subsection (8).

(5) In this section, 'the disabled person concerned' means—

(a)   in the case of arrangements for determining to whom employment should be offered, any disabled person who is, or has notified the employer that he may be, an applicant for that employment;
(b)   in any other case, a disabled person who is—
       (i) an applicant for the employment concerned; or
       (ii) an employee of the employer concerned.

(6) Nothing in this section imposes any duty on an employer in relation to a disabled person if the employer does not know, and could not reasonably be expected to know—

(a)   in the case of an applicant or potential applicant, that the disabled person concerned is, or may be, an applicant for the employment; or
(b)   in any case, that that person has a disability and is likely to be affected in the way mentioned in subsection (1).

(7) Subject to the provisions of this section, nothing in this Part is to be taken to require an employer to treat a disabled person more favourably than he treats or would treat others.

(8) Regulations may make provision, for the purposes of subsection (1)—

(a)   as to circumstances in which arrangements are, or a physical feature is, to be taken to have the effect mentioned in that subsection;
(b)   as to circumstances in which arrangements are not, or a physical feature is not, to be taken to have that effect;
(c)   as to circumstances in which it is reasonable for an employer to have to take steps of a prescribed description;
(d)   as to steps which it is always reasonable for an employer to have to take;
(e)   as to circumstances in which it is not reasonable for an employer to have to take steps of a prescribed description;
(f)   as to steps which it is never reasonable for an employer to have to take;
(g)   as to things which are to be treated as physical features;
(h)   as to things which are not to be treated as such features.

(9) Regulations made under subsection (8) (c), (d), (e) or (f) may, in particular, make provision by reference to the cost of taking the steps concerned.

(10) Regulations may make provision adding to the duty imposed on employers by this section, including provision of a kind which may be made under subsection (8).

(11) This section does not apply in relation to any benefits under an occupational pension scheme or any other benefit payable in money or money's worth under a scheme or arrangement for the benefit of employees in respect of—

(a)   termination of service;
(b)   retirement, old age or death;
(c)   accident, injury, sickness or invalidity; or
(d)   any other prescribed matter.

(12) This section imposes duties only for the purpose of determining whether an employer has discriminated against a disabled person; and accordingly a breach of any such duty is not actionable as such.

7   Exemption for small businesses

(1) Nothing in this Part applies in relation to an employer who has fewer than 15 employees.

(2) The Secretary of State may by order amend subsection (1) by substituting a different number (not greater than 20) for the number for the time being specified there.

(3) Before making an order under subsection (2) the Secretary of State shall consult—

(a)   the Disability Rights Commission;
(b)   such organisations representing the interests of employers as he considers appropriate; and
(c)   such organisations representing the interests of disabled persons in employment or seeking employment as he considers appropriate.

(4) The Secretary of State shall, before laying an order under this section before Parliament, publish a summary of the views expressed to him in his consultations.

Amendments – Amended by Disability Discrimination (Exemption for Small Employers) Order 1998, SI 1998/2618, art 2; Disability Rights Commission Act 1999, s 11.

Enforcement etc.

8   Enforcement, remedies and procedure

(1) A complaint by any person that another person—

(a)   has discriminated against him in a way which is unlawful under this Part, or
(b)   is, by virtue of section 57 or 58, to be treated as having discriminated against him in such a way,

may be presented to an employment tribunal.

(2) Where an employment tribunal finds that a complaint presented to it under this section is well-founded, it shall take such of the following steps as it considers just and equitable—

(a)   making a declaration as to the rights of the complainant and the respondent in relation to the matters to which the complaint relates;
(b)   ordering the respondent to pay compensation to the complainant;
(c)   recommending that the respondent take, within a specified period, action appearing to the tribunal to be reasonable, in all the circumstances of the case, for the purpose of obviating or reducing the adverse effect on the complainant of any matter to which the complaint relates.

(3) Where a tribunal orders compensation under subsection (2)(b), the amount of the compensation shall be calculated by applying the principles applicable to the calculation of damages in claims in tort or (in Scotland) in reparation for breach of statutory duty.

(4) For the avoidance of doubt it is hereby declared that compensation in respect of discrimination in a way which is unlawful under this Part may include compensation for injury to feelings whether or not it includes compensation under any other head.

(5) If the respondent to a complaint fails, without reasonable justification, to comply with a recommendation made by an employment tribunal under subsection (2)(c) the tribunal may, if it thinks if just and equitable to do so—

(a)   increase the amount of compensation required to be paid to the complainant in respect of the complaint, where an order was made under subsection (2)(b); or

(b)   make an order under subsection (2)(b).

(6) Regulations may make provision—

(a)   for enabling a tribunal, where an amount of compensation falls to be awarded under subsection (2)(b), to include in the award interest on that amount; and

(b)   specifying, for cases where a tribunal decides that an award is to include an amount in respect of interest, the manner in which and the periods and rate by reference to which the interest is to be determined.

(7) Regulations may modify the operation of any order made under section 14 of the Employment Tribunals Act 1996 (power to make provision as to interest on sums payable in pursuance of employment tribunal decisions) to the extent that it relates to an award of compensation under subsection (2)(b).

(8) Part I of Schedule 3 makes further provision about the enforcement of this Part and about procedure.

Amendments – Amended by Employment Tribunals Act 1996, s 43, Sch 1, para 12(1), (2); Employment Rights (Dispute Resolution) Act 1998, s 1(2)(a), (c).

---

9   Validity of certain agreements

(1) Any term in a contract of employment or other agreement is void so far as it purports to—

(a)   require a person to do anything which would contravene any provision of, or made under, this Part;

(b)   exclude or limit the operation of any provision of this Part; or

(c)   prevent any person from presenting a complaint to an employment tribunal under this Part.

(2) Paragraphs (b) and (c) of subsection (1) do not apply to an agreement not to institute proceedings under section 8(1), or to an agreement not to continue such proceedings, if—

(a)   a conciliation officer has acted under [section 18 of the Employment Tribunals Act 1996] in relation to the matter; or

(b)   the conditions set out in subsection (3) are satisfied.

(3) The conditions are that—

(a)　the complainant must have received advice from a relevant independent adviser as to the terms and effect of the proposed agreement (and in particular its effect on his ability to pursue his complaint before an employment tribunal);

(b)　when the adviser gave the advice there must have been in force a contract of insurance, or an indemnity provided for members of a professional body, covering the risk of a claim by the complainant in respect of loss arising in consequence of the advice; and

(c)　the agreement must be in writing, relate to the particular complaint, identify the adviser and state that the conditions are satisfied.

(4) A person is a relevant independent adviser for the purposes of subsection (3)(a)—

(a)　if he is a qualified lawyer,

(b)　if he is an officer, official, employee or member of an independent trade union who has been certified in writing by the trade union as competent to give advice and as authorised to do so on behalf of the trade union,

(c)　if he works at an advice centre (whether as an employee or a volunteer) and has been certified in writing by the centre as competent to give advice and as authorised to do so on behalf of the centre, or

(d)　if he is a person of a description specified in an order made by the Secretary of State.

(4A) But a person is not a relevant independent adviser for the purposes of subsection (3)(a) in relation to the complainant—

(a)　if he is, is employed by or is acting in the matter for the other party or a person who is connected with the other party,

(b)　in the case of a person within subsection (4)(b) or (c), if the trade union or advice centre is the other party or a person who is connected with the other party,

(c)　in the case of a person within subsection (4)(c), if the complainant makes a payment for the advice received from him, or

(d)　in the case of a person of a description specified in an order under subsection (4)(d), if any condition specified in the order in relation to the giving of advice by persons of that description is not satisfied.

(4B) In subsection (4)(a) 'qualified lawyer' means—

(a)　as respects England and Wales, a barrister (whether in practice as such or employed to give legal advice), a solicitor who holds a practising certificate, or a person other than a barrister or solicitor who is an authorised advocate or authorised litigator (within the meaning of the Courts and Legal Services Act 1990), and

(b)　as respects Scotland, an advocate (whether in practice as such or employed to give legal advice), or a solicitor who holds a practising certificate.

(4C) In subsection (4)(b) 'independent trade union' has the same meaning as in the Trade Union and Labour Relations (Consolidation) Act 1992.

(5) For the purposes of subsection (4A) any two persons are to be treated as connected—

(a)　if one is a company of which the other (directly or indirectly) has control, or

(b)   if both are companies of which a third person (directly or indirectly) has control.

(6) An agreement under which the parties agree to submit a dispute to arbitration—

(a)   shall be regarded for the purposes of subsection (2) as being an agreement not to institute, or an agreement not to continue, proceedings if—
       (i) the dispute is covered by a scheme having effect by virtue of an order under section 212A of the Trade Union and Labour Relations (Consolidation) Act 1992, and
       (ii) the agreement is to submit it to arbitration in accordance with the scheme, but
(b)   shall be regarded as neither being nor including such an agreement in any other case.

Amendments – Amended by Employment Tribunals Act 1996, s 43, Sch 1, para 12(1), (3); Employment Rights (Dispute Resolution) Act 1998, ss 1(2)(a), (c), 8(4), 9(1), (2)(d), 10(1), (2)(d), 15, Sch 1, para 11.

---

10   Charities and support for particular groups of persons

(1) Nothing in this Part—

(a)   affects any charitable instrument which provides for conferring benefits on one or more categories of person determined by reference to any physical or mental capacity; or
(b)   makes unlawful any act done by a charity or recognised body in pursuance of any of its charitable purposes, so far as those purposes are connected with persons so determined.

(2) Nothing in this Part prevents—

(a)   a person who provides supported employment from treating members of a particular group of disabled persons more favourably than other persons in providing such employment; or
(b)   the Secretary of State from agreeing to arrangements for the provision of supported employment which will, or may, have that effect.

(3) In this section—

'charitable instrument' means an enactment or other instrument (whenever taking effect) so far as it relates to charitable purposes;
'charity' has the same meaning as in the Charities Act 1993;
'recognised body' means a body which is a recognised body for the purposes of Part I of the Law Reform (Miscellaneous Provisions) (Scotland) Act 1990; and
'supported employment' means facilities provided, or in respect of which payments are made, under section 15 of the Disabled Persons (Employment) Act 1944.

(4) In the application of this section to England and Wales, 'charitable purposes' means purposes which are exclusively charitable according to the law of England and Wales.

(5) In the application of this section to Scotland, 'charitable purposes' shall be construed in the same way as if it were contained in the Income Tax Acts.

11   Advertisements suggesting that employers will discriminate against disabled persons

(1) This section applies where—

(a)   a disabled person has applied for employment with an employer;

(b)   the employer has refused to offer, or has deliberately not offered, him the employment;

(c)   the disabled person has presented a complaint under section 8 against the employer;

(d)   the employer has advertised the employment (whether before or after the disabled person applied for it); and

(e)   the advertisement indicated, or might reasonably be understood to have indicated, that any application for the advertised employment would, or might, be determined to any extent by reference to—

    (i)   the successful applicant not having any disability or any category of disability which includes the disabled person's disability; or

    (ii)   the employer's reluctance to take any action of a kind mentioned in section 6.

(2) The tribunal hearing the complaint shall assume, unless the contrary is shown, that the employer's reason for refusing to offer, or deliberately not offering, the employment to the complainant was related to the complainant's disability.

(3) In this section 'advertisement' includes every form of advertisement or notice, whether to the public or not.

Discrimination by other persons

12   Discrimination against contract workers

(1) It is unlawful for a principal, in relation to contract work, to discriminate against a disabled person—

(a)   in the terms on which he allows him to do that work;

(b)   by not allowing him to do it or continue to do it;

(c)   in the way he affords him access to any benefits or by refusing or deliberately omitting to afford him access to them; or

(d)   by subjecting him to any other detriment.

(2) Subsection (1) does not apply to benefits of any description if the principal is concerned with the provision (whether or not for payment) of benefits of that description to the public, or to a section of the public which includes the contract worker in question, unless that provision differs in a material respect from the provision of the benefits by the principal to contract workers.

(3) The provisions of this Part (other than subsections (1) to (3) of section 4) apply to any principal, in relation to contract work, as if he were, or would be, the employer of the contract worker and as if any contract worker supplied to do work for him were an employee of his.

(4) In the case of an act which constitutes discrimination by virtue of section 55, this section also applies to discrimination against a person who is not disabled.

(5) This section applies only in relation to contract work done at an establishment in Great Britain (the provisions of section 68 about the meaning of 'employment at an establishment in Great Britain' applying for the purposes of this subsection with the appropriate modifications).

(6) In this section—

'principal' means a person ('A') who makes work available for doing by individuals who are employed by another person who supplies them under a contract made with A;

'contract work' means work so made available; and
'contract worker' means any individual who is supplied to the principal under such a
    contract.

13   Discrimination by trade organisations

(1) It is unlawful for a trade organisation to discriminate against a disabled person—

(a)   in the terms on which it is prepared to admit him to membership of the
       organisation; or
(b)   by refusing to accept, or deliberately not accepting, his application for
       membership.

(2) It is unlawful for a trade organisation, in the case of a disabled person who is a
member of the organisation, to discriminate against him—

(a)   in the way it affords him access to any benefits or by refusing or deliberately
       omitting to afford him access to them;
(b)   by depriving him of membership, or varying the terms on which he is a
       member; or
(c)   by subjecting him to any other detriment.

(3) In the case of an act which constitutes discrimination by virtue of section 55, this
section also applies to discrimination against a person who is not disabled.

(4) In this section 'trade organisation' means an organisation of workers, an
organisation of employers or any other organisation whose members carry on a
particular profession or trade for the purposes of which the organisation exists.

14   Meaning of 'discrimination' in relation to trade organisations

(1) For the purposes of this Part, a trade organisation discriminates against a disabled
person if—

(a)   for a reason which relates to the disabled person's disability, it treats him less
       favourably than it treats or would treat others to whom that reason does not or
       would not apply; and
(b)   it cannot show that the treatment in question is justified.

(2) For the purposes of this Part, a trade organisation also discriminates against a
disabled person if—

(a)   it fails to comply with a section 15 duty imposed on it in relation to the disabled
       person; and
(b)   it cannot show that its failure to comply with that duty is justified.

(3) Subject to subsection (5), for the purposes of subsection (1) treatment is justified if,
but only if, the reason for it is both material to the circumstances of the particular case
and substantial.

(4) For the purposes of subsection (2), failure to comply with a section 15 duty is
justified if, but only if, the reason for the failure is both material to the circumstances of
the particular case and substantial.

(5) If, in a case falling within subsection (1), the trade organisation is under a section 15
duty in relation to the disabled person concerned but fails wtihout justification to

comply with that duty, its treatment of that person cannot be justified under subsection (3) unless the treatment would have been justified even if the organisation had complied with the section 15 duty.

(6) Regulations may make provision, for purposes of this section, as to circumstances in which—

(a)   treatment is to be taken to be justified;
(b)   failure to comply with a section 15 duty is to be taken to be justified;
(c)   treatment is to be taken not to be justified;
(d)   failure to comply with a section 15 duty is to be taken not to be justified.

15   Duty of trade organisation to make adjustments

(1) Where—

(a)   any arrangements made by or on behalf of a trade organisation, or
(b)   any physical feature of premises occupied by the organisation,

place the disabled person concerned at a substantial disadvantage in comparison with persons who are not disabled, it is the duty of the organisation to take such steps as it is reasonable, in all the circumstances of the case, for it to have to take in order to prevent the arrangements or feature having that effect.

(2) Subsection (1)(a) applies only in relation to—

(a)   arrangements for determining who should become or remain a member of the organisation;
(b)   any term, condition or arrangements on which membership or any benefit is offered or afforded.

(3) In determining whether it is reasonable for a trade organisation to have to take a particular step in order to comply with subsection (1), regard shall be had, in particular, to—

(a)   the extent to which taking the step would prevent the effect in question;
(b)   the extent to which it is practicable for the organisation to take the step;
(c)   the financial and other costs which would be incurred by the organisation in taking the step and the extent to which taking it would disrupt any of its activities;
(d)   the extent of the organisation's financial and other resources;
(e)   the availability to the organisation of financial or other assistance with respect to taking the step.

This subsection is subject to any provision of regulations made under subsection (7).

(4) In this section 'the disabled person concerned' means—

(a)   in the case of arrangements for determining to whom membership should be offered, any disabled person who is, or has notified the organisation that he may be, an applicant for membership;
(b)   in any other case, a disabled person who is—
   (i) an applicant for membership; or
   (ii) a member of the organisation.

(5) Nothing in this section imposes any duty on an organisation in relation to a disabled person if the organisation does not know, and could not reasonably be expected to know that the disabled person concerned—

(a)   is, or may be, an applicant for membership; or
(b)   has a disability and is likely to be affected in the way mentioned in subsection (1).

(6) Subject to the provisions of this section, nothing in this Part is to be taken to require a trade organisation to treat a disabled person more favourably than it treats or would treat others.

(7) Regulations may make provision for the purposes of subsection (1) as to any of the matters mentioned in paragraphs (a) to (h) of section 6(8) (the references in those paragraphs to an employer being read for these purposes as references to a trade organisation).

(8) Subsection (9) of section 6 applies in relation to such regulations as it applies in relation to regulations made under section 6(8).

(9) Regulations may make provision adding to the duty imposed on trade organisations by this section, including provision of a kind which may be made under subsection (7).

(10) This section imposes duties only for the purpose of determining whether a trade organisation has discriminated against a disabled person; and accordingly a breach of any such duty is not actionable as such.

Premises occupied under leases

16   Alterations to premises occupied under leases

(1) This section applies where—

(a)   an employer or trade organisation ('the occupier') occupies premises under a lease;
(b)   but for this section, the occupier would not be entitled to make a particular alteration to the premises; and
(c)   the alteration is one which the occupier proposes to make in order to comply with a section 6 duty or section 15 duty.

(2) Except to the extent to which it expressly so provides, the lease shall have effect by virtue of this subsection as if it provided—

(a)   for the occupier to be entitled to make the alteration with the written consent of the lessor;
(b)   for the occupier to have to make a written application to the lessor for consent if he wishes to make the alteration;
(c)   if such an application is made, for the lessor not to withhold his consent unreasonably; and
(d)   for the lessor to be entitled to make his consent subject to reasonable conditions.

(3) In this section—

'lease' includes a tenancy, sub-lease or sub-tenancy and an agreement for a lease, tenancy, sub-lease or sub-tenancy; and
'sub-lease' and 'sub-tenancy' have such meaning as may be prescribed.

(4) If the terms and conditions of a lease—

(a)   impose conditions which are to apply if the occupier alters the premises, or
(b)   entitle the lessor to impose conditions when consenting to the occupier's altering the premises,

the occupier is to be treated for the purposes of subsection (1) as not being entitled to make the alteration.

(5) Part I of Schedule 4 supplements the provisions of this section.

Occupational pension schemes and insurance services

17   Occupational pension schemes

(1) Every occupational pension scheme shall be taken to include a provision ('a non-discrimination rule')—

(a)   relating to the terms on which—
        (i) persons become members of the scheme; and
        (ii) members of the scheme are treated; and
(b)   requiring the trustees or managers of the scheme to refrain from any act or omission which, if done in relation to a person by an employer, would amount to unlawful discrimination against that person for the purposes of this Part.

(2) The other provisions of the scheme are to have effect subject to the non-discrimination rule.

(3) Without prejudice to section 67, regulations under this Part may—

(a)   with respect to trustees or managers of occupational pension schemes make different provision from that made with respect to employers; or
(b)   make provision modifying the application to such trustees or managers of any regulations made under this Part, or of any provisions of this Part so far as they apply to employers.

(4) In determining, for the purposes of this section, whether an act or omission would amount to unlawful discrimination if done by an employer, any provision made under subsection (3) shall be applied as if it applied in relation to the notional employer.

18   Insurance services

(1) This section applies where a provider of insurance services ('the insurer') enters into arrangements with an employer under which the employer's employees, or a class of his employees—

(a)   receive insurance services provided by the insurer; or
(b)   are given an opportunity to receive such services.

(2) The insurer is to be taken, for the purposes of this Part, to discriminate unlawfully against a disabled person who is a relevant employee if he acts in relation to that employee in a way which would be unlawful discrimination for the purposes of Part III if—

(a)   he were providing the service in question to members of the public; and
(b)   the employee was provided with, or was trying to secure the provision of, that service as a member of the public.

(3) In this section—

'insurance services' means services of a prescribed description for the provision of benefits in respect of—
(a)   termination of service;
(b)   retirement, old age or death;
(c)   accident, injury, sickness or invalidity; or

  (d) any other prescribed matter; and

'relevant employee' means—

  (a) in the case of an arrangement which applies to employees of the employer in question, an employee of his;

  (b) in the case of an arrangement which applies to a class of employees of the employer, an employee who is in that class.

(4) For the purposes of the definition of 'relevant employee' in subsection (3), 'employee', in relation to an employer, includes a person who has applied for, or is contemplating applying for, employment by that employer or (as the case may be) employment by him in the class in question.

PART III

DISCRIMINATION IN OTHER AREAS

Goods, facilities and services

19 Discrimination in relation to goods, facilities and services

(1) It is unlawful for a provider of services to discriminate against a disabled person—

  (a) in refusing to provide, or deliberately not providing, to the disabled person any service which he provides, or is prepared to provide, to members of the public;

  (b) in failing to comply with any duty imposed on him by section 21 in circumstances in which the effect of that failure is to make it impossible or unreasonably difficult for the disabled person to make use of any such service;

  (c) in the standard of service which he provides to the disabled person or the manner in which he provides it to him; or

  (d) in the terms on which he provides a service to the disabled person.

(2) For the purposes of this section and sections 20 and 21—

  (a) the provision of services includes the provision of any goods or facilities;

  (b) a person is 'a provider of services' if he is concerned with the provision, in the United Kingdom, of services to the public or to a section of the public; and

  (c) it is irrelevant whether a service is provided on payment or without payment.

(3) The following are examples of services to which this section and sections 20 and 21 apply—

  (a) access to and use of any place which members of the public are permitted to enter;

  (b) access to and use of means of communication;

  (c) access to and use of information services;

  (d) accommodation in a hotel, boarding house or other similar establishment;

  (e) facilities by way of banking or insurance or for grants, loans, credit or finance;

  (f) facilities for entertainment, recreation or refreshment;

  (g) facilities provided by employment agencies or under section 2 of the Employment and Training Act 1973;

  (h) the services of any profession or trade, or any local or other public authority.

(4) In the case of an act which constitutes discrimination by virtue of section 55, this section also applies to discrimination against a person who is not disabled.

(5) Except in such circumstances as may be prescribed, this section and sections 20 and 21 do not apply to—

- (a) education which is funded, or secured, by a relevant body or provided at—
  - (i) an establishment which is funded by such a body or by a Minister of the Crown; or
  - (ii) any other establishment which is a school as defined in section 4(1) and (2) of the Education Act 1996 or section 135(1) of the Education (Scotland) Act 1980;
- (b) any service so far as it consists of the use of any means of transport; or
- (c) such other services as may be prescribed.

(6) In subsection (5) 'relevant body' means—

- (a) a local education authority in England and Wales;
- (b) an education authority in Scotland;
- (c) the Funding Agency for Schools;
- (d) the Schools Funding Council for Wales;
- (e) the Further Education Funding Council for England;
- (f) the Further Education Funding Council for Wales;
- (g) the Higher Education Funding Council for England;
- (h) the Scottish Higher Education Funding Council;
- (i) the Higher Education Funding Council for Wales;
- (j) the Teacher Training Agency;
- (k) a voluntary organisation; or
- (l) a body of a prescribed kind.

Amendment – Amended by Education Act 1996, s 582(1), Sch 37, Pt I, para 129.

---

20   Meaning of 'discrimination'

(1) For the purposes of section 19, a provider of services discriminates against a disabled person if—

- (a) for a reason which relates to the disabled person's disability, he treats him less favourably than he treats or would treat others to whom that reason does not or would not apply; and
- (b) he cannot show that the treatment in question is justified.

(2) For the purposes of section 19, a provider of services also discriminates against a disabled person if—

- (a) he fails to comply with a section 21 duty imposed on him in relation to the disabled person; and
- (b) he cannot show that his failure to comply with that duty is justified.

(3) For the purposes of this section, treatment is justified only if—

- (a) in the opinion of the provider of services, one or more of the conditions mentioned in subsection (4) are satisfied; and
- (b) it is reasonable, in all the circumstances of the case, for him to hold that opinion.

(4) The conditions are that—

(a)   in any case, the treatment is necessary in order not to endanger the health or safety of any person (which may include that of the disabled person);

(b)   in any case, the disabled person is incapable of entering into an enforceable agreement, or of giving an informed consent, and for that reason the treatment is reasonable in that case;

(c)   in a case falling with section 19(1)(a), the treatment is necessary because the provider of services would otherwise be unable to provide the service to members of the public;

(d)   in a case falling within section 19(1)(c) or (d), the treatment is necessary in order for the provider of services to be able to provide the service to the disabled person or to other members of the public;

(e)   in a case falling within section 19(1)(d), the difference in the terms on which the service is provided to the disabled person and those on which it is provided to other members of the public reflects the greater cost to the provider of services in providing the service to the disabled person.

(5) Any increase in the cost of providing a service to a disabled person which results from compliance by a provider of services with a section 21 duty shall be disregarded for the purposes of subsection (4)(e).

(6) Regulations may make provision, for purposes of this section, as to circumstances in which—

(a)   it is reasonable for a provider of services to hold the opinion mentioned in subsection (3)(a);

(b)   it is not reasonable for a provider of services to hold that opinion.

(7) Regulations may make provision for subsection (4)(b) not to apply in prescribed circumstances where—

(a)   a person is acting for a disabled person under a power of attorney;

(b)   functions conferred by or under Part VII of the Mental Health Act 1983 are exercisable in relation to a disabled person's property or affairs; or

(c)   powers are exercisable in Scotland in relation to a disabled person's property or affairs in consequence of the appointment of a curator bonis, tutor or judicial factor.

(8) Regulations may make provision, for purposes of this section, as to circumstances (other than those mentioned in subsection (4)) in which treatment is to be taken to be justified.

(9) In subsections (3), (4) and (8) 'treatment' includes failure to comply with a section 21 duty.

21   Duty of providers of services to make adjustments

(1) Where a provider of services has a practice, policy or procedure which makes it impossible or unreasonably difficult for disabled persons to make use of a service which he provides, or is prepared to provide, to other members of the public, it is his duty to take such steps as it is reasonable, in all the circumstances of the case, for him to have to take in order to change that practice, policy or procedure so that it no longer has that effect.

(2) Where a physical feature (for example, one arising from the design or construction of a building or the approach or access to premises) makes it impossible or

unreasonably difficult for disabled persons to make use of such a service, it is the duty of the provider of that service to take such steps as it is reasonable, in all the circumstances of the case, for him to have to take in order to—

(a)   remove the feature;

(b)   alter it so that it no longer has that effect;

(c)   provide a reasonable means of avoiding the feature; or

(d)   provide a reasonable alternative method of making the service in question available to disabled persons.

(3) Regulations may prescribe—

(a)   matters which are to be taken into account in determining whether any provision of a kind mentioned in subsection (2)(c) or (d) is reasonable; and

(b)   categories of providers of services to whom subsection (2) does not apply.

(4) Where an auxiliary aid or service (for example, the provision of information on audio tape or of a sign language interpreter) would—

(a)   enable disabled persons to make use of a service which a provider of services provides, or is prepared to provide, to members of the public, or

(b)   facilitate the use by disabled persons of such a service,

it is the duty of the provider of that service to take such steps as it is reasonable, in all the circumstances of the case, for him to have to take in order to provide that auxiliary aid or service.

(5) Regulations may make provision, for the purposes of this section—

(a)   as to circumstances in which it is reasonable for a provider of services to have to take steps of a prescribed description;

(b)   as to circumstances in which it is not reasonable for a provider of services to have to take steps of a prescribed description;

(c)   as to what is to be included within the meaning of 'practice, policy or procedure';

(d)   as to what is not to be included within the meaning of that expression;

(e)   as to things which are to be treated as physical features;

(f)   as to things which are not to be treated as such features;

(g)   as to things which are to be treated as auxiliary aids or services;

(h)   as to things which are not to be treated as auxiliary aids or services.

(6) Nothing in this section requires a provider of services to take any steps which would fundamentally alter the nature of the service in question or the nature of his trade, profession or business.

(7) Nothing in this section requires a provider of services to take any steps which would cause him to incur expenditure exceeding the prescribed maximum.

(8) Regulations under subsection (7) may provide for the prescribed maximum to be calculated by reference to—

(a)   aggregate amounts of expenditure incurred in relation to different cases;

(b)   prescribed periods;

(c)   services of a prescribed description;

(d)   premises of a prescribed description; or

(e)   such other criteria as may be prescribed.

(9) Regulations may provide, for the purposes of subsection (7), for expenditure incurred by one provider of services to be treated as incurred by another.

(10) This section imposes duties only for the purpose of determining whether a provider of services has discriminated against a disabled person; and accordingly a breach of any such duty is not actionable as such.

Premises

22   Discrimination in relation to premises

(1) It is unlawful for a person with power to dispose of any premises to discriminate against a disabled person—

    (a)   in the terms on which he offers to dispose of those premises to the disabled person;

    (b)   by refusing to dispose of those premises to the disabled person; or

    (c)   in his treatment of the disabled person in relation to any list of persons in need of premises of that description.

(2) Subsection (1) does not apply to a person who owns an estate or interest in the premises and wholly occupies them unless, for the purpose of disposing of the premises, he—

    (a)   use the services of an estate agent, or

    (b)   publishes an advertisement or causes an advertisement to be published.

(3) It is unlawful for a person managing any premises to discriminate against a disabled person occupying those premises—

    (a)   in the way he permits the disabled person to make use of any benefits or facilities;

    (b)   by refusing or deliberately omitting to permit the disabled person to make use of any benefits or facilities; or

    (c)   by evicting the disabled person, or subjecting him to any other detriment.

(4) It is unlawful for any person whose licence or consent is required for the disposal of any premises comprised in, or (in Scotland) the subject of, a tenancy to discriminate against a disabled person by withholding his licence or consent for the disposal of the premises to the disabled person.

(5) Subsection (4) applies to tenancies created before as well as after the passing of this Act.

(6) In this section—

    'advertisement' includes every form of advertisement or notice, whether to the public or not;

    'dispose', in relation to premises, includes granting a right to occupy the premises, and, in relation to premises comprised in, or (in Scotland) the subject of, a tenancy, includes—

        (a)   assigning the tenancy, and

        (b)   sub-letting or parting with possession of the premises or any part of the premises;

    and 'disposal' shall be construed accordingly;

    'estate agent' means a person who, by way of profession or trade, provides services for the purpose of finding premises for persons seeking to acquire them or assisting in the disposal of premises; and

    'tenancy' means a tenancy created—

    (a)   by a lease or sub-lease,

    (b)   by an agreement for a lease or sub-lease,

    (c)   by a tenancy agreement, or

    (d)   in pursuance of any enactment.

(7) In the case of an act which constitutes discrimination by virtue of section 55, this section also applies to discrimination against a person who is not disabled.

(8) This section applies only in relation to premises in the United Kingdom.

23   Exemption for small dwellings

(1) Where the conditions mentioned in subsection (2) are satisfied, subsection (1), (3) or (as the case may be) (4) of section 22 does not apply.

(2) The conditions are that—

    (a)   the relevant occupier resides, and intends to continue to reside, on the premises;

    (b)   the relevant occupier shares accommodation on the premises with persons who reside on the premises and are not members of his household;

    (c)   the shared accommodation is not storage accommodation or a means of access; and

    (d)   the premises are small premises.

(3) For the purposes of this section, premises are 'small premises' if they fall within subsection (4) or (5).

(4) Premises fall within this subsection if—

    (a)   only the relevant occupier and members of his household reside in the accommodation occupied by him;

    (b)   the premises comprise, in addition to the accommodation occupied by the relevant occupier, residential accommodation for at least one other household;

    (c)   the residential accommodation for each other household is let, or available for letting, on a separate tenancy or similar agreement; and

    (d)   there are not normally more than two such other households.

(5) Premises fall within this subsection if there is not normally residential accommodation on the premises for more than six persons in addition to the relevant occupier and any members of his household.

(6) For the purposes of this section 'the relevant occupier' means—

    (a)   in a case falling within section 22(1), the person with power to dispose of the premises, or a near relative of his;

    (b)   in a case falling within section 22(4), the person whose licence or consent is required for the disposal of the premises, or a near relative of his.

(7) For the purposes of this section—

    'near relative' means a person's spouse, partner, parent, child, grandparent, grandchild, or brother or sister (whether of full or half blood or by affinity); and

    'partner' means the other member of a couple consisting of a man and a woman who are not married to each other but are living together as husband and wife.

24   Meaning of 'discrimination'

(1) For the purposes of section 22, a person ('A') discriminates against a disabled person if—

(a)   for a reason which relates to the disabled person's disability, he treats him less favourably than he treats or would treat others to whom that reason does not or would not apply; and

(b)   he cannot show that the treatment in question is justified.

(2) For the purposes of this section, treatment is justified only if—

(a)   in A's opinion, one or more of the conditions mentioned in subsection (3) are satisfied; and

(b)   it is reasonable, in all the circumstances of the case, for him to hold that opinion.

(3) The conditions are that—

(a)   in any case, the treatment is necessary in order not to endanger the health or safety of any person (which may include that of the disabled person);

(b)   in any case, the disabled person is incapable of entering into an enforceable agreement, or of giving an informed consent, and for that reason the treatment is reasonable in that case;

(c)   in a case falling within section 22(3)(a), the treatment is necessary in order for the disabled person or the occupiers of other premises forming part of the building to make use of the benefit or facility;

(d)   in a case falling within section 22(3)(b), the treatment is necessary in order for the occupiers of other premises forming part of the building to make use of the benefit or facility.

(4) Regulations may make provision, for purposes of this section, as to circumstances in which—

(a)   it is reasonable for a person to hold the opinion mentioned in subsection 2(a);

(b)   it is not reasonable for a person to hold that opinion.

(5) Regulations may make provision, for purposes of this section, as to circumstances (other than those mentioned in subsection (3)) in which treatment is to be taken to be justified.

Enforcement, etc.

25   Enforcement, remedies and procedure

(1) A claim by any person that another person—

(a)   has discriminated against him in a way which is unlawful under this Part; or

(b)   is by virtue of section 57 or 58 to be treated as having discriminated against him in such a way,

may be made the subject of civil proceedings in the same way as any other claim in tort or (in Scotland) in reparation for breach of statutory duty.

(2) For the avoidance of doubt it is hereby declared that damages in respect of discrimination in a way which is unlawful under this Part may include compensation for injury to feelings whether or not they include compensation under any other head.

(3) Proceedings in England and Wales shall be brought only in a county court.

(4) Proceedings in Scotland shall be brought only in a sheriff court.

(5) The remedies available in such proceedings are those which are available in the High Court or (as the case may be) the Court of Session.

(6) Part II of Schedule 3 makes further provision about the enforcement of this Part and about procedure.

26 Validity and revision of certain agreements

(1) Any term in a contract for the provision of goods, facilities or services or in any other agreement is void so far as it purports to—

(a) require a person to do anything which would contravene any provision of, or made under, this Part,

(b) exclude or limit the operation of any provision of this Part, or

(c) prevent any person from making a claim under this Part.

(2) Paragraphs (b) and (c) of subsection (1) do not apply to an agreement settling a claim to which section 25 applies.

(3) On the application of any person interested in an agreement to which subsection (1) applies, a county court or a sheriff court may make such order as it thinks just for modifying the agreement to take account of the effect of subsection (1).

(4) No such order shall be made unless all persons affected have been—

(a) given notice of the application; and

(b) afforded an opportunity to make representations to the court.

(5) Subsection (4) applies subject to any rules of court providing for that notice to be dispensed with.

(6) An order under subsection (3) may include provision as respects any period before the making of the order.

27 Alterations to premises occupied under leases

(1) This section applies where—

(a) a provider of services ('the occupier') occupies premises under a lease;

(b) but for this section, he would not be entitled to make a particular alteration to the premises; and

(c) the alteration is one which the occupier proposes to make in order to comply with a section 21 duty.

(2) Except to the extent to which it expressly so provides, the lease shall have effect by virtue of this subsection as if it provided—

(a) for the occupier to be entitled to make the alteration with the written consent of the lessor;

(b) for the occupier to have to make a written application to the lessor for consent if he wishes to make the alteration;

(c) if such an application is made, for the lessor not to withhold his consent unreasonably; and

(d) for the lessor to be entitled to make his consent subject to reasonable conditions.

(3) In this section—

'lease' includes a tenancy, sub-lease or sub-tenancy and an agreement for a lease, tenancy, sub-lease or sub-tenancy; and 'sub-lease' and 'sub-tenancy' have such meaning as may be prescribed.

(4) If the terms and conditions of a lease—

(a)   impose conditions which are to apply if the occupier alters the premises, or

(b)   entitle the lessor to impose conditions when consenting to the occupier's altering the premises,

the occupier is to be treated for the purposes of subsection (1) as not being entitled to make the alteration.

(5) Part II of Schedule 4 supplements the provisions of this section.

28   Conciliation of disputes

(1) The Commission may make arrangements with any other person for the provision of conciliation services by, or by persons appointed by, that person in relation to disputes arising under this Part.

(2) In deciding what arrangements (if any) to make, the Commission shall have regard to the desirability of securing, so far as reasonably practicable, that conciliation services are available for all disputes arising under this Part which the parties may wish to refer to conciliation.

(3) No member or employee of the Commission may provide conciliation services in relation to disputes arising under this Part.

(4) The Commission shall ensure that any arrangements under this section include appropriate safeguards to prevent the disclosure to members or employees of the Commission of information obtained by a person in connection with the provision of conciliation services in pursuance of the arrangements.

(5) Subsection (4) does not apply to information relating to a dispute which is disclosed with the consent of the parties to that dispute.

(6) Subsection (4) does not apply to information which—

(a)   is not identifiable with a particular dispute or a particular person; and

(b)   is reasonably required by the Commission for the purpose of monitoring the operation of the arrangements concerned.

(7) Anything communicated to a person while providing conciliation services in pursuance of any arrangements under this section is not admissible in evidence in any proceedings except with the consent of the person who communicated it to that person.

(8) In this section 'conciliation services' means advice and assistance provided by a conciliator to the parties to a dispute with a view to promoting its settlement otherwise than through the courts.

Amendment – Substituted by Disability Rights Commission Act 1999, s 10.

PART IV

EDUCATION

29   Education of disabled persons

(1), (2) (*repealed*)

(3) In section 1 of the Education Act 1994 (establishment of the Teacher Training Agency) add, at the end—

'(4) In exercising their functions, the Teacher Training Agency shall have regard to the requirements of persons who are disabled persons for the purposes of the Disability Discrimination Act 1995.'

Amendment – Amended by Education Act 1996, s 582(2), Sch 38, Pt I.

---

30   Further and higher education of disabled persons

(1) The Further and Higher Education Act 1992 is amended as set out in subsections (2) to (6).

(2) In section 5 (administration of funds by further education funding councils), in subsection (6)(b), after 'may' insert ', subject to subsection (7A) below,'.

(3) After section 5(7) insert—

'(7A) Without prejudice to the power to impose conditions given by subsection (6)(b) above, the conditions subject to which a council gives financial support under this section to the governing body of an institution within the further education sector—

(a)   shall require the governing body to publish disability statements at such intervals as may be prescribed; and

(b)   may include conditions relating to the provision made, or to be made, by the institution with respect to disabled persons.

(7B) For the purposes of subsection (7A) above—

"disability statement" means a statement containing information of a prescribed description about the provision of facilities for education made by the institution in respect of disabled persons;

"disabled persons" means persons who are disabled persons for the purposes of the Disability Discrimination Act 1995; and

"prescribed" means prescribed by regulations.'

(4) In section 8 (supplementary functions) add, at the end—

'(6) As soon as is reasonably practicable after the end of its financial year, each council shall make a written report to the Secretary of State on—

(a)   the progress made during the year to which the report relates in the provision of further education for disabled students in their area; and

(b)   their plans for the future provision of further education for disabled students in their area.

(7) In subsection (6) above—

"disabled students" means students who are disabled persons for the purposes of the Disability Discrimination Act 1995; and

"financial year" means the period of twelve months ending with 31st March 1997 and each successive period of twelve months.'

(5) In section 62 (establishment of higher education funding councils), after subsection (7) insert—

'(7A) In exercising their functions, each council shall have regard to the requirements of disabled persons.

(7B) In subsection (7A) "disabled persons" means persons who are disabled persons for the purposes of the Disability Discrimination Act 1995.'

(6) In section 65 (administration of funds by higher education funding councils), after subsection (4) insert—

'(4A) Without prejudice to the power to impose conditions given by subsection (3) above, the conditions subject to which a council makes grants, loans or other payments under this section to the governing body of a higher education institution shall require the governing body to publish disability statements at such intervals as may be specified.

(4B) For the purposes of subsection (4A) above—

"disability statement" means a statement containing information of a specified description about the provision of facilities for education and research made by the institution in respect of persons who are disabled persons for the purposes of the Disability Discrimination Act 1995; and

"specified" means specified in the conditions subject to which grants, loans or other payments are made by a council under this section.'

(7)–(9) (*repealed*)

Amendment – Amended by Education Act 1996, s 582(2), Sch 38, Pt I.

---

31 Further and higher education of disabled persons: Scotland

(1) The Further and Higher Education (Scotland) Act 1992 is amended as follows.

(2) In section 37 (establishment of Scottish Higher Education Funding Council) after subsection (4) insert—

'(4A) In exercising their functions, the Council shall have regard to the requirements of disabled persons.

(4B) In subsection (4A) above, "disabled persons" means persons who are disabled persons for the purpose of the Disability Discrimination Act 1995.'

(3) In section 40 (administration of funds by the Council), after subsection (4) insert—

'(5) Without prejudice to the power to impose conditions given by subsection (3) above, the conditions subject to which the Council make grants, loans or other payments under this section to the governing body of an institution within the higher education sector shall require the governing body to publish disability statements at such intervals as may be specified.

(6) For the purposes of subsection (5) above—

"disability statement" means a statement containing information of a specified description about the provision of facilities for education and research made by the institution in respect of persons who are disabled persons for the purpose of the Disability Discrimination Act 1995; and

"specified" means specified in the conditions subject to which grants, loans or other payments are made by the Council under this section.'

PART V

PUBLIC TRANSPORT

Taxis

32 Taxi accessibility regulations

(1) The Secretary of State may make regulations ('taxi accessibility regulations') for the purpose of securing that it is possible—

   (a)   for disabled persons—
- (i) to get into and out of taxis in safety;
- (ii) to be carried in taxis in safety and in reasonable comfort; and

   (b)   for disabled persons in wheelchairs—
- (i) to be conveyed in safety into and out of taxis while remaining in their wheelchairs; and
- (ii) to be carried in taxis in safety and in reasonable comfort while remaining in their wheelchairs.

(2) Taxi accessibility regulations may, in particular—

   (a)   require any regulated taxi to conform with provisions of the regulations as to—
- (i) the size of any door opening which is for the use of passengers;
- (ii) the floor area of the passenger compartment;
- (iii) the amount of headroom in the passenger compartment;
- (iv) the fitting of restraining devices designed to ensure the stability of a wheelchair while the taxi is moving;

   (b)   require the driver of any regulated taxi which is plying for hire, or which has been hired, to comply with provisions of the regulations as to the carrying of ramps or other devices designed to facilitate the loading and unloading of wheelchairs;

   (c)   require the driver of any regulated taxi in which a disabled person who is in a wheelchair is being carried (while remaining in his wheelchair) to comply with provisions of the regulations as to the position in which the wheelchair is to be secured.

(3) The driver of a regulated taxi which is plying for hire, or which has been hired, is guilty of an offence if—

   (a)   he fails to comply with any requirement imposed on him by the regulations; or

   (b)   the taxi fails to conform with any provision of the regulations with which it is required to conform.

(4) A person who is guilty of such an offence is liable, on summary conviction, to a fine not exceeding level 3 on the standard scale.

(5) In this section—

'passenger compartment' has such meaning as may be prescribed;
'regulated taxi' means any taxi to which the regulations are expressed to apply;
'taxi' means a vehicle licensed under—
- (a) section 37 of the Town Police Clauses Act 1847, or
- (b) section 6 of the Metropolitan Public Carriage Act 1869,

but does not include a taxi which is drawn by a horse or other animal.

33   Designated transport facilities

(1) In this section 'a franchise agreement' means a contract entered into by the operator of a designated transport facility for the provision by the other party to the contract of hire car services—

   (a)   for members of the public using any part of the transport facility; and

   (b)   which involve vehicles entering any part of that facility.

(2) The Secretary of State may by regulations provide for the application of any taxi provision in relation to—

   (a)   vehicles used for the provision of services under a franchise agreement; or

   (b)   the drivers of such vehicles.

(3) Any regulations under subsection (2) may apply any taxi provision with such modifications as the Secretary of State considers appropriate.

(4) In this section—

'designated' means designated for the purposes of this section by an order made by the Secretary of State;

'hire car' has such meaning as may be prescribed;

'operator', in relation to a transport facility, means any person who is concerned with the management or operation of the facility;

'taxi provision' means any provision of—

    (a)   this Act, or

    (b)   regulations made in pursuance of section 20(2A) of the Civic Government (Scotland) Act 1982,

which applies in relation to taxis or the drivers of taxis; and

'transport facility' means any premises which form part of any port, airport, railway station or bus station.

34 New licences conditional on compliance with taxi accessibility regulations

(1) No licensing authority shall grant a licence for a taxi to ply for hire unless the vehicle conforms with those provisions of the taxi accessibility regulations with which it will be required to conform if licensed.

(2) Subsection (1) does not apply if such a licence was in force with respect to the vehicle at any time during the period of 28 days immediately before the day on which the licence is granted.

(3) The Secretary of State may by order provide for subsection (2) to cease to have effect on such date as may be specified in the order.

(4) Separate orders may be made under subsection (3) with respect to different areas or localities.

35 Exemption from taxi accessibility regulations

(1) The Secretary of State may make regulations ('exemption regulations') for the purpose of enabling any relevant licensing authority to apply to him for an order (an 'exemption order') exempting the authority from the requirements of section 34.

(2) Exemption regulations may, in particular, make provision requiring a licensing authority proposing to apply for an exemption order—

    (a)   to carry out such consultations as may be prescribed;

    (b)   to publish the proposal in the prescribed manner;

    (c)   to consider any representations made to it about the proposal, before applying for the order;

    (d)   to make its application in the prescribed form.

(3) A licensing authority may apply for an exemption order only if it is satisfied—

    (a)   that, having regard to the circumstances prevailing in its area, it would be inappropriate for the requirements of section 34 to apply; and

    (b)   that the application of section 34 would result in an unacceptable reduction in the number of taxis in its area.

(4) After considering any application for an exemption order and consulting the Disabled Persons Transport Advisory Committee and such other persons as he considers appropriate, the Secretary of State may—

(a)   make an exemption order in the terms of the application;
(b)   make an exemption order in such other terms as he considers appropriate; or
(c)   refuse to make an exemption order.

(5) The Secretary of State may by regulations ('swivel seat regulations') make provision requiring any exempt taxi plying for hire in an area in respect of which an exemption order is in force to conform with provisions of the regulations as to the fitting and use of swivel seats.

(6) The Secretary of State may by regulations make provision with respect to swivel seat regulations similar to that made by section 34 with respect to taxi accessibility regulations.

(7) In this section—

'exempt taxi' means a taxi in relation to which section 34(1) would apply if the exemption order were not in force;
'relevant licensing authority' means a licensing authority responsible for licensing taxis in any area of England and Wales other than the area to which the Metropolitan Public Carriage Act 1869 applies; and
'swivel seats' has such meaning as may be prescribed.

36   Carrying of passengers in wheelchairs

(1) This section imposes duties on the driver of a regulated taxi which has been hired—

(a)   by or for a disabled person who is in a wheelchair; or
(b)   by a person who wishes such a disabled person to accompany him in the taxi.

(2) In this section—

'carry' means carry in the taxi concerned; and
'the passenger' means the disabled person concerned.

(3) The duties are—

(a)   to carry the passenger while he remains in his wheelchair;
(b)   not to make any additional charge for doing so;
(c)   if the passenger chooses to sit in a passenger seat, to carry the wheelchair;
(d)   to take such steps as are necessary to ensure that the passenger is carried in safety and in reasonable comfort;
(e)   to give such assistance as may be reasonably required—
      (i)   to enable the passenger to get into or out of the taxi;
      (ii) if the passenger wishes to remain in his wheelchair, to enable him to be conveyed into and out of the taxi while in his wheelchair;
      (iii) to load the passenger's luggage into or out of the taxi;
      (iv) if the passenger does not wish to remain in his wheelchair, to load the wheelchair into or out of the taxi.

(4) Nothing in this section is to be taken to require the driver of any taxi—

(a)   except in the case of a taxi of a prescribed description, to carry more than one person in a wheelchair, or more than one wheelchair, on any one journey; or
(b)   to carry any person in circumstances in which it would otherwise be lawful for him to refuse to carry that person.

(5) A driver of a regulated taxi who fails to comply with any duty imposed on him by this section is guilty of an offence and liable, on summary conviction, to a fine not exceeding level 3 on the standard scale.

(6) In any proceedings for an offence under this section, it is a defence for the accused to show that, even though at the time of the alleged offence the taxi conformed with those provisions of the taxi accessibility regulations with which it was required to conform, it would not have been possible for the wheelchair in question to be carried in safety in the taxi.

(7) If the licensing authority is satisfied that it is appropriate to exempt a person from the duties imposed by this section—

   (a)   on medical grounds, or
   (b)   on the ground that his physical condition makes it impossible or unreasonably
         difficult for him to comply with the duties imposed on drivers by this section,

it shall issue him with a certificate of exemption.

(8) A certificate of exemption shall be issued for such period as may be specified in the certificate.

(9) The driver of a regulated taxi is exempt from the duties imposed by this section if—

   (a)   a certificate of exemption issued to him under this section is in force; and
   (b)   the prescribed notice of his exemption is exhibited on the taxi in the prescribed
         manner.

37   Carrying of guide dogs and hearing dogs

(1) This section imposes duties on the driver of a taxi which has been hired—

   (a)   by or for a disabled person who is accompanied by his guide dog or hearing
         dog, or
   (b)   by a person who wishes such a disabled person to accompany him in the taxi.

(2) The disabled person is referred to in this section as 'the passenger'.

(3) The duties are—

   (a)   to carry the passenger's dog and allow it to remain with the passenger; and
   (b)   not to make any additional charge for doing so.

(4) A driver of a taxi who fails to comply with any duty imposed on him by this section is guilty of an offence and liable, on summary conviction, to a fine not exceeding level 3 on the standard scale.

(5) If the licensing authority is satisfied that it is appropriate on medical grounds to exempt a person from the duties imposed by this section, it shall issue him with a certificate of exemption.

(6) In determining whether to issue a certificate of exemption, the licensing authority shall, in particular, have regard to the physical characteristics of the taxi which the applicant drives or those of any kind of taxi in relation to which he requires the certificate.

(7) A certificate of exemption shall be issued—

   (a)   with respect to a specified taxi or a specified kind of taxi; and
   (b)   for such period as may be specified in the certificate.

(8) The driver of a taxi is exempt from the duties imposed by this section if—

   (a)   a certificate of exemption issued to him under this section is in force with
         respect to the taxi; and
   (b)   the prescribed notice of his exemption is exhibited on the taxi in the prescribed
         manner.

(9) The Secretary of State may, for the purposes of this section, prescribe any other category of dog trained to assist a disabled person who has a disability of a prescribed kind.

(10) This section applies in relation to any such prescribed category of dog as it applies in relation to guide dogs.

(11) In this section—

'guide dog' means a dog which has been trained to guide a blind person; and
'hearing dog' means a dog which has been trained to assist a deaf person.

38   Appeal against refusal of exemption certificate

(1) Any person who is aggrieved by the refusal of a licensing authority to issue an exemption certificate under section 36 or 37 may appeal to the appropriate court before the end of the period of 28 days beginning with the date of the refusal.

(2) On an appeal to it under this section, the court may direct the licensing authority concerned to issue the appropriate certificate of exemption to have effect for such period as may be specified in the direction.

(3) 'Appropriate court' means the magistrates' court for the petty sessions area in which the licensing authority has its principal office.

39   Requirements as to disabled passengers in Scotland

(1) Part II of the Civic Government (Scotland) Act 1982 (licensing and regulation) is amended as follows.

(2) In subsection (4) of section 10 (suitability of vehicle for use as taxi)—

(a)   after 'authority' insert '—(a)'; and
(b)   at the end add '; and
      (b) as not being so suitable if it does not so comply.'

(3) In section 20 (regulations relating to taxis etc.) after subsection (2) insert—

'(2A) Without prejudice to the generality of subsections (1) and (2) above, regulations under those subsections may make such provision as appears to the Secretary of State to be necessary or expedient in relation to the carrying in taxis of disabled persons (within the meaning of section 1(2) of the Disability Discrimination Act 1995) and such provision may in particular prescribe—
      (a)   requirements as to the carriage of wheelchairs, guide dogs, hearing dogs and other categories of dog;
      (b)   a date from which any such provision is to apply and the extent to which it is to apply; and
      (c)   the circumstances in which an exemption from such provision may be granted in respect of any taxi or taxi driver,
and in this subsection—
      "guide dog" means a dog which has been trained to guide a blind person;
      "hearing dog" means a dog which has been trained to assist a deaf person; and
      "other categories of dog" means such other categories of dog as the Secretary of State may prescribe, trained to assist disabled persons who have disabilities of such kinds as he may prescribe.'

40   PSV accessibility regulations

(1) The Secretary of State may make regulations ('PSV accessibility regulations') for the purpose of securing that it is possible for disabled persons—

(a)   to get on to and off regulated public service vehicles in safety and without unreasonable difficulty (and, in the case of disabled persons in wheelchairs, to do so while remaining in their wheelchairs); and

(b)   to be carried in such vehicles in safety and in reasonable comfort.

(2) PSV accessibility regulations may, in particular, make provision as to the construction, use and maintenance of regulated public service vehicles including provision as to—

(a)   the fitting of equipment to vehicles;

(b)   equipment to be carried by vehicles;

(c)   the design of equipment to be fitted to, or carried by, vehicles;

(d)   the fitting and use of restraining devices designed to ensure the stability of wheelchairs while vehicles are moving;

(e)   the position in which wheelchairs are to be secured while vehicles are moving.

(3) Any person who—

(a)   contravenes or fails to comply with any provision of the PSV accessibility regulations,

(b)   uses on a road a regulated public service vehicle which does not conform with any provision of the regulations with which it is required to conform, or

(c)   causes or permits to be used on a road such a regulated public service vehicle,

is guilty of an offence.

(4) A person who is guilty of such an offence is liable, on summary conviction, to a fine not exceeding level 4 on the standard scale.

(5) In this section—

'public service vehicle' means a vehicle which is—
(a)   adapted to carry more than eight passengers; and
(b)   a public service vehicle for the purposes of the Public Passenger Vehicles Act 1981;
'regulated public service vehicle' means any public service vehicle to which the PSV accessibility regulations are expressed to apply.

(6) Different provision may be made in regulations under this section—

(a)   as respects different classes or descriptions of vehicle;

(b)   as respects the same class or description of vehicle in different circumstances.

(7) Before making any regulations under this section or section 41 or 42 the Secretary of State shall consult the Disabled Persons Transport Advisory Committee and such other representative organisations as he thinks fit.

41   Accessibility certificates

(1) A regulated public service vehicle shall not be used on a road unless—

(a)   a vehicle examiner has issued a certificate (an 'accessibility certificate') that such provisions of the PSV accessibility regulations as may be prescribed are satisfied in respect of the vehicle; or

(b)   an approval certificate has been issued under section 42 in respect of the vehicle.

(2) The Secretary of State may make regulations—

(a)   with respect to applications for, and the issue of, accessibility certificates;

(b)   providing for the examination of vehicles in respect of which applications have been made;

(c)   with respect to the issue of copies of accessibility certificates in place of certificates which have been lost or destroyed.

(3) If a regulated public service vehicle is used in contravention of this section, the operator of the vehicle is guilty of an offence and liable on summary conviction to a fine not exceeding level 4 on the standard scale.

(4) In this section 'operator' has the same meaning as in the Public Passenger Vehicles Act 1981.

42   Approval certificates

(1) Where the Secretary of State is satisfied that such provisions of the PSV accessibility regulations as may be prescribed for the purposes of section 41 are satisfied in respect of a particular vehicle he may approve the vehicle for the purposes of this section.

(2) A vehicle which has been so approved is referred to in this section as a 'type vehicle'.

(3) Subsection (4) applies where a declaration in the prescribed form has been made by an authorised person that a particular vehicle conforms in design, construction and equipment with a type vehicle.

(4) A vehicle examiner may, after examining (if he thinks fit) the vehicle to which the declaration applies, issue a certificate in the prescribed form ('an approval certificate') that it conforms to the type vehicle.

(5) The Secretary of State may make regulations—

(a)   with respect to applications for, and grants of, approval under subsection (1);

(b)   with respect to applications for, and the issue of, approval certificates;

(c)   providing for the examination of vehicles in respect of which applications have been made;

(d)   with respect to the issue of copies of approval certificates in place of certificates which have been lost or destroyed.

(6) The Secretary of State may at any time withdraw his approval of a type vehicle.

(7) Where an approval is withdrawn—

(a)   no further approval certificates shall be issued by reference to the type vehicle; but

(b)   any approval certificate issued by reference to the type vehicle before the withdrawal shall continue to have effect for the purposes of section 41.

(8) In subsection (3) 'authorised person' means a person authorised by the Secretary of State for the purposes of that subsection.

43   Special authorisations

(1) The Secretary of State may by order authorise the use on roads of—

(a)   any regulated public service vehicle of a class or description specified by the order, or

(b)   any regulated public service vehicle which is so specified,

and nothing in section 40, 41, or 42 prevents the use of any vehicle in accordance with the order.

(2) Any such authorisation may be given subject to such restrictions and conditions as may be specified by or under the order.

(3) The Secretary of State may by order make provision for the purpose of securing that, subject to such restrictions and conditions as may be specified by or under the order, provisions of the PSV accessibility regulations apply to regulated public service vehicles of a description specified by the order subject to such modifications or exceptions as may be specified by the order.

44   Reviews and appeals

(1) Subsection (2) applies where—

(a)   the Secretary of State refuses an application for the approval of a vehicle under section 42(1); and
(b)   before the end of the prescribed period, the applicant asks the Secretary of State to review the decision and pays any fee fixed under section 45;

(2) The Secretary of State shall—

(a)   review the decision; and
(b)   in doing so, consider any representations made to him in writing, before the end of the prescribed period, by the applicant.

(3) A person applying for an accessibility certificate or an approval certificate may appeal to the Secretary of State against the refusal of a vehicle examiner to issue such a certificate.

(4) An appeal must be made within the prescribed time and in the prescribed manner.

(5) Regulations may make provision as to the procedure to be followed in connection with appeals.

(6) On the determination of an appeal, the Secretary of State may—

(a)   confirm, vary or reverse the decision appealed against;
(b)   give such directions as he thinks fit to the vehicle examiner for giving effect to his decision.

45   Fees

(1) Such fees, payable at such times, as may be prescribed may be charged by the Secretary of State in respect of—

(a)   applications for, and grants of, approval under section 42(1);
(b)   applications for, and the issue of, accessibility certificates and approval certificates;
(c)   copies of such certificates;
(d)   reviews and appeals under section 44.

(2) Any such fees received by the Secretary of State shall be paid by him into the Consolidated Fund.

(3) Regulations under subsection (1) may make provision for the repayment of fees, in whole or in part, in such circumstances as may be prescribed.

(4) Before making any regulations under subsection (1) the Secretary of State shall consult such representative organisations as he thinks fit.

Rail vehicles

46   Rail vehicle accessibility regulations

(1) The Secretary of State may make regulations ('rail vehicle accessibility regulations') for the purpose of securing that it is possible—

   (a)   for disabled persons—
         (i) to get on to and off regulated rail vehicles in safety and without unreasonable difficulty;
        (ii) to be carried in such vehicles in safety and in reasonable comfort; and
   (b)   for disabled persons in wheelchairs—
         (i) to get on to and off such vehicles in safety and without unreasonable difficulty while remaining in their wheelchairs, and
        (ii) to be carried in such vehicles in safety and in reasonable comfort while remaining in their wheelchairs.

(2) Rail vehicle accessibility regulations may, in particular, make provision as to the construction, use and maintenance of regulated rail vehicles including provision as to—

   (a)   the fitting of equipment to vehicles;
   (b)   equipment to be carried by vehicles;
   (c)   the design of equipment to be fitted to, or carried by, vehicles;
   (d)   the use of equipment fitted to, or carried by, vehicles;
   (e)   the toilet facilities to be provided in vehicles;
   (f)   the location and floor area of the wheelchair accommodation to be provided in vehicles;
   (g)   assistance to be given to disabled persons.

(3) If a regulated rail vehicle which does not conform with any provision of the rail vehicle accessibility regulations with which it is required to conform is used for carriage, the operator of the vehicle is guilty of an offence.

(4) A person who is guilty of such an offence is liable, on summary conviction, to a fine not exceeding level 4 on the standard scale.

(5) Different provision may be made in rail vehicle accessibility regulations—

   (a)   as respects different classes or descriptions of rail vehicle;
   (b)   as respects the same class or description of rail vehicle in different circumstances;
   (c)   as respects different networks.

(6) In this section—

   'network' means any permanent way or other means of guiding or supporting rail vehicles or any section of it;
   'operator', in relation to any rail vehicle, means the person having the management of that vehicle;

'rail vehicle' means a vehicle—
- (a)   constructed or adapted to carry passengers on any railway, tramway or prescribed system; and
- (b)   first brought into use, or belonging to a class of vehicle first brought into use, after 31st December 1998;

'regulated rail vehicle' means any rail vehicle to which the rail vehicle accessibility regulations are expressed to apply; and

'wheelchair accommodation' has such meaning as may be prescribed.

(7) In subsection (6)—

'prescribed system' means a system using a prescribed mode of guided transport ('guided transport' having the same meaning as in the Transport and Works Act 1992); and

'railway' and 'tramway' have the same meaning as in that Act.

(8) The Secretary of State may by regulations make provision as to the time when a rail vehicle, or a class of rail vehicle, is to be treated, for the purposes of this section, as first brought into use.

(9) Regulations under subsection (8) may include provision for disregarding periods of testing and other prescribed periods of use.

(10) For the purposes of this section and section 47, a person uses a vehicle for carriage if he uses it for the carriage of members of the public for hire or reward at separate fares.

(11) Before making any regulations under subsection (1) or section 47 the Secretary of State shall consult the Disabled Persons Transport Advisory Committee and such other representative organisations as he thinks fit.

47   Exemption from rail vehicle accessibility regulations

(1) The Secretary of State may by order (an 'exemption order') authorise the use for carriage of any regulated rail vehicle of a specified description, or in specified circumstances, even though that vehicle does not conform with the provisions of the rail vehicle accessibility regulations with which it is required to conform.

(2) Regulations may make provision with respect to exemption orders including, in particular, provision as to—

- (a)   the persons by whom applications for exemption orders may be made;
- (b)   the form in which such applications are to be made;
- (c)   information to be supplied in connection with such applications;
- (d)   the period for which exemption orders are to continue in force;
- (e)   the revocation of exemption orders.

(3) After considering any application for an exemption order and consulting the Disabled Persons Transport Advisory Committee and such other persons as he considers appropriate, the Secretary of State may—

- (a)   make an exemption order in the terms of the application;
- (b)   make an exemption order in such other terms as he considers appropriate;
- (c)   refuse to make an exemption order.

(4) An exemption order may be made subject to such restrictions and conditions as may be specified.

(5) In this section 'specified' means specified in an exemption order.

Supplemental

48   Offences by bodies corporate etc.

(1) Where an offence under section 40 or 46 committed by a body corporate is committed with the consent or connivance of, or is attributable to any neglect on the part of, a director, manager, secretary or other similar officer of the body, or a person purporting to act in such a capacity, he as well as the body corporate is guilty of the offence.

(2) In subsection (1) 'director' , in relation to a body corporate whose affairs are managed by its members, means a member of the body corporate.

(3) Where, in Scotland, an offence under section 40 or 46 committed by a partnership or by an unincorporated association other than a partnership is committed with the consent or connivance of, or is attributable to any neglect on the part of, a partner in the partnership of (as the case may be) a person concerned in the management or control of the association, he, as well as the partnership or association, is guilty of the offence.

49   Forgery and false statements

(1) In this section 'relevant document' means—

(a)   a certificate of exemption issued under section 36 or 37;
(b)   a notice of a kind mentioned in section 36(9)(b) or 37(8)(b);
(c)   an accessibility certificate; or
(d)   an approval certificate.

(2) A person is guilty of an offence if, with intent to deceive, he—

(a)   forges, alters or uses a relevant document;
(b)   lends a relevant document to any other person;
(c)   allows a relevant document to be used by any other person; or
(d)   makes or has in his possession any document which closely resembles a relevant document.

(3) A person who is guilty of an offence under subsection (2) is liable—

(a)   on summary conviction, to a fine not exceeding the statutory maximum;
(b)   on conviction on indictment, to imprisonment for a term not exceeding two years or to a fine or to both.

(4) A person who knowingly makes a false statement for the purpose of obtaining an accessibility certificate or an approval certificate is guilty of an offence and liable on summary conviction to a fine not exceeding level 4 on the standard scale.

PART VI

THE NATIONAL DISABILITY COUNCIL

50   The National Disability Council

(1) There shall be a body to be known as the National Disability Council (but in this Act referred to as 'the Council').

(2) It shall be the duty of the Council to advise the Secretary of State, either on its own initiative or when asked to do so by the Secretary of State—

(a)   on matters relevant to the elimination of discrimination against disabled persons and persons who have had a disability;

(b)   on measures which are likely to reduce or eliminate such discrimination; and

(c)   on matters related to the operation of this Act or of provisions made under this Act.

(3) The Secretary of State may by order confer additional functions on the Council.

(4) The power conferred by subsection (3) does not include power to confer on the Council any functions with respect to the investigation of any complaint which may be the subject of proceedings under this Act.

(5) In discharging its duties under this section, the Council shall in particular have regard to—

(a)   the extent and nature of the benefits which would be likely to result from the implementation of any recommendation which it makes; and

(b)   the likely cost of implementing any such recommendation.

(6) Where the Council makes any recommendation in the discharge of any of its functions under this section it shall, if it is reasonably practicable to do so, make an assessment of—

(a)   the likely cost of implementing the recommendation; and

(b)   the likely financial benefits which would result from implementing it.

(7) Where the Council proposes to give the Secretary of State advice on a matter, it shall before doing so—

(a)   consult any body—
    (i) established by any enactment or by a Minister of the Crown for the purpose of giving advice in relation to disability, or any aspect of disability; and
    (ii) having functions in relation to the matter to which the advice relates;

(b)   consult such other persons as it considers appropriate; and

(c)   have regard to any representations made to it as a result of any such consultations.

(8) Schedule 5 makes further provision with respect to the Council, including provision about its membership.

(9) The power conferred on the Council by subsection (2) to give advice on its own initiative does not include power to give advice—

(a)   by virtue of paragraph (a) or (b), in respect of any matter which relates to the operation of any provision of or arrangements made under—
    (i) the Disabled Persons (Employment) Acts 1944 and 1958;
    (ii) (*repealed*)
    (iii) the Employment Rights Act 1996; or
    (iv) section 2(3) of the Enterprise and New Towns (Scotland) Act 1990; or

(b)   by virtue of paragraph (c), in respect of any matter arising under Part II or section 53, 54, 56 or 61.

(10) Subsection (9) shall not have effect at any time when there is neither a national advisory council established under section 17(1)(a) of the Disabled Persons (Employment) Act 1944 nor any person appointed to act generally under section 60(1) of this Act.

Amendments – Amended by Employment Rights Act 1996, s 240, Sch 1, para 69(1), (2); Employment Rights (Northern Ireland) Order 1996, SI 1996/1919 (NI 16), art 257, Sch 3; prospectively repealed by Disability Rights Commission Act 1999, s 14(2), Sch 5 as from a day to be appointed.

51 Codes of practice prepared by the Council

(1) It shall be the duty of the Council, when asked to do so by the Secretary of State—

   (a)   to prepare proposals for a code of practice dealing with the matters to which the Secretary of State's request relates; or
   (b)   to review a code and, if it considers it appropriate, propose alterations.

(2) The Secretary of State may, in accordance with the procedural provisions of section 52, issue codes of practice in response to proposals made by the Council under this section.

(3) A failure on the part of any person to observe any provision of a code does not of itself make that person liable to any proceedings.

(4) A code is admissible in evidence in any proceedings under this Act before an employment tribunal, a county court or a sheriff court.

(5) If any provision of a code appears to a tribunal or court to be relevant to any question arising in any proceedings under this Act, it shall be taken into account in determining that question.

(6) In this section and section 52 'code' means a code issued by the Secretary of State under this section and includes a code which has been altered and re-issued.

Amendments – Amended by Employment Rights (Dispute Resolution) Act 1998, s 1(2)(a); prospectively repealed by Disability Rights Commission Act 1999, s 14(2), Sch 5 as from a day to be appointed.

52 Further provision about codes issued under section 51

(1) In this section 'proposal' means a proposal made by the Council to the Secretary of State under section 51.

(2) In preparing any proposal, the Council shall consult—

   (a)   such persons (if any) as the Secretary of State has specified in making his request to the Council; and
   (b)   such other persons (if any) as the Council considers appropriate.

(3) Before making any proposal, the Council shall publish a draft, consider any representations made to it about the draft and, if it thinks it appropriate, modify its proposal in the light of any of those representations.

(4) Where the Council makes any proposal, the Secretary of State may—

   (a)   approve it;
   (b)   approve it subject to such modifications as he considers appropriate; or
   (c)   refuse to approve it.

(5) Where the Secretary of State approves any proposal (with or without modifications), he shall prepare a draft of the proposed code and lay it before each House of Parliament.

(6) If, within the 40-day period, either House resolves not to approve the draft, the Secretary of State shall take no further steps in relation to the proposed code.

(7) If no such resolution is made within the 40-day period, the Secretary of State shall issue the code in the form of his draft.

(8) The code shall come into force on such date as the Secretary of State may appoint by order.

(9) Subsection (6) does not prevent a new draft of the proposed code from being laid before Parliament.

(10) If the Secretary of State refuses to approve a proposal, he shall give the Council a written statement of his reasons for not approving it.

(11) The Secretary of State may by order revoke a code.

(12) In this section '40-day period', in relation to the draft of a proposed code, means—

    (a)   if the draft is laid before one House on a day later than the day on which it is laid before the other House, the period of 40 days beginning with the later of the two days, and

    (b)   in any other case, the period of 40 days beginning with the day on which the draft is laid before each House,

no account being taken of any period during which Parliament is dissolved or prorogued or during which both Houses are adjourned for more than four days.

Amendment – Prospectively repealed by Disability Rights Commission Act 1999, s 14(2), Sch 5 as from a day to be appointed.

PART VII

SUPPLEMENTAL

53   Codes of practice prepared by the Secretary of State

(1) The Secretary of State may issue codes of practice containing such practical guidance as he considers appropriate with a view to—

    (a)   eliminating discrimination in the field of employment against disabled persons and persons who have had a disability; or

    (b)   encouraging good practice in relation to the employment of disabled persons and persons who have had a disability.

(2) The Secretary of State may from time to time revise the whole or any part of a code and re-issue it.

(3) Without prejudice to subsection (1), a code may include practical guidance as to—

    (a)   the circumstances in which it would be reasonable, having regard in particular to the costs involved, for a person to be expected to make adjustments in favour of a disabled person or a person who has had a disability; or

    (b)   what steps it is reasonably practicable for employers to take for the purpose of preventing their employees from doing, in the course of their employment, anything which is made unlawful by this Act.

(4) A failure on the part of any person to observe any provision of a code does not of itself make that person liable to any proceedings.

(5) A code is admissible in evidence in any proceedings under this Act before an employment tribunal, a county court or a sheriff court.

(6) If any provision of a code appears to a tribunal or court to be relevant to any question arising in any proceedings under this Act, it shall be taken into account in determining that question.

(7) In this section and section 54 'code' means a code issued by the Secretary of State under this section and includes a code which has been revised and re-issued.

(8) In subsection (1)(a), 'discrimination in the field of employment' includes discrimination of a kind mentioned in section 12 or 13.

(9) In subsections (1)(b) and (3), 'employment' includes contract work (as defined by section 12(6)).

Amendments – Amended by Employment Rights (Dispute Resolution) Act 1998, s 1(2)(a); prospectively repealed by Disability Rights Commission Act 1999, s 14(2), Sch 5 as from a day to be appointed.

53A Codes of practice

(1) The Disability Rights Commission may prepare and issue codes of practice giving practical guidance—

   (a)   to employers, service providers or other persons to whom provisions of Part II or Part III apply on how to avoid discrimination or on any other matter relating to the operation of those provisions in relation to them; or

   (b)   to any persons on any other matter, with a view to—
      (i) promoting the equalisation of opportunities for disabled persons and persons who have had a disability, or
      (ii) encouraging good practice regarding the treatment of such persons,
   in any field of activity regulated by any provision of Part II or Part III.

(2) The Commission shall, when requested to do so by the Secretary of State, prepare a code of practice dealing with the matters specified in the request.

(3) In preparing a code of practice the Commission shall carry out such consultations as it considers appropriate (which shall include the publication for public consultation of proposals relating to the code).

(4) The Commission may not issue a code of practice unless—

   (a)   a draft of it has been submitted to and approved by the Secretary of State and laid by him before both Houses of Parliament; and

   (b)   the 40-day period has elapsed without either House resolving not to approve the draft.

(5) If the Secretary of State does not approve a draft code of practice submitted to him he shall give the Commission a written statement of his reasons.

(6) A code of practice issued by the Commission—

   (a)   shall come into effect on such day as the Secretary of State may by order appoint;

   (b)   may be revised in whole or part, and re-issued, by the Commission; and

   (c)   may be revoked by an order made by the Secretary of State at the request of the Commission.

(7) Where the Commission proposes to revise a code of practice—

   (a)   it shall comply with subsection (3) in relation to the revisions; and

   (b)   the other provisions of this section apply to the revised code of practice as they apply to a new code of practice.

(8) Failure to observe any provision of a code of practice does not of itself make a person liable to any proceedings, but any provision of a code which appears to a court or tribunal to be relevant to any question arising in any proceedings under Part II or Part III shall be taken into account in determining that question.

(9) In this section—

'code of practice' means a code of practice under this section;
'discrimination' means anything which is unlawful discrimination for the purposes of any provision of Part II or Part III; and
'40-day period' has the same meaning in relation to a draft code of practice as it has in section 3 in relation to draft guidance.

Amendment – Inserted by Disability Rights Commission Act 1999, s 9(1) as from a day to be appointed.

54   Further provision about codes issued under section 53

(1) In preparing a draft of any code under section 53, the Secretary of State shall consult such organisations representing the interests of employers or of disabled persons in, or seeking, employment as he considers appropriate.

(2) Where the Secretary of State proposes to issue a code, he shall publish a draft of it, consider any representations that are made to him about the draft and, if he thinks it appropriate, modify his proposals in the light of any of those representations.

(3) If the Secretary of State decides to proceed with a proposed code, he shall lay a draft of it before each House of Parliament.

(4) If, within the 40-day period, either House resolves not to approve the draft, the Secretary of State shall take no further steps in relation to the proposed code.

(5) If no such resolution is made within the 40-day period, the Secretary of State shall issue the code in the form of his draft.

(6) The code shall come into force on such date as the Secretary of State may appoint by order.

(7) Subsection (4) does not prevent a new draft of the proposed code from being laid before Parliament.

(8) The Secretary of State may by order revoke a code.

(9) In this section '40-day period', in relation to the draft of a proposed code, means—

(a)   if the draft is laid before one House on a day later than the day on which it is laid before the other House, the period of 40 days beginning with the later of the two days, and
(b)   in any other case, the period of 40 days beginning with the day on which the draft is laid before each House,

no account being taken of any period during which Parliament is dissolved or prorogued or during which both Houses are adjourned for more than four days.

Amendment – Prospectively repealed by Disability Rights Commission Act 1999, s 14(2), Sch 5 as from a day to be appointed.

55   Victimisation

(1) For the purposes of Part II or Part III, a person ('A') discriminates against another person ('B') if—

(a)   he treats B less favourably than he treats or would treat other persons whose circumstances are the same as B's; and

(b)   he does so for a reason mentioned in subsection (2).

(2) The reasons are that—

(a)   B has—
   (i)   brought proceedings against A or any other person under this Act; or
   (ii) given evidence or information in connection with such proceedings brought by any person; or
   (iii) otherwise done anything under this Act in relation to A or any other person; or
   (iv) alleged that A or any other person has (whether or not the allegation so states) contravened this Act; or

(b)   A believes or suspects that B has done or intends to do any of those things.

(3) Where B is a disabled person, or a person who has had a disability, the disability in question shall be disregarded in comparing his circumstances with those of any other person for the purposes of subsection (1)(a).

(4) Subsection (1) does not apply to treatment of a person because of an allegation made by him if the allegation was false and not made in good faith.

56   Help for persons suffering discrimination

(1) For the purposes of this section—

(a)   a person who considers that he may have been discriminated against, in contravention of any provision of Part II, is referred to as 'the complainant'; and

(b)   a person against whom the complainant may decide to make, or has made, a complaint under Part II is referred to as 'the respondent'.

(2) The Secretary of State shall, with a view to helping the complainant to decide whether to make a complaint against the respondent and, if he does so, to formulate and present his case in the most effective manner, by order prescribe—

(a)   forms by which the complainant may question the respondent on his reasons for doing any relevant act, or on any other matter which is or may be relevant; and

(b)   forms by which the respondent may if he so wishes reply to any questions.

(3) Where the complainant questions the respondent in accordance with forms prescribed by an order under subsection (2)—

(a)   the question, and any reply by the respondent (whether in accordance with such an order or not), shall be admissible as evidence in any proceedings under Part II;

(b)   if it appears to the tribunal in any such proceedings—
   (i)   that the respondent deliberately, and without reasonable excuse, omitted to reply within a reasonable period, or

(ii) that the respondent's reply is evasive or equivocal,

it may draw any inference which it considers it just and equitable to draw, including an inference that the respondent has contravened a provision of Part II.

(4) The Secretary of State may by order prescribe—

(a) the period within which questions must be duly served in order to be admissible under subsection (3)(a); and

(b) the manner in which a question, and any reply by the respondent, may be duly served.

(5) This section is without prejudice to any other enactment or rule of law regulating interlocutory and preliminary matters in proceedings before an employment tribunal, and has effect subject to any enactment or rule of law regulating the admissibility of evidence in such proceedings.

Amendment – Amended by Employment Rights (Dispute Resolution) Act 1998, s 1(2)(a).

---

57 Aiding unlawful acts

(1) A person who knowingly aids another person to do an act made unlawful by this Act is to be treated for the purposes of this Act as himself doing the same kind of unlawful act.

(2) For the purposes of subsection (1), an employee or agent for whose act the employer or principal is liable under section 58 (or would be so liable but for section 58(5)) shall be taken to have aided the employer or principal to do the act.

(3) For the purposes of this section, a person does not knowingly aid another to do an unlawful act if—

(a) he acts in reliance on a statement made to him by that other person that, because of any provision of this Act, the act would not be unlawful; and

(b) it is reasonable for him to rely on the statement.

(4) A person who knowingly or recklessly makes such a statement which is false or misleading in a material respect is guilty of an offence.

(5) Any person guilty of an offence under subsection (4) shall be liable on summary conviction to a fine not exceeding level 5 on the standard scale.

58 Liability of employers and principals

(1) Anything done by a person in the course of his employment shall be treated for the purposes of this Act as also done by his employer, whether or not it was done with the employer's knowledge or approval.

(2) Anything done by a person as agent for another person with the authority of that other person shall be treated for the purposes of this Act as also done by that other person.

(3) Subsection (2) applies whether the authority was—

(a) express or implied; or

(b)   given before or after the act in question was done.

(4) Subsections (1) and (2) do not apply in relation to an offence under section 57(4).

(5) In proceedings under this Act against any person in respect of an act alleged to have been done by an employee of his, it shall be a defence for that person to prove that he took such steps as were reasonably practicable to prevent the employee from—

(a)   doing that act; or
(b)   doing, in the course of his employment, acts of that description.

59   Statutory authority and national security etc.

(1) Nothing in this Act makes unlawful any act done—

(a)   in pursuance of any enactment; or
(b)   in pursuance of any instrument made by a Minister of the Crown under any enactment; or
(c)   to comply with any condition or requirement imposed by a Minister of the Crown (whether before or after the passing of this Act) by virtue of any enactment.

(2) In subsection (1) 'enactment' includes one passed or made after the date on which this Act is passed and 'instrument' includes one made after that date.

(3) Nothing in this Act makes unlawful any act done for the purpose of safeguarding national security.

PART VIII

MISCELLANEOUS

60   Appointment by Secretary of State of advisers

(1) The Secretary of State may appoint such persons as he thinks fit to advise or assist him in connection with matters relating to the employment of disabled persons and persons who have had a disability.

(2) Persons may be appointed by the Secretary of State to act generally or in relation to a particular area or locality.

(3) The Secretary of State may pay to any person appointed under this section such allowances and compensation for loss of earnings as he considers appropriate.

(4) The approval of the Treasury is required for any payment under this section.

(5) In subsection (1) 'employment' includes self-employment.

(6) The Secretary of State may by order—

(a)   provide for section 17 of, and Schedule 2 to, the Disabled Persons (Employment) Act 1944 (national advisory council and district advisory committees) to cease to have effect—
        (i) so far as concerns the national advisory council; or
        (ii) so far as concerns district advisory committees; or
(b)   repeal that section and Schedule.

(7) At any time before the coming into force of an order under paragraph (b) of subsection (6), section 17 of the Act of 1944 shall have effect as if in subsection (1), after

'disabled persons' in each case there were inserted ', and persons who have had a disability,' and as if at the end of the section there were added—

  '(3) For the purposes of this section—
    (a)   a person is a disabled person if he is a disabled person for the purposes of the Disability Discrimination Act 1995; and
    (b)   "disability" has the same meaning as in that Act.'

(8) At any time before the coming into force of an order under paragraph (a) (i) or (b) of subsection (6), section 16 of the Chronically Sick and Disabled Persons Act 1970 (which extends the functions of the national advisory council) shall have effect as if after 'disabled persons' in each case there were inserted ', and persons who have had a disability,' and as if at the end of the section there were added—

  '(2) For the purposes of this section—
    (a)   a person is a disabled person if he is a disabled person for the purposes of the Disability Discrimination Act 1995; and
    (b)   "disability" has the same meaning as in that Act.'

61 Amendment of Disabled Persons (Employment) Act 1944

(1) Section 15 of the Disabled Persons (Employment) Act 1944 (which gives the Secretary of State power to make arrangements for the provision of supported employment) is amended as set out in subsections (2) to (5).

(2) In subsection (1)—

  (a)   for 'persons registered as handicapped by disablement' substitute 'disabled persons';
  (b)   for 'their disablement' substitute 'their disability'; and
  (c)   for 'are not subject to disablement' substitute 'do not have a disability'.

(3) In subsection (2), for the words from 'any of one or more companies' to 'so required and prohibited' substitute 'any company, association or body'.

(4) After subsection (2) insert—

  '(2A) The only kind of company which the Minister himself may form in exercising his powers under this section is a company which is—
    (a)   required by its constitution to apply its profits, if any, or other income in promoting its objects; and
    (b)   prohibited by its constitution from paying any dividend to its members.'

(5) After subsection (5) insert—

  '(5A) For the purposes of this section—
    (a)   a person is a disabled person if he is a disabled person for the purposes of the Disability Discrimination Act 1995; and
    (b)   "disability" has the same meaning as in that Act.'

(6) The provisions of section 16 (preference to be given under section 15 of that Act to ex-service men and women) shall become subsection (1) of that section and at the end insert—

  'and whose disability is due to that service.

  (2) For the purposes of subsection (1) of this section, a disabled person's disability shall be treated as due to service of a particular kind only in such circumstances as may be prescribed.'

(7) The following provisions of the Act of 1944 shall cease to have effect—

(a)   section 1 (definition of 'disabled person');
(b)   sections 6 to 8 (the register of disabled persons);
(c)   sections 9 to 11 (obligations on employers with substantial staffs to employ a quota of registered persons);
(d)   section 12 (the designated employment scheme for persons registered as handicapped by disablement);
(e)   section 13 (interpretation of provisions repealed by this Act);
(f)   section 14 (records to be kept by employers);
(g)   section 19 (proceedings in relation to offences); and
(h)   section 21 (application as respects place of employment, and nationality).

(8) Any provision of subordinate legislation in which 'disabled person' is defined by reference to the Act of 1944 shall be construed as if that expression had the same meaning as in this Act.

(9) Subsection (8) does not prevent the further amendment of any such provision by subordinate legislation.

* * * *

64   Application to Crown etc.

(1) This Act applies—

(a)   to an act done by or for purposes of a Minister of the Crown or government department, or
(b)   to an act done on behalf of the Crown by a statutory body, or a person holding a statutory office,

as it applies to an act done by a private person.

(2) Subject to subsection (5), Part II applies to service—

(a)   for purposes of a Minister of the Crown or government department, other than service of a person holding a statutory office, or
(b)   on behalf of the Crown for purposes of a person holding a statutory office or purposes of a statutory body,

as it applies to employment by a private person.

(3) The provisions of Parts II to IV of the 1947 Act apply to proceedings against the Crown under this Act as they apply to Crown proceedings in England and Wales; but section 20 of that Act (removal of proceedings from county court to High Court) does not apply.

(4) The provisions of Part V of the 1947 Act apply to proceedings against the Crown under this Act as they apply to proceedings in Scotland which by virtue of that Part are treated as civil proceedings by or against the Crown; but the proviso to section 44 of that Act (removal of proceedings from the sheriff court to the Court of Session) does not apply.

(5) Part II does not apply to service—

(a)   as a member of the Ministry of Defence Police, the British Transport Police, the Royal Parks Constabulary or the United Kingdom Atomic Energy Authority Constabulary;
(b)   as a prison officer; or
(c)   for purposes of a Minister of the Crown or government department having functions with respect to defence as a person who is or may be required by his terms of service to engage in fire fighting.

(6) Part II does not apply to service as a member of a fire brigade who is or may be required by his terms of service to engage in fire fighting.

(7) It is hereby declared (for the avoidance of doubt) that Part II does not apply to service in any of the naval, military or air forces of the Crown.

(8) In this section—

'the 1947 Act' means the Crown Proceedings Act 1947;
'British Transport Police' means the constables appointed, or deemed to have been appointed, under section 53 of the British Transport Commission Act 1949;
'Crown proceedings' means proceedings which, by virtue of section 23 of the 1947 Act, are treated for the purposes of Part II of that Act as civil proceedings by or against the Crown;
'fire brigade' means a fire brigade maintained in pursuance of the Fire Services Act 1947;
'Ministry of Defence Police' means the force established under section 1 of the Ministry of Defence Police Act 1987;
'prison officer' means a person who is a prison officer within the meaning of section 127 of the Criminal Justice and Public Order Act 1994, apart from those who are custody officers within the meaning of Part I of that Act;
'Royal Parks Constabulary' means the park constables appointed under the Parks Regulation Act 1872;
'service for purposes of a Minister of the Crown or government department' does not include service in any office for the time being mentioned in Schedule 2 (Ministerial offices) to the House of Commons Disqualification Act 1975;
'statutory body' means a body set up by or under an enactment;
'statutory office' means an office so set up; and
'United Kingdom Atomic Energy Authority Constabulary' means the special constables appointed under section 3 of the Special Constables Act 1923 on the nomination of the United Kingdom Atomic Energy Authority.

65   Application to Parliament

(1) This Act applies to an act done by or for purposes of the House of Lords or the House of Commons as it applies to an act done by a private person.

(2) For the purposes of the application of Part II in relation to the House of Commons, the Corporate Officer of that House shall be treated as the employer of a person who is (or would be) a relevant member of the House of Commons staff for the purposes of section 195 of the Employment Rights Act 1996.

(3) Except as provided in subsection (4), for the purposes of the application of sections 19 to 21, the provider of services is—

(a)   as respects the House of Lords, the Corporate Officer of that House; and
(b)   as respects the House of Commons, the Corporate Officer of that House.

(4) Where the service in question is access to and use of any place in the Palace of Westminster which members of the public are permitted to enter, the Corporate Officers of both Houses jointly are the provider of that service.

(5) Nothing in any rule of law or the law or practice of Parliament prevents proceedings being instituted before an employment tribunal under Part II or before any court under Part III.

Amendments – Amended by Employment Rights Act 1996, s 240, Sch 1, para 69(1), (3); Employment Rights (Dispute Resolution) Act 1998, s 1(2)(a).

66   Government appointments outside Part II

(1) Subject to regulations under subsection (3), this section applies to any appointment made by a Minister of the Crown or government department to an office or post where Part II does not apply in relation to the appointment.

(2) In making the appointment, and in making arrangements for determining to whom the office or post should be offered, the Minister of the Crown or government department shall not act in a way which would contravene Part II if he or the department were the employer for the purposes of this Act.

(3) Regulations may provide for this section not to apply to such appointments as may be prescribed.

67   Regulations and orders

(1) Any power under this Act to make regulations or orders shall be exercisable by statutory instrument.

(2) Any such power may be exercised to make different provision for different cases, including different provision for different areas or localities.

(3) Any such power includes power—

   (a)   to make such incidental, supplemental, consequential or transitional provision as appears to the Secretary of State to be expedient; and
   (b)   to provide for a person to exercise a discretion in dealing with any matter.

(4) No order shall be made under section 50(3) unless a draft of the statutory instrument containing the order has been laid before Parliament and approved by a resolution of each House.

(5) Any other statutory instrument made under this Act, other than one made under section 3(9), 52(8), 54(6) or 70(3), shall be subject to annulment in pursuance of a resolution of either House of Parliament.

(6) Subsection (1) does not require an order under section 43 which applies only to a specified vehicle, or to vehicles of a specified person, to be made by statutory instrument but such an order shall be as capable of being amended or revoked as an order which is made by statutory instrument.

(7) Nothing in section 34(4), 40(6) or 46(5) affects the powers conferred by subsections (2) and (3).

Amendment – Prospectively amended by Disability Rights Commission Act 1999, s 14(1), Sch 4, para 3(1), (2) as from a day to be appointed.

68   Interpretation

(1) In this Act—

   'accessibility certificate' means a certificate issued under section 41(1)(a);

'act' includes a deliberate omission;

'approval certificate' means a certificate issued under section 42(4);

'benefits', in Part II, has the meaning given in section 4(4);

'conciliation officer' means a person designated under section 211 of the Trade Union and Labour Relations (Consolidation) Act 1992;

'employment' means, subject to any prescribed provision, employment under a contract of service or of apprenticeship or a contract personally to do any work, and related expressions are to be construed accordingly;

'employment at an establishment in Great Britain' is to be construed in accordance with subsections (2) to (5);

'enactment' includes subordinate legislation and any Order in Council;

'licensing authority' means—

(a)   in relation to the area to which the Metropolitan Public Carriage Act 1869 applies, the Secretary of State or the holder of any office for the time being designated by the Secretary of State; or

(b)   in relation to any other area in England and Wales, the authority responsible for licensing taxis in that area;

'mental impairment' does not have the same meaning as in the Mental Health Act 1983 or the Mental Health (Scotland) Act 1984 but the fact that an impairment would be a mental impairment for the purposes of either of those Acts does not prevent it from being a mental impairment for the purposes of this Act;

'Minister of the Crown' includes the Treasury;

'occupational pension scheme' has the same meaning as in the Pension Schemes Act 1993;

'premises' includes land of any description;

'prescribed' means prescribed by regulations;

'profession' includes any vocation or occupation;

'provider of services' has the meaning given in section 19(2)(b);

'public service vehicle' and 'regulated public service vehicle' have the meaning given in section 40;

'PSV accessibility regulations' means regulations made under section 40(1);

'rail vehicle' and 'regulated rail vehicle' have the meaning given in section 46;

'rail vehicle accessibility regulations' means regulations made under section 46(1);

'regulations' means regulations made by the Secretary of State;

'section 6 duty' means any duty imposed by or under section 6;

'section 15 duty' means any duty imposed by or under section 15;

'section 21 duty' means any duty imposed by or under section 21;

'subordinate legislation' has the same meaning as in section 21 of the Interpretation Act 1978;

'taxi' and 'regulated taxi' have the meaning given in section 32;

'taxi accessibility regulations' means regulations made under section 32(1);

'trade' includes any business;

'trade organisation' has the meaning given in section 13;

'vehicle examiner' means an examiner appointed under section 66A of the Road Traffic Act 1988.

(2) Where an employee does his work wholly outside Great Britain, his employment is not to be treated as being work at an establishment in Great Britain.

(3) Except in prescribed cases, employment on board a ship, aircraft or hovercraft is to be regarded as not being employment at an establishment in Great Britain.

(4) Employment of a prescribed kind, or in prescribed circumstances, is to be regarded as not being employment at an establishment in Great Britain.

(5) Where work is not done at an establishment it shall be treated as done—

(a)   at the establishment from which it is done; or

(b)   where it is not done from any establishment, at the establishment with which it has the closest connection.

Amendment – Amended by Equal Opportunities (Employment Legislation) (Territorial Limits) Regulations 1999, SI 1999/3163, reg 4.

69   Financial provisions

(1) There shall be paid out of money provided by Parliament—

(a)   any expenditure incurred by a Minister of the Crown under this Act;

(b)   any increase attributable to this Act in the sums payable out of money so provided under or by virtue of any other enactment.

70   Short title, commencement, extent etc.

(1) This Act may be cited as the Disability Discrimination Act 1995.

(2) This section (apart from subsections (4), (5) and (7)) comes into force on the passing of this Act.

(3) The other provisions of this Act come into force on such day as the Secretary of State may by order appoint and different days may be appointed for different purposes.

(4) Schedule 6 makes consequential amendments.

(5) The repeals set out in Schedule 7 shall have effect.

(6) This Act extends to Northern Ireland, but in their application to Northern Ireland the provisions of this Act mentioned in Schedule 8 shall have effect subject to the modifications set out in that Schedule.

(7) In Part II of Schedule 1 to the House of Commons Disqualification Act 1975 and in Part II of Schedule 1 to the Northern Ireland Assembly Disqualification Act 1975 (bodies whose members are disqualified) in each case insert at the appropriate places—

'The National Disability Council.'
'The Northern Ireland Disability Council.'

(8) Consultations which are required by any provision of this Act to be held by the Secretary of State may be held by him before the coming into force of that provision.

Amendment – Prospectively amended by Disability Rights Commission Act 1999, s 14(2), Sch 5 as from a day to be appointed.

SCHEDULES

SCHEDULE 1

PROVISIONS SUPPLEMENTING SECTION 1

Section 1(1)

Impairment

1   (1) 'Mental impairment' includes an impairment resulting from or consisting of a mental illness only if the illness is a clinically well-recognised illness.

(2) Regulations may make provision, for the purposes of this Act—

(a)   for conditions of a prescribed description to be treated as amounting to impairments;

(b)   for conditions of a prescribed description to be treated as not amounting to impairments.

(3) Regulations made under sub-paragraph (2) may make provision as to the meaning of 'condition' for the purposes of those regulations.

Long-term effects

2   (1) The effect of an impairment is a long-term effect if—

(a)   it has lasted at least 12 months;

(b)   the period for which it lasts is likely to be at least 12 months; or

(c)   it is likely to last for the rest of the life of the person affected.

(2) Where an impairment ceases to have a substantial adverse effect on a person's ability to carry out normal day-to-day activities, it is to be treated as continuing to have that effect if that effect is likely to recur.

(3) For the purposes of sub-paragraph (2), the likelihood of an effect recurring shall be disregarded in prescribed circumstances.

(4) Regulations may prescribe circumstances in which, for the purposes of this Act—

(a)   an effect which would not otherwise be a long-term effect is to be treated as such an effect; or

(b)   an effect which would otherwise be a long-term effect is to be treated as not being such an effect.

Severe disfigurement

3   (1) An impairment which consists of a severe disfigurement is to be treated as having a substantial adverse effect on the ability of the person concerned to carry out normal day-to-day activities.

(2) Regulations may provide that in prescribed circumstances a severe disfigurement is not to be treated as having that effect.

(3) Regulations under sub-paragraph (2) may, in particular, make provision with respect to deliberately acquired disfigurements.

Normal day-to-day activities

4   (1) An impairment is to be taken to affect the ability of the person concerned to carry out normal day-to-day activities only if it affects one of the following—

(a)   mobility;
(b)   manual dexterity;
(c)   physical co-ordination;
(d)   continence;
(e)   ability to lift, carry or otherwise move everyday objects;
(f)   speech, hearing or eyesight;
(g)   memory or ability to concentrate, learn or understand; or
(h)   perception of the risk of physical danger.

(2) Regulations may prescribe—

(a)   circumstances in which an impairment which does not have an effect falling within sub-paragraph (1) is to be taken to affect the ability of the person concerned to carry out normal day-to-day activities;
(b)   circumstances in which an impairment which has an effect falling within sub-paragraph (1) is to be taken not to affect the ability of the person concerned to carry out normal day-to-day activities.

Substantial adverse effects

5   Regulations may make provision for the purposes of this Act—

(a)   for an effect of a prescribed kind on the ability of a person to carry out normal day-to-day activities to be treated as a substantial adverse effect;
(b)   for an effect of a prescribed kind on the ability of a person to carry out normal day-to-day activities to be treated as not being a substantial adverse effect.

Effect of medical treatment

6   (1) An impairment which would be likely to have a substantial adverse effect on the ability of the person concerned to carry out normal day-to-day activities, but for the fact that measures are being taken to treat or correct it, is to be treated as having that effect.

(2) In sub-paragraph (1) 'measures' includes, in particular, medical treatment and the use of a prosthesis or other aid.

(3) Sub-paragraph (1) does not apply—

(a)   in relation to the impairment of a person's sight, to the extent that the impairment is, in his case, correctable by spectacles or contact lenses or in such other ways as may be prescribed; or
(b)   in relation to such other impairments as may be prescribed, in such circumstances as may be prescribed.

Persons deemed to be disabled

7   (1) Sub-paragraph (2) applies to any person whose name is, both on 12th January 1995 and on the date when this paragraph comes into force, in the register of disabled persons maintained under section 6 of the Disabled Persons (Employment) Act 1944.

(2) That person is to be deemed—

(a) during the initial period, to have a disability, and hence to be a disabled person; and

(b) afterwards, to have had a disability and hence to have been a disabled person during that period.

(3) A certificate of registration shall be conclusive evidence, in relation to the person with respect to whom it was issued, of the matters certified.

(4) Unless the contrary is shown, any document purporting to be a certificate of registration shall be taken to be such a certificate and to have been validly issued.

(5) Regulations may provide for prescribed descriptions of person to be deemed to have disabilities, and hence to be disabled persons, for the purposes of this Act.

(6) Regulations may prescribe circumstances in which a person who has been deemed to be a disabled person by the provisions of sub-paragraph (1) or regulations made under sub-paragraph (5) is to be treated as no longer being deemed to be such a person.

(7) In this paragraph—

'certificate of registration' means a certificate issued under regulations made under section 6 of the Act of 1944; and

'initial period' means the period of three years beginning with the date on which this paragraph comes into force.

Progressive conditions

8 (1) Where—

(a) a person has a progressive condition (such as cancer, multiple sclerosis or muscular dystrophy or infection by the human immunodeficiency virus),

(b) as a result of that condition, he has an impairment which has (or had) an effect on his ability to carry out normal day-to-day activities, but

(c) that effect is not (or was not) a substantial adverse effect,

he shall be taken to have an impairment which has such a substantial adverse effect if the condition is likely to result in his having such an impairment.

(2) Regulations may make provision, for the purposes of this paragraph—

(a) for conditions of a prescribed description to be treated as being progressive;

(b) for conditions of a prescribed description to be treated as not being progressive.

SCHEDULE 2

PAST DISABILITIES

Section 2(2)

1 The modifications referred to in section 2 are as follows.

2 References in Parts II and III to a disabled person are to be read as references to a person who has had a disability.

3 In section 6(1), after 'not disabled' insert 'and who have not had a disability'.

4 In section 6(6), for 'has' substitute 'has had'.

5 For paragraph 2(1) to (3) of Schedule 1, substitute—

'(1) The effect of an impairment is a long-term effect if it has lasted for at least 12 months.

(2) Where an impairment ceases to have a substantial adverse effect on a person's ability to carry out normal day-to-day activities, it is to be treated as continuing to have that effect if that effect recurs.

(3) For the purposes of sub-paragraph (2), the recurrence of an effect shall be disregarded in prescribed circumstances.'

SCHEDULE 3

ENFORCEMENT AND PROCEDURE

Sections 8(8) and 25(6)

PART I

EMPLOYMENT

Conciliation

1   (*repealed*)

Restriction on proceedings for breach of Part II

2   (1) Except as provided by section 8, no civil or criminal proceedings may be brought against any person in respect of an act merely because the act is unlawful under Part II.

(2) Sub-paragraph (1) does not prevent the making of an application for judicial review.

Period within which proceedings must be brought

3   (1) An employment tribunal shall not consider a complaint under section 8 unless it is presented before the end of the period of three months beginning when the act complained of was done.

(2) A tribunal may consider any such complaint which is out of time if, in all the circumstances of the case, it considers that it is just and equitable to do so.

(3) For the purposes of sub-paragraph (1)—

   (a)   where an unlawful act of discrimination is attributable to a term in a contract, that act is to be treated as extending throughout the duration of the contract;
   (b)   any act extending over a period shall be treated as done at the end of that period; and
   (c)   a deliberate omission shall be treated as done when the person in question decided upon it.

(4) In the absence of evidence establishing the contrary, a person shall be taken for the purposes of this paragraph to decide upon an omission—

   (a)   when he does an act inconsistent with doing the omitted act; or
   (b)   if he has done no such inconsistent act, when the period expires within which he might reasonably have been expected to do the omitted act if it was to be done.

Evidence

4 (1) In any proceedings under section 8, a certificate signed by or on behalf of a Minister of the Crown and certifying—

(a) that any conditions or requirements specified in the certificate were imposed by a Minister of the Crown and were in operation at a time or throughout a time so specified, or

(b) that an act specified in the certificate was done for the purpose of safeguarding national security,

shall be conclusive evidence of the matters certified.

(2) A document purporting to be such a certificate shall be received in evidence and, unless the contrary is proved, be deemed to be such a certificate.

PART II

DISCRIMINATION IN OTHER AREAS

Restriction on proceedings for breach of Part III

5 (1) Except as provided by section 25 no civil or criminal proceedings may be brought against any person in respect of an act merely because the act is unlawful under Part III.

(2) Sub-paragraph (1) does not prevent the making of an application for judicial review.

Period within which proceedings must be brought

6 (1) A county court or a sheriff court shall not consider a claim under section 25 unless proceedings in respect of the claim are instituted before the end of the period of six months beginning when the act complained of was done.

(2) Where, in relation to proceedings or prospective proceedings under section 25, a person appointed in connection with arrangements under section 28 is approached before the end of the period of six months mentioned in sub-paragraph (1), the period allowed by that sub-paragraph shall be extended by two months.

(3) A court may consider any claim under section 25 which is out of time if, in all the circumstances of the case, it considers that it is just and equitable to do so.

(4) For the purposes of sub-paragraph (1)—

(a) where an unlawful act of discrimination is attributable to a term in a contract, that act is to be treated as extending throughout the duration of the contract;

(b) any act extending over a period shall be treated as done at the end of that period; and

(c) a deliberate omission shall be treated as done when the person in question decided upon it.

(5) In the absence of evidence establishing the contrary, a person shall be taken for the purposes of this paragraph to decide upon an omission—

(a) when he does an act inconsistent with doing the omitted act; or

(b) if he has done no such inconsistent act, when the period expires within which he might reasonably have been expected to do the omitted act if it was to be done.

Compensation for injury to feelings

7 In any proceedings under section 25, the amount of any damages awarded as compensation for injury to feelings shall not exceed the prescribed amount.

Evidence

8 (1) In any proceedings under section 25, a certificate signed by or on behalf of a Minister of the Crown and certifying—

(a) that any conditions or requirements specified in the certificate were imposed by a Minister of the Crown and were in operation at a time or throughout a time so specified, or

(b) that an act specified in the certificate was done for the purpose of safeguarding national security,

shall be conclusive evidence of the matters certified.

(2) A document purporting to be such a certificate shall be received in evidence and, unless the contrary is proved, be deemed to be such a certificate.

Amendments – Amended by Employment Tribunals Act 1996, s 45, Sch 3, Pt I; Industrial Tribunals (Northern Ireland) Order 1996, SI 1996/1921 (NI 18), art 28(1), Sch 3; Employment Rights (Dispute Resolution) Act 1998, s 1(2)(a); prospectively amended by Disability Rights Commission Act 1999, s 14(1), Sch 4, para 3(1), (3) and Employment Relations Act 1999, ss 41, 44, Sch 8, para 7, Sch 9, Pt 12 as from a day to be appointed.

SCHEDULE 4

PREMISES OCCUPIED UNDER LEASES

Sections 16(5) and 27(5)

PART I

OCCUPATION BY EMPLOYER OR TRADE ORGANISATION

Failure to obtain consent to alteration

1 If any question arises as to whether the occupier has failed to comply with the section 6 or section 15 duty, by failing to make a particular alteration to the premises, any constraint attributable to the fact that he occupies the premises under a lease is to be ignored unless he has applied to the lessor in writing for consent to the making of the alteration.

Joining lessors in proceedings under section 8

2 (1) In any proceedings under section 8, in a case to which section 16 applies, the complainant or the occupier may ask the tribunal hearing the complaint to direct that the lessor be joined or sisted as a party to the proceedings.

(2) The request shall be granted if it is made before the hearing of the complaint begins.

(3) The tribunal may refuse the request if it is made after the hearing of the complaint begins.

(4) The request may not be granted if it is made after the tribunal has determined the complaint.

(5) Where a lessor has been so joined or sisted as a party to the proceedings, the tribunal may determine—

  (a)   whether the lessor has—
           (i) refused consent to the alteration, or
           (ii) consented subject to one or more conditions, and
  (b)   if so, whether the refusal or any of the conditions was unreasonable.

(6) If, under sub-paragraph (5), the tribunal determines that the refusal or any of the conditions was unreasonable it may take one or more of the following steps—

  (a)   make such declaration as it considers appropriate;
  (b)   make an order authorising the occupier to make the alteration specified in the order;
  (c)   order the lessor to pay compensation to the complainant.

(7) An order under sub-paragraph (6)(b) may require the occupier to comply with conditions specified in the order.

(8) Any step taken by the tribunal under sub-paragraph (6) may be in substitution for, or in addition to, any step taken by the tribunal under section 8(2).

(9) If the tribunal orders the lessor to pay compensation it may not make an order under section 8(2) ordering the occupier to do so.

Regulations

3   Regulations may make provision as to circumstances in which—

  (a)   a lessor is to be taken, for the purposes of section 16 of this Part of this Schedule to have—
           (i)   withheld his consent;
           (ii) withheld his consent unreasonably;
           (iii) acted reasonably in withholding his consent;
  (b)   a condition subject to which a lessor has given his consent is to be taken to be reasonable;
  (c)   a condition subject to which a lessor has given his consent is to be taken to be unreasonable.

Sub-leases etc.

4   The Secretary of State may by regulations make provision supplementing, or modifying, the provision made by section 16 or any provision made by or under this Part of this Schedule in relation to cases where the occupier occupies premises under a sub-lease or sub-tenancy.

PART II

OCCUPATION BY PROVIDER OF SERVICES

Failure to obtain consent to alteration

5   If any question arises as to whether the occupier has failed to comply with the section 21 duty, by failing to make a particular alteration to premises, any constraint attributable to the fact that he occupies the premises under a lease is to be ignored unless he has applied to the lessor in writing for consent to the making of the alteration.

Reference to court

6 (1) If the occupier has applied in writing to the lessor for consent to the alteration and—

(a) that consent has been refused, or
(b) the lessor has made his consent subject to one or more conditions,

the occupier or a disabled person who has an interest in the proposed alteration to the premises being made, may refer the matter to a county court or, in Scotland, to the sheriff.

(2) In the following provisions of this Schedule 'court' includes 'sheriff'.

(3) On such a reference the court shall determine whether the lessor's refusal was unreasonable or (as the case may be) whether the condition is, or any of the conditions are, unreasonable.

(4) If the court determines—

(a) that the lessor's refusal was unreasonable, or
(b) that the condition is, or any of the conditions are, unreasonable,

it may make such declaration as it considers appropriate or an order authorising the occupier to make the alteration specified in the order.

(5) An order under sub-paragraph (4) may require the occupier to comply with conditions specified in the order.

Joining lessors in proceedings under section 25

7 (1) In any proceedings on a claim under section 25, in a case to which this Part of this Schedule applies, the plaintiff, the pursuer or the occupier concerned may ask the court to direct that the lessor be joined or sisted as a party to the proceedings.

(2) The request shall be granted if it is made before the hearing of the claim begins.

(3) The court may refuse the request if it is made after the hearing of the claim begins.

(4) The request may not be granted if it is made after the court has determined the claim.

(5) Where a lessor has been so joined or sisted as a party to the proceedings, the court may determine—

(a) whether the lessor has—
(i) refused consent to the alteration, or
(ii) consented subject to one or more conditions, and
(b) if so, whether the refusal or any of the conditions was unreasonable.

(6) If, under sub-paragraph (5), the court determines that the refusal or any of the conditions was unreasonable it may take one or more of the following steps—

(a) make such declaration as it considers appropriate;
(b) make an order authorising the occupier to make the alteration specified in the order;

(c)   order the lessor to pay compensation to the complainant.

(7) An order under sub-paragraph (6)(b) may require the occupier to comply with conditions specified in the order.

(8) If the court orders the lessor to pay compensation it may not order the occupier to do so.

Regulations

8   Regulations may make provision as to circumstances in which—

(a)   a lessor is to be taken, for the purposes of section 27 and this Part of this Schedule to have—
(i)   withheld his consent;
(ii) withheld his consent unreasonably;
(iii) acted unreasonably in withholding his consent;
(b)   a condition subject to which a lessor has given his consent is to be taken to be reasonable;
(c)   a condition subject to which a lessor has given his consent is to be taken to be unreasonable.

Sub-leases etc.

9   The Secretary of State may by regulations make provision supplementing, or modifying, the provision made by section 27 or any provision made by or under this Part of this Schedule in relation to cases where the occupier occupies premises under a sub-lease or sub-tenancy.

SCHEDULE 5

THE NATIONAL DISABILITY COUNCIL

Section 50(8)

Status

1   (1) The Council shall be a body corporate.

(2) The Council is not the servant or agent of the Crown and does not enjoy any status, immunity or privilege of the Crown.

Procedure

2   The Council has power to regulate its own procedure (including power to determine its quorum).

Membership

3   (1) The Council shall consist of at least 10, but not more than 20, members.

(2) In this Schedule 'member', except in sub-paragraph (5)(b), means a member of the Council.

(3) Each member shall be appointed by the Secretary of State.

(3A) One of the members shall be a person who appears to the Secretary of State to have special knowledge of Scotland.

(4) The Secretary of State shall appoint one member to be chairman of the Council and another member to be its deputy chairman.

(5) The members shall be appointed from among persons who, in the opinion of the Secretary of State—

   (a)   have knowledge or experience of the needs of disabled persons or the needs of a particular group, or particular groups, of disabled persons;
   (b)   have knowledge or experience of the needs of persons who have had a disability or the needs of a particular group, or particular groups, of such persons; or
   (c)   are members of, or otherwise represent, professional bodies or bodies which represent industry or other business interests.

(6) Before appointing any member, the Secretary of State shall consult such persons as he considers appropriate.

(7) In exercising his powers of appointment, the Secretary of State shall try to secure that at all times at least half the membership of the Council consists of disabled persons, persons who have had a disability or the parents or guardians of disabled persons.

Term of office of members

4   (1) Each member shall be appointed for a term which does not exceed five years but shall otherwise hold and vacate his office in accordance with the terms of his appointment.

(2) A person shall not be prevented from being appointed as a member merely because he has previously been a member.

(3) Any member may at any time resign his office by written notice given to the Secretary of State.

(4) Regulations may make provision for the Secretary of State to remove a member from his office in such circumstances as may be prescribed.

Remuneration

5   (1) The Secretary of State may pay such remuneration or expenses to any member as he considers appropriate.

(2) The approval of the Treasury is required for any payment made under this paragraph.

Staff

6   The Secretary of State shall provide the Council with such staff as he considers appropriate.

Supplementary regulation-making power

7   The Secretary of State may by regulations make provision—

   (a)   as to the provision of information to the Council by the Secretary of State;

(b)   as to the commissioning by the Secretary of State of research to be undertaken on behalf of the Council;

(c)   as to the circumstances in which and conditions subject to which the Council may appoint any person as an adviser;

(d)   as to the payment by the Secretary of State, with the approval of the Treasury, of expenses incurred by the Council.

Annual report

8   (1) As soon as is practicable after the end of each financial year, the Council shall report to the Secretary of State on its activities during the financial year to which the report relates.

(2) The Secretary of State shall lay a copy of every annual report of the Council before each House of Parliament and shall arrange for such further publication of the report as he considers appropriate.

Amendments – Amended by Scotland Act 1998 (Modification of Functions) Order 1999, SI 1999/1756, arts 2, 8, Sch, para 18; prospectively repealed by Disability Rights Commission Act 1999, s 14(2), Sch 5 as from a day to be appointed.

SCHEDULE 6

CONSEQUENTIAL AMENDMENTS

Section 70(4)
1–3   (*repealed*)

Companies Act 1985 (c. 6)

4   In paragraph 9 of Schedule 7 to the Companies Act 1985 (disclosure in directors' report of company policy in relation to disabled persons), in the definition of 'disabled person' in sub-paragraph (4)(b), for 'Disabled Persons (Employment) Act 1944' substitute 'Disability Discrimination Act 1995'.

Local Government and Housing Act 1989 (c. 42)

5   In section 7 of the Local Government and Housing Act 1989 (all staff of a local authority etc. to be appointed on merit), in subsection (2)—

(a)   paragraph (a) shall be omitted;

(b)   the word 'and' at the end of paragraph (d) shall be omitted; and

(c)   after paragraph (e) insert—
   '; and
      (f)   sections 5 and 6 of the Disability Discrimination Act 1995 (meaning of discrimination and duty to make adjustments).'

Enterprise and New Towns (Scotland) Act 1990 (c. 35)

6   In section 16 of the Enterprise and New Towns (Scotland) Act 1990 (duty of certain Scottish bodies to give preference to ex-service men and women in exercising powers to select disabled persons for training), in subsection (2), for 'said Act of 1944' substitute 'Disability Discrimination Act 1995'.

Amendments – Amended by Employment Rights Act 1996, s 242, Sch 3, Pt I; Employment Tribunals Act 1996, s 45, Sch 3, Pt I; Employment Rights (Northern Ireland) Order 1996, SI 1996/1919 (NI 16), art 257, Sch 3.

SCHEDULE 7

REPEALS

Section 70(5)

Chapter	Short title	Extent of repeal
7 & 8 Geo. 6 c. 10.	The Disabled Persons (Employment) Act 1944.	Section 1. Sections 6 to 14. Section 19. Section 21. Section 22(4).
6 & 7 Eliz. 2 c. 33.	The Disabled Persons (Employment) Act 1958.	Section 2.
1970 c. 44.	The Chronically Sick and Disabled Persons Act 1970.	Section 16.
1978 c. 44.	The Employment Protection (Consolidation) Act 1978.	In Schedule 13, in paragraph 20(3), the word "or" in the definitions of "relevant complaint of dismissal" and "relevant conciliation powers".
1989 c. 42.	The Local Government and Housing Act 1989.	In section 7(2), paragraph (a) and the word "and" at the end of paragraph (d).
1993 c. 62.	The Education Act 1993.	In section 161(5), the words from "and in this subsection" to the end.

SCHEDULE 8

MODIFICATIONS OF THIS ACT IN ITS APPLICATION TO NORTHERN IRELAND

Section 70(6)

1 In its application to Northern Ireland this Act shall have effect subject to the following modifications.

2 (1) In section 3(1) for 'Secretary of State' substitute 'Department'.

(2) In section 3 for subsections (4) to (12) substitute—

'(4) In preparing a draft of any guidance, the Department shall consult such persons as it considers appropriate.

(5) Where the Department proposes to issue any guidance, the Department shall publish a draft of it, consider any representations that are made to the Department about the draft and, if the Department thinks it appropriate, modify its proposals in the light of any of those representations.

(6) If the Department decides to proceed with any proposed guidance, the Department shall lay a draft of it before the Assembly.

(7) If, within the statutory period, the Assembly resolves not to approve the draft, the Department shall take no further steps in relation to the proposed guidance.

(8) If no such resolution is made within the statutory period, the Department shall issue the guidance in the form of its draft.

(9) The guidance shall come into force on such date as the Department may by order appoint.

(10) Subsection (7) does not prevent a new draft of the proposed guidance being laid before the Assembly.

(11) The Department may—
  (a) from time to time revise the whole or any part of any guidance and re-issue it;
  (b) by order revoke any guidance.

(12) In this section—
   "the Department" means the Office of the First Minister and Deputy First Minister;
   "guidance" means guidance issued by the Department under this section and includes guidance which has been revised and re-issued;
   "statutory period" has the meaning assigned to it by section 41(2) of the Interpretation Act (Northern Ireland) 1954.'

3 In section 4(6) for 'Great Britain' substitute 'Northern Ireland'.

4 (1) In section 7(2) for 'Secretary of State' substitute 'Office of the First Minister and Deputy First Minister'.

(2) In section 7(4) to (10) for 'Secretary of State' wherever it occurs substitute 'Office of the First Minister and Deputy First Minister', for 'he' and 'him' wherever they occur substitute 'it' and for 'his' wherever it occurs substitute 'its'.

(3) In section 7(9) for 'Parliament' substitute 'the Assembly'.

5 (1) In section 8(3) omit 'or (in Scotland) in reparation'.

(2) In section 8(7) for 'paragraph 6A of Schedule 9 to the Employment Protection (Consolidation) Act 1978' substitute 'Article 16 of the Industrial Tribunals (Northern Ireland) Order 1996'.

6 (1) In section 9(2)(a) for 'a conciliation officer' substitute 'the Agency'.

(2) (*repealed*)

7 (1) In section 10(1)(b) omit 'or recognised body'.

(2) In section 10(2)(b) for 'Secretary of State' substitute 'Department of Higher and Further Education, Training and Employment'.

(3) In section 10(3) in the definition of 'charity' for '1993' substitute '(Northern Ireland) 1964', omit the definition of 'recognised body' and in the definition of 'supported employment' for 'Act 1944' substitute 'Act (Northern Ireland) 1945'.

(4) In section 10(4) for 'England and Wales' where it twice occurs substitute 'Northern Ireland'.

(5) Omit section 10(5).

8 In section 12(5) for 'Great Britain' where it twice occurs substitute 'Northern Ireland'.

9 (1) In section 19(3)(g) for 'section 2 of the Employment and Training Act 1973' substitute 'sections 1 and 2 of the Employment and Training Act (Northern Ireland) 1950'.

(2) In section 19(5) for paragraph (a) substitute—

'(a) education which is funded, or secured, by a relevant body or provided at—
    (i) an establishment which is funded by such a body or by the Department of Education for Northern Ireland; or
    (ii) any other establishment which is a school within the meaning of the Education and Libraries (Northern Ireland) Order 1986;'.

(3) For section 19(6) substitute—

'(6) In subsection (5) "relevant body" means—
    (a) an education and library board;
    (b) a voluntary organisation; or
    (c) a body of a prescribed kind.'.

10 In section 20(7) for paragraphs (b) and (c) substitute '; or

    (b) functions conferred by or under Part VIII of the Mental Health (Northern Ireland) Order 1986 are exercisable in relation to a disabled person's property or affairs.'.

11 In section 22(4) and (6) omit 'or (in Scotland) the subject of'.

12 (1) In section 25(1) omit 'or (in Scotland) in reparation'.

(2) In section 25(3) for 'England and Wales' substitute 'Northern Ireland'.

(3) Omit section 25(4).

(4) In section 25(5) omit the words from 'or' to the end.

13 In section 26(3) omit 'or a sheriff court'.

14 (1) In section 28 for 'Secretary of State' wherever it occurs substitute 'Office of the First Minister and Deputy First Minister'.

(2) In section 28(3) and (4) for 'he' substitute 'it'.

(3) In section 28(5) for 'Treasury' substitute 'Department of Finance and Personnel in Northern Ireland'.

15 Omit sections 29, 30 and 31.

16 (1) In section 32(1) for 'Secretary of State' substitute 'Department of the Environment'.

(2) In section 32(5) for the definition of 'taxi' substitute—

' "taxi" means a vehicle which—
  (a) is licensed under Article 61 of the Road Traffic (Northern Ireland) Order 1981 to stand or ply for hire; and
  (b) seats not more than 8 passengers in addition to the driver'.

17 In section 33, for 'Secretary of State', wherever it occurs, substitute 'Department of the Environment'.

18 For section 34 substitute—

'34 New licences conditional on compliance with accessibility taxi regulations

(1) The Department of the Environment shall not grant a public service vehicle licence under Article 61 of the Road Traffic (Northern Ireland) Order 1981 for a taxi unless the vehicle conforms with those provisions of the taxi accessibility regulations with which it will be required to confirm if licensed.

(2) Subsection (1) does not apply if such a licence was in force with respect to the vehicle at any time during the period of 28 days immediately before the day on which the licence is granted.

(3) The Department of the Environment may by order provide for subsection (2) to cease to have effect on such date as may be specified in the order.'.

19 Omit section 35.

20 In section 36(7) for 'licensing authority' substitute 'Department of the Environment'.

21 (1) In section 37(5) and (6) for 'licensing authority' substitute 'Department of the Environment'.

(2) In section 37(9) for 'Secretary of State' substitute 'Department of the Environment'.

22 (1) In section 38(1) for 'a licensing authority' substitute 'the Department of the Environment'.

(2) In section 38(2) for 'licensing authority concerned' substitute 'Department of the Environment'.

(3) In section 38(3) for the words from 'the magistrates' court' to the end substitute 'a court of summary jurisdiction acting for the petty sessions district in which the aggrieved person resides'.

23 Omit section 39.

24 (1) In section 40 for 'Secretary of State' wherever it occurs substitute 'Department of the Environment'.

(2) In section 40(5) for the definition of 'public service vehicle' substitute—

' "public service vehicle" means a vehicle which—
  (a) seats more than 8 passengers in addition to the driver; and
  (b) is a public service vehicle for the purposes of the Road Traffic (Northern Ireland) Order 1981;'.

(3) In section 40(7) for the words for 'the Disabled' to the end substitute 'such representative organisations as it thinks fit'.

25 (1) In section 41(2) for 'Secretary of State' substitute 'Department of the Environment'.

(2) In section 41 for subsections (3) and (4) substitute—

'(3) Any person who uses a regulated public service vehicle in contravention of this section is guilty of an offence and liable on summary conviction to a fine not exceeding level 4 on the standard scale.'.

26 (1) In section 42 for 'Secretary of State' wherever it occurs substitute 'Department of the Environment'.

(2) In section 42(1) for 'he' substitute 'it'.

(3) In section 42(6) for 'his' substitute 'its'.

27 In section 43 for 'Secretary of State' wherever it occurs substitute 'Department of the Environment'.

28 (1) In section 44 for 'Secretary of State' wherever it occurs substitute 'Department of the Environment'.

(2) In section 44(2) for 'him' substitute 'it'.

(3) In section 44(6) for 'he' substitute 'it' and for 'his' substitute 'its'.

29 (1) In section 45 for 'Secretary of State' wherever it occurs substitute 'Department of the Environment'.

(2) In section 45(2) for 'him' substitute 'it' and at the end add 'of Northern Ireland'.

(3) In section 45(4) for 'he' substitute 'it'.

30 (1) In section 46 for 'Secretary of State' wherever it occurs substitute 'Department for Regional Development'.

(2) In section 46(6) in the definition of 'rail vehicle' for the words 'on any railway, tramway or prescribed system' substitute 'by rail'.

(3) Omit section 46(7).

(4) In section 46(11) for the words from 'the Disabled' to the end substitute 'such representative organisations as it thinks fit'.

31 (1) In section 47 for 'Secretary of State' wherever it occurs substitute 'Department for Regional Development'.

(2) In section 47(3) for the words 'the Disabled Persons Transport Advisory Committee and such other persons as he' substitute 'such persons as it' and for 'he' substitute 'it'.

32 Omit section 48(3).

33 (1) In sections 50 to 52 for 'the Council' substitute, in each place, the 'Equality Commission for Northern Ireland'.

(1A) Section 50(1) shall have no effect.

(2) In section 50(2) for 'Secretary of State' in the first place where it occurs substitute 'a Northern Ireland department' and in the other place where it occurs substitute 'that department'.

(3) In section 50(3) for 'Secretary of State' substitute 'Office of the First Minister and Deputy First Minister'.

(4) In section 50(7) for 'Secretary of State' substitute 'a Northern Ireland department' and after 'Crown' insert 'or a Northern Ireland department'.

(5) In section 50(9)(a) for sub-paragraphs (i) to (iv) substitute—

    '(i)   the Disabled Persons (Employment) Act (Northern Ireland) 1945;
    (ii) the Contracts of Employment and Redundancy Payments Act (Northern Ireland) 1965;
    (iii) the Employment and Training Act (Northern Ireland) 1950;
    (iv) the Employment Rights (Northern Ireland) Order 1996; or'.

(6) In section 50(10) for the words from 'time when' to the end substitute 'time when—

    (a)   there are no committees in existence under section 17 of the Disabled Persons (Employment) Act (Northern Ireland) 1945; and
    (b)   there is no person appointed to act generally under section 60(1) of this Act.'.

34   (1) In section 51(1) for 'the Secretary of State' substitute 'any Northern Ireland department' and for 'the Secretary of State's' substitute 'that department's'.

(2) In section 51(2) for 'The Secretary of State' substitute 'A Northern Ireland department'.

(3) In section 51(4) for 'a county court or a sheriff court' substitute 'or a county court'.

(4) In section 51(6) for 'the Secretary of State' substitute 'a Northern Ireland department'.

35   For section 52 substitute—

'52   Further provisions about codes issued under section 51

(1) In this section—
    "proposal" means a proposal made by the Equality Commission for Northern Ireland to a Northern Ireland department under section 51;
    "responsible department"—
        (a)   in relation to a proposal, means the Northern Ireland department to which the proposal is made,
        (b)   in relation to a code, means the Northern Ireland department by which the code is issued; and
    "statutory period" has the meaning assigned to it by section 41(2) of the Interpretation Act (Northern Ireland) 1954.

(2) In preparing any proposal, the Equality Commission for Northern Ireland shall consult—
    (a)   such persons (if any) as the responsible department has specified in making its request to the Equality Commission for Northern Ireland; and
    (b)   such other persons (if any) as the Equality Commission for Northern Ireland considers appropriate.

(3) Before making any proposal the Equality Commission for Northern Ireland shall publish a draft, consider any representations made to it about the draft and, if it thinks it appropriate, modify its proposal in the light of any of those representations.

(4) Where the Equality Commission for Northern Ireland makes any proposal, the responsible department may—

(a) approve it;

(b) approve it subject to such modifications as that department thinks appropriate; or

(c) refuse to approve it.

(5) Where the responsible department approves any proposal (with or without modifications) that department shall prepare a draft of the proposed code and lay it before the Assembly.

(6) If, within the statutory period, the Assembly resolves not to approve the draft, the responsible department shall take no further steps in relation to the proposed code.

(7) If no such resolution is made within the statutory period, the responsible department shall issue the code in the form of its draft.

(8) The code shall come into force on such date as the responsible department may appoint by order.

(9) Subsection (6) does not prevent a new draft of the proposed code from being laid before the Assembly.

(10) If the responsible department refuses to approve a proposal, that department shall give the Council a written statement of the department's reasons for not approving it.

(11) The responsible department may by order revoke a code.'.

36 (1) In section 53 for 'Secretary of State' wherever it occurs substitute 'Office of the First Minister and Deputy First Minister'.

(2) In section 53(1) for 'he' substitute 'it'.

(3) In section 53(3) for 'a county court or a sheriff court' substitute 'or a county court'.

37 For section 54 substitute—

'54 Further provisions about codes issued under section 53

(1) In preparing a draft of any code under section 53, the Department shall consult such organisations representing the interests of employers or of disabled persons in, or seeking, employment as the Department considers appropriate.

(2) Where the Department proposes to issue a code, the Department shall publish a draft of the code, consider any representations that are made to the Department about the draft and, if the Department thinks it appropriate, modify its proposals in the light of any of those representations.

(3) If the Department decides to proceed with the code, the Department shall lay a draft of it before the Assembly.

(4) If, within the statutory period, the Assembly resolves not to approve the draft, the Department shall take no further steps in relation to the proposed code.

(5) If no such resolution is made within the statutory period, the Department shall issue the code in the form of its draft.

(6) The code shall come into force on such date as the Department may appoint by order.

(7) Subsection (4) does not prevent a new draft of the proposed code from being laid before the Assembly.

(8) The Department may by order revoke a code.

(9) In this section—
"the Department" means the Office of the First Minister and Deputy First Minister; and
"statutory period" has the meaning assigned to it by section 41(2) of the Interpretation Act (Northern Ireland) 1954.'.

38 In section 56(2) and (4) for 'Secretary of State' substitute 'Office of the First Minister and Deputy First Minister'.

39 In section 59(1) after 'Crown' where it twice occurs insert 'or a Northern Ireland department'.

40 (1) In section 60(1) to (3) for 'Secretary of State' wherever it occurs substitute 'Office of the First Minister and Deputy First Minister' and for 'he' and 'him' wherever they occur substitute 'it'.

(2) In section 60(4) for 'Treasury' substitute 'Department of Finance and Personnel in Northern Ireland'.

(3) For section 60(6) substitute—

'(6) The Office of the First Minister and Deputy First Minister may by order repeal section 17 of, and Schedule 2 to, the Disabled Persons (Employment) Act (Northern Ireland) 1945 (district advisory committees).'.

(4) In section 60(7) omit 'paragraph (b) of', for '1944' substitute '1945' and omit 'in each case'.

(5) In section 60, omit subsection (8).

41 For section 61 substitute—

'61   Amendments of Disabled Persons (Employment) Act (Northern Ireland) 1945

(1) Section 15 of the Disabled Persons (Employment) Act (Northern Ireland) 1945 (which gives the Office of the First Minister and Deputy First Minister power to make arrangements for the provision of supported employment) is amended as set out in subsection (2) to (5).

(2) In subsection (1)—
  (a)   for "persons registered as handicapped by disablement" substitute "disabled persons";
  (b)   for "their disablement" substitute "their disability"; and
  (c)   for "are not subject to disablement" substitute "do not have a disability".

(3) In subsection (2) for the words from "any of one or more companies" to "so required and prohibited" substitute "any company, association or body".

(4) After subsection (2) insert—

"(2A) The only kind of company which the Department itself may form in exercising its powers under this section is a company which is—
  (a)   required by its constitution to apply its profits, if any, or other income in promoting its objects; and
  (b)   prohibited by its constitution from paying any dividend to its members.".

(5) After subsection (5) insert—

"(5A) For the purposes of this section—

(a)   a person is a disabled person if he is a disabled person for the purposes of the Disability Discrimination Act 1995; and

(b)   'disability' has the same meaning as in that Act.".

(6) The provisions of section 16 of the Act of 1945 (preference to be given under section 15 of that Act to ex-service men and women) shall become subsection (1) of that section and at the end insert—

"and whose disability is due to that service.

(2) For the purposes of subsection (1) of this section, a disabled person's disability shall be treated as due to service of a particular kind only in such circumstances as may be prescribed."

(7) The following provisions of the Act of 1945 shall cease to have effect—

(a)   section 1 (definition of "disabled person");

(b)   sections 2 to 4 (training for disabled persons);

(c)   sections 6 to 8 (the register of disabled persons);

(d)   sections 9 to 11 (obligations on employers with substantial staffs to employ quota of registered persons);

(e)   section 12 (the designated employment scheme for persons registered as handicapped by disablement);

(f)   section 13 (interpretation of provisions repealed by this Act);

(g)   section 14 (records to be kept by employer);

(h)   section 19 (proceedings in relation to offences);

(j)   sections 21 and 22 (supplementary).

(8) Any statutory provision in which "disabled person" is defined by reference to the Act of 1945 shall be construed as if that expression had the same meaning as in this Act.'.

42   (*repealed*)

43   Omit section 63.

44   (1) In section 64(3) for 'England and Wales' substitute 'Northern Ireland'.

(2) Omit section 64(4).

(3) In section 64(5)(a) omit the words from ', the British' to the end.

(4) In section 64(8)—

(a)   omit the definitions of 'British Transport Police', 'Royal Parks Constabulary' and 'United Kingdom Atomic Energy Authority Constabulary';

(b)   in the definition of 'the 1947 Act' at the end add 'as it applies both in relation to the Crown in right of Her Majesty's Government in Northern Ireland and in relation to the Crown in right of Her Majesty's Government in the United Kingdom';

(c)   in the definition of 'fire brigade' for the words from 'means' to the end substitute 'has the same meaning as in the Fire Services (Northern Ireland) Order 1984';

(d)   in the definition of 'prison officer' for the words from 'means' to the end substitute 'means any individual who holds any post, otherwise than as a medical officer, to which he has been appointed under section 2(2) of the Prison Act (Northern Ireland) 1953 or who is a prison custody officer within the meaning of Chapter III of Part VIII of the Criminal Justice and Public Order Act 1994';

    (e)   in the definition of 'service for purposes of a Minister of the Crown or government department' at the end add 'or service as the head of a Northern Ireland department'.

45   Omit section 65.

46   For section 67 substitute—

'67   Regulations and orders etc.

(1) Any power under this Act to make regulations or orders shall be exercisable by statutory rule for the purposes of the Statutory Rules (Northern Ireland) Order 1979.

(2) Any such power may be exercised to make different provision for different cases, including different provision for different areas or localities.

(3) Any such power, includes power—
    (a)   to make such incidental, supplementary, consequential or transitional provision as appears to the Northern Ireland department exercising the power to be expedient; and
    (b)   to provide for a person to exercise a discretion in dealing with any matter.

(4) No order shall be made under section 50(3) unless a draft of the order has been laid before and approved by a resolution of the Assembly.

(5) Any other order made under this Act, other than an order under section 3(9), 52(8), 54(6) or 70(3), and any regulations made under this Act shall be subject to negative resolution within the meaning of section 41(6) of the Interpretation Act (Northern Ireland) 1954 as if they were statutory instruments within the meaning of that Act.

(6) Section 41(3) of the Interpretation Act (Northern Ireland) 1954 shall apply in relation to any instrument or document which by virtue of this Act is required to be laid before the Assembly as if it were a statutory instrument or statutory document within the meaning of that Act.

(7) Subsection (1) does not require an order under section 43 which applies only to a specified vehicle, or to vehicles of a specified person, to be made by statutory rule.

(8) Nothing in section 40(6) or 46(5) affects the powers conferred by subsections (2) and (3).'

47   (1) For section 68(1) substitute—

'(1) In this Act—
    "accessibility certificate" means a certificate issued under section 41(1)(a);
    "act" includes a deliberate omission;
    "the Agency" means the Labour Relations Agency;
    "approval certificate" means a certificate issued under section 42(4);
    "the Assembly" means the Northern Ireland Assembly;
    "benefits", in Part II, has the meaning given in section 4(4);
    "the Department of Economic Development" means the Office of the First Minister and Deputy First Minister in Northern Ireland;
    "the Department of the Environment" means the Department of the Environment for Northern Ireland;

"the Department of Health and Social Services" means the Office of the First Minister and Deputy First Minister for Northern Ireland;

"employment" means, subject to any prescribed provision, employment under a contract of service or of apprenticeship or a contract personally to do work and related expressions are to be construed accordingly;

"employment at an establishment in Northern Ireland" is to be construed in accordance with subsections (2) to (5);

"enactment" means any statutory provision within the meaning of section 1(f) of the Interpretation Act (Northern Ireland) 1954;

"government department" means a Northern Ireland department or a department of the Government of the United Kingdom;

"Minister of the Crown" includes the Treasury;

"Northern Ireland department" includes (except in sections 51 and 52) the head of a Northern Ireland department;

"occupational pension scheme" has the same meaning as in the Pension Schemes (Northern Ireland) Act 1993;

"premises", includes land of any description;

"prescribed" means prescribed by regulations;

"profession" includes any vocation or occupation;

"provider of services" has the meaning given in section 19(2)(b);

"public service vehicle" and "regulated public service vehicle" have the meaning given in section 40;

"PSV accessibility regulations" means regulations made under section 40(1);

"rail vehicle" and "regulated rail vehicle" have the meaning given in section 46;

"rail vehicle accessibility regulations" means regulations made under section 46(1);

"regulations" means—

(a)   in Parts I and II of this Act, section 66, the definition of "employment" above and subsections (3) and (4) below, regulations made by the Department of Economic Development;

(b)   in Part V of this Act, regulations made by the Department of the Environment;

(c)   in any other provision of this Act, regulations made by the Department of Health and Social Services.

"section 6 duty" means any duty imposed by or under section 6;

"section 15 duty" means any duty imposed by or under section 15;

"section 21 duty" means any duty imposed by or under section 21;

"taxi" and "regulated taxi" have the meaning given in section 32;

"taxi accessibility regulations" means regulations made under section 32(1);

"trade" includes any business;

"trade organisation" has the meaning given in section 13;

"vehicle examiner" means an officer of the Department of the Environment authorised by that Department for the purposes of sections 41 and 42.'.

(2) In section 68—

(a)   for subsection (2) substitute—
'(2) Where an employee does his work wholly outside Northern Ireland, his employment is not to be treated as being work at an establishment in Northern Ireland.'; and

(b)   in subsections (3) and (4) for 'Great Britain' wherever it occurs substitute 'Northern Ireland'.

48 (1) In section 70(3) for 'Secretary of State' substitute 'Office of the First Minister and Deputy First Minister'.

(2) In section 70(8) for 'the Secretary of State' substitute 'a Northern Ireland department' and for 'him' substitute 'it'.

49 (1) In Schedule 1 in paragraph 7(1) for 'Act 1944' substitute 'Act (Northern Ireland) 1945'.

(2) In Schedule 1 in paragraph 7(7) for '1944' substitute '1945'.

50 (1) (*repealed*)

(2) In Schedule 3 for paragraph 4(1) substitute—

'(1) In any proceedings under section 8—
   (a)   a certificate signed by or on behalf of a Minister of the Crown or a Northern Ireland department and certifying that any conditions or requirements specified in the certificate were imposed by that Minister or that department (as the case may be) and were in operation at a time or throughout a time so specified; or
   (b)   a certificate signed by or on behalf of the Secretary of State and certifying that an act specified in the certificate was done for the purpose of safeguarding national security,
shall be conclusive evidence of the matters certified.'.

(3) In Schedule 3 in paragraph 6(1) omit 'or a sheriff court'.

(4) In Schedule 3 for paragraph 8(1) substitute—

'(1) In any proceedings under section 25—
   (a)   a certificate signed by or on behalf of a Minister of the Crown or a Northern Ireland department and certifying that any conditions or requirements specified in the certificate were imposed by that Minister or that department (as the case may be) and were in operation at a time or throughout a time so specified; or
   (b)   a certificate signed by or on behalf of the Secretary of State and certifying that an act specified in the certificate was done for the purpose of safeguarding national security,
shall be conclusive evidence of the matters certified.'.

51 (1) In Schedule 4 in paragraphs 2(1) and (5) and 7(1) and (5) omit 'or sisted'.

(2) In Schedule 4 in paragraph 4 for 'Secretary of State' substitute 'Office of the First Minister and Deputy First Minister'.

(3) In Schedule 4 in paragraph 6(1) omit 'or, in Scotland, to the sheriff'.

(4) In Schedule 4 omit paragraph 6(2).

(5) In Schedule 4 in paragraph 9 for 'Secretary of State' substitute 'Office of the First Minister and Deputy First Minister'.

52 (1) Schedule 5, except paragraph 7(a) to (c), shall have no effect.

(2) In paragraph 7(a) to (c), for 'Secretary of State' wherever it occurs substitute 'Department of Health and Social Services'.

53 For Schedules 6 and 7 substitute—

'SCHEDULE 6

CONSEQUENTIAL AMENDMENTS

The Industrial Relations (Northern Ireland) Order 1976 (NI 16)

1   In Article 68(6) of the Industrial Relations (Northern Ireland) Order 1976 (reinstatement or re-engagement of dismissed employees)—

(a)   in the definition of 'relevant complaint of dismissal', omit 'or' and at the end insert 'or a complaint under section 8 of the Disability Discrimination Act 1995 arising out of a dismissal';

(b)   in the definition of 'relevant conciliation powers' omit 'or' and at the end insert 'or paragraph 1 of Schedule 3 to the Disability Discrimination Act 1995';

(c)   in the definition of 'relevant compromise contract' for 'or Article' substitute 'Article' and at the end insert 'or section 9(2) of the Disability Discrimination Act 1995'.

The Companies (Northern Ireland) Order 1986 (NI 6)

3   In paragraph 9 of Schedule 7 to the Companies (Northern Ireland) Order 1986 (disclosure in directors' report of company policy in relation to disabled persons) in the definition of 'disabled person' in sub-paragraph (4)(b) for 'Disabled Persons (Employment) Act (Northern Ireland) 1945' substitute 'Disability Discrimination Act 1995'.

SCHEDULE 7

REPEALS

Chapter	Short Title	Extent of repeal
1945 c. 6 (N.I.)	The Disabled Persons (Employment) Act (Northern Ireland) 1945.	Sections 1 to 4. Sections 6 to 14. In section 16 the words "vocational training and industrial rehabilitation courses and", the words "courses and" and the words from "and in selecting" to "engagement". Section 19. Section 21. Section 22.
1960 c. 4 (N.I.)	The Disabled Persons (Employment) Act (Northern Ireland) 1960.	The whole Act.
1976 NI16	The Industrial Relations (Northern Ireland) Order 1976.	In Article 68(6) the word "or" in the definitions of "relevant complaint of dismissal" and "relevant conciliation powers".'.

Amendments – Amended by Employment Rights (Northern Ireland) Order 1996, SI 1996/1919 (NI 16), art 255, Sch 1; Industrial Tribunals (Northern Ireland) Order 1996, SI 1996/1921 (NI 18), art 28(1), Sch 3; Northern Ireland Act 1998, s 99, Sch 13, para 16; Employment Rights (Dispute Resolution) (Northern Ireland) Order 1998, SI 1998/1265 (NI 8), art 16, Sch 2; Departments (Transfer and Assignment of Functions) Order (Northern Ireland) 1999, SR 1999/481, arts 4, 6(d), 8(a), Schs 2, 4, 6; Equal Opportunities (Employment Legislation) (Territorial Limits) Regulations (Northern Ireland) 2000, SR 2000/8, reg 3.

Appendix II

DISABILITY RIGHTS COMMISSION ACT 1999
(1999 c. 17)

ARRANGEMENT OF SECTIONS

Section	Page
1 The Disability Rights Commission	309
2 General functions	310
3 Formal investigations	310
4 Non-discrimination notices	311
5 Agreements in lieu of enforcement action	311
6 Persistent discrimination	313
7 Assistance in relation to proceedings	313
8 Recovery of expenses of providing assistance	314
9 Codes of practice	314
10 Conciliation of disputes under Part III of the 1995 Act	316
11 Procedure for amending s 7(1) of the 1995 Act	316
12 Regulations	317
13 Interpretation	317
14 Consequential amendments and repeals	317
15 Crown application	317
16 Short title, commencement and extent	317

SCHEDULES:

	Page
Schedule 1—Constitution etc	318
Schedule 2—Additional commissioners	321
Schedule 3—Formal investigations and non-discrimination notices	321
Part I—Conduct of formal investigations	321
Part II—Non-discrimination notices	324
Part III—Action plans	326
Part IV—Supplementary	329
Schedule 4—Minor and consequential amendments	331
Schedule 5—Repeals	332

An Act to establish a Disability Rights Commission and make provision as to its functions; and for connected purposes. [27th July 1999]

1 The Disability Rights Commission

(1) There shall be a body known as the Disability Rights Commission (referred to in this Act as 'the Commission').

(2) The Secretary of State shall pay to the Commission such sums as he thinks fit to enable it to meet its expenses.

(3) Schedule 1 (the Commission's constitution and related matters) has effect.

(4) The National Disability Council (which is superseded by the Commission) is abolished.

2   General functions

(1) The Commission shall have the following duties—

- (a)   to work towards the elimination of discrimination against disabled persons;
- (b)   to promote the equalisation of opportunities for disabled persons;
- (c)   to take such steps as it considers appropriate with a view to encouraging good practice in the treatment of disabled persons; and
- (d)   to keep under review the working of the Disability Discrimination Act 1995 (referred to in this Act as 'the 1995 Act') and this Act.

(2) The Commission may, for any purpose connected with the performance of its functions—

- (a)   make proposals or give other advice to any Minister of the Crown as to any aspect of the law or a proposed change to the law;
- (b)   make proposals or give other advice to any Government agency or other public authority as to the practical application of any law;
- (c)   undertake, or arrange for or support (whether financially or otherwise), the carrying out of research or the provision of advice or information.

Nothing in this subsection is to be regarded as limiting the Commission's powers.

(3) The Commission shall make proposals or give other advice under subsection (2)(a) on any matter specified in a request from a Minister of the Crown.

(4) The Commission may make charges for facilities or services made available by it for any purpose.

(5) In this section—

'disabled persons' includes persons who have had a disability;
'discrimination' means anything which is discrimination for the purposes of any provision of Part II or Part III of the 1995 Act; and
'the law' includes Community law and the international obligations of the United Kingdom.

3   Formal investigations

(1) The Commission may decide to conduct a formal investigation for any purpose connected with the performance of its duties under section 2(1).

(2) The Commission shall conduct a formal investigation if directed to do so by the Secretary of State for any such purpose.

(3) The Commission may at any time decide to stop or to suspend the conduct of a formal investigation; but any such decision requires the approval of the Secretary of State if the investigation is being conducted in pursuance of a direction under subsection (2).

(4) The Commission may, as respects any formal investigation which it has decided or been directed to conduct—

- (a)   nominate one or more commissioners, with or without one or more additional commissioners appointed for the purposes of the investigation, to conduct the investigation on its behalf; and
- (b)   authorise those persons to exercise such of its functions in relation to the investigation (which may include drawing up or revising terms of reference) as it may determine.

(5) Schedule 2 (appointment and tenure of office of additional commissioners) and Schedule 3 (so far as relating to the conduct of formal investigations) have effect.

4 Non-discrimination notices

(1) If in the course of a formal investigation the Commission is satisfied that a person has committed or is committing an unlawful act, it may serve on him a notice (referred to in this Act as a non-discrimination notice) which—

   (a)   gives details of the unlawful act which the Commission has found that he has committed or is committing; and
   (b)   requires him not to commit any further unlawful acts of the same kind (and, if the finding is that he is committing an unlawful act, to cease doing so).

(2) The notice may include recommendations to the person concerned as to action which the Commission considers he could reasonably be expected to take with a view to complying with the requirement mentioned in subsection (1)(b).

(3) The notice may require the person concerned—

   (a)   to propose an adequate action plan (subject to and in accordance with Part III of Schedule 3) with a view to securing compliance with the requirement mentioned in subsection (1)(b); and
   (b)   once an action plan proposed by him has become final, to take any action which—
          (i) is specified in the plan; and
          (ii) he has not already taken,
          at the time or times specified in the plan.

(4) For the purposes of subsection (3)—

   (a)   an action plan is a document drawn up by the person concerned specifying action (including action he has already taken) intended to change anything in his practices, policies, procedures or other arrangements which—
          (i) caused or contributed to the commission of the unlawful act concerned; or
          (ii) is liable to cause or contribute to a failure to comply with the requirement mentioned in subsection (1)(b); and
   (b)   an action plan is adequate if the action specified in it would be sufficient to ensure, within a reasonable time, that he is not prevented from complying with that requirement by anything in his practices, policies, procedures or other arrangements;

and the action specified in an action plan may include ceasing an activity or taking continuing action over a period.

(5) In this section 'unlawful act' means an act which is unlawful discrimination for the purposes of any provision of Part II or Part III of the 1995 Act or any other unlawful act of a description prescribed for the purposes of this section.

(6) Schedule 3 (so far as relating to non-discrimination notices and action plans) has effect.

5 Agreements in lieu of enforcement action

(1) If the Commission has reason to believe that a person has committed or is committing an unlawful act, it may (subject to sectoin 3(3)) enter into an agreement in

writing under this section with that person on the assumption that that belief is well founded (whether or not that person admits that he committed or is committing the act in question).

(2) An agreement under this section is one by which—

(a)   the Commission undertakes not to take any relevant enforcement action in relation to the unlawful act in question; and

(b)   the person concerned undertakes—

(i) not to commit any further unlawful acts of the same kind (and, where appropriate, to cease committing the unlawful act in question); and

(ii) to take such action (which may include ceasing an activity or taking continuing action over any period) as may be specified in the agreement.

(3) Those undertakings are binding on the parties to the agreement; but undertakings under subsection (2)(b) are enforceable by the Commission only as provided by subsection (8).

(4) For the purposes of subsection (2)(a), 'relevant enforcement action' means—

(a)   beginning a formal investigation into the commission by the person concerned of the unlawful act in question;

(b)   if such an investigation has begun (whether or not the investigation is confined to that matter), taking any further steps in the investigation of that matter; and

(c)   taking any steps, or further steps, with a view to the issue of a non-discrimination notice based on the commission of the unlawful act in question.

(5) The action specified in an undertaking under subsection (2)(b)(ii) must be action intended to change anything in the practices, policies, procedures or other arrangements of the person concerned which—

(a)   caused or contributed to the commission of the unlawful act in question; or

(b)   is liable to cause or contribute to a failure to comply with his undertaking under subsection (2)(b)(i).

(6) An agreement under this section—

(a)   may include terms providing for incidental or supplementary matters (including the termination of the agreement, or the right of either party to terminate it, in certain circumstances); and

(b)   may be varied or revoked by agreement of the parties.

(7) An agreement under this section may not include any provisions other than terms mentioned in subsections (2) and (6)(a) unless their inclusion is authorised by regulations made by the Secretary of State for the purposes of this section; but any provisions so authorised are not enforceable by the Commission under subsection (8).

(8) The Commission may apply to a county court or by summary application to the sheriff for an order under this subsection if—

(a)   the other party to an agreement under this section has failed to comply with any undertaking under subsection (2)(b); or

(b)   the Commission has reasonable cause to believe that he intends not to comply with any such undertaking.

(9) An order under subsection (8) is an order requiring the other party to comply with the undertaking or with such directions for the same purpose as are contained in the order.

(10) Nothing in this section affects the Commission's powers to settle or compromise legal proceedings of any description.

(11) In this section 'unlawful act' means an act which is unlawful for the purposes of any provision of Part II or Part III of the 1995 Act or any other unlawful act of a description prescribed for the purposes of this section.

(12) Schedule 3 (so far as relating to agreements under this section) has effect.

6   Persistent discrimination

(1) This section applies during the period of five years beginning on the date on which—

   (a)   a non-discrimination notice served on a person,

   (b)   a finding by a court or tribunal in proceedings under section 8 or 25 of the 1995 Act that a person has committed an act which is unlawful discrimination for the purposes of any provision of Part II or Part III of that Act, or

   (c)   a finding by a court or tribunal in any other proceedings that a person has committed an act of a description prescribed under subsection (4)(b),

has become final.

(2) If during that period it appears to the Commission that unless restrained the person concerned is likely to do one or more unlawful acts, the Commission may apply to a county court for an injunction, or to the sheriff for interdict, restraining him from doing so.

(3) The court, if satisfied that the application is well-founded, may grant the injunction or interdict in the terms applied for or in more limited terms.

(4) In this section 'unlawful act' means an act which is unlawful discrimination for the purposes of any provision of Part II or Part III of the 1995 Act or any other unlawful act of a description prescribed for the purposes of this section.

(5) A finding of a court or tribunal becomes final for the purposes of this section when an appeal against it is dismissed, withdrawn or abandoned or when the time for appealing expires without an appeal having been brought.

7   Assistance in relation to proceedings

(1) This section applies to—

   (a)   proceedings which an individual has brought or proposes to bring under section 8 or 25 of the 1995 Act (complaints and claims about unlawful discrimination under Parts II and III); and

   (b)   proceedings of a description prescribed for the purposes of this subsection, being proceedings in which an individual who has or has had a disability relies or proposes to rely on a matter relating to that disability.

(2) Where the individual concerned applies to the Commission for assistance in relation to any proceedings to which this section applies, the Commission may grant the application on any of the following grounds—

   (a)   that the case raises a question of principle;

   (b)   that it is unreasonable to expect the applicant to deal with the case unaided (because of its complexity, because of the applicant's position in relation to another party or for some other reason);

(c)   that there is some other special consideration which makes it appropriate for the Commission to provide assistance.

(3) If the Commission grants an application, it may—

(a)   provide or arrange for the provision of legal advice;
(b)   arrange for legal or other representation (which may include any assistance usually given by a solicitor or counsel);
(c)   seek to procure the settlement of any dispute;
(d)   provide or arrange for the provision of any other assistance which it thinks appropriate.

(4) Subsection (3)(b) does not affect the law and practice as to who may represent a person in relation to any proceedings.

(5) The Commission may authorise any employee of the Commission to exercise such of its functions under this section as it may determine.

8   Recovery of expenses of providing assistance

(1) This section applies where—

(a)   the Commission has given an individual assistance under section 7 in relation to any proceedings; and
(b)   any costs or expenses (however described) have become payable to him by another person in respect of the matter in connection with which the assistance is given.

(2) A sum equal to any expenses incurred by the Commission in providing the assistance shall be a first charge for the benefit of the Commission on the costs or expenses concerned.

(3) It is immaterial for the purposes of this section whether the costs or expenses concerned are payable by virtue of a decision of a court or tribunal, an agreement arrived at to avoid proceedings or to bring them to an end, or otherwise.

(4) The charge created by this section is subject to—

(a)   any charge under the Legal Aid Act 1988 and any provision in that Act for payment of any sum to the Legal Aid Board; and
(b)   any charge or obligation for payment in priority to other debts under the Legal Aid (Scotland) Act 1986 and any provision in that Act for payment of any sum into the Scottish Legal Aid Fund.

(5) Provision may be made by regulations made by the Secretary of State for the determination of the expenses of the Commission in cases where this section applies.

9   Codes of practice

(1) The following section shall be inserted at the beginning of Part VII of the 1995 Act (supplemental)—

'53A   Codes of practice

(1) The Disability Rights Commission may prepare and issue codes of practice giving practical guidance—

(a)   to employers, service providers or other persons to whom provisions of Part II or Part III apply on how to avoid discrimination or on any other matter relating to the operation of those provisions in relation to them; or

(b)   to any persons on any other matter, with a view to—

    (i)   promoting the equalisation of opportunities for disabled persons and persons who have had a disability, or

    (ii)   encouraging good practice regarding the treatment of such persons,

    in any field of activity regulated by any provision of Part II or Part III.

(2) The Commission shall, when requested to do so by the Secretary of State, prepare a code of practice dealing with the matters specified in the request.

(3) In preparing a code of practice the Commission shall carry out such consultations as it considers appropriate (which shall include the publication for public consultation of proposals relating to the code).

(4) The Commission may not issue a code of practice unless—

(a)   a draft of it has been submitted to and approved by the Secretary of State and laid by him before both Houses of Parliament; and

(b)   the 40 day period has elapsed without either House resolving not to approve the draft.

(5) If the Secretary of State does not approve a draft code of practice submitted to him he shall give the Commission a written statement of his reasons.

(6) A code of practice issued by the Commission—

(a)   shall come into effect on such day as the Secretary of State may by order appoint;

(b)   may be revised in whole or part, and re-issued, by the Commission; and

(c)   may be revoked by an order made by the Secretary of State at the request of the Commission.

(7) Where the Commission proposes to revise a code of practice—

(a)   it shall comply with subsection (3) in relation to the revisions; and

(b)   the other provisions of this section apply to the revised code of practice as they apply to a new code of practice.

(8) Failure to observe any provision of a code of practice does not of itself make a person liable to any proceedings, but any provision of a code which appears to a court or tribunal to be relevant to any question arising in any proceedings under Part II or Part III shall be taken into account in determining that question.

(9) In this section—

"code of practice" means a code of practice under this section;

"discrimination" means anything which is unlawful discrimination for the purposes of any provision of Part II or Part III; and

"40 day period" has the same meaning in relation to a draft code of practice as it has in section 3 in relation to draft guidance.'

(2) The Commission may treat any consultation undertaken by the National Disability Council under section 52(2) of the 1995 Act as being as effective for the purposes of section 53A(3) of that Act as if it had been undertaken by the Commission.

(3) Nothing in this section affects the Commission's powers apart from this section to give practical guidance on matters connected with its functions.

10   Conciliation of disputes under Part III of the 1995 Act

For section 28 of the 1995 Act (arrangements by the Secretary of State with a view to the settlement of disputes under Part III) there shall be substituted the following section—

'28   Conciliation of disputes

(1) The Commission may make arrangements with any other person for the provision of conciliation services by, or by persons appointed by, that person in relation to disputes arising under this Part.

(2) In deciding what arrangements (if any) to make, the Commission shall have regard to the desirability of securing, so far as reasonably practicable, that conciliation services are available for all disputes arising under this Part which the parties may wish to refer to conciliation.

(3) No member or employee of the Commission may provide conciliation services in relation to disputes arising under this Part.

(4) The Commission shall ensure that any arrangements under this section include appropriate safeguards to prevent the disclosure to members or employees of the Commission of information obtained by a person in connection with the provision of conciliation services in pursuance of the arrangements.

(5) Subsection (4) does not apply to information relating to a dispute which is disclosed with the consent of the parties to that dispute.

(6) Subsection (4) does not apply to information which—
    (a)   is not identifiable with a particular dispute or a particular person; and
    (b)   is reasonably required by the Commission for the purpose of monitoring the operation of the arrangements concerned.

(7) Anything communicated to a person while providing conciliation services in pursuance of any arrangements under this section is not admissible in evidence in any proceedings except with the consent of the person who communicated it to that person.

(8) In this section 'conciliation services' means advice and assistance provided by a conciliator to the parties to a dispute with a view to promoting its settlement otherwise than through the courts.'

11   Procedure for amending s 7(1) of the 1995 Act

For subsections (3) to (10) of section 7 of the 1995 Act (exemption for small businesses) there shall be substituted the following subsections—

'(3) Before making an order under subsection (2) the Secretary of State shall consult—
    (a)   the Disability Rights Commission;
    (b)   such organisations representing the interests of employers as he considers appropriate; and
    (c)   such organisations representing the interests of disabled persons in employment or seeking employment as he considers appropriate.

(4) The Secretary of State shall, before laying an order under this section before Parliament, publish a summary of the views expressed to him in his consultations.'

12 Regulations

(1) Any power under this Act to make regulations is exercisable by statutory instrument.

(2) Any such regulations may make—

   (a)   different provision for different cases or areas;
   (b)   provision enabling a person to exercise a discretion in dealing with any matter; and
   (c)   incidental, supplemental, consequential or transitional provision.

(3) A statutory instrument containing any such regulations shall be subject to annulment in pursuance of a resolution of either House of Parliament.

13 Interpretation

(1) In this Act—

   'Commission' means the Disability Rights Commission;
   'final', in relation to a non-discrimination notice, has the meaning given by paragraph 11 of Schedule 3;
   'formal investigation' means an investigation under section 3;
   'non-discrimination notice' means a notice under section 4;
   'notice' means notice in writing;
   'prescribed' means prescribed in regulations made by the Secretary of State; and
   'the 1995 Act' means the Disability Discrimination Act 1995.

(2) Expressions used in this Act which are defined for the purposes of the 1995 Act have the same meaning in this Act as in that Act.

14 Consequential amendments and repeals

(1) Schedule 4 (minor and consequential amendments) has effect.

(2) The enactments mentioned in Schedule 5 are repealed to the extent specified.

15 Crown application

This Act binds the Crown (but does not affect Her Majesty in her private capacity or in right of Her Duchy of Lancaster or the Duke of Cornwall).

16 Short title, commencement and extent

(1) This Act may be cited as the Disability Rights Commission Act 1999.

(2) This Act (apart from this section) shall come into force on such day as the Secretary of State may by order made by statutory instrument appoint; and different days may be appointed for different purposes.

(3) An order under subsection (2) may contain transitional provisions and savings relating to the provisions brought into force by the order.

(4) The following provisions extend to Northern Ireland—

   (a)   section 14(1), in relation to paragraphs 1, 2 and 4 of Schedule 4; and
   (b)   section 14(2), in relation to the repeal of words in the House of Commons Disqualification Act 1975, the Northern Ireland Assembly Disqualification Act 1975 and section 70(7) of the 1995 Act.

(5) Except as mentioned in subsection (4), this Act does not extend to Northern Ireland.

SCHEDULES

SCHEDULE 1   Section 1(3)

CONSTITUTION ETC

Status

1 (1) The Commission is a body corporate.

(2) The Commission is not the servant or agent of the Crown, it does not enjoy any status, immunity or privilege of the Crown and its property is not to be regarded as property of or as held on behalf of the Crown.

Membership

2 (1) The Commission shall consist of not less than 10 and not more than 15 commissioners appointed by the Secretary of State.

(2) The Secretary of State may appoint as a commissioner a person who is not disabled and has not had a disability only if satisfied that after the appointment more than half of the commissioners will be disabled persons or persons who have had a disability.

(3) Sub-paragraph (2) shall not apply in respect of the first three appointments under this paragraph.

Tenure of office of commissioners

3 (1) A commissioner shall hold and vacate office in accordance with the terms of his appointment.

(2) A person shall not be appointed a commissioner for less than two or more than five years; but a person who has served as a commissioner may be reappointed.

4 A commissioner may resign by notice in writing to the Secretary of State.

5 The Secretary of State may terminate the appointment of a commissioner if satisfied that—

- (a) without the consent of the chairman he has failed to attend meetings of the Commission during a continuous period of six months beginning not earlier than nine months before the termination;
- (b) he has become bankrupt, has had his estate sequestrated or has made a composition or arrangement with, or granted a trust deed for, his creditors; or
- (c) he is otherwise unable or unfit to carry out his functions as a commissioner.

Tenure of office of chairman and deputy chairmen

6 (1) The Secretary of State shall appoint one commissioner as chairman of the Commission and either one or two other commissioners as deputy chairmen.

(2) The Secretary of State shall exercise his powers of appointment under this paragraph with a view to securing that at least one of the persons holding office as chairman or deputy chairman is a disabled person or a person who has had a disability.

7 A person appointed as chairman or deputy chairman—

(a) shall hold and vacate that office in accordance with the terms of his appointment,

(b) may resign that office by notice in writing to the Secretary of State, and

(c) shall cease to hold that office if he ceases to be a commissioner.

Remuneration, pensions etc. of commissioners

8 The Commission may—

(a) pay to any commissioner such remuneration or expenses; and

(b) pay, or make provision for the payment of, such sums by way of pensions, allowances or gratuities to or in respect of any commissioner,

as the Secretary of State may determine.

9 If the Secretary of State determines that there are special circumstances which make it right that a person who has ceased to be a commissioner should receive compensation, the Secretary of State may direct the Commission to pay that person such sum by way of compensation as the Secretary of State may determine.

Staff

10 (1) The Commission shall have—

(a) a chief executive appointed by the Commission, subject to the approval of the Secretary of State; and

(b) such other employees as the Commission may appoint, subject to the approval of the Secretary of State as to numbers and terms and conditions of service.

(2) The first appointment of a chief executive shall be made by the Secretary of State.

11 (1) Employment with the Commission shall be included among the kinds of employment to which a scheme under section 1 of the Superannuation Act 1972 may apply, and accordingly in Schedule 1 to that Act (in which those kinds of employment are listed) at the end of the list of Royal Commissions and other Commissions there shall be inserted—

'Disability Rights Commission.'

(2) The Commission shall pay to the Minister for the Civil Service, at such times as he may direct, such sums as he may determine in respect of the increase attributable to sub-paragraph (1) in the sums payable out of money provided by Parliament under that Act.

Proceedings etc.

12 (1) The Commission may regulate its own procedure (including quorum).

(2) The quorum for meetings of the Commission shall in the first instance be determined by a meeting of the Commission attended by at least five commissioners.

13 The validity of any proceedings of the Commission is not affected by a vacancy among the commissioners or by a defect in the appointment of a commissioner.

Delegation

14 (1) The Commission may authorise any committee of the Commission or any commissioner to exercise such of its functions (other than functions relating to the conduct of a formal investigation) as it may determine.

(2) This paragraph does not affect any power of the Commission to authorise its employees to do anything on its behalf.

Accounts

15 (1) The Commission shall—

(a) keep proper accounts and proper records in relation to the accounts,

(b) prepare a statement of accounts in respect of each accounting year, and

(c) send copies of the statement to the Secretary of State and the Comptroller and Auditor General not later than the 31st August following the end of the accounting year to which it relates.

(2) The Comptroller and Auditor General shall examine, certify and report on the statement of accounts and shall lay copies of the statement and of his report before each House of Parliament.

(3) The Commission's accounting year is the twelve months ending with 31st March.

(4) The Commission's first accounting year shall be the period of not more than 12 months beginning with the Commission's establishment and ending with 31st March.

Annual reports

16 (1) As soon as practicable after the end of each accounting year the Commission shall submit to the Secretary of State a report on its activities during that year.

(2) The report shall include (among other things)—

(a) a report on anything done by the Commission, in the performance of its functions under section 2(1)(a) to (c), jointly or otherwise in co-operation with any other organisation;

(b) a general survey of developments in matters within the scope of the Commission's functions; and

(c) proposals for the Commission's activities in the current year.

(3) The Secretary of State shall lay a copy of the report before Parliament and arrange for such further publication of it as he considers appropriate.

List of consultees

17 (1) The Commission shall maintain a list of the organisations it has consulted generally for the purposes of any of its functions.

(2) An organisation may be removed from the list if it has not been consulted generally in the 12 months preceding its removal.

(3) For the purposes of sub-paragraphs (1) and (2), consultation is general unless it relates only—

(a) to an investigation to which paragraph 3 of Schedule 3 applies,

(b) to assistance under section 7, or

(c)   otherwise to a particular individual or individuals.

(4) The Commission shall make the list available to the public in whatever way it considers appropriate (subject to any charge it may impose).

SCHEDULE 2   Section 3(5)

ADDITIONAL COMMISSIONERS

1   (1) The Commission may, with the approval of the Secretary of State, appoint one or more individuals as additional commissioners for the purposes of a formal investigation.

(2) An additional commissioner is not the servant or agent of the Crown.

2   (1) An additional commissioner shall hold and vacate office in accordance with the terms of his appointment (and may be re-appointed).

(2) The Commission may not alter the terms of appointment of an additional commissioner except with his consent and the approval of the Secretary of State.

3   The Commission may—

(a)   pay such remuneration or expenses to any additional commissioner as the Secretary of State may determine, and

(b)   pay, or make provision for the payment of, such sums by way of pensions, allowances or gratuities to or in respect of any additional commissioner as the Secretary of State may determine.

4   (1) An additional commissioner may resign by notice in writing to the Commission.

(2) The Commission may, with the approval of the Secretary of State, terminate the appointment of an additional commissioner if satisfied that—

(a)   without reasonable excuse he has failed to carry out his duties during a continuous period of three months beginning not earlier than six months before the termination;

(b)   he has become bankrupt, has had his estate sequestrated or has made a composition or arrangement with, or granted a trust deed for, his creditors; or

(c)   he is otherwise unable or unfit to carry out his duties.

(3) The appointment of an additional commissioner shall otherwise terminate at the conclusion of the investigation for which he was appointed.

5   If the Secretary of State determines that there are special circumstances which make it right that a person who has ceased to be an additional commissioner should receive compensation, the Secretary of State may direct the Commission to pay that person such sum by way of compensation as the Secretary of State may determine.

SCHEDULE 3   Sections 3(5), 4(6) and 5(12)

FORMAL INVESTIGATIONS AND NON-DISCRIMINATION NOTICES

PART I

CONDUCT OF FORMAL INVESTIGATIONS

Introductory

1   (1) This Part of this Schedule applies to a formal investigation which the Commission has decided or has been directed to conduct.

(2) Any subsequent action required or authorised by this Part of this Schedule (or by Part IV of this Schedule) to be taken by the Commission in relation to the conduct of a formal investigation may be taken, so far as they are authorised to do so, by persons nominated under section 3(4) for the purposes of the investigation.

Terms of reference and preliminary notices

2   (1) The Commission shall not take any steps in the conduct of a formal investigation until—

  (a)   terms of reference for the investigation have been drawn up; and
  (b)   notice of the holding of the investigation and the terms of reference has been served or published as required by sub-paragraph (3) or (4).

(2) The terms of reference for the investigation shall be drawn up (and may be revised)—

  (a)   if the investigation is held at the direction of the Secretary of State, by the Secretary of State after consulting the Commission; and
  (b)   in any other case, by the Commission.

(3) Where the terms of reference confine the investigation to activities of one or more named persons, notice of the holding of the investigation and the terms of reference shall be served on each of those persons.

(4) Where the terms of reference do not confine the investigation to activities of one or more named persons, notice of the holding of the investigation and the terms of reference shall be published in such manner as appears to the Commission appropriate to bring it to the attention of persons likely to be affected by it.

(5) If the terms of reference are revised, this paragraph applies again in relation to the revised investigation and its terms of reference.

Investigation of unlawful acts etc.

3   (1) This paragraph applies where the Commission proposes to investigate in the course of a formal investigation (whether or not the investigation has already begun) whether—

  (a)   a person has committed or is committing any unlawful act;
  (b)   any requirement imposed by a non-discrimination notice served on a person (including a requirement to take action specified in an action plan) has been or is being complied with;
  (c)   any undertaking given by a person in an agreement made with the Commission under section 5 is being or has been complied with.

(2) The Commission may not investigate any such matter unless the terms of reference of the investigation confine it to the activities of one or more named persons (and the person concerned is one of those persons).

(3) The Commission may not investigate whether a person has committed or is committing any unlawful act unless—

  (a)   it has reason to believe that the person concerned may have committed or may be committing the act in question, or

(b)   that matter is to be investigated in the course of a formal investigation into his compliance with any requirement or undertaking mentioned in sub-paragraph (1)(b) or (c).

(4) The Commission shall serve a notice on the person concerned offering him the opportunity to make written and oral representations about the matters being investigated.

(5) If the Commission is investigating whether the person concerned has committed or is committing any unlawful act (otherwise than in the course of a formal investigation into his compliance with any requirement or undertaking mentioned in sub-paragraph (1)(b) or (c)) the Commission shall include in the notice required by sub-paragraph (4) a statement informing that person that the Commission has reason to believe that he may have committed or may be committing any unlawful act.

(6) The Commission shall not make any findings in relation to any matter mentioned in sub-paragraph (1) without giving the person concerned or his representative a reasonable opportunity to make written and oral representations.

(7) The Commission may refuse to receive oral representations made on behalf of the person concerned by a person (not being counsel or a solicitor) to whom the Commission reasonably objects as being unsuitable.

(8) If the Commission refuses to receive oral representations from a person under sub-paragraph (7), it shall give reasons in writing for its objection.

(9) A notice required by sub-paragraph (4) may be included in a notice required by paragraph 2(3).

(10) In this paragraph 'unlawful act' means an act which is unlawful discrimination for the purposes of any provision of Part II or Part III of the 1995 Act or any other unlawful act of a description prescribed for the purposes of this paragraph.

Power to obtain information

4   (1) For the purposes of a formal investigation the Commission may serve a notice on any person requiring him—

(a)   to give such written information as may be described in the notice; or
(b)   to attend and give oral information about any matter specified in the notice, and to produce all documents in his possession or control relating to any such matter.

(2) A notice under this paragraph may only be served on the written authority of the Secretary of State unless the terms of reference confine the investigation to the activities of one or more named persons and the person being served is one of those persons.

(3) A person may not be required by a notice under this paragraph—

(a)   to give information, or produce a document, which he could not be compelled to give in evidence, or produce, in civil proceedings before the High Court or the Court of Session; or
(b)   to attend at any place unless the necessary expenses of his journey to and from that place are paid or tendered to him.

5   (1) The Commission may apply to a county court or by summary application to the sheriff for an order under this paragraph if—

(a)   a person has been served with a notice under paragraph 4; and

(b)   he fails to comply with it or the Commission has reasonable cause to believe that he intends not to comply with it.

(2) An order under this paragraph is an order requiring the person concerned to comply with the notice or with such directions for the same purpose as may be contained in the order.

6 (1) The Commission may make recommendations in the light of its findings in a formal investigation.

(2) The recommendations may be—

(a)   recommendations to any person for changes in his policies or procedures, or as to any other matter, with a view to promoting the equalisation of opportunities for disabled persons or persons who have had a disability, or

(b)   recommendations to the Secretary of State, for changes in the law or otherwise.

(3) The Commission may make such recommendations before the conclusion of the investigation concerned.

Reports

7 (1) The Commission shall prepare a report of its findings in any formal investigation.

(2) The Commission shall exclude from such a report any matter which relates to an individual's private affairs or any person's business interests if—

(a)   publication of that matter might, in the Commission's opinion, prejudicially affect that individual or person, and

(b)   its exclusion is consistent with the Commission's duties and the object of the report.

(3) The report of an investigation carried out at the direction of the Secretary of State shall be published by the Secretary of State or, if the Secretary of State so directs, by the Commission.

(4) The report of any other investigation shall be published by the Commission.

(5) Nothing in this paragraph affects the Commission's power to issue a non-discrimination notice before a report is prepared or published.

PART II

NON-DISCRIMINATION NOTICES

Procedure for issuing and appealing against non-discrimination notices

8 (1) The Commission shall not issue a non-discrimination notice addressed to any person unless it has complied with the requirements of this paragraph.

(2) The Commission shall serve on the person concerned a notice—

(a)   informing him that the Commission is considering issuing a non-discrimination notice and of the grounds for doing so,

(b)   offering him the opportunity to make written and oral representations.

(3) The Commission shall give the person concerned or his representative the opportunity of making oral and written representations within a period specified in the notice of not less than 28 days.

(4) The Commission may refuse to receive oral representations made on behalf of the person concerned by a person (not being counsel or a solicitor) to whom the Commission reasonably objects as being unsuitable.

(5) If the Commission refuses to receive oral representations from a person under sub-paragraph (4), it shall give reasons in writing for its objection.

9   On issuing a non-discrimination notice, the Commission shall serve a copy on the person to whom it is addressed.

Appeal against non-discrimination notice

10   (1) A person on whom a non-discrimination notice is served may, within the period of six weeks beginning on the day after the day on which the notice is served on him, appeal against any requirement imposed by the notice under section 4(1)(b) or (3).

(2) An appeal under this paragraph lies—

(a)   to an employment tribunal, so far as the requirement relates to acts within the tribunal's jurisdiction; and
(b)   to a county court or a sheriff court, so far as the requirement relates to acts which are not within the jurisdiction of an employment tribunal.

(3) The court or tribunal may quash or, in Scotland, recall any requirement appealed against—

(a)   if it considers the requirement to be unreasonable; or
(b)   in the case of a requirement imposed under section 4(1)(b), if it considers that the Commission's finding that the person concerned had committed or is committing the unlawful act in question was based on an incorrect finding of fact.

(4) On quashing or recalling a requirement, the court or tribunal may direct that the non-discrimination notice shall have effect with such modifications as it considers appropriate.

(5) The modifications which may be included in such a direction include—

(a)   the substitution of a requirement in different terms; and
(b)   in the case of a requirement imposed under section 4(1)(b), modifications to the details given under section 4(1)(a) so far as necessary to describe any unlawful act on which the requirement could properly have been based.

(6) Sub-paragraph (1) does not apply to any modifications contained in a direction under sub-paragraph (4).

(7) If the court or tribunal allows an appeal under this paragraph without quashing or recalling the whole of the non-discrimination notice, the Commission may by notice to the person concerned vary the non-discrimination notice—

(a)   by revoking or altering any recommendation included in pursuance of the Commission's power under section 4(2); or
(b)   by making new recommendations in pursuance of that power.

11   For the purposes of this Act a non-discrimination notice becomes final when—

(a)   an appeal under paragraph 10 is dismissed, withdrawn or abandoned or the time for appealing expires without an appeal having been brought; or

(b)   an appeal under that paragraph is allowed without the whole notice being quashed or, in Scotland, recalled.

Enforcement of non-discrimination notice

12 (1) This paragraph applies during the period of five years beginning on the date on which a non-discrimination notice served on a person has become final.

(2) During that period the Commission may apply to a county court or by summary application to the sheriff for an order under this paragraph, if—

(a)   it appears to the Commission that the person concerned has failed to comply with any requirement imposed by the notice under section 4(1)(b); or

(b)   the Commission has reasonable cause to believe that he intends not to comply with any such requirement.

(3) An order under this paragraph is an order requiring the person concerned to comply with the requirement or with such directions for the same purpose as are contained in the order.

Register of non-discrimination notices

13 (1) The Commission shall maintain a register of non-discrimination notices which have become final.

(2) The Commission shall, in the case of notices which impose a requirement to propose an action plan, note on the register the date on which any action plan proposed by the person concerned has become final.

(3) The Commission shall arrange for—

(a)   the register to be available for inspection at all reasonable times, and

(b)   certified copies of any entry to be provided if required by any person.

(4) The Commission shall publish those arrangements in such manner as it considers appropriate to bring them to the attention of persons likely to be interested.

PART III

ACTION PLANS

Introductory

14 (1) This Part of this Schedule applies where a person ('P') has been served with a non-discrimination notice which has become final and includes a requirement for him to propose an action plan.

(2) In this Part 'adequate' in relation to a proposed action plan means adequate (as defined in section 4(4)(b)) for the purposes of the requirement mentioned in section 4(1)(b).

The first proposed action plan

15 (1) P must serve his proposed action plan on the Commission within such period as may be specified in the non-discrimination notice.

(2) If P fails to do so, the Commission may apply to a county court or by way of summary application to the sheriff for an order directing him to serve his proposed action plan within such period as the order may specify.

(3) If P serves a proposed action plan on the Commission in response to the non-discrimination notice, or to an order under sub-paragraph (2), the action plan shall become final at the end of the prescribed period, unless the Commission has given notice to P under paragraph 16.

Revision of first proposed action plan at invitation of Commission

16   (1) If the Commission considers that a proposed action plan served on it is not an adequate action plan, the Commission may give notice to P—

(a)   stating its view that the plan is not adequate; and
(b)   inviting him to serve on the Commission a revised action plan which is adequate, within such period as may be specified in the notice.

(2) A notice under this paragraph may include recommendations as to action which the Commission considers might be included in an adequate action plan.

(3) If P serves a revised proposed action plan on the Commission in response to a notice under this paragraph, it shall supersede the previous proposed action plan and become final at the end of the prescribed period, unless the Commission has applied for an order under paragraph 17.

(4) If P does not serve a revised action plan in response to a notice under this paragraph, the action plan previously served on the Commission shall become final at the end of the prescribed period, unless the Commission has applied for an order under paragraph 17.

Action by Commission as respects inadequate action plan

17   (1) If the Commission considers that a proposed action plan served on it is not an adequate action plan it may apply to the county court or by way of summary application to the sheriff for an order under this paragraph.

(2) The Commission may not make an application under this paragraph in relation to the first proposed action plan served on it by P (even where it was served in compliance with an order of the court under paragraph 15(2)) unless—

(a)   a notice under paragraph 16 has been served on P in relation to that proposed action plan; and
(b)   P has not served a revised action plan on the Commission in response to it within the period specified in the notice under paragraph 16(1)(b).

(3) An order under this paragraph is an order—

(a)   declaring that the proposed action plan in question is not an adequate action plan;
(b)   requiring P to revise his proposals and serve on the Commission an adequate action plan within such period as the order may specify; and
(c)   containing such directions (if any) as the court considers appropriate as to the action which should be specified in the adequate action plan required by the order.

(4) If on an application under this paragraph the court does not make an order, the proposed action plan in question shall become final at the end of the prescribed period.

18 (1) This paragraph applies where an order of the court under paragraph 17 ('the order') requires P to serve an adequate action plan on the Commission.

(2) If, in response to the order, P serves an action plan on the Commission, that action plan shall become final at the end of the prescribed period unless the Commission has applied to a county court or, in Scotland, to the sheriff to enforce the order on the ground that the plan does not comply with the order (and any directions under paragraph 17(3)(c)).

(3) Where an application is made as mentioned in sub-paragraph (2)—

    (a)   if the Commission withdraws its application, the action plan in question shall become final at the end of the prescribed period;

    (b)   if the court considers that the action plan in question complies with the order, that action plan shall become final at the end of the prescribed period.

Variation of action plans

19 An action plan which has become final may be varied by agreement in writing between the Commission and P.

Enforcement of action plans

20 (1) This paragraph applies during the period of five years beginning on the date on which an action plan drawn up by P becomes final.

(2) If during that period the Commission considers that P has failed to comply with the requirement under section 4(3)(b) to carry out any action specified in the action plan, the Commission may apply to a county court or by summary application to the sheriff for an order under this paragraph.

(3) An order under this paragraph is an order requiring P to comply with that requirement or with such directions for the same purpose as are contained in the order.

Power to obtain information

21 (1) For the purposes of determining whether—

    (a)   an action plan proposed by P is an adequate action plan; or

    (b)   P has complied or is complying with the requirement to take the action specified in an action plan which has become final,

the Commission may serve a notice on any person requiring him to give such information in writing, or copies of documents in his possession or control, relating to those matters as may be described in the notice.

(2) A person may not be required by a notice under this paragraph to give information, or produce a document, which he could not be compelled to give in evidence or produce in civil proceedings before the High Court or the Court of Session.

(3) The Commission may apply to a county court or by summary application to the sheriff for an order under this sub-paragraph if a person has been served with a notice under this paragraph and fails to comply with it.

(4) An order under sub-paragraph (3) is an order requiring the person concerned to comply with the notice or with such directions for the same purpose as may be contained in the order.

PART IV

SUPPLEMENTARY

Restriction on disclosure of information

22   (1) No information given to the Commission by any person ('the informant') in connection with—

(a)   a formal investigation; or

(b)   the exercise of any of its functions in relation to non-discrimination notices, action plans and agreements under section 5,

shall be disclosed by the Commission or by any person who is or has been a commissioner, an additional commissioner or an employee of the Commission.

(2) Sub-paragraph (1) does not apply to any disclosure made—

(a)   on the order of a court,

(b)   with the informant's consent,

(c)   in the form of a summary or other general statement published by the Commission which does not identify the informant or any other person to whom the information relates,

(d)   in a report of the investigation published by the Commission,

(e)   to a commissioner, an additional commissioner or an employee of the Commission, or, so far as is necessary for the proper performance of the Commission's functions, to other persons, or

(f)   for the purpose of any civil proceedings to which the Commission is a party, or of any criminal proceedings.

(3) A person who discloses information contrary to sub-paragraph (1) is guilty of an offence and liable on summary conviction to a fine not exceeding level 5 on the standard scale.

Enforcement of court orders

23   (1) This paragraph applies to any order made by a county court or the sheriff under section 5(8) or under any provision of this Schedule.

(2) Section 55 of the County Courts Act 1984 (penalty for failure to give evidence) shall have effect in relation to a failure to comply with an order made by a county court to which this paragraph applies with the following modifications—

(a)   for subsection (1) there shall be substituted—

'(1) Any person who fails without reasonable excuse to comply with an order made by a county court under section 5(8) of or any provision of Schedule 3 to the Disability Rights Commission Act 1999 shall forfeit such fine as the judge may direct.';

(b)   subsection (3) shall be omitted (but without prejudice to the operation of paragraph 4(3)(b) of this Schedule); and

(c)   in subsection (4), for the words 'the party injured by the refusal or neglect' there shall be substituted the words 'the Disability Rights Commission for expenses incurred or wasted in consequence of the failure to comply with the order concerned'.

(3) Where the sheriff finds a person to be in contempt of court in respect of the failure of a person to comply with an order made by the sheriff to which this paragraph applies—

(a)   notwithstanding section 15 of the Contempt of Court Act 1981, the sheriff shall not commit the person to prison; and

(b)   the sheriff may grant decree in favour of the Commission for such amount of any fine imposed for the contempt as appears to the sheriff to be appropriate in respect of the expense incurred or wasted by the Commission (including the expenses of any proceedings under this Schedule) in consequence of the failure to comply with the order.

(4) If the Commission applies to a county court or, in Scotland, to the sheriff to enforce an order to which this paragraph applies, the court may modify the order.

Offences

24   (1) A person who—

(a)   deliberately alters, suppresses, conceals or destroys a document to which a notice under paragraph 4 or 21, or an order under paragraph 5 or 21(3), relates; or

(b)   in complying with—

   (i)   a notice under paragraph 4 or 21;
   (ii) a non-discrimination notice;
   (iii) an agreement under section 5; or
   (iv) an order of a court under section 5(8) or under any provision of this Schedule,

makes any statement which he knows to be false or misleading in a material particular or recklessly makes a statement which is false or misleading in a material particular,

is guilty of an offence and liable on summary conviction to a fine not exceeding level 5 on the standard scale.

(2) Proceedings for an offence under this paragraph may (without prejudice to any jurisdiction exercisable apart from this sub-paragraph) be instituted—

(a)   against any person at any place at which he has an office or other place of business;

(b)   against an individual at any place where he resides, or at which he is for the time being.

Service of notices

25   (1) Any notice required or authorised by any provision of this Schedule to be served on a person may be served by delivering it to him, by leaving it at his proper address or by sending it by post to him at that address.

(2) Any such notice may—

(a)   in the case of a body corporate, be served on the secretary or clerk of that body;

(b)   in the case of a partnership, be served on any partner or a person having control or management of the partnership business;

(c)   in the case of an unincorporated association (other than a partnership), may be served on any member of its governing body.

(3) For the purposes of this paragraph and section 7 of the Interpretation Act 1978 (service of documents) in its application to this paragraph, the proper address of any person is—

(a)   in the case of a body corporate, its secretary or clerk, the address of its registered or principal office in the United Kingdom;

(b)   in the case of an unincorporated association (other than a partnership) or a member of its governing body, its principal office in the United Kingdom;

(c)   in any other case, his usual or last-known address (whether of his residence or of a place where he carries on business or is employed).

Regulations

26 The Secretary of State may make regulations making provision—

(a)   supplementing Part I or II of this Schedule in connection with any matter concerned with the conduct of formal investigations or the procedure for issuing non-discrimination notices; or

(b)   amending Part III of this Schedule in relation to the procedures for finalising action plans.

SCHEDULE 4   Section 14(1)

MINOR AND CONSEQUENTIAL AMENDMENTS

House of Commons Disqualification Act 1975 (c. 25)

1   In Part II of Schedule 1 to the House of Commons Disqualification Act 1975 (bodies whose members are disqualified) there shall be inserted at the appropriate place the words 'The Disability Rights Commission'.

Northern Ireland Assembly Disqualification Act 1975 (c. 26)

2   In Part II of Schedule 1 to the Northern Ireland Assembly Disqualification Act 1975 (bodies whose members are disqualified) there shall be inserted at the appropriate place the words 'The Disability Rights Commission'.

Disability Discrimination Act 1995 (c. 50)

3   (1) The Disability Discrimination Act 1995 shall be amended as follows.

(2) In section 67(5) (orders not subject to annulment) for '52(8), 54(6)' substitute '53A(6)(a)'.

(3) In Schedule 3 (enforcement and procedure under Parts II and III), in paragraph 6(2), for the words from 'a person' to 'approached' there shall be substituted 'the dispute concerned is referred for conciliation in pursuance of arrangements under section 28'.

Scotland Act 1998 (c. 46)

4   In Part III of Schedule 5 to the Scotland Act 1998 (reserved bodies), in paragraph 3(2)(c), for the words 'the National Disability Council' there shall be substituted 'the Disability Rights Commission'.

SCHEDULE 5   Section 14(2)

REPEALS

Chapter	Short title	Extent of repeal
1975 c. 24.	House of Commons Disqualification Act 1975.	In Part II of Schedule 1, the entry relating to the National Disability Council.
1975 c. 25.	Northern Ireland Assembly Disqualification Act 1975.	In Part II of Schedule 1, the entry relating to the National Disability Council.
1995 c. 50.	Disability Discrimination Act 1995.	Sections 50 to 54. In section 70(7), the words 'The National Disability Council'. Schedule 5.

INDEX

References are to paragraph numbers.

ACAS   10.3.12, 10.3.14, 10.3.16, *see also* Conciliation

Access to goods and services   5.2.1, *see also* Services, etc, provision of

Access to premises
building regulations, made under   3.6.15
employment discrimination   3.6.8
services provision, and   5.2.1, 5.5.1, 5.5.7
trade organisation   4.5.3, 4.5.6

Access to public transport   8.1.5, *see also* Transport

Accommodation agency   6.2.5, 6.2.13

Act of Parliament
see also Legislation
act done in pursuance of   10.2.8–10.2.11

Action plan, *see* Disability Rights Commission

Actuarial evidence, *see* Evidence, expert

Adjustments duty   3.6, 6.3.1–6.3.3
advice, failure to take   3.6.14
allocation of duties, by   3.6.11
alternative methods, consideration of   3.6.15
arrangements placing person at
disadvantage   3.6.4, 3.6.6, 3.6.7
'arrangements'   3.6.6, 3.6.7
dismissal process   3.6.7, 3.6.13
limits on scope   3.6.7
carer's needs as part of   3.4.18
circumstances triggering   3.6.4
contract work   3.9.5, 3.9.7–3.9.9
example   3.9.9
costs   3.6.12, 3.6.14, 3.6.16–3.6.18
resources of employer   3.6.16, 3.6.18
disabled employee/applicant, owed to   3.6.19
Code of Practice   3.6.20
employer's knowledge   3.6.19
disapplication of   3.7.4, 3.7.7, 3.8.7
evidence of disability   3.6.20

failure in   3.4.1, 3.6.3, 3.6.22
discrimination element   3.6.22
justification for   3.5.7, 3.6.3, 3.6.5, 3.6.22
result of, showing   3.6.3
unjustifiable   3.6.23
guidance on approach   3.6.5, 3.6.11
homeworker   3.6.8
individualised duty   3.6.9
leasehold premises, *see* Leasehold premises
more than one adjustment   3.6.16
need for   3.6.2
pay, performance-related   3.6.10, 3.6.17
physical features of premises placing person at disadvantage   3.6.4, 3.6.8
access, *see* Access to premises
adjustment to premises   3.6.11
'building'   3.6.8
employer's premises, limited to   3.6.8
relevant features   3.6.8
unreasonable alteration   3.6.15
positive discrimination
distinguished   3.6.1
reasonableness   3.6.5, 3.6.14–3.6.18
building Regs, and   3.6.15
Code   3.6.16
factors   3.6.16, 3.6.17
illustrations   3.6.16–3.6.18
test of   3.6.14
service provider, *see* Services, etc, provision of
steps to take   3.6.11
'substantial disadvantage'   3.6.9, 3.6.10
comparators   3.6.9
trade organisation, *see* Trade organisation
working hours   3.6.11, 3.6.12

Advertisement   3.3.2, 3.4.14–3.4.17
    definition   3.4.17
    discriminatory   3.4.14–3.4.16
    reasonable health requirements
        3.4.17
Adviser
    'relevant independent' for
        compromise   10.3.16–10.3.18
        meaning   10.3.17
        negligence   10.3.18
Aesthetic appearance   2.5.10
Agent
    unlawful discrimination by   10.2.7,
        10.3.7
Agreement
    see also Compromise agreement;
        Conciliation; Settlement
    void   10.3.15, 10.4.7
Agreement in lieu of enforcement, *see*
    Disability Rights Commission
Agricultural wages   3.5.9
Aid (auxiliary)
    see also Equipment; Interpreter;
        Prosthesis; Wheelchair
    provision as 'adjustment'
        employer, by   3.6.11, 3.6.12
        service provider, by   5.5.1, 5.5.2,
            5.5.12–5.5.14
Aiding unlawful act
    complaint against person for
        10.3.7
    liability for   10.2.1, 10.2.2
Aircraft   3.2.5, 8.1.5, 8.5
    non-statutory code   8.5.1
Airport   8.5.1
    hire car   8.2.14, 8.2.15
Alcohol addiction   2.3.3
Allergic rhinitis   2.3.3, 2.5.5
Alternative dispute resolution   4.7.1,
    see also Conciliation
Alzheimer's disease   2.5.9
Appeal   3.10.1, 10.3.8
    non-discrimination notice, against
        9.2.21, 9.2.22
    EAT, to, restricted reporting order
        10.3.24
Application form   3.3.12, 3.6.6
Arrangements
    employment discrimination
        disadvantaging disabled person, *see*
            Adjustments duty
        meaning and scope, *see* Adjustments
            duty; Recruitment
    trade organisation   4.5.1

Armed forces   3.2.12, 4.2.3, 9.5.4
    ex-service personnel   3.11.2
Attorney, power of   5.6.9
Australia   1.1.2
Aviation, *see* Aircraft; Airport

Banking services   5.2.1, *see also*
    Services, etc, provision of
Benefits
    see also Insurance benefits; Pension,
        occupational
    contract worker, for   3.9.3
    employment   3.3.6, 3.3.7
        adjustment duty, disapplication
            of   3.8.7
        provision to public   3.3.9–3.3.11
    leasehold premises, use of 'benefits or
        facilities'   6.2.5
    trade organisation membership
        4.3.4
Birth mark   2.5.10
Blindness, *see* Eyesight impairment
Boat, *see* Ferry; Ship
Body corporate
    DRC as   9.2.2
    liability for unlawful act of
        employee   10.2.2
    PSV offence, liability   8.3.8
    rail vehicle offence, liability   8.4.6
    service on   9.2.38
        questionnaire   10.3.3
Body-piercing   2.5.11
Broadcasting services   5.2.2, *see also*
    Services, etc, provision of
Building
    definition   3.6.8, 5.5.8, *see also*
        Adjustments duty
Bulimia   2.3.8
Burns   2.5.10
Bus
    hire cars at bus stations   8.2.14,
        8.2.15
    vehicle accessibility, *see* Public service
        vehicle

Canada   1.1.2
Cancer   2.5.7, 2.9, *see also* Terminal
    illness
Car
    company, provision of   3.3.6
    parking space
        dedicated, as adjustment   3.6.12,
            5.5.11

Car – *cont*
  parking space – *cont*
    leasehold premises   6.2.5
    provision   3.3.6
Carer   3.4.18
Charity   3.2.13
Child
  education, *see* Education services
  under six, with impairment   2.4.4
Chronic fatigue syndrome   2.3.8
Civil proceedings   10.4
Club, private members'   5.2.7
Coach
  vehicle accessibility, *see* Public service
    vehicle
Code of Practice   9.3
  current procedure, DRC
    preparation   9.3.4–9.3.6
    approval of draft by Parliament
      9.3.5
    consultations   9.3.5
    revision/re-issue   9.3.5
  Employment   3.1.2, 3.2.8, 3.3.3
  failure to comply   9.3.6
  Goods, Facilities, Services and
    Premises, access rights   5.1.3
  original procedure   9.3.1, 9.3.2
  sex and race discrimination   9.3.3
College
  exclusion from Part III provisions
    7.2.3, 7.2.8, 7.3.1, *see also*
    Education services
  further education, *see* Further
    education college
Commencement   3.1.2
  services etc provision, implementation
    timetable   5.1.2, 5.5.7
  trade organisation provisions
    4.5.1, 4.5.3
  treatment prior to   3.4.8
Commercial lease   6.2.10, 6.3.3, *see*
  also Leasehold premises
Communication services   5.2.1, *see*
  also Services, etc, provision of
Community council employment
  3.12
Community services   7.2.5
Compensation   10.3.28–10.3.32, *see*
  also Remedies
Complaint, *see* Employment tribunal
Complainant
  see also Employment tribunal
  employee   10.3

Compromise agreement   3.10.2,
  10.3.15–10.3.20
  validity, conditions   10.3.16–10.3.20
    advice from 'relevant independent
      adviser'   10.3.16–10.3.18
    insurance or indemnity cover
      10.3.19
    writing, agreement in   10.3.20
Conciliation   3.10.1, 3.10.2, 10.3.12–
  10.3.20
  agreement, form and effect of
    10.3.14
  conciliation officer
    inadmissibility of communications
      with   10.3.13, 10.4.5
    role   10.3.12, 10.3.13
  DRC arrangements for   10.4.5
  extension of provision for   10.4.5
Consent
  lessor's to alterations, *see* Leasehold
    premises
Continence
  impairment affecting   2.4.1
Contract
  see also Agreement
  incapacity, and justification
    defence   5.6.8, 5.6.9, 6.2.15
  void term   3.10.2
Contract work   3.2.3, 3.9
  commencement of provisions
    affecting   3.1.2
  discrimination against disabled
    worker   3.9.1–3.9.6
    adjustment duty   3.9.5, 3.9.7–
      3.9.9
    benefits provided to public   3.9.4
    categories   3.9.3
    EAT case   3.9.2
    hirer   3.9.6, 3.9.7
    justification defence   3.9.5
    'principal'   3.9.1
    remedies   3.10
    scope   3.9.5, 3.9.6
    small business exemption   3.9.5
Corporation, *see* Body corporate
Cost
  adjustment, of, *see* Adjustment duty
  increased, by service provider
    5.6.12, 5.6.13
  indemnity for DRC   9.2.36
County court proceedings   10.4
Criminal offence
  DRC powers, relating to   9.2.37

Criminal offence – *cont*
  PSV accessibility, *see* Public service
      vehicle
  rail vehicle accessibility, *see* Rail travel
  taxi accessibility, *see* Taxi
Crown
  application of Act to acts and
      omissions   9.5.1
    employment field   9.5.2
  civil servants, position of   9.5.2
  condition imposed by, act in
      pursuance of   10.2.8–10.2.11
    certification   10.2.11
  prison officer, *see* Prison officer
  'statutory body' and 'office'   9.5.2,
      9.5.3

Day-to-day activities, *see* Disability
Deafness   2.3.7, 2.4.1
  see also Interpreter
  hearing aid   2.5.13
  induction loop   5.5.1, 5.5.13
Declaration of rights   10.3.27, 10.4.11
Deemed disabled, *see* Disabled person
Defence, *see* Justification
Deposit
  goods or facilities, for   5.6.16
  tenancy or occupation of premises,
      for   6.2.16
Depression   2.3.6
Detriment
  contract worker subjected to   3.9.3
  employee subjected to   3.3.8
  property manager subjecting person
      to   6.2.6
Diabetes   2.5.13
Disability
  'ability to carry out day-to-day
      activities'   2.4–2.4.5
    affected activities, list   2.4.1
    child under six   2.4.4
    effect on complainant central
      2.4.2
  definition   2.1.2–2.1.4, 2.2–2.6
    guidance, *see* Guidance
    reform proposed   2.9
  generic   2.3.8
  'impairment'   2.3
    expert evidence   2.3.5
    Guidance   2.3.2, 2.3.4
    mental   2.3.4–2.3.6, 2.3.8
    physical   2.3.3, 2.3.7, 2.3.8
    sensory   2.3.7
    WHO definition   2.3.1

'long-term' adverse effect   2.6–
    2.6.4
  Guidance   2.6.3, 2.6.4, 9.4.1,
      9.4.2
  legislative provision   2.6.1, 2.6.4
mild or trivial complaint or
    condition   2.4.3, 2.5.2
mitigation of effects   2.5.4
past, *see* Past disability
remediation by treatment, device etc,
    see Medical treatment
short-term   2.6.1, 2.9
'substantial' adverse effect   2.5–
    2.5.15
  corrective measures, see Medical
      treatment
  cumulative effect   2.5.3
  Guidance   2.5.1–2.5.3
  modification of behaviour to avoid
      effect   2.5.4
  progressive conditions, *see*
      Progressive condition
  recurring condition   2.5.5, 2.5.6
  severe disfigurement   2.5.10,
      2.5.11
  substantial   2.5.2, 2.5.3
  time taken to do activity,
      relevance   2.5.3
Disability Rights Commission
  action plan   9.2.24–9.2.30
    'adequate'   9.2.24, 9.2.26, 9.2.27,
        9.2.28
    court action by DRC   9.2.25,
        9.2.27–9.2.30
    enforcement of   9.2.29, 9.2.30
    final   9.2.25, 9.2.26, 9.2.27,
        9.2.28
    first   9.2.25, 9.2.26
    inadequate   9.2.27
    information or copy documents
        request   9.2.30
    requirement   9.2.24
    revised   9.2.26, 9.2.27
  agreement in lieu of enforcement
      action   9.2.31–9.2.33
    compliance investigation   9.2.12
    enforcement   9.2.33, 9.2.37
    no investigation or non-
        discrimination notice   9.2.32
    termination or variation   9.2.33
    undertakings   9.2.32, 9.2.33
  annual report   9.2.8
  assistance of individuals with
      proceedings   9.2.9–9.2.11

Disability Rights Commission – *cont*
  assistance of individuals with
    proceedings – *cont*
    expenses as charge   9.2.11
    legal advice and representation
      9.2.10
  chairman and deputy   9.2.5
  chief executive   9.2.3
  codes of practice, preparation
    9.3.4, *see also* Code of Practice
  commissioners   9.2.4, 9.2.5
    additional, appointment and
      tenure   9.2.13
    appointment and termination of
      appointment   9.2.4
    vacancy, and validity of
      proceedings   9.2.7
  conciliation arrangements   10.4.5
  consultation with (small business
    threshold)   3.2.11
  costs and expenses for   9.2.36
  court order enforcement   9.2.36
  criminal offences relating to
    powers   9.2.37
  disclosure by   9.2.35
  establishment   9.1.3, 9.2.1
  fine   9.2.36
  formal investigation, *see* Investigation
  functions   9.2.1, 9.2.6–9.2.8
  information request   9.2.17, 9.2.30
    document concealment etc
      9.2.37
    restriction on disclosure by DRC
      9.2.35
  injunction application   9.2.34
  misleading statement to   9.2.37
  non-discrimination notice, *see* Non-
    discrimination notice
  powers   9.2.6, 9.2.7, 9.2.12 *et seq*
    delegation   9.2.7
    persistent discrimination, in cases
      of   9.2.34
  recommendations   9.2.18
  report, *see* Investigation
  representations to   9.2.16, 9.2.19
  service of notices   9.2.38
  staff   9.2.3
  status   9.2.2
Disability Rights Task Force, *see* Task
  Force
Disabled person
  burden of proof   2.1.4
  deemed for Act   2.1.3, 2.7
  definition   2.1.2–2.1.4, 2.2

  approach of court   2.2.2
    see also Disability
  newly disabled   3.6.13
  registered disabled person   2.1.3,
    2.7.1, 2.7.2
  relationship with, action by person
    with   10.1.7
  supported employment   3.2.14,
    3.2.15
Discrimination
  see also Justification; Less favourable
    treatment
  adjustments duty failure as   3.4.1,
    3.6.3, 3.6.22
  association, by   3.4.18
  meaning
    employment provisions, for   3.4
    services, etc, provision, for   5.4
    trade organisation provisions,
      for   4.4
  occupational pension benefits, as
    to   3.7, *see also* Pension,
    occupational
  persistent, DRC powers   9.2.34
  remedies, *see* Remedies
  unlawful acts
    legal liability, *see* Liability
    summary   10.1.2
Disfigurement, severe   2.5.10, 2.5.11
Dismissal   3.3.8, 3.3.15, 3.6.13
  adjustments duty, application to
    3.6.7
  unfair dismissal protection and
    discrimination, relationship
    of   3.6.13
Drug
  addiction   2.3.3
  medically prescribed   2.3.3
Dwellinghouse, disposal of   6.2.10–
  6.2.12

Education services   7.1 *et seq*
  examination and assessment
    services   7.2.5, 7.2.7
  exclusion from Part III   5.2.9, 7.1.1,
    7.2.1–7.2.8
    private and State exclusion   7.2.2
    Regulations, scope   7.2.5–7.2.8
    services provision exclusion
      7.2.3
  local education authorities   7.2.2,
    7.2.6, 7.3.11
  non-educational provision by school,
    etc   7.2.4, 7.2.8

Education services – *cont*
  policy-making   7.3
    further education colleges, *see*
        Further education college
    integration of disabled pupils
        7.3.3
    scope of provisions   7.3.1
    special educational needs children,
        annual report   7.3.2, 7.3.3
    Teacher Training Agency   7.3.4
  research   7.2.7
  student unions   7.2.8
  Task Force recommendations
        7.2.9
  universities, *see* University
  voluntary organisation, provision
        by   7.2.7
  youth and community services
        7.2.5
Employee
  complaint by   10.3, *see also*
        Employment tribunal;
        Questionnaire, statutory
  discrimination against, *see*
        Employment, discrimination in
  liability, aiding unlawful act   10.2.2,
        10.2.4, 10.2.5
Employer
  adjustments duty, *see* Adjustments duty
  knowledge of disability
    adjustments duty   3.6.19
    less favourable treatment
        3.4.10–3.4.13
  leasehold premises, alterations to, *see*
        Leasehold premises
  liability, *see* Liability
  prohibition on discrimination by, *see*
        Employment, discrimination in
  vicarious liability   10.2.4
Employers' association, *see* Trade
        organisation
Employment agency   5.2.1
Employment Appeal Tribunal, *see* Appeal
Employment, discrimination in   3.1 *et
        seq*
  adjustments, making reasonable, *see*
        Adjustments duty
  arrangements for offering
        employment, *see* Recruitment
  benefits   3.3.6, 3.3.7, 3.3.9
  Code of Practice   3.1.2, 3.2.8, 3.3.3
  commencement of provisions
        affecting   3.1.2
  'discrimination'   3.4

  association, by   3.4.18
  indirect   3.4.2, 3.5.1
  justification, *see* Justification
  less favourable treatment, *see* Less
        favourable treatment
  dismissal or other detriment   3.3.8
  'employment'   3.2.3, 3.2.4
  'establishment in GB'   3.2.5
  exclusions/exemptions   3.2.6–
        3.2.15, 3.3.9, 9.5.2–9.5.4
  grievance procedure, use of
        10.3.13
  opportunities, access to   3.3.6, 3.3.7
  pre-employment health screening
        3.3.12–3.3.15
    health-related questions in
        application form   3.3.12
    reform recommended   3.13
    see also Medical examination
  post-employment   3.3.8
  prohibition   3.2, 3.3
    acts prohibited   3.3.2–3.3.8
    scope   3.2.1, 3.3
    territorial scope   3.2.1
  promotion, transfer and training
        3.3.6, 3.3.7
  refusal of employment   3.3.4
  remedies   3.10
  selection, *see* Recruitment
  sex/race discrimination compared
        3.1, 3.4.1, 3.4.5, 3.5.1
  small business exclusion, *see* Small
        business
  terms of offer   3.3.3, 3.3.5, 3.7.1
  vicarious liability of employer, *see*
        Liability
Employment tribunal   10.3.7–10.3.11
  appeal from   3.10.1, 10.3.8
  appeal to, on non-discrimination
        notice   9.2.21, 9.2.22
  commencement of proceedings
        10.3.8
  complaint to, alterations to leasehold
        premises   6.3.14, 6.3.16
  complaint to, employment/contract
        work discrimination   3.10.1
  compensation and damages
        3.10.1
  declaration or recommendation
        3.10.1
  time-limit   3.10.1
  complaint to, general   10.3.7–
        10.3.11

Employment tribunal – *cont*
  conciliation agreement, effect on
    10.3.14
  copy complaint to ACAS   10.3.12
  DDA 1995 covers   10.3.8
  decision   10.3.8, 10.3.25
    extended reasons   10.3.25
  evidence   10.3.4
    publicity restriction, *see* Restricted
      reporting order
  hearing   10.3.25
  originating application   10.3.8
  questionnaire   10.3.4–10.3.6
  remedies, *see* Remedies
  time-limit   10.3.9–10.3.11
    contracts, calculating for   10.3.10
    extension of   10.3.11
    omission, when starts to run for
      10.3.10
    out of time   10.3.11
Enforcement   3.10
  see also Remedies
  action plan, *see* Disability Rights
    Commission
  non-discrimination notice   9.2.23
Entertainment services   5.2.1
Epilepsy   2.3.8, 2.5.13
Equipment
  employer's duty   3.6.8, 3.6.11
  service provider's duty   5.5.8
  use of own/charity's   3.6.18
'Establishment in GB'   3.2.5
Estate agent
  management of premises   6.2.13,
    see also Leasehold premises
  sale by   6.2.9
European Convention on Human
    Rights   1.1.3
European law   1.1.4
Eviction
  protection from   6.2.6
Evidence
  conciliation communications,
    inadmissibility   10.3.13, 10.4.5
  publicity restriction, *see* Restricted
    reporting order
  questionnaire answers   10.3.4
Evidence, expert   2.3.5, 2.4.2
  compensation assessment, for
    10.3.28
  insurance, for   3.8.3
  pension scheme, for   3.7.6
Eyesight impairment   2.3.7, 2.4.1
  auxiliary aids   5.5.13
  colour-blindness   2.4.3

  information on tape   5.5.1, 5.5.13
  minor impairment   2.5.2
  lighting adjustment   5.5.11
    PSVs, on   8.3.6
    rail vehicles   8.4.3
  spectacle use   2.5.15

Facilities, *see* Services, etc, provision of
Factory   6.2.10, *see also* Leasehold
    premises
Feelings, injury to   10.3.31, 10.4.10
Ferry   8.1.5, 8.5.1
Finance and credit services   5.2.1
Fire brigade   3.2.12, 9.5.4
Fire regulations   5.6.7
Flat, *see* Leasehold premises
Furniture and fittings
  employer's duty   3.6.8
  service provider's duty   5.5.8
Further education college   7.3.5–
    7.3.9
  disabled/learning disabled students
    disability statements   7.3.7, 7.3.8
    funding councils   7.3.6, 7.3.7,
      7.3.10
    redress for student   7.3.9
    strategic plans for   7.3.6
  Government approach   7.3.5

Genetic risk   2.5.9
Goods, provision of, *see* Services, etc,
    provision of
Government
  approach to disability discrimination
    in 90s   1.1.1
  service provision by   5.2.2
Government department
  application of Act to acts and
    omissions   9.5, *see also* Crown
Green Paper   1.1.6, 5.1.1, 5.4.9, 5.5.6,
    7.2.1, 8.1.1
Grievance procedure, use of   10.3.13
Guarantee
  less favourable treatment in respect
    of   5.6.15
Guidance
  consultation duty   9.4.3
  draft   9.4.3
    approval by Parliament and final
      issue   9.4.4
    representations on draft   9.4.3
  legal status of   2.1.2

Guidance – *cont*
  'disability', on meaning   9.4
    illustrating and exemplifying
      9.4.2
    impairment, whether has long-term
      adverse effect   9.4.1, 9.4.2
    power of Secretary of State to issue
      9.4
    revocation   9.4.1
Guide dog   5.4.9, 5.5.6
Guides   7.2.5

HIV   2.5.7, 2.5.8, 2.9
Harassment   3.3.8, 6.2.6
Health insurance, *see* Insurance benefits
Health or safety risk
  justifying less favourable treatment
    3.5.2, 5.6.7, 6.2.15
Health screening   3.3.12, 3.3.13
  see also Medical examination
  reform recommended   3.13
Healthcare   3.3.6
Hearing impairment, *see* Deafness
Helicopter   8.5.1
Higher education institution, *see*
  University
Hire car   8.2.14, 8.2.15
Hirer, *see* Contract work
Holiday facilities   5.2.1, 5.2.5, *see also*
  Services, etc, provision of
Hotel services   5.2.1, *see also* Services,
  etc, provision of
Hours of work
  adjustment to   3.6.11, 3.6.12
Hovercraft   3.2.5
Huntingdon's chorea   2.5.9

Impairment, *see* Disability
Indirect discrimination   3.4.2, 3.5.1,
  5.4.9, 5.6.2
Induction procedure   3.3.5
Information, *see* Disability Rights
  Commission
Injunction   9.2.34, 10.4.11
Institutions, see Disability Rights
  Commission; National Disability
  Council
Insurance benefits (employment)
  3.3.6, 3.8
  adjustments duty disapplied   3.8.7
  employer discriminating   3.8.6,
    3.8.7
    justification   3.8.6

insurance company providing
  3.8.1, 3.8.2
  complaint by disabled person
    3.8.4
  discrimination provision   3.8.3,
    3.8.4
  'insurance services'   3.8.3, 3.8.5
  permanent health insurance
    benefits   3.8.5
Insurance services, *see* Services, etc,
  provision of
Interest   10.3.32
International legal standards   1.1.3
Interpreter
  provision of   3.6.11, 3.6.12, 5.5.13
Interview   3.3.2
  adjustments duty   3.6.6
  disability-related questions   3.6.20
Investigation
  DRC, formal   9.2.12–9.2.18
    circumstances for   9.2.12
    commissioners for   9.2.13
    criminal offences   9.2.37
    information request and order
      9.2.17, 9.2.37
    non-discrimination notice, service
      of, *see* Non-discrimination
      notice
    procedure   9.2.13
    recommendations from findings
      9.2.18
    report of findings   9.2.18, 9.2.35
    representations   9.2.16, 9.2.19
    scope   9.2.15
    service   9.2.14, 9.2.16, 9.2.38
    terms of reference   9.2.14, 9.2.15
Ireland   1.1.2

Justification   3.5
  adjustments duty
    failure, justification of   3.5.3,
      3.5.6, 3.5.7, 3.6.3, 3.6.22
    must be addressed first   3.2.23
  agricultural wages   3.5.9
  burden of proof   3.5.1
  health risk   3.5.2
  limitations   3.2.23
  legislative test   3.5.3–3.5.5
    balance of interests   3.5.6
    cases   3.5.6, 3.5.7
    circumstances of case   3.5.4
    Code of Practice   3.5.5
    'material' and 'substantial'
      3.5.4, 3.5.5, 3.5.7, 3.6.22, 3.6.23

Justification – *cont*
  legislative test – *cont*
    sequence for establishing   3.5.6
  occupational pension, of less
      favourable treatment as to
      3.7.2
  particular defence   3.5.3
  pay, performance-related, for   3.5.8
  premises, discrimination as to
      6.2.14–6.2.16
  service provider, by   5.6, *see also*
      Services, etc, provision of
  sex/race defence distinguished
      3.5.1
  trade organisation discrimination, *see*
      Trade organisation

Knowledge of disability
  adjustments duty   3.6.19, 4.5.4
  less favourable treatment, for
      3.4.10–3.4.13
    conflicting EAT decisions
        3.4.13, 5.4.7
  objective test   5.4.7
  services provision   5.4.6–5.4.8

Land   5.5.8, 6.2.10
Landlord, discrimination by, *see*
    Leasehold premises
Lawyer
  advice for compromise agreement
      10.3.17
Learning ability
  impairment affecting   2.4.1
Learning disability   2.3.4, 2.3.6, 7.3.6
Leasehold premises   6.1 *et seq*
  alterations to   6.1.2, 6.3.3–6.3.8
    compensation award   6.3.14
    consent and conditions   6.3.6,
        6.3.7, 6.3.9–6.3.12, 6.3.16,
        6.3.18
    employer's/trade organisation's
        duty   6.3.1, 6.3.3–6.3.5,
        6.3.9–6.3.14
    failure to obtain consent   6.3.13
    justification   6.3.13
    'lease'   6.3.5
    lessor as party to proceedings
        6.3.14, 6.3.17
    remedies   6.3.13, 6.3.14
    service provider's duty   6.3.2,
        6.3.3–6.3.5, 6.3.15–6.3.18

    statutory term implied into lease
        6.3.6–6.3.8
    'sub-lease'   6.3.5, 6.3.7
    term in lease forbidding   6.3.4,
        6.3.6
    unreasonably withheld consent
        6.3.11, 6.3.14, 6.3.16
  deposit   6.2.16
  discrimination   6.2.13–6.2.18
    background   6.2.13
    justification conditions   6.2.14–
        6.2.16
    less favourable treatment   6.2.14,
        6.2.15
  disposal of premises, unlawful acts of
      landlord etc   6.1.1, 6.2.1–6.2.8,
      6.3.19
    adjustments, no duty   6.3.2,
        6.3.19
    'disposal'   6.2.8
    licence or consent, withholding
        of   6.2.7
    local authority or housing
        association lists   6.2.4, 6.2.17
    'person with power to dispose'
        6.2.8
    refusal   6.2.3
    rent and other terms of disposal
        6.2.2
  manager or agency   6.2.13
    discrimination as to 'benefits or
        facilities'   6.2.5, 6.2.15
    eviction or other detriment
        6.2.6
    harassment by   6.2.6
    service provider, as   6.2.13
  'premises'   6.2.10
    small   6.2.11
  remedies   6.2.18
  small dwelling exemption   6.2.11,
      6.2.12
    'relevant occupier' on premises
        6.2.12
  victimisation   6.2.17
Left-handedness   2.4.3
Legal advice/representation
  provision by DRC   9.2.10
Legal proceedings   5.2.2
  see also Employment tribunal; Services,
      etc, provision of
  assistance of DRC   9.2.9–9.2.11
Legislation
  act done in pursuance of   10.2.8,
      10.2.9

Legislation – *cont*
　background to　　1.1
　enactment　　1.1.7
　Green Paper, *see* Green Paper
　overview　　1.2
　private members' bills　　1.1.5
　subordinate　　10.2.8
　territorial scope　　1.2.1
　White Paper, *see* White Paper
Less favourable treatment　　3.4.1,
　　3.4.3–3.4.8
　'but for' test　　3.4.4
　claim separate from adjustments duty
　　failure claim　　3.6.3
　comparator　　3.4.4–3.4.8
　　another disabled person　　3.4.6
　　CA approach　　3.4.8
　　test for　　3.4.7, 3.4.8
　concept　　3.4.3
　defence, *see* Justification
　discriminatory advertisement
　　3.4.14–3.4.17
　premises, in respect of　　6.2.14
　reason for treatment　　3.4.8, 3.4.9–
　　3.4.13, 3.5.2
　　employer's knowledge　　3.4.10–
　　　3.4.13
　　presumption　　3.4.16
　　relating to disability　　3.4.9,
　　　3.4.10, 3.6.23, 4.4.3
　　wide interpretation　　3.4.10,
　　　3.4.13
　service provider, by, *see* Services, etc,
　　provision of
　trade organisation discrimination
　　4.4.2, 4.4.3
　treatment prior to DDA 1995　　3.4.5
Liability　　10.2
　agent　　10.2.7
　aiding unlawful acts　　10.2.2
　　company employee　　10.2.2
　　defence　　10.2.3
　company liability　　10.2.2
　employee　　10.2.2, 10.2.4, 10.2.5
　employer, vicarious liability　　3.2.2,
　　10.2.1, 10.2.4–10.2.6
　　complaint　　10.3.7
　　defence　　10.2.6
　　'in course of employment', act done
　　　in　　10.2.5
　national security exception　　10.2.12
　principal, vicarious liability　　10.2.1,
　　10.2.7, 10.3.7

statutory authority exception
　　10.2.8–10.2.11
　certificate of imposition by
　　Crown　　10.2.11
　example, future legislation
　　10.2.10
　'in pursuance of' enactment etc
　　10.2.9
Licence　　6.2.8, *see also* Leasehold
　premises
Lifting/carrying ability
　impairment affecting　　2.4.1
Lighting　　5.5.11, 8.3.6, 8.4.3
Local authority
　employment　　3.12
　　positive action　　3.12.2
　housing list　　6.2.4, 6.2.17
　services etc provision　　5.2.1, 5.2.4
　　home care services, case on
　　　5.4.5
Local education authority　　7.2.2,
　7.2.6
　disability statements　　7.3.11

ME (chronic fatigue syndrome)　　2.3.8
Manager of premises, *see* Leasehold
　premises
Manual dexterity
　impairment affecting　　2.4.1
Meals　　3.3.6
Medical evidence, *see* Evidence, expert;
　Medical examination
Medical examination　　3.3.12–3.3.15
　adjustments
　　duty, where standards too high
　　　3.6.6
　　to determine need/type　　3.3.14,
　　　3.6.20
　'arrangement' for offering
　　employment　　3.3.13
　Code of Practice guidance　　3.3.14,
　　3.3.15
　singling out disabled person　　3.3.15
Medical and health services　　5.2.2, *see*
　also Services, etc, provision of
Medical treatment
　see also Prosthesis
　absence for, employer allowing
　　3.6.11
　impairment controlled, etc, by
　　2.3.2, 2.4.2, 2.5.12–2.5.15
　　examples　　2.5.13
　　Guidance　　2.5.14
　　legislative approach to　　2.5.13,
　　　2.5.14

Memory/concentration
  impairment affecting   2.4.1
Mental illness   2.3.5, 2.4.5, 2.9
Mental impairment   2.3.4–2.3.6, 2.3.8
  capacity to contract   5.6.8, 5.6.9,
    6.2.15
Minicab   8.2.14, 8.2.15
Misleading information   9.2.37
Misleading statement   10.2.3
Mobility
  impairment affecting   2.4.1
Mobility clause   3.6.6
Multiple sclerosis   2.5.7, 2.5.9
Muscular dystrophy   2.5.7

National Advisory Council on the
    Employment of Disabled People
  establishment and
    disestablishment   9.1.2
National Disability Council   1.2.1, 9.1
  codes of practice   9.3.1, 9.3.2
  establishment   9.1.1
  functions   9.1.1–9.1.3
    limitations   9.1.3
  superseded by DRC   9.2.1, *see also*
    Disability Rights Commission
National security
  act to safeguard   10.2.12
New Zealand   1.1.2
Newspaper, *see* Restricted reporting
    order
Nicotine addiction   2.3.3
Non-discrimination notice   9.2.19–
    9.2.23
  action plan requirement   9.2.24 *et
    seq*, *see also* Disability Rights
    Commission
  appeal   9.2.21
    requirement or whole quashed
      9.2.21–9.2.23
    time for   9.2.21
  compliance investigation   9.2.12,
    9.2.15
  details in   9.2.20
  enforcement
    order   9.2.23
    penalties   9.2.36
    period   9.2.23, 9.2.34
  final   9.2.23
  procedural requirements   9.2.19
  service   9.2.19, 9.2.20, 9.2.38
Northern Ireland   2.7.1, 3.2.1, 3.2.5
  Labour Relations Agency   10.3.12

taxis   8.2.16

Occupational pension, *see* Pension,
    occupational
Offer of employment
  refusal of   3.3.4
  terms of   3.3.3, 3.3.5, 3.7.1
Office block   6.2.10, *see also*
    Leasehold premises
Omission, time-limit for   10.3.10
Orders   9.7
Organisation   5.2.7, *see also* Trade
    organisation
Originating application   10.3.8

Parish council employment   3.12
Parliament
  application of DDA 1995 to act or
    omission   9.6.1
  employer, who is   9.6.2
  service provider, who is   9.6.2
Partnership   3.2.4
Past disability   2.6.4, 2.7.2, 2.8
  consistency of treatment   2.8.1
  determination as if Act in force
    2.8.2
  what must be shown   2.8.3
Pay
  agricultural, permit for lower than
    minimum   3.5.9
  lost, compensation for   10.3.30,
    10.3.36
  performance-related
    justification defence   3.5.8
  'substantial disadvantage' for
    adjustments duty, and
    3.6.10, 3.6.17
Pension, occupational   3.3.6, 3.7
  access right   3.7.6
  Code of Practice   3.7.7
  less favourable treatment in access,
    terms etc   3.7.1–3.7.4
    adjustments duty disapplied
      3.7.4
    contributions same but benefits
      not   3.7.3, 3.7.4
    cost factor   3.7.2
    justification   3.7.2, 3.7.3
  trustees' decisions, and 'non-
    discrimination rule'   3.7.5–
    3.7.7
    adjustments duty disapplied
      3.7.7

Pension, occupational – *cont*
  trustees' decisions, and 'non-
      discrimination rule' – *cont*
    complaint method   3.7.7
    justification   3.7.7
    liability   3.7.7
    overriding rule   3.7.6
    regulations, power for   3.7.8
Physical co-ordination
  impairment affecting   2.4.1
Physical features of premises
  disadvantaging disabled person, *see*
      Adjustments duty
Physical impairment   2.3.3, 2.3.7,
  2.3.8
Police   3.2.12, 4.2.3, 9.5.4
Prison officer   3.2.12, 4.2.3, 9.5.4
Premises
  see also Adjustments duty
  discrimination as to   6.2.13–6.2.18
    meaning for   6.2.10
    remedies   10.4, *see also* Remedies
  see also Leasehold premises
Professional organisation
  membership issues, *see* Trade
      organisation
  services, etc, provision   5.2.1, 5.2.2
Progressive condition   2.5.7–2.5.9,
  2.6.3
  future effect of present condition
      2.5.9
  predisposition or genetic risk   2.5.9
  symptoms must manifest   2.5.8
Promotion   3.3.6
  arrangements for, adjustments
      duty   3.6.6
  refusal   3.3.15, 3.4.4
Property
  sale or other disposal   6.2.8, 6.2.9,
    see also Leasehold premises
Property management agency   6.2.5
Prosthesis   2.3.2, 2.5.12, 2.5.13
Psychiatric impairment   2.3.4
Psychological counselling   2.5.13
Psychological impairment   2.3.4
Psychopathic disorder   2.3.6
Public, provision of benefit, service, etc,
    to   3.3.9–3.3.11, 3.9.4, 5.2.5, 5.2.7
Public sector   9.5
Public service vehicle   8.1.5, 8.3
  accessibility   8.3.3 *et seq*
    certificate, *see* 'accessibility
        certificates' and 'type approval'
        below

construction, use and maintenance
      provisions   8.3.5
    draft Regs   8.3.5, 8.3.19
    equipment, devices, priority seats
        etc   8.3.5
    exemptions, *see* 'exemption' *below*
    failure to conform   8.3.7
    lighting/colour contrast   8.3.6
    new vehicles, limited to   8.3.1
    purpose of regs   8.3.3
    regional variations   8.3.4
  accessibility certificates   8.3.9–
      8.3.12
    applications, lost certificates etc
        8.3.10
    approval of vehicle types   8.3.11,
        8.3.12
    issue requirement   8.3.9
  codes of practice   8.3.6
  criminal offences   8.3.7, 8.3.9,
      8.3.15
    corporate body and officer's
        liability   8.3.8
  exemption   8.3.16, 8.3.17
    authorisation order   8.3.17
    special authorisation   8.3.16
  help from staff   8.3.6
  implementation   8.3.4, 8.3.18
    amended timetable   8.3.19
    proposed dates for various
        vehicles   8.3.18
  lifts   8.3.5
  meaning   8.3.2
  ramps   8.3.5
  'regulated public service vehicle'
      8.3.4
  sensorily impaired travellers   8.3.6
  type approval
    certificate   8.3.13
    certificate withdrawal   8.3.14
    'type vehicle'   8.3.11
  wheelchair users   8.3.3, 8.3.5,
      8.3.19
Public transport, *see* Public service
    vehicle; Transport
Publicity restriction, *see* Restricted
    reporting order

Questionnaire, statutory   10.3.1–
    10.3.6
  admissibility   10.3.4
  adverse inference from non-
      completion   10.3.5
  form   10.3.2, 10.3.3

Questionnaire, statutory – *cont*
  service and reply   10.3.2, 10.3.3–
    10.3.5
  sex and race discrimination, use in
    10.3.1
  without prejudice   10.3.6
Quota scheme
  repeal   3.1.3, 3.11.1, 3.12.1

Radio, *see* Restricted reporting order
Rail travel   8.1.5, 8.4
  accessibility   8.4.2–8.4.11
    boarding devices, lifts and
      ramps   8.4.4
    catering facilities   8.4.4
    equipment and toilet facilities
      8.4.3, 8.4.4
    exemption   8.4.10
    exemption applications and
      revocations   8.4.11
    lighting/colour contrast   8.4.3
    new vehicles, limited to   8.4.7,
      8.4.9
    priority seating   8.4.4
    purpose of regs   8.4.2
    scope   8.4.7–8.4.9
    summary of provisions   8.4.4
    variations between 'networks'
      8.4.5
  announcements   8.4.4
  background to provisions   8.4.1
  criminal offences   8.4.6
    body corporate and officer's
      liability   8.4.6
  hire cars at station   8.2.14, 8.2.15
  magnetic levitation systems   8.4.7
  monorail   8.4.7
  'rail vehicle'   8.4.9
  'railway'   8.4.8
  'regulated rail vehicle'   8.4.3, 8.4.7
  sensorily impaired travellers   8.4.3
  Task Force recommendations
    8.4.9
  telephones   8.4.4
  tramway, *see* Tramcar
  underground   8.4.5
  wheelchair users   8.4.2
Ramp
  PSV, in   8.3.5
  rail vehicle   8.4.4
  taxi, in   8.2.3
Reasonable adjustments, *see* Adjustments
  duty

Recommendation   10.3.37–10.3.40
  failure to comply   10.3.40
  power, limits   10.3.38, 10.3.39
  'reasonable' action, for   10.3.37
Recreation services   5.2.1, 5.3.2, 5.3.3
Recruitment   3.2.1–3.3.5, 3.4.2
  'arrangements'   3.3.2, 3.3.13, 3.4.2,
    3.6.6, *see also* Adjustments duty
  health screening   3.3.12–3.3.15
  induction procedure   3.3.5
  refusal of offer of employment
    3.3.4
  terms of offer   3.3.3, 3.3.5, 3.7.1
Recurring condition   2.5.5, 2.5.6
  past disability   2.6.4, 2.8.1
  steps to prevent recurrence   2.5.6
Reform
  'disability', to   2.9, 3.13
  employment discrimination
    provisions   3.13
Refreshment services   5.2.1, 5.3.3
Registered disabled person
  deemed disabled for Act   2.7.1,
    2.7.2
  repeal of register   3.11.1
Regulations   9.7
Remedies   3.10, 10.3.26–10.3.40
  compensation   10.3.28–10.3.32
    aggravated damages   10.3.31
    employment discrimination case
      10.3.29
    guidance on assessment   10.3.28
    heads of damage   10.3.30
    higher additional award   10.3.34
    increase, failure in recommended
      action   10.3.40
    injury to feelings   10.3.31
    interest   10.3.32
    loss of earnings   10.3.30, 10.3.36
    mitigation of loss   10.3.30
    unfair dismissal compensation, and,
      see Unfair dismissal
  declaration of rights   10.3.27
  employment tribunal powers
    10.3.26
  recommendations, *see*
    Recommendation
  services and premises cases   10.4
    conciliation   10.4.5, 10.4.6
    county court claim   10.4.1
    damages and compensation
      10.4.10, 10.4.11
    declaration or injunction
      10.4.11

Remedies – *cont*
  services and premises cases – *cont*
    injury to feelings   10.4.10
    settlement   10.4.7–10.4.9
    time-limit   10.4.2, 10.4.3, 10.4.6
  Task Force recommendations
    10.3.41
Rent   6.2.2
Reserved occupations
  repeal   3.1.3
Restaurant   5.2.1, 5.2.8, 5.3.3, 5.5.11,
  see also Services, etc, provision of
Restricted reporting order   10.3.21–
  10.3.24
  appeal to EAT   10.3.24
  duration   10.3.23
  effect   10.3.22
  liability for breach   10.3.23
  'written publication'   10.3.22
Risk of physical danger
  impairment affecting perception
    2.4.1

Scar   2.5.11
Schizophrenia   2.3.6
School   7.2.3, 7.3.1–7.3.3, *see also*
  Education services
Scotland   6.2.7, 6.3.9, 6.3.17, 7.2.6,
  7.3.6
  higher education funding   7.3.13
  interdict application by DRC
    9.2.34
  partner's liability
    PSVs   8.3.8
    rail vehicle   8.4.6
  sheriff's court proceedings   10.4.1,
    10.4.2
  taxis   8.2.16
Scouts   7.2.5
Secretary of State
  DCR's recommendations to   9.2.18
  Guidance, issue of, *see* Guidance
  job opportunities, power under 1944
    Act   3.11.2
  regulations and orders, power
    9.7.1
Selection
  arrangements for, adjustments
    duty   3.6.6
  criteria   3.3.2
Sensory impairment   2.3.7
Service (notices)
  body corporate   9.2.38, 10.3.3

DRC   9.2.38, *see also* Investigation,
  formal
non-discrimination notice   9.2.19,
  9.2.20, 9.2.38
questionnaire   10.3.2, 10.3.3–10.3.5
unincorporated association, on
  9.2.38
Services, etc, provision of   3.3.11, 5.1
  et seq
  adjustment duty   5.5, 6.3.2
    anticipatory and evolving duty
      5.5.4
    cost factor   5.5.3
    failure   5.1.4, 5.3.5, 5.5.2
    'impossible or reasonably difficult'
      to use service   5.5.2, 5.5.3,
      5.5.5
    justification of failure, *see*
      'justification' *below*
    physical features, *see* 'physical
      features impeding access' *below*
    'practice, policy or procedure'
      5.5.5, 5.5.6
    reasonable steps   5.5.3, 5.5.5
  auxiliary aid or service, duties
    5.5.12–5.5.14
    commencement of duty   5.5.14
    examples   5.5.13
    permanent alteration to physical
      fabric, restriction   5.5.14
  background to legislation   5.1.1
  Code of Practice   5.1.3, 5.2.1,
    5.2.7, 5.5.3, 5.5.4, 5.5.6
  consumer, disabled person only
    as   5.2.8
  cost   5.6.12, 5.6.13
  deposit, level of refund   5.6.16
  'discrimination'   5.4
    adjustment failure   5.4.1, 5.5.2,
      see also 'adjustment duty' *above*
    indirect   5.4.9
    less favourable treatment, *see* 'less
      favourable treatment' *below*
  discrimination prohibition   5.1.4,
    5.3
    refusal of service   5.3.2, 5.4.2,
      5.4.5, 5.6.10
    standard or manner   5.3.3,
      5.6.11
    terms of service provision   5.3.4
  goods and facilities, what
    constitutes   3.3.11, 5.2.3
  guarantee   5.6.15

Services, etc, provision of – *cont*
  implementation timetable   5.1.2,
    5.5.7, 5.5.14
  insurance services   5.2.1
    less favourable treatment where
      additional risk   5.6.14
  justification   5.4.2, 5.4.8, 5.6
    background to defence of   5.6.1–
      5.6.3
    burden of proof   5.6.5
    conditions for defence   5.6.6–
      5.6.13
    reasonableness   5.6.5
    subjective-objective dual test
      5.6.4, 5.6.5
  labelling, instructions, etc   5.2.6
  less favourable treatment   5.4.1–
    5.4.8
    case (home care services
      charges)   5.4.5
    comparator   5.4.3
    justification, *see* 'justification' *above*
    knowledge issue   5.4.6–5.4.8
    positive discrimination   5.4.2
    reason relating to disability
      5.4.2, 5.4.4, 5.4.5
  physical features impeding access
    5.5.7–5.5.11
    exemption from duty, power
      5.5.10
    'physical feature'   5.5.8
    removal, alteration etc, duty
      5.5.7
    steps to be taken   5.5.9, 5.5.11
  refusal of service   5.3.2, 5.4.2, 5.4.5
    necessary to provide service at
      all   5.6.10
  remedies   5.7.1, 10.4, *see also*
    Remedies
  service provider
    manufacturers and designers,
      position of   5.2.6
    meaning and scope   5.2.4, 5.2.5,
      6.2.13
    more than one   5.2.4
    public, service provision to
      5.2.5, 5.2.7
  services, what constitutes   3.3.11,
    5.2
    example list   5.2.1
    exclusions   5.2.9
    scope   5.2.1, 5.2.2
    with or without payment   5.2.1
  settlement   10.4.7–10.4.9

standard of service   5.3.3, 5.6.11
  territorial scope   5.2.5
Settlement   10.3.15, 10.4.7–10.4.9, *see
  also* Compromise agreement;
  Conciliation
Ship   3.2.5, 8.5
  shipping industry, guidance on
    access   8.5.1
Shop   5.2.1, 5.3.4, *see also* Services,
  etc, provision of
Sight, *see* Eyesight impairment
Sign language, *see* Interpreter
Signs   5.5.11
Small business
  exclusion from Act   3.2.6–3.2.11
    alteration of threshold   3.2.9
    associated employers/groups
      3.2.8
    consultation requirement   3.2.11
    contract work   3.9.5
    review of threshold displaced
      3.2.10, 3.2.11
    seasonal or temporary workers
      3.2.6, 3.2.7
    threshold   3.2.6–3.2.9
Small dwelling   6.2.11, 6.2.12
Smoking, *see* Nicotine addiction
Special educational needs   7.3.2,
  7.3.3
Speech   2.3.7, 2.4.1
Statutory agreement (in lieu of
  enforcement proceedings), *see*
  Disability Rights Commission
'Statutory body' and 'office'   9.5.2,
  9.5.3
Student, *see* Education services
Supervision, provision of   3.6.11
Supported employment
  person providing, exemption for
    3.2.14, 3.2.15

Task Force   1.1.7, 9.5.4
  Disability Rights Commission,
    development of   9.1.3
  recommendations   10.3.41
    'disability' definition, for reform
      to   2.9
    education services   7.2.9
    pre-employment health
      screening   3.13
    public transport disabled
      provision   8.1.3, 8.5.1
    railway travel   8.4.9
Tattoo   2.5.11

Taxi   8.1.5, 8.2
  accessibility   8.2
    failure to comply with regs   8.2.3
    implementation   8.2.17
  criminal offences   8.2.3, 8.2.9,
    8.2.10, 8.2.12
  driver's duties   8.2.9–8.2.13
    assistance   8.2.9
    charges   8.2.9
    dogs   8.2.12, 8.2.13
    lawfulness, limitations as result
      of   8.2.10
    medical exemption   8.2.11,
      8.2.13
  exemption   8.2.7, 8.2.8
  hire cars at transport terminus
    8.2.14, 8.2.15
  guide/hearing dogs   8.2.12
    exemption certificate   8.2.13
  newly licensed vehicles   8.2.1, 8.2.5
  ramp   8.2.3
  relicensing   8.2.5
  swivel-seats   8.2.8
  'taxi'   8.2.4
  viability of trade   8.2.5–8.2.7
  wheelchair users   8.2.1, 8.2.2, 8.2.3,
    8.2.9–8.2.11, *see also* 'driver's
    duties' *above*
Teacher Training Agency   7.3.4
Television, *see* Restricted reporting order
Tenancy   6.2.10, *see also* Leasehold
  premises
Terminal illness   2.6.2
Termination of employment
  see also Dismissal
  adjustments to avoid   3.6.7
Terms of employment   3.3.3, 3.3.5,
  3.7.1
Terms of service provision   5.3.4
Territorial scope   3.2.1, 3.2.5, 5.2.5
Theatre   5.2.1, 5.3.2, 5.3.3
Time-limit
  claim in county court (services/
    premises case)   10.4.2, 10.4.3,
    10.4.6
  complaint, for (employment case)
    10.3.9–10.3.11
Trade organisation   4.1 *et seq*, 5.2.7
  adjustments duty   4.4.4, 4.5
    'arrangements', scope   4.5.2
  ballots and election provision,
    relation with   4.5.7, 4.5.8
  commencement of provisions
    4.5.1, 4.5.3

  cost factor   4.5.5
  failure   4.5.1, 4.6.3
  leasehold premises, *see* Leasehold
    premises
  must be addressed first   4.6.2
  particular duty to disabled
    person   4.5.1, 4.5.4
  physical features of premises
    4.5.3
  reasonable steps   4.5.5, 4.5.6
  'discrimination'   4.4, 4.6.1
    circumstances for   4.4.1
  discrimination prohibitions
    benefits of membership   4.3.4
    membership applications   4.1.3,
      4.3.2, 4.3.3
    outline   4.1.1, 4.1.2, 4.3.1
  employers', organisation of   4.2.1,
    4.2.5
  employers' association   4.2.5
  justification 'defence'   4.6
    examples   4.6.4
    limitations   4.6.2, 4.6.3
    'material' and 'substantial'   4.6.2
  less favourable treatment   4.4.2,
    4.4.3, 4.6.2
  reason relating to disability   4.4.3
  meaning   4.2
  profession or trade, organisation
    for   4.2.6, 4.2.7
  bodies issuing qualifications etc
    4.2.7
  Code of Practice   4.2.6, 4.2.7
  remedies   4.7, *see also* Remedies
  victimisation   4.4.5
  workers, organisation of   4.2.1–
    4.2.4
    'organisation'   4.2.4
    trade union   4.2.2
    'worker'   4.2.3
Trade union
  advice for compromise agreement
    from official, etc   10.3.17
  discrimination provisions, *see* Trade
    organisation
Training (employment)
  disabled person, for, under
    adjustments duty   3.6.11
  opportunities   3.3.6, 3.3.10
Training facilities   5.2.1, *see also*
  Services, etc, provision of
Tramcar   8.4.4, 8.4.5, 8.4.7
  'tramway'   8.4.8
Transfer   3.3.6

Transport   8.1 *et seq*
  accessibility, Government power
    8.1.5
  aeroplane, *see* Aircraft; Airport
  breakdown services   8.1.3
  'designated transport facility'
    8.2.14
  Disabled Persons Transport Advisory
    Committee   8.2.2, 8.2.7
  employment   8.1.4
  exclusion from Part III   5.2.9, 8.1.2,
    8.1.3, 8.5.1
  facilities subject to anti-discrimination
    provisions   8.1.2
  hire cars   8.2.14, 8.2.15
  minicabs   8.2.4, 8.2.14, 8.2.15
  PSVs, *see* Public service vehicles
  rail vehicle, *see* Rail travel
  ships, *see* Ferry; Ship
  Task Force recommendations
    8.1.3
  taxis, *see* Taxi
  tramcar   8.4.4, 8.4.5
Travel, *see* Transport
Treatment, *see* Medical treatment

Underground railway   8.4.5
Unfair dismissal
  compensation, relation with
      discrimination compensation
      10.3.33–10.3.36
    higher additional award   10.3.34
    loss of earnings   10.3.36
    no double award   10.3.35
    statutory maximum   10.3.36
  protection   3.6.13
Unincorporated association
  service on   9.2.38
United Nations   1.1.3
United States of America   1.1.2, 1.1.5
University
  exclusion from Part III   7.2.1–7.2.3,
    7.2.8
  policy-making   7.3.1, 7.3.5, 7.3.12–
    7.3.17
    current policy, information on
      7.3.15, 7.3.16
    disability statements   7.3.12–
      7.3.17
    effect of provisions   7.3.17

  regard to disabled persons'
      requirements   7.3.12
    strategic planning   7.3.14
Unlawful discrimination, *see*
  Discrimination
Usher syndrome   2.5.9

Ventilation   5.5.11
Vicarious liability   3.2.2
  see also Liability
  agent's acts, for   10.2.7
  employee's acts, for   10.2.4–10.2.6
Victimisation   10.1.4–10.1.8
  cause of action from   10.1.4
  complainant not 'disabled person'
    10.1.7
  forms of   10.1.5, 10.1.6
    examples   10.1.8
  premises, relating to   6.2.17
  trade organisation, by   4.4.5

Wage, *see* Pay
Wales
  higher education funding   7.3.13
Wheelchair
  bus or coach, use on, *see* Public service
    vehicle
  rail vehicle, use on, *see* Rail travel
  person's use of, and 'disability'
    2.5.12
  service provider
    adjustments duty   5.5.10, 5.5.11
    discrimination against user
      5.3.3, 5.5.6
  taxi use
    accessibility   8.2.1, 8.2.2, 8.2.3
    driver's duties   8.2.9–8.2.11, *see
      also* Taxi
White Paper   1.1.6, 5.1.1, 5.4.9, 5.5.1,
  5.5.6, 7.2.1, 8.1.1
World Health Organization
  impairment definition   2.3.1
Worsening condition   3.4.10, *see also*
  Progressive condition

Youth services   7.2.5